I0091121

DEED ABSTRACTS OF
TRYON, LINCOLN & RUTHERFORD COUNTIES
NORTH CAROLINA
1769-1786
TRYON COUNTY WILLS & ESTATES

ABSTRACTED BY:
    BRENT HOLCOMB, C.R.S.
PUBLISHED BY:
    SOUTHERN HISTORICAL PRESS

Copyright 1977 by:

The Rev. Silas Emmett Lucas, Jr.

All rights reserved. No part of this publication may be reproduced,
stored in a retrieval system or transmitted in any form or by any
means without the prior written permission of the publisher.

Please Direct All Correspondence and Book Orders to:
Southern Historical Press, Inc.
PO Box 1267
375 West Broad Street
Greenville, SC 29602-1267
or
southernhistoricalpress@gmail.com

ISBN #0-89308-047-0

CONTENTS

Introduction

Approximate Boundaries of Tryon County at Its Formation (Map)

Index

Early maps showing Tryon County

INTRODUCTION

Tryon County was formed from Mecklenburg County in 1769, Mecklenburg having been formed from Anson County in 1763. At its formation, Tryon County extended north to Earl Granville's line and west to the Indian line of 1767 (a portion of which is now the line between Greenville and Spartanburg Counties, South Carolina.). The eastern boundary was the Catawba River. Tryon County included all or part of the North Carolina counties of Lincoln, Gaston, Cleveland, Rutherford, Henderson, Polk, Burke and McDowell and the South Carolina counties of York, Chester, Union, Cherokee, Spartanburg, Greenville, Laurens and Newberry. While no land grants from Tryon County may have fallen as far south as Laurens or Newberry counties, the lands which were granted earlier from Mecklenburg and Anson counties came under the jurisdiction of Tryon County, e. g. the deed from Jacob and Mary Pennington to Alexander Lockart, page 28 (372-375) and the deed from John and Martha Dickinson to John Patton, page 32 (433).

The first courts of Tryon County were held in what is now York County, South Carolina. The court house site was moved into present Gaston County, North Carolina, when the border survey of 1772 determined the other site to be in South Carolina. When the border survey was made, the South Carolina county system as we know it was not yet set up. The Tryon County lands south of the border were then in Craven or Berkley (sometimes spelled Barkley) counties and/or Camden or Ninety Six District, or occasionally St. Mark's Parish was used for location. After the border survey, the lands formerly granted by North Carolina were registered in the South Carolina Land Memorials and often called "North Patents." South Carolina issued new grants for some of these lands, e. g., the grant to Giles Connel, S. C. Royal Grants, Vol. 33, p. 208, and the grant to James Gibbs, S. C. Royal Grants, Vol. 33, p. 252.

The few remaining wills and estate papers from Tryon County are in the North Carolina Archives filed with the Lincoln County records. All those pertaining to Tryon County are abstracted here as well as the lists of wills and estates from the Secretary of State's papers.

The copies of the Tryon deeds abstracted here are those in the Lincoln County Court House--Lincoln Volumes 1 and 2. While some of the original deed books are extant, they are not complete and some are in poor condition. However, they have been compared to the Lincoln copies, and the Lincoln copies are quite accurate and legible. There are some gaps in the deeds, but this does not signify that any recorded deeds have been lost. These gaps correspond with gaps in the Minutes of the Court of Pleas and Quarter Sessions. Apparently, the court did not function at certain times for one reason or another.

The Lincoln deeds are abstracted here to the end of Volume 2 (1786). Tryon County was abolished in 1779 to form Lincoln and Rutherford Counites. The Rutherford Deeds are abstracted for the same period, Volume A-d actually going on to 1787. This will take the Rutherford abstracts up to the point where Mrs. Caroline Davis began her work. As would be expected, some Tryon deeds were recorded late, after Lincoln and Rutherford Counties were formed. What may not be expected are the occasional deeds involving South Carolina lands recorded in these counties.

These deeds, wills and estates should provide many missing links for the researcher working on the Carolina frontier. This is a continuation of my abstracts of records of Anson and Mecklenburg Counties soon to be completed.

Brent H. Holcomb, G. R. S.
Clinton, South Carolina
October 8, 1976

APPROXIMATE BOUNDARIES OF TRYON COUNTY
AT ITS FORMATION

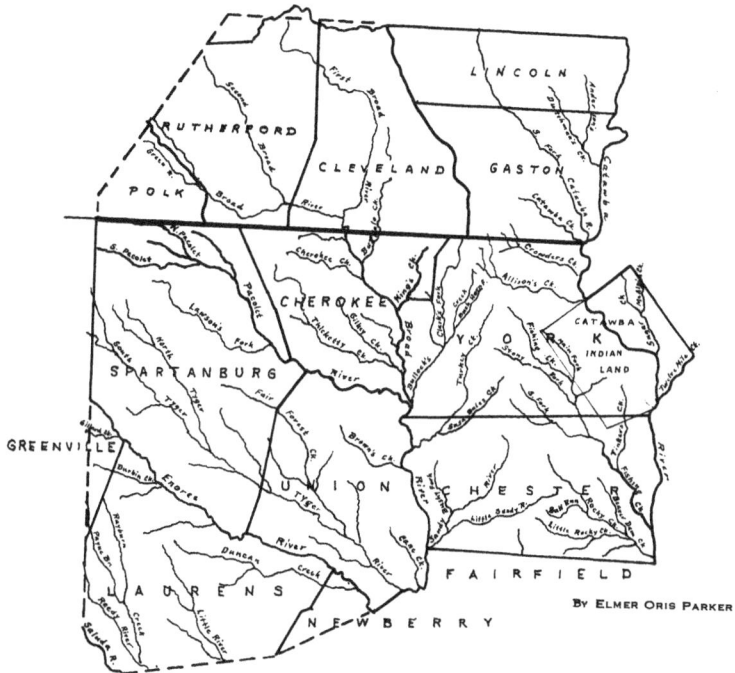

By Elmer Oris Parker

Pp. 1-2: 10 Apr 1769, THOMAS MITCHEL & wf AGNESS of Mecklenburg Co., to AARON LOCKHART
of same, (lease s5, release Ł 600 SC money)...100 A on N side Broad River
including his mill and improvement, granted to THOMAS MITCHEL 28 Apr 1768...THOMAS
MITCHEL (SEAL), AGNES MITCHEL ('Ħ) (SEAL), Wit: THOMAS DAVIS, JOHN MILES, and one
German signature. Rec. April term 1769.

Pp. 3-4: 1 Sept 1768, CASPER SLEGER & wf ELIZABETH of Mecklenburg Co., to ARCHIBALD
ELLIOT of same, for Ł 5 NC money...1/2 of tract between the waters of Catawba
River and Fishing Creek, 768 A, granted to sd. SLEGER 25 Sept 1754...CASPER SLEGER
(SEAL), ELIZABETH SLEGER (X) (SEAL), Wit: CASPER CLUB, JAMES CLARK. Rec. Apr term 1769.

Page 5: 21 Apr 1769, JOHN SLOAN Junior of Mecklenburg Co., to JOHN HUGGINS Junior of
Rowan Co., for Ł 18 proc. money...150 A in Tryon County on the So side of So
fork of Catawba River on one of the head branches of Long Creek, joining and above
THOMAS WELSHES land, granted to sd. JOHN SLOAN 26 Sept 1766...JOHN SLOAN (SEAL), Wit:
JAMES AUBUY, JOSEPH GILBREATH. Rec. Apr. term 1769.

Page 6: 18 Apr 1769, FRANCIS BEATTY of Mecklenburg Co., to JOHN BEEMAN of Tryon Co., for
Ł 27 proc. money...350 A on Indian Creek between the land that formerly belonged
to AARON MOORE and THOMAS ROBINSONs land, granted to sd. BEATTY 6 Apr 1765...FRANCIS
BEATY (SEAL), Wit: CHRISTOPHER CARPENTER (+), JAMES PATTEY. Rec. Apr. term 1769.

Pp. 6-7: 26 Apr 1769, JOHN SARTAIN of Tryon Co., Yeoman, to THOMAS WADE of Craven Co.,
S. C., Merchant, for Ł 60 proc. money...land on both sides McIntires Creek including
the mill and improvements, 100 A granted to sd. JOHN SARTAIN 9 Apr 1768...JOHN SARTAIN
(SEAL), Wit: WM YANCEY, JOHN FONDREN. Rec. Apr. term 1769.

Pp. 7-8: 16 Jan 1769, CHRISTIAN CARPENTER of Tryon Co., planter, to JOSEPH GOODE of same,
for Ł 40 proc. money...300 A on both sides of Knob Creek near the Cherokee path
granted to sd. CARPENTER 29 Apr 1768...CHRISTIAN CARPENTER (ȧ) (SEAL), Wit: DAVID
JENKINS, and a German signature. Rec. Apr. term 1769.

Pp. 8-9: 25 Jan 1769, JAMES MILLER of Tryon Co., Yeoman, to WILLIAM SHARP of Mecklenburg
Co., for Ł 6 s 5 proc. money...land on South fork of White Oak, a branch of
Green River above JAMES BLYTHS survey...250[?] A granted to sd. MILLER 22 Dec 1768...
JAMES MILLER (SEAL), Wit: JOHN YOUNG, JNO. MOORE. Rec. Apr. term 1769.

Pp. 9-10: 24 Apr 1769, PATRICK LAFFITY & wf PRUDENCE of Mecklenburg Co., to ROBERT
McCURDY of same, for Ł 28 proc. money...150 A on both sides Beaverdam, a branch
of Broad River...PATRICK LAFFERTY (P) (SEAL), PRUDENCE LAFFERTY (♂) (SEAL), Wit:
SAMUEL FULTON, JOHN FULTON. Rec. Apr. term 1769.

Pp. 10-11: 25 Nov 1768, JAMES McAFEE & wf MARGARET of Mecklenburg Co., to THOMAS POLK of
same, farmer, for Ł 50 proc. money...land on the main fork of Kings Creek
near the land of JOHN KUYKENDALL, deceased, being the place formerly surveyed for JOHN
MOORE, 300 A granted to FRANCIS BEATY 19 Apr 1763, conveyed to JOHN HARDEN, and from him
to sd. McAFEE...JAMES McAFEE (X) (SEAL), MARGARET McAFEE (X) (SEAL), Wit: ROBERT McAFEE,
JOHN TAGERT. Rec. Apr. term 1769.

Pp. 11-12: 27 Apr 1769, JOHN HARTNESS of Tryon Co., planter, to WILLIAM McCULLOH of Rowan
Co., for Ł 38 proc. money...200 A on E side Bullocks Creek on Smiths branch...
JOHN HARTNESS (Ⱶ) (SEAL), Wit: JOHN NUCKOLS, WILLIAM GARDNER. Rec. Apr. term 1769.

Pp. 12-13: 27 Aug 1768, JACOB COBRON of Mecklenburg Co., planter, to CHARLES McCLEAN of
same, for Ł 150 proc. money...300 A on W side Catawba, on a branch of the N
fork of Crowders Creek, granted 16 Nov 1764 to sd. COBRON...JACOB COBRON (SEAL), Wit:
JOHN WILSON, JOHN FONDREN, JAMES TEMPLETON. Rec. Apr. term 1769.

Page 13: 22 July 1768, CHARLES McKNIGHT & wf JENNET of Mecklenburg Co., to WILLIAM BYERS
of same, for Ł 70 proc. money...land granted to sd. McKNIGHT 30 Aug 1763...
CHARLES McKNIGHT (SEAL), JENNET McKNIGHT (X) (SEAL), Wit: CHARLES McCLAIN, ALEXANDER
COULTER, ABRAHAM CLAMINS. Rec. Apr. term 1769.

Page 14: 5 Apr 1769, JOHN MILLER & wf MARGARET of Tryon Co., Yeoman, to MARTIN OTTS of
same, for Ł 10 proc. money...land on N side Tiger River on Wards Branch including the forks of the branch, adj. CHARLES MOORE, granted to sd. JNO. MILLER 24 Oct 1767
...JOHN MILLER (SEAL), MARGARET MILLER (X) (SEAL), Wit: MOSES CUTTER, AGNES CUTTER (X)
CHS. MOORE. Rec. Apr. term 1769.

Pp. 15-16: 25 Jan 1768, WILLIAM GLOVER BISHOP of Mecklenburg Co., planter, to WILLIAM
BARRON of same, Cooper, for Ł 20 NC money...100 A including the easternmost
branch of Turky Creek...WILLIAM GLOVER BISHOP (SEAL), LUCY GLOVER BISHOP (X). Wit:
THOMAS BARRON, JOHN GLOVER. Rec. Apr. term 1769.

Pp. 16-17: 19 Apr 1769, ANDREW SPROT & wf MARY of Mecklenburg Co., to JOSEPH BIGGER of
Tryon Co., for Ł 60 proc. money...land in Tryon Co., on S side Catawba River,
230 A granted to ROBERT LEEPER 20 Mar 1755 by Gov. Dobbs, conveyed to WILLIAM McCULLOH...
ANDREW SPROT (SEAL), MARY SPROT (X) (SEAL), Wit: SAML MOORE, THOS POLK. Rec. Apr. term
1769.

Pp. 17-18: 7 Jan 1769, PETER CULP of Craven Co., SC, planter, to HENRY CULP of same, for
Ł 200 SC money...land in Mecklenburg Co., originally granted to THOMAS Mc-
CLELAND and legally conveyed unto the sd. PETER CULP, proved in open court and recorded
in the Clerks office the October Court 1766, entered in the register's office, 19 Feb
1767, on stony fork of Fishing Creek adj. WILLIAM HANNA's survey, 190 A...PETER CULP (SEAL)
Wit: ARCHIBALD ELLIOT (AE), HUGH WHITESIDES. Rec. Apr. term 1769.

Pp. 18-19: 15 Sept 1768, JOHN THOMAS of Craven Co., SC, to WILLIAM BARRIN of Mecklenburg
Co., for Ł 10 proc. money...land on the waters of Broad River on a branch of
Turkey Creek about a mile and a half below JOHN GARVINs land, 100 A, granted to sd. JOHN
THOMAS 26 Oct 1767...JOHN THOMAS (SEAL), Wit: JAMES MESKELLY, JOHN GORDON, DAVID GORDON.
Rec. Apr.term 1769.

Pp. 19-20: 27 Aug 1768, JACOB COBRON of Mecklenburg Co., planter, to CHARLES McCLEAN of
same, for Ł 100 proc. money...240 A on both sides the north fork of Crowders
Creek adj. JOHN WALKERS corner...JACOB COBRON (SEAL), Wit: JOHN WILSON, JOHN JORDEN, JAMES
TEMPLETON. Rec. Apr. term 1769.

Pp. 20-21: 25 Feb 1769, ANDREW ARMOR of Tryon Co., to ANDREW PATRICK of same, for Ł 17
s 10...145 A on S side Catawba River, on the waters of little Catawba Creek,
adj. JAMES CRAIG, and OZBURNS old survey...ANDREW ARMOUR (SEAL), Wit: JOHN STONE, ANDREW
GOFORTH, JOSHUA PATRICK. Rec. Apr. term 1769.

Pp. 21-22: 3 Feb 1769, JOHN RIGGS of Tryon Co., to THOMAS BRANDON of same, for Ł 93...
300 A on Bullocks Creek, adj. McADOU, GUYAN MOORE, granted to sd. RIGGS 25
Apr 1767...JOHN RIGGS (‡) (SEAL), Wit: FRANCIS TRAVERSE, DANIEL TRAVERS. Rec. Apr. term
1769.

Pp. 22-23: 17 Jan 1769, JOHN BENNET & wf AGNESS of Tryon Co., to WILLIAM ANDERSON, farmer,
of same, for Ł 5 proc. money...300 A, granted 29 Apr 1768...JOHN BENNET (SEAL),
AGNESS BENNET (X) (SEAL), Wit: DAVID JENKINS, FREDERICK HAMBRIGHT. Rec. Apr. term 1769.

Pp. 23-24: 18 Apr 1769, PATRICK LAVERTY & wf PRUDENCE of Tryon Co., to JOHN FULTON of same,
for Ł 14...100 A on a branch of Broad River, granted 25 Apr 1768...PATRICK
LAFFERTY (X) (SEAL), PRUDENCE LAFFERTY (X) (SEAL), Wit: SAMUEL FULTON, ROBERT McCURDY.
Rec. Apr. term 1769.

Pp. 24-25: 2 Mar 1768, JAMES WALKER & wf ELIZABETH of Mecklenburg Co., to JAMES CAMPBEL
of same, for Ł 40 proc. money...land on main branch of Turkey Creek including
the land he lives on, 155 A...JAMES WALKER (X) (SEAL), ELIZABETH WALKER (X) (SEAL), Wit:
JOSEPH BROWN (B), ABRAHAM WALKER (⋀). Rec. Apr. term 1769.

Pp. 25-26: 16 Dec 1768, EPHRAIM McCLAIN, Blacksmith, & wf ELIZABETH of Mecklenburg Co., to
RICHARD VENABLES, of Cumberland Co., Pa., for Ł 100 proc. money...220 A on
both sides middle fork of Crowders Creek...EPHRAIM McCLAIN (SEAL), ELIZABETH McCLAIN (X)
(SEAL), Wit: JOHN JORDAN, JOHN VENABLES, JOHN BARBER. Rec. Apr. term 1769.

Pp. 26-27: 20 Oct 1768, DAVID VANCE & wf RUTH of Mecklenburg Co., planter, to THOMAS
GARVIN, of same, for Ł 5 proc. money...100 A on a branch of Turkey Creek...
DAVID VANCE (SEAL), RUTH VANCE (SEAL), Wit: JOHN GARVIN, JEAN VANCE (X). Rec. Apr. term
1769.

Pp. 27-28: 6 June 1768, PETER KUKENDALL & ABRAM KUYKENDALL of Mecklenburg Co., to JAMES
YOUNG, for Ł 40...part of tract upon Fishing Creek, now in possession of sd.
JAMES YOUNG, between JAMES YOUNG and JOHN _____...granted 30 Apr 1753 to GEORGE CATHEY,
then made over to ABRAHAM KUYKENDALL 22 Apr 1763...PETER KUYKENDAL (SEAL), ABRAM KUYKEN-
DAL (SEAL), Wit: JAMES RISK, ____ WINBORNE, ROBERT McMINN. Rec. Apr. term 1769.

Pp. 28-29: 26 Apr 1769, DAVID WATSON of Tryon Co., planter, to JOHN WATSON of same, cordwainer, for Ł 100 proc. money...200 A on N side Broad River on the middle fork
of Bullocks Creek, part of 340 A...DAVID WATSON (SEAL), Wit: JOHN WILSON, THOMAS GARVIN.
Rec. Apr. term 1769.

Pp. 29-30: 23 Mar 1769, JOHN McKENNY of Tryon Co., to JOHN THOMPSON of same, for Ł 50 proc.
money...440 A on little beaverdam creek, a fork of Bullocks Creek, granted to
sd. McKENNY 27 Apr 1767...JOHN McKENNY (SEAL), Wit: JOHN PATTERSON, SAML DAVISON, BENJAMIN
HAWS[?]. Rec. Apr. term 1769.

Pp. 30-31: 6 June 1768, ABRAM KUYKENDAL of Mecklenburg Co., to PETER KUYKENDAL of same,
for Ł 5 proc. money...63 A on S side Fishing Creek adj. PETER KUYKENDOL old
survey...ABRAHAM KUYKENDOL (SEAL), Wit: JAMES YOUNG, JAMES RISK, DENNY WINBORNE. Rec.
Apr. term 1769.

Pp. 31-32: 20 Oct 1768, JOHN GARVIN & wf MARTHA of Mecklenburg Co., to THOMAS GARVIN of
same, [amount not stated]....150 A on head waters of Turkey Creek...JOHN
GARVIN (SEAL), MARTHA GARVIN (/) (SEAL), Wit: JAMES MISKELLY, THOMAS HANNA (✗). Rec.
Apr. term 1769.

Pp. 32-33: 7 Feb 1769, BENAJAH PENETON of Tryon Co., farmer, to THOMAS BARRIN of same,
farmer, for Ł 30 NC money...300 A on waters of Rocky Allisons Creek adj. RUSK,
JAMES McCALIN...BENAJAH PENETON (SEAL), Wit: SAMUEL WATSON, ALEXANDER STEVENSON. Rec.
Apr. term 1769.

Pp. 33-34: 20 Apr 1769, JOHN MILLER & WILLIAM NEELY of Tryon Co., to JOHN YOUNG of same,
...a grant to ROBERT MILLER 18 Nov 1752, and by virtue of his will, sd. MILLER
& NEELY do seel for Ł 50 NC money to JOHN YOUNG, 50 A, part of 800 A, adj. to land of
JOHN MILLER...JOHN MILLER (SEAL), WILLIAM NELLY (SEAL), Wit: JAMES YOUNG, JOSEPH BOGS,
JOSEPH WALLACE, AARON BOGS. Rec. Apr. term 1769.

Pp. 34-35: 26 Apr 1769, JAMES WATSON & wf JEAN of Tryon Co., to JEAN IRVIN of same, for
Ł 70...tract on Allisons Creek adj. JOHN McKNIGHT, ALEXANDER, including the old
Beaverdam, 315 A sold to WATSON by JOHN McCULLOH 24 Sept 1768...JAMES WATSON (SEAL), JEAN
WATSON (SEAL), Wit: JAMES HANNA, WILLIAM ADAMS, IBNI[?] BRYSON. Rec. Apr. term 1769.

Pp. 35-36: 18 Feb 1769, WILLIAM McDOWEL & wf ELEANOR of Mecklenburg Co., to WILLIAM
STEPHENSON of same, for Ł 29 proc. money...land on Allisons Creek adj. ROBERT
McDOWEL, 150 A...WILLIAM McDOWEL (SEAL), ELEANOR McDOWEL (⟩) (SEAL), Wit: PETER JOHNSTON,
ALEXR. STEPHENSON. Rec. Apr. term 1769.

Page 36: July Term 1769. North Carolina, Meck. County: This day came before me one of
his Majestys Justice of the peace for said county COLONEL JOHN CLARK and made
oath by the Holy Evangelist of Almighty God that a certain red oak which is dead in the
first corner tree Like the Patent of four hundred acres of land joining to JOHN ARMSTRONG
Obertien[?] of the No side of the said Fork of Cataba River now in the possession of
NICHOLAS FRYDAY Sworn before me the 27th day of February 1768. JOHN CLARK, Wit: NICHOLAS
SHRAM, PHILLIP RUDISALE, JOHN ROTZKOUPT.

Pp. 36-37: 1 June 1769, JOHN BIGGER of Mecklenburg Co., planter, to ARCHIBALD McNEAL of
same, for Ł 20 proc. money...land in Tryon Co., on E side of Indian Creek near
HUGH POLLOCKs land, on the line of a survey said to be McANCRUMS land on the head of
Leonards Fork, opposite the mouth of the buffalo Branch, granted to sd. BIGGER, 5 May
1769, 400 A...JOHN BIGGER (ʃ) (SEAL), CATHRIN BIGGER (0) (SEAL), Wit: PETER JOHNSTON,
MATTHEW BIGGER. Rec. July term 1769.

Pp. 37-38: 9 May 1769, THOMAS RAINEY & BENJAMIN PHILLIPS of Tryon Co., to JOHN FONDREN of
same, for Ł 10 proc. money...the remainder of a tract granted to sd. RAINEY &
PHILLIPS 26 Oct 1767 adj. ROBERT CARR, ISAAC KELLOUGS, RICHARD SADLER, and JOHN FONDREN,
150 A...THOS RAINEY (SEAL), BENJN. PHILLIPS (SEAL), Wit: JNO. GORDON, DAVID GORDON,
BENJN. RAINEY. Rec. July term 1769.

Pp. 38-39: 31 May 1769, JOHN McCULLOH of Tryon Co., to GEORGE PATTERSON of same, for Ł 130
proc. money...325 A on S side Catawba River on both sides of Allison Creek,
part of a tract conveyed by ANDREW ALLISON to sd. McCULLOH 25 Jan 1762...JOHN McCULLOH
(SEAL), Wit: EZEKIEL POLK, ROBERT PATRICK. Rec. July term 1769.

Pp. 39-40: 27 Apr 1769, ZACHARIAH BULLOCK and JOHN FONDREN of Tryon Co., to WM HENRY of
same, for Ł 10 proc. money...300 A on S fork Fishing Creek, on or near ROBERT
CARRs line...ZACHARIAH BULLOCK (SEAL), JOHN FONDREN (SEAL), Wit: JNO. KNUCKOLS, ROB: SWANN

Rec. July term 1769.

Pp. 40-41: 29 July 1768, ROBERT BISHOP of Mecklenburg Co., to JOHN SHIN of same, for Ⴠ 80
          proc. money...100 A on S side Packlet, including half the river a mile above
the Scul Shoals, including all the land granted to sd. BISHOP by Gov. Tryon, 26 Sept 1766
...ROBERT BISHOP (SEAL), Wit: ZACHARIAH BULLOCK, JAMES STEEN, JAMES COOK. Rec. July term
1769.

Pp. 41-42: 7 Feb 1769, WILLIAM BARNET of Mecklenburg Co., to WILLIAM CRONICAL of same, for
          Ⴠ 150...400 A in Tryon Co., in the forks of the Catauba River on both sides of
the waggon Road, adj. WM PATTERSON, granted to sd. BARNET 23 Feb 1754...WILLIAM BARNETT
(SEAL), Wit: JOHN BEAK, ARCHD. McNEAL. Rec. July term 1769.

Page 42: 24 July 1769, HARDY GLOVER of Tryon Co., to JOAB MITCHEL of same, for Ⴠ 50 proc.
          money...600 A on both sides Sandy Run...HARDY GLOVER (SEAL), Wit: JOHN HAIL,
CHARLES ROBINSON. Rec. July term 1769.

Pp. 42-43: 24 Jan 1769, HENRY FERGUSON of Tryon Co., to ADAM CARRUTH of same, for Ⴠ 30...
          200 A on an east branch of Long Creek adj. MOOR, McCARTY, granted to sd. FERGU-
SON __ Dec 1768...HENRY FERGUSON (SEAL), Wit: FREDERICK HAMBRIGHT, DAVID JENKINS, JOHN
LOW. Rec. July term 1769.

Pp. 43-44: 20 Sept 1768, JOHN WEBB of Orange Co., N. C., planter, to HUGH QUIN of Tryon
          Co., for Ⴠ 35 proc. money...300 A in Tryon Co., on S side Green River and on
N fork White Oak Creek including the forks of sd. creek above BLACKWELLs, granted 24 Oct
1767...JOHN WEBB (SEAL), SARAH WEBB (X) (SEAL), Wit: JAMES CAPSHAW, JAMES BYAS, PETER QUIN.
Rec. July term 1769.

Page 44: Powers of Atty Bills of Sale &C.
          CHARLES ROBINSON to JOHN PARKS, 12 head of cattle, two cows mark'd crop in right
ear and slit in the left and one do. crop in the right ear and swallow frok in the left...
3 May 1769, CHARLES ROBERSON[sic]. Wit: JOSH: FARGUSON, ROBERT COLEMAN. Rec. July term
1769.

Page 45: DANIEL HIGDON of Tryon Co., to JOAB MITCHEL of same, 22 head of cattle, some
          marked and branded..22 July 1769...DANIEL HIGDON (SEAL), Wit: JOHN HAILE, CHARLES
ROBERSON. Rec. July term 1769.
          WILLIAM MILLS of Tryon Co., for love and good will, to my son JESSE MILLS of same,
20 head of cattle, three breeding mares, one feather bed, three dishes, eight and five
pounds proc. money...18 July 1769...WILLIAM MILLS (A) (SEAL), Wit: THORNEAS GORE, JOHN
GORE. Rec. July term 1769.

Pp. 45-46: North Carolina, Tryon County: JOHN LINDSEY of Berkley Co., S. C., for natural
          love and affection to my Brother ISAAC LINDSEYs children...to EZEKIEL LINDSEY
one lite Gray marbed three B's...to MARY LINDSEY a cow and calf...to JEMIMA LINDSEY
red cow and heifer calf...17 July 1769...JOHN LINDSEY (SEAL), Wit: BENJAMIN THOMPSON,
JAMES COLE. Rec. July term 1769.

Pp. 46-47: 25 July 1769, SAMUEL JOHNSTON of Tryon Co., to JAMES COOK, planter, of same,
          for Ⴠ 40 proc. money...300 A on Cathys Creek of 2nd Broad River, adj. McCARTY,
granted to sd. JOHNSTON 26 Oct 1767...SAMUEL JOHNSTON (SEAL), Wit: ROBERT W. WHARTEN, JOHN
TERREL. Rec. July term 1769.

Pp. 47-48: 20 May 1769, JOAB MITCHEL of Tryon Co., to ROBERT WILKINS of same, for Ⴠ 50
          proc. money...300 A on both sides S fork Packlet...JOAB MITCHEL (M) (SEAL),
Wit: DAVID ROBERSON, WILLIAM WILKINS, ISAM LEE (+). Rec. July term 1769.

Pp. 48-49: 2 Sept 1768, JOEL BLACKWEL of Tryon Co., to HUGH QUIN of same, for Ⴠ 100 proc.
          money...300 A on both sides the north and middle fork of White Oak Creek,
granted 26 Oct 1767...JOEL BLACKWEL (X), HENRIETTA BLACKWELL (—); Wit: JAMES BUYOS,
JOSEPH GREEN (Ⴕ), PRESTON HAMPTON. Rec. July term 1769.

Pp. 49-50: 19 Oct 1768, WILLIAM SHERRIL of Cravin [sic] Co., S. C., planter, to ROBERT
          HARPER of Mecklenburg Co., for Ⴠ 50 proc. money...200 A on N side Broad River,
on a creek thereof...WILLIAM SHERRILL (W), Wit: JOHN BLAKENEY, JOHN LEDBETTER, FREDERICK
LEDBETTER. Provided the corner tree is found, I do acknowledge the said deed...19 Oct
1768, WILLIAM SHERILL (W), Wit: JAMES BLAKENEY. Rec. July term 1769.

Pp. 50-51: 20 Dec 1768, JOHN INCRAM of New Hanover Co., Merchant, to JOHN LUSK of Mecklenburg Co., for ₤ 20 proc. money...300 A on shady branch of Clarks Creek adj.
HUGH WILLSON...JOHN ANCRUM (SEAL), Wit: ROBERT HARRIS JR., JAS. BLYTHE. Rec. July term
1769.

Page 51: 23 Jan 1769, WILLIAM SIMS of N. C., surveyor, to PERREGREEN MAGNUS, planter, for
₤ 5 proc. money...land in Tryon Co., on both sides a large fork of Buffalow Creek
300 A, granted __ Dec 1769[sic]...WILLIAM SIMS (SEAL), Wit: THOMAS WELCH, GEORGE WATTS.
Rec. July term 1769.

Page 52: 19 June 1769, OWEN CARTER & wf MARY of Parish of St. George, Prov. of Georgia, to
JOHN STEEN of Tryon Co., for ₤ 200 proc. money...300 A on a branch of Broad River
called Thickety Creek...OWEN CARTER (O) (SEAL), MARY CARTER (ᗡ) (SEAL), Wit: JAMES
WALKER (‡), EPHRAIM LEDBETTER, ELIZABETH RORE (E). Rec. July term 1769.

Pp. 52-53: 24 July 1769, JOAB MITCHELL of Tryon Co., to JOHN BUCKHAM of same, for ₤ 100
proc. money...478 A on both sides Packlet River...JOAB MITCHEL (M), Wit: JOHN
HAILE, CHARLES ROBERSON. Rec. July term 1769.

Pp. 53-54: 22 July 1769, JOAB MITCHELL of Tryon Co., planter, to DAVID ROBINSON of same,
for ₤ 115 proc. money...250 A on both sides Mill Creek of Packlet River adj.
HUGHEYs line...JOAB MITCHEL (M), Wit: JOHN HAILE, DAVID ROBERSON, DANIEL HEYDON. Rec.
July term 1769.

Pp. 54-55: 1 Oct 1768, JOHN BOUN of Tryon Co., to HUGH QUINN of same, for ₤ 30 proc. money
...200 A on E side Broad River on both sides the suck branch waters of Mountain
Creek, granted 3 June 1767...JOHN BOUN (SEAL), Wit: JOHN FONDREN, JAMES CAPSHAW. Rec.
July term 1769.

Pp. 55-57: 17 June 1769, ROBERT GORDEN & wf MARY of Tryon Co., to JOHN WOODS of same, for
250 A on N side Allisons Creek including a shoal about a mile and a half below
the cedar flat...ROBERT GORDON (SEAL), MARY GORDON (Ꮞ) (SEAL), Wit: HENRY GORDON, JAMES
DAVIES. Rec. July term 1769.

Page 58: 6 Dec 1768, CHRISTOPHER GUIE & wf MARGARET of Mecklenburg Co., to ULRICK CROWDER
of same, for ₤ 28 ...200 A on the long branch of Killians Creek above the first
shoal and above JOSEPH SAILERS place...CHRISTOPHER GUIE (SEAL), MARGARET GUIE (ᒷ) (SEAL),
Wit: JACOB FORNEY, WILLIAM BARRY, MILES ABERNATHY. Rec. July term 1769.

Pp. 58-59: 28 Mar 1769, WILLIAM SIMS and WILLIAM MARCHBANKS of Tryon Co., to ROBERT MOORE
of same, for ₤ 50 proc. money...400 A on both sides Gouches branch of Turkey
Creek, granted 25 Apr 1767...WILLIAM SIMS (SEAL), WILLIAM MARCHBANKS (SEAL), Wit: JOHN
KENIDY, JOHN CLOY, PATRICK MOORE. Rec. July term 1769.

Pp. 59-60: 26 July 1769, JOHN STANFORD of Tryon Co., to GEORGE TUBS of same, for ₤ 75...
land on main Broad River including a large Island at the Ninety Islands [sic],
150 A granted to THOMAS HOOPER 27 Apr 1767...JOHN STANFORD (SEAL), SARY STANFORD (S) (SEAL)
Wit: HUGH QUINN (H), JAMES FORSYTH. Rec. July term 1769.

Pp. 60-61: 26 July 1769, JOSEPH HARDEN of Tryon Co., to JOHN MULINAX   of same, for
₤ 10 proc. money...land on Kings Creek about a mile above JOHN HARDINs adj.
JOHN McKELMURRYS on the west side of Jumping branch...200 A...JOSEPH HARDEN (SEAL), Wit:
PETER JOHNSTON, GEORGE POTS. Rec. July term 1769.

Pp. 61-62: 3 Apr 1769, PETER DUNCAN of Tryon Co., to THOMAS JONES of same, for ₤ 80 proc.
money...300 A on second Broad River including his improvement...PETER DUNCAN
(SEAL), Wit: WM SLACK, GEORGE BALL, JOHN WALKER. Rec. July term 1769.

Pp. 62-63: 1 Apr 1769, RABOURT FARES, late of Mecklenburg Co., cordwainer, & JAMES WAT-
SON of same, for one waggon and hind gears being valued at ₤ 25 proc. money...
200 A on waters of Allisons Creek adj. SAMUEL WATSON, SIMBERRALS[sic] line...JAMES WATSON
(SEAL), JEAN WATSON (SEAL), Wit: JAMES REAH, WILLIAM WATSON. Rec. July term 1769.

Pp. 63-64: 20 July 1769, ROBERT BLACKBURN of Tryon Co., farmer, & wf MARTHA, to THOMAS
WELCH of same, for ₤ 10...land adj. GRESSIMORE, PETER SUMMY, 150 A...ROBERT
BLACKBURN (SEAL), MARTHA BLACKBURN (SEAL), Wit: ALEXANDER LOCKHART, JAMES LOCKHART. Rec.
July term 1769.

Pp. 64-65: 21 Apr 1768, JEREMIAH ROUTH of Mecklenburg Co., to JOSEPH CLARK of same, for
₤ 40 proc. money...200 A on both sides Green River, granted to ROUTH 25 Sept

1766...JEREMIAH ROUTH (SEAL), MARGARET ROUTH (M) (SEAL), Wit: EDWARD BISHOP, RICHARD POWELL, EDWARD ROUTH. Rec. July term 1769.

Pp. 65-66: 19 May 1769, HUGH QUIN of Tryon Co., to MENARTER SAUNDERS of Maklin [Mecklen-
burg ??] Co., Colony of Virginia, for Ḷ 40 proc. money...200 A on E side Broad
River, granted 30 Oct 1765...HUGH QUINN (H), MARGARET QUINN (O), Wit: GEO. BLANTON,
WILLIAM GRISSOM. Rec. July term 1769.

Pp. 66-67: 30 Dec 1768, JOHN STANFORD of Tryon Co., to ESSEX CAPSHAW of s ame, for Ḷ 25...
the upper half of a tract on main broad river including a large shoal at the
ninety nine Islands, granted to THOMAS HOOPER 27 Apr 1767, 150 A...JOHN STANFORD (SEAL),
SARAH STANFORD (L) (SEAL), Wit: JAMES CAPSHAW, HUGH QUINN (H), JOSEPH GREEN (‡). Rec.
July term 1769.

Pp. 67-68: 21 July 1769, HUGH QUINN of Tryon Co., to CHARLES CAUTHEN of same, for Ḷ 40...
land on Main broad river, on the south side adj. BEATIES line, 400 A granted
__ Oct 1767...HUGH QUINN, MARGARET QUINN (M), Wit: DAVID DICKEY, WM. PARKER (+), Rec.
July term 1769.

Pp. 68-69: __ Feb 1768, JOHN MILLER & wf MARGARET of Mecklenburg Co., planter, to MOSES
COTTER of same, for Ḷ 30 proc. money...400 A on north fork of Little river
above PATT. CAMPBELs survey, the upper half of plantation sd. MILLER lives on, granted to
sd. MILLER 3 Sept 1753...JOHN MILLER (SEAL), MARGARET MILLER (SEAL), Wit: JAMS. McELWEAN,
FRANCIS PRINCE, THOS COLLINS. Rec. July term 1769.

Pp. 69-71: 25 July 1769, WILLIAM ADEAR & wf MARY of Tryon Co., to DAVID STARRET of Cumberland Co., Pa., (lease s5, release Ḷ 20 proc. money)...285 A, p art of a tract
of 575 A where the sd. ADEAR now lives, granted to ABRAHAM KUYKENDALL 27 Mar 1753, conveyed
to sd. ADEAR 16 & 17 May 1754....WM ADEAR (SEAL), MARY ADEAR (SEAL), Wit: SAMUEL NEISBETT,
JAMES WILLIAMSON. Rec. July term 1769.

Pp. 71-72: 26 Sept 1768, MOSES FERGUSON of Mecklenburg Co., Schoolmaster, to JAMES FERGUSON
late of Mecklenburg Co., farmer, for Ḷ 20...land on both sides Allisons Creek,
adj. WILLIAM PATRICK, originally granted to HEZEKIAH ALEXANDER 9 Nov 1764, and conveyed
by him to sd. MOSES FERGUSON...MOSES FERGUSON (SEAL), Wit: ROBERT FERGUSON, JEAN FARIS (N).
Rec. July term 1769.

Page 78: 14 Jan 1769, JOHN MAYER & wf SARAH of Tryon Co., to ANDREW HEYELL of same, for
Ḷ 20 proc. money...270 A granted to sd. MEYER 26 Oct 1767 on both sides little
long creek adj. DONISON HOWISES line...JOHN MAIER (M), SARAH MAIER (O), Wit: JOHN RITZ-
HOUPT, JOHN HEYEL, SAMUEL MARTIN. Rec. July term 1769.

Page 74: __ Feb 1769, JOHN GERRAD of Mecklenburg Co., to WILLIAM McKOWN of same, for Ḷ 20
...land on E side Broad River, on N side Bullocks Creek adj. DANIEL RICHARDSON,
granted to sd. GERRAD 29 Apr 1768, ...JOHN GERRAD (SEAL), Wit: NATH. CLARK, JOHN McLADIN,
GIDEON GERRAD (X). Rec. July term 1769.

Pp. 75-76: 12 July 1769, THOMAS JOHNSTON of Tryon Co., to JOHN McFADING SR. of same, for
Ḷ30 proc. money...land on N side Broad River, on both sides Mountain Creek,300
A...THOMAS JOHNSTON (SEAL), MARY JOHNSTON (O) (SEAL), Wit: THOMAS ROBINSON, JOHN MEGUIRE,
JOHN WALKER. Rec. July term 1769.

Pp. 75-77: 25 July 1769, JOHN WALKER & wf ELIZABETH of Tryon Co., to WILLIAM BARR of Rowan
Co., (lease s5, release Ḷ 55)...250 A on both sides Catheys Creek of 2nd Broad
River, granted to sd. WALKER, patent # 161, 26 Sept 1766...JOHN WALKER (SEAL), ELIZABETH
WALKER (SEAL), Wit: JOHN JOHNSTON, JOHN GERRAD, JOHN McTEER. Rec. July term 1769.

Pp. 77-78: 11 Mar 1769, ABRAHAM KUYKENDALL of Tryon Co., to JAMES ARMSTRONG of Orange Co.,
N. C., for Ḷ 225 proc. money...land on S side Fishing Creek adj. JAMES YOUNG,
333 A granted to sd. KUYKENDALL, 22 Apr 1763...ABRAHAM KUYKENDALL (A) (SEAL), Wit: PETER
KUYKENDALL, JOHN GORDEN, DAVID GORDEN. Rec. July term 1769.

Page 79: 27 Mar 1769, WILLIAM ARMSTRONG & wf MARGARET of Mecklenburg Co., to JACOB SIDES
of same, for Ḷ 50 NC money...200 A on branches of Leepers Creek adj. JOHN ARMSTRONG
...WILLIAM ARMSTRONG (A) (SEAL), MARGARET ARMSTRONG (M) (SEAL), Wit: GEORGE POOF, LEONARD
SAILOR. Rec. July term 1769.

Pp. 79-80: 4 Oct 1768, DANIEL McCARTY and WILLIAM SIMS of Mecklenburg Co., to GARRAT VAN-
ZANT of same, for Ḷ 36 proc. money...400 A on both sides S fork Cataba adj.
JACOB CAUSNER, including the place where sd. VANZANT now lives, near HAYLES line...DANIEL

McCARTY (SEAL), WILLIAM SIMS (SEAL), Wit: THOMAS TEVILION, GEORGE P_?. Rec. July term 1769.

Pp. 80-81: 26 July 1769, WILLIAM McKOWN of Tryon Co., to THOMAS WADE of Craven Co., S. C., for ₺ 35 proc. money...190 A on Broad River including an Island, adj. DANIEL RICHARDSON on Bullocks Creek, granted to JOHN GARROT 29 Apr 1768, conveyed by him to sd. McKOWN....WILLIAM McKOWN (SEAL), Wit: BENJAMIN THOMPSON, GEORGE McKOWN. Rec. July term 1769.

Pp. 81-82: 1 June 1768, GEORGE HEATHERLY of S. C., to WILLIAM YANCEY of Mecklenburg Co., for ₺ 20 proc. money...100 A on E side Broad River...GEORGE HEATHERLY (C), Wit: AUSTIN YANCEY, MADISON HUNT (H), SAMUEL HEATHERLY (/). Rec. July term 1769.

Pp. 82-83: 15 June 1768, MICAJAH PENNINGTON & wf RACHEL of Mecklenburg Co., to WILLIAM COLE, for ₺ 15...land granted 6 Apr 17__ to sd. MICAJAH PENNINGTON, 152 A on a branch of Fishing Creek adj. BENAJAH PENNINGTON....MICAJAH PENNINGTON (SEAL), RACHEL PENNINGTON (I) (SEAL), Wit: WILLIAM McMURRY, WM. MOORE, ANN MOORE. Rec. July term 1769.

Pp. 83-84: 8 July 1768, THOMAS RAINY & BENJAMIN RAINY of Mecklenburg Co., to THOMAS BROWN of same, for ₺ 20 proc. money...on middle ground between the waters of Sandy River and a south branch of the south fork of Fishing Creek, 500 A granted to sd. RAINEYS 8 Apr 1768...THOS RAINY (SEAL), BENJAMIN RAINY (SEAL), Wit: WM ADEAR, JAMES MOORE, THOMAS BERRY (4), Rec. July term 1769.

Pp. 84-85: 30 Aug 1768, HUGH MOORE of Mecklenburg Co., to JOSEPH COLLINS of same, for s 50...400 A on both sides Thicketty Creek, granted to sd. MOORE 27 Apr 1768... HUGH MOORE (SEAL), Wit: ZACHARIAH BULLOCK, DAVID BROWN (X). Rec. July term 1769.

Page 85: 7 June 1769, JOHN WILLIAMS of Granville Co., N. C., Attorney, to JOHN WALKER of Tryon Co., planter, for s5 proc. money...300 A on both sides Catheys Creek, granted to sd. WILLIAMS 26 Oct 1767...JOHN WILLIAMS (SEAL), Wit: LEN. HENLY BULLOCK, WILLIAM SIMS. Rec. July term 1769.

Page 86: 27 Oct 1769, JOHN WADE of Tryon Co., planter, to JOHN SADLER of same, for ₺ 70 proc. money...land on waters of Turkey Creek adj. WADES Old Store, 300 A... JOHN WADE (SEAL), Wit: JAMES FORSYTH, JAMES MURPHY. Rec. Oct. term 1769.

Pp. 86-87: 23 Oct 1769, JOHN STANDFORD of Tryon Co., to ESSEX CAPSHAW of same, son of FRANCIS CAPSHAW decd, and ELIZABETH his now relict, for natural love to his half brother sd. ESSEX CAPSHAW...half of tract on N side Main Broad River, granted to THOMAS HOOPER, 27 Apr 1767...JOHN STANFORD (SEAL), SARAH STANFORD (D) (SEAL), Wit: PETER QUIN, WILLIAM LOGAN. Rec. Oct. term 1769.

Pp. 87-88: 20 Sept 1767, ANDREW McNABB of Mecklenburg Co., to ROBERT McNABB of same, for ₺ 5 sterling...land on S fork Fishing Creek, 210 A, part of 400 A granted to sd. ANDREW__ Apr 1753...ANDREW McNABB, MARGARET McNABB (X)., Wit: ROBERT DAY, SAML DAY. Rec. Oct. term 1769.

Pp. 88-89: 23 Dec 1768, the HON. LEWIS HENRY DeROSSET of New Hanover Co., to HUGH POLLOCK of Mecklenburg Co., for ₺ 80 proc. money...land in Tryon County, formerly Anson, later Mecklenburg, on branches of Indian Creek, a South branch of the S fork of Catawba River adj. THOMAS REYNOLDS, DAVID HUDLESTON...LEWIS DeROSSET (SEAL), Wit: WILL REED, WILLIAM SIMS. Rec. Oct. term 1769.

Page 89: 27 Aug 1769, HUGH POLLOCK of Mecklenburg Co., to JAMES FOSTER of same, for ₺ 50 proc. money...land on Indian Creek, adj. THOMAS REYNOLDS, DAVID HUDLESTON, 450 A [same property as in preceding deed]...HUGH POLLOCK (SEAL), Wit: THOS. POLK, JOHN TAGERT. Rec. Oct. term 1769.

Page 90: 28 Mar 1769, WILLIAM COAL of Tryon Co., to MICHAEL STATEN, for ₺ 20...land granted to sd. COAL, 15 June 1768, on a branch of Fishing Creek, 150 A...WILLIAM COAL (Θ), Wit: JAMES YOUNG, JOHN DUNCAN, JAMES DUNCAN. Rec. Oct. term 1769.

Pp. 90-91: 28 July 1769, JOHN RUSSEL JR. of Tryon Co., to THOMAS WADE of Craven Co., S. C., for ₺ 50 proc. money...land on E side Broad River above WILLIAM LOVEs land, including an improvement which HENRY SMITH bought of MICHAEL TAYLOR, 100 A granted to HENRY SMITH 30 Oct 1765...JOHN RUSSEL (Ŧ) (SEAL), Wit: HENRY SMITH, ABRAHAM SMITH. Rec. Oct. term 1769.

Pp. 91-93: 13 June 1769, EDWARD LACEY of Tryon Co., to JOSHUA LACY and REUBIN LACY, for
Ł 50 ... 300 A on S fork Fishing Creek adj. MATHIAS ANDERS, SAMUEL GAY, JOHN
MOORE...granted to sd. EDWARD LACY 29 Apr 1768...EDWARD LACEY (SEAL), Wit : OLIVER
WALLACE, JOHN GARVIN. Rec. Oct. term 1769.

Page 93: 6 Sept 1769, ULRICK CROWDER & wf CATERINA of Tryon Co., to JOHN LINEBARGER of
same, for Ł 20 proc. money...200 A granted to CHRISTOPHER GRICE[sic] 6 Apr 1765,
on long branch of Killians Creek above JOSEHH SAILORS place...ULRICK CROWDER (SEAL),
CATARINA CROWDER (CC), Wit: JOHN RITZHOUPT, and a German signature.

Page 94: 2 Aug 1769, NICHOLAS GRANDORFF of Tryon Co., to FREDERICK WIRTERNBURG of same,
for Ł 11 proc. money...400 A granted to sd. GRANDORFF 26 Oct 1767 including the
head of Pinch Gut, waters of Hagers Fork, adj. LAWRENCE VEBURN [?]...JNO. MICHLAS.
GRANDORFF (4), Wit: JOHN RITZHOUPT, MATTHIAS BARRINGER. Rec. Oct. term 1769.

Pp. 94-95: 1 Apr 1769, PETER KUYKENDALL of Tryon Co., to JOHN CUNDAN of same, for Ł 45
...400 A on N side Fishing Creek adj. HUMPHREYs land, BEALLs corner...PETER
KUYKENDALL (SEAL), Wit: JAMES YOUNG, JOHN PRICE. Rec. Oct. term 1769.

Pp. 95-96: 5 Nov 1768, PETER LINEBARGER of Mecklenburg Co., farmer, to LODERWICK LINE-
BURGER of same, for Ł 21...200 A on E side Kuykendalls Creek...PETER LINEBURGER
(∅), Wit: DAVID JENKINS, JAMES COZART. Rec. Oct. term 1769.

Pp. 96-97: 24 Apr 1769, JAMES WYATT & BEHMILEER[?] his wife of Tryon Co., to DANIEL WYATT
of same, for Ł 12 s 5 proc. money...100 A on E side S fork Catawba River adj.
sd. JAS. WYATTs line, part of a patent to JAMES WYATT of 392 A...JAMES WYATT, BEHETHELEM
WYATT (X), Wit: PATRICK McDAVID, JOHN LOW, GEO. LUMKIN. Rec. Oct. term 1769.

Pp. 97-98: 13 Sept 1768, NICHOLAS FISHER of Tryon Co., planter, to JOHN STANDFORD of same,
for Ł20 proc. money...land on both sides Bull Creek about a mile from the mouth
adj. ROBERT HUMPHRIES line, 200 A granted 25 Apr 1767...NICHOLAS FISHER, ELIZABETH FISHER
(X), Wit: JAMES CAPSHAW, HUGH QUIN (H), HOSEPH GREEN (‡). Recż Oct. term 1769.

Pp. 98-99: 8 Mar 1769, THOMAS BLACK of Mecklenburg Co., to RICHARD WARD of same, for Ł 10
proc. money...250 A on both sides first broad River, part of a patent to sd.
BLACK 29 Apr 1768, adj. SHAWs line......THOMAS BLACK (T), Wit: WILLIAM SIMES[?], STEPHEN
LANGFORD, JOHN MOORE. Rec. Oct. term 1769.

Pp. 99-102: 18 & 19 Aug 1769, ROBERT LOVE of Craven Co., S. C. to SAMUEL BARNET of Tryon
Co., (lease sł0, release Ł210)...land in Tryon Co., formerly Anson County, on
N side Broad River, on Bullocks Creek bounded on all sides by vacant land...400 A....
ROBERT LOVE (0) (SEAL), VIOLET LOVE (0) (SEAL), Wit: THOS GILLHAM JR., JACOB BARNET.
Rec. Oct. term 1769.

Pp. 102-103: 7 Sept 1766, ROBERT McCLENACHAN & wf ELIZABETH of Mecklenburg Co., to JAMES
PATTON of Parish of St. Marks, Craven Co., S. C., gentleman, for Ł 50 NC
money...219 A on N side Catawba River, adj. to sd. river and THOMAS WILLIAMS...ROBT
McCLENACHAN (SEAL), ELIZ McCLENACHAN (SEAL), Wit: JNO SMITH, WM HAGGINS, SAML THOMPSON.
Rec. Oct. term 1769.

Pp. 103-105: 15 Sept 1755[sic], CHARLES ANDERSON & wf ELIZABETH of Mecklenburg Co., to
JAMES PATTON of St. Marks Parish, Craven Co., S. C., for 18 Pistols...land
on E side Catawba River adj. ROBERT McCLENACHAN, JOHN SILLERS[?]...granted to ROBERT
McCLENACHAN for 939 A, 24 Sept 1754, numbered 1190, conveyed to DANIEL McGLAUGHLIN, then
to JAMES MILLER, then to CHARLES ANDERSON, ___ July 1764...CHAS. ANDERSON (SEAL), ELIZA.
ANDERSON (SEAL), Wit: JNO. SMITH, WM HAGGINS, ROBT. McCLENACHAN. Rec. Oct. term 1769.
[The date of this deed is obviously in error, as evidenced by the chain
of title and the facts that Mecklenburg County was not formed until 1762,
and St. Marks Parish was not created until 1757.]

Pp. 105-106: 10 Sept 1765, CHARLES ANDERSON of Mecklenburg Co., Gentleman, to JAMES PATTON
of St. Marks Parish, Craven Co., S. C., for Ł 30 NC money...land on W side
Catawba River, adj. THOMAS WILLIAMS, granted to ROBERT McCLENACHAN for 939 A, 24 Sept
1754...conveyed to sd. CHARLES ANDERSON 14 July 1764...CHARLES ANDE RSON (SEAL), ELIZA.
ANDERSON (SEAL), Wit: JNO. SMITH, WM HAGGINS, ROBERT McCLENACHAN. Rec. Oct. term 1769.

Pp. 106-107: 26 Aug 1769, JOHN JORDAN of Tryon Co., to EZEKIEL POLK of same, for Ł 35 proc.
money...56 A on a south branch of Allisons Creek, part of a tract sold to
JORDAN by CHARLES McCLEAN 7 July 1768...JOHN JORDAN (SEAL), Wit: JNO. BARKER, THOS HENRY
(T). [Rec. date not stated.]

Pp. 107-108: 15 Jan 1770, HENRY HILDEBRAND & wf MARY of Tryon Co., to JOHN WAGGERLIN of
same, for ℔ 30 proc. money...land on W side of the South fork of Cataba on
waters of Howards Creek adj. POTTS corner, REINHARDs line, WELSHES line, 300 A...HENRY
HILDEBRAND, MARY HILDEBRAND (M), Wit: WILL REED, JAMES WITHEROW (⅟), FREDERICK WISE.
Rec. Jan. term 1770.

Pp. 108-109: 27 Sept 1769, JOHN LUSK & wf SARAH of Tryon Co., to GEORGE HEFENER of same,
for ℔ 10 proc. money...land on Pinch Gut, waters of Clarks Creek adj. JOHN
ALEXANDER, 10 A, part of 196 1/2 A granted to sd. LUSK __ Apr 1769...JOHN LUSK (SEAL),
SARAH LUSK (S) (SEAL), Wit: WILL REED, WM BARNETT. Rec. Jan. term 1770.

Pp. 109-110: ____ 1769, MARTIN DILLINGER of Tryon Co., farmer, to PETER COSNER of same,
yeoman, for ℔ 20...200 A on S side Sides' branch...MARTIN DILLINGER (SEAL),
Wit: JACOB COSTNER, DAVID JENKINS. Rec. Jan. term 1770.

Pp. 110-111: 30 Oct 1769, JOHN POTTS of Tryon Co., to CHRISTIAN REINHARDT of same, for
℔ 50 proc. money...land in Tryon Co., (formerly Anson), on waters of S fork
of Catawba River on Fishers Creek, now call'd Howards Creek, 260 A granted to SAMUEL
HAYWARD 30 Aug 1753, and at the decease of sd. SAMUEL HEYWARD, fell to JOHN POTTS, the
proper and lawful heir...JOHN POTTS (SEAL), Wit: JAMES ROBINSON, WILL REED. Rec. Jan.
term 1770.

Pp. 111-112: 24 Apr 1769, JACOB JOHNSON & wf SUSANNAH of Tryon Co., to PATRICK McDADE of
same, for ℔ 40 proc. money...100 A where the sd. McDADE now lives...on the
South Fork [?]...JACOB JOHNSTON(SEAL), SUSANNAH JOHNSTON (⌐) (SEAL), Wit: GEORGE LAMPKIN,
DAVID ALEXANDER. Rec. Jan. term 1770.

Page 112: 23 Sept 1769, GEORGE LAMPKIN of Tryon Co., to JOHN LOW of same, for ℔ 15 proc.
money...land on both sides Long Creek, granted to THOMAS RAY 20 Oct 1767, sold
by RAY to LAMPKIN, 100 A...GEORGE LAMPKIN (SEAL), Wit: JAMES WYAT, JOHN DULIN (R). Rec.
Jan. term 1770.

Page 113: 26 Dec 1769, NICHOLAS FRY & wf ELIZABETH of Tryon Co., to PHILIP FRY of same,
for ℔ 20 proc. money...land on both sides Clarks Creek, granted to sd. NICHOLAS
FRY, 21 Dec 1763...NICHOLAS FRY (NF) (SEAL), ELIZABETH FRY (Θ), Wit: WILL REED, FRAS.
McBRIDE. Rec. Jan. term 1770.

Pp. 113-114: JOHN CATHEY and JANE ERWIN, both of Prov. of N. C., to JAMES PATTERSON of
Tryon Co., ...; ℔ 120 proc. money to be paid ot sd. PATTERSON of his attorney
dated 8 May 1769, condition of the obligation, the sd. PATTERSON having bought a tract
on W side S fork Catawba River, known as HUGH IRWINs plantation...JNO. CATHEY (SEAL),
JEAN IRWIN (SEAL), Test. ALEXR. PATTERSON, HENDRY HENDRY. Rec. Jan. term 1770.

Pp. 114-115: 1 Oct 1769, JOHN NEAVE & wf EVE of Mecklenburg Co., to WILLIAM COONS of same,
for ℔ 30...land on both sides of the cane branch of Clarks Creek, 396 A,
granted 25 Apr 1767...JOHN NEAVE (SEAL), EVE NEAVE (X) (SEAL), Wit: JOHN McDOWELL, JOSEPH
DOBSON, JOSEPH McDOWELL, GEORGE BROCK. Rec. Jan. term 1770.

Pp. 115-116: 7 Sept 1768, RICHARD HENDERSON of Granville Co., N. C., to JOHN CLARK of
Mecklenburg Co., for ℔ 10 proc. money...600 A on both sides North fork of
Pacolet, adj. MARGARET CAMPBELL, JOHN WILSON...RICHD HENDERSON (SEAL), Wit: ZACHH. BULLOCK,
JOHN NICHOLS. Proven in Rowan County by RICHARD HENDERSON before M. HOWARD, C. J.
[No rec. date].

Pp. 116-117: 8 Sept 1768, JOHN CLARK of Mecklenburg Co., to JOHN POTTS of same, for ℔ 10
proc. money...600 A on North fork of Packolet adj. MARGARET CAMPBELL, JOHN
WILSON...JOHN CLARK (SEAL), Wit: ZACH. BULLOCK, JNO. NICHOLS. Proven in Salisbury
District, N. C. by JOHN CLARK before RICHARD HENDERSON.

Page 117: 19 Aug 1769, DANIEL WARLOCK & wf BARBARA of Tryon Co., to HENRY HILDEBRAND of
same, for ℔ 50 proc. money...land granted to sd. DANIEL WARLOCK 3 Sept 1753,
1000 A adj. DERICK WISE, PHILIP WARLOCK, 200 A, part of sd. 1000 A....DANIEL WARLOCK (SEAL),
BARBARA WARLOCK (C) (SEAL), Wit: WILL REED, PETER NEOMLAIER[?]. Re c. Jan. term 1770.

Page 118: 20 Dec 1769, DANIEL WARLICK & wf BARBARA of Tryon Co., to NICHOLAS WARLOCK of
same, for ℔ 50 proc. money...land on both sides the mill creek, adj. the land
he now lives on, 200 A granted 27 Oct 1767...DANIEL WARLOG (SEAL), BARBARA WARLICK (C)
(SEAL), Wit: WILL REED, PETER MEMBAN. Rec. Jan. term 1770.

Page 119: 19 Jan 1770, JOHN MILLER & wf JEAN of Tryon Co., to ROBERT SIMONTON of same,
          planter, for Ⱡ 5 proc. money...land on a branch of Turkey Creek, being the place
where HUGH SAGRIFF did live on, 100 A granted to sd. JOHN MILLER 4 May 1769....JOHN MILLER
(X) (SEAL), JEAN MILLER (1) (SEAL), Wit: PETER JOHNSTON, JOHN DONALD. Rec. Jan. term 1770.

Pp. 119-120: 19 Aug 1769, DANIEL WARLICK & wf BARBARA of Tryon Co., to NICHOLAS WARLOCK of
            same, for Ⱡ 55 proc. money...land on S fork Catawba River, including JEREMIAH
POTTS' improvements, 200 A...DANIEL WARLIG, BARBARA WARLICK (C), Wit: WILL REED, PETER
MEMBAIES[?]. Rec. Jan. term 1770.

Pp. 120-121: 16 Dec 1769, DANIEL WARLICK & wf BARBARA of Tryon Co., to DAVID RAMSOUR of
            same, for Ⱡ 50 proc. money...278 A granted to sd. WARLICK 23 Dec 1768...
DANIEL WARLICK (SEAL), BARBARA WARLICK (C) (SEAL), Wit: WILL REED, PETER MUMBAIES[?].
Rec. Jan. term 1770.

Pp. 121-122: DANIEL WARLICK & wf BARBARA to VALENTINE WARLICK of Tryon Co., for Ⱡ 50...
            land on S fork Catawba River, between TYREE HARRIS and ANDREW LAMBERT,
granted to sd. DANIEL 28 Mar 1757, 260 A...DANIEL WARLICK, BARBARA WARLICK (C), Wit:
WILL REED, PETER MOMBAIR. Rec. Jan. term 1770.   Deed dated 16 Dec 1769.

Pp. 122-123: 16 Dec 1769, DANIEL WARLICK & wf BARBARA to VALENTINE WARLICK, for Ⱡ 50 proc.
            money...land on N side Clarks Creek adj. BEAVERS line, adj. DANIEL WARLICKs
old open line, adj. DAVID RAMSOURs part...DANIEL WARLICK (SEAL), BARBARA WARLICK (C)
(SEAL), Wit: WILL REED, PETER MEMBAIN. Rec. Jan. term 1770.

Pp. 123-124: 16 Dec 1769, DANIEL & BARBARA WARLICK to ELIZABETH WARLICK, for Ⱡ 50 proc.
            money...land on Howards fork, part of a grant to sd. DANIEL 10 Apr 1761...
DANIEL WARLICK (SEAL), BARBARY WARLICK (C) (SEAL), Wit: WILL REED, PETER MORNBAIER.
Rec. Jan. term 1770.

Page 125: 28 Oct 1769, OLIVER WALLACE of Tryon Co., to JOHN ELLIS, for Ⱡ 70 proc. money...
          400 A on both sides Jumping branch, granted to sd. WALLACE 28 Apr 1768...
OLIVER WALLACE (SEAL), Wit: SAML McCULLOH, JNO. ANDERSON, JOSEPH BOGGS. Rec. Jan. term
1770.

Pp. 126-127: 20 Dec 1769, DANIEL WARLICK & wf BARBARA to MARTIN SHUFORD of Tryon Co., for
            Ⱡ 50 proc. money...land on waters of Howards Creek adj. DANIEL WARLICKs line
part of 400 A, part of the same tract part which was sold to ELIZABETH WARLICK...DANIEL
WARLICK (SEAL), BARBARA WARLICK (C) (SEAL), Wit: WILL REED, PETER MOMBAIER. Rec.
Jan. term 1770.

Pp. 127-128: 19 Aug 1769, DANIEL WARLICK & wf BARBARA to MARTIN SHUFORD of Tryon Co., for
            Ⱡ 50 proc. money...land on waters of Howards Creek adj. corner of old tract
where he now lives, 50 A granted to EZRA ALEXANDER 22 Dec 1768, adj. HENRY BULLINGER, conveyed to sd. WARLICK 11 Jan 1769...DANIEL WARLICK (SEAL), BARBARA WARLICK (C) (SEAL), Wit:
WILL REED, PETER MOMBAIR. Rec. Jan. term 1770.

Pp. 128-129: 16 Dec 1769, DANIEL WARLICK & wf BARBARA to BARBARA WARLICK of Tryon Co., for
             Ⱡ 50...land on both sides Potts' Creek adj. FREDERICK WISE, PHILIP WARLICK...
500 A...DANIEL WARLICK (SEAL), BARBARA WARLICK (C) (SEAL), Wit: WILL REED, PETER MOMBAIN.
Rec. Jan. term 1770.

Pp. 129-130: 19 Aug 1769, DANIEL WARLICK & wf BARBARA to FREDERICK WISE of Tryon Co., for
             Ⱡ 40 proc. money...land adj. PHILIP WARLICK, granted to DANIEL WARLICK, 3
Sept 1753, 1000 A...DANIEL WARLICK (SEAL), BARBARA WARLICK (C) (SEAL), Wit: PETER MEMBAIN,
WILL REED. Rec. Jan. term 1770.

Pp. 130-131: 31 Oct 1769, EZEKIEL SMITH of Tryon Co., to WILLIAM TWITTY of same, for Ⱡ 60
             proc. money...land on N side Broad River adj. and between JOHN WRIGHTS and
LILLERS[?] JOHNSONS line including his improvements...EZEKIEL SMITH (X) (SEAL), Wit: JONAS
BEDFORD, MILES HART[?]. Rec. Jan. Term 1770.

Pp. 131-132: 2 Dec 1769, WILLIAM ANDERSON of Tryon Co., to JOHN HOYLE of same, for Ⱡ 42
             s 10...280 A on both sides Little Long Creek including WABRIG CARPENTERs
ford, adj. JOHN MYERS corner, JOHN HOYLES line...250 A of which was granted to WM ANDERSON
19[?] Oct 1767...WILLIAM ANDERSON (W) (SEAL), Wit: WM MOORE, JOHN SCOTT, JAMES CUNNINGHAM
Rec. Jan. Term 1770.

Pp. 132-133: 24 Jan 1770, JOHN WALKER Esqr., of Tryon Co., to WILLIAM BARR of Rowan Co.,
             for Ⱡ 30 proc. money...300 A(excepting so much as may be found to run into

the tract where WILLIAM WRAY now lives, formerly the property of SAMUEL COBRON, on both
sides Catheys Creek of 2nd Broad River above WILLIAM RAYS, granted to JOHN WILLIAMS JUR.,
26 Oct 1767, sold by WILLIAMS to sd. WALKER 7 June 1769...JOHN WALKER (SEAL), Wit:
CHRISTIAN CARPENTER (C≠). Rec. Jan. Term 1770.

Pp. 133-134: 24 Jan 176_, DAVID WATSON of Tryon Co., planter, to WILLIAM WATSON of same,
            for Ⱡ 20...land on middle fork of Bullocks Creek, near JAMES WILSONS land...
200 A granted to DAVID WATSON 18 Nov 1764...DAVID WATSON (SEAL), Wit: JNO. CUMINS, JOHN
CHAMBERS. Rec. Jan. term 1770.

Page 134: 9 Sept 1769, JOHN HOYLE of Tryon Co., farmer, & wf MARGARET to CONROD KINDER of
          same, for Ⱡ 10 proc. money...220 A adj. PETER HOYLE...JOHN HOYLE (SEAL), MARGAR-
ET HOYLE (X) (SEAL), Wit: GARRIT VANZANT, JACOB COSTNER. Rec. Jan. Term 1770.

Page 135: 5 Jan 1770, SAMUEL WILSON of Granville Co., S. C., son and heir of SAML WILSON,
          late of Mecklenburg Co., N. C., to JACOB HOSS of Tryon Co., planter, for Ⱡ 100
money of Great Britain...400 A on S side Clarks Creek at the mouth of Fishers Creek...
SAMUEL WILSON (SEAL), JACOB HOSS (SEAL), Wit: JNO. LEWIS BAIRD, DAV. CRAIGE, JOHN DUNN.
Rec. Jan. Term 1770.

Pp. 135-136: 2 Nov 1769, JANE IRWIN, Widow, of Mecklenburg Co., relict of Hugh Irwin, decd.,
            to JAMES PATTERSON of Tryon Co., for Ⱡ 60 proc. money...239 A on W side S
fork Catawba, known as HUGH IRWINS plantation at the forks of Fishing Creek containing
HUGH IRWINS improvements...land conveyed in fee simple by DAVID MACKEY unto the said
JANE IRWIN, as appears of record by deed 3 Dec 1767, as in the records of Rowan & Mecklen-
burg may appear...JANE IRWIN (SEAL), Wit: JNO. BREVARD, WM. PATTERSON, JONATHAN GULLICK.
Rec. Jan. Term 1770.

Page 137: 29 Feb 1768, THOMAS BEATY of Mecklenburg Co., to WILLIAM BEATY & ABEL BEATY, for
          Ⱡ 50 ...land granted to JOHN BEATY __ Jan 1754, sold to sd. THOMAS BEATY 1 Jan
1756...THOMAS BEATY (SEAL), MARGARET BEATY (SEAL), Wit: ROBT McCASLAND, HUGH CATHY (8),
SAML. HUNTER (S). Rec. Jan. term 1770.

Page 138: 2 July 1769, JAMES FOSTER of Mecklenburg Co., to THOMAS ADAMS of Charlestown,
          for Ⱡ 1000 proc. money...200 A on the head waters of Bullocks Creek, also 200
A on Long Creek, also 300 A on Kings Creek, also land on the mouth of Cubs [Creb?] Creek,
several patents granted to JAMES FOSTER...total 2260 A...JAS FOSTER (SEAL), Wit: ELIZABETH
LeFAVOR, JAMES FORSYTHE. Rec. Jan. Term 1770.

Pp. 138-139: 27 Dec 1769, ROBERT McREE & wf MARGARET of Mecklenburg Co., to JOHN THOMPSON
            of same, for Ⱡ 40 proc. money...land on SW side of N fork Tager River, 300
A...ROBERT McREE (SEAL), MARGARET McREE (SEAL), Wit: THOS NUTT[?], WM BERRYHILL, ALEXANDER
McREE. Rec. Jan. term 1770.

Pp. 139-140: 29 Aug 1769, THOMAS WILLIAMSON & wf REBECCA of Tryon Co., to THOMAS BARTON,
            for Ⱡ 10 proc. money...land on Packolet River between the forks including an
improvement he bought of JAMES GREEN, 140 A granted to sd. WILLIAMSON 25 Apr 1767...THOMAS
WILLIAMSON (SEAL), REBECCA WILLIAMSON (X) (SEAL), Wit: JOHN WILLIAMSON (ᘐ), ROBT.
NELLRON[?]. Rec. Jan. term 1770.

Pp. 140-141: 20 May 1769, MARMADUKE DAURAUGH & wf ISABELLA of Craven Co., S. C., to WILLIAM
            MINTER of same, for Ⱡ 5...land on E side of Broad River, on Turkey Creek, 200
A near JAMES CAMPBELLs line, granted __ Dec 1768...MARMADUKE DAURAUGH (c) (SEAL), ISABELL
DAURAUGH (ᔑ) (SEAL), Wit: FRANCIS TRAVERSE, EDWARD LACEY, JAMES MILES. Rec. Jan. term
1770.

Pp. 142-144: 6 & 7 Jan 1769, JOHN POTTS & wf MARY of Tryon Co., to NICHOLAS CLAY of
            CUMBERLAND CO., PA., (lease s5, release Ⱡ 20 proc. mon ey)...land on S side
S fork Catawba River, adj. his own land on the S side Potts Creek, granted to THOMAS
POTTS decd, father of sd. JOHN POTTS, being the eldest son of sd. THOMAS POTTS, granted
30 Aug 1753...JOHN POTTS (SEAL), MARY POTTS (M) (SEAL), Wit: WILL REED, JACOB FORNEY[signed
in German], JAMES ROBINSON. Rec. Jan. Term 1770.

Pp. 144-146: 6 & 7 Jan 1769, JOHN & MARY POTTS to NICHOLAS CLAY (lease s5, release Ⱡ 100)
            ...456 A on S side S fork Catawba, including his deceased fathers improvements
...granted to sd. JOHN POTTS 19 Apr 1763...JOHN POTTS (SEAL), MARY POTTS (M) (SEAL), Wit:
WILL REED, JACOB _____[German signature], JAMES ROBINSON. Rec. Jan. term 1770.

Pp. 146-148: 11 & 12 Sept 1769, MATTHIAS BEAVER & wf SUSANNAH of Mecklenburg Co., to
            FREDERICK MISKEL of Tryon Co., (lease s5, release Ⱡ 9)...land on N side of

Pinch Gut, 400 A, including GEORGE DAYS improvements, granted 15 Feb 1764, on the N side JACOB AUGUAR[?]...MATTHIAS BEAVER (SEAL), SUSANNA BEAVER ( ) (SEAL), Wit: JOHN TAGERT, JOHN BEATY. Rec. Jan. term 1770.

Pp. 148-150: 23 Jan 1770, ZACHARIAH BELL of Craven Co., S. C., to WILLIAM McADOU of same, for Ł 40...land on E side Broad River, on waters of Bullocks Creek on Tius Branch, CHARLES TUIS corner, adj. land BELL bought of JOHN WHERRY, 150 A granted to sd. BELL, 30 Oct 1763...ZACHARIAH BELL (SEAL), Wit: WILLIAM McADOU, DAVID McADOU. Rec. Jan. Term 1770.

Pp. 150-151: 20 Aug 1769, WILLIAM HENRY & wf ISABELLA of Tryon Co., to ROBT ABERNATHY of same, for Ł 80 proc. money...land on W side Catawba River, granted to sd. WM HENRY 28 Feb 1754, at the Tuckasege Ford, adj. ANDREW McNABB, 300 A...WM. HENRY (SEAL), ISABELLA HENRY (SEAL), Wit: GEORGE LAMPKINS, JACOB JOHNSON, JAMES McCORD. Rec. Jan. Term 1770.

Page 151: 20 Mar 1769, HEZEKIAH PIGG & wf ELIZABETH of Tryon Co., to JAMES FORSYTHE of Mecklenburg Co., for Ł 60 proc. money...161 A on N side Broad River joining below JOHN STANDFORDs land, adj. JOHN STANFORDS corner...HEZEKIAH PIGG (SEAL), ELIZABETH PIGG (Ł) (SEAL), Wit: GEO. BLANTON. ISHAM PEOPLES (Ŧ), JOHN MYERS (X). Rec. Jan. Term 1770.

Pp. 151-153: 8 Feb 1768, MOSES WYLIE of Mecklenburg Co., planter, to ABRAHAM BELEW of same, planter, for Ł 30 sterling...150 A granted to MOSES WYLIE 27 Apr 1767 on both sides the Dutchmans or Crowders [should read Cowdens] Creek, falling into the No. side of Tygar River...MOSES WYLIE (SEAL), Wit: JAMES McELWEAN, CHAS. MOORE. Rec. Jan. term 1770.

Page 153: 12 Dec 1769, SIMON KUYKENDALL of Tryon Co., to JAMES MILLIGAN of same, for Ł 40 proc. money...land granted to JAMES KUYKENDA_L, 1 Apr ____, 300 A on S side Catawba on Kuykendalls Creek...SIMON KUYKENDALL, Wit: JOHN GORDON, JAMES HANNA. Rec. Jan. term 1770.

Page 154: 23 Aug 1769, WILLIAM WYAT of Tryon Co., to JOHN LOW of same, for Ł 15 proc. money ...land on both sides Rudisals Creek, adj. RUDISALS line, 100 A granted to sd. WILLIAM WYATT 29 Aug 1768...WILLIAM WYATT (SEAL), Wit: GEORGE LAMPKINS, JNO. McELROY, PETER LAMKIN. Rec. Jan. Term 1770.

Pp. 154-155: 25 Jan 1770, THOMAS CHILDERS & wf URDICE of Tryon Co., to PEREGREENE MAGNIS of same, for Ł 45 proc. money...250 A on both sides Buffalo Creek adj. REYNOLDS lower line and FRANCIS BEATYs line...THOMAS CHILDERS (T), URADICE CHILDERS (U), Wit: WAIGHTSELL AVERY, GEORGE WATT. Rec. Jan. term 1770.

Pp. 155-156: 14 Nov 1769, JOHN ARMSTRONG & wf MARY of Tryon Co., to JAMES CARSON, for Ł 30 proc. money...116 A on both sides Leopards Creek, granted to HANCE ADAM SNIDER, 200 A and resurveyed, conveyed by L & R to sd. ARMSTRONG...JNO. ARMSTRONG (SEAL), MARY ARMSTRONG (SEAL), Wit: GEORGE RUTLEGE, SAML RANKIN. Rec. Jan. Term 1770.

Pp. 156-157: 5 Aug 1768, WM WRAY of Mecklenburg Co., to WILLIAM MOORE of same, for Ł 90 proc. money...land on both sides the north fork of Crowders Creek, 272 A, granted 16 Nov 1764...WILLIAM WRAY (SEAL), Wit: JAMES BAIRD, DANIEL DENVER[?] (⊃). Rec. Jan. Term 1770.

Pp. 157-158: 15 Sept 1769, JOHN LOW of Tryon Co., to WILLIAM WYATT of same, for Ł 45 proc. money...land on both sides little long creek, about 4 miles up the same, on the west side of the Catawba River, granted to sd. LOW 29 Apr 1768...JOHN LOW (SEAL), Wit: GEORGE LAMKIN, JAMES WYATT, PATRICK McDAVID. Rec. Jan. Term 1770.

Pp. 158-159: 16 Nov 1769, JOSEPH CARROL & THOS CARROL of Tryon Co., to JAMES LOGAN of same, for Ł 20 proc. money...300 A on both sides little Catawba Creek, granted to sd. JOSEPH & THOS....JOSEPH CARROL (SEAL), THOMAS CARROL (SEAL), Wit: JOHN VENABLES, JOSEPH CARROL, SAML CARROL. Rec. Jan. Term 1770.

Pp. 159-160: 10 Apr 1769, RICHARD WARD & wf MARY, late of Mecklenburg Co., to WILLIAM STOCKTON of same, planter, for Ł 200 proc. money...land in Mecklenburg Co., on both sides first Little Broad River, granted to THOMAS BLACK 29 Apr 1768, 251 A adj. SHAW...RICHARD WARD (SEAL), MARY WARD (X) (SEAL), Wit: ROBERT COLLENWOOD, WILLIAM SHEPHERD, ABRAHAM FORD[??]. Rec. Jan. Term 1770.

Pp. 160-161: 6 Mar 1769, NICHOLAS TRY & wf ELIZABETH of Tryon Co., to JOHN SHUFORD of same,
for Ł 20 proc. money...land granted to sd. FRY 26 Oct 1767, between his new
survey and LEGANIERS land on W side S fork Catawba including the broad meadow...NICHOLAS
FRY (SEAL), ELIZABETH FRY (F) (SEAL), Wit: WILL REED, HENRY RIDER[?]. Rec. Jan. Term 1770.

Pp. 161-162: 4 Aug 1769, JAMES SMITH of Tryon Co., weaver, to HUGH CUMMINGS of same, for
Ł 27 proc. money...200 A, part of a tract of 300 A, in Tryon Co., formerly
Mecklenburg, on N side Broad River, on Buckners fork of Bullocks Creek...JAMES SMITH
(SEAL), Wit: JNO. CUMMING, MARY WILSON (B), Rec. Jan. Term 1770.

Pp. 162-163: 16 Jan 1769, THOMAS RAY of Prov. of Georgia, County of _____, to CORNELIUS
McCARTY of Tryon Co., for Ł 10...land on both sides NOLANDS branch, adj.
ANDREW NOLAND, 100 A granted to sd. THOMAS RAY, 26 Oct 1767...THOS RAY (SEAL), Wit: GEORGE
LAMKIN, JNO. LOW, DANIEL WYAT (X). Rec. Jan. Term 1770.

Pp. 163-164: 24 Apr 1769, JAMES WYATT & wf BEHELHELUM [sic] of Tryon Co., to JOHN WYATT of
same, for Ł 10 proc. money...100 A on E side S fork Cataba adj. PETER BOSSES
line, part of 392 A granted to sd. WYATT..JAMES WYATT (SEAL), BEHELHLEM WYATT (X) (SEAL),
Wit: PATRICK McDAVID, JOHN LOW, GEORGE LAMKIN. Rec. Jan. Term 1770.

Pp. 164-165: 6 Mar 1769, JOHN SHUFORD & wf CLARA of Tryon Co., to MARTIN SHUFORD, for Ł 10
proc. money...299 A on S side S fork Catawba adj. sd. JOHN SHUFORD, by the
branch on which sd. MARTIN SHUFORD now lives, granted to SAMUEL WILKINS 27 Sept 1751...
JOHN SHUFORD (SEAL), CLARA SHUFORD (X) (SEAL), Wit: WILL REED, HENRY RIDER.

Pp. 165-166: 10 Jan 1770, HENRY HILDEBRAND of Tryon Co., farmer, to CHRISTIAN REINHART of
same, for Ł 10 proc. money...land adj. POTTS, granted to sd. HILDEBRAND 22
Dec 1768...HENRY HILDEBRAND (SEAL), Wit: DANIEL WARLICK, JOHANNES _____[German signature].
Rec. Jan. Term 1770.

Pp. 166-167: 4 Oct 1769, HENRY JACOBS of Tryon Co., farmer, & wf SUSANNA to MICHAEL
RUDISELL, of same, for Ł 27 proc. money...land adj. AB RAHAM KEENER, 486 A
granted 4 Sept 1767...HENRY JACOBS (1) (SEAL), SUSANNAH JACOBS (V) (SEAL), Wit: ROBERT
BLACKBURN, JOHN DEAL. Rec. Jan. Term 1770.

Pp. 167-168: 24 July 1769, JAMES MOORE of Tryon Co., Sadler, to DAVID LEECH of same, for
Ł 65...226 A on S fork Fishing Creek, granted __ Dec 1763...JAS MOORE (SEAL),
RACHEL MOORE (SEAL), Wit: JOHN MOORE, SAML RAINY. Rec. Jan. Term 1770.

Pp. 168-169: 14 Oct 1769, JOHN MORRIS of Tryon Co., to WILLIAM GILBERTS of same, for Ł 45
...land adj. CLEATON, granted 26 Sept 1766, to RICHARD WARD, conveyed to sd.
MORRIS, 3 June 1769...JOHN MORRIS (SEAL), Wit: JOHN WALKER (Jurate), PHILIP PRICE, THOMAS
SIMMONDS[?], Rec. Jan. Term 1770.

Pp. 169-170: 3 June 1769, RICHARD WARD to JOHN MORRIS, for Ł 33...land on S fork of Camp
Creek adj. CLATONs land, 185 A...RICHARD WARD (SEAL), Wit: WM WRAY, JOHN
JOHNSTON, WM CRAIG. Rec. Jan. Term 1770.

Page 171: 15 Jan 1770, WILLIAM GASTON of Tryon Co., planter, to ROBERT GILLS of same, for
Ł 150 proc. money...land granted to WILLIAM LOVE, the date of the letters of
administration granted to JAMES LOVE on estates of WILLIAM LOVE decd, April 17, 1756...on
N side Broad River, and the date of JAMES LOVE's will to JANET LOVE now the wife of WM
GASTON, 27 Apr 1760...land on a branch of Moores Creek, 600 A...WILLIAM GASTON (SEAL),
JENNET GASTON (Ŧ) (SEAL), Wit: FRANCIS TRAVERSE, GEO. GILL. Rec. Jan. Term 1770.
[N. B. The will of the above mentioned WILLIAM LOVE is recorded in Anson
County, N. C.Will Book 1, page 20 (N. C. Archives # C. R. 005.801.1.) The
will of the above mentioned JAMES LOVE is recorded in Charleston, S. C.
Wills, Vol. PP, pp. 291-292.]

Pp. 172-173: 22 Jan 1770, MAJOR TEMPLE & wf MARY of Tryon Co., to JAMES PATTERSON of same,
for Ł 70...land on a branch of Allisons Creek a little above WM. McDOWELS,
near the waggon Road, 150 A a part of a grant to sd. MAJOR TEMPLE 26 Oct 1767...MAJOR
TEMPLE (SEAL), MARY TEMPLE (SEAL), Wit: ALEXANDER KENIDY, THOS POLK. Rec. Jan. Term 1770.

Pp. 173-174: 26 Apr 1770, JOHN HARDIN of Tryon Co., Farmer, to WM JOHNSTON of Albemarle
Co., Virginia, for Ł 20 proc. money...200 A on Jumping Branch of Kings Creek
...JOHN HARDIN (SEAL), Wit: THOMAS POLK, ROBT. GORDON. Rec. Apr. Term 1770.

Pp. 174-176: _____ 1768, WILLIAM NEELY of Mecklenburg Co., to JOHN CARROL of same, for
Ł 58 proc. money...land on W side Catawba, on S side N fork of Fishing Creek

granted to sd. NEELY 14 May 1768...WILLIAM NEELY (SEAL), Wit: JOHN ANDERSON, THOS Mc-
WHORTER.[Lease has HANCE McWHORTER]. Rec. Apr. Term 1770.

Pp. 176-177: 30 Dec 1769, FREDERICK RAPPER of Rowan Co., to DANIEL WILL of Tryon Co., for
ᵵ 15 proc. money...200 A on both sides of middle Creek, the upper end of a
tract of 400 A granted to sd. FREDERICK RAPPER, 23 Dec 1768...FREDERICK RAPPER (SEAL),
Wit: GEO. LAMKIN, LEONARD SAILOR (X), and two German signatures. Rec. April term 1770.

Pp. 177-178: 30 Dec 1769, FREDERICK RAPPER & wf CATHARINE of Rowan Co., to FREDERICK
TINKLER of Tryon Co., for ᵵ 15 proc. money...200 A on Middle Creek, granted
to sd. RAPPER 23 Dec 1768...FREDERICK RAPPER (SEAL), KATHARINE RAPPER (SEAL), Wit: GEORGE
LAMPKIN, LEONARD SAILER (X), and two German signatures. Rec. Apr. Term 1770.

Pp. 178-179: 3 June 1769, DAVID ROBERSON of Tryon Co., to WILLIAM GLOVER BISHOP of same,
for ᵵ 50 proc. money...land on N side Broad River on waters of Turkey Creek,
on both sides the waggon road including Wades old Store house adj. JNO. KELLYs line, JNO
WADEs line, JAMES HANNAS line...DAVID ROBERSON (SEAL), Wit: JOHN WADE, DRURY GLOVER, WM.
McKOWN. Rec. April Term 1770.

Pp. 179-180: 22 Jan 1770, WILLIAM HILLHOUSE of Craven Co., S. C., planter, to ARCHIBALD
ROBINSON of Tryon Co., for ᵵ 26 proc. money...450 A granted to MATHEW FLOYD,
deeded by him to sd. HILLHOUSE, adj. FANNINGS[?] line...WILLIAM HILLHOUSE (SEAL), Wit:
STEWARD BROWN, JOHN HILLHOUSE, JAMES HILLHOUSE. Rec. Apr. Term 1770.

Pp. 180-181: 22 Mar 1770, GEORGE MOORE of Tryon Co., to JOHN HANEY of same, for ᵵ 30 proc.
money...135 A that sd. GEORGE MOORE now lives on...GEORGE MOORE (W) (SEAL),
Wit: SUNCOCK[?] CANNON, RICHARD HUGHES, RUSSELL CANNON (X). Rec. Apr. Term 1770.

Page 181: 23 Apr 1770, FRANCIS ADAMS of Tryon Co., farmer, to GEORGE COX of same, for ᵵ 50
proc. money...50 A including the mill on Kings Creek, formerly sold to sd. ADAMS
...FRANCIS ADAMS (SEAL), Wit: WM LURK, DAVID ADAMS. Rec. Apr. Term 1770.

Page 182: 20 Feb 1770, FRANCIS BEATY & JOHN BEATY of Mecklenburg Co., farmers, to JAMES
TATE of same, for ᵵ 80 proc. money...640 A on both sides first little Broad River
...FRANCIS BEATY (SEAL), JOHN BEATY (SEAL), Wit: JAMES PULLEY, JAMES BEATY. Rec. Apr.
Term 1770.

Pp. 182-183: 16 Jan 1770, JOHN WOOLING CARPENTER of Tryon Co., to THOMAS COSTNER, farmer,
of same, for ᵵ 15 proc. money...land on Costners branch, adj. JACOB COSTNER,
300 A...JNO WOOLING CARPENTER (SEAL), Wit: HENRY MARTIN[?], JACOB COSTNER. Rec. Apr.
Term 1770.

Pp. 183-184: 17 Apr 1770, HEZEKIAH COLLINS of Tryon Co., to ISAAC COLLINS of same, for
ᵵ 2 proc. money...land on E side Kings Creek below the Milstone Branch near
MOOREs land, 200 A...HEZEKIAH COLLINS (⨍) (SEAL), Wit: FRANCIS ADAMS, JOHN CAIRNS. Rec.
Apr. Term 1770.

Pp. 184-185: 3[?] Feb 1770, JAMES McKEE of Mecklenburg Co., planter, to FRANCIS BEATY of
same, for ᵵ 22 proc. money...200 A adj. W side Catawba River, adj. originally
BENJN. HARDINS corner, now FRANCIS BEATIES...JAMES McKEE (SEAL), Wit: JAMES BEATY, THOMAS
BEATEY. Rec. Apr. Term 1770.

Pp. 185-186: 10 Mar 1770, JAMES TATE of Mecklenburg Co., to FRANCIS BEATY of same, for
ᵵ 90 proc. money...640 A on both sides Little broad River including the mouth
of Hickory Creek...JAMES TATE (SEAL), Wit: JAMES BEATY, JAMES PATTY. Rec. Apr. Term 1770.

Pp. 186-187: 30 Mar 1770, FRANCIS BEATY of Mecklenburg Co., gent., to JAMES BEATY of same,
for ᵵ 200 proc. money...318 A whereon BENJN. HARDIN did formerly dwell adj.
W side Cataba, below the Tuckasege ford adj. CATHEYs line...FRANCIS BEATY (SEAL), Wit:
FRANCES ARMSTRONG, JAMES PALLEY [PATTEY?]. Rec. Apr. Term 1770.

Pp. 187-188: 1 Dec 1769, JOHN SHARP of Rowan Co., to ALEXANDER McCARTER of Tryon Co., for
ᵵ 10 proc. money...land on both branches North Fork Tyger River below ROBT.
MILLERs land...JOHN SHARP (SEAL), Wit: WILLIAM SHARP, WALTER SHARP. Rec. Apr. Term 1770.

Pp. 188-190: 21 Feb 1770, ANDREW HESLIP of Tryon Co., planter, to JOHN HESLIP of Tryon Co.,
for natural love & affection...land adj. S side Catawba River apposite to
CHUSICKS land...60 A granted to THOMAS ROBERTSON 4 Apr 1752, and also granted to EDWARD
GIVINS & wf AGNESS unto JAMES HUGGINS by L & R, 19 & 20 Apr 1759, then to sd. ANDREW HESLIP
22 Oct 1761...ANDREW HESLIP (SEAL), Wit: ANDREW HAMPTON, BENJAMIN HIDER. Rec. Apr. Term

1770.

Pp. 190-191: 25 Nov 1769, ZECHARIAH ROUTH of Tryon Co., to MICHAEL HOYLE of same, for ₤ 3
proc. money...170 A on N side Long Creek adj. MICHAEL HOYLE, STANDLEY,
granted to sd. ZACHEUS RUTH [sic] 9 Dec 1768...ZACHEUS ROUTH (SEAL), Wit: THOS NEEL,
FREDERICK HAMBRIGHT, JOHN ROBINSON. Rec. Apr. Term 1770.

Pp. 191-192: 27 Mar 1768, JOHN McKNIT ALEXANDER of Mecklenburg Co., to SAMUEL SHARP of
Cecil County, Maryland, for ₤ 5 s 10 proc. money...land on N side Green River,
on both sides Walnut Creek adj. JOHN FIFERs upper line, 200 A granted to sd. ALEXANDER
29 Apr 1768 [sic]...JNO McKN. ALEXANDER (SEAL), Wit: WILLIAM TEMPLE, WILLIAM SHARP.
Rec. Apr. Term 1770.

Pp. 192-193: 3 May 1770, JAMES MEANS & wf RACHEL of Berkly Co., S. C., farmer, to WILLIAM
MEANS of Tryon Co., N. C.,for ₤ 10 sterling...300 A on N side Fairforest on
Michels [Mitchells] branch adj. Mitchells Line, granted to sd. JAMES MEANS 25 Apr 1767...
JAMES MEANS (T) (SEAL), RACHEL MEANS (O) (SEAL), Wit: JEAMS McLEWEAN, GEORGE PARK. Rec.
Apr. Term 1770.

Pp. 193-194: 20 Mar 1770, FRANCIS BEATY of Mecklenburg Co., to GEORGE TROUT of Tryon Co.,
for ₤ 30 proc. money...land on both sides the sholy branch of Muddy fork of
Buffalow Creek including the three forks a few poles above BENJAMIN SHAWs old place and
near FRANCIS BEATYS lowest ridge place, land granted to JAMES KELLY, then to FRANCIS BEATY
22 May 1767...FRANCIS BEATY (SEAL), Wit: JAMES TATE, JAMES PULLEY[?], GEORGE WATTS. Rec.
Apr. Term 1770.

Pp. 194-195: 9 Apr 1770, JAMES DOUGHERTY of Tryon Co., farmer, to JOHN COLLENS of same,
Wheelwright, for ₤ 20 proc. money...200 A on both sides Maple branch of
Mountain Creek below BETMANNs survey...JAMES DOUGHERTY (SEAL), Wit: FRANCIS ADAMS, ISAAC
COLLINS. Rec. Apr. Term 1770.

Pp. 195-196: 22 July 1769, THOMAS WELSH & wf ANNE of Tryon Co., planter, to REV. JOHN
FREDERICK DOUBBER , for ₤ 15 proc. money...300 A on N side Beaver Dam Creek,
waters of S fork Catawba...THOMAS WELCH (SEAL), AGNIS WELCH (1) (SEAL), Wit: JOHN
BEEMAN, ROBERT GUNTLEY [GWALTNEY?]. Rec. Apr. Term 1770.

Pp. 196-197: 21 Feb 1770, ROBERT ABERNATHY & wf SARAH of Tryon Co., to ULRICH CROWDER of
same, for ₤ 20 proc. money...land on both sides Lepers Creek...ROBERT
ABERNATHY (SEAL), SARAH ABERNATHY (SEAL), Wit: TWO GERMAN SIGNATURES. Rec. Apr. Term 1770.

Pp. 197-198: 27 Mar 1770, GABRIEL BROWN JUNER & ANNY BROWN his wife of Craven Co., S. C.,
planters, to JACOB BROWN of same, for ₤ 10 sterling...land on W side Broad
River on South fork of Browns Creek adj. WILSONs line, granted _____ 1769...GABRIEL
BROWN (X) (SEAL), ANNY [AMY?] BROWN (X) (SEAL), Wit: JOHN NUCKOLS, SHADRACH PORTER. Rec.
Apr. Term 1770.

Pp. 198-199: 30 Mar 1770, ALEXANDER KILLPATRICK of Tryon Co., to JOSEPH MOORE of same, for
₤ 5 proc. money...land on both sides N fork Pacolet, 200 A...ALEXANDER KILL-
PATRICK (SEAL), Wit: JOHN HAIL, JAMES McGRAW, JOHN PORTER. Rec. Apr. term 1770.

Pp. 199-200: 3 Jan 1770, ALEXANDER McINTER of Tryon Co., to JOHN LUSK of same, for ₤ 10
s 10...land on both sides First Little Broad River, 200 A granted _____ 1766
...ALEXANDER McONTIER (SEAL), JANET McONTIER (SEAL), Wit: JAS. COLLINS, JAS. McONTIR, JAS.
SWAFFER. [Rec. date not stated.]

Pp. 200-201: 10 Mar 1770, JOHN SEAGLE SENR of Tryon Co., planter, to JOHN SEAGLE JR.,
planter, for ₤ 50...150 A on head waters of Duarts Creek...JOHN SEAGLE
(SEAL), Wit: THOMAS NEEL, JAMES JOHNSON, PAUL WISENANT. Rec. Apr. Term 1770.

Pp. 201-202: 12 Mar 1770, MARY FEEMSTER of Tryon Co., widow, to SAMUEL FEMSTER her son of
same, for s 35....patent granted to JOHN CLARK by MATHEW ROWAN, 400 A on
S side Broad, Anson County at time of original grant...JOHN CLARK did sell to JOHN FEMSTER
150 A, part of sd. 400 A, adj. WILLIAM LOVEs line...sd. JOHN FEMSTER did make unto his
loving mother MARY FEMSTER title...MARY FEEMSTER (SEAL), Wit: ARCHA. ROBISON, THOS.
CROSBY, SARAH ROBISON. Rec. Apr. Term 1770.

Pp. 202-20 5: 7 June 1769, JAMES GORDEN & wf ANN of Tryon Co., to JAMES DUFF of same, for
(lease s5, release ₤ 20 proc. money)...150 A on both sides Beaver Dam Creek,
adj. BEATIES upper line...JAMES GORDON (SEAL), ANN GORDON (//) (SEAL), Wit: JOHN ROBIN-
SON, WILLIAM ADAMS. Rec. Apr. Term 1770.

Page 205: 27 Jan 1770, GEORGE SIGHTS & wf SUSANNA of Tryon Co., to ADAM SIGHTS of same,
        for s5 proc. money...200 A on S side Catawba on N side of S fork of Sd. River...
adj. LAWRENCE SNAPPS line, on branch of Leppers[sic] Creek...GEORGE SIGHTS (c ʃ) (SEAL),
SUSANNA SIGHTS (X) (SEAL), Wit: PAUL WISSENHUNT (P), MILES ABERNATHY. Rec. April term
1770.

Page 206: 6 June 1768, PETER KUYKENDAL of Mecklenburg Co., to JOHN STALIONS of same, for
        Ł 245 proc. money...290 A on Fishing Creek, part of three sundry tracts...
PETER KUYKENDAL (SEAL), Wit: JAMES YOUNG, JAMES KURK, DAMSEY WINBORNE. Rec. April term
1770.

Pp. 206-207: 18 Aug 1769, RICHARD WARD of Tryon Co., to JOHN McDANIEL for Ł 12...200 A
        on Indian Creek adj. MONEYS land...RICHARD WARD (SEAL), Wit: JOHN BEEMAN,
CHRISTY CARPENTER (Cℤ) Rec. April term 1770.

Pp. 207-208: 27 Mar 1770, FRANCIS BEATY of Mecklenburg Co., Gent., to JAMES PALLEY of same,
        for Ł 90...land on both sides Long Creek, a branch of S fork Cataba on both
sides of the Great Road including GEO. FROUTS' improvement, adj. THOS WALCHES corner,
granted to sd. BEATY 19 Apr 1763....FRANCIS BEATY (SEAL), Wit: JAMES TATE, JAMES BEATY,
JOHN BEATY. [Rec. date not given.]

Page 209: 30 Mar 1770, JAMES BEATY of Mecklenburg Co., planter, to FRANCIS BEATEY of same,
        for Ł 50 proc. money...300 A on both sides Hickory Creek adj. JOHN & FRANCIS
BEATIES corner...granted to JAMES BEATY, 30 Oct 1765...JAMES BEATY (SEAL), Wit: JAMES
TATE, FRANCES ARMSTRONG, JAMES PALLEY. Rec. April Term 1770.

Pp. 209-210: 28 May 1768, THOMAS MORGAN of Mecklenburg Co, to DEMSY WINBURN of same, for
        Ł 20 proc. money...75 A, part of a tract on Fishing Creek adj. land lately
purchased by JOHN HALENS [STALENS?] of PETER KUYKENDAL, part of tract granted to THOMAS
BEATY and conveyed to sd. THOMAS MORGAN...THOMAS MORGAN (T) (SEAL), Wit: JAMES STALLING,
JOHN STALIONS (Ŧ), JOHN McCULLICK. Rec. April Term 1770.

Pp. 210-211: 2 Apr 1770, FRANCIS DODDS & wf AGNES of Tryon Co, to HENRY LEECH of same,
        for Ł 12 s10...land on both sides S fork of Tyger River as surveyed by
WILLIAM DICKSON, granted to sd. DODS by patent 24 Oct 1767...FRANCIS DODS (SEAL), AGNES
DODS (SEAL), Wit: JOHN LOVIK[?], DAVID ANDERSON. Rec. April Term 1770.

Pp. 211-212: 25 Oct 1769, WILLIAM ADAMS of Tryon Co., planter, to PHILIP HENSON of same.
        for Ł5 proc. money on Wm ROBINS Creek, on the side of the North fork of
Broad River, including BARTLETT HENSONS[?] Camps...200 A granted to sd. WM ADAMS, Dec
1768...WILLIAM ADAMS (SEAL), Wit: WM SHARP, HENRY CLARK. Rec. April Term 1770.

Pp. 212-213: WILLIAM BOGAN for Ł40 pd. by JOHN TAGERT, ESQR...12 head of neat cattle,
        etc. [gives cattle marks]...20 Mar 1770...WM BOGGAN (SEAL), Wit: ROBERT
LEEPER, JAMES PATRICK. Rec. April Term 1770.

Pp. 213-214: 22 Dec 1769, ZACHARIAH BELL of Cravin Co., S. C., to PATRICK ROBINSON, for
        Ł 50...land in Tryon Co. on N side Broad River on Bullocks Creek and the long
watery brench adj. LOVE, granted to MOSES McCARTER for 300 A, 26 Sept 1766...ZACHARIAH
BELL (SEAL), MARAIET[?] BELL (M) (SEAL), Wit: ARCH ROBINSON, ANDREW LEATHEM, JAMES BEEL.
Rec. April Term 1770.

Pp. 214-215: 29 Mar 1770, JOHN FOSTER of Tryon Co., to WILLIAM YOUNG of same, for Ł 30
        s 13 d4 proc. money...land on Harrises Creek, a branch of Fairforest a little
above JOHN DAVIS survey, granted to sd. FOSTER 5 May 1769...JOHN FOSTER (SEAL), ANN
FOSTER (A) (SEAL), Wit: JAMES McLEWEAN, JOSEPH KELSO. Rec. Apr. term 1770.

Pp. 215-216: 20 July 1768, ROBERT LOVE of Mecklenburg Co., to THOMAS WADE of Craven Co.,
        S. C., for Ł 300 proc. money...land on N side Broad River on Bullocks Creek,
being the place ABRAHAM SUMMERFORD now live on, which place is known as Wades old Store,
being the upper part of that tract...granted to ROBERT LOVE by patent 17 May 1755,
375 A...ROBERT LOVE (O) (SEAL), Wit: JAMES LOVE, JOHN BROWN. Rec. Apr. term 1770.

Page 217: 26 June 1770, JAMES WILSON, brother and heir of WILLIAM WILSON, late of Anson
        Co., decd., & UNITY wf of sd. JAMES WILSON, to WILLIAM TEMPLE COLES of Rowan
Co, for Ł 100...200 A granted to WILLIAM WILSON 18 Nov 1752 ...JAMES WILSON (SEAL),
UNITY WILSON (O) (SEAL), Wit: JOHN FFIFER, DAVID DAVIDSON. Rec. July Term 1770.

Page 218: 28 July 1770, HANCE McWHORTER of Tryon Co., to JOHN BARTON of same, for Ł 90
        proc. money...245 A on both sides Crowders Creek adj. McCLEAN...HANCE McWHORTER

(SEAL), Wit: JOHN WILSON, DANA NISBET. Rec. July Term 1770.

Pp. 218-219: 8 Sept 1769, JOHN STANLEY in Georgia to BOSTIN BEST of Tryon Co, for Ł 30
proc. money...177 A granted to sd. STANLEY 22 Dec 1768 on both sides Long
Creek adj. RUTHS line, DAVID STANLEYs corner, BENNETS line...JOHN STANLEY (+++) (SEAL),
Wit: JOHN LOW, DAVID STANDLEY (D). Rec. July Term 1770.

Pp. 219-220: 10 Sept 1768, ALEXR KILPATRICK of Mecklenburg Co., planter, to JACOB WOMACK
for Ł 83 proc. money...300 A on So side of Green River on both sides of White
Oak Creek about a mile above the cherokee path, granted 25 Sept 1766...ALEXANDER KILPATRICK
(SEAL), Wit: THOS STEWARD (/), THOMAS THOR[?], VALENTINE McCANT ( ). Rec. July Term 1770.

Pp. 220-221: 1 Dec 1768, EDWARD HOGAN of Mecklenburg Co., to JOHN MOORE of same, for Ł
90 proc. money...200 A on West side Broad River on Doctors Creek adj.
COBRONS old line including sd. HOGANs improvement by an old school house branch...origin-
ally granted to JOHN BEATY, conveyed to sd. HOGAN by L & R 8 & 9 March [no year given]...
EDWARD HOGAN ( ) (SEAL), Wit: WILLIAM MOORE, JOHN SCOTT. Rec. July Term 1770.

Pp. 221-222: EZEKIEL SMITH of Tryon Co., for love, good will and affection to MARY BURTIN,
daughter of ELIZABETH BURTIN of same...negro woman Flora and cattle...23
July 1770...EZEKIEL SMITH (X) (SEAL), Wit: SAMUEL RICHARDSON, JOHN RICHARDSON. Rec. July
Term 1770i

Pp. 222-223: 20 July 1770, JAMES McBEE of Tryon Co. to JOHN WEEDINGHAM of same, for Ł 40
proc. money...500 A on S side Pacolet River on the Reedy branch including an
improvement he bought of CHARLES PARK...JAMES McBEE (SEAL), Wit: JAMES STEEN, ROBERT LOONY,
REUBIN SAFOLD. Rec. July Term 1770.

Pp. 223-224: 14 June 1770, FRANCIS BEATY of Mecklenburg Co., planter, to WILLIAM TATE of
Tryon Co, for Ł 80 proc. money...318 A on West side Broad River opposite
the mouth of Buffalo Creek, granted to sd. BEATY 26 Aug[?] 1770...FRANCIS BEATY (SEAL),
Wit: JOHN BEATY, JAMES PULLEY[?]. Rec. July Term 1770.

Page 224: EZEKIEL SMITH of Tryon Co for good will and affection to WILLIAM BASSET of same
...gift of cattle...23 July 1770...EZEKIEL SMITH (X) (SEAL), Wit: SAMUEL
RICHARDSON, JOHN RICHARDSON. Rec. July Term 1770.

Pp. 224-225: EZEKIEL SMITH of Tryon Co for good will and affection to SARAH BURTIN daughter
of ELIZABETH BURTIN of same...gift of cattle...EZEKIEL SMITH (X) (SEAL), Wit:
SAMUEL RICHARDSON, JOHN RICHARDSON. Rec. July Term 1770.

Page 225: EZEKIEL SMITH of Tryon Co., for good will and affection to ESTHER BURTIN daughter of ELIZABETH BURTIN of same...gift of cattle...23 July 1770. EZEKIEL SMITH
(X) (SEAL), Wit: SAMUEL RICHARDSON, JOHN RICHARDSON. Rec. July Term 1770.

Pp. 225-226: 20 July 1769, JAS STEEN of Tryon Co to JOHN STEEN of same, for Ł 120 proc.
money...400 A on S side Broad river on Neals Creek...JAMES STEEN (SEAL), Wit:
ROBERT LUSK, MR. MICHAEL GRAHAM, ROBERT LUNEY. Rec. July Term 1770.

Pp. 226-227: 18 Feb 1770, WILLIAM YANCEY of Tryon Co to BENJAMIN TURNER of same, for Ł 30
proc. money...100 A on East side Broad River...WILLIAM YANCEY (SEAL), SOPHIA
YANCEY (SEAL), Wit: MATTHIAS DAVID TURNER, WILLIAM ELLIS. Rec. July Term 1770.

Pp. 227-228: 20 Apr 1770, PHILIP HINSON of Tryon Co., to ABRAHAM CLEMENTS of same, for
Ł 60 proc. money...100 A on West side Broad River adj. THOMAS HOOPER, inclu-
ding a little island...PHILIP HINSON (X) (SEAL), Wit: Wit: JONAS BEDFORD, JNO. SUTTON,
JOSHUA MORGAN, Rec. July Term 1770.

Pp. 228-229: 1 Sept 1769, WILLIAM GLENN & wf JENET of Tryon Co to JOHN GILLESPIE of same,
for Ł 6 proc. money...land on S side S Fork Catawba, 200 A, granted to sd.
GLENN 23 Apr 1767...WILLIAM GLENN (φ), JANET GLENN (8). Wit: GEORGE EWING, PATRICK Mc-
DAVID, THO. HENDERSON. Rec. July Term 170.

PAGE 229: ----- 1770, JOHN McFADDIN of Tryon Co., for JOHN TURNER of same, for Ł 100 proc.
money...300 A on Mcfaddins creek of second Broad River...JOHN McFADDIN (SEAL),
Wit: WM YANCEY, ROBERT McMECAN. Rec. July Term 1770.

Page 230: THOMAS DICKSON of Tryon Co., planter, for love, good will and affection to
my loving cousin BENJAMIN DICKSON of same...220 A on Knob branch of Crowders
Creek adj. RANKINS...25 July 1770...THOMAS DICKSON (SEAL), Wit: GEORGE SADLER, JAMES BRAN-
DON. Rec. July Term 1770.

Pp. 230-231: 2 July 1770, JAMES BRIDGES of Tryon Co., to WILLIAM TWITTY of same, for Ƚ 60
proc. money...375 A on both sides Thicketty Creek including the mouth of
Memkins[?] Creek, adj. THOMAS BALMS corner, HOWARDS line...JAMES BRIDGES (SEAL), Wit:
JONAS BEDFORD, MILES HART. Rec. July Term 1770.

Pp.231-232: 7 Aug 1769, PHILIP HINSTON [sic] of Tryon Co., Yeoman, to JOHN SCOTT of same,
yeoman, for Ƚ 40 proc. money...land on N side Green River on both sides Walnut Creek adj. REYNOLDS line, 100 A granted 29 Apr 1768...PHILIP HINSTON (X) (SEAL), Wit:
WILLM CLEGHORN, JAMES MILLER. Rec. July Term 1770.

Pp. 232-233: 5 July 1770, STEPHEN JONES of Tryon Co., to JOHN JOHNSTON, half brother of
sd. STEPHEN JONES, of same, for natural love and affection...150 A, being the
westward part of land granted to sd. STEPHEN for 300 A adj. ZACHARIAH BULLOCK & ANDW.
JONES...STEPHEN JONES (SEAL), Wit: JAMES FORSYTH, ANDREW JONES. Rec. July Term 1770.

Pp. 233-234: 17 June 1770, JOHN COLLINS of Tryon Co., Wheelright, to HEZEKIAH COLLINS of
same, forƚ 10...150 A, part of a tract granted to JOHN COLLINS 1768, on both
sides Kings Creek...JOHN COLLINS (.Ħ) (SEAL), Wit: FRANCIS ADAMS, MARY (W) ADAMS. Rec.
July Term 1770.

Pp. 234-235: 13 July 1770, ROBERT ABERNATHY JUNR of Tryon Co., yeoman, to WILLIAM MOORE
of same, Gentn., for Ƚ 5 proc. money...102 A granted to sd. ABERNATHY 5 May
1769 on branches of Dutchmans Creek adj. WM. MOORES corner, CARROLS line...ROBERT ABER-
NATHY (SEAL), Wit: DAVID ALEXANDER, WILLIAM LAMKIN, ANN ABERNATHY. Rec. July Term 1770.

Pp. 235-236: 16 May 1770, JAMES HOWARD of Tryon Co., to THOMAS WADE Esq. of South Carolina
[no county given], for Ƚ 50 proc. money...250 A adj. ALEXR KILPATRICK whereon JOSEPH MOORE now lives, adj. ELIZABETH CLARKs line...JAMES HOWARD (SEAL), Wit: JNO
NICKOLDS, DAVID ROBERSON. Rec. July Term 1770.

Pp. 236-237: 11 Oct 1769, MOSES WHITELY of Tryon Co., to NICHOLAS FISHER of same, for Ƚ17
proc. money...200 A on first little Broad River adj. JOHN GEADYS [GRADYS?]
...MOSES WHITELY (SEAL), Wit: WM. YANCY, ANTHONY TURNER, AARON BURRISON. Rec. July Term
1770.

Page 237: June 15, 1770, This day appeared JOHN FONDRON and JAMES COLLINS, chosen by
JACOB MONEY of the one part and SOLOMON BEASON of the other part...cattle sale
...Sworn before JAS. McENTIRE. Rec. July Term 1770.

Pp. 237-238: 10 Dec 1769, ANDREW McNABB of Tryon Co., to JEMIMA SHARP of Mecklenburg Co.,
for Ƚ 5 proc. money... land on both sides N fork of Crowders Creek, 100 A
granted to sd. McNABB 29 Apr 1768 adj. SAMUEL GINGLES, JAMES BALDRIDGE, JOHN MARTIN...
ANDREW McNABB (SEAL), Wit: JOHN BARBER, ROBT. LATTIMORE. Rec. July Term 1770.

Pp. 238-239: 26 July 1770, WILLIAM HENRY of Tryon Co., to OLIVER WALLACE of same, for Ƚ
118 proc. money...land on S fork Fishing Creek adj. ROBERT KERR, including
his former survey and OLIVER WALLACES improvement, adj. WILLIAM DICKSON, 488 A...WILLIAM
HENRY (SEAL), Wit: JAMES ALCORN[??], WM WRAY. Rec. July Term 1770.

Pp. 239-240: 23 Apr 1770, HUGH QUIN of Tryon Co., & wf MARGARET to WILLIAM CAPSHAW of
same, for Ƚ 60 proc. money...land on S side Green River on North fork of
White Oak Creek including the forks of said creek above JOHN BLACKWELs survey, formerly
granted to JOHN WEBB, 24 Oct 1767, and by him conveyed to sd. HUGH QUIN...HUGH QUINN (H)
(SEAL), MARGARET QUINN (M) (SEAL), Wit: WM SUMMER[?], HARDY GLOVER, JAMES CAPSHAW. Rec.
July Term 1770.

Pp. 240-241: 11 July 1770, JAMES COZART of Tryon Co., planter, to GEORGE RUTLEDGE of same
for Ƚ 20 proc money...land on both sides of white Walnut Creek below the _?_
of north fork of Broad River, 300 A...JAMES COZART (SEAL), Wit: JAMES RUTLEDGE, SUSANNA
RUTLEDGE (X). Rec. July Term 1770.

Pp. 241-242: 25 May 1769, WILLIAM TWITTY of Tryon Co., to WILLIAM SAFFOLD of same, for Ƚ
5 proc. money...200 A on both sides of Bullocks Creek of Thicketty adj. HUGH
MOORES line...WILLIAM TWITTY (SEAL), Wit: WM. SAFOLD, REUBIN SAFFOLD, DAVID SAFFOLD. Rec.
July Term 1770.

Pp. 242-243: 2 June 1770, JOHN BARNS & wf RACHEL of Tryon Co., to BARBARA BARNS for s5...
81 A, granted 28 Apr 1768...JOHN BARNS (B) (SEAL), RACHEL BARNS (R) (SEAL),
Wit: THEOPHILUS FAVER, ESSIX CAPSHAW, REUBEN FAVOUR. Rec. July Term 1770.

Page 243: CHARLES MOORE of Tryon Co., for natural love and affection to son in law
ANDREW BARRY of same...land on both sides Tyger River known as Lawsons Creek
adj. HUGH LAWSON, the plantation sd. ANDREW BARRY now lives on 300 A granted to sd.
MOORE 26 Oct 1767...20 July 1770...CHAS. MOORE (SEAL), Wit: NATHL. MILLER, MARTIN OTT,
THOS. McCULLOH. Rec. July term 1770.

Page 244: 5 July 1770, STEPHEN JONES of Tryon Co., to ANDREW JONES, son of sd. STEPHEN,
for natural love and affection...1/2 of tract on Thicketty Creek, 150 A,
part of 300 A granted to sd. STEPHEN JONES adj. JOHN NICHOLS...STEPHEN JONES (SEAL),
Wit: JAMES FORSYTH, ANDREW JONES. Rec. July Term 1770.

Pp. 244-245: 20 July 1770, JOHN FULTON of Tryon Co., to JAMES DERVINE of same, for
Ł 20...100 A on a branch of Broad River...JOHN FULTON (SEAL), Wit: ROBERT
McCURDY, DAVID PORTER. Rec. July Term 1770.

Pp. 245-246: 11 Nov 1769, JAMES BRIDGES of Tryon Co., to YERBY[?] DUBERRY for Ł 100
proc. money...150 A on muddy fork of Bullocks Creek of Thicketty Creek...
JAMES BRIDGES ( ), Wit: WM. SAFFOLD, SARAH SAFFOLD, DANIEL SAFFOLD. Rec. July Term 1770.

Pp. 246-247: 21 July 1770, JOHN STANFORD & wf SARAH of Tryon Co., to GEORGE BLANTON of
same for Ł 30 proc. money...land on E side Broad River, 168 A, granted to
STANFORD __ April 1768...JOHN STANFORD ( ), SARAH STANFORD (O) (). Wit: WM. TALE[?],
WILLIAM ARNCE[?]. Rec. July Term 1770.

Pp. 247-248: 28 June 1769, JOSEPH DOOLITTLE of Tryon Co., to HEZEKIAH PIGG of same for
Ł 50...land on both sides of Doolittles Creek, 200 a...JOSEPH DOOLITTLE (℃)
Wit: GEORGE BLANTON, JOHNSON PEOPLES (Ŧ). Rec. July TErm 1770.

Pp. 248-249: 23 April 1770, ALEXANDER McINTIRE & wf JANE of Tryon Co., to JOHN LUSK of
same, for Ł ____...land on both sides Little Broad River, 300 A, granted
to sd. McINTIRE, April 1770...ALEXANDER McINTIRE (SEAL), JENNET McINTIRE (SEAL), Wit:
GEO. BLANTON, JOSEPH COLLINS. Rec. July Term 1770.

Page 249: 22 May 1769, WILLIAM TWITTY of Tryon Co., planter, to WILLIAM WILKINS of same,
for Ł 10 s 5 proc. money...200 A on ridge between Pacolet and Thicketty, granted 29 Apr 1767...WILLIAM TWITTY (SEAL), Wit: PAT MOORE, CHARLES ROBINSON, JAMES BRIDGES.

Pp. 250-251: 14 May 1770, MICHAEL RUDISEL of Tryon Co., farmer, & wf CATHARINE, for Ł 45
proc. money, pd. by JACOB BAKER of same...486 A adj. ABRAHAM KEENER, granted
to HENRY JACOBS 14 Sept 1767...MICHAEL RUDISEL ( ), CATHARINE RUSISEL (X) (), Wit:
JOHANNES _____ [German signature], ROBERT BLACKBURN. Rec. July term 1770.

Pp. 251-252: 25 July 1770, JAMES COZART of Tryon Co., to JAMES LOGAN of same, for Ł 78
proc. money...land on both sides Little Cataba, 200 A adj. above HUGH
BERRYs line, granted to sd. COZART, 16 Dec 1769...JAMES COZART (SEAL), Wit: ABEL BEATY,
ALEXR. ROBINSON. Rec. July term 1770.

Pp. 252-253: 21 July 1770, THOMAS BRANDON & wf ELIZABETH of Tryon Co., to JOHN FULTON of
same, for Ł 18 proc. money...land on N side Broad River, on Bullocks Creek,
adj. GUYAN MOORE, granted to sd. BRANDON 25 Apr 1767, 88 A...THOS BRANDON (SEAL),
ELIZABETH BRANDON (SEAL), Wit: SAMUEL FULTON, DAVID McDEW[?]. Rec. July Term 1770.

Pp. 253-254: 4 June 1770, JOHN ALEXANDER & wf ELIZABETH to GEORGE LUTES and JACOB LUTES
all of Tryon Co., for Ł 150 proc. money...land on a branch of Clarks Creek,
called Pinch Gut, 400 A granted to SAMUEL YOUNG 31 Mar 1755, and by YOUNG conveyed to
ALEXANDER 12 Apr 1755...JOHN ALEXANDER (SELA), ELIZABETH ALEXANDER (A) (SEAL), Wit:
ROBERT BLACKBURN, JOSEPH SCOTT. Rec. July Term 1770.

Pp. 254-255: 14 Feb 1770, JOHN ARMSTRONG & wf MARY of Tryon Co., to DAVID ABERNATHY of
same, for Ł 100...land on both sides Lepers Creek, 275 A...JOHN ARMSTRONG
(SEAL), MARY ARMSTRONG (SEAL), Wit: MILES ABERNATHY, BENJAMIN ARMSTRONG, ROBERT ABERNATHY.
Rec. July Term 1770.

Pp. 255-256: 15 Nov 1769, THOMAS RANEY of Tryon Co., to ROBERT ROBERSON of same, for Ł5
...land on Fishing Creek adj. WILLIAM HENRY, granted 26 Oct 1767....THOS.
RANEY (SEAL), Wit: JAMES YOUNG, AGNES YOUNG. Rec. July Term 1770.

Pp. 256-257: 28 May 1770, WILLIAM WRIGHT of Tryon Co., to MOSES WRIGHT for Ł 55...600 A
granted to sd. WRIGHT by MATHEW ROWAN, President of the Council, land on
N side Broad River on Turkey Creek...WILLIAM WRIGHT (SEAL), Wit: ARTUR HICKLIN, THOMAS
CLELAHIN[?]. Rec. July Term 1770.

Pp. 257-259: 23 July 1770, WILLIAM McADOW of Craven Co., S. C. to DAVID McADOW of same, for ₺ 20 proc. money...159 A on E side Broad River, on waters of Bullocks Creek, Tius branch, adj. land ZACHARIAH BELL bought of JOHN WHERRY, part of 150 A granted to ZACHARIAH BELL 13 Oct 1765. conveyed to sd. McADOW, 23 Feb 1770...WM. McADOU (SEAL), Wit: JOHN FULTON, JAMES McADOU. Proven July Term 1770.

Pp. 259-260: 14 July 1770, GEORGE WRIGHT of Craven Co., S. C. St. Mark's Parish, to MOSES WRIGHT, for ₺ 200 current money of S. C....600 A granted to WILLIAM WRIGHT, by Mathew Rowan, originally in Anson Co., on N side Broad River on a creek now called Turkey Creek, which land the sd. GEORGE WRIGHT had of the sd. WILLIAM WRIGHT by a will ...GEORGE WRIGHT (SEAL), Wit: JAMES CARA[?], WM. THOMPSON, ABY THOMPSON, WILLIAM WRIGHT. Proven July Term 1770.

Pp. 260-261: 11 Feb 1769, JOHN KIMBER of Mecklenburg Co., to JOHN McMICHAEL of same, for ₺ 30 proc. money...land on both sides Allisons Creek adj. Indian line... granted to sd. JOHN KIMBRE 29 Apr 1768...JOHN KIMBRE (X) (SEAL), Wit: JOHN GORDON, JABEZ EVANS, DAVID GORDON. Proven July term 1770.

Pp. 261-262: 23 Dec 1768, GILES CONNELL of Barkley[sic] Co., S. C., to ZACHARIAH GIBBS of Tryon Co, for ₺ 500 lawful money of S. C....200 A on a Reedy Branch of Fair Forest adj. GILES TOLLOTS line, granted to sd. CONNELL, 23 Dec 1768...GILES CONNELL (SEAL), Wit: WM. NEAVIL, WM. SAFOLD, JOHN WILLIAMSON (X). Proven July Term 1770.

Page 262: 19 ___ 1770, ELIZABETH McWHARTOR to THOMAS DRAPER, for ₺ 250 S. C. money...150 A on S side Pacolett River, part of 200 A granted to sd. ELEANOR McWHARTON, 26 Sept 1766...ELENOR McWHARTER (9) (SEAL), Wit: Z. GIBBS, ROBT McWHARTOR. Proven July term 1770.

Pp. 263-264: 25 July 1769, SAMUEL DAVIDSON of Tryon Co..from CURTIS CALDWELL for ₺ 100 proc. money...land on both sides Broad River and both sides Bullocks Creek adj. WRIGHTS line, CALDWELLs corner...GEORGE COWENS line, granted to sd. CALDWELL, 28 Apr 1768 ...CARTIS CALDWELL (C) (SEAL), Wit: BENJAMIN HAWES, NEWBERRY STOCKTON. Proven July term 1770.

Pp. 264-265: 19 May 1770, GEORGE HEFFNER of Tryon Co & wf ANNA to GEORGE LUTES, for ₺ 85 ...land adj. JOHN ALEXANDER, FREDERICK MARKLE, 400 A, granted 27 Dec 1768 to sd. HEFFNER...GEORGE HAFFNER (SEAL), ANNA HEFFNER (X) (SEAL), Wit: JOHN SICKMAN[?] (⌀), JOHN BLACKBURN. Proven July term 1770.

Pp. 264-265: 10 Feb 1770, WILLIAM WILLINGBURG of Rowan Co., to JOHN SHNIDER of same, for ₺ ___...350 A in Mecklenburg Co., adj. WHISNANTS[?] line, adj. JOSEPH & COMIA WILLINGBURG, granted to sd. WILLIAM WILLINGBURG, 28 Apr 1768....WILLIAM WILLINGBURG (X) Wit: JOSEPH WILLINGBURG (X). GEORGE ASSNE[?] [German signature?]. Proved July term 1770.

Pp. 266-269: 2 Jan 1768, BENJAMIN RAINY of Mecklenburgh Co., Yeoman, to ANDW. CALLEY, of same (lease s5, release ₺ 40)...330 A in Meck. Co on south side of Fishing Creek, adj. WM HANNA, JAMES HANNA, JAMES SAUING [should be YOUNG]...ALEXR. LEWIS... THOMAS McMURRAY line..., granted 25 Apr 1767, grant rec. in Book No. 12....BENJAMIN RAINEY (SEAL), Wit: RICHARD BALL, ROBERT ROBERSON (R), WILLIAM BROWN. Rec. July Term 1770.

Page 269: ROBERT WILKINS of Tryon Co., for natural love to son ALEXR. WILKINS...negro Dina...for s5 proc. money...ROBERT WILKINS (R), [no date]. Wit: JOHN NUCKOLS, PAT. MOORE. Rec. July Term 1770.

Pp. 269-270: 23 July 1770, NICHOLAS WELSH & wf ELIZABETH of Tryon, to FREDERICK WISE of same, for ₺ 30 proc money...adj. DANIEL WARLOCK, WILLIAMS, 190 A...NICHOLAS WELSH, ELIZABETH WELSH (E), Wit: WILLIAM DEARMAN (O), MARGARET WELSH (M), Proven July Term 1770.

Pp. 270-272: 25 Apr 1770, WILLIAM WRAY of Tryon Co., to LODERICK WRAY, 300 A on both sides Catheys Creek of Second Broad River...consideration ₺ 150...WILLIAM WRAY (SEAL) Wit: WILLIAM HENRY, THOMAS DICKSON. Rec. July Term 1770.

Pp. 272-273: 3 Aug 1767, CURTIS COLWELL of Mecklenburg Co., planter, to SAML DAVISON, Carpenter, for ₺ 50 proc. money...land on both sides Bullocks Creek, granted to COLWELL, 13 Oct 1765, 150 A...CURTIS COLWELL (X) (SEAL), Wit: HENRY CLARK, GEORGE COWEN, EZEKIEL GILHAM.

Page 273: 21 July 1770, DAVID LEECH & wf PRUDENCE of Tryon Co., to RICHARD SADLER for ₺ 25 N. C. proc. money...land on middle branch of fork of Fishing Creek, granted

21 Dec 1763 to JAS. MOORE, 200 A, part of sd. grant...DAVID LEECH (SEAL), PRUDENCE LEECH (SEAL), Wit: THOS. RAINY, SAML RAINEY. HENRY LEECH. Proven July Term 1770.

Page 274: 24 Apr 1770, JAMES LOGAN of Tryon Co., planter, to GEORGE GILL, clockmaker[?], of same, for ₤ 4 s15 d8 proc. money...land granted to sd. LOGAN 4 May 1769 on waters of Fishing Creek adj. GEORGE GILLs land he now lives on...JAMES LOGAN (SEAL), Wit: BENJAMIN PHILLIPS, HENRY LEECH. Proven July Term 1770.

Pp. 275-276: 7 Nov 1769, THOS RAINEY & wf ANN of Tryon Co., NC, to RICHARD SADLER of same, for ₤ 69...land that THOMAS RAINEY now lives on, on middle fork of Fishing Creek, 150 A granted 15 Nov 1764...THOMAS RAINEY (SEAL), ANN RAINEY (0) (SEAL), Wit: JAMES YOUNG, JOHN MOORE, DAVID LEECH. ANN RAINEY ack. deed 17 July 1770, before JOHN GORDON, JP. Proven July Term 1770.

Pp. 276-277: 6 Oct 1768[?], THOMAS RAINEY of Mecklenburg Co., to SAML RAINEY of same, for ₤ 50 proc. money...land on middle branch of south fork of fishing Creek adj. land where he now lives, granted to sd. THOMAS RAINEY, 17 Nov 1764...THOS RAINEY (SEAL), ANN RAINEY (0) (SEAL), Wit: RACHEL RAINEY (0), BENJAMIN RAINEY. BENJN. PHILIPS.

Pp. 277-278: 20 July 1770, JOHN RAMSEY & AGNES his wife of Tryon Co., to RICHARD JONES of same, for ₤ 62...land on W side Killions Creek, 38 A, part of 100 A granted to ANDW. KILLIAN, 30 Sept 1749, conveyed by sd. KILLIAN to RAMSEY...JOHN RAMSEY (0) (SEAL), AGNES RAMSEY (X) (SEAL), Wit: THOMAS BEATY, ABEL BEATY. Proven July Term 1770.

Pp. 278-279: 22 Dec 1770, MOSES McCARTER to WILLM BOLDING, both of Tryon Co., for ₤ 60 proc. money...land on Susey Boles branch of Turkey Creek, near McNETT ALEXRS. land, granted to sd. McCARTER, 4 May 1769, 250 A...MOSES McCARTER (SEAL), Wit: ROBERT HARPER, ALEXR. HARPER. Rec. Jan. Term 1771.

Pp. 279-280: 10 Jan 1770, WILLIAM SHARP of Rowan Co., yeoman, to THOMAS SHARP SENR, of Cecil Co., Prov. of Maryland, for ₤ 10 s 10 proc. money...land on E side Main Broad River on both sides THOMAS DILLS Creek, crossing the creek and RICHARDSONS path, sd. DILLS [GILLS?] line...308 A, granted to WM. SHARP by patent 25 Apr 1767... WILLIAM SHARP (SEAL), Wit: WALTER SHARP, SARAH THOMPSON. Rec. Oct. Term 1770.

Pp. 280-281: 8 Aug 1770, JOHN CONNER of Tryon Co., to HUGH QUINN of same, for ₤ 23 proc. money...land on N side Little Broad River, 200 A, granted 20 Oct 1767...JOHN CONNER (SEAL), Wit: PETER QUINN, HARDY GLOVER, WILLIAM PARKER (ᒣ). Rec. Oct. term 1770.

Pp. 281-283: 26 & 27 Sept 1770, DERRICK RAMSOEUR of Tryon Co., to BOSTIAN CLINE of same, for (lease s5, release ₤ 50 proc, money)...land on S fork Cataba, part of a larger tract, granted to PETER BROYAL, 3 Sept 1753, conveyed to sd. RAMSEUR by sd. BROYAL, 3 June 1758, estimated 200 A...DERRICK RAMSOUR (X) (SEAL), Wit: WILL REED, JACOB RAMSEUR, JAMES HUSTON. Proven Oct. term 1770.

Pp. 283-285: 26 & 27 Sept 1770, DERRICK RAMSEUR of Tryon Co., to JACOB CARPENTER of same, (lease s5, release ₤ 50 proc. money)...land on S fork Cataba, granted to PETER BROYAL, 3 Sept 1753...DERICK RAMSEUR (X) (SEAL), Wit: JACOB RAMSEOUR, WILL REED, JAMES HUSTON. Rec. Oct. term 1770.

Pp. 285-286: _____ 1770, MICHAEL MASTER & wf MARGARET of Tryon Co., to PETER LINEBURGER for ₤ _____...land on N branch of Clarks Creek, adj. GEORGE POSSES, granted to sd. MICHAEL MASTER 23 Dec 1768...MICHAEL MASTER (M) (SEAL), MARGARET MASTER (+) (SEAL), Wit: GEORGE DICK, _____ MAISTER (Ɫ M) [German signature]. Proven Oct. term 1770. [Court minutes for Oct. term record a deed from MICHAL MASTIN & MARY his wife to PETER LINEBERGER, proved by HENRY MASTIN.]

Pp. 286-287: 7 Aug 1764, JOHN BALAM, alias BAÚM[?], & wf MAGDALINE of Buck Co., Town of Reading, Pennsylvania, to JACOB WEIDNER of Craven Co., S. C., planter, for ₤ 14 Va. money...land on S side Broad River, on Thicketty Creek below McPETERS land, 400 A, a whole survey granted 11 May 1753...JOHANNES BAÚM [German signature], (SEAL), Wit: JAMES WHITEHEAD JUNR., SUSANNAH WHITEHEAD, JOSHUA BRADLEY, Jurate. Proven Oct. term 1770. [The grant for the above mentioned tract is in the name of HONES BALAM File #166(788); Gr. #275; Bk. 2, p. 56(10, 375), Anson County, N. C., and was resurveyed 3 July 1767, File #023, Mecklenburg Co., N. C.]

Pp. 287-288: 25 Sept 1770, SAML COBURN & wf MARGARET of Tryon Co., to JAMES COBURN of
    same, for Ŀ40...400 A on S side S fork Cataba River, adj. JOSEPH WISHARD,
adj. river...SAMUEL COBURN (+) (SEAL), MARGARET COBURN (SEAL), Wit: WILLIAM MOORE, JOHN
BENNET, ALEXANDER MOORE. Proved Oct. term 1770.

Pp. 288-289: 26 July 1770, FRANCIS ADAMS of Tryon Co., to HENRY TURNER of same, for Ŀ 10
    proc. money...100 A on E side Broad River on both sides of Kings Creek...
FRANCIS ADAMS (SEAL), Wit: DAVID ADAMS, WILLIAM SIMPSON. Rec. Oct. term 1770.

Pp. 289-290: 31 Aug 1770, ROBERT CALLDERWOOD & wf ELIZABETH, formerly ELIZABETH FREELAND,
    of Tryon Co., to PETER AKER of same, planter, of same, for Ŀ 100...on both
sides of a north branch of Beaverdam Creek, adj. CHRISLEY AKERS, formerly JOSEPH GREENS,
by survey 300 A, granted 10 Apr 1761, granted to sd. ELIZABETH FREELAND...ROBERT CALLDER-
WOOD (SEAL), ELIZABETH CALLDERWOOD (⌒ J) (SEAL), Wit: WILLIAM STOCKTON, BENJAMIN GARDEN
[?], Jurate. Rec. Oct. term 1770.

Pp. 290-291: 25 Oct 1770, JOHN PATTON of Tryon Co., to JOSEPH SMITH of same, for Ŀ 10
    sterl.,...200 A in Tryon Co., formerly Mecklenburg Co., on S side Allisons
Creek adj. JOHN KERR, JOHN TAGERT...JOHN PATTON (SEAL), Wit: RICHD BARRY, JOHN TAGERT,
FRANCIS McBRIDE. Rec. Oct. term 1770.

Pp. 291-292: 22 Jan 1770, ARCHIBALD ROBINSON & wf SARAH of Tryon Co., tO WILLIAM ROBINSON
    of same, for Ŀ 26 proc. money...450 A which ARCHIBALD ROBINSON bought of
WILLIAM HILLHOUSE, granted to MATTHEW FLOYD in 1754, bought of sd. FLOYD by WILLIAM
HILLHOUSE, 350 A out of sd. 450 A tract...ARCHIBALD ROBINSON (SEAL), SARAH ROBINSON (SEAL),
Wit: JAMES WILLSON, WILLIAM REDMAN, JAMES SCOTT. Rec. Oct. term 1770.

Pp. 292-293: 18 Oct 1770, JOHN SARTAIN of Tryon Co., to ZECHARIAH BULLOCK of same, for
    Ŀ 5 proc. money...200 A on S fork of Pacalet...JNO. SARTAIN (SEAL), Wit:
JOHN WADE, JAS. COLLINS, Jurate, WM. YANCEY. Rec. Oct. term 1770.

Pp. 293-294: 9 June 1770, THOMAS LOVELATTY of Tryon Co., to MARSHAL LOVELATTY of same, for
    s5 proc. money...200 A, part of a grant to sd. THOMAS LOVELATTY, 26 Sept
1766....THOS LAVELATTY (SEAL), Wit: JNO NICKELS, Jurate.

Pp. 294-295: 11 Oct 1770, ISRAEL PATTERSON of Tryon Co., to ANDREW PATTERSON of same, for
    Ŀ 5proc. money...land on both sides of the right hand forks of Turkies [sic]
Creek, the whole content of a grant to sd. ISRAEL PATTERSON, 6 Apr 1770, 250 A...ISRAEL
PATTERSON (I), Wit: WILLIAM DAVIS, JOHN BRYSON. Rec. Oct. term 1770.

Pp. 295-296: 15 Mar 1770, ZACHA. BULLOCK of Tryon Co., to GEORGE COWEN of same, for
    Ŀ 30 current money...land on N side of Broad River below ELIZABETH YOUNGs
land, 300 A, granted 28 Apr 1768...ZACH. BULLOCK (SEAL), Wit: ROBERT WILLSON, JACOB
GARDNER. Rec. Oct. term 1770.

Pp. 296-297: 7 Feb 1764, JAMES HENDERSON of Rowan Co., to JAMES MUCKLEROY of Mecklenburg
    Co., for Ŀ 40 proc. money...200 A granted to JOHN DICKY by Mathew Rowan,
__ Feb 1754, on S side Fairforest, on Sugar Creek, conveyed by JOHN DICKEY to sd. HENDER-
SON by deed ...JAMES HENDERSON (SEAL), Wit: WILLIAM WOFFORD, WILLIAM NORRIMAN[?], JOHN
BLASINGAME. Rec. Oct. term 1770.

Pp. 297-298: 16 Feb 1770, ROBERT SWANN & wf MARTHEW of Tryon Co., to MATTHEW COWAN of
    same, for Ŀ 15 proc. money...200 A granted to sd. ROBERT SWANN, 27 Apr 1767
...ROBT SWANN (SEAL), MARTHEW SWANN (SEAL), Wit: ANDREW COWAN, Jurate, SAMUEL SWANN. Rec.
Oct term 1770.

Pp. 298-299: 18 Aug 1770, JOHN MILLER & wf JEAN of Tryon Co., to WILLIAM WILLIAMSON of
    same, for Ŀ 20 proc. money...land on the dividing ridge between Love's
and Burlison's forks of Turkey Creek including the improvements said WILLIAMSON now lives
on adj. GEORGE RUTLEDGE, granted to sd. JOHN MILLER 16 Dec 1769...JOHN MILLER (SEAL) (8),
JEAN MILLER (1) (SEAL), Wit: PETER JOHNSTON, JOHN ROSS (∓). Rec. Oct. term 1770.

Pp. 299-300: 22 Mar 1770, PETER HOWARD of Tryon Co., to JOHN WADE of same, for Ŀ 20
    proc. money...land on a small branch of Pacolet River called Island Creek...
PETER HOWARD (SEAL), Wit: ZACHA. BULLOCK, Jurate, JOAB MITCHELL (M), VARDRY McBEE. Rec.
Oct. term 1770.

Pp. 300-301: 22 Sept 1770, MICHAEL HOYLE of Tryon Co., to JOSEPH SHELL of same, for Ŀ 25
    NC currency...land on Beaverdam Branch of Mountain Creek, granted to JACOB
COOK, 21 Dec 1760[?], 200 A, conveyed by COOK to MICHAEL HOIL....MICHAEL HOYLE (SEAL),

[German signature]. MARGRETHA HOYLE (X) (SEAL) [German signature]. Wit:PETER ZIMMERMAN [German signature], AARON BIGGERSTAFF. Rec. Oct term 1770. [Court minutes show that deed was proved by PETER CARPENTER, ZIMMERMAN is German for Carpenter.]

Pp. 301-302: 22 Oct 1770, GEORGE RUTLEDGE of Tryon Co., planter, to his son JAMES RUT-LEDGE of same, for s5 sterl.,300 A in three parcels...(1) 125 A on South side Catawba, adj. JAMES ARMSTRONG, granted unto JAMES ARMSTRONG decd. 23 Feb 1754 & also 75 A, being part of another tract, on Kuykendalls Creek, part of 300 A granted to JAMES ARMSTRONG decd, 30 Aug 1753...100 A on branches of Leepers Creek, granted to sd. GEORGE RUTLEDGE, 4 May 1769...GEORGE RUTLEDGE (SEAL), Wit: WILLIAM MOORE, Jurate; SAMUEL RAN-KIN. Rec. Oct. Ct. 1770.

Pp. 302-303: 12 Mar 1770, JAMES FANNING of Tryon Co., to JOSEPH ENGLAND of same, for ₤ 5 proc. money...land on E side Broad River on the High Shoal branch of Kings Creek above JOHN McNEAT ALEXANDER & FREDERICK HAMBRIGHT, 300 A, granted to JAS. FANNING, 26 Oct 1767...JAMES FANNING (SEAL), Wit: JAMES LOGIN, JOHN McMICHAEL. Rec. Oct. term 1770.

Pp. 303-305: 19 Feb 1770, JAMES WOODS & JOHN LYON, both of Tryon Co., to HUGH QUINN of same...whereas JOHN LYON by his letter of attorney bearing date 6 Oct 1769 rec. in _____ [Rowan?] County Court...also did sell unto sd. LYONS property in counties of Cumberland, Bladen, & Anson, Mecklenburg and Tryon in the province or in the province of South Carolina, giving unto sd. JAMES WOODS full power of attorney...now, for ₤ 40 pd. by HUGH QUINN, land that tract on the South side of Enoree River, on Rocky Creek above the shoals, now in the province of S. C., 600 A...JAS. WOODS (SEAL), Wit: JOHN TAGERT, GARRET WHITE, JOSEPH COLLINS. Rec. Oct. term 1770.

Pp. 305-306: 11 Sept 1770, ANDREW HESLEP of Tryon Co., to JOHN HASLEP of same, for s5 sterl., land on W side Catawba, adj. his own land including his own and MICAJAH PENNINGTONs improvements, opposite EDWARD CHUSICKS, SAMUEL WILSONS, the planta-tion on which the sd. ANDREW now lives, 390 A, including a survey formerly made for THOMAS ROBINSON, granted to sd. HASLEP, 16 Nov 1764...ANDREW HESLEP (SEAL), Wit: THOMAS HASLEP, HENRY HENRY. Rec. Oct. term 1770.

Pp. 306-307: 25 Oct 1770, JACOB WEIDNER of Tryon Co., to DAVID ROBERSON of same, for ₤ 30 proc. money...400 A on both sides Thicketty Creek, below McPETERS granted to HONY BALAM 11 May 1753...JACOB WEIDNER (SEAL), Wit: ROBT LUNEY, JOHN NICHOLS, ROBT. WILKINS. Rec. Oct term 1770.

Pp. 307-308: 7 Aug 1770, RICHARD GULLICK & wf MARY of Tryon Co., to JOSEPH NEEL of same, for ₤ 6 s 10 sterl...land on both sides the N fork of Mill Creek, 150 A... RICHARD GULLICK (SEAL), MARY GULLICK (SEAL), Wit: THOS NEEL, Jurate, PRESTON GOFORTH, ANDREW GOFORTH. Rec. Oct. term 1770.

Pp. 308-309: 2 June 1768, JAMES YOUNG of Mecklenburg Co., to PETER KUYKENDALL of same, for s 20...land on fishing Creek, granted 4 Sept 1753 to JOSEPH MILLICAN, then made over by him to his brother WILLIAM by will at his death, and then made by deed unto sd. JAMES YOUNG, 4 Dec 1764...JAMES YOUNG (SEAL), Wit: JAMES RISK, DEMSY WINBORNE, JOHN STALION (‡). Rec. Oct. term 1770.

Pp. 309-310: 23 Jan 1770, JAMES WOODS, attorney for JOHN LYON of Wilmington, by power of attorney recorded in Hanover County, N. C., to JOHN WOODS...400 A, formerly Anson, now Tryon County, land on south branch of GILSHOT THOMAS Creek...JAS. WOODS (SEAL), Wit: JOHN WALKER, ELIZABETH WALKER, JOHN WALKER JUNIOR. Recd. of JOHN WOODS, one negro wench, it being the consideration mentioned in the deed. Rec. Oct. term 1770.

Pp. 311-312: 21 July 1770, WILLIAM WHALEY of Craven Co., S. C., to WILLIAM STUART of Tryon County, for ₤ 34 proc. money...land on waters of Rocky Allisons Creek, adj. his own, SAMUEL WATSON, DANIEL SHAW, SIMONTON, & SIMRIL, Indian line, granted 6 May 1769, 285 A...WM. WHALEY (SEAL), Wit: THOS NEEL, Jurate, WILLIAM WILSON, SAMUEL WATSON. Rec. Oct. term 1770.

Pp. 312-313: 22 Oct 1770, WM. DAVIS of Tryon Co., to ANDREW COWAN of same, for ₤ 10 proc. money...150 on both sides Beaver Dam Creek of Bullocks Creek, adj. NIGHT... WILLIAM DAVIS (SEAL), MARY DAVIS (SEAL), Wit: MATTHEW COWAN, ANDREW PETERSON. Rec. Oct. term 1770.

Page 313: 28 Feb 1770, JOHN SLOAN of Mecklenburg Co., to THOMAS HOWE of same, for ₤ 33 proc. money...150 A on head of Clemmons Branch, adj. ALEXANDER McGINTY, granted to sd. SLOAN 15 Sept 1766...JOHN SLOAN (SEAL), Wit: JOHN CARRUTH, JOSEPH RICHEY. Rec. Oct. term 1770.

Page 314: 17 Aug 1770, SIMON KUYKENAL of Tryon Co., to BENJAMIN KUYKENDAL of same, for
Ʊ 70 proc. money...land on S fork Fishing Creek adj. JOSEPH KUYKENDAL, 285 A,
part of a tract granted to JOHN KUYKENDAL, 15 Aug 1753...SIMON KUYKENDAL (SEAL), Wit:
PETER JOHNSTON, JOSEPH KUYKENDAL. Rec. Oct. term 1770.

Page 315: 16 Aug 1770, SIMON KUYKENDAL to JOSEPH KUYKENDAL, for Ʊ 70 proc. money...185 A,
part of a tract granted to JOHN KUYKENDAL, 30 Aug 1753, adj. JAMES WILLIAMSON
...SIMON KUYKENDAL (SEAL), Wit: PETER JOHNSTON, BENJAMIN KUYKENDAL. Rec. Oct. term 1770.

Page 316: 6 Oct 1770, JOHN FONDREN of Tryon Co., to JAMES HANNA of same, for Ʊ 84 proc.
money...land on both sides of main branch of Rockey Creek about two miles from
the Saluda Road, 300 A...JOHN FONDREN (SEAL), Wit: JOHN GORDON, Jurate; CATHREN GORDON,
DA. GORDON. Rec. Oct term 1770.

Pp. 317-318: 22 Jan 1771, WILLIAM WATSON & wf VIOLET of Tryon Co., to WILLIAM ADEAR of
same, for Ʊ 75 proc. money...land on waters of fishing Creek adj. his own
line, 262 A, granted 4 May 1769...WILLIAM WATSON (SEAL), VIOLET WATSON (SEAL), Wit:
JOHN PRICE, Jurate: ROBT ADAMS, JOHN THOMPSON. Rec. Jan. term 1771.

Pp. 318-319: 14 Jan 1771, WM. GLOVER BISHOP of Tryon Co., to JOHN WALLACE of same, for
Ʊ 25 proc. money...land on N side Broad River, waters of Turkey Creek, adj.
both sides of the waggon road including Wade's old store house, adj. JOHN KELLY, JOHN
WADE, JAMES HANNA, JAMES McNABB...WM. GLOVER BISHOP, LUCY GLOVER BISHOP (+). Wit: JOHN
MOORE, THOS RANEY, BENJ. PHILLIPS. Rec. Jan. term 1771.

Pp. 319-320: 10 Dec 1770, THOS WELCH of Tryon Co., Yeoman, & wf RACHEL, to WILLIAM
BARRUCH of same, yeoman, for Ʊ 3Ʊ proc. money...land on N fork Howards
Creek between JOHN POTTS & HILDEBRAND, 200 A, granted to sd. WELCH, 3 Dec 1768...THOMAS
WELCH (T) (SEAL), RACHEL WELCH (X) (SEAL), Wit: MARTHA BLACKBURN, ROBERT BLACKBURN. Rec.
Jan. term 1771.

Page 320: 17 Jan 1771, WM. SHARP of Rowan Co., to MATTHEW HARPER of Tryon Co., for Ʊ 15
proc. money...300 A on both sides Culb Creek, granted to ROBT HENDERSON, 29
Apr 1768...WM. SHARP (SEAL), Wit: FRANCIS PRINCE[?], JOSEPH JONES.

Page 321: 22 Jan 1771, NATHANIEL JEFFREYS of Tryon Co., to DAVID GEORGE of same, for
Ʊ 200 proc. money...600 A on S side Broad River about 3 miles below GABRIEL
BROWNS...NATHL JEFFREYS (V) (SEAL), Wit: JNO NICHOLS, JNO. QUIN. Rec. Jan. term 1771.

Pp. 321-322: 21 Jan 1771, JOHN PRINCE of Tryon Co., to FRANCIS PRINCE of same, for
Ʊ 5 proc. money...land on branches of north fork of Tyger River, being
part of a tract granted to sd. JOHN PRINCE, 20 Apr 1768 adj. JOHN NISBETT, 256 A...JOHN
PRINCE (SEAL), Wit: JOHN MILLER, JOSEPH KELER. Rec. Jan. term 1771.

Pp. 322-323: GEORGE BOUNDS of Tryon Co., for natural love & affection to my loving son in
law FRANCIS PRINCE and my daughter SARAH PRINCE, wife of sd. FRANCIS...negro
Hannah & negro Ben & others...21 Jan 1771...GEORGE BOUNDS (SEAL), Wit: JOHN MILLER, JOSEPH
KELLER. Rec. Jan. term 1771.

Page 323: 2 Feb 1771, JOHN FONDREN of Tryon Co., to JAMES MURPHY, WILLIAM ADAIR, HANCE
McWHIRTER, ALEXANDER LOVE, JOHN PRICE & HENDRY NEELY, all of Tryon Co., for s5
current money of N.C....unto the sd. Representatives and their successors, of the
congregation of Bethesda...land on north side of the branch commonly known as Buckeys[?]
branch, 10 A...JOHN FONDREN (SEAL), Wit: JOHN ROBINSON, WILLIAM HANNA (W). Rec. Jan. term
1771.

Pp. 323-324: 11 Aug 1770, SAMUEL RICHARDSON & wf MARY of Tryon Co., to JOHN STANFORD of
same, for Ʊ 45...157 A on E side Broad River, patent dated 27 Apr 1767...SAM-
UEL RICHARDSON (SEAL), MARY RICHARDSON (M) (SEAL), Wit: WILLIAM CAPSHAW, JOHN NABOURS (Ŧ).
Rec. Jan. term 1771.

Pp. 324-326: 22 Jan 1770, JOHN THOMSONof Rowan Co., to ALEXANDER HEMPHILL of Tryon Co.,
for Ʊ 50...400 A in County of Mecklenburg according to the patent, but now
changed to County of Tryon on the Callibash Branch of Allisons Creek adj. HENRY JOHNSON,
granted to sd. THOMPSON, 28 Oct 1765...JOHN THOMSON (SEAL), Wit: ROBERT ADAMS, JOSEPH
HARDIN, ROBERT McAFEE. Rec. Jan. term 1771.

Pp. 326-328: 21 Apr 1769, SAMUEL & LIDDY CANNON his wife of Craven County, S. C. to
WILLIAM LEE of same, for Ʊ 10...land in Craven County, S. C., formerly
Anson County, N. C., on the N side Little River now Called Tygar River above ye mouth of

fairforest, granted to SAMUEL CANNON by North Carolina patent, 31 Aug 1753, 240 A...
SAML CANNON (SEAL), LYDIA CANNON (SEAL), Wit: JAS WHIGHT, JAMES ORR, MICHEAL LEE, Jurate.
Rec. Jan. term 1771.

Pp. 328-329: WILLIAM MOORE of Tryon Co., to ALEXR GILLELAND of same, 2 Oct 1770, for
           Ŀ 100 proc. money...272 A granted to SAML COBURN, 16 Nov 1764, sold by
COBURN to WILLIAM WRAY and by WRAY to WILLIAM MOORE, on both sides North fork of Crowders
Creek adj. and above JACOB COBURNS line...WILLIAM MOORE (SEAL), DAVID ALEXANDER, Jurate;
GEORGE LAMKIN, JOHN SCOTT. Rec. Jan. term 1771.

Pp. 329-330: 24 Jan 1771, WM SIMS of Tryon Co., to THOMAS WELCH of same, for s 24 proc.
           money...146 A on both sides of a branch of Long Creek adj. THOMAS WALSH,
granted to MATHEW FLOYD 25 Apr 1767...WILLIAM SIMS (SEAL), Rec. Jan. term 1771.

Pp. 330-331: 20 Oct 1770, WILLIAM SIMS of Tryon Co., to JOHN STANFORD of same, for Ŀ 80
           proc. money...land on Broad River at BEATYS corner, about 1/4 mile below
the mouth of Hickory Creek, thence down 1st little Broad River...162 A...WILLIAM SIMS
(SEAL), Wit: HENRY HOLLMAN, JAMES CAPSHAW, JAS. WOODS. Rec. Jan. term 1771.

Page 331: 15 Oct 1770, JOSEPH WHITE of Anson County, to MATHEW HARPER of Tryon Co., for
        Ŀ 40...land on W side Broad River, on a branch thereof called the South fork
of Pacolet, including the mouth of a Creek called Cub Creek between two tracts of land
surveyed for JAMES HUTCHINS, 640 A, granted to sd. JOSEPH WHITE, 25 Apr 1767...JOSEPH
WHITE (SEAL), EVERLIA WHITE (+) (SEAL), Wit: MATTHEW HARPER, ROBERT HARPER, Jurate. Rec.
Jan. term 1771.

Page 332: 22 Oct 1770, GEORGE PATTERSON of Tryon Co., to THOMAS PATTERSON & JAMES PATTER-
        SON of same, for Ŀ 130 proc. money...land on S side Catawba River on both sides
Allisons Creek, 325 A, conveyed by ANDREW ALLISON to JOHN McCULLOH, 25 Jan 1762, then by
McCULLOH to sd. GEORGE PATTERSON by deed 21 May 1769...GEORGE PATTERSON (SEAL), Wit:
SAMUEL BARNES, WILLIAM GARDNER, jurate. Rec. Jan term 1771.

Pp. 332-333: 4 Jan 1771, WM. WALLACE & THOMAS WALLACE his son of Tryon Co., to DAVID
           PORTER of same...THOMAS WALLACE to be apprentice to sd. PORTER to be taught
the art, trade or mistery of Cooper to serve him 14 years....WILLIAM WALLACE (+) (SEAL),
DAVID PORTER (SEAL), Wit: FRANCIS ADAMS, WILL REBD. Rec. Jan. term 1771.

Pp. 333-334: 7 Sept 1770, GEORGE COX of Tryon Co., Millwright, to JOSEPH GREEN of same
           farmer, for Ŀ 50 proc. money...50 A including the Mill on Kings Creek that
was formerly the property of FRANCIS ADAMS...GEORGE COX (GC) (SEAL), Wit: FRANCIS
ADAMS, Jurate; JACOB RANDALL. Rec. Jan. term 1771.

Pp. 334-335: 12 Dec 1770, GEORGE BLANTON of Tryon Co, to JINSWELL[?] WOOD of same, for
           Ŀ 40...168 A a grant made Apr 1768, on main Broad River...GEO. BLANTON
(SEAL), SUSANAH BLANTON (+) (SEAL), Wit: WILLIAM TATE, Jurate; LAZAROUS WOOD. Rec. Jan.
term 1771.

Pp. 335-336: 6 Aug 1770, WILLIAM DULANY of Tryon Co., yeoman, to MICHAEL GRINDSTAFF of
           same, for Ŀ 60 proc. money...land on Bells Creek, including the mouth of Bulls
fork, 640 A, patent to sd. DULANY 5 Apr 1765...WILLIAM DULANY (SFAL), MARY DULANY (M)
(SEAL), Wit: ROBERT BLACKBURN, Juate; MARTHA BLACKBURN. Rec. Jan. term 1771.

Pp. 336-337: 20 Sept 1770, JOHN PEARSON of Tryon Co., planter, to THOMAS CLARK of same,
           planter, for Ŀ 12 current money of NC...land on waters of N branch of Alli-
sons Creek...adj. DAVISONS line, the NW part of a patent of 114 A granted to sd. JOHN
PEARSON, 20 Sept 1770...JOHN PERSON (Ŧ P) (SEAL), Wit: THOMAS JEANS, Jurate: WM. McCLEŀ
MURRY. Rec. Jan. term 1771.

Pp. 337-338: 22 July 1769, JACOB GARDNER of Tryon Co., to GARRET MORRIS of same, for
           Ŀ 30 proc. money of NC...land on the heads of the S fork of Jumping branch
of Kings Creek, including four springs, granted 20 Sept 1766...JACOB GARDNER (SEAL), MARY
GARDNER (U) (SEAL), Wit: ROBERT WILLSON, JOHN McMILLIN. Rec. Jan. term 1771.

Pp. 338-339: 10 June 1770, JOHN SLOAN of Mecklenburg Co., planter, to JOHN BENNET of
           Tryon Co., for Ŀ 20 proc. money...134 A, granted to sd. SLOAN 25 Apr 1767,
adj. THOMAS HENRY, on both sides Long Creek...JOHN SLOAN (SEAL), Wit: DANIEL McCARTY,
Jurate; JAMES COOK. Rec. Jan. term 1771.

Pp. 339-340: 24 Jan 1771, WM. SHARP of Rowan Co., yeoman, to JOHN WALKER of Tryon Co.,
           for Ŀ 25 proc. money...land on both sides Cedar Creek between McDOWELLS and

SMITHS, 200 A granted to sd. WM. SHARP 22 Dec 1770...WM. SHARP (SEAL), Wit: CHARLES Mc-LANE, JNO. NUCKOLS. Rec. Jan. term 1771.

Pp. 340-341: 13 Jan 1771, GEORGE DICKEY of Tryon Co., planter, to JOHN McFADIN, planter, of same, for Ŀ 40 proc. money...land on E side main Broad River on both sides Mountain Creek, 300 A, granted 22 Dec 1768...GEORGE DICKEY (SEAL), Wit: JOHN WALKER, THOMAS JEAN. Rec. Jan. term 1771.

Page 341: 30 Oct 1770, MATTHEW FLOYD of Tryon Co., planter, to WILLIAM SIMS of same, for Ŀ 10 proc. money...400 A granted to sd. FLOYD, 25 Apr 1767, on both sides long creek aboves THOS. WELCHES...MATTHEW FLOYD (SEAL), Wit: JOSEPH NEAL, NICHOLAS NEAL (X), Jurate: Rec. Jan. Term 1771.

Page 342: 17 Aug 1770, JACOB WOMACK of Tryon Co., & wf SARAH to JAMES CAPSHAW of same, for Ŀ 150 proc. money...land on S side Green River about a mile above the Cherokee path, granted to GEORGE ALEXANDER 5 Sept 1766, conveyed to ALEXR KIRKPATRICK [sic], by him conveyed to JACOB WOMACK, 300 A...JACOB WOMACK (SEAL), SARAH WOMACK (SEAL), Wit: WILLIAM CAPSHAW, Jurate; JOSEPH GUEST[?] (+). Rec. Jan. term 1771.

Page 343: 25 July 1769, JOHN McNIT ALEXANDER of Mecklenburg Co., to FRANCIS TRAVERS of Tryon Co., for Ŀ 12...land on waters of Susy Bowls Branch, 150 A, granted to sd. ALEXANDER 26 Sept 1767...JNO. MCK. ALEXANDER (SEAL), Wit: ROBT HARPER, GARRET MORRIS, Jurate. Rec. Jan. term 1771.

Pp. 343-344: 8 Jan 1770, HENRY VARNER of Tryon Co., planter, to WILLIAM VARNER of same, for Ŀ 40 proc. money...268 A granted to sd. HENRY VERNER 29 Apr 1768, on the north fork of Crowders Creek adj. JOHN WALKER...HENRY VERNOR (H) (SEAL), REBECA VERNER (SEAL), Wit: ALEXANDER GILLELAND, Jurate; JOHN ALEXANDER, JOHN VERNER. Rec. Jan. term 1771.

Pp. 344-345: 27 Feb 1769, WILLIAM McCONNELL of Peters Township in Cumberland Co., Penn-sylvania, to THOMAS PATTON of Tryon Co., N. C., for Ŀ 30...258 A, part of 434 A granted to sd. McCONNELL 31 Mar 1753, on N side Allisons Creek including the sd. THOMAS PATTONs improvements...WILLIAM McCONNELL (SEAL), Wit: JAMES BEATEY, Jurate: FRANCIS ARMSTRONG. Rec. Jan. term 1771.

Pp. 345-346: MARTIN ARMSTRONG of Tryon Co., for Ŀ 45 proc. money of NC, to PETER KUYKIN-DAL of same, yeoman...land adj. Indian Land (Claimed by the Catawbas)... 2 Jan 1771...MARTIN ARMSTRONG (SEAL), Wit: TIMOTHY RIGGS, Jurate; JAMES SWAFFAR. Rec. Jan. term 1771.

Pp. 346-347: 24 Jan 1771, JOHN MOFFET of Tryon Co., yeoman, to ABRAHAM McCORCLE of same, for Ŀ 17 s 12 d 6 proc. money...200 A on both sides Rockey Allisons Creek, adj. between the lands of ROBERT SHAW, JOHN HENRY, granted to sd. MOFFET, 25 Apr 1767... JOHN MOFFET (SEAL), Wit: WM. SHARP, WILLIAM ADAMS. Rec. Jan. term 1771.

Pp. 347-348: ROBERT HUMPHRISS of Tryon Co., Yeoman, for Ŀ 170 pd. by ABRAHAM KUYKENDAL of same, yeoman...land on Buffalo Creek, 333 A...ROBERT HUMPHRIES (H) (SEAL), Wit: TIMOTHY RIGGS, Jurate: ROBERT M.MINN [McMINN?], DANIEL SHIPMAN. Rec. Jan. term 1771.

Pp. 348-349: 9 Oct 1770, JOHN CLARK of Tryon Co., to JOHN McGREW of same, for Ŀ 5 proc. money...land in Tryon County on the North fork of Packlet, 200 A adj. MARGARET CAMPBELL, including sd. CLARKS improvement...JNO. CLARK (SEAL), Wit: JAS. McBEE, JOHN POTTS, Jurate. Rec. Jan. term 1771.

Pp. 349-351: 7 Aug 1770, WILLIAM WILLSON & wf JANE of Craven Co., S. C. to NATHL JEFFERIES of Broad River, County and province afrsd., for Ŀ 200 current money of S. C. ...all that plantation, 600 A, in Anson Co., N. C. on S side Broad River about 3 miles below GABRIEL BROWN's land...WILLIAM WILLSON (W) (SEAL), JANE WILSON (Ŧ) (SEAL), Wit: PETER NANCE, JOHN STEDMAN (O). Rec. Jan. term 1771.

Pp. 351-353: 19 Sept 1770, [Lease and release], ANDREW WOODS & wf MARGARET of Botetourt Co., Colony of Virginia, to JAMES STAFFORD & DAN ALEXANDER, of Mecklenburg Co., N. C. (lease s5, release Ŀ 10)...land on S side Catawba, on a branch of Fishing Creek adj. GEORGE CATHEY, granted to sd. WOODS by patent 31 Mar 1753, 400 A...ANDREW WOODS (SEAL), MARTHA WOODS (SEAL), Wit: WM. WALLACE, GARET WILSON. Rec. Jan. term 1771.

Pp. 353-354: 30 Dec 1769, DANIEL PLUMER & wf MARY of fairforest settlement in the Prov. of S. C., to JOSEPH BREED JUNR of Tryon Co.,.., for Ŀ 25...100 A on N side Fair Forest, granted to SAMUEL YOUNG, 1753, for 520 A, then in Anson County, now Tryon...

sold by sd. SAMUEL YOUNG to DANIEL PLUMMER, 2 Dec 1764, rec. in Mecklenburg County Court, Jan. term 1765...DANIEL PLUMMER (SEAL), MARY PLUMMER (X) (SEAL), Wit: BENNEY BELUE, Jurate; WILLIAM PLUMMER (W). Rec. Jan. term 1771.

Pp. 354-355: 25 Jan 1771, JOHN CATHEY & wf MARY of Mecklenburg Co., to WILLIAM FALLS of Tryon Co., whereas GEORGE the third, by his Agents conveyed & make over by deed into JOHN CAUTHEY, 150 A by deed bearing date 5 Apr 1765, now for ₤ 50 proc. money, land on second Broad River, adj. above ROBERTSONs land...JOHN CATHEY (SEAL), MAREY CATHY (**?**) (SEAL), Wit: ALEXR. McLEAN, HENRY WRIGHT. Rec. Jan. term 1771.

Pp. 355-356: 22 Jan 1771, CHRISTIAN MOONEY of Tryon Co., to JOSEPH HARDIN of same, for ₤ 25 proc. money...200 A on both sides Knob Creek below the Cherokee path, including the forks...CHRISTIAN MOONEY (X) (SEAL), Wit: ROBERT McAFEE, JOHN PATTON, Jurate; ANDREW McNABB. Rec. Jan. term 1771.

Pp. 356-357: 25 July 1769, JOHN McNIT ALEXANDER of Mecklenburg County, to DAVID REED of Tryon Co., for ₤ 15...land on both sides Susy Bowles Branch, including STEPHEN WRIGHTS old improvement, 100 A granted to sd. ALEXANDER 13 Oct 1765...JNO. McK. ALEXANDER (SEAL), Wit: ROBT HARPER, GARRET MORRIS, Jurate. Rec. Jan. term 1771.

Pp. 357-358: 12 Aug 1770, JOHN MACKELMURRY of Prov. of Georgia, planter, to JOHN PATTON of Tryon Co., for ₤ 30 proc. money...250 A, on S side Catawba on both sides CHARLES MOORES branch of Allisons Creek adj. WM. HANNA, DAVISON, JOHN WILLSON...JOHN MULKELMORRY (SEAL), Wit: JOHN POTTS, Jurate; JAMES POTTS, WILLIAM BEARD. Rec. Jan. term 1771.

Pp. 358-359: 22 Jan 1771, DAVID HUDDLESTONE of Tryon Co., to WILLIAM SMART of same, for ₤ 25...240 A, on both sides Camp Branch adj. WARDS line....DAVID HUDDLESTON (**𝒹H**) (SEAL), Wit: ALEXANDER McGAUGHY, WILLIAM HUDDLESTON. Rec. Jan. term 1771.

Pp. 360-361: 30 Dec 1769, DANIEL PLUMMER & wf MARY of fair forest settlement in Prov. of S. C. to RENEY BELUE of fair forest Settlement in Tryon County, Prov. of N. C., for ₤ 300 S. C. money...land on N side fair forest, part of a grant to SAMUEL YOUNG, 520 A, 1753, lying in Anson County, afterwards in Mecklenburg County, now in Tryon County, on both sides Fair Forest...DANIEL PLUMMER (SEAL), MARY PLUMMER (X) (SEAL), Wit: JOSEPH BREED, Jurate: WILLIAM PLUMMER (W).

Page 361: 24 Oct 1769, WILLIAM HANNA & wf JANE of Tryon Co., to GEORGE SADLER of same, for ₤ 30...land on waters of fishing creek, being a part of the tract the sd. WILLIAM HANNA lives upon, and was made over to him 22 Dec 1768, Nu. 322 by patent, 100 A...WILLIAM HANA (SEAL), JANE HANNA (M) (SAEL), Wit: THOMAS CLARK, Jurate: RICHARD SADLER, JOHN SADLER. Rec. Jan. term 1771.

Pp. 361-363: 30 Aug 1769, JAMES HANNA & wf JANE of Tryon Co., to THOMAS KILLOUGH of same, for ₤ 60 proc. money...land on head waters of a Branch of Turky Creek, being the land sd. JAMES HANNAH bought of EPHRAIM McLEAN, 300 A granted to sd. JAMES HANNA, 28 Oct 1765...JAMES HANNAH (SEAL), JANE HANNA (O) (SEAL), Wit: WILLIAM HANNA, JOS. WALLACE, Jurate; ISAAC KILLOUGH. Rec. Jan. term 1771.

Pp. 363-365: 8 Aug 1770, HUGH QUIN & wf MARGARET of Tryon Co., to GEORGE BLANTON for ₤ 40 proc. money...200 A on S side Broad River on Cherokee Creek, granted 24 Sept 1754...HUGH QUIN (H) (SEAL), MARGARET QUIN (X) (SEAL), Wit: JOHN TAGERT, JOHN STANFORD, Jurate; Jan. term 1771.

Pp. 365-366: 22 Jan 1771, WILLIAM BRATTON & wf MARTHA of Tryon Co., to WILLIAM ADEAR, for ₤ 40 NC money...land on waters of S fork fishing Creek adj. ROBERT KERS, 200 A, adj. CRAFTS corner, McCLEANS land, granted to sd. BRATTON 4 May 1769...WILLIAM BRATTON (SEAL), MARTHA BRATTON (W) (SEAL), Wit: JOHN PRICE, Jurate; GEORGE SADLER, WILLIAM MANAHAN. Rec. Jan. term 1771.

Pp. 366-368: 18 Feb 1771, JAMES WOOD, late of Philadelphia, Pennsylvania, to HENRY WRIGHT of Rowan Co., N. C., for s 20...land in Tryon Co., on W side Catawba... PETER HARPILLs line on Andersons Branch of Fishers Creek, including the poplar springs, southward of the So Fork of Catawba, granted to ARCHIBALD MACLAINE, 30 Apr 1762, but now in possession of JAMES WOODs, by virtue of power of attorney from ARCHIBALD MACLAINE, bearing date New Hanover Court, 1769, 250 A...JAMES WOODS (SEAL), Wit: MOSES WINSLEY, ALEXR McLEAN. Rec. April term 1771.

Pp. 368-370: 5 Apr 1771, JOHN DAVISON & wf RUTH of Tryon Co., to HENRY GOOD of Cicell Co.,
Prov. of Maryland, (lease __, release ₺ 80 proc. money)...land on S fork
Fishing Creek adj. his own and McNABBs lines...ANDREW McNABBS corner, granted to EPHRAIM
McLEAN, 16 Nov 1764...JOHN DAVIDSON (SEAL), RUTH DAVIDSON (SEAL), Wit: ANDREW LOVE,
Jurate; JOHN DAVIDSON. Rec. Apr. term 1771.

Pp. 370-372: 1 Feb 1770, JOHN FLEMING & wf ELISABETH of Tryon Co., to JOHN TURNER of
same, for ₺ 45 proc. money...297 A on waters of Allisons Creek adj. JOHN
McNITT ALEXANDER & JOHN BUCHANAN, granted to sd. FLEMING, 4 May 1769...JOHN FLEMING (SEAL),
ELISABETH FLEMING (+) (SEAL), Wit: WILLIAM STEVENSON, JAMES McCALL. Rec. Apr term 1771.

Pp. 372-375: 24 Dec 1770, JACOB PENINGTON & wf MARY of Berkley Co., S. C., to ALEXR
LOCKART of Tryon Co., N. C. (lease s5, release ₺ 300)...300 A in the County
of Mecklenburg, on S side Broad River on Kings River[now Enoree--BHH], above WILLIAM
FERGUSONs land, including the Great Cane Bottom, granted to sd. ALEXR LOCKART, 23 Feb
1754...JACOB PENNINGTON (SEAL), MARY PENNINGTON (SEAL), Wit: NATHANAEL HILLIN, JOHN
PENINGTON. Proven by JOHN PENINGTON before ROBERT BLACKBURN, J. P.. Rec. Apr term 1771.

Pp. 375-377: 16 Feb 1771, HERMAN KOLB of Tryon Co., to FRANCIS TRAVES[sic] and JAMES
MILES of same, for (lease s5, release ₺ 50)...200 A on E side Turkey Creek
adj. between ROBERT DICKSON & ROBERT ADAMS...HERMON KOLB (SEAL), FEEPHA KOLB ; Wit:
JAS. FOWLER, JOHN KIDD. Rec. Apr. term 1771.

Pp. 377-378: 21 Feb 1770, GABRIEL BROWN JUNR to GABRIEL BROWN SENR, for ₺ 100...land on
Browns Creek adj. WILLSON, 100 A...GABRIEL BROWN (X) (SEAL), Wit: THO.
FLETCHALL, JOHN BAPTISTEAR (₺), STEWARD BROWN. Rec. Apr. term 1771.

Pp. 378-379: 28 Apr 1770, WILLIAM HAGAR of Tryon Co., to JONATHAN HODGSON, of same, for
₺ 35 proc. money...land on So side Catawba River, part of tract whereon
GEORGE HEAGER liveth, 200 A granted to GEORGE HEAGER, then conveyed to sd. WM. HEAGER
by Lease & Release, 9 Apr 1750...WILLIAM HEAGER (SEAL), ELISABETH HEAGER (1) (SEAL),
Wit: WILLIAM RAMSAY, JACOB SIDES (X), HENRY HENDRY. Rec. Apr. term 1771.

Pp. 379-380: 23 Apr 1771, DERICK RAMSOUR of Tryon Co., to NICHOLAS FRIDAY SENR of same,
for ₺ 56 proc. money...land on N side S fork Cataba River on Piney Old
Field branch, being two tracts of land formerly granted to sd. DERICK RAMSOUR, one bearing date 24 Sept 1754, the other 26 Oct 1767...DERICK RAMSOUR (X) (SEAL), Wit: HENRY
HOLLMAN Jurate, JACOB RAMSOUR. Rec. Apr. term 1771.

Pp. 380-381: 11 Feb 1771, GEORGE MIELE[?] WISENHAUNT of Tryon Co. to CHRISTIAN CARPENTER
of same, for s5 sterl....150 A granted to CHRISTIAN CARPENTER & GEORGE
MIELE WISENHUNT by patent, on both sides main Buffalo Creek Near three Mile below the
Cherokee path, patent dated 22 Apr 1767...WISENHUNT releasing his interest...GEORG
WISNANT[?] [German signature]. Wit: ERNST _____ [German signature], JOHANNES ZIMMERMAN
[German signature], _____ [German signature]. Proved by ADAM WISENHAUNT. Rec. Apr.
term 1771.

Pp. 381-382: 18 Apr 1771, VALENTINE MAUNEY of Tryon Co., to MICHAEL FLADDERMILLER of
same, for s5 sterl...200 A on a branch of Leonhards fork, granted to sd.
MAUNEY, 25 Apr 1767...VALENTINE MAUNY (SEAL), CATHARINA MAUNEY (0) (SEAL), Wit: ADAM
WISENAND, Jurate [German signature], CATHARINE CHRISTINA HOOFMANN (X), _____ BEST [German
signature]. Rec. Apr. term 1771.

Page 383: 11 Mar 1770, ABRAHAM CLEMENT of Tryon Co., to BARELET HENSON of same, for ₺ 75
proc. money...100 A adj. Wt side of Broad River adj. THOMAS HOPERS upper line
including a little Island, formerly conveyed by a deed from PHILIP HENSON to sd. CLEMENTS
...ABRAHAM CLEMENTS (0) (SEAL), Wit: JOHN McKINNEY, Jurate; ALEXANDER TURNER. Rec. Apr.
term 1771.

Page 384: 8 Apr 1771, ALEXANDER REYNOLDS of Tryon Co. to RICHD. REYNOLDS of same, for
₺ 50 proc. money...land on Buffalow Creek that runs into Broad River, formerly
conveyed to sd. ALEXANDER REYNOLDS by deed from THOS. REYNOLDS & wf MARY, 18 Jan 1759,
granted to sd. THOS REYNOLDS...ALEXANDER REYNOLDS (A) (SEAL), Wit: TIMOTHY RIGGS, HENRY
REYNOLD. Rec. Apr. term 1771.

Page 385: 5 Feb 1771, AARON BIGGERSTAFF & wf MARY of Tryon Co. to PHILIP KENSYLLER, for
₺ 74...land on NE side of S fork Catawba, on the path between AARON BIGGERSTAFF
and DERICK RAMSOUR, granted to FRANCIS BEATY 16 Nov 1764, conveyed from BEATY to sd.
AARON BIGGERSTAFF...AARON BIGGERSTAFF (SEAL), MARY BIGGERSTAFF (N) (SEAL), Wit: WILLIAM
RAMSAY, Jurate; DAVID RAMSAY. Rec. Apr. term 1771.

Pp. 386-387: _____, JOHN HALL & wf PRUDENCE of Tryon Co., to JOHN KIMBRO, for _____...
land on both sides Rocky Allisons Creek, adj. JAMES STEVINSONS corner,
200 A granted to sd. HALL 28 Apr 1768...also adj. WALTER DAVIS...JOHN HALL (Seal)
PRUDENCE HALL (SEAL), Wit: MOSES THOMPSON, ALEXANDER McWHORTER, JONATHAN FITCHELL. Rec.
Apr. term 1771.

Pp. 387-388: 12 Nov 1770, SAMUEL WATSON & wf ELISABETH of N. C. to ARCHIBALD BARRON of
same, for Ł 20 proc. money...land on waters of Rocky Allisons Creek adj.
and between New Survey SIMRAL & the Indian lands, granted to sd. WATSON 27 Apr 1767...
SAMUEL WATSON (SEAL), ELISABETH WATSON (SEAL), Wit: JOHN HALL, RICHARD BERRY. Rec. Apr.
term 1771.

Pp. 388-389: 24 Apr 1771, ROBERT ADAMS of Tryon Co., to JAMES ADAMS his son of same, for
love good will and affection...land on Allisons Creek, 300 A, part of a
tract now belonging to sd. ROBT. ADAMS...ROBT. ADAMS (SEAL), Wit: FRANS. ADAMS, JAMES
HENDRY. Rec. Apr. term 1771.

Pp. 389-390: 12 Nov 1770, SAML. WATSON & wf ELISABETH of Tryon Co., to ARCHIBALD BARRON
of same, for Ł 10 proc. money...land on waters of Rocky Allisons Creek adj.
SIMONTON, SIMERAL & his own land, part of Archibald Barrons improvements, 250 A,
granted to sd. SAML WATSON, 28 Apr 1768...SAMUEL WATSON (SEAL), ELIZABETH WATSON (SEAL),
Wit: JOHN HALL, RICHARD BERRY. Rec. Apr. term 1771.

Pp. 390-391: 18 Aug 1768, ROBERT WALTER of Mecklenburg Co., planter, to GEORGE RUTLEDGE
of same, planter, for Ł 30 proc. money...land on Leepers Creek including
improvements adj. HOGANS line...ROBERT WALTER (SEAL), Wit: SAMUEL JOHNSTON, JAMES
RUTLEDGE, Jurate. Rec. Apr. term 1771.

Pp. 391-392: 21 Mar 1771, JOHN LUSK of Tryon Co., farmer, and JAMES WILSON of same,
yeoman...for Ł 35 proc. money pd. by JAMES WILSON...land on Shady Branch of
Clarks Creek adj. HUGH MILLES Corner, granted 19 Apr 1763 to JOHN ANCRUM, and for Ł 25
proc. money sold by sd. JOHN LUSK, Dec 1769...JOHN LUSK (SEAL), SARAH LUSK (S) (SEAL),
Wit: JONATHAN GILKEY, Jurate; ROBT. BLACKBURN. Rec. Apr. term 1771.

Page 392: 19 May 1770, STOPHAL VALSAD[sic]Yeoman & wf MARY, to GEORGE HEFFENER of Tryon
Co., for Ł 20 proc. money...land on both sides Pinch Gut Creek adj. JOHN ALEX-
ANDERS corner, 150 A, granted to sd. VALSOD, 29 Apr 1768...CHRISTERH. WALBERT (SEAL),
MARY WALBERT (+) (SEAL), Wit: WILLIAM BOST[?] (W), Jurate; GEORG _____ [German signature].
Rec. Apr. term 1771.

Pp. 393-395: 27 May 1771, WILLIAM BOLDINGS of Tryon Co., to MOSES McCARTER of same,
for Ł 250 proc. money...land on Susey Bolds Branch...WILLIAM BOLDING (SEAL),
Wit: WM. MILBANK, Jurate; CATHERINE MILBANK (X). Rec. Apr. term 1771.

Pp. 395-396: 18 Dec 1769, JAMES MAHAN of Tryon Co. to WILLIAM HANNA of same, for Ł 20
N. C. money...land on Stony Fork of Fishing Creek, adj. WM. HANN JUR., &
CULP, 250 A, granted to sd. MAHAN, 22 Dec 1768...JAMES MAHAN (Ŧ) (SEAL), Wit: OLIVER
WALLACE, ALEXANDER MCELHENEY, JAMES HANNA, Jurate. Rec. Apr. term 1771.

Pp. 396-397: 20 Apr 1771, ALEXR. HAMPHILL of Tryon Co., to SAML HEMPHILL of same, for
Ł 65 proc. money...land on Callabash Branch of Allisons Creek adj. HENRY
JOHNSTON, 400 A...ALEXR. HEMPHILL (SEAL), Wit: JOHN DUNCAN, JOHN GARVIN. Rec. Apr. term
1771.

Pp. 397-398: 24 Apr 1771, JOHN BAIRD of Tryon Co., to ADAM BAIRD, his Own Son of same,
for Tender regard, Love and good will...land on little Catawba, part of the
land sd. JOHN now lives on, granted to JONATHAN NEWMAN, 7 Apr 1752, and made over to
sd. JOHN BAIRD, by L & R, 10 Sept 1762...JOHN BAIRD (SEAL), Wit: JOSEPH BRADNER. Rec.
Apr. term 1771.

Pp. 398-399: 15 Sept 1770, NICHOLAS WHISTLEHAUNT of Prov. of S. C. to PETER WHISTLENANT
of same, for Ł 40...400 A in Tryon Co, on a branch of Clarks Creek...
NICHOLAS WISENANT (X) (SEAL), Wit: EZEK. POLK, MARY POLK. Rec. Apr. term 1771.

Pp. 399-400: 13 Mar 1771, ABRAHAM WOMACK of Tryon Co., to JAMES FLEMING of same, for
Ł 18 s 10 proc. money...land granted to JOHN LARGE, conveyed by him to
JAMES ARMOR, then to DINISH DYER, then to LEONARD DOZER, then to JOHN STROUD, then to
ABRAHAM WOMACK, 26 Mar 1770...ABRAHAM WOMACK (SEAL), ELIZABETH WOMACK (E) (SEAL), Wit:
JAMES PRICE, HENRY HENDRY, THOMAS BEATY, Jurate. Rec. Apr. term 1771.

Pp. 400-401: 26 Feb 1771, ABRAHAM HOLLINGSWORTH of Parish of St. Mark, Prov. of S. C.,
planter, to JAMES HAWKINS, planter of parish and prov. aforesd., for ₺ 150
So. currency...145 A in county of Mecklenburg, on S side Broad River on both sides of
Cane Creek, granted 11 Aug 1763...ABRM. HOLLINSWORTH (SEAL), EMEY[?] HOLLINGSWORTH
(SEAL), Wit: ELIAS HOLLINSWORTH J. P., JOHN HAWKINS, Jurate; ISAAC FREIGER[?] (₺).
Rec. Apr. term 1771.

Pp. 401-402: 16 June 1770, JACOB GARDNER of Tryon Co., to BARNET BURNS of same, for
₺ 20 proc. money...100 A granted 22 Apr 1767...JACOB GARDNER (SEAL), Wit:
JOHN BARNS, PETER JONES, MOSES BARNES. Rec. Apr. term 1771.

Pp. 402-403: 20 Feb 1771, JOHN LUSK, SARAH LUSK & WM. BARNET of Tryon Co., to THOMAS
MARIN for ₺ 30 proc. money...186 A in Fitzgeralds Creek adj. ALEXANDER,
SIMON SHERSES...JOHN LUSK (SEAL), SARAH LUSK (S) (SEAL), WILLIAM BARNET (SEAL), Wit:
NICHOLAS FISHER, Jurate, JO. SARTAIN, WILLIAM LUSK. Rec. Apr. term 1771.

Pp. 403-404: 6 Oct 1770, CHARLES QUAIL of Craven Co., S. C., to THOS MITCHEL of same,
for ₺ 200 proc. money...land on N side Broad River on a branch of Bullocks
Creek, 250 A, granted to sd. QUAIL 1763...CHARLES QUYEL (SEAL), Wit: JOHN GRESSET, AARON
LOCKERT, Jurate; EDWARD GRIFFIN (X). Rec. Apr. term 1771.

Pp. 404-405: 22 Apr 1770, FRANCIS GUTHREY & wf FRANCES of Tryon Co., to JAMES PURSLEY of
same, for ₺ 15 proc. money...land on Allisons Creek adj. JOHN HENRY,
JOHN BUCHANAN, 132 A granted to sd. GUTHREY 4 May 1769...FRANCIS GUTHREY (SEAL), FRANCES
GUTHREY (O) (SEAL), Wit: WILLIAM SWENSON,   ALEXANDER STEVENSON, Jurate. Rec. Apr.
term 1771.

Pp. 405-406: JOHN BEEMAN of Tryon Co., for ₺ 30 proc. money pd. by PETER ACKER of same...
350 A on Indian Creek, granted to FRANCIS BEATTY 6 Apr 1765...JOHN BEEMAN
(SEAL), MARGET BEEMAN (SEAL), Wit: TIMOTHY RIGGS, Jurate; JOHANN _____ [German signa-
ture]. Rec. Apr. term 1771

Pp. 406-407: 25 Jan 1769, ORSIMUS[?] RUPERT of Towan Co., Farmer, to DAVID JENKINS of
same, for ₺ 15...tract of land which he holds of the most westerly end of
a tract which DANIEL McCARTY sold unto DAVID JENKINS & JAMES COZORT, about 50 A...
part of a tract of 500 A, granted to ORSIMUS RUPART, 21 Apr 1764 on long Creek in the
County of Mecklenburg on the S side of S fork Catawba River...ERASMUS RUPERT (SEAL),
Wit: SARAH COGDALE (X), NICHOLAS FRIDIG [German signature], jurate. Rec. Apr. term 1771.

Pp. 407-408: 24 Apr 1771, MATTHEW BIGGER of Tryon Co., to JOSEPH HOWE of same, for ₺ 45
proc. money...land on W side Crowders Creek adj. the land sd. HOWE now
lives on...49 A...MATTHEW BIGGER (SEAL), Wit: WILLIAM PATRICK, BENJAMIN DAVIDSON,
THOMAS CAMPBELL. Rec. Apr. term 1771.

Pp. 408-409: 28 Apr 1770, WILLIAM HAGER of Tryon Co., to JONATHAN HODGSON & LEVI HODG-
SON, both of same, for love & affection to them...100 A on S side Catawba
River on Killions Creek above HEAGERS land, granted to sd. HEAGER, 23 Feb 1754...WILLIAM
HEAGER(SEAL), ELIZABETH HEGGAR (A) (SEAL), Wit: WILLIAM RAMSEY, JACOB SIDES (X), HENRY
HENDRY. Rec. Apr. term 1771.

Pp. 409-410: 22 Nov 1770, ROBERT SWANN of Tryon Co., planter, to JAMES TEMPLETON of
same, for ₺ 75 proc. money...240 A on a branch of Bullocks Creek adj.
LAUGHLIN...ROBT SWANN (SEAL), Wit: DAVID NISBIT, MATTHEW PORTER. Rec. Apr. term 1771.

Pp. 410-411: 9 Apr 1771, JAMES ARMOR, JAMES ALLCORN & wf KATHERINE of Tryon Co., planters, to WM. ARMSTRONG of same, for ₺ 22 proc. money...land on SW side
Catawba River, on both sides Beaver dam Creek adj. land of JAMES CAMPBELL & JAMES ARMOR
including sd. JAMES ALLCORNS improvements...near MR. CAMPBELLs garden, part of a tract
granted to JOHN THOMAS...JAMES ARMOR (SEAL), JAMES ALLCORN (SEAL), CATHARINE ALL
(O) (SEAL), Wit: JOHN BEATY, FRANCIS ARMSTRONG, Jurate; ROBT ARMSTRONG. Rec. Apr. term
1771.

Pp. 411-412: 18 Feb 1770, MATTHEW PORTER & wf MARY of Tryon Co., to JAMES PORTER of
same, for ₺ 20 proc. money...300 A on Turkey Creek adj. DAVID BYERS,
granted 22 Dec 1769...MATTHEW PORTER (SEAL), MARY PORTER (M) (SEAL), Wit: DAVID BYERS,
Jurate; JOHN BRYSON. Rec. Apr. term 1771.

Pp. 412-413: 20 Jan 1771, THOMAS BLACK & wf ELIZABETH of Tryon Co., for s5 sterl., pd.
by ROBERT COLLINSWOOD...land on both sides little broad river above CONAWAYs
land, 150 A granted to sd. THOMAS BLACK, 23 Apr 1767...THOMAS BLACK (T) (SEAL), ELIZABETH

BLACK (E) (SEAL), Wit: WILLIAM GRAHAM, BENJAMIN HARDIN, Jurate; THOS HUGHS. Rec. Apr.
term 1771.

Pp. 413-414: 11 Mar 1771, JOHN MITCHELL of Craven Co., S. C. to MATTHEW TROY of Rowan Co.
for Ь 65 proc. money...land in Tryon Co., on S side S fork Catawba River
on S side Long Creek about two miles above the mouth of sd. Creek, 250 A...JOHN MITCHELL
(SEAL), ELIZABETH MITCHELL (SEAL), Wit: JOHN DUNN, CHRISTOPHER BEEKMAN. 11 Mar 177_,
ELIZABETH MITCHELL, wife of JOHN, relinquished dower, before DANL. LITTLE, J. P. Rec.
date not given.

Pp. 414-415: 21 July 1770, WM PATTERSON & wf ELISABETH of Tryon Co., to ROBERT ELDER
from Virginia, now of Tryon Co.,for sum of Ь 10, proc. money.,...land on
S side Catawba adj. BEATY, CATHY, 92 A granted to ROGER COOK, 30 Oct 1765, conveyed to
FREDERICK HAMBRIGHT, then to sd. PATTERSON...WILLIAM PATTERSON (SEAL), ELISABETH PATTER-
SON (SEAL), Wit: ALEXANDER PATTERSON, Jurate; FRANCIS BEATEY, JAMES PALLEY[?]. Rec.
Apr. term 1771.

Pp. 415-416: 21 July 1770, WM PATTERSON & wf ELISABETH to ROBERT ELDER for Ь 30 proc.
money...400 A on W side Catawba River including improvements made by FREDER-
ICK HAMBRIGHT, RODGER COOK & sd. WM. PATTERSON, part of tract conveyed by SAML YOUNG to
JOHN KUYKENDALL, to FREDERICK HAMBRIGHT, and conveyed by HAMBRIGHT & wf SARAH to RODGER
COOK, then back to sd. HAMBRIGHT, then to WILLIAM PATTERSON. Same signatures and wit.
Rec. Apr. term 1771.

Pp. 416-417: 26 Oct 1770, ALEX KYLE of Tryon Co., to JOHN SLOAN JUNR & JAMES CARUTH of
Mecklenburg Co., for Ь 45 proc. money...200 A on both sides Muddy Fork of
Buffalo Creek including the Old Mill Shoals, granted to ALEXR KYLE 25 Apr 1767...ALEXAN-
DER KYLE (∩) (SEAL), Wit: JAMES SENTER, ANN MURPHY, Jurate; Rec. Apr. term 1771.

Pp. 417-418: 2 Mar 1770, JAMES McELWEAN of Tryon Co., to DANEL BUSH of Tryon Co., for Ь
115 current of S. C....land on head of Mill Creek & the branches of Fairforest granted unto JAMES McELWEAN, by Gov. Tryon, 25 Apr 1767, 190 A adj. MITCHELL...
JAMES McELWEAN (SEAL), Wit: CHRISTOPHER COLEMAN, Jurate; JOHN FORD. Rec. Apr. term 1771.

Pp. 418-419: 21 Feb 1771, ROBERT WILKINS of Tryon Co., & wf SUSANNAH to GEORGE BLANTON
of same, for Ь 75 proc. money...land on So Fork of Pacolet by a small
branch, granted to JOHN CRAWFORD __ Sept 1769...ROBERT WILKINS (R) (SEAL), SUSANAH
WILKINS (X) (SEAL), Wit: PENSWELL WOOD, Jurate; HENRY BATES (+), JOHN SNEED (Є). Rec.
Apr. term 1771.

Pp. 419-420: 30 Dec 1769, THOMAS RAY of Prov. of Ga., to GEORGE LAMPHIN of Tryon Co.,
for Ь 10...land on both sides Long Creek, granted to sd. RAY 26 Oct 1767,
100 A...THOS RAY (SEAL), Wit: JOHN LOW, Jurate; CORNELIUS McCARTY (Ↄ), DANIEL WYATT
(DY). Rec. Apr. term 1771.

Pp. 420-421: 15 Dec 1769, WILLIAM RUNNALDS of Tryon Co., to ALEXR RUNNALDS of same, for
Ь 50 proc. money...land on N side Indian Creek, 200 A adj. THOS RUNNOLDS...
WILLIAM RUNNALDS (W) (SEAL), HANNAH RUNOLDS (1) (SEAL), Wit: JOHN RIZHAUPT, J; JOHN
RUNOLDS (---), Rec. Apr. term 1771.

Pp. 421-422: 24 Apr 1771, DAVID DAVIES of Tryon Co., to JOSEPH BRADNER of same, for Ь 10
procl. money...66 A on W side Catawba, granted to MICHAEL DICKSON, 26 Mar
1763...DAVID DAVIES (SEAL), Wit: THOS NEEL, ALEXANDER FAKINS. Rec. Apr. term 1771.

Pp. 422-423: 21 Aug 1769, JOAB MITCHEL of Tryon Co., to JOHN GRANDAL of same, for Ь 30
proc. money...land on N side Packolat River, 100 A adj. HUGHS, ELLETS...
JOAB MITCHEL (M) (SEAL), Wit: JOHN HAILE, CHARLES BLACKWELL. Rec. Apr. term 1771.

Pp. 423-426: 9 Sept 1763, MATTHEW FLOYD of Mecklenburg Co., to JAMES & JOSEPH KOLB of
same, (lease s5, release Ь 20 proc. money)...land on E side Broad River, on
a branch of Turkey Creek adj. THOS HARRIS, 200 A...MAT FLOYD (SEAL), SARAH FLOYD; Wit:
HERMAN KOLB, JAMES BROWN. Rec. July term 1771.

Pp. 426-429: 31 Aug & 1 Sept 1769, JOHN DICKINSON of Augusta Co., Colony of Virginia, to
JOHN PATTON of Tryon Co., (lease s5, release Ь 100 Va. money)...900 A, in
Tryon, formerly Anson Co., on the So fork of Sandy River on the N side Broad River, in-
cluding Improvements Bought of JOHN STEWART...JOHN DICKINSON(SEAL), MARTHA DICKINSON
(SEAL), Wit: SAMUEL ADAMS, Jurate; ROBERT JOHNSTON, JOHN HUMPHREYS. Rec. July term 1771.

Page 429: 7 Apr 1770, WM. SIMS of Tryon Co., to ISAAC EDWARDS of Brunswick Co., for s5
            sterl., land on both sides little broad river, including the mouth of Sandy[?]
Run and an improvement made by GEORGE HATHERLY, granted to WM. SIMS for 300 A, 20 Sept
1766...WILLIAM SIMS (SEAL), Wit: JOHN ROGERS, PETERJOHNSTON, Jurate. Rec. July term 1771.

Pp. 429-430: 24 Dec 1768, PETER JOHNSTON of Mecklenburg Co., to the HONL. ROBERT PALMER
            ESQ. Surveyor General for the Prov. afrsd. by ₺ 5 proc. money...land in
Tryon Co., on both sides Fair Forest Creek, 300 A, granted to sd. JOHNSTON 23 Dec 1768...
PETER JOHNSTON (SEAL), Wit: ZACH BULLOCK, JESSE BENTON. Rec. July term 1771.

Page 431: 23 July 1771, JOHN KYMBEL of Tryon Co., to JOHN CARSON of Mecklenburg Co., for
            ₺ 10 proc. money...land on both sides big Allisons Creek adj. WILLIAM PATRICK...
JOHN KIMBOLE (X) (SEAL), MARY KIMBOLE (X) (SEAL), Wit: MOSES FERGUSON, THOS McMURRY (X),
ALBERT FERGUSON JUNR. Rec. July term 1771.

Page 432: 21 July 1771, DAVID McREE of Mecklenburg Co., to JOHN CORSON of same, for ₺ 20
            proc. money...land in Tryon Co., on both sides Buffalow Creek of broad River
above JAMES KELLEYs land, 200 A...DAVID McCREE (SEAL), Wit: PETER JOHNSTON, Jurate; JOHN
McREE. Rec. July term 1771.

Page 433: 29 Aug 1769, JOHN DICKINSON of Augusta Co., Va., to JOHN PATTON of Tryon Co.,
            for s5 sterl., land on S side Broad River on both sides Kings River, 600 A....
JOHN DICKINSON (SEAL), MARTHA DICKINSON (SEAL), Wit: SAMUEL ADAMS, Jurate: ROBERT JOHN-
STON, JOHN HUMPHREYS. [Kings River is now Enoree River.]

Pp. 433-436: 13 Aug 1769, JOHN DICKINSON to JOHN PATTON, for ₺ 100...land on S side Broad
            River on both sides Kings River, 600 A...JOHN DICKINSON (SEAL), MARTHA
DICKINSON (SEAL), Wit: SAMUEL ADAMS, Jurate; JOHN HUMPHREYS, ROBERT JOHNSTON. Rec.
July Term 1771. [The above two instruments are apparently lease & release.]

Pp. 436-437: 12 Mar 1771, DAVID CROCKATT of Tryon Co., to WILLIAM PATTERSON, for ₺ 50
            proc. money...land that he purchased the day before the date hereof of
THOMAS YATES, 150 A on Coburn[?] Creek...DAVID CROCKATT (SEAL)_ Wit: ALEXANDER PETERSON,
Jurate; JOHN BEATY. Rec. July term 1771.

Pp. 437-438: 23 Jan 1771, WILLIAM ADAMS of Tryon Co., planter, to THOMAS PRICE of same,
            planter, for ₺ 5 proc. money...122 A granted to sd. ADAMS on N side S fork
Crowders Creek above JAMES ALEXANDERS land, at the sound bottom...WILLIAM ADAMS (SEAL),
Wit: JOHN McK. ALEXANDER, WM. SHARP. Rec. July term 1771.

Pp. 438-439: 12 July 1771, JACOB SHATELEY of Tryon Co., to MICHAEL WILLIAMS of same, for
            ₺ 25 proc. money...land on both sides Hoyls Mill Creek of the So Fork of
Catawba River, 150 A granted to sd. JACOB SHETLY, 29 Apr 1768...JACOB SHÖTL[?] [German
signature]. Wit: ROBT BLACKBURN, Jurate; MARTHA BLACKBURN. Rec. July term 1771.

Pp. 439-440: 24 Feb 1770, JOHN IRWIN & wf MARY of Collecton [sic] County, South Carolina,
            Sadler, to JONATHAN PARKER of Granville County, South Carolina, planter,
for ₺ 55 NC money...300 A in Tryon County on a branch of Tyger River called Fair Forest
Creek, including sd. PARKERs improvement...JOHN IRWIN (SEAL), MARY IRWIN (M) (SEAL),
Wit: ROBT IRWIN, Jurate; EDWD McGARRY, JOHN BLACKSTOCK. Rec. July term 1771.

Pp. 440-442: 20 Aug 1768, JAMES HANNAH & wf JANE of Tryon Co., to ROBERT KILLOUGH of same,
            for ₺ 35 proc. money...land on head Branch of the So Fork of Fishing Creek,
on the So. side of the Waggon Road, formerly surveyed for JOHN WADE adj. sd. HANNAH,
BALL, 146 A granted to sd. JAMES HANNAH 26 Oct 1767...JAS. HANNA (SEAL), JANE HANNA (O)
(SEAL), Wit: THOMAS KILLOUGH, Jurate; WILLIAM HANNA, MARTHA HANNA (M).Rec. July term 1771.

Page 442: 5 Apr 1771, JACOB GARDNER of Tryon Co., to ISIAH PARKER of Mecklenburg, yeoman,
            for ₺ 5 proc. money...land in Tryon Co., on W side Broad River on both sides
Allisons Creek, adj. WILSON, PARKER, granted to WILLIAM JOHNSTON, 26 Oct 1767, & by
him conveyed to sd. JACOB GARDNER 15 Oct 1768...JACOB GARDNER (SEAL), Wit: JNO. McK.
ALEXANDER, JANE ALEXANDER. Rec. July term 1771.

Page 443: 22 July 1771, PHILIP CLONINGER of Tryon Co., to ADAM CLONINGER, for ₺ 40...200
            A on both sides Seegles Creek, adj. THOS BEATY...PHILIP CLONINGER (SEAL), Wit:
MICHAEL RUDISIL [German signature], Jurate; JACOB COSTNER, JACOB ____ [German signature].
Rec. July ter 1771.

Pp. 443-444: 23 July 1771, WILLIAM SIMS of Tryon Co., NC to CHRISTIAN WEAVER of same, for Ł 20 proc. money...land on S side S fork Cataba River adj. AARON BIGGER-STAFF, SAMUEL BIGGERSTAFF, 200 A granted to sd. SIMS 9 Apr 1770...WILLIAM SIMS (SEAL), Wit: JOHN DUNN, Jurate; BROMFIELD RIDLEY. Rec. July Term 1771.

Pp. 444-447: __ Sept 1767, THOMAS COHUNE & wf MARY of Mecklenburg Co., to JAMES WILSON of same, (lease s5, release Ł 150)...land on E side S fork Catawba River, adj. sd. JAMES WILSON...THOMAS COHUNE (SEAL), MARY COHUNE (N) (SEAL), Wit: JAMES McAFEE, ROBERT BLACKBURN, Jurate; WILL REED. Rec. July term 1771.

Pp. 447-448: 15 Nov 1770, JOHN WALLACE & wf HANNAH of Tryon Co., to WILLIAM CALLEY of same, for Ł 129...land on S side Catawba River and on the So Fork of Fishing Creek, granted to WILLIAM MOORE 8 Apr 1754, 300 A...JOHN WALLACE (SEAL), HANNAH WALLACE (H) (SEAL), Wit: THOMAS FAIRLEY (ㄱ), JAMES BRICE. Rec. date not given.

Pp. 449-450: 12 Feb 1771, MOSES FERGUSON & wf MARTHA of Tryon Co., to THOS. McMURRY of same, for Ł 65 proc. money...land on W side Catawba River, on the waters of Rocky Allisons Creek, 171 A adj. McFADEN, sd. FERGUSON, part of a grant to WALTER DAVIS, 6 Apr 1765...MOSES FERGUSON (SEAL), MARTHA FERGUSON (O) (SEAL), Wit: DANIEL SHAW, Jurate; PATRICK SHAW, WILLIAM McMURREY. Rec. July Court 1771.

Pp. 450-451: THOMAS REYNOLDS SENR. to THOMAS REYNOLDS JUNR., for Ł 50 NC money...land on both sides Indian Creek, adj. JOHN REYNOLDS, HENRY REYNOLDS, granted to THOMAS REYNOLDS SENR, 30 Aug 1753...5 July 1771...THOMAS REYNOLDS (SEAL) (T). Wit: TIMOTHY RIGGS, JOHN REYNOLDS (ł), Jurate. Rec. July term 1771.

Pp. 451-452: 23 July 1771, SAML COBURN of Tryon Co., to WILLIAM EAKINS of same, for Ł 20 proc. money...land on a branch of Allisons Creek adj. PATRICKS line, 150 A, part of a grant to sd. COBURN, 5 May 1769...SAMUEL COBURN (SEAL) (X). Wit: WILL REED, ANDREW NEAL. Rec. July term 1771.

Pp. 452-453: 21 July 1770, HUGH BARRY of Tryon Co., to JOHN BARRY of same, for Ł 40 NC proc. money...land on N side Broad River on McDonnels Creek, adj. JAMES BYERS, granted to THOMAS RAINEY...300 A...HUGH BARRY (SEAL), Wit: JAMES SIMRAL, CHS. MOORE. ANDREW BARRY, Jurate. Rec. July term 1771.

Pp. 453-454: 8 Jan 1771, THOS RAINEY of Tryon Co., to BENJAMIN PHILLIPS of Craven County, SC, for Ł 20 proc. money...land on S Fork of Fishing Creek joining DAVID-SONS line, granted to sd. RAINEY 18 Nov 1764...THOS. RAINEY (SEAL), Wit: RACHEL RAINEY (3), MARY RAINEY, THOMAS REYNOLDS. Rec. July term 1771.

Pp. 454-455: 11 Mar 1771, THOS YEATS of Berkley County, SC to DAVID CROCKET of Tryon Co., for Ł 10 current money of this province...land in Tryon Co., on S side Catawba River adj. ABM. SCOTT, granted to JNO. KILLIAN __ Sept 1759...THOS. YEATS (SEAL), Wit: JOHN BEATY, FRANCIS BEATY. Rec. July term 1771.

Pp. 455-456: 24 Apr 1771, JOHN McKNITT ALEXANDER of Mecklenburg Co., to JAMES DAVIS of Tryon Co., for Ł 20 proc. money...land on W side of Catawba River between Crowders and Allisons Creeks on a little branch called Beaver Dam Creek, granted to sd. ALEXANDER [date not given]...JNO. MCK. ALEXANDER (SEAL), No wit. Rec. July term 1771.

Pp. 457-458: 10 Dec 1770, WILLIAM DICKSON of Duplin Co., N. C. to JAMES HANNA of Tryon Co., for Ł 100 proc. money...land in Tryon Co., formerly Mecklenburg, on the waters of Fishing Creek & Turkey Creek joining WM. HENRY's, EDWARD LACEY's, JAMES McNABB's, PRICES, JOHN THOMASES, JOHN FONDRENs lines...540 A, granted to SD. WILLIAM DICKSON, 25 Oct 1766, also another tract on Stoney Fork of Fishing Creek, adj. THOMAS PRICE, JOHN THOMAS, & his own lines of the above granted land, 130 A granted 26 Oct 1767...WILLIAM DICKSON (SEAL), Wit: PETER JOHNSTON, Jurate; JOSEPH DICKSON. Rec. July term 1771.

Pp. 458-459: 18 May 1771, DAVID PORTER & wf JEAN of Tryon Co., to JAMES PORTER of same, for Ł 40 proc. money...land granted to sd. DAVID PORTER, 27 Apr 1771...DAVID PORTER (SEAL), JANE PORTER (SEAL), Wit: DAVID BYERS, NICHOLAS WALTON, Jurate. Rec. July term 1771.

Pp. 459-460: 24 July 1771, JOHN McKNIT ALEXANDER of Mecklenburg Co., to DAVID THOMPSON of Tryon Co., for Ł 5 proc. money...land in Tryon Co. on waters of DAVID WATSONs spring branch of Bullock's Creek, 138 A...JNO. McK. ALEXANDER (SEAL), Wit: None. Rec. July term 1771.

Pp. 460-461: 18 Mar 1771, JOHN WITHROW of Tryon Co., to JOHN COUNTS of same, for ₺ 35
           proc. money...300 A on both sides Cane Creek, on the side of a mountain,
granted to sd. WITHROW 26 Apr 1768...JOHN WITHROW (W) (SEAL), Wit: JOHN WALKER, Jurate;
WILLIAM HENRY. Rec. July term 1771.

Pp. 461-462: PETER ACHER of Tryon Co., for ₺ 30 proc. money pd. by JOHN BEEMAN of same...
           150 A on both sides Robinsons Creek...7 Feb 1771...PETER ACRE (+) (SEAL),
BARBARA ACRE (O) (SEAL), Wit: TIMOTHY RIGGS, JOHANNES _____ [German signature].

Pp. 462-463: 22 July 1771, PETER BLOUNT of Tryon Co., planter, to JACOB HUFSTADLER of
           same, for ₺ 5 proc. money...200 A on the branches of Long Creek, adj.
MICHAEL HUSTALIN[?]...granted to sd. PETER BLOUNT, 9 Apr 1770...PETER BLOUNT (PB) (SEAL),
Wit: _____ [German signature], LORENTZ KEISER, Jurate [German signature],
VALLENTINE MAUNY. Rec. July term 1771.

Pp. 463-464: 25 July, 1771, PETER JOHNSTON of Mecklenburg Co., to ROBERT BRATTON of
           Tryon Co., for ₺ 5 proc. money...land on waters of Turkey Creek, joining
the land sd. BRATTON lives on, adj. MISKELLY...PETER JOHNSTON, Wit: DAVID WATSON, THOMAS
BARRON. Rec. July term 1771.

Pp. 464-465: 23 Oct 1771, MARSHALL LOVELATTEY of Tryon Co., to JOHN LOVELATTEY of same,
           for ₺ 20 proc. money...land on Abbensons Creek, adj. THOMAS LOVELATTYs
corner, 200 A...MARSHAL LOVELATTY (M) (SEAL), Wit: HENRY SMITH, Jurate; GIDEON SMITH.
Rec. July term 1771.

Pp. 465-466: 22 July 1771, JOHN LOVE of Broad River, & wf MARTHA, of South Carolina, to
           THOMAS WADE of Craven County, S. C., for ₺ 16 NC money...land in Tryon
County on S side Broad River, above the mouth of Thicketty Creek, 400 A...JOHN LOVE
(SEAL), MARTHA LOVE (SEAL), Wit: JAMES HAMILTON, Jurate; JOHN GILLISPIE. Rec. July term
1771.

Pp. 466-467: 14 Feb 1771, JOHN McK. ALEXANDER of Mecklenburg Co., to FRANCIS GILMORE of
           same, for ₺ 25 proc. money...land in Tryon Co., on Duharts Creek, adj.
NATHL. HENDERSON, DAVIES, 156 A granted to sd. ALEXANDER, 29 Nov 1764...JNO. McK. ALEXAN-
DER (SEAL), Wit: WILLIAM THOMPSON, JOHN STEWART (ꕉ). Rec. July term 1771.

Pp. 467-468: 29 June 1771, NICHOLAS FRIDAY of Tryon Co., to MICHAEL QUICKLE of same, for
           ₺ 25 proc. money...land on N side S fork Catawba River, 150 A..._____
FRIDIG [German signature] (Seal), Wit: MICHAEL KILLIAN[?] [German signature]; NICHOLAS
FRITAG JUNR., Jurate [German signature]. Rec. July term 1771.

Pp. 468-469: 11 Dec 1770, THOMAS McMURRY & wf NANCY of Tryon Co., to GEORGE STANLEY of
           same, for ₺ 140...185 A, granted 6 Apr 1765...THOMAS McMURRY (X) (SEAL),
NANCY MURRY (N) (SEAL), Wit: JOHN ANDERSON, Jurate; ANGUS[?] YOUNG (O). Rec. July term
1771.

Pp. 469-470: 24 July 1771, JOHN PATTON of Tryon Co., to JOHN SMITH of same, for ₺ 100
           proc. money...land on S side Allisons Creek, a branch of Catawba River
including the improvement on sd. tract, 245 A...JOHN PATTON (SEAL), Wit: FRANS. ADAMS,
JAS. ALLCORN, Jurate; JAMES WILLSON[?]. Rec. July term 1771.

Page 471: 24 June 1771, JAMES CLARK of Mecklenburg Co., to JAMES ALCORN of Tryon Co.,
           for ₺ 85 proc. money...250 A on Allisons Creek, granted by deed to sd. JAMES
CLARK 14 Oct 1763 by one JOSEPH CLARK, being granted by patent to sd. JOSEPH CLARK 29
Mar 1753 by Mathew Rowan, ...JAMES CLARK (SEAL), Wit: JOHN BEARD JR., JOHN SMITH, Jurate;
GEO. DENNY[?]. Rec. July term 1771.

Pp. 472-473: 22 July 1771, WILLIAM JONES of Tryon Co., to BENJAMIN ELLICE of same, for
           ₺ 19 proc. money...250 A on both sides Buffalo Creek, granted to sd. JONES
23 Dec 1768...WILLIAM JONES (SEAL), Wit: PERREGREEN MACKNESS, Jurate; WILLIAM MACKNESS.
Rec. July term 1771.

Pp. 473-474: 12 July 1770, PETER JOHNSTON of Mecklenburg Co., to SAMUEL GAY of Tryon Co.,
           for ₺ 20 proc. money...land on waters of S fork Fishing Creek adj. BENJAMIN
PHILLIPS, JAMES MURPHREY, granted to sd. JOHNSTON 16 Dec 1769-..PETER JOHNSTON (SEAL),
Wit: HUGH BRATTON, Jurate; WILLIAM PATRICK.Rec. July term 1771.

Pp. 474-475: 6 June 1771, BOSTON CLINE JR. of Tryon Co., to JACOB CARPENTER of same, for
           ₺ 50 proc. money...land on S fork Catawba River, on E side & on Clarks Creek
granted to PETER BROYAL, 1753, 3 Sept, conveyed by sd. BROYAL to DERICK RAMSOUR, 3 June

1758, and by RAMSEUR to BOSTON CLINE, 6 Dec 1770, 250 A..._____ [German signature]
(SEAL), MARGARET CLINE (+) (SEAL), Wit: JACOB RAMSOUR, ROBT BLACKBURN, Jurate. Rec.
July term 1771.

Pp. 475-476: 23 Jan 1771, JOHN WADE of Tryon Co., to ABRAHAM SMITH of same, for Ƚ 100
...land on E side Broad River, on Bullocks Creek on Lows[?] Branch, 300 A...
JOHN WADE (SEAL), Wit: HENRY CLARK, NATHL. CLARK, Jurate. Rec. July term 1771.

Pp. 476-477: 27 Dec 1770, JOHN RAMSAY & wf AGNES, ALEXANDER BALDRIDGE & wf JANE, of Tryon
Co., to THOMAS PRICE of same, for Ƚ 58 proc. money...land on both sides
Allisons Creek, now Crowders Creek adj. ALLISONS corner(now BALDRIDGES corner)...granted
to JAMES ALEXANDER 18 Nov 1752, and by him conveyed to sd. JOHN RAMSEY & ALEXANDER BALD-
RIDGE, 1 May 1765, 346 A...JOHN RAMSEY (0) (SEAL), AGNES RAMSEY (+) (SEAL), ALEXR.
BALDRIDGE (SEAL), JANE BALDRIDGE (SEAL), Wit: RICHD BARRY, Jurate; JOHN HUD, MOSES HENDRY.
Rec. July term 1771.

Pp. 477-478: 6 Mar 1771, THOMAS YATES of Berkly County, SC, to WILLIAM CROCKET of Tryon
Co., for Ƚ 16...land on Shulands[?] Creek, adj. WM. CATHEY, SITES, KINCAIDs,
RAMSEYS, granted to THOMAS YEATS, ___ Dec 1768...THOMAS YEATES (SEAL), Wit: JOHN HILL,
Jurate; JAMES JOHNSTON, JOHN CROCKATT. Rec. July term 1771.

Pp. 478-479: 8 Dec 1770, FRANCIS BEATY of Mecklenburg Co., to CHRISTIAN MOONEY of Tryon
Co., for Ƚ 50 proc. money...350 A on waters of Beaver Dam Creek, on the
waggon road about 3 miles above PETER ACKERs, granted to BEATTY 21 Dec 1763...FRANCIS
BEATY (SEAL), Wit: DAVID MILLER, Jurate; THOMAS RICHEY, JOHN BEATY. Rec. July term 1771.

Pp. 479-480: 20 May 1771, BENJAMIN TURNER of Tryon Co., planter, to JOHN NEIGHBORS of
Tryon Co., planter, for Ƚ 35 proc. money...land on E side Broad River
below the mouth of Little Broad River, 100 A...BENJAMIN TURNER (B) (SEAL), Wit: STEPHEN
SHELTON, Jurate; JOHN TURNER, Rec. July term 1771.

Pp. 480-481: THOMAS REYNOLDS SENR of Tryon Co., for Ƚ 50 pd. by THOMAS REYNOLDS JUNR...
200 A on Indian Creek...5 July 1771...THOMAS REYNOLDS (+) (SEAL), Wit:
TIMOTHY RIGGS, JOHN REYNOLDS (Ŧ) Jurate. Rec. July term 1771.

Pp. 481-483: 4 Feb 1771, JOHN HILL & wf JEAN (JANE) of Tryon Co., planter, to THOMAS
ESPY of same, for Ƚ 5 sterling...land adj. JAMES ORMOND on S fork Catawba
on long Creek...350 A, granted to one MEEK, 17 May 1754, conveyed from Meek to HILL...
JOHN HILL (SEAL), JEAN HILL (0) (SEAL), Wit: ROBERT EWART, JAMES COBURN, DAVID CROCKATT.
Proven July Court. [For the deed from MEEK to JOHN HILL, see my Mecklenburg County,
North CarolinaDeed Abstracts, Vol. I, 1763-1768, p. 54].

Pp. 483-484: 16 June 1771, THOS HARROD of Tryon Co., & Parish of St. Thomas, to JOHN
OAKS of same, for Ƚ 20 NC money...land granted to sd. HARROD, 1765, on both
sides Buffalow Creek, 275 A, adj. JAMES GREEN...THOMAS HARROD (SEAL), Wit: JOHN LOGIN,
JAS. McENTIRE, Jurate. Rec. July term 1771.

Pp. 484-485: 29 Jan 1771, RICHARD HICKS of Tryon Co., planter, to JOHN FOSTER of same,
for Ƚ 56 proc. money...200 A on N side Broad River, adj. RICHARD CRUNKS
corner, at the mouth of dry creek...RICHARD HIC (SEAL), Wit: ARCHIBALD ROBISON, SAMUEL
BARNET, JOHN WALERSON. Rec. July term 1771.

Pp. 485-486: 16 Oct 1771, JOHN McELLILY of Mecklenburg Co., weaver, to JOHN PENNY of
same, for Ƚ 5 proc. money...land in Tryon Co., on S side S fork Fishing
Creek, adj. SAMUEL MONROW, 200 A granted to sd. McELLILY 9 Apr 1770...JOHN McELLILEY
(SEAL), Wit: JOHN PHIFER, SAMUEL PATTON, Jurate. Rec. Oct. term 1771. [The grant to
which reference is made was issued out of Mecklenburg County, rather than Tryon. See
my North Carolina Land Grants in South Carolina Volume II: Anson & Mecklenburg Counties,
1749-1770, p. 60.]

Pp. 486-487: 18 Oct 1771, JOHN PENNY of Mecklenburg Co., to MOSES ALEXANDER of same, for
Ƚ 30 proc. money...land on S fork Fishing Creek, adj. SAMUEL MONROW, granted
to JOHN McELLILY 9 Apr 1770...200 A...JOHN PENNY (SEAL), Wit: THOS POLK, SAMUEL PATTON,
Jurate. Rec. Oct. term 1771.

Pp. 487-488: EZEK SMITH of Tryon Co., to ELIZABETH BURTON, daughter of ELIZABETH BURTON,
of same...deed of gift for 20 cattle [marks given]...EZEKIEL SMITH (✝).
(SEAL), Wit: EZEK POLK, FRANCS. ADAMS. Rec. Oct. term 1771.

Pp. 488-489: 19 July 1771, JAMES CARSON & wf MARY of Tryon Co., to DAVID ABERNATHY of
same, for one waggon & Ⱡ 6 NC money...land on S side Catawba River, on
both sides Lepers Creek adj. JOHN ARMSTRONG, 116 A...JAMES CARSON (SEAL), MARY CARSON
(+) (SEAL), Wit: DAVID CROCKETT,ROBERT ABERNATHY. Rec. Oct. term 1771.

Pp. 490-491: 18 Oct 1771, LAWRENCE KOIZER SENR of Tryon Co., to JOSEPH KOISER of same,
for s5...land on a branch of long creek near to MICHAEL HOFSTEDLARS land,
250 A...LORENZ KEISER (SEAL), [German signature]. Wit: VALLENTINE MAUNEY, LORENZ KEISER,
Jurate. [German signature]. Rec. Oct. term 1771.

Pp. 491-492: 10 Aug 1771, JOHN WYATT of Tryon Co., to BOSTON BESS of same, for Ⱡ 40
proc. money...100 A on E side S fork Catawba, 100 A, part of 392 A granted
to JAMES WYATT...JOHN WYAT (ᑎ) (SEAL), Wit: JOHN RITZHAUPT, Jurate; JOHN HEYEL. Rec.
Oct. term 1771.

Page 492: ANDREW HASLEP of Tryon Co., planter, for and in consideration of a deed of
conveyance to be executed in one month by THOMAS HASLEP, my son, for 390 A
where I now live, I give to my sd. son one road gelding 3 yrs. old, & other cattle, &
all appeara1[sic] of my son JOHN HASLEP decd, 40 bu. of INdian corn...25 Oct 1771...
ANDREW HESLEP (SEAL), Wit: JOHN DUNN, HUGH JENKINS, ALEXR. MARTIN. Rec. Oct. term.

Pp. 492-493: 19 Jan 1768, DAVID ALEXANDER of Mecklenburg Co., to SAMUEL RANKIN of same,
for Ⱡ 80 proc. money...land on Kuykendalls Creek, 150 A granted to JOHN
ARMSTRONG in 1762, 25 Apr...DAVID ALEXANDER (SEAL), Wit: WILLIAM MOORE[?], THOS RAY.
Rec. Oct term 1771.

Pp. 494-495: 11 Oct 1771, DAVID THOMPSON of Gryon Co., to JAMES SMITH for Ⱡ 50 proc.
money...138 A in Tryon Co., formerly part of Mecklenburg Co., on the waters
of DAVID WATSONs Spring branch that leads into Bullocks Creek, granted to JOHN McKNIT
ALEXANDER 6 Apr 1765...DAVID THOMPSON (SEAL), Wit: ONSLOW BARRATT, Jurate; JOHN ELMER[?]
Rec. Oct. term 1771.

Page 495: 22 Apr 1770, DANIEL McCARTY of Tryon Co., to sons DANIEL & JOHN McCARTY, for
s5 sterling...cattle, plates, etc...DANIEL McCARTY (SEAL), Wit: EDGENIAH BUR-
GIN (B), WILLIAM ANDERSON (A). Rec. Oct term 1771.

Pp. 496-497: 22 June 1771, JNO. COLLINS & wf PHEBE of Tryon Co., Wheelright, to DAVID
GEORGE of same, farmer, for Ⱡ 20 proc. money...200 A on Mountain Creek
below JOHN BETMANs survey...JOHN COLLINS (ₕₕₕ) (SEAL), Wit: JOHN CARRIER[?], Jurate;
HEZEKIAH COLLINS (H). Rec. Oct term 1771.

Pp. 497-498: 28 Aug 1769, ROBERT RUSSELL of Mecklenburg Co., to DAVID BRUTON of Tryon
Co., for Ⱡ 35...land on S side Tyger River, on a fork of Antiquorum Creek,
now known as Fergusons Creek, Tyger River formerly known as Little River adj. JAMES
RUSSELL, 317 A...ROBERT RUSSEL (SEAL), Wit: MOSES ALEXANDER, Jurate; WILL ALEXANDER.
Rec. Oct. term 1771.

Pp. 498-499: 21 Oct 1771, SAMUEL DAVISON of Tryon Co., to JOHN BRYSON of same, for Ⱡ 20
proc. money...land on both sides Turkey Creek, adj. JAMES BRISON, the whole
content of a patent to sd. DAVISON 26 Sept 1766...SAMUEL DAVISON (SEAL), Wit: SAML ADAMS,
DAVD. GORDON. Rec. Oct. term 1771.

Pp. 499-500: 22 Oct 1771, THOMAS BULLION of Tryon Co., to ZACHARIAH GIBBS of Fair Forrest
in same co., for Ⱡ 25 proc. money...200 A on Buffalo Lick Creek, granted 16
Dec 1769...THOMAS BULLION (SEAL), Wit: RICHARD PRICE, ESSIX CAPSHAW, Jurate. Rec. Oct.
term 1771.

Pp. 500-501: 10 Dec 1770, SAML FULTON of Cravan Co., S. C. to JAMES DAVIDSON of Rowan
Co., N. C., for Ⱡ 150 proc. money...land on both sides Bullocks Creek, adj.
RIGGS, MCADOU, 319 A, granted unto sd. SAMUEL FULTON, 29 Apr 1768...SAMUEL FULTON (SEAL),
Wit: JOHN DAVIDSON, Jurate; BENJAMIN DAVIDSON, NATHL EWING. Rec. Oct. term 1771.

Pp. 501-502: 15 May 1771, GILES FILLET [TILLET?] of Pacolate River in Tryon Co., to JOHN
GIBBS SENR of Fair forest settlement in same county, for Ⱡ 100 proc. money...
640 A on both sides Fair Forrest, granted 22 Dec 1769...GILES FILLET (SEAL), Wit:
ZACHARIAH GIBBS, Jurate; JOHN THOMAS, J[?] GIFFORD[?]. Rec. Oct term 1771.

Pp. 502-503: 11 __ 1770, JAMES MILLICAN of Tryon Co., to JNO McKNITT ALEXANDER for Ⱡ 5
proc. money...land on N side Broad River, nearly joining below the mouth of
Floyds Creek a little below CANNONs land & above WILSONS improvement, 150 A granted 29

Apr 1768...JAMES MILLICAN (M) (SEAL), Wit: DAVID MOORE, Jurate; ROBERT MONROE. Rec. Oct. term 1771.

Pp. 503-504: 31 July 1771, HUGH QUIN & wf MARGARET of Tryon Co., to WILLIAM CAPSHAW of
        same, for ₺ 50 proc. money...100 A on S side Green River, part of 200 A
granted to JOEL BLACKWELL, 26 Oct 1767...HUGH WUIN (H) (SEAL), MARGET QUIN (Γ) (SEAL),
Wit: WILLIAM TATE, ESSIX CAPSHAW, Jurate: THOMAS HICKS (T). Rec. Oct. term 1771

Pp. 504-506: 9 Sept 1771, JAMES ENDSLEY of Rowan Co., N. C., to JOHN MORRIS of Tryon Co.,
        for ₺ 5 proc. money...land on N side Mountain Creek, adj. ANDREW HAMPTONs
lower tract...250 A...JAMES ENDSLEY (SEAL), Wit: ANDREW HAMPTON, Jurate; JOHN ENDSLEY,
JOHN BLECKLY. Rec. Oct term 1771.

Pp. 506-507: 13 May 1771, JOHN McCOLLOH of Rowan Co., to JOHN SMITH of Tryon Co., for
        ₺ 5 sterling...126 A on the dividing ridge between Allisons Creek and Fishing
Creek adj. JOHN McELMURRY...JNO. McCULLOH (SEAL), Wit: WM. JOHNSON, GEORGE WINTERS (X),
CALLPURNA[?] WINTERS[?]. Rec. Oct term 1771.

Pp. 507-508: 15 July 1771, JOHN COLLINS & wf PHEBE of Tryon Co., to FRANCIS ROSS, farmer,
        of same, for ₺ 50 proc. money...120 A, part of a grant to sd. COLLINS in
1768 on both sides Kings Creek...JOHN COLLINS (HH) (SEAL), PHEBE COLLINS (ح) (SEAL),
Wit: WM. MILBANK, Jurate: HEZEKYE COLLINS (H). Rec. Oct term 1771.

Page 508: 22 Oct 1771, ROBERT ADAMS of Tryon Co., to ANDREW CAMPBELL of same, for ₺ 18
        proc. money...land adj. JAMES CAMPBELL, 50 A, part of land granted to ADAMS
2 Apr 1753...ROBERT ADAMS (SEAL), Wit: JAMES CAMPBELL, Jurate: JAMES PATTERSON. Rec. Oct
term 1771.

Pp. 509-510: 28 Jan 1772, ROBERT KER & wf HANNAH of Meck., to JOHN SWAIN of Rowan Co.,
        for ₺ 140 proc money...land in Tryon Co., one tract on both sides the South
fork of Fishing Creek, adj. WM. HENRY, 400 A granted to sd. KER 25 Sept 1754, resurveyed
22 Sept 1766... another tract adj. to above tract adj. WIDOW KUYKENDALL & WM HENRY, 62
A, granted to ROBERT CARR (SEAL), HANNAH KER (ح) (SEAL), Wit: WM. SWAN, Jurate: JNO.
McK. ALEXANDER. Rec. January term 1772.

Pp. 510-511: 29 Jan 1772, JOHN LUSK of Tryon Co., farmer to JACOB LUTES of same, yeoman,
        for ₺ 20 lawful proc. money...186 A on w side Pinch Gut creek adj. SIMON
HOISES [HORSES?], ALEXANDER, HEPNER, granted to JOHN LUSK & WILLIAM BARNET 5 May 1769,
and conveyed to THOMAS WARREN (WARRIN) by deed and then to JOHN LUSK...JOHN LUSK (SEAL),
Wit: MATTHEW WILLSON, ROBT. BLACKBURN, Jurate: Rec. Jan. term 1772.

Pp. 511-512: 27 Jan 1772, JOHN WALLACE & wf HANNAH of Tryon Co., to WILLIAM BARREN of
        same, for ₺ 46 proc. money...land on both sides Mill Creek including Wades
Old Store, 200 A adj. JOHN KELLY...JOHN WALLACE (SEAL), HANNAH WALLACE (H) (SEAL), Wit:
ROBT BRATTON, Jurate: GEORGE SADLER, BENJ. PHILLIPS. Rec. Jan. term 1772.

Pp. 512-513: 15 Aug 1771, JOHN STROUD of Tryon Co., to ROSANNAH REDDICK of same, for ₺ 25
        proc. money...land granted to JOHN LARGE 25 Sept 1754, sold by him to JAMES
ARMOR, then to DINISH[?] DYER, then to LEONARD DOZER then to JOHN STROUD, on S side Catawba
adj. WM. HAGER, Jonstons Creek, JOHN CAMRIES line, WILLIAM LITTLE...JOHN STROUD (X)
(SEAL), Wit: ROBERT CHERRY, SAMUEL COBURN (+), Jurate. Rec. Jan.term 1772.

Pp. 513-514: 23 Apr 1771, SAMUEL ADAMS of Tryon Co., to JOHN PRICE of same, for ₺ 25 proc.
        money...300 A, part of a tract granted to sd. SAMUEL ADAMS 5 May 1769...
SAMUEL ADAMS (SEAL), Wit: JOSEPH HARDIN, JOHN CARR, JOHN POTTER. Rec. Jan. term 1772.

Pp. 514-515: 22 Jan 1772, NICHOLAS WELSH of Tryon Co. & wf ELIZABETH, to JACOB YERLY of
        same, for ₺ 130 proc. money...land on S side S Fork Catawba, 178 A granted to
AVINTON SHERRILL 28 Mar 1755, adj. SPROTS, THOS. POTTS, conveyed by SHERRILL to WILLIAM
WELSH, 22 Jan 1756, and to the above named NICHOLAS WELSH, 15 July 1765...NICHOLAS WELSH
(SEAL), ELIZABETH WELSH (E) (SEAL), Wit: THOMAS WELSH (T), Jurt., GEORGE DAVIES (X). Rec.
Jan. term 1772. [For the deed from AVINTON SHERRILL to WILLIAM WELSH, see my
Anson Co., NC Deed Abstracts, I, p. 12.]

Pp. 515-516: 25 Oct 1771, PETER JOHNSTON of Mecklenburg Co., N.C. to RICHARD PRICE of same,
        for ₺ 5 proc. money;...600 A including RICHARD PRICEs improvement, adj. GEORGE
JULIAN...PETER JOHNSTON (SEAL), Wit: SAML ADAMS, Jurate, THOS WADE. Rec. Jan term 1772.

Pp. 516-517: 17 Aug 1771, DERRICK RAMSOUR of Tryon Co., to CHRISTIAN REINHARDT of same, for
        ₺ 40 proc. money...land on E side Clarks Creek adj. sd. RAMSOURS, 100 A, part

of two tracts, granted 19 Apr 1763 and 16 Dec 1769...DERRICK RAMSOUR (X) (SEAL), Wit: HENRY HOLLMAN, ROBT. BLACKBURN. Rec. Jan term 1772.

Page 517: JACOB MAUNEY sells to MAUDLIN COUP five cows & calves, etc.27 Dec 1771...JACOB M____ (SEAL), Wit: JOHN TAGERT, JOHN OAK (O). Rec.·Jan term 1772. Also wit. JAMES McAFFEE.

Page 518: 5 Oct 1771, THOMAS LINN of Tryon Co., planter, for Ŀ 50 proc. money, to JOHN OAKS...250 A including THOMAS LINNs improvement...THOMAS LINN (TL) (SEAL), MARY LINN (ᕋ) (SEAL). Wit: ROBT McAFFEE, Jurate; JOHN ELLIS. Rec. Jan term 1772.

Pp. 518-519: 5 July 1771, DAVID ROBERSON of Tryon Co., to JAMES STEEN JUNR. of same, for Ŀ 200 proc. money...land on both sides Mill Creek, a So. branch of Pacolate River, 250 A adj. HUGHYs, part of a tract of land surveyed for the use of JOAB MITCHELL, and conveyed to sd. ROBERSON with a mill on said land...DAVID ROBERSON (SEAL), Wit: WM. SAFOLD JUR., Jurate; IRBY DISBERY. Rec. Jan. term 1772.

Pp. 519-520: 27 Oct 1771, JOSEPH NEAL of Broad River in Tryon Co., planter, to WILLIAM SMITH of Broad River, co. aforesd., for Ŀ 30 proc. money...land on both sides of a branch of Broad River, known by the name of Kings Creek, 100 A granted to JOSEPH NEAL, 5 May 1769...JOSEPH NEAL (SEAL), Wit: JACOB RANDALL, Jurate; GEORGE JULIAN. Rec. Jan term 1772.

Page 521: 28 Oct 1770, THOMAS WADE of Craven Co., S. C. to WILLIAM MOORELL[?], for Ŀ 50 proc. money...land on N side Broad river, about one mile above Smiths ford, 100 A granted to HENRY SMITH, and conveyed to JOHN RUSSELL JUR. and then to THOMAS WADE... THOS. WADE (SEAL), Wit: JACOB RANDALL, Jurate; WILLIAM SMITH.Rec. Jan. term 1772.

Page 522: RICHARD REYNOLDS of Tryon Co., for Ŀ 50 proc. money of N. C. pd. by HENRY LANDERS of same...land on Buffalow Creek that runs into broad river, 250 A...RICHARD REYNOLDS (R) (SEAL), ELIZABETH REYNOLDS (O) (SEAL), Wit: TIMOTHY RIGGS, Jurate; CHRISTIAN GOODRIGHT (C). Rec. Jan. term 1772.

Page 523: 28 Oct 1770, THOMAS WADE of Craven Co., S. C., to WILLIAM MORRIS of Guilford Co., N. C., for Ŀ 80 proc. money...land in Tryon Co. on No side Broad River on Howards [sic], 250 A granted to WM. BOFFIN 17 Nov 1764, conveyed by sd. WM. BOGAN to sd. THOMAS WADE...THOS. WADE (SEAL), Wit: WILLIAM SMITH, JACOB RANDALL, Jurate; Rec. Jan. term 1772.

Pp. 524-525: 6 Sept 1771, JAS. WRIGHT & WM. WRIGHT of Tryon Co., to WM. BYERS of Tryon Co., for Ŀ 200 proc. money...land on waters of Bullocks Creek formerly called Wrights Creek on N side Broad River, 535 A...JAMES WRIGHT (SEAL), WILLIAM WRIGHT (SEAL), Wit: CHARLES McLEAN, Jurate: WILLIAM HALL. Rec. Jan. term 1772.

Pp. 525-7:27 Nov 1768, PETER STUTS & wf ELIZABETH of Mecklenburg Co., to·CONRADE MINGS, for Ŀ 12 s 10...400 A granted to sd. STUT by deed 15[?] Oct 1765, on branches of Clarks Creek adj. ANTHONEYs line...PETER STUTS (X) (SEAL), ELIZABETH STUTS (X) (SEAL), Wit: ABRAHAM ANTHONY, _____ [German signature]. Rec. Jan. term 1772.

Pp. 527-530: 14 & 15 Sept 1771, SAMUEL WILSON of Craven Co., S. C., to JACOB ANTHONY of· Tryon Co., N. C., for (lease s10, release Ŀ 20 proc. money)...200 A granted to SAMUEL WILSON, 8 Apr 1768, on both sides Henry WHITNERS fork of the S fork of Catawba ...SAML. WILLSON (SEAL), SARAH WILLSON (SEAL), Wit: JOHN MULL (J M), Jurate; JOHN REED (R). Rec. Jan. term 1772.

Pp. 530-532: 27 & 28 Jan 1772, ADAM SIGHTS & wf SUSANNAH of Tryon Co., Taylor, to GEORGE SIGHTS of same, (lease s5, release Ŀ 75)...200 A on S side Catawba on the N side of the S fork of sd. river adj. LAWRENCE SNAPP,.on the N branch of Leapharts Creek, land which was conveyed to sd. SIGHTS by a certain TILLINGER, 2 Sept 1757, the same being granted to the sd. MARTIN TILLINGER 28 Mar 1755...ADAM SIGHTS (X) (SEAL), SUSANNA SIGHTS (X) (SEAL), Wit: LEMUEL SAUNDERS: GEORGE SITES[??], [German signature], Jurate. Rec. Jan. term 1772.[For the deed from TILLINGER to SIGHTS, see my Anson Co., Deed Abstracts, I, p.53]

Pp. 532-534: 20 May 1771, PAUL ANTHONY & wf FRONY of Rowan Co., to CHRISTIAN CHURCHES, Luteran & Presbyterian of the State aforesd.[?] commonly called the South fork, for Ŀ 2 N. C. money...10 A adj. PAUL ANTHONY, granted to sd. PAUL ANTHONY 25 Apr 1767... to the said two churches...._____ [German signature], (SEAL), FRONY ANTHONY (F) (SEAL) Wit: (1) _____[at least partial German signature], (2) JOHANNES GÄZHER [?] [German signature], (3) EZZRELL WINSLER[?] [German signature], (4) JOHN MULL, (5) JOHANNES EALN [?] [German signature], (6) ABRAHAM ANTHONEY, (7) JACOB ANTONY, (8) JOHANNES _____ [German signature]. Rec. Jan term 1772.

Pp. 534-536: 21 Dec 1771, ADAM OVERWINTER of Tryon Co., to GEORGE WILFONG for Ł 22...
250 A on waters of S fork Catawba..._____ OVERWINTER (SEAL), BETS[?]
OVERWINTER (SEAL), Wit: HUBNET[?] GANG, EDWARD[?] GANG. Rec. Jan. term 1772.

Page 536: 23 Nov 1771, THOMAS WELCH of Tryon Co., to EDWARD HAMPTON of same, for Ł 5 proc.
money...land on Indian Creek, a branch of Catawba River, 200 A...THOMAS WELCH
(T) (SEAL), RACHEL WELCH, Wit: GEORGE DAVIS, Jurate; SARY DAVIS. Rec. Jan term 1772.

Pp. 536-538: 31 May 1771, HENRY WHITNER & wf CATHERINE of Tryon Co., to JOHN MOYL for Ł -
...land adj. WHITNER, granted to WHITNER or HENRY WIDENER, 29 Sept 1750[?]...
HEINRICH _____ [German signature] (SEAL), CATARIANA WEIDNER (SEAL), Wit: _____
[German signature], ABRAHAM ANTHONY. Rec. Jan. term 1772.

Pp. 538-539: 31 Jan 1771, PERRYGREEN MAGNESS of Tryon Co., to JOHN CARSON of same, for
Ł 30 proc. money...300 A...PERRYGREEN MACKNESS (SEAL), Wit: WM. YANCEY,
JOSEPH DICKSON. Rec. Jan. term 1772.

Pp. 539-540: 25 Jan 1772, JAMES McENTIRE of Tryon Co., to BENJAMIN ELLIS of same, for
300 A on S side First Broad River adj. BEATIES line...JAS. McENTIRE (SEAL),
Wit: ROBERT McAFEE, Jurate; WILLIAM GREEN. Rec. Jan. term 1772.

Pp. 540-541: 25 Oct 1770, JOSEPH SCOTT & wf MARY of Rowan Co., to ALEXANDER WILLIS of
Tryon Co., for Ł 25...land on S side Catawba, 200 A adj. JOHNSON, BOLDRIDGE
...JOSEPH SCOTT (SEAL), MARY SCOTT (F) (SEAL), Wit: JAMES JOHNSTON, Jurate; THOMAS SCOTT,
Rec. Jan. term 1772.

Pp. 541-542: 15 Aug 1771, JAMES REED of Granville Co., S. C., to HENRY BARKLEY of Rowan
Co., N. C., for Ł 40 proc. money...300 A on both sides north fork of little
Broad River adj. FRACIS BEATY, HENRY THOMPSON...JAMES REED (EAL), Wit: JAMES FINLEY, JOHN
REED, Jurate; Rec. Jan. term 1772.

Pp. 542-543: 16 Oct 1771, WILLIAM DIAMENT & wf MARY of Tryon Co., to FREDERIC WISE of same,
for Ł 14 proc. money...land on S side S fork Catawba, on S side Potts Creek,
adj. his own land, in line of the old tract of 1000 A...400 A formerly granted to JOHN
POTTS...the sd. 1000 A tract granted to DANIEL WARLOCK and conveyed by him to FREDERIC
WISE...WILLIAM DIAMENT (0) (SEAL), MARY DIAMENT (0) (SEAL), Wit: FRANCIS McBRIDE, LEONARD
PATTERSON. Rec. Jan. term 1772.

Pp. 543-545: 3 Jan 1772, NATHANIEL MILLER of prov. of NC, to JOSEPH THOMSON of same prov.,
for Ł 32...200 A on the So Branch of the No Fork of Tygar River above ROBERT
MILLERS land, the whole contents of a patent granted to DAVID DAVIS, 25 Sept 1766...
NATHANIEL MILLER (SEAL), Wit: NEVIL WAYLAND, ALEXANDER MaCARTER, Jurate. Rec. Jan. term
1772.

Page 545: 15 Oct 1771, JOSEPH DOBSON of Tryon Co., to JOHN FISHER of same, for Ł 20...
land on HENRY WEIDNERs fork of S fork Cataba, 200 A, granted to sd. DOBSON, 28
Apr 1768...JOSEPH DOBSON (SEAL), Wit: JOHN MELL, Jurate; JOHN DOBSON, Rec. Jan term 1772.

Pp. 545-547: 6 Sept 1771, THOMAS BEATY & wf MARGARET of Tryon Co., to JOHN FLEMING and
JOHN McCLURE of Rowan Co., for Ł 50...400 A on N fork of Main Broad River,
granted to THOMAS BEATY 16 Nov 1764...THOMAS BEATY (SEAL), MARGARET BETTY (SEAL), Wit:
JAMES FINLEY, DAVID CHERRY, Rec. Jan. term 1772.

Pp. 547-548: 9 Apr 1771, JOANNA HUMPHRIES of Tryon Co., to ROBERT CHERRY, farmer, for Ł 48
proc. money...200 A on S side Catawba, part of 950 A granted to LEONARD KILIAN,
30 Sept 1749, sold by KILION & wf MARY to GEORGE BROWN, 1 Jan 1754, then to JOHN WATKINS,
20 July 1757, then to JOANNA UMPHRIES 25 Oct 1764...JOANNA UMPHRIES (𝒹) (SEAL), Wit:
JAMES FINLEY, THOMAS BEATY, Jurate. Rec. Jan. term 1772.

Pp. 548-549: 25 Jan 1772, BENJAMIN ELLIS of Tryon Co., to JAMES McENTIRE for Ł 30...250 A
on both sides of Buffalow Creek about a mile above BEATIES land...BENJAMIN
ELLIS (𝖂) (SEAL), Wit: ROBERT McAFEE, Jurate; WM. GREEN.

Pp. 549-550: 1 Sept 1771, AARON BURLESON of Tryon Co., to JOHN METEER of same, for Ł 40...
200 A...AARON BURLESON (SEAL), Wit: DAVID WILKINS, Jurate; ROBERT McMINN. Rec.
Jan. term 1772.

Pp. 550-551: 7 July 1771, JOHN ISON of Tryon Co., to WILLIAM CARPENTER of same, for Ł 100
...300 A on first little broad river, including the sd. JOHN ISONs improvements
adj. WILLIS, granted to ISON, 16 Dec 1769...JOHN ISON (𝒥) (SEAL), Wit: BENJAMIN HARDIN,
Jurate; EDWARD ISON. Rec. Jan term 1772.

Pp. 551-552: 29 Jan 1772, GEORGE SIDES of Tryon Co., to GEORGE WILFONG & PETER MULL of
same, for Ł _____ proc. money...all that land which GEORGE SIDES took up, gr.
26 Oct 1767, 200 A on N side S fork Catawba adj. HENRY WHITNER & FISHERS...GEORGE SEITZ (GS)
[German signature], Wit: JACOB ANTOHNY, Jurate; PHILLIP MARION[?], Rec. Jan. term 1772.

Pp. 552-553: 17 Aug 1771, ANDREW HADDOCK of Tryon Co., to MICHAEL KELLER of same, for Ł 20
proc. money...land on N side S fork Catawba adj. RAMSOURS, 150 A granted to
sd. HADDOCK 4 May 1769..._____ [German signature] (SEAL), Wit:[Two German signatures.]
Rec. Jan term 1772.

Pp. 553-555: 5 Mar 1770, ALEXR. DICKSON of Duplin Co., N. C., to EDWARD DICKSON of same,
for Ł 60 proc. money...land in Tryon Co., on both sides Lawsons fork of
Pacolette including a small improvement above JAMES ALEXANDERS land, granted to ALEXANDER
DICKSON, 23 Apr 1767...ALEXANDER DICKSON (SEAL), Wit: JOHN DICKSON, JAMES DICKSON, Rec.
Jan. term 1772.

Pp. 555-556: 13 Dec. 1771, PHILIP ADAMS & CATRINE his wife of Tryon Co., to MELCHER
HEVENER of Frederic Co., Md., for Ł 130...350 A granted to sd. PHILIP ADAMS
30 Oct 1765...PHILLIP ADAMS (SEAL), CATRIN ADAMS (X) (SEAL), Wit: ABRAHAM ANTHONEY, _____
_____ [German signature], and ADAM ACHERT (X). Rec. Jan. term 1772.

Pp. 556-557: 13 Jan 1772, PETER WHISTLEHUNT of Tryon Co., to JOHN SWRIES[?] for Ł 60 proc.
money...200 A on Clarks Creek, part of 600 A granted to JACOB AGNER, 27 Apr
1764, sold by sd. AGNER to NICHOLAS WHISTLEHUNT by deed 15 June 1765, by NICHOLAS to sd.
PETER...PETER WHISTLEHUNT (P) (SEAL), Wit: _____ FISHER[?] [German signature], JOHANNES
WILL, HENRY HENGRY. Rec. Jan. term 1772. [For deed from JACOB AGNER to NICHOLAS WHISTLE-
HUNT, see my Mecklenburg County, N. C. DEEDS I, P. 48.]

Pp. 557-558: 24 Jan 1772, JOHN LINEBARGER of Tryon Co., to JOHN CON [COX?] for Ł 55 proc.
money...200 A, granted to CHRISTOPHER GRICE[?], 6 Apr 1765, and conveyed to
UBUY CROWDER and from sd. CROWDER to JNO. LINEBARGER, on the long branch of Killians Creek
above the first shoal and above JOS. SAILORS place...JOHANNES LEINBERGER [German signature]
(SEAL), ISABELLE LINEBARGER (X), Wit: FRANCIS McKORKLE, _____ [German signature]. Rec.
Jan. term 1772.

Pp. 559-560: 28 Jan 1772, ADAM SIGHTS of Tryon Co., to GEORGE SIGHTS of same, for Ł 20
...100 A on branches of Leepers Creek, granted 25 Apr 1768...ADAM SIGHTS (X)
(SEAL), Wit: LEMUEL SAUNDERS, GEORGE SEITS[?] [German signature]. Rec. Jan. term 1772.

Pp. 560-561: 2 Oct 1771, WILLIAM DAVIS & wf MARY of Tryon Co., to ROBERT DICKEY of same,
for Ł 30...land on Beaver Dam fork of Bullocks Creek including an improvement
...150 A granted to sd. WILLIAM DAVIS, 6 May 1769...WILLIAM DAVIS (SEAL), MARY DAVIS (X)
(SEAL), Wit: JOHN DICKEY, GEORGE DICKEY, ANDREW COWAN. Rec. Jan. term 1772.

Pp. 562-563: 8 Jan 1772, JAMES MOORE & wf MARY of Tryon Co., to GEORGE SIGMAN of same, for
Ł 30...288 A on a branch of Leyles's Creek between JONASES[?] & CLINES,
granted to sd. JAMES MOORE 28 Apr 1768...JAMES MOORE (SEAL), MARY MOORE (SEAL), Wit:
JOHN[?] FISHER, RICHART COLAT. Rec. Jan. term 1772.

Pp. 563-564: 7 Jan 1772, JOHN REED & wf MARTHA of Tryon Co., to JAMES FINLEY of same, for
Ł 50 proc. money...300 A on S side Catawba, part of 660 A granted to JOHN
BEATY & THOMAS BEATY 24 Sept 1754[?], and by them conveyed to JOHN CONNELLY, then to sd.
JOHN REED...adj. THOMAS BEATY...JOHN REED (SEAL), MARTHA REED (SEAL), Wit: MARY FLEMING
(X), MARTHA REED (X). Rec. Jan. term 1772.

Pp. 564-565: 5 Mar 1770, EDWARD DICKSON of Duplin Co., N. C., to ALEXR DICKSON of same,
for Ł 30 proc. money...land on S side Moores Creek, a branch of Broad River
and on the north side of a branch called SUSY[BOLES] including the popler[sic] spring,
300 A granted to ROBERT DICKSON, 19 Apr 1763...EDWARD DICKSON (SEAL), Wit: JOHN DICKSON,
JAMES DICKSON, JOSEPH DICKSON. Rec. Jan. term 1772.

Pp. 565-566: THOMAS REYNOLDS of Tryon Co., Yeoman, for maintainance the remainder of my
life to be done by HENRY REYNOLDS of same place...two tracts of land in Tryon
Co., the first on both sides of Indian Creek, adj. HENRY REYNOLDS corner, granted to sd.
THOS REYNOLDS 30 Aug 1753 & another tract of 200 A....27 Jan 1772...THOS REYNOLDS (X) (SEAL),
Wit: TIMOTHY RIGGS, JAMES DOHERTY (I). Rec. Jan. term 1772.

Pp. 566-567: ALEXANDER REYNOLDS of Tryon Co., Yeoman, for Ł 30 proc. money pd. by THOMAS
REYNOLDS SENR of same, Yeoman...land on N side Indian Creek, adj. THOMAS REY-
NOLDS line, 200 A...19 Nov 1771...ALEXANDER REYNOLDS(A) (SEAL), Wit: TIMOTHY RIGGS, HENRY
REYNOLDS (+). Rec. Jan. term 1772.

Pp. 567-568: 30 Oct 1771, THOS HESLEP of Tryon Co., to ANDREW HESLEP of same, in consideration of a Roan Gelding three years old, one brown mare three years old, one sorrel horse, cows & calves, & all the wearing belonging to JOHN HESLEY decd., forty bushels of Indian corn, one bed quilt & bed stead paid to the sd. THOMAS HASLEP...390 A, being the plantation now occupied by sd. ANDREW including a survey formerly made for THOMAS ROBINSON, originally granted to sd. ANDREW HESLEP 16 Nov 1764, and by him sold to JOHN HASLEP his son, and now sold back to his father the said ANDREW HASLEP...THOMAS HESLEP (SEAL), Wit: WILLIAM LAWING, DANIEL DUOUR[?] (D). Rec. Jan. term 1772.

Pp. 568-569: 27 Dec 1771, ALEXANDER McENTIRE & wf JANET of Tryon Co., to JAMES COLLINS SENR., for Ł 35 proc. money...200 A on both sides Buffalow Creek...ALEXANDER McENTIRE (SEAL), JANET McTIRE (SEAL), Wit: ROBERT McAFEE, JACOB COLLINS, WM. GREEN. Rec. Jan. term 1772.

Pp. 569-570: 11 July 1771, CHARLES HARRITON of Tryon Co., to WM. JOHNSTON of same, for Ł 60 proc. money...land on both sides Sandy Run, a branch of Broad River, 200 A...CHARLES HARRINTON (X) (SEAL), ELISABETH HARRINTON (X) (SEAL), Wit: JOSHUA RITOUR, EDWARD DICAF JUNIOR, EDWARD DICAF SINIOR. Rec. Jan. term 1772.

Pp. 571-572: 13 Jan 1772, PETER MULL of Tryon Co., to JOHN MYERS of same, for Ł 65...land on N side S fork Catawba adj. THOMAS WHITNERS, 200 A granted to sd. PETER MULL, 22 Apr 1763...PETER MOLL [partial German signature] (SEAL), Wit: THO. POLK, JACOB ANTOHNY. Rec. Jan. term 1772.

Pp. 571-572: 28 JAN 1772, WILLIAM BYERS of Tryon Co., to DAVID PORTER of same, for Ł 100 ...land on main fork of Bullocks Creek, formerly call'd Wrights creek, being 1/2 of tract containing 270 A purchased of JAMES & WILLIAM WRIGHT...WILLIAM BYERS (SEAL), Wit: CHARLES McLEAN, WILLIAM SIMS, JOSEPH DICKSON. Rec. Jan. term 1772.

Pp. 572-573: 25 Nov 1771, WILLM. HANNA & wf JANE to WILLIAM BARRENHILL of same, for Ł 75 proc. money...land on a branch on the S side Allisons creek between WM. DAVIDSONS & JOHN MACKELMURRYS new survey, 340 A, granted to sd. HANNA 16 Apr 1765...WILLIAM HANNA (W) (SEAL), JANE HANNA (2) (SEAL), Wit: ROBERT FLEMING, JOHN GREEN, SAML ADAMS. Rec. Jan. term 1772.

Page 573: WILLIAM JOINER of Tryon Co., for Ł 60 proc. money pd. by WILLIAM SAFFOLD JR.... one negro Hall[?] aged about 10 years, one other male slave named Tom about Seven years, a smale slave Granville aged about seven years, a male slave Abram about four years, female Lucey about 17 years, female Agga aged about 6 years...1 Sept 1770... WILLIAM JOYNIER (SEAL), Wit: WM. SUMNAR[?], JAMES FORSYTH. Rec. Jan. term 1772.

Pp. 573-574: WILLIAM JOINER of Tryon Co., appoint WILLIAM SAFFOLD JUNR., my lawful attorney...[concerning slaves named in preceding deed]...1 Sept 1770...WILLIAM JOYNER (SEAL), Wit: WM. SUMNER, JAMES FORSYTH. Rec. Jan. term 1772.

Pp. 574-575: JOHN JOHNSON and MATTHEW WILSON personally appeared ....JOSHUA JONES told them that through divers temptations on his way that she knew him to be in the bottom field she would come and push him as if she meant to push him in the fire, and he would then throw her down and she would turn upon him & ride him...if she would continue to throw such temptation in his way for the future he would be dam'd but he would __?__ the said MARGARET and a certain GEORGE ROSS would be out at night by themselves and he believed her to be a damned whore. 8 Jan 1772. ROBT BLACKBURN.
    I, JOSHUA JONES, the subscriber do hereby acknowledge that I unjustly & maliciously report the defamatory above related and that I never knew any thing unbecoming or immodest to the sd. MARGARET WILLSON...8 Jan 1772...JOSHUA JONES (ᔕᔭ) (SEAL), Wit: JOHN COSNER[?]. Rec. Jan. term 1772.

Page 575: WILLIAM WRAY of Tryon Co., for Ł 100 pd. by JOHN TAGERT of same...negro female slave Dinah...1 Feb 1772...WM.WRAY (SEAL), Wit: JAMES FORSYTHE, ALEXR. ERWIN. Rec. Jan. term 1772.

Pp. 575-577: 13 & 14 Feb 1772, WILLIAM PATRICK & wf MARY of Tryon Co., to JOSEPH GUYTON of same (lease s5, release Ł 67)...land adj. HENDERSON, land granted to sd. PATRICK 25 Apr 1767, adj. McCULLOH, JAMES MOORE...WILLIAM PATRICK (SEAL), MARY PATRICK (C) (SEAL), Wit: THOS. NEEL, ROBT HARRIS, JOHN PATRICK. Rec. April term 1772.

Pp. 577-580: 4 Jan 1772, DAVID DAVIS & wf ELENOR of Tryon Co., farmer, to HENRY HARTEL of same (lease s5, release Ł 40)...200 A granted to DAVID DAVIS, 28 Oct 1767 on both sides N fork Tyger River adj. JONATHAN NEWMANS upper line on the So side of sd. fork...DAVID DAVIS (D) (SEAL), ELINOR DAVIS (W) (SEAL), Wit: NEVIL WAYLAND, FRANCIS

PRINCE. Rec. April term 1772.

Pp. 580-581: 4 Feb 1771, JAMES KELLY of Tryon Co., to JAMES McENTIRE of same, for ₺ 20
            proc. money...land on both sides Buffalow Creek, 200 A...JAMES KELLY (‡)
(SEAL), Wit: None. Rec. April term 1772.

Pp. 581-582: 24 Mar 1772, ANDREW COWAN of Tryon Co., Waggon Maker, to DAVID PORTER or same,
            for ₺ 50 proc. money...land on both sides Beaver Dam Creek of Bullocks Creek,
150 A adj. WRIGHTS line...ANDW. COWAN (SEAL), Wit: EZEK. POLK, WILLIAM BYERS, SAML. WILL-
SON. Rec. Jan. term 1772. [probably error, should be April term.]

Pp. 582-583: 1 Nov 1771, BARNET BARNS of Tryon Co., to MATTHEW PORTER of same, for ₺ 20...
            land on waters of Allisons Creek [Abbisons?] Creek, on West side of Broad
River, 100 A including my improvement...BARNET BARNS (B) (SEAL), Wit: HUGH QUINN (H),
JOSEPH NEAL. Rec. April term 1772.

Pp. 583-584: 8 Nov 1771, ABRAHAM SCOTT & wf MARGARY of Rowan Co., to CHARLES WILLIAMS JUNR.,
            of Dinwiddie Co., Va., for ₺ 100 proc. money...250 A on S side Catawba, part
of a tract of 1000 A granted to JOHN KILION, 30 SEpt 1759...ABRM. SCOTT (SEAL), Wit:
GEORGE LAMKIN, ROBT ABERNATHY, JAMES ABERNATHY. Rec. April term 1772.

Page 584: 28 Apr 1772, JACOB GREEN of Tryon Co., to FREELOVE GREEN, daughter of sd. JACOB
            GREEN, for natural love & affection...200 A on N side Pacolet River adj. WALLIS
HIX, KING...JACOB GREEN (SEAL), Wit: WM. YANCEY, JOHN MAGUIRE. Rec. April term 1772.

Page 585: 27 Dec 1770, ROBERT McCASLAND of Tryon Co., to JAMES POLLY of same, for ₺ 10
            proc. money...200 A on waters of Kuykendalls Creek, including where sd. McCASLAND
built a house, granted to sd. ROBT. McCASLAND 25 Apr 1767...ROBT. McCASLAND (SEAL), Wit:
JAMES ALLEN, JOHN BEATTY, WALLACE BEATY. Rec. April term 1772.

Page 586: 7 Apr 1772, JAMES PALLEY of Tryon Co., weaver, to JAMES WHITE of Chester Co.,
            Pennsylvania, for ₺ 92 proc. money...land on a So Branch of the So Fork of the
Catawba, alone his other line, adj. MICHAEL HOFSTETLER...on Lond[?] Creek granted to
FRANCIS BEATY 19 Apr 1763, conveyed to sd. JAMES 29 Mar 1770...JAMES PALLEY (SEAL), Wit:
JAMES ALLEN, ROBT. BLACKBURN.

Pp. 586-588: 1 Dec 1771, HUGH QUINN & wf MARGARET of Sugar Creek, Prov. of N. C., to
            GEORGE DICKINSON of Charlestown, Prov. of S. C., for ₺ 700 SC money...land on
E side Broad River adj. sd. QUINN, granted to WALKER, then sold to RICHARD, then to JOHN
STANFORD, then to sd. QUINN...HUGH QUINN (H) (SEAL), MARGARET QUINN (X) (SEAL), Wit:
GLASS CASTON, THOMAS HICKS (T). Rec. April term 1772.

Page 588: WILLIAM REED of Mecklenburg Co., for ₺ 40 pd. by MOSES CRAWFORD of Tryon Co...
            land on Jacobs River, being a So fork of the So fork of the Catawba River,
three miles above the Indian old ford, 300 A...WILL REED (SEAL), Wit: ROBT. BLACKBURN,
TIMOTHY RIGGS. Rec. April term 1772.

Page 589: 14 Oct 1771, JACOB COBRON of Tryon Co., to ELIAS MORGIN of Brunswick Co., Va.,
            for ₺ 70...200 A on a branch of Broad River...JACOB COBURN (SEAL), Wit: JOHN
MORGAN, HART.[?] HONNICUTT. Rec. April term 1772.

Page 590: 18 Apr 1772, JOHN TURNER of Tryon Co., to JOHN ASHWORTH of same, for ₺ 100 proc.
            money...300 A on McFaddens Creek on Second Broad River, including the said
improvements where ASHWORTH now lives...JOHN TURNER (SEAL), Wit: WILLIAM YANCEY, SOPHIA
YANCEY. Rec. April term 1772.

Pp. 590-591: ___ Oct 1770, MICHAEL HECKELMAN & wf ELIZABETH of Tryon Co., to SAML. MARTIN
            of same, for ₺ 10...land on both sides Anderson Mountain Creek, granted to
sd. HECKELMAN 22 Dec 1768, adj. SAILORS line...MICHAEL HECKELMAN (X) (SEAL), ELIZABETH
HECKELMAN (X) (SEAL), Wit: ISAAC LECLARE[?], HENRY LOLLER. Rec. April term 1772.

Pp. 592-593: 15 Feb 1772, GEORGE POTTS of Tryon Co., yeoman, to PETER CARPENTER of same,
            Blacksmith, whereas sd. POTTS stands justly indebted to sd. CARPENTER for
₺ 40 NC money, by one certain sum bearing date with this same indenture with lawful
interest upon the 15 Feb 1774...200 A on Potts Buffalow Creek, on S side Guthreys branch
...GEORGE POTTS (+) (SEAL), Wit: JAMES COZART. Rec. April term 1772.

Pp. 593-594: 23 Apr 1772, ABRAHAM KUYKENDALL of Tryon Co., planter, to BAPTIST SCOTT, for
            ₺ 70 proc. money...300 A on S side Catawba, opporsite the great Shoals, gran-
ted to MARTIN SHUCKMAN[?] by patent 23 Feb 1754, conveyed to sd. KUYKENDALL 27 Aug 1757...
ABRAHAM KUYKENDALL (A) (SEAL), Wit: WILLIAM HENRY, JAMES EDENS (‡), JOHN KUYKENDALL. Rec.

April term 1772.

Pp. 594-595: 28 Apr 1772, MOSES MOORE of Tryon County, planter to JOSEPH LAWRENCE of
same, planter, for Ꝉ 100 proc. money...204 A on both sides Camp Creek adj.
BROWNS line, MOORES line...granted 6 Oct 1765...MOSES MOOR (SEAL), Wit: THOS. POLK,
FRAS. ADAMS. Rec. April term 1772.

Page 595: 27 April 1772, JOHN PATTON of Tryon Co., planter, to JOHN HOPE of same, planter,
for Ꝉ 60...land on S side Cataba on both sides CHARLES MOORES branch of Allisons
Creek, 250 A adj. WILLIAM HANNAH, DAVIDSON, JOHN WILSON...JOHN PATTON (SEAL), Wit:
JOSEPH HARDIN, JAMES THOMPSON, JOHN SMITH. Rec. April term 1772.

Pp. 596-597: 27 Feb 1772, JOHN HOWELL of St. Pauls Parish, Georgia, to PETER PATTYPOOL
of Tryon Co., for Ꝉ 70 proc. money...202 A on Black Walnut Creek, otherwise
Mitchells Creek, a branch of Fair Forrest, granted 26 Mar 1755...JOHN HOWELL (SEAL),
Wit: JEREMIAH ROUTH, ELISABETH CARSON. Rec. April term 1772.
[For reference to plat and grant for the tract mentioned, see my North Carolina Land
Grants in South Carolina, Vol II, p. 11]

Pp. 597-598: North Carolina: 7 Nov 1771, JOHN BROWN, late of Rowan Co., yeoman &
FRANCIS McKORKLE & wf SARAH of same, to JOHN WORK of same, yeoman, for Ꝉ 70
proc. money...400 A on both sides second Broad River at the mouth of Camp Creek about 2
miles below MOSES MOORES & adj. to MOSES & AARON MOORES...JOHN BROWN (SEAL), FRANCIS
McCORKEL (SEAL), SARAH McCORKEL (SEAL), Wit: JAMES BYARES, BENJAMIN McFARLIN. Rec. April
term 1772.

Page 598: 28 Apr 1772, WILLIAM RAMSEY of Tryon Co., farmer, to JOHN KRAPS of same, for Ꝉ
32 proc. money...land on Leonards fork of Indian Creek adj. SAMUEL HOWARD, decd.
300 A granted to sd. RAMSEY 16 Apr 1765...WILLIAM RAMSEY (SEAL), Wit: JAMES WRIGHT,
DAVID RAMSEY. Rec. April term 1772.

Pp. 599-600: 27 Apr 1772, DERRICK RAMSOUR of Tryon Co., planter, to JACOB RAMSOUR of same,
for Ꝉ 250...land in the fork of S fork Catawba & Clarks Creek, 600 A
conveyed by ANDREW LAMBETH by L & R 11 Aug 1758 & recorded in
Rowan County & a tract adj. to it, granted to RAMSOUR 17 Apr 1753, 200 A, & another tract
granted 6 Apr 1765,100 A and another granted 29 Apr 1768, all which patents are enrolled
in the Secretary Generals Office, total 960 A...DERRICK RAMSOUR (X) (SEAL), Wit: ADOLPH
REEP [RUP?] [German signature], JOHN DUNN. Rec. April term 1772.
[For deed from ANDREW LAMBETH(LAMBERT) to DERRICK RAMSOUR, see Rowan Co., N. C. Deed
Abstracts, Vol. I, p. 3, by Mrs. Stahle Linn, Jr.]

Page 600: 28 Apr 1772, DERRICK RAMSOUR to DAVID RAMSOUR, son of sd. DERRICK, for Ꝉ 250...
600 A on N side S fork Catawba...DERRICK RAMSOUR (X) (SEAL), Wit: ADOLPH REEP
(RUP?), JOHN DUNN. Rec. April term 1772.

Page 601: 30 Apr 1772, JACOB RAMSOUR of Tryon Co., planter, to DAVID RAMSOUR of same,
for Ꝉ 100 proc. money...land on N side S fork Catawba River, adj. lines of
the late HENRY RAMSOUR, decd, adj. WELCHES line & another tract adj. to it...total 280 A
...JACOB RAMSOUR (SEAL), Wit: JOHN DILLINGER, JOHN DUNN, JACOB COBURN. Rec. April term
1772.

Page 602: 27 Apr 1772, JACOB RAMSOUR & DAVID RAMSOUR, surviving Heirs & Legatees of HENRY
RAMSOUR, decd, and JOHN RAMSOUR decd, for Ꝉ 200 to DERRICK RAMSOUR of Tryon
Co....land on N side S fork Catawba, 600 A granted to DAVID JONES, Sheriff in virtue of
his office to HENRY RAMSOUR, now decd, & bequeathed to JOHN RAMSOUR decd, & his surviving
brothers JACOB & DAVID...JACOB RAMSOUR (SEAL), DAVID RAMSOUR (SEAL), Wit: ADOLPH REEP
(RUP?), JOHN DUNN. Rec. Apr. term 1772.

Pp. 602-603: JACOB & DAVID RAMSOUR, both of Tryon Co., planters, bound to DERRICK RAM-
SOUR for the sum of Ꝉ 1000...27 Apr 1772, 960 A...do promise to provide
yearly during his natural life, Ꝉ 15 proc. money, 25 bu. sheat, 25 bu. Indian corn, 50
1kbs. good butter, 400 weight of good beef & 1/6 profit of the fruit trees, 30 lbs. sugar,
3 lbs. Bohea tea & 2 lbs. coffee, 12 gallons of whiskey, 4 bu. malt, 1 bu. salt...
JACOB RAMSOUR (SEAL), DAVID RAMSOUR (SEAL), Wit: ADOLPH REEP (RUP?), JOHN DUNN. Rec.
April term 1772.

Page 604: DERRICK RAMSOUR of Tryon Co., planter, for Ꝉ 20 proc. money, pd. by JACOB &
DAVID RAMSOUR, my two sons...lands where I now live, & all stock, etc...DERRICK
RAMSOUR (X) (SEAL), Wit: ADOLPH REEP (RUP?), JOHN DUNN. Rec. April term 1772.

Pp. 604-605: JAMES ALEXANDER of Tryon Co., to JOHN TAGERT, one bay horse, black mare, & other cattle & stock (enumerated), for Ŀ 50...JAMES ALEXANDER (SEAL), Wit: WM. HENRY, ANDW. PATRICK. W. AVERY, Atty. Rec. April term 1772.

Pp. 605-607: 20 & 21 Apr 1772, JOHN ALLEN, cooper of Granville Co., S. C. to PETER ARRAND of Craven Co., S. C., for (lease s5, release Ŀ 250)...land in Tryon Co., on N side S fork Catawba, 600 A, granted 7 May 1754...JOHN ALLEN (SEAL), Wit: PETER BELLER, THOMAS CHADWICK. Rec. July term 1772.

Pp. 607-609: 24 Apr 1771, JOHN TAGERT, high sheriff of Tryon Co., to FRANCIS ADAMS of same county...by virtue and in obedience to his commission given to him... whereas judgement was lately received in the inferior court of please & Quarter Sessions by FRANCIS ADAMS for the recovery of Ŀ 4 proc. money in debt, also Ŀ 2 s 17 & d6 by your deputy WILLIAM YANCEY returned on the writ of attachment, for Ŀ 6 tract sold by sd. JOHN TAGERT, sheriff to FRANCIS ADAMS, the property of HENRY TURNER, including the improvement that DAVID COX formerly lived on, 100 A on both sides Kings Creek...JOHN TAGERT Shff (SEAL), Wit: THOMAS CLARK, ROBT. LUSK. Rec. July term 1772.

Pp. 609-610: 3 Oct 1771, ROBERT ABERNATHY & wf ANN of Tryon Co., to JOHN ALSTON of Wake Co., N. C., for Ŀ 80 proc. money...300 A on W side Catawba, and on both sides of a branch falling into the Catawba River, a little below the Tuccaseegee Ford, granted to WILLIAM HENRY, and by him conveyed to ROBERT ABERNATHY JUR., patent bearing date 25 Feb 1754...ROBERT ABERNATHY (SEAL), ANN ABERNATHY (SEAL), Wit: PHILIP ALSTON, WILLIAM LAMKIN, GEORGE LAMKIN. Rec. July term 1772.

Pp. 610-611: 10 Oct 1771, FRANCIS BEATEY of Mecklenburg Co., surveyor, to PHILIP ALSTON, Gunsmith, of Tryon Co., for Ŀ 200 proc. money...land in fork of Catawba River by the waggon road, adj. JOHN CATHEY, THOS. HENRY, BOLES, McNABBS, 600 A, the substance of three patents, 300 A granted to GEORGE SCALES, 6 Apr 1753, conveyed to FRANCIS BEATY by deed, 20 & 21 Dec 1762, and 250 A granted to SAMUEL YOUNG, 20 Oct 1758, conveyed to sd. FRANCIS BEATY 28 May 1761, and 50 A granted to sd. BEATY 16 Dec 1769... FRANCIS BEATEY (SEAL), Wit: GEORGE LAMKIN, JAMES PALLEG[?]. Rec. July term 1772.

Pp. 611-612: 26 Oct 1771, MATTHEW FLOYD of Tryon Co., to JOHN McKNITT ALEXANDER of Mecklenburg Co., for Ŀ 70 proc. money...170 A granted to FLOYD, 25 Apr 1767, on the river bank, on the W side Broad river including the improvements where sd. FLOYD now dwells, adj. WILLIAM McMULLENS...MATHEW FLOYD (SEAL), Wit: FRAS. ADAMS, SAML. SPENCER. Rec. July term 1772.

Pp. 612-614: 14 Jun 1771, GEO. CLAYTON of Tryon Co., to GEORGE BLACK of same, (lease s5, release Ŀ 35 proc. money)...land in the forks of the Broad River and in the forks of <u>Second Broad River</u> above MOSES MOORES upper entry including the two branches of the beaver dam, 460 A granted to sd. CLAYTON 16 Apr 1765...SARAH CLAYTON, GEORGE CLAYTON (SEAL), Wit: JAMES WITHROW (丰). Rec. July term 1772.

Pp. 614-615: 31 July 1770, THOMAS DICKSON of Tryon Co., to HUGH BRYSON of same, [amt. of money not given]...300 A on waters of Crowders Creek adj. TATES corner... ROBT. TATES old entry[?]...THOMAS DICKSON (SEAL), Wit: MATTHEW DICKSON, JOHN THOMPSON. Rec. July term 1772.

Pp. 615-616: 27 July 1772, ISAAC HINTON of Tryon Co., to JAMES BUCKHANNON of same, for Ŀ 15...50 A on N side Hintons Creek, granted to sd. HINTON16 Nov 1764... ISAAC HINTON (X) (SEAL), Wit: JAMES WHITESIDES, JACOB WILLIS. Réc. July term 1772.

Pp. 616-617: 19 June 1772, ADAM DICK of Tryon Co., to GEO. DICK of same, for Ŀ 20 proc. money...land on S side Catawba River on the waters of Killians Creek, 141 A, part of a grant to sd. ADAM DICK, 14 Nov 1771....ADAM DICK (SEAL), Wit: MATHIAS PETERSON, GEORGE REAL. Rec. July term 1772.

Pp. 617-618: 21 Oct 1771, SAMUEL COBURN of Tryon Co., to JOHN DOZER of same, for Ŀ 20 proc. money...100 A on S side Catawba, adj. JOSEPH WISHARTS, JAMES COBURNS, JOHN COBURNS, SAMUEL COBURNS, part of a patent to sd. SAMUEL COBURN for 176 A 6 Oct 1767 ...SAMUEL COBURN (+) (SEAL), Wit: DAVID CROCKATT JUNR., DAVID CROCKATT SENR. Rec. July term 1772.

Pp. 618-619: 25 June 1772, MATHIAS PETERSON of Tryon Co., to MICHAEL ENGLE of same, for Ŀ 12 proc. money...land on waters of Killians Creek adj. PHILIP EREHARTS... 250 A, part of a grant to sd. MATHIAS PETERSON 18 Apr 1771...MATHIAS PETERSON (SEAL), Wit: HEINRICH _____ [German signature], MARTIN SHUTTS, ANDREW PETERSON. Rec. July term 1772.

Pp. 619-620: 28 Jan 1772, REES PRICE of Tryon Co., to WILLIAM EDGAR of same, for ₺ 5 proc.
money...200 A granted to JOHN HILL 26 Sept 1766 & from HILL conveyed to PRICE
27 Dec 1770...on both sides Crowders Creek, on S side S fork Catawba adj. JOHN CRAGE...
REES PRICE (SEAL), Wit: JAMES RAMSEY, THOMAS PRICE, ARCHALL EDGER. Rec. July term 1772.

Pp. 620-621: _____ 1772, JOHN GALLESPY of Tryon Co., to THOMAS GALLESPY of _____ Co.,
same prov., for ₺ 10 proc., for ₺ 10 proc. money...200 A on both sides Muddy fork of Buffalo
Creek, adj. BEATIES line, granted to sd. JOHN GALLESPY 22 Dec 1768...JOHN GELLESPIE (SEAL),
Wit: PATRICK McDAVID, and one German signature. Rec. July term 1772.

Page 621: 23 July 1772, ABRM. ALEXANDER of Mecklenburg Co., to NATHANIEL HENDERSON of
Tryon Co., for ₺ 20 proc. money...150 A on Duharts Creek to the south of ABRM.
ALEXANDERs and near NATHANIEL HENDERSON, granted to sd. ALEXANDER 9 Nov 1764...ABRM.
ALEXANDER (SEAL), Wit: JOHN MOORE, WM. MUCKELMURRY. Rec. July term 1772.

Page 622: 15 Apr 1772, THOMAS BEATY of Rowan Co., planter, to DAVID HODSON of Tryon Co.,
for ₺ 72 proc. money...400 A on W side Catabo above JOHN BEATIES, granted to
FRANCIS BEATY 24 Apr 1762 and conveyed to sd. THOMAS BEATY...THOMAS BEATY (SEAL), Wit:
ABEL BEATY, THOMAS BEATY. Rec. July term 1772.

Page 623: MARGARET WILLIS to her son WILLIAM HANNAH...gift of cattle & other items (listed)
when sd. HANNAH shall arrive at 21 years old...11 Feb 1772...MARGARET WILLIS
(+) (SEAL), Wit: JAMES BUCHANAN, ELEXND. COYL. Rec. July term 1772.

Pp. 623-624: 24 Jan 1772, LYLLIUS JOHNSON of Tryon Co., to JAMES KELLY of same, for ₺ 50
...72 A on W side Main Broad River adj. EZEKIEL SMITH, granted to her by
patent 24 Oct 1767...LYLLIUS JOHNSON (O) (SEAL), Wit: JONAS BEDFORD, WILLIAM TWITTY,
WILLIAM CLEGHORN.

Pp. 624-625: 18 Oct 1771, THOMAS WARRIN of Tryon Co., to JOHNLUSK of same, for ₺ 30...186
A on a branch of Pinch gut, a branch of Clarks Creek adj. SIMEON HOFFES
[HOSSES?]...granted 5 May 1769...THOMAS WARRIN (SEAL), Wit: WILLIAM PARKER (9), WILLIAM
LOGAN (L), HENRY BALES (X). Rec. July term 1772.

Pp. 625-626: 9 Oct 1771, JACOB SEITS & wf MARY of Tryon Co., to JOHN McELROY of same, for
₺ 30 proc. money...250 A on W side Catawba, on head of Beaverdam branch of
MATHEW ARMSTRONGS little creek, granted to sd. SEITS 28 Apr 1768...JACOB SEITS (SEAL),
MARY SEITS (∧) (SEAL), Wit: WILLIAM MOORE, WILLIAM CATHEY. Rec. July term 1772.

Page 626: 29 July 1772, PETER WATKINS to JOHN McKINNY, both of Tryon Co., for ₺ 50...
land on both sides of McKinnys Creek of Broad River, 100 A granted 14 Nov 1771
...PETER WATKINS (SEAL), Wit: WILLIAM CAPSHAW, ALEXANDER COULTER. Rec. July term 1772.

Pp. 626-627: 25 Jan 1772, AGNES NEVANS of Rowan Co., to ALEXANDER McGAUGHEY of Tryon Co.,
yeoman, for ₺ 29... land in Tryon Co. [acreage not given]...AGNESS NEVINS
(+) (SEAL), Wit: JAMES MARTIN, HENREY NEVINS. Rec. July term 1772.

Pp. 627-628: 20 May 1772, THOMAS LOVELATTY & wf HANNA of Tryon Co., to ROBT. McMULLEN
of same, for ₺ 65 proc. money...200 A on Indian Camp Cr-ek, a fork of Abit-
tons Creek, waters of Broad River, part of 400 A granted 26 Spet 1766...THOS LOVELATTY
(SEAL), HANNAH LOVELATTY (h) (SEAL), Wit: ROBT LUSK, ABM. SMITH. Rec. July term 1772.

Pp. 628-629: 7 June 1772, ALEXANDER McGAUGHEY of Tryon Co., Yeoman, to ROBT. McMURRY of
Mecklenburg Co., yeoman, for ₺ 30 NC money...land on both sides Catheys Creek,
below WRAYs land...ALEXANDER McGAUGHY (SEAL), RACHEL McGAUGHEY (O) (SEAL), Wit: JOHN
DEVENY, SAMUEL McMURRY. Rec. July term 1772.

Pp. 629-630: 3 Feb 1772, EDMD BISHOP & wf ANNY[?] of Tryon Co., to JOHN MILLER of same,
for consideration of another tract of land made over to sd. EDMD BISHOP &
wf AMY...land on middle fork of Turkey Creek, granted to sd. BISHOP 25 Sept 1766 adj.
JOHN MILLER...EDMUND BISHOP (2) (SEAL), EME BISHOP (O) (SEAL), Wit: GEORGE ROSS, THOMAS
GERVIN, JAMES KELLEY. Rec. July term 1772.

Pp. 630-631: 16 July 1770, ROBERT PATRICK of Tryon Co., to JOHN PATRICK of same, for s 1
sterling...land on W side Catawba, above the mouth of the S fork, adj. WM.
RATCHFORD, JOSEPH CARROLLS & TYREE HARRISS, including his own improvements...ROBERT
PATRICK (R) (SEAL), Wit: JOHN HOWE, ANDREW ARMOR, THOS NEAL. Rec. July term 1772.

Pp. 631-632: 27 Dec 1770, JOHN HILL & wf JANE of Tryon Co., to REESE PRICE JUR. of Mecklenburg Co., for ₺ 5 proc. money...200 A granted to sd. HILL 26 Sept 1766
land on both sides Crowders Creek on S side S fork Catawba...JOHN HILL (SEAL), JANE HILL

(SEAL), Wit: RICHD BARRY, JOHN LAWSON, THOMAS PRICE. Rec. July term 1772.

Pp. 632-633: 5 Mar 1772, JAMES PATTERSON, SARAH PATTERSON, THOMAS PATTERSON & MARY
          PATTERSON of Tryon Co., to JOHN PATTERSON of same, for Ь 180 proc. money...
land on S side Catawba River on both sides Allisons Creek, 325 A, part of land conveyed by
ANDREW ALLISON to JOHN McCULLOH, 25 Jan 1762, conveyed by McCULLOH to GEORGE PATTERSON,
21 May 1769, and from GEORGE PATTERSON to sd. JAMES PATTERSON & THOMAS PATTERSON, and now
to JOHN PATTERSON...THOMAS PATTERSON (SEAL), JAMES PATTERSON (SEAL), MARY PATTERSON (1)
(SEAL), SARAH PATTERSON (X) (SEAL), Wit: ROBERT DONALDSON, GEORGE PLEMON. Rec. July
term 1772.

Pp. 633-634: 28 Mar 1772, ROBERT ARMSTRONG of Tryon Co., to JAMES PATTERSON of same, for
          Ь 20 proc. money...land on waters of Allisons Creek, adj. GEORGE RENICKS,
CAMPBELL, part of 400 A granted to WILLIAM PATRICK 16 Nov 1764, conveyed to sd. ARMSTRONG
by L. & R. on 11 & 12 Jan[?] 1765, 120 A...ROBERT ARMSTRONG (SEAL), AGNESS ARMSTRONG (a)
Wit: JAS. PALLEY, JAMES RITCHEY. Rec. July term 1772.

Pp. 634-635: 1 July 1772, PETER STOODS & wf ELIZABETH of Tryon Co., planter, to FRANCIS
          PALMER of same, for Ь 120 proc. money...land on both sides Mackling Creek,
500 A...PETER STOTZ[?] [German signature], ELIZABETH _____ (⊕) [German signature]. Wit:
CHRISTOPHER BECKMAN, MATHIAS BETERINGER. Rec. July term 1772.

Page 635: 11 Feb 1772, WILLIAM REED of Mecklenburg Co., to ANSON REYNOLDS of Tryon Co.,
          for Ь 31 s 10 proc. money of N. C....land on Jacobs River, a S fork of S fork
Catawba River including the rich bottom, 200 A granted to sd. WILLIAM REED, 25 Apr 1767...
WILL REED (SEAL), Wit: _____ [German signature], JESSE REYNOLDS, JAMES CRAWFORD (O).
Rec. July term 1772.

Page 636: 1 Apr 1772, ANDREW GOFORTH of Tryon Co., planter, to JAMES RAMSEY of same, for
          Ь 40 proc. money...136 A on S side Crowders Creek, granted to sd. GOFORTH 14
Nov 1771, adj. WM. ADAMS, JAMES RAMSEY...ANDREW GOFORTH (SEAL), ELIZABETH GOFORTH (C)
(SEAL), Wit: THOMAS PRICE, JANE McLEOD[?] (O). Rec. July term 1772.

Pp. 636-637: 20 May 1772, MOSES WHITELY of Tryon Co., farmer to FRANCIS SHUB for Ь 40....
          land on Clarks Creek adj. WILLIAM WALSHES including his own improvements,
167[?] A granted to sd. WHITELY, 6 Apr 1765...MOSES WHITELY (SEAL), Wit: SAML ADAMS,
ROBT. BLACKBURN. Rec. July term 1772.

Pp. 637-638: 27 July 1772, JOHN POTTS & wf MARY of Tryon Co., to PAUL TOWNSEND of Charles-
          town, Prov. of So. Carolina, for Ь 200 s 15 d 4 proc. money...south half of
land sd. POTTS now lives on, on both sides North fork of Pacolet River on the S side of
sd. RIVER, adj. MARGARET CAMPBELLS line, JOHN WILSONS corner, 600 A, 300 A taken off the
lower end...JOHN POTTS (SEAL), MARY POTTS (M) (SEAL), Wit: DAVID GRIGG, JAMES CAPSHAW,
JOHN MEGREU, ARTHUR ROGERS. Rec. July term 1772.

Pp. 638-639: 25 July 1772, JOHN WOODS of Tryon Co., planter, to BENJAMIN VAUGHN of same,
          for Ь 20...the upward half of the plantation he lives on, granted to sd.
WOODS 22 Dec 1770, on N side N fork Pacolet...JOHN WOOD (SEAL), SOPHIA WOODS (+) (SEAL),
Wit: MILES HART, ALEXANDER COULTER, DAVID DICKEY. Rec. Jluy term 1772.

Pp. 639-640: 30 July 1772, JAMES WILSON of Tryon Co., farmer from?WM. WILSON of same,
          cordwainer...land on branches of Clarks Creek adj. MATHEW WILSON, ANDERSON,
200 A granted to JAMES WILSON 18 Apr 1771...WILLIAM WILSON (SEAL), Wit: ROBT BLACKBURN,
GODARD BRUTEL[?] (X). Rec. July term 1772.

Pp. 640-641: 5 Oct 1771, NICHOLAS FISHER & wf ELIZABETH of Tryon Co., to THOMAS WARREN
          of same, for Ь 40 "like money"...200 A on first Broad River, adj. JOHN GRADEY,
granted 22 Sept 1765...NICHOLAS FISHER (SEAL), ELIZABETH FISHER (X) (SEAL), Wit: JOHN
LUSK, JOHN STANFORD, JEAN BRADLY.

Pp. 641-642: 5 May 1772, JOHN STANFORD & wf SARAH of Tryon Co., to THOMAS WARREN of same,
          for Ь 70 like money...land on both sides Buffalo Creek about a mile from the
mouth adj. ROBERT HUMPHRES, 200 A, granted 25 Apr 1767...JOHN STANFORD (SEAL), SARY STAN-
FORD (O) (SEAL), Wit: JOHN LOGIN, JOSEPH WARRIN, HUGH QUINN (H). Rec. July term 1772.

Pp. 642-643: 10 July 1772, HUGH BEATEY of Rowan Co., farmer, to WILLIAM WHITESIDES JUNR.,
          of Tryon Co., for Ь 100 proc. money...land on both sides of little Broad
River, 200 A granted to sd. BEATEY 6 Apr 1765...HUGH BEATEY (SEAL), Wit: JACOB WILLIS,
BENJAMIN BRACKET (B). Rec. July term 1772.

Pp. 643-644: 10 July 1772, HUGH BEATEY of Rowan Co., to JAMES WHITESIDE of Tryon Co., for
Ł 100 proc. money...land on both sides of first little Broad River...100 A,
part of 300 A, granted to sd. HUGH BEATEY 26 May 1765...HUGH BEATEY (SEAL), Wit: JACOB
WILLIS, BENJAMIN BRACKET (B). Rec. July term 1772.

Pp. 644-645: 31 July 1772, JOHN OAKES of Tryon Co., to WILLIAM WRAY of same, for Ł 50
proc. money...275 A granted to THOMAS HOWARD 1765, adj. JOSEPH GREENS...on
both sides Buffalo Creek...JOHN OAKES (O)(SEAL), Wit: JOHN TAGERT, ROBT. McCASLAND. Rec.
July term 1772.

Page 645: 11 July 1772, JOHN McENTIRE & wf RACHEL of Tryon Co., to GEORGE WIGGINTON of
same, for Ł 30 s 12...land on both sides first little broad river adj. THOMAS
BLACK, 100 A granted to JOHN McENTIRE 4 May 1770...JOHN McENTIRE (SEAL), RACHEL McENTIRE
(SEAL), Wit: JAS. McENTIRE, NICHOLAS FISHER. Rec. July term 1772.

Page 646:   OCTOBER COURT 1772. ANDREW NEEL Register.
23 Oct 1772, ABRAHAM KEENER & wf ULA of Tryon Co. to JAMES ABERNATHY of same,
for Ł 60...land on both sides Leeper Creek, adj. ABM. KEENERS line,280 A, part of 450 A
granted unto GASPER KEENER on 20 May 1754...ABRAHAM KEENER (SEAL), ULA KEENER (X) (SEAL)_
Wit: WILLIAM MOORE, ROBT. ABERNATHY, MILES ABERNATHY. Rec. Oct. term 1772.

Page 647: 31 Aug 1772, BENJAMIN SHAW of Tryon Co., to JOHN ALEXANDER of same, for Ł 75
proc. money...land on both sides first little Broad River including the forks,
granted to sd. SHAW 26 Sept 1766...BENJAMIN SHAW (SEAL), Wit: MARTHA BLACKBURN, ROBT.
BLACKBURN. Rec. Oct. term 1772.

Pp. 647-648: 7 Mar 1772, GEORGE LAMKIN & wf HANNAH of Tryon Co., to WM. ALSTON of same,
for Ł 60 proc. money...land on S side Catawba River near FRANCIS BEATIES
land adj. WIDOW McKENDRICKS granted to ROBT SCOTT 21 Dec 1763...GEORGE LAMKIN (SEAL), Wit:
JOHN ALSTON, JOHN ALSTON, PHILIP ALSTON. Rec. Oct. term 1772.

Pp. 648-649: 3 Oct 1772, JOSEPH DAVIS of Tryon Co., planter, to WM. ALSTON of same, for
Ł 40 proc. money...93 A on both sides Dutchmans Creek known by the name of
DAVIS mill place, part of a grant to JOSEPH DAVIS (decd) 6 May 1769...JOSEPH DAVIS (J)
(SEAL), Wit: GEORGE LAMKIN, JOHN ROSS, NATHAN DAVIS. Rec. Oct. term 1772.

Pp. 649-650: 5 Oct 1772, SAML YOUNG of Rowan Co., to JOHN ALSTON of Tryon Co., for Ł 46
s 5 proc. money...250 A on S side Catawba River nigh to the Tucasege Ford
adj. ANDREW McNABBS, WM. HENRY, SAMUEL COBRUNS & JUDITH COBURNS old lines, granted to sd.
YOUNG 26 Nov 1757...SAML. YOUNG (SEAL), Wit: JNO. KIRKCONNELL, JOHN McELROY, JOSEPH JOR-
DAN. Rec. Oct. term 1772.

Pp. 650-651: 27 Mar 1772, ANDW. McNABB & wf MARGARET of Tryon Co., to JOHN ALSTON of same,
for Ł 120 proc. money...130 A on S side Catawba River adj. his own, SAML.
YOUNG, & KELLYS land, granted to sd. ANDW. McNABB 5 Apr 1765...ANDREW McNABB (SEAL),
MARGARET McNABB (O) (SELA), Wit: WM. ALSTON, JOHN ALSTON, JOHN BROWN Skrimshire. Rec.
Oct. term 1772.

Pp. 651-652: 27 Mar 1772, ANDW. McNABB & wf MARGARET to JOHN ALSTON for Ł 20 proc. money
300 A on S side Catawba River, part of a tract of land formerly WM. HENRYS
granted to sd. HENRY 25 Feb 1754 & by deed made to ANDREW McNABB 16 Aug 1760...ANDREW
McNABB (SEAL), MARGARET McNABB (O) (SEAL), Wit: WM. ALSTON, JOHN ALSTON. Rec. Oct. term
1772.

Pp. 652-653: 7 July 1772, JOHN NICHOLS of Tryon Co., Bricklayer, to JAMES COZART of same,
planter, for Ł 10 proc. money...land on both sides Long Creek adj. MOORES,
being the land where sd. JAMES COZART now lives..JNO. NICHOLS (SEAL), Wit: FREDERICK
HAMBRIGHT, JAMES DUFF, JOSEPH CLARK. Rec. Oct. term 1772.

Pp. 653-654: 23 Mar 1772, DAVID JENKINS of Tryon Co., to JAMES COZART of same, yeoman,
for Ł 40 NC money...land adj. MOORES, 52 A part of a larger tract of land
which CRASSIMUS RUPER in his life time granted to DAVID JENKINS by lease bearing date
15 Jan 1769 recorded in the Registers office in Tryon County afsd. in book No. __...
DAVID JENKINS (SEAL), Wit: FREDERICK HAMBRIGHT, SARAH HAMBRIGHT (⬤) Rec. Oct. term 1772.

Pp. 654-655: 29 Aug 1772, GEORGE PEE of Tryon Co., to EDWARD CALLEHAN for Ł 30 proc. money
...land on both sides Hunting Creek adj. THOS. ROBINSONS including where
WALKELS [sic] road crosses the creek adj. SAML WITHROW, 200 A granted to GEORGE PEE 25
Apr 1765...GEORGE PEE (SEAL), Wit: JOHN MOORE, ANDW NEEL. Rec. Oct. term 1772.

Pp. 655-656: 30 June 1772, JAMES ANDEREWS of Tryon Co., to WM. CALLAHAM of same, for ₤ 33
s 15...land on both sides Hunting Creek, below WITHROWs land, 200 A granted
9 Apr 1770...JAMES ANDEREWS (SEAL), Wit: JACOB NICKOLS, EDWARD CALLAHAN (O). Rec. Oct.
term 1772.

Pp. 656-657: 20 Sept 1772, JOHN POTTS of Tryon Co., to NICHOLAS CLAY of same, for ₤ 25...
land granted to JOHN POTTS 22 Dec 1768, adj. to sd. CLAY, adj. corner of the
school House land...JOHN POTTS (SEAL), Wit: ALEXR. IRWIN, WILLIAM CUMBERLAND. Rec. Oct.
term 1772.

Page 657: 24 Oct 1772, NICHOLAS WELCH, planter, & wf ELIZABETH to JOHN CUSTER, Black smith,
for ₤ 40 proc. money...land on both sides Buffalo Branch of Indian Creek adj.
land surveyed for JACOB BEEK [BECK?], 300 A granted to sd. WELCH, 20 May 1772...NICHOLAS
WELSH (SEAL), ELIZABETH WELSH (E) (SEAL), Wit: NICOLAS _____ [German signature], HENRY
WORTMAN. Rec. Oct. term 1772.

Page 658: 11 Aug 1772, JACOB COBRON of Tryon Co., to JOHN STROUD of same, for ₤ 60 proc.
money...land on S side Catawba River adj. SAML COBORNS & GEORGE CATHEYS, 300
A granted 30 Aug 1753 to JNO. COBORN...JACOB COBRUN (SEAL), Wit: ROBERT EWART, JOHN HILL,
DAVID CROCKET. Rec. Oct. term 1772.

Page 659: 12 Sept 1772, MATTHIAS BEHRINGER & GEORGE POPE of Tryon Co., planters, to PHILIP
HENRY GRADER of same, for ₤ 9 proc. money...land on a branch of Clarks Creek
adj. PETER STUDS, NICHOLAS FRYS & GEORGE POPE including the School House, 60 A...MATHIAS
BEHRINGER (SEAL), GEORGE _____ [German signature] (SEAL), Wit: CHRISTOPHER BECKMAN, JOHANN
BAPTIST _____ [German signature]. Rec. Oct. term 1772.

Pp. 659-660: 19 Oct 1772, JOHN KINCADE of Tryon Co., to WM. KINCAID of same, for ₤ 100
proc. money...150 A on Killinas mill Creek adj. KILLION, and KINKADE, formerly KILLIONS...JOHN KINCADE (O) (SEAL), Wit: DAVID CROCKATT, WILLIAM CROCKETT.. Rec.
Oct. term 1772.

Pp. 660-661: 10 Oct 1772, GEORGE WIGINTON & wf ELIZABETH of Tryon Co., to ALEXANDER
KOYL of same, for ₤ 30 proc. money...land on both sides little broad river
adj. THOMAS BLACK, 100 A bought of JOHN McTYRE[?] patent dated 14 May 1771...GEORGE
WIGENTON (SEAL), ELIZABETH WIGGENTON (E) (SEAL), Wit: JAMES BUCKHANNAN, JACOB WILLIS.
Rec. Oct. term 1772.

Pp. 661-662: 21 Oct 1772, JACOB HUFSTATLER of Tryon Co., to ANDW KELLER of same, planter,
for ₤ 15 proc. money...200 A on branches of Long Creek adj. MICHAEL HUFSTET-
LER, granted to PETER PLUNT 9 Apr 1770...JACOB HUFSTATLER (h) (SEAL), _____ [German
signature]. Wit: WILLIAM SIMS, LORENTZ KEISER [German signature], GEO. MICHEL WISNANT,
[German signature]. Rec. Oct. term 1772.

Pp. 662-663: 20 Oct 1772, JOHN McTIER of Tryon Co., to ROBERT LEE of same, for s 10
sterling...land on both sides south fork of sandy Run of Broad River, 200 A
...JOHN McTIER (SEAL), Wit: TIMOTHY RIGGS, ABEL LEE (A). Rec. Oct. term 1772.

Page 663: 5 Jan 1772, DANIEL SHIPMAN of Tryon Co., to ABEL LEE of same, for s 5 sterling...
land on both sides middle fork of sandy Run, 100 A...DANIEL SHIPMAN (D) (SEAL),
Wit: ROBERT LEE, JEREMIAH GATE (X). Rec. Oct. term 1772.

Pp. 663-664: 14 Nov 1771, ROBERT SCOTT of Mecklenburg Co., to GEORGE LAMKIN of Tryon Co.,
for ₤ 36 proc. money...land on W side Catawba River near FRANCIS BEATIES
adj. WIDOW McKENDRICKS, 100 A, granted to sd. ROBERT SCOTT 21 Dec 1763...ROBERT SCOOT (ϴ)
Wit: WILLIAM LAMKIN, JAMES SCOTT, JOSEPH MOFEY (+). Rec. Oct term 1772.

Pp. 664-665: 29 Oct 1772, NICHOLAS WARLOCK of Tryon Co., to his brother LEWIS WARLICK of
same, for ₤ 10 proc. money...land on W side S fork Catawba, 200 A adj.
DANIEL WARLOCK decd, McELWEAN, granted to DANIEL WARLICK decd, 3 Apr 1752...NICHOLAS WAR-
LICH (SEAL) [German siganture], BARBARA WARLOCK (B) (SEAL), Wit: HENRY HILDEBRAND, VALEN-
TINE WARLOCK (X), WM. SHARP. Rec. Oct. term 1772.

Pp. 665-666: 6 June 1772, MATTHEW ARMSTRONG & BENJAMIN ARMSTRONG of Tryon Co., to GARRET
WILL of same, for ₤ 100 proc. money...land on both sides Leepers Creek,
granted to ROBERT LEEPER, conveyed to JAS. ARMSTRONG, and the sd. ARMSTRONG by his L. W.
& T. gave the land to his sons MATTHEW & BENJAMIN...BENJAMIN ARMSTRONG (SEAL), MATTHEW
ARMSTRONG (SEAL), Wit: JACOB SEETS, GEORGE LAMKIN, PETER CUNTZ[German signature]. Rec.
Oct. term 1772.

Pp. 666-667: 29 Oct 1772, JOHN PFIFER & wf CATHERINE of Mecklenburg Co., to CHRISTOPHER
WALBERT of same, for ₺ ___ proc. money...land on both sides of Walnut Creek
of Green Rivef about two miles above THOMAS REYNOLDS, 200 A granted to sd. JOHN PFIFER
18 Apr 1771...JOHN PIFER (SEAL), CATERINA PFIFER [German? signature] (SEAL), Wit: HARKLES
KRUNKNIGHT, CHARLES FERGUSON. Rec. Oct. term 1772.

Pp. 667-668: 21 Oct 1772, LAWRENCE KYZER of Tryon Co., planter, to MICHAEL WESENANT,
Blacksmith of same, for ₺ 8 proc. money...[grantee later referred to as
GEORGE MICHAEL WISENANT]...45 A on branches of Long Creek adj. HAGER, HAMFIT...LORENTZ
KEISER [German signatûre] (SEAL), Wit: ___ WISENOUNT [German signature], JACOB HUFSTATLER
(h), WILLIAM SIMS. Rec. Oct. term 1772.

JANUARY SESSION 1773.
Pp. 668-669: 3 Oct 1771, JOHN SHARP of Rowan Co., yeoman to JOHN ALLISON of same, for
₺ 30 proc. money...land on S branch of North Fork of Tyger River, about a
mile above ALEXANDER McCARTERS land...300 A granted to JOHN SHARP, 26 Oct 1767...JOHN
SHARP (SEAL), Wit: WM. SHARP JUNR., JOHN KING. Rec. Jany Session 1773.

Pp. 669-670: 4 Dec 1772, JAMES MARLIN & wf AGNIS of Rowan Co., to SAMUEL ANDREWS of same,
for ₺ 25...470 A in the forks of Cane Creek, being a branch of 2nd Broad
River near MOSES MOORES & HUDDLESTONS lands adj. JOHN CARSONS place, granted to JAMES
MARLIN 6 Apr 1765...JAMES MARLIN (SEAL), AGNESS MARLIN (A) (SEAL), Wit: WILLIAM BARR,
JOHN MARLIN. Rec. Jan. term 1773.

Pp. 670-671: 13 May 1765, ALEXR. McALISTER & wf MARGARET of York County, Pennsylvania,
to JOHN BALDRIDGE of Lancaster County, same prov., for ₺ 75 Pa. currency...
land in Mecklenburg Co., N. C. on S side of Catawba River on Indian Camp Creek taking in
the Indian old fields on the so. side of the said creek, granted to ANDREW ALLISON, 3
Apr 1752, and conveyed by him by L & R to sd. ALEXR McCALISTER 17 Dec 1754...ALEXANDER
McALISTER (SEAL), MARGARET McALISTER (SEAL), Wit: JOHN RAMSEY (0), JAMES RAMSEY. Rec.
Jan. term 1773. [for the deed from ALISON to McALISTER, see my Anson County, N. C. Deed
Abstracts, Vol I:1749-1757, p. 37].

Pp. 671-672: 9 Feb 1771, JOSEPH DAVIS of Tryon Co., to NATHAN DAVIS of same, for ₺ 20...
93 1/2 A on W side Dutchmans Creek, on the road leading from Tuckaseegee
to a drain falling into Beaver dam Creek by SIMON KUYKENDALLS, granted to JOSEPH DAVIS
6 May 1769...JOSEPH DAVIS (J) (SEAL), Wit: GEORGE LAMPKIN, WILLIAM MASSEY. Rec. Jan. term
1773.

Pp. 672-673: 19 Jan 1773, WILLIAM ANDERSON of Tryon Co., to JOHN DELLINGER of same, for
₺ 27 s 14 proc. money...land including the shoal of Indian Creek adj. JOHN
ALEXANDER...WILLIAM ANDERSON (A) (SEAL), Wit: ALEXANDER LOCKHART, ROBT. BLACKBURN. Rec.
Jan term 1773.

Page 673: 1 Jan 1773, DANIEL DEVOUR of Tryon Co., to JOSEPH ENGLAND of same, for ₺ 50
proc. money...mares, and other cattle [marks included]...DANIEL DEVOUR (0)
(SEAL), Wit: DANIEL SINGLETON, WILLIAM McKINA (+). Rec. Jan.term 1773.

Page 674: 23 Aug 1768, SAMUEL GIVENS of Mecklenburg Co, yeoman, to WILLIAM FLACK of same,
for ₺ 4 s10 proc. money...100 A on Camp Creek or long branch thereon adj.
SAMUEL GIVENS...SAMUEL GIVENS (SEAL), Wit: JOHN WALKER, ARON MOORE (0), JOSEPH CURRY. Rec.
Jan term 1773.

Pp. 674-675: 26 Jan 1773, PRESTON GOFORTH of Tryon Co., to WILLIAM GOFORTH SEN. of same,
for and in consideration of tender years and good will to sd. WILLIAM his
son...200 A granted to sd. PRESTON GOFORTH...PRESTON GOFORTH (X) (SEAL), Wit: GEORGE
DOHERTY, WM. BERRY, JOHN GOFORTH. Rec. Jan. term 1773.

Pp. 675-677: 17 Nov 1772, DANIEL McCARTY of Tryon Co., & wf AGNIS, to ANDREW GOFORTH &
RICHARD GULLICK, all of same place, yeomen, for ₺ 70 proc. money...300 A...
DANIEL McCARTY (SEAL), AGNIS McCARTY (K) (SEAL), Wit: DAVID JENKINS, JOHN WELLS (+++)
Rec. Jan. term 1773.

Page 677: 12 Dec 1772, MARGARET WILLIS & WILLIAM WILLIS both of Tryon Co., to WILLIAM
HANNAH, for s 5 sterling...land on Stantons Creek running in first little Broad
River, 250 A...WILLIAM WILLIS (SEAL), MARGARET WILLIS (X) (SEAL), Wit:BENJAMIN HARDIN,
JAMES BUCKHANNAN. Rec. Jan. term 1773.

Pp. 677-678: 10 Jan 1770, JAMES LOGAN of Tryon Co., to JOHN HUGGINS of same, for ₺ 10
proc. money...200 A on little Catawba, part of 300 A surveyed to HUGH BERRY,

and granted to sd. BERRY, 25 Apr 1767, ...JAMES LOGAN (SEAL), Wit: ROBERT CARRUTH, JEREMIAH SMITH, MARGARET CALDWELL. Rec. Jan. term 1773.

Pp. 678-679: 4 July 1771, ANDREW HAMPTON & wf KATHERINE of Tryon Co., to SAML. JOHNSTON of same, for ₺ 80...land on N side Dutchmans Creek adj. ABRAHAM KUYKENDALL, JAMES KUYKENDALL, 280 A granted to MARY KUYKENDALL, now wife of MARTIN ARMSTRONG, who conveyed the same to ANDREW HAMPTON by a single deed, dated 25 Nov 1763, and was granted 26 Mar 1755...ANDREW HAMPTON (SEAL), KATHRINE HAMPTON (O) (SEAL), Wit: PATRICK McDAVID, JAMES MILLIKIN (M), JOHN McELROY. Rec. Jan. term 1773. [For the deed from ARMSTRONG to HAMPTON, see my Mecklenburg County, North Carolina Deed Abstracts, Vol. I, p. 50.]

Page 680: 1 Dec 1770, THOMAS REYNOLDS of Tryon Co., to AMBROSE MILLS of same, for ₺ 100 proc. money...land on both sides Green River including the mouth of Walnut Creek by the upper end of a small Island above the mouth of the creek, 640 A granted 25 Sept 1760...THOMAS REYNOLDS (+) (SEAL), Wit: WILLIAM MILLS, MOSE MOORE, HENRY REYNOLDS (+). Rec. Jan. term 1773.

Pp. 680-681: JAMES GRAHAM of Tryon Co., sold to JAMES MILLIKEN three milch cows & other cattle [marks included]...25 Oct 1772...JAMES GRAHAN (SEAL), Wit: SAMUEL JOHNSTON, ANDW MILLICAN, WILLIAM MOORE. Rec. Jan. term 1773.

Pp. 681-682: 27 Jan 1773, THOMAS ROBENSON of Tryon Co., to MOSES MOORE of same, for ₺ 50 proc. money...land on both sides Indian Creek, being a So. branch of the So. Fork of Catawba, being part of 600 A whereon sd. MOSES MOORE lived & was granted to RICHARD REYNOLDS, 28 Mar 1755 and afterwards conveyed to sd. MOSES MOORE...adj. DAVIDSONS line...THOMAS ROBINSON (SEAL), Wit: THOS POLK, MOSES WHITELY. Rec. Jan. term 1773. [For the deed from RICHARD REYNOLDS to MOSES MOORE, See my Anson County, N. C. Deed Abstracts, Vol I, p. 47.]

Pp. 682-683: 21 Aug 1772, WM. BATSELL of Tryon Co., to JAMES MILLER of same, for ₺ 48 proc. money...land on both sides of broad river including his improvement, including the mouth of two creeks...WILLIAM BATSELL (M) (SEAL), Wit: JONAS BEDFORD, WILLIAM CLEGHORN, EDWARD HOGAN (S). Rec. Jan. term 1773.

Pp. 683-684: 11 Aug 1772, JOHN McELROY & wf MARY of Tryon Co., to JAMES McNIGHT of Rowan Co., for ₺ 50 proc. money...250 A on W side Catawba adj. MATTHEW ARMSTRONGs little creek, granted to JACOB SEITS 28 Apr 1768...JOHN McELROY (SEAL), MARY McELROY (SEAL), Wit: JACOB SEITS, PATRICK McDAVID, JOHN GILLESPIE. Rec. Jan. term 1773.

Pp. 684-685: 1 Aug 1772, AARON BURLISON of Tryon Co., to ROBERT McMINN of same, for ₺ 50 proc. money...100 A on both sides Sandy Run & N side Broad River...AARON BURLISON (SEAL), Wit: TIMOTHY RIGGS, JAS. BUCHANAN. Rec. Jan.term 1773.

Pp. 685-686: 12 Jan 1773, JONATHAN NEWMAN of Mecklenburg Co., planter to CHARLES McLEAN of Tryon Co., for ₺ 150 proc. money...300 A on N fork Crowders Creek, above JACOB COBRONS, granted to sd. NEWMAN, 25 Oct 1765...JONATHAN NEWMAN (SEAL), Wit: SIMON COZART, DAVID ALEXANDER, ANDREW GOFORTH. Rec. Jan. term 1773.

Pp. 686-687: 12 Jan 1773, JONATHAN NEWMAN to CHARLES McLEAN for ₺ 150 proc. money...300 A on the upper fork of Crowders Creek adj. JACOB COBRON, at the foot of the N side of the little mountain , granted to NEWMAN 25 Apr 1764...[same wit as above]. Rec. Jan. term 1773.

Page 687: 1 Dec 1772, DAVID RAMSEY of Tryon Co., to WILLIAM RAMSEY of same, planter, for ₺ 16 proc. money...160 A on S side S Fork Catawba...granted to sd. DAVID RAMSEY 6 Apr 1765...DAVID RAMSEY (SEAL), Wit: JOHN ALEXANDER, JOHN ALEXANDER. Rec. Jan. term 1773.

Page 688: 24 Dec 1772, HENRY DELLINGER of Tryon Co., & wf HANNAH to MARTIN SHUTTS, for ₺ 10 proc. money...land on head waters of Leepers Creek on Lick Run adj. JOHN DELLINGER, 300 A granted to sd. HENRY DELLINGER 1 Apr 1765...HEINRICH DELLINGER [German signature] (SEAL), HANNAH DELLINGER (H) (SEAL), Wit: _____ [German signature], CHARLES [??] FROCHLICKE. Rec. Jan. term 1773.

Pp. 688-689: 26 Dec 1772, JAMES WYATT & wf BETHLEHEM of Tryon Co., to ZECHARIAH SPENCER of Delaware County, Maryland, for ₺ 26 proc. money...land on S side S fork Catawba...193 A adj. HUGH BERRY, granted to sd. JAMES WYATT 26 Oct 1767...JAMES WYATT (SEAL), BETHELEM WYATT (X) (SEAL), Wit: AND NEEL, WILLIAM SPENCER, JOHN DUNWOODY[?]. Rec. Jan. term 1773.

Pp. 689-690: 29 Jan 1772, ROBERT HENDERSON of Mecklenburg Co., planter, to WILLIAM SHARP of Rowan Co., for Ł 5 proc. money...land on So side the So. Fork of Packlet on a creek called Cub Creek including some Beaver Dams, 300 A granted to ROBERT HENDERSON...ROBERT HENDERSON (SEAL), Wit: W. AVERY, JNO. McK. ALEXANDER. Rec. Jan. term 1773.

Pp. 690-691: N. C. Tryon County: JAMES KELLY sold for Ł 80 to LEONARD SAILOR, a negro Priscilla, aged 11...27 Jan 1773...JAMES KELLY (Ŧ) (SEAL), Wit:AARON BIGGER-STAFF. Rec. Jan. term 1773.

Page 691: 18 Dec 1772, GEORGE MICHAEL WISENANT & wf of Tryon Co., to NICHOLAS THIRTER for Ł 53...land on the branches of Long Creek, granted to sd. WISENANT 30 Oct 1765...GEORG MICHEL WYSNANT [German signature] (SEAL), NANCEY WISENHUNT (Ŧ) (SEAL), Wit: PETER AKER (+), VALLENTINE MAUNEY, AND. NEEL, THOS POLK. Rec. Jan. term 1773.

Page 692: 26 Jan 1773, GEORGE MICHAEL WISENHAUNT to NICHOLAS THIRTER, for Ł 8 proc. money ...45 A on branches of long creek, part of a larger quantity granted to LAWRENCE KYZER, 9 Oct 1764...GEORG MICHEL WHISNANT [German signature] (SEAL), Wit: AND NEEL, VALLENTINE MAUNY, THOS POLK. Rec. Jan. term 1773.

Pp. 692-693: 19 Aug 1772, EZEKIEL SMITH of Tryon Co., planter, to WILLIAM TWITTY of same, for Ł 100 proc. money...land on both sides Broad River, including his im-provements...EZEKIEL SMITH (X) (SEAL), Wit: JONAS BEDFORD, THOS BRANTLEY, JAMES GRAY. Rec. Jan. term 1773.

Pp. 693-694: 22 Dec 1772, HUGH QUINN of Craven County, Prov. of S. C., to CHARLES TICE of same, for Ł 50 proc. money...200 A on first little Broad River...HUGH QUINN (H) (SEAL), Wit: JOHN TAGERT, JAS. McCLINE[?], JOSEPH JORDAN. Rec. Jan. term 1773.

Pp. 694-695: 23 ___ 1772, JOHN REED of Tryon Co., to ABRAHAM WAMMOCK of same, for s 5 sterling...land on W side Catawba River, granted to JOHN BEATY, then conveyed to JOHN REED, 160 A...JOHN REED (SEAL), MARTHA REED (SEAL), Wit: ABEL BEATTY, JNO. BEATY. Rec. Jan. term 1773.

Pp. 695-696:   April Court Anno Dom. 1774.
        8 Apr 1773, JOHN ALSTON of Tryon Co., to WM ALSTON of same, for Ł 20 proc. money...300 A, part of a grant to WILLIAM HENRY, 28 Feb 1754...JOHN ALSTON (SEAL), Wit: JNO. KIRKENDALL, WILLIAM MASSEY. Rec. April term 1774.

Pp. 696-697: 8 Apr 1773, JOHN ALSTON to WILLIAM ALSTON, for Ł 50 proc. money...250 A adj. ANDREW McNABB, WILLIAM HENRY, SAML COBURN, & JUDITH COBURN, it being a survey formerly made to SAMUEL YOUNG, 26 Nov 1757...JOHN ALSTON (SEAL), Wit: JOHN KIRK-CONELL, WILLIAM MASSEY. Rec. Apr. term 1774.

Pp. 697-698: 8 Apr 1773, JOHN ALSTON & wf ELIZABETH to WILLIAM ALSTON, for Ł 80 proc. money...300 A on W side Catawba River, a little below the Tuckaseage Ford, granted to JOHN ALSTON by ROBERT ABERNATHY JNR. by indenture dated 3 Oct 1771, patent bearing date 28 Feb 1754...JOHN ALSTON (SEAL), [Same wit as above]. Rec. Apr. term 1774.

Pp. 698-699: 8 Apr 1773, JOHN ALSTON to WILLIAM ALSTON for Ł ___ proc. money...land on both sides S fork Catawba adj. ROBT PALMER, ALSTON, including the broken islands...JOHN ALSTON (SEAL), Wit: JNO. KIRKCONNELL, WILLIAM NICHOLAS (W). Rec. Apr. term 1774.

Pp. 699-700: 8 Apr 1773, JOHN ALSTON to WILLIAM ALSTON, for Ł 123 proc. money...130 A on S side Catawba River adj. SAMUEL YOUNG, granted to ANDREW McNABB 6 Apr 1765...JOHN ALSTON (SEAL), Wit: JOHN KIRKCONELL, WILLIAM MASSEY. Rec. Apr. term 1774.

Pp. 700-701: 3 Sept 1772, SAMUEL COBUN of Tryon Co., to PHILIP ALSTON...SAMUEL COBUN & wf MARGARET, for Ł 350 proc. money pd. by sd. PHILIP ALSTON...land on S side of the N branch of Catawba River adj. GEORGE CATHEY, 400 A...SAMUEL COBURN (X) (SEAL), MARGARET COBURN (SEAL), Wit: GEORGE LAMKIN, JOHN ALSTON, JOHN SKRIMSHIRE. Rec. Apr. term 1774.

Pp. 701-702: GEORGE LAMKIN & wf HANNAH of Tryon Co., to ROBERT ABERNATHY JUNR. of same, for Ł 50 proc. money...dated ___ 1774...200 A on branches of Leepers Creek adj. ABERNATHY, BALDRIDGE, granted to sd. GEORGE LAMKIN, 18 Apr 1771...GEORGE LAMKIN (SEAL), HANNAH LAMKIN (SEAL), Wit: JOHANNA ____, PETER CUNTZ[?] [German signature]. Rec. Apr. term 1774.

Pp. 702-703: 26 Jan 1773, SAML RANKIN & wf ELEN of Tryon Co., to PHILIP ALSTON of same,
        for Ł 100 proc. money...200 A on the branches of Dutchmans Creet of Catawba
River adj. his own line, granted to SAML RANKIN 22 Dec 1768...SAMUEL RANKIN (SEAL), Wit:
JAMES COBUN, JOHN McCARLY, JOHN ALSTON. Rec. Apr. term 1774.

Pp. 703-704: 26 Mar 1773, SAMUEL RANKIN of Tryon Co., to PHILIP ALSTON of same, for Ł 100
        proc. money...land on Kuykendalls Creek adj. JAMES ARMSTRONG, 150 A granted
to JNO. ARMSTRONG 25 Apr 1762...SAMUEL RANKIN (SEAL), ELENDER RANKIN (O) (SEAL), Wit:
JOHN ALSTON, ELLET DAVIS (E), WM. ALSTON. Rec. Apr. term 1774.

Pp. 704-705: 26 Jan 1773, SAMUEL RANKIN & wf ELEN of Tryon Co., to PHILIP ALSTON, for Ł
        100 proc. money...275 A on Kuykendalls Creek, granted to JAMES ARMSTRONG
2 Oct 1751...SAMUEL RANKIN (SEAL), Wit: JAMES COBUN, JOHN McCARTY, JOHN ALSTON. Rec.
Apr. term 1774.

Pp. 705-706: 8 Oct 1773, ANDREW ROBISON & wf MARGARET of Prov. of N. C.,Blacksmith, to
        HUGH BARRY of Prov. of S. C. yeoman, for Ł 70 proc. money...150 A granted to
WILLIAM GLEGHORN, 24 Apr 1762, conveyed by him to sd. ANDREW ROBISON, 24 Sept 1762, on W
side S fork Catawba at the mouth of Duharts Creek...ANDREW ROBISON (SEAL), MARGRIT ROBI-
SON (SEAL), Wit: RICHD BARRY, WILLIAM SHIELDS, GEO[?] ELLIOT. Rec. Apr. term 1774.

Pp. 706-707: 16 Dec 1773, JOHN BEARD SENR of Tryon Co., to WM. BEARD his son of Frederick
        Co., Maryland, for Ł 100 proc. money...land on both sides Broad River inclu-
ding the mouth of a small creek on the No side of said River by EZEKIEL SMITHs upper line,
250 A...JOHN BEARD (SEAL), FRANCES BEARD (Θ) (SEAL), Wit: JNO. KIRKCONELL, ADAM BAIRD.
Rec. Apr. term 1774.

Pp. 707-708: 23 Apr 1774, JOHN GULLICK & wf ELIZABETH of Tryon Co., to JOHN BRYSON (BRISON)
        of same, for Ł 70 proc. money...300 A on S side little Catawba adj. DAVID
JOHN, SAMUEL GINGLES, granted to sd. GULLICK 26 Sept 1766....JOHN GULLICK (SEAL), ELIZA-
BETH GULLICK (X). Rec. JAMES PATTERSON, ALEXANDER PATTERSON, WM. BERRY. Rec. April term
1774.

Pp. 708-709: 14 Dec 1772, WM. WILKINS of Tryon Co., farmer, to SAMUEL BLACKBURN of same,
        yeoman, for Ł 55 proc. money pd. to sd. JOHN WILKINS...land on both sides
Beaver Dam Creek of broad River including sd. WILKINS improvements, granted to JOHN WIL-
KINS 10 Dec 1769...JOHN WILKINS (±) (SEAL), Wit: MARTIN SHUTTS, ROBT BLACKBURN, MARTHA
BLACKBURN. Rec. Apr. term 1774.

Page 709: 13 Dec 1771, HUGH MILLS of Botetourt Co., Colony of Virginia, to JOHN BOYD of
        Tryon Co., N. C., for Ł 50 NC money, 350 A on shady branch of Clarks Creek
adj. DANIEL WARBRIGHTS, granted to sd. MILLS 10 Apr 1761...HUGH MILLS (SEAL), Wit: WILLIAM
RAMSEY, JOSEPH LOVE, JOHN ANDREW. Rec. Apr. term 1774.

Pp. 709-710: 2 Nov 1773, JOHN McKENNY of Tryon Co., to JOEL BLACKWELL of same, for Ł 50
        proc. money...land on S side Broad River 170 A...JOHN McKINNY (SEAL), Wit:
JONAS BEDFORD, RICHD. HIX. Rec. Apr. term 1774.

Pp. 710-711: 2 Dec 1773, ELIZABETH BIGGERSTAFF widow to her son BENJAMIN BIGGERSTAFF,
        for Ł 50 NC money...land on the first large creek above the Indian path on
the north side of second Broad River including the first large meadow below and joining
the mountain, 100 A, granted to THOMAS ROBINS 16 Nov 1764...ELIZABETH BIGGERSTAFF (+)
(SEAL), Wit: JOHN BEEMAN, AARON BIGGERSTAFF. Rec. Apr. term 1774.

Pp. 711-712: 23 Nov 1773, JAMES COZART of Tryon Co., to JAMES BELL of same, for Ł 30 proc.
        money...300 A on both sides of Walnut Creek below the cove of the No fork
of Broad River...JAMES COZART (SEAL), Wit: FREDERICK HAMBRIGHT, ANDREW HEYEL. Reç. Apr.
term 1774.

Pp. 712-713: 30 Jan 1774, MOSES HENDRY of Craven County, N. C., to HUGH BRYSON of same,
        for Ł 40 proc. money...150 A granted to WILLIAM HENRY his father, being heir
at law, on both sides of Crowders Creek adj. McLEAN...MOSES HENDRY (SEAL), Wit: JOHN
ROBINSON, THOMAS BULLIN, WILLIAM ROBINSON (X). Rec. Apr. term 1774.

Pp. 713-714: 25 May 1773, PHILLIP HENRY GRADER of Tryon Co., to HENRY BULLINGER, NICHOLAS
        FRY, PETER EIGART[?], JOHN SHUFORT, MARTIN COTTER [COLTER?], FREDERICK
MARKLE, MICHAEL GRINDSTAFF, WILLIAM DEAL & JOHN DEAL, all of co. and prov. aforesd., for
Ł 11 d 6 proc. money...land to be set apart for a school House for the use of the public
& on a branch of Clarks Creek adj. FRANCIS PALMER, NICHOLAS FRY, & GEORGE POPEs lands,
including the School House...& for a meeting house for the good of the public, 60 A...
PHILIPPE HENRY GRETHER (SEAL), Wit: CHRISTOPHER BECKMAN, JOHN SITSER (+), Rec. Apr. term

1774.

Pp. 714-715: 2 June 1773, JAMES McDANIEL of Tryon Co., to SAML COBURN of same, for ₺ 50
    proc. money...land on a branch of little Dutchmans Creek of Catawba...
JAMES McDANIEL(SEAL), Wit: JOHN WALKER, JOHN McCLEAIN, FELIX WALKER. Rec. Apr. term 1774.

Pp. 715-716: 23 Oct 1773, PAUL WISINHUNT of Tryon Co., to JOHN DELLINGER of same, for
    ₺ 100...land on N side S fork Catawba, on a creek called Hoyles Creek, 300
A granted 26 Mar 1755 to EDWARD BOLE, and since conveyed by different grants to divers
persons by patent & other conveyances...PAUL WIZANDAUNT (PW), Wit: JOHN HOYEL, LUDWIG[?]
_____ [German signature], JOHN DUNN. Rec. Apr. term 1774.

Page 716: 27 Apr 1773, JACOB FORNEY & PAUL WIZANDAUNT of Tryon Co., to DEVIL CRITES of
    Tryon Co., for ₺ 20 proc. money...75 A on Killions Creek, adj. FORNEY, MICHAEL
SITES, granted to JACOB FORNEY, PAUL WIZANHAUNT, & DEVIL CRITES for 225 A, 9 Apr 1770...
JACOB FORNEY (SEAL), PAUL WIZANDAUNT (SEAL) (PW), Wit: GEORGE LAMKIN, JOHANNES WILL[?]
[German signature], HENRY HERGETRITE[?]. Rec. Apr. term 1774.

Page 717: 29 Apr 1774, JOHN SLOAN SR. of Mecklenburg Co., to JOHN CARUTH of same, for
    ₺ 10 proc. money...land on both sides lick fork of Indian Creek above & adj.
to HUGH POLLOCK, granted 16 Dec 1769...JOHN SLOAN (SEAL), Wit: WM. CAPPELS, JAMES ASTON.
Rec. Apr. term 1774.

Pp. 717-718: 10 Aug 1773, JOHN McDOWELL of Rowan Co., to WM. CLEGHORN of Tryon Co., for
    ₺ 400 proc. money...land on both sides N fork Main Broad River above the
mouth of first creek that empties in on the No side of the No fork above the Indian
path...400 A granted to sd. JOHN McDOWELL 16 Nov 1764...JOHN McDOWELL (SEAL), Wit: JOHN
WALKER, WILLIAM GILBERT, SAML MOORE. Rec. Apr. term 1774.

Pp. 718-719: 1 Nov 1773, JOHN SLOAN SR. of Mecklenburg to ADAM CARUTH of same, for ₺ 20
    proc. money...land granted to JOHN SLOAN JR. __ May 1772 on both sides of
little Catawba...JOHN SLOAN (SEAL), Wit: WILLIAM CAPPLES, ALEXANDER CARRUTH. Rec. Apr.
term 1774.

Pp. 719-720: 22 July 1773, JAMES HEMPHILL & wf SUSANNAH of Rowan Co., to THOMAS COSTNER[?]
    of Tryon Co., for ₺ 51 s 10 proc. money...300 A in Tryon Co., formerly
Anson, on S side South Fork Catawba on a branch of Long Creek, granted to sd. JAMES
HEMPHILL, 28 Mar 1755...JAMES HEMPHILL (SEAL), SHUSANAH HEMPHILL (SEAL), Wit: SAML.
YOUNG, PETER SEITES (+). Rec. Apr. term 1774.

Pp. 720-721: 27 Jan 1773, JAMES COZART of Tryon Co., to PETER CARPENTER of same, for
    ₺ 50 proc. money...200 A on little long Creek near four miles up the same
on the West side of Catawba River, granted to JOHN LOVE 29 Apr 1768...JAMES COZART
(SEAL), Wit: THOS POLK, VALLENTINE MAUNEY. Rec. Apr. term 1774.

Pp. 721-722: 1 Apr 1773, HENRY VERNOR of Mecklenburg Co., to JOHN DUNWOODY of Cumberland
    Co., Pa., for ₺ 50 proc. money...land in Tryon Co., on N fork Crowders Creek,
286 A, part of a grant to JACOB COBURN 9 Nov 1764...HENER VERNER (SEAL), Wit: AND. NEEL,
PETER JOHNSTON. Rec. Apr. term 1774.

Pp. 722-723: 26 Apr 1774, WILLIAM McGAUGHEY to WM. DUNN, both of Tryon Co., for ₺ 40
    proc. money...land on both sides Flat branch of Far[?] Camp Creek, 200 A...
WILLIAM McGAUGHEY (O) (SEAL), MARY McGAUGHY (W) (SEAL), Wit: FELIX WALKER. Rec. Apr.
term 1774.

Pp. 723-724: 11 Oct 1773, PHILIP EREHART of Tryon Co., formerly Mecklenburg, to JACOB
    DEVALD of Guilford Co., for ₺ 28 proc. money...land on Teddy Branch of
Killions Creek, part of a grant to sd. PHILIP EREHART 28 Apr 1768...PHILIP EREHART
(SEAL), Wit: ADAM DICK, PHILIP[?] CLONINGER[?] [German signature], _____ [German sign.]
_____ DELLINGER, [German signature]. Rec. Apr. term 1774.

Pp. 724-725: 22 Mar 1774, WILLIAM ALSTON of Tryon Co., to ROBERT ALEXANDER of same, for
    ₺ 125 proc. money...land on W side Catawba River on both sides of the great
road that leads to the Quaker Meadows, it being a place the sd. WILLIAM ALSTON formerly
kept store on, & on a branch of McNabbs Creek adj. JAMES HENDERSON, part of one patent
to WILLIAM GLAGHORN, and also one granted to JAMES HENDERSON, and part of a patent
granted to GEORGE LAMKIN including 178 A...WM. ALSTON (SEAL), Wit: JOHN GILLIAM, FRANCIS
GAS CARGIN[?].

Pp. 725-726: 1 June 1773, ROBERT ELDER of Tryon Co., to DAVID ELDER of same, for ₺ 100
                proc. money...land adj. W side Catawba River adj. ROBERT ARMSTRONG, conveyed
by SAMUEL YOUNG to JOHN KUYKENDAL, dced, and JOSEPH HARDEN and afterwards conveyed by
HARDEN to FREDERICK HAMBRIGHT, then to WILLIAM PATTERSON, then to ROBERT ELDER, 200 A...
ROBERT ELDER (N) (SEAL), Wit: ROBT. ARMSTRONG, SAMUEL ELDER. Rec. Apr. term 1774.

Pp. 726-727: 18 Sept 1773, JOSEPH CLARK of South Carolina & Parish of St. Mark's, Black-
                smith, to SAMUEL FRENCH of Tryon Co., planter, for ₺ 60 proc. money...land
on both sides Green River, on a small branch above the cherokee ford, N side of the
River, granted 200 A to JOSEPH CLARK, 25 Sept 1766...JOSEPH CLARK (SEAL), Wit:JOHN
FRENCH, WILLIAM WILEY (4). Rec. Apr. term 1774.

Page 727: 26 Feb 1774, LEMUEL SAUNDERS & wf MARTHA of Tryon Co., to JAMES FREEMAN of
                same, for ₺ 10 s 4...land on waters of Killians Creek adj. PHILIP EREHART, 125
A conveyed by them to a certain MICHAEL ENGLE, and granted to MATHIAS PETERSON 18 Apr
1771...LEMUEL SAUNDERS (SEAL), MARTHA SAUNDERS (SEAL), Wit: JOHN RUDSEL, MICHEL RUDISILI
[German signature]. Rec. Apr. term 1774.

Page 728: 27 July 1772, JOHN McDANIEL of Rowan Co., planter, to WM. FAULIFT[?] of same,
                for ₺ 30 proc. money...land on a branch of Indian Creek, granted to RICHARD
WARD 29 Sept 1766, 200 A...JOHN McDANIEL (SEAL), Wit: JAMES WITHROW, DAVID ELIOT[??].
Rec. Apr. term 1774.

Pp. 728-729: 26 May 1773, ALEXANDER DICKSON of Duplin Co., N. C. to ANDREW FOSTER of
                Tryon Co., for ₺ 21 proc. money...land on waters of Crowders Creek, in the
fork of the bridge branch & west side of the little mountain called Bairds Mountain,
granted to sd. DICKSON 18 Apr 1771...ALEXANDER DICKSON (SEAL), Wit: JONATHAN GULLICK, WM.
BERRY. Rec. Apr. term 1774.

Pp. 729-730: 23 Oct 1773, PAUL WIZENHAUNT & DEVOL CRITES of Tryon Co., to JACOB FORNEY
                for ₺ 20 proc. money...75 A on doctors Branch of Killians Creek, granted
to JACOB FORNEY, PAUL WIZENHAUNT, & DEVOL CRITES, 9 Apr 1770...PAUL WIZENHUNT (PW)
(SEAL), DEVOL CRITES (+) (SEAL), Wit: GEORGE LAMKIN, JOHANNES DILL, HENRY HERGETAOLD[?]
Rec. Apr. term 1774.

Page 730: ALEXANDER KYLE of Tryon Co., for love, goodwill & affection, my brother and
                sister, GEORGE & MARY FREELAND of same...100 A, part of my father land inclu-
ding his own improvements...11 Apr 1774...ALEXANDER KYLE (A) (SEAL), Wit: JOHN DUNN,
JAMES JOHNSTON. Rec. Apr. term 1774.

Pp.730-731: 16 Feb 1773, JAMES McCOARD of Mecklenburg Co., waggon maker, to FRANCIS
                GASKINS of Tryon Co., for ₺ 25 proc. money...land on W side Catawba River,
on doctors creek, 150 A near the lands of WM. MOORE ESQR, granted 28 Apr 1765 to sd.
JAMES McCORD...JAMES McCOARD (SEAL), Wit: JOSEPH GALBREATH, WILLIAM ALSTON, JOHN ALSTON.

Pp. 731-732: 10 Aug 1773, THOMAS WELSH & wf RACHEL of Rowan Co., to HENRY GROSS of same,
                yeoman, for ₺ 112 proc. money..,land in county of formerly Anson, now Rowan,
adj. lands formerly HENRY ROBINSON now DAVID RAMSOUR, 300 A granted to sd. WELSH, 10
Apr 1761...THOMAS WELCH (T) (SEAL), RACHEL WELCH (R) (SEAL), Wit: ALEXANDER LOCKHART,
ROBERT BLACKBURN. Rec. Apr. term 1774.

Pp. 732-733: 18 Feb 1774, VALENTINE WARLOCK of Tryon Co., & wf CATHERINE, to CHRISTIAN
                GROSS of same, yeoman, for ₺ 130 proc. money...land in county of Rowan,
formerly Tryon, on N side of S fork Catawba on both sides Clarks Creek, 275 A, adj.
McAFEEs line, granted to DANL. WARLICK by patent 28 Mar 1751 & 23 Dec 1765, by DANIEL
conveyed unto sd. VALENTINE WARLICK, 16 Oct 1769..._____ [German signature], CATHERINE
WARLOCK (X) (SEAL), Wit: GEORGE WHISENHUNT (V), ROBERT BLACKBURN. Rec. Apr. term 1774.

Pp. 733-734: 10 Aug 1773, THOS. WELCH & wf RACHEL of Rowan Co., to HENRY GROSS of same,
                yeoman, for ₺ 58 proc. money...land on Et. side of S fork Catawba, adj.
lands formerly belonging to JAMES McAFEE, CRISMANS, PETER SUMMY, THOMAS WELCHs line, 150
A...granted unto ROBERT BLACKBURN, 28 Apr 1768, and conveyed to THOS WELCH...THOMAS WELCH
(T) (SEAL), RACHEL WELCH (R) (SEAL), Wit: ALEXANDER LOCKHART, ROBERT BLACKBURN. Rec.
Apr. term 1774.

Pp. 734-735: 15 Sept 1772, WILLM. WRAY of Tryon Co., to WILLIAM GILBERT of same, for ₺
                260...300 A on both sides Catheys Creek, a S fork of Second Broad River,
granted to GEORGE CATHEY, and conveyed by deed to SAMUEL COBURN, then by deed 20 July
1765...WM. WRAY (SEAL), Wit: JAMES COOK, JOHN MORRIS (+), ALEXANDER COULTER. Rec.
Apr. term 1774.

Page 735: 26 Sept 1773, JACOB COBUN of Tryon Co., to WILLIAM HENRY of same, for Ƚ 100 proc. money...335 A on both sides second Broad river adj. WALKERs corner... JACOB COBUN (SEAL), Wit: JOHN WALKER, JAMES COOK, JONATHAN HAMPTON.

Page 736: 27 Apr 1774, SAMUEL JACK of Mecklenburg Co., to WM. HENRY of Tryon Co., for Ƚ 50 proc. money...tract below the cove of the north fork of Broad River, 300 A...SAML JACK (SEAL), Wit: THO POLK, JOHN WALKER. Rec. Apr. term 1774.

Pp. 736-737: 26 Sept 1773, JACOB COBRON of Tryon Co., to WM. HENRY of same, for Ƚ 40 proc. money...land adj. JACOB COBUNS corner, WALKERS line on N side second Broad River...JACOB COBUN (SEAL), Wit: JOHN WALKER, JAMES COOK, JONATHAN HAMPTON. Rec. Apr. term 1774.

Pp. 737-738: 13 Feb 1773, MOSES HENDRY of Cravan County, South Carolina,Millwright, to JOHN HENRY of Tryon Co., N. C., for s 5...250 A granted to WILLIAM HENRY, 25 Apr 1768, and deeded to sd. MOSES by heirship, on both sides of Crowders Creek...MOSES HENDRY (SEAL), Wit: JOHN ROBINSON, JOHN DICKEY. Rec. Apr. term 1774.

Page 738: 7 Feb 1773, MOSES HENDRY of Craven County, S. C., millright, to PHILIP HENRY of Tryon Co., N. C., for s 5 proc. money...100 A granted to WILLIAM HENRY 22 Dec. 1768 and devolved to sd. MOSES by heirship...MOSES HENDRY (SEAL), Wit: JOHN COBURN, JOHN DICKEY. Rec. Apr. term 1774.

Page 739: 26 Apr 1774, LEWIS WEIDNER & wf BARBARA of Tryon Co., to RUDOEPH HOOZER[?] of same, for Ƚ 20 proc. money...150 A on branches of Beaver Dam Creek granted to LEWIS WEIDNER 18 Apr 1771...LUTWIG WIETNER [German signature] (SEAL), BARBARA WIDNER (X) (SEAL), Wit: VALLENTINE MAUNEY, ___ _____ [German signtaure]. Rec. Apr. term 1774.

Pp. 739-740: 26 Apr 1774, LEWIS WEIDNER to RUDOLPH HOOZER, for Ƚ 40 proc. money...124 A on east branches of Beaver Dam Creek adj. DOULBARD, granted 30 Dec 1773... LUTWIG WEIDNER [Germ. signature] (SEAL), Wit: VALLENTINE MAUNY, ____ ____ [Germ. signature], Rec. Apr. term 1774.

Pp. 740-741: 30 Jan 1773, JOHN(JOHANNES)KRASto JACOB HOILE, farmer, both of Tryon Co., for Ƚ 5 proc. money...land on Leonards fork of Indian Creek adj. SAML. KEYSER[??], granted to WILLIAM RAMSEY by patent, 1 Apr 1765, conveyed to sd. JOHN KRASS 28 Apr 1772...JOHANNES ___SS [German signature] (SEAL), Wit: DAVID RAMSEY, _____, WILLIAM RAMSEY.

Pp. 741-742: 14 Jan 1774, CORNELIUS McCARTY of Tryon Co., to THOMAS HAWKINS of same, for Ƚ 40...100 A granted by patent to THOMAS RAY, 6 Oct 1765...Niuluns[?] branch ...CORNELIUS McCARTY (C) (SEAL), WINE McCARTY (+) (SEAL), Wit: GEORGE LAMKIN, JOHN MOORE, ELLET[?] DAVIS, MARY BIRD (MB). Rec. Apr. term 1774.

Pp. 742-743: 24 May 1773, PHILIP ALSTON of Tryon Co., to JAMES JOHNSTON of same, for Ƚ 160 proc. money...land on the waggon road, corner to JOHN CATHEYs, McNABB... 100 A...PHILIP ALSTON (SEAL), Wit: WM. ALSTON, WILLIAM PORTER, JAMES COBUN. Rec. Apr. term 1774.

Page 743: 24 May 1773, PHILIP ALSTON to JAMES JOHNSTON, for Ƚ 50 proc. money...land on Kuykendalls Creek adj. JAMES ARMSTRONG...granted to JOHN ARMSTRONG by patent ____ 1762, 28 Apr...150 A...PHILIP ALSTON (SEAL), Wit: WM. ALSTON, RICHARD WALKER, WILL-IAM PORTER. Rec. apr. term 1774.

Page 744: 24 May 1773, PHILIP ALSTON to JAMES JOHNSTON, for Ƚ 350 proc. money...400 A on S side N branch of Catawba River adj. GEORGE CATHEY...PHILIP ALSTON (SEAL) [Same wit as preceding]. Rec. Apr. term 1774.

Pp. 744-745: 24 May 1773, PHILIP ALSTON to JAMES JOHNSTON, for Ƚ 50 proc. money...land in the fork of the Catawba River, on Kuykendalls Creek, a branch of Dutch-mans Creek...225 A granted to sd. PHILIP ALSTON by SAMUEL RANKIN by indenture dated 26 Jan 1773...PHILIP ALSTON (SEAL), Wit: WM. ALSTON, WILLIAM PORTER, JAMES COBUN. Rec. Apr. term 1774.

Pp. 745-746: 28 Apr 1774, PETER COSTNER & wf MOLLY of Tryon Co., to ROBERT JOHNSTON of same, for Ƚ 40 proc. money...200 A on Sides branch, granted to MARTIN DELLINGER 28 Apr 1768...PETER COSTNER (P) (SEAL), MOLLY COSTNER (+) (SEAL), Wit: GEORGE LAMKIN, JACOB CASTNER. Rec. Apr. term 1774.

Pp. 746-747: 21 June 1771, JOHN BENNET of Tryon Co., to JOSEPH JENKINS of same, for ₺ 40
          proc. money...land adj. DAVID STANLEY, JOHN STANLEY...JOHN BENNET (SEAL),
Wit: FREDERICK HAMBRIGHT, ABRAM. LANDEF[?]. Rec. Apr. term 1774.

Pp. 747-748: 18 Aug 1773, MICHAEL PLATTNER of Rowan Co., to JEWATT HUNTSUCKER of same,
          planter, for ₺ 120 proc. money...land granted in Mecklenburg, since fallen
into Rowan County and on both sides Liles' Creek adj. POPEs corner, 385 A...MICHEL
PLATTNER (SEAL), _____ [German signature], Wit: _____, _____ [both German signautures],
Rec. Apr. term 1774.

Pp. 748-749: 24 Mar 1773, GARRET WELLS of Tryon Co., & wf BARBARA to HUGH JENKINS of
          Rowan Co., for ₺ 150 proc. money...land on Killians Creek, 320 A...GERHARDT
[?] WILL [German signature] (SEAL), BARBARA WILL [German signature] (SEAL), Wit: DAVID
JENKINS, JACOB WILL, to GARRET; JOSEPH JENKINS wit. to BARBARA WILLS. Rec. Apr. term
1774.

Pp. 749-750: 27 Apr 1774, JAMES BELL of Mecklenburg Co., to SAMUEL JACK of same, for ₺
          60...300 A on both sides of White Walnut Creek below the cove of the No
fork of Broad River, granted to JAMES COZART __ Dec 1769...JAMES BELL (SEAL), Wit: THOS.
POLK, WM. GILBERT. Rec. Apr. term 1774.

Page 750: 21 Mar 1774, LEONARD KILLION of Tryon Co., to MATTHEW KILLION his son of same,
          for s 5 sterling...land on both sides of Little Creek on Catawba River at or
near HENNINGS line, 270 A...LEONARD KILLION (LK) (SEAL), Wit: JNO KIRKCONELL, JNO.
RIGGS.

Page 751: 26 July 1773, JAMES COZART of Tryon Co., to JAMES LOGAN for ₺ 10...200 A on
          Little Catawba Creek adj. LOGAN, part of 300 A granted to COZART...JAMES COZART
(SEAL), Wit: FREDERICK HAMBRIGHT, WM. VERNER, JEREMIAH SMITH. Rec. Apr. term 1774.

Pp. 751-752: 18 May 1773, JAMES MITCHEL of Tryon Co., to JAMES LOGAN, for ₺ 50 proc.
          money...land supposed to be in Rowan County on Jacobs River, a So. fork of
So. fork Catawba...JAMES MITCHEL (SEAL), Wit: JOHN HUGGINS, MARGARET HUGGINS (M), THOS.
MITCHELL. Rec. Apr. term 1774.

Pp. 752-753: 19 Apr 1774, PHILIP CLORINGER of Tryon Co., to CHRISTINA LIKE of Guilford
          Co., for ₺ 50 proc. money...land on Seeglar Creek of Catawba River, 200 A
adj. his own line, granted to PHILIP CORRINER 25 Jan 1773..._____ [German signature]
(SEAL), Wit: ADAM DICK, and two German signatures. Rec. Apr. term 1774.

Page 753: 24 Apr 1774, ALEXANDER REYNOLDS & wf MARY of Tryon Co., to JOHN LANDERS[?],
          for ₺ 10 sterling...land on S side Indian Creek adj. THOMAS WALKERS line, 200
A...ALEXANDER REYNOLDS (A) (SEAL), MARYAN REYNOLDS (W) (SEAL), Wit: MEDDERT HURT[?] (H),
WILLIAM WILS (X). Rec. Apr. term 1774.

Page 754: 24 Apr 1774, THOMAS REYNOLDS & wf MARTHA of Tryon Co., to HENRY LANDERS,
          for ₺ 60 NC money...land on corn field fork of Indian Creek, 200 A...THOMAS
REYNOLDS (T) (SEAL), MARTHA REYNOLDS (M) (SEAL), Wit: MEDDER HUNT (H), WILLIAM WELS (+).
Rec. Apr. term 1774.

Pp. 754-755: 30 Mar 1774, NICHOLAS WELSH of Tryon Co., & wf ELIZABETH to JAMES LOCKART
          of Rowan Co., for ₺ 20 proc. money...land on Clarks Creek adj. JOHN MILLS
Est. in the county formerly Anson, now Rowan, granted to NICHOLAS WELCH, 15 Nov 1762...
NICHOLAS WELSH (SEAL), ELIZABETH WELSH (E) (SEAL), Wit: ROBT BLACKBURN, HENRY GROSS.
Rec. Apr. term 1774.

Page 756: 24 Mar 1774, JAMES HENDERSON of Tryon Co., to WILLIAM MASSEY of same, for ₺
          80 proc. money paid to sd. JAMES HENDERSON & wf VIOLET...216 A on W side Cataw-
ba adj. McKENDRICK, HENDERSON, part of two patents, one granted to WILLIAM GLAGHORN, the
other to JAMES HENDERSON...JAMES HENDERSON (SEAL), Wit: GEORGE LAMKIN, WM. ALSTON. Rec.
Apr. term 1774.

Pp. 756-757: 29 Mar 1773, ANSON REYNOLDS of Tryon Co., to JAMES MITCHELL of same, for
          ₺ 45 proc. money...land on Jacobs River, a S fork of S fork Catawba, in the
county of Tryon, now Rowan, granted to WM. REED 23 Apr 1767, 200 A...ANSON REYNOLDS
(SEAL), Wit: JESSE REYNOLDS, THOMAS ALLEY, JAMES ALLY. Rec. Apr. term 1774.

Pp. 757-758: 15 May 1773, NICHOLAS BRADWAY of Tryon Co., to JOHN McKINNEY of same, for
          ₺ 50 NC money...land on W side Broad River, 170 A granted to sd. NICHOLAS
BRADWAY 27 May 1772...NICHOLAS BROADWAY (SEAL), Wit: WILLIAM McFARSON (.), JONAS
BRADAWAY. Rec. Apr. term 1774.

Pp. 758-759: 24 Oct 1772, ALEXANDER McGAUGHY & wf RACHEL of Tryon Co., to SAML McMURRY
          of same, for Ŀ 5 proc. money...200 A granted to sd. MCGAUGHY 24 Dec 1770,
on both sides Fan[?] Camp of Second Broad River above WARDs land...ALEXR McGAUGHY, (SEAL),
RACHEL McGAUGHY (0) (SEAL), Wit: WILLIAM DUNN, JOHN DEVENEY. Rec. Apr. term 1774.

Pp. 759-760: 30 Nov 1770, BENJAMIN BIGGERSTAFF to PETER MARSHALL, both of Tryon Co., for
          Ŀ 40 proc. money...land on N side S fork Catawba, 100 A, granted to sd.
BIGGERSTAFF, 18 Apr 1771...BENJAMIN BIGGERSTAFF (B) (SEAL), MARY BIGGERSTAFF (M) (SEAL),
Wit: PETER ZIMMERMAN, GEORG[?] ZIMMERMAN [both partial German signatures]. Rec. Apr.
term 1774.

Pp. 760-761: 30 Nov 1773, SAMUEL BIGGERSTAFF & BENJAMIN BIGGERSTAFF to PETER MARSHALL
          for Ŀ 50...land on N side S fork Catawba opposite the long shoals, 320 A,
granted to PETER OYSTER 23 Feb 1754, & conveyed by him to SAMUEL BIGGERSTAFF, and afterward at his decease, made over by his last will & testament unto his sons BENJAMIN &
SAMUEL...SAMUEL BIGGERSTAFF (SEAL), BENJAMIN BIGGERSTAFF (B) (SEAL), MARY BIGGERSTAFF
(M) (SEAL), Wit: PETER ZIMMERMAN, GEORGE[?] ZIMMERMAN. [Rec. date not given].

Pp. 761-762: 22 Apr 1774, LEWIS WEIDNER of Tryon Co., to VALENTINE MAUNY of same, for
          Ŀ 10 proc. money...100 A on both sides Indian Creek near & below the
waggon Ford, granted to sd. LEWIS WEIDNER 10 Dec 1769...LUTWIG WEITNER [German signature]
(SEAL), Wit: MICHEL HEYLE[?] [German signature], _____ WISNANT[?] [German signature].

Pp. 762-763: 1 Jan 1774, NATHAN ALDRICH & wf ROSAMOND of Tryon Co., to ROBERT MILLER of
          same, for Ŀ 35 proc. money...100 A on branches of Little Catawba Creek adj.
BERRY...land granted to sd. ALDRIGE, by patent 9 Apr 1770...NATHANIEL ALDRIGE (X) (SEAL),
ROSAMOND ALDRIGE (X) (SEAL), Wit: JOHN McGUINN (J), GEORGE POU, JONATHAN GULLICK.

Page 763: 24 Oct 1772, JAMES BLACK of Tryon Co., to SAML McMURRY of same, for Ŀ 5 proc.
          money...220 A granted to JAMES BLACK 9 Apr 1770, on Catheys Creek of 2nd Broad
River...JAMES BLACK (SEAL), Wit: ALEXR McGAUGHY, JOHN DEVENY, FELIX WALKER. Rec. Apr.
term 1774.

Page 764: 24 Oct 1772, PETER JOHNSTON of Mecklenburg Co., to JAMES NICHOLS of Tryon Co.,
          for Ŀ 20 proc. money...land on S side Allisons Creek adj. ROBERT McDOWELL,
on both [sides] of the waggon road...near JOHN BLACKS corner...JOHN YOUNGS land...granted
to sd. PETER JOHNSTON, 6 Dec 1771...PETER JOHNSTON (SEAL), Wit: WILL KENNON, SAML SPEN-
CER. Rec. Apr. term 1774. [For reference to grant to PETER JOHNSTON, see my North
Carolina Land Grants in South Carolina, Vol. I, p. 12.

Pp. 764-765: 10 Sept 1773, WILLIAM GILBERT of Tryon Co., to ROBERT PORTER of same, for
          Ŀ 20...land on S side Carnes[?] Creek granted to sd. GILBERT 15 May 1771...
BLACKS Line...WM. GILBERT (SEAL), Wit: JOSEPH DOBSON, WM. WRAY, JOHN MORRISS (X). Rec.
Apr. term 1774.

Pp. 165-766: 5 Jan 1773, WILLIAM GILBERT to ROBERT PORTER, for Ŀ 150...land on S fork
          Camp Creek, 200 A breaking into CLAYTONs line...WILLIAM GILBERT (SEAL), Wit:
JOSEPH DOBSON, WM. WRAY, LODERWICK WRAY. Rec. Apr. term 1774.

Pp. 766-767: 16 Oct 1773, JAMES BELL of Mecklenburg Co., to WM. PATTERSON of same, for
          Ŀ 50 proc. money...200 A in Tryon Co., on Catheys Creek of Second Broad
River, about 3/4 mile from WM. WRAYs land, granted to BELL by deed bearing dated 25 Jan
1773...JAMES BELL (SEAL), Wit: THO. POLK, JNO. KIRKCONELL. Rec. Apr. term 1774.

Page 767: 23 Aug 1773, JOHN OAKS of Tryon Co., to JONATHAN PRICE, Sadler of same, for Ŀ
          100 proc. money250 A on a branch of Kings Creek including sd. JOHN OAKS improve-
ment...JOHN OAKS (0) (SEAL), Wit: SIMON KUYKENDAL, REBECCA KUYKENDALL (R), ELIZABETH
WINBORNE(W) (?). [Rec. date not given.]

Page 768: 1 Oct 1772, WM. KEVAN of Tryon Co., yeoman, to THOMAS PERKINS of same, farmer,
          for Ŀ 5 proc. money...100 A adj. KEVANS corner...[name appears to be REVAN
later in deed]...WILLIAM REVAN (R) (SEAL), Wit: FREDERICK HAMBRIGHT, DAVID JENKINS. Rec.
App. term 1774

Pp. 768-769: 23 Aug 1773, THOMAS HENRY of Tryon Co., Joiner, to CHRISTIAN REINHARDT of
          same, for Ŀ 40 s 10 proc. money...land on S side S fork Catawba, 300 A
granted to sd. THOMAS HENRY by FRANCIS BEATY by indenture 26 Jan 1764...THOMAS HENRY
(SEAL), Wit: WM. ALSTON, DAN HUNTER, _____ _____ [German signature], Rec. Apr. term 1774.

Pp. 769-770: 21 Aug 1773, GEORGE FINK & wf MARY of Tryon Co., to GEORGE REEL of same, for Ł 40...land on both sides mill branch of Leepers Creek, adj. SNAPS land, 300 A, granted 22 Dec 1768...GEORG FINK [German signature] (SEAL), MARY FINK (X) (SEAL), Wit: LEMUEL SAUNDERS, WILLIAM TANKERSLY (WT). Rec. Apr. term 1774.

Pp. 770-771: 9 Apr 1773, PHILIP ALSON[sic] of Tryon Co., to JAMES RUTLEDGE of same, for Ł 50 proc. money...100 A on W side Catawba adj. GEO. RUTLEDGE...PHILIP ALSTON (SEAL), Wit: JNO. KIRKCONNEL, WM. NICHOLAS (W). Rec. Apr. term 1774.

Pp. 771-772: 26 Feb 1773, JAMES ANDREWS of Rowan Co., planter, to WILLM. ROBERTSON of Rowan Co., for Ł 30 proc. money...200 A on both sides Hunting Creek of Second Broad River adj. GEORGE POEs line...JAMES ANDREWS (SEAL), Wit: JOHN WALKER, FELIX WALKER, JOSEPH DOBSON. Rec. Apr. term 1774.

Pp. 772-773: 28 Mar 1772, ALEXANDER GILLILAND of Tryon Co., planter, to SAML RANKIN for Ł 60 proc. money...land granted to JOHN WALKER, 26 Sept 1766, 202 A on a branch of Crowders Creek adj. COBURNS corner...ALEXANDER GILLILAND (SEAL), Wit: DAVID ALEXANDER, WILLIAM VERNER. Rec. Apr. term 1774.

Pp. 773-774: 6 July 1773, SAMUEL COBURN of Tryon Co., to WILLIAM SMITH JUNR., of same, for Ł 20 proc. money...land on both sides of Duharts Creek of the waters of Catawba, granted to SAMUEL COBRON for 150 A...SAMUEL COBURN (+) (SEAL), Wit: GEORGE LAMKIN, HANNAH LAMKIN (H). Rec. Apr. term 1774.

Pp. 774-775: 28 Dec 1773, MOSES CRAWFORD & wf JEAN of Rowan Co., to GEORGE SEELY of same, for Ł 50...land purchased of WM. REED by deed 1 Feb 1772, granted 25 Apr 1767, 300 A on Jacobs Fork, being a fork of South Fork of Catawba River about 3 miles above the Indian old field...MOSES CRAFFORD (SEAL), JEAN CRAWFORD (O) (SEAL), Wit: ALEXR ERWIN, JOHN ORR. Rec. Apr. term 1774.

Pp. 775-776: 4 May 1773, GEORGE POFF of Tryon Co., to GEORGE SIGHTS of same, for Ł 7... land on E side S fork Catawba adj. PETER MULL, JAMES ROBINSON, WHITLEY, 400 A granted by patent 25 Apr 1768...GEORGE POFF (SEAL), Wit: LEMUEL SAUNDERS, JAMES FREEMAN (Ŧ). Rec. Apr. term 1774.

Pp. 776-777: 26 Apr 1773, MICHAEL ENGL & wf BARBARY of Tryon Co., to LEMUEL SAUNDERS of same, for Ł 20 proc. money...land on S side Catawba River on waters of Killions Creek adj. PHILIP EREHARTS line, 250 A, conveyed by MATHEW PATTERSON 25 June 1772, and granted to sd. PATTERSON 18 Apr 1771...MICHEL ENGLE (M) (SEAL), BARBARA ENGLE (E) (SEAL), Wit: JOHN RIDISEIL, MICHEL RUDISILI [German signature]. Rec. Apr. term 1774.

Pp. 777-778: 28 Apr 1774, HENRY HILDEBRAND of Rowan Co., to ADAM SMITH of Tryon Co., for Ł 25...land in Tryon Co., formerly Mecklenburg, on both sides Howards Creek below NICHOLAS FRIDAYS land inclduing the shoals on sd. creek, 300 A granted to PETER HAVENER, 29 Apr 1768...and conveyed unto HILDEBRAND 21 Oct 1768...HENRY HILDEBRAND (SEAL), Wit: JESSE WILLIAMSON, DAVID RAMSOUR. Rec. Apr. term 1774.

Pp. 778-779: 24 Mar 1773, PAUL WIZENHAUNT & wf CATHERINE of Tryon Co., to MICHAEL SITS of same, for Ł 30 proc. money...200 A on a S branch of Killions Creek, granted to JACOB SITS 23 Dec 1763...PAUL WIZENHUNT (PW), CATHARINE WIZENHUNT (+), Wit: JACOB SEITS, GEORG SEITS[??] [German signature], Rec. Apr. term 1774.

Pp. 779-780: 26 July 1773, SAMUEL COBURN of Tryon Co., to WILLIAM SMITH, for Ł 20 proc. money...land on the cattail branch of little Dutchmans Creek, waters of Catawba, granted to JAMES McDANIEL 200 A 22 May 1772...SAML COBURN (+) (SEAL), Wit: GEORGE LAMKIN, GEORGE LAMKIN JUR., WILLIAM SMITH. Rec. Apr. term 1774.

Pp. 780-781: 6 Mar 1773, SAMUEL KUYKENDALL of Tryon Co., to JOHN TAYLOR of same, for Ł 250 proc. money...land on the Indian path about two miles from JACOB KUYKENDALL, on Leepers Creek, 314 A granted to SAML COBRON, 31 Mar 1753...SAMUEL KUYKENDALL (SEAL), Wit: NATHAN DAVIS, JONATHAN KUYKENDALL. Rec. Apr.term 1774.

Pp. 781-782: 24 Apr 1774, JOHN McFADDEN, planter, of Tryon Co., to ROBERT TAYLOR, planter, of same, for Ł 100 proc. money...100 A on E side Main Broad River, both sides of Mountain Creek, granted to GEORGE DICKEY by patent 22 Dec 1768...JOHN McFADDIN (Ŧ), Wit: JOSEPH BUFFINGTON, VALENTINE MAUNEY. Rec. Apr. term 1774.

Pp. 782-783: WILLIAM BALDRIDGE of Tryon Co., to JOHN TUCKER, for divers causes and considerations, all my lands that lieth in the crest of Leopards Creek, whereon the sd. TUCKER now liveth the land that JOHN BALRIDG bought of JOHN ARMSTRONG, adj.

JACOB SIDES, RICHARD JONES, DAVID ABERNATHY...1 July 1773...WILLIAM BALDRIDGE (SEAL),
Wit: JAMES ABERNATHY, WILLIAM BERRY. Rec. Apr. term 1774.

Pp. 783-784: 14 Oct 1773, JACOB FORNEY and DAVOL CRITES of Tryon Co., to PAUL WISENHUNT
                of same, for Ł _?_ ...land on waters of Leepers Creek, granted to sd.
FORNEY, CRITES & WISENHUNT 7 Apr 1770...JACOB FORNEY (SEAL), DEVOL CRITES (+), Wit:
JACOB SEITS, JOHANNES WILL, Rec. Apr. term 1774.

Page 784: 24 Mar 1773, JACOB SIETS of Tryon Co., to GARRET WILL of same, for Ł 18 proc.
                money...38 A on Leepers Creek, granted to WM ARMSTRONG by patent 29 Apr 1768...
JACOB SEITS (SEAL), Wit: GEORGE SEITS, JACOB WILL. Rec. Apr. term 1774.

Page 785:   GARRET WILL of Tryon Co., for love and affection to my son JOHN WILL...174
                A on both sides Leepers Creek of Catawba, adj. RUTLEDGE, JACOB SEITS, part
of a grant to ROBERT LEEPER..._____ 1773...GERHARDT WILL [German signature] (SEAL), Wit:
_____ [German signature], JACOB WILL. Rec. Apr. term 1774.

Pp. 785-787: _____ Apr 1773, JAMES McENTIRE of Tryon Co., Yeoman & wf, to GEORGE WISEN-
                HAUNT of same, for Ł 25 proc. money...land, 200 A granted unto JAMES KELLY,
27 Sept 1766, and for Ł 20 conveyed to sd. JAMES McENTIE 4 Feb 1771...JAS. McENTIRE (SEAL),
ANN McENTIRE (SEAL), Wit: WILLIAM BOOTH, WILLIAM GREEN. Rec. Apr. term 1774.

Pp. 787-788: 16 Apr 1773, THOMAS GALLESPIE of Tryon Co., to PAUL WISENHUNT of same, for
                Ł 40 proc. money...land on N side S fork Catawba, 300 A, on Hoils Creek
about four miles above sd. HOIL, granted 1 Apr 1759 to[BOYL?]...THOMAS GILLESPE (SEAL),
Wit: JACOB SEITS, MARGET CLUB (X). Rec. Apr. term 1774.

Pp. 788-789: 12 Nov 1773, JOHN WALKER & wf ELIZABETH of Tryon Co., to JONES WILLIAMS of
                same, for Ł 100...land on both sides Cedar Creek between McDOWELS and
SMITHS, 200 A granted to WILLIAM SHARP, 22 Dec 1768...JOHN WALKER (SEAL), ELISABETH
WALKER (SEAL), Wit: THOMAS MORRESS, JOHN MORRIS, JOHN DEVENY. Rec. Apr. term 1774.

Pp. 789-790: 22 Aug 1773, ADAM WISENANT of Tryon Co., to PHILIP WISENANT and his children
                for his good will unto his children[?]...100 unto my son PHILIP WISENANT
during his lifetime and after his disease[sic] it shall belong to the sd. PHILIPs children...land on two branches of Indian Creek that empties into Leonard fork adj. HARRILLS
survey, granted to WM. MOORE by patent 16 Nov 1764...ADAM WYSENANT [German signature]
(SEAL), Wit: VALLENTINE MAUNY, THOMAS MAXWELL. Rec. Apr. term 1774.

Pp. 790-791: 26 Apr 1774, ADAM WISENANT to GEORGE MIELS[?] WISENANT, both of Tryon Co.,
                for Ł 5 proc. money...200 A on waters of Indian Creek adj. his own land,
granted to ADAM WISENANT by patent 14 Nov 1771...ADAM WISENANT [German sign]. (SEAL),
Wit: VALLENTINE MAUNY, ____ WYSENAUNT [German sign].

Pp. 791-792: 26 Apr 1774, ADAM WISENHUNT of Tryon Co., to GEORGE MICHAEL WISENANT, for
                Ł 50 proc. money...land on two branches of Leonards fork of Indian Creek,
200 A adj. to 100 A granted to PHILIP WISENANT and his children by sd. ADAM...[same
signatures and wit. as preceding]. Rec. Apr. term 1774.

Pp. 792-793: 27 Jan 1773, MOSES MOORE of Tryon Co., to JOHN WITHROW of same, for Ł 5
                proc. money...150 A conveyed to sd. MOSES MOORE 23 Dec 1750...MOSES MOORE
(SEAL), Wit: JAMES WITHROW, MARK WHITEKER. Rec. Apr. term 1774.

Pp. 793-794: 29 Apr 1774, JACOB CARPENTER of Tryon Co., to JOHN WHITESIDES, hatter, of
                same, for Ł 40 proc. money...land on both sides first broad River above
JACOB COBURNS land adj. HUGH BEATYS, ROBT ARMSTRONG, granted to sd. JACOB CARPENTER by
patent 5 May 1769...JACOB ZIMMERMAN (SEAL), Wit: DAVID RAMSEY, JOSEPH LAWENCE. Rec.
Apr. term 1774.

Page 794: 26 Apr 1774, ALEXANDER KYLE to THOMAS BLACK, both of Tryon Co., for Ł 27 proc.
                money...land on both sides first little Broad River below sd. BLACKS land,
100 A sd. KYLE bought of GEORGE WIGGENTON, by a patent 24 May 1771...ALEXANDER KYLE
(A) (SEAL), Wit: JOHN DUNN. Rec. Apr. term 1774.

Page 795: JULY COURT 1774.
                26 Sept 1772, THOMAS PULLIAM of Tryon Co., to JOHN ASHLEY of same, for Ł 50
                proc. money...200 A adj. POOLIAMS corner, WARDS[?] line, part of a grant to
JOHN CLARK, 25 Sept 1766...THOMAS PULLIAM (SEAL), Wit: JAMES WOODS, JOHN SUTTON, JAMES
McFARLIN. Rec. July term 1774.

Page 796: 10 June 1774, THOMAS POLK of Mecklenburg Co., to JOHN BEARD of Tryon Co., for
ь 164 proc. money...land on S side Catawba on Crowders Creek known as SAMUEL
COBURNS camp, 220 A granted 3 Apr 1753 to JOHN LITTLE...THOS POLK (SEAL), Wit: JOSEPH
DOWNS, R. BROWNFIELD. Rec. July term 1774.

Page 797: 25 July 1774, JOHN BEARD & wf FRANCES of Tryon Co., to JAMES BEARD their son
of same, for love & good will &c....land on SW side S fork Catawba River next
below HUGH BARNS, JOHN ARMSTRONG, near the Waggon ford, including the improvements made
by WILLIAM McDOWELL and ADAM CRAIN JONES, 150 A granted unto FRANCIS BEATY 28 Apr 1764
...conveyed by BEATY & wf MARTHA by L & R unto ADAM CRAIN JONES and by deed of L & R to
sd. JOHN BEARD...JOHN BEARD (SEAL), FRANCES BEARD (F) (SEAL), Wit: ANDW. NEEL, ROBERT
BAIRD. Rec. July term 1774.

Pp. 798-799: 29 July 1771, JOHN McKNITT ALEXANDER of Mecklenburg Co., to JOHN BLACK of
Tryon Co., for ь 35 proc. money...land on both sides Allisons Creek inclu-
ding PEANS Cabin & Mill Seat, 300 A granted to sd. ALEXANDER 9 Nov 1764...JNO. McKNITT
ALEXANDER (SEAL), Wit: CATHARIN ALEXANDER. JOHN SCOTT. Rec. July term 1774.

END OF VOLUME I.

VOLUME 2

Page 1: 2 July 1774, ELIAS MORGIN of Tryon Co., to JOHN BATTLE of Sussex Co., Prov. of
        Virginia, for Ъ 180 proc. money...200 A on a branch of Broad River including an
improvement made by GEORGE FRELAND adj. HUDDLESTONs line...ELIAS MORGIN (SEAL), Wit:
UEL LAMKIN, DANIEL SINGLETON, MOSES WHITELY. Rec. July term 1774.

Pp. 1-2: 11 Apr 1772, ABRAHAM SCOTT of Rowan Co., planter, to JOHN BUCHANNAN of Mecklen-
        burg Co., for Ъ 50 sterling money of Great Britain...land on S side Catawba on a
branch of Fishing Creek, north of WILLIAM PRICES survey...granted to THOMAS BETTY [BEATY]
28 Mar 1755, 290 A, conveyed by BETTY to sd. SCOTT 4 Jan 1764...ABRAHAM SCOTT (SEAL), Wit:
WILLIAM LATTA, HUGH McHAFEY, THOMAS FLMING [?], JOHN COBUN. Rec. July term 1774.

Pp. 2-3: CHRISTOPHER WALBERT of Meclenburg[sic] Co., farmer, for Ъ 16 NC money to MATHIAS
        BEAVER, one waggon and harness, three black norses branded CW WC 3...19 Jan 1773
...CHRISTOPHER WALBARD (SEAL), Wit: ROBERT ALLEN, JOHN RICE. Rec. July term 1774.

Pp. 3-4: 23 July 1774, JAMES COLLINS of Tryon Co., to JACOB COLLINS of same, for Ъ 50 NC
        money...land on E side Buffalo Creek, 100 A...JAMES COLLINS (I) (SEAL),
BATHIAH COLLINS (𝓰) Wit: ROBT McAFEE, JAMES CROW, ABRAHAM COLLINS. Rec. July term 1774.

Pp. 4-5: 5 July 1774, JOHN POTTS of Tryon Co., to JAMES CHEEK of same, for Ъ 300 proc.
        money...land on both sides N fork Pacolet River adj. PAUL TOWNSENDS, granted to
RICHARD HENDERSON, 26 Oct 1767...JOHN POTTS (SEAL), Wit: WM. HANNAN (W), JOHN DENKINS
(↻), JNO. EARLE. Rec. July term 1774.

Pp. 5-6: 3 Mar 1774, JAMES COOK of Tryon Co., to JAMES COOK for Ъ 20proc. money...land
        where sd. JAMES COOK now liveth...150 A on Catheys Creek, formerly belonging to
SAMUEL JOHNSTON...JAMES COOK JUNR (SEAL), Wit: WILLIAM HENRY, JOHN COOK, JOHN PRICE,
THOMAS COOK. Rec. July term 1774.

Pp. 6-7: 25 July 1774, JOHN McENTIRE of Tryon Co., to JAMES DOUGHERTY, for Ъ 40 NC money
        ...land on E side little Broad River including THOMAS WILLIAMS improvement, 200
A...JOHN M TIER (SEAL), Wit: SAMUEL WILKINS, THOMAS CAMPBELL, THOMAS NEEL. Rec. July
term 1774.

Pp. 7-8: 25 July 1772, JOHN DEVENY & wf MARY of Tryon Co., to JAMES DOWDLE of Mecklenburg
        Co., for Ƀ 5 proc. money...100 A granted to sd. JOHN DEVENY, 25 Nov 1771 on a
branch of fare camp creek adj. WM. McGAHAHs line...JOHN DEVENY (SEAL), MARY DEVENY (O)
(SEAL), Wit: ALEXR McGAUGHY, WILLIAM SMART. Rec. July term 1774.

Pp. 8-9: 22 Dec 1772, MOSES McCARLEY of Berkley Co., South Carolina, to JOHN DEVENY of
        Tryon Co., for Ъ 5 proc. money...200 A on both sides Camp Creek, adj. WILLIAM
SMART,CLEATON, 200 A granted to sd. McCARLEY 28 Apr 1768...MOSES McCARLEY (SEAL), Wit:
ALEXR McGAUGHY, DAVID HUDDLESTONE (D). Rec. July term 1774.

Page 9: GEORGE SEALEY of Rowan Co., bound unto MOSES CRAWFORD of same, for Ъ 500...14 May
        1774...the condition of this obligation is to clear title for 300 A on Jacobs
River bought of WM. REED...GEORGE SEALY (G) (SEAL), Wit: TIMOTHY RIGGS, EDWARD SHIPMAN
(𝓛𝓷). Rec. July term 1774.

Pp. 9-10: ROBERT DAVIS of Tryon Co., yeoman, for consideration of my comfortable maintainance during the rest of my life and for love and good will that I bear to my son
THOMAS DAVIS of same county...land on little broad river, part of tract whereon I now live
patent dated 9 Apr 1770 adj. WILLIAM WILLINS line...24 May 1773...ROBERT DAVIS (SEAL),
Wit: JAMES ALLEY, ROBERT DAVIS JR. (R), ELIZABETH DAVIS (+). [Rec. date not given.]

Pp. 10-11: 2 Mar 1774, WILLIAM WRAY of Rowan Co., to WILLM GREEN of County of Camden and
        Prov. of South Carolina, for Ъ 15 proc. money...275 A, part of a tract of land
granted to THOMAS HARRED[?] in 1765 on both sides of Buffalo Creek in Tryon Co, adj. sd.
GREENs line...WM. WRAY (SEAL), Wit: ROBT CORN, LODEWICK WRAY, JOHN OAKS (O). Rec. July
term 1774.

Pp. 11-12: Sir, This with my best respects to you and your bedfellow and family, I
        understand that my son ABEL is gone to be married to your daughter and I am
very well pleased as what you will give them is unknown is unknown[sic] to me as yet, I
desire that you will send them hence and not let them stay for everything is going to
less for want of some to take care. Sir my desire is that you may come a long a see the
country & the place that your daughter has got, your sons can tell you there is many[?]
your family or wifes that ever could command the like. So I desire that if you will give

them anything be generous, or if not keep all and send her to me, I will make her welcome and I will make her worth Eight Hundred pounds of my own estate then with my best respects to you and your bedfellow and family not forgoetting the Doctor & his wife This is all that offers from you old friend.   JOHN BEATTY.
To Mr. ARCHIBALD GRAHAM.
N. C. Tryon Co., July court 1774, The within letter was proved in open court by the oath of WILLIAM GRAHAM...AND. NEEL, C. C.

Pp. 12-13: 19 Jan 1774, ANDREW LEWIS of Botetourt, Colony of Virginia, to WILLIAM
          GRAHAM of Pittsylvania Co., Colony aforesd., for Ⱡ 100 Va. money...land on
Buffaloe Creek, granted to THOMAS REYNOLDS 20 Aug 1753, 400 A...ANDW. LEWIS (SEAL),
Wit: WILLIAM NEELLY, JAMES NEELLY, JOHN GRAHAM. Rec. July term 1774.

Pp. 13-14: 29 Sept 1772, JOHN STROUD of Tryon Co., to JOHN HILL of same, for Ⱡ 21 proc.
          money...land on S side Catawba adj. the SW side of JOHN HILLs plantation, 100
A, part of that place commonly known by the name of GEORGE BEALLS plantation, granted
to JOHN COBURN 30 Aug 1753, now the sd. JOHN COBURN dying and likwise his brother
ISAAC COBURN, their brother who hath sold and conveyed the sd. land to sd. JOHN STROWD...
JOHN STROUD (+) (SEAL), MARTHA STROUD (X) (SEAL), Wit: JAMES COBUN, JOHN CRISWELL, JAMES
DOUGHERTY. Rec. July term 1774.

Pp. 14-16: 26 Sept 1773, HENRY HOLLMAN of County of Philadelphia, Prov. of Pa., farmer,
          to ANTHONY HOLMAN of same place, yeoman, for s 5 sterling...225 A in county
of Rowan, formerly Mecklenburg adj. JAMES WILSON, THOMAS COBURN[or CAHOON?]...sd. tract
conveyed by JAS. McAFEE & wf MARGARET to JOHN BRADLEY, 9 & 10 Sept 1767, and by BRADLEY
& his wife MARTHA to HENRY HOLMAN SEN. by L & R 12 & 13 Oct 1767...HENRY HOLLMAN (H)
(SEAL), Wit: ABRAM. MARKLEY, HENRY HOLLMAN. Rec. July term 1774.

Pp. 16-17: 25 July 1774, JOHN STANFORD of Tryon Co., to ABRAHAM HARGESS of Tryon Co.,
          for Ⱡ 2 proc. money...land granted to MOSES WHITLEY 22 Dec 1768, and by
him conveyed to NICHOLAS FISHER, then to THOMAS WARREN, 200 A on S side of first little
broad River, where GRADYS crosses the sd. river at a big Rocky Hill, adj. JOHN GRADYES
corner...JOHN STANFORD (SEAL), Wit: WILLIAM CAPSHAW, JOHN FISHER (1), GEORGE TUB (H).
Rec. July term 1774.

Pp. 17-18: 27 July 1774, MOSES MOORE of Tryon Co., to JOHN HARMAN of same, for Ⱡ 120
          proc. money...land on S side of Reynolds or Indian Creek, commonly call'd
camp Creek including his own improvement, 350 A, granted to DAVID HUDDLESTONE 10 Apr
1761...MOSES MOORE (m) (SEAL), Wit: ALEXR. MARTIN. Rec. July term 1774.

Pp. 18-19: __ Dec 1772, JOSHUA HIGHTOWER of Tryon Co., to GEORGE HARRIS of same, for
          Ⱡ 20 proc. money...land on Buck Creek of first little broad river including
his improvements...200 A...JOSHUA HIGHTOWER (+) (SEAL), Wit: WILLIAM GREEN, JOHN McTIER,
DRUSSILLA GREEN. Rec. July term 1774.

Pp. 19-20: 25 July 1774, STEPHEN SHELTON of Tryon Co., planter, to SAML HUNTER of same,
          for Ⱡ 10 proc. money...150 A on N side little broad river, part of 400 A
granted to STEPHEN SHELTON 22 May 1772...STEPHEN SHELTON (SEAL), Wit: DAVID DICKEY,
JOHN SCOTT. Rec. July term 1774.

Pp. 20-21: 20 July 1774, HENRY VERNOR of Tryon Co., to PETER NORMAN of Craven County,
          So. Carolina, for Ⱡ 50 SC money...100 A on both sides N fork of Crowders
Creek...HENRY VERNOR (h) (SEAL), Wit: CHARLES McLEAN, MATTHEW ROBERTSON. Rec. July
term 1774.

Pp. 21-22: 21 July 1774, DAVID GEORGE of Tryon Co., planter, to SAML HUNTER of same,
          for Ⱡ 40...land on both sides of little Broad River on or near JOHN BEARDs
line, 200 A granted to sd. GEORGE 22 Jan 1773...DAVID GEORGE (+) (SEAL), Wit: JONATHAN
HAMPTON, ANDW HAMPTON. [Rec. date not given.]

Pp. 22-23: 18 Nov 1772, WILLIAM SHARP of Rowan Co., to EDWARD HOGAN of Tryon Co., for
          Ⱡ 20 proc. money...land on both sides Green River between WHITESIDES and
REYNOLDS, 100 A granted to JAS. CRAWFORD, 22 Dec 1768, and from him to sd. SHARP 10 Apr
1769...WM. SHARP (SEAL), Wit: DAVID DICKEY, ADM. SIMONTON. Rec. July term 1774.

Page 23: 24 May 1773, PHILIP ALSTON of Tryon Co., to JAMES JOHNSTON of same, for Ⱡ 50
          proc. money...land in the fork of the Catawba River and on a branch of
Dutchmans Creek, 200 A granted to sd. ALSTON by SAML RANKINS by indenture 26 Jan 1773...
PHILIP ALSTON (SEAL), Wit: WM. ALSTON, JAMES COBUN, WILLIAM PORTER. Rec. July term 1774.

Page 24: 22 July 1774, WILLIAM CROCKET of Tryon Co., to WILLIAM KING of same, planter, for ₤ 45 proc. money...land on the branches of Keailands[sic] Creek, adj. WM. CATHEY, 160 A, granted to THOMAS by patent 22 Dec 1768...WILLIAM CROCKET (SEAL), Wit: DAVID ABERNATHY, WILLIAM KINGHAID. Rec. July term 1774.

Pp. 24-25: 8 Dec 1773, JONATHAN PRICE of Tryon Co., to REBECCA KUYKENDALL of same, for ₤ 6 proc. money...20 A on a branch of Kings Creek...JONTH. PRICE (SEAL), MARY PRICE (SEAL), Wit: JACOB MONY, SARAH KUYKENDALL. Rec. July term 1774.

Pp. 25-26: 11 Sept 1773, SAMUEL COBURN of Tryon Co., to GEORGE LAMKIN of same, for ₤ 15 proc. money...165 A on W side Catawba River adj. SAML McCOMBS, JNO. RICHMOND, granted for SAML COBURN 26 Oct 1767...SAMUEL COBURN (X) (SEAL), Wit: UEL LAMKIN, JOSEPH MASEY (T), JAMES COBURN. Rec. July term 1774.

Pp. 26-27: 17 Mar 1773, WILLIAM JOHNSTON of Tryon Co., to WM. LAUFIELD[?] of same, for ₤ 80 proc. money...land on both sides of Sandy Run of Broad River, granted to CHARLES ARRINGTON, 200 A..[later name appears to be WM. LACEFIELD]...WILLIAM JOHNSON (SEAL), REBECCA JOHNSON (X) (SEAL), Wit: JOSEPH COLLINS, EDWARD DICUS (X), SAML CIMBOL (X) [probably KIMBRELL]. Rec. July term 1774.

Pp. 27-28: 1 Aug 1772, FRANCIS McCORKLE & wf SARAH of Rowan Co., to PETER LINEBURGER of Tryon Co., for [am.t not stated]...land on waters of Mountain Creek in the head branches of Halls fork, 200 A, granted to sd. McCORKLE 18 May 1771...adj. to sd. McCORKLE...FRANCIS McCORKLE (SEAL), SARAH McCORKLE (SEAL), Wit: LEONARD LEALER[?] (1), LATTIS LITTLE (O-her mark). Rec. July term 1774.

Pp. 28-29: 26 July 1774, JOHN McLEAN of Tryon Co., to JOHN MORRIS of same, for ₤ 200 proc. money...land on Mountain Creek, 200 A below ANDREW HAMPTONS...JOHN McLEAIN (SEAL), JENNY McLEAIN (SEAL), Wit: JAMES MILLER. Rec. July term 1774.

Pp. 29-30: 13 June 1774, EPHRAIM McLEAN of Tryon Co., to JOHN McLEAN of same, for ₤ 20 proc. money...200 A on Mountain Creek below ANDREW HAMPTONS survey [same tract in preceding deed]...EPHRAIM McLEAN (SEAL), Wit: ARCHD. McCALLISTER, CHARLES McLEAN. Rec. July term 1774.

Pp. 30-31: 9 July 1772, NICHOLAS EDRINGTON & wf RHODA of Rowan Co., to JOHN DOWELL of same, for ₤ 150...land on N side Broad River on the main No. Fork of Kings Creek, 600 A granted to JNO EDRINGTON 30 Aug 1753...NICHOLAS EDINGTON (SEAL), RHODA EDINGTON (R) (SEAL), Wit: JOSEPH DOBSON, THOMAS McDOWELL, JOS. McDOWELL. Name appears in memorandum as JOHN McDOWELL[grantee]...Rec. July term 1774.

Pp. 31-32: 26 Apr 1774, PERRY GREEN MAGNES of Tryon Co., to WM. MAGNESS of same, for ____...land on both sides of the Patent bearing date 6 May 1769 adj. BEATIES, obtained by a deed from THOMAS CHILDERS & UNUDICE CHILDERS...PERYGREN MACKNYS (SEAL), Wit: AND NEEL. Rec. July term 1774.

Pp. 32-33: _____ 1773, JAMES KELLY of Tryon Co., to JAMES MURPHY of same, for ₤ 9 s 10 proc. money...land on N fork of Buffalo Creek adj. FRANCIS BEATTIES land... JAMES KELLY (SEAL), Wit: WILLIAM MURPHY, ALLECKSANDER HILL. Rec. July term 1774.

Pp. 33-34: 27 Apr 1774, DAVID HUDDLESTON of Tryon Co., to MOSES MOORE of same, for ₤ 100 proc. money...land on the So branch of Reynolds or Indian Creek, commonly call'd Camp Branch including his own improvements...350 A granted 10 Apr 1761 to sd. HUDDLESTON...DAVID HUDDLESTON (DH), Wit: JOHN WALKER, JOSEPH LAWRENCE, JOHN COOK. Rec. July term 1774.

Pp. 34-35: 20 Dec 1772, JOHN HIGHTOWER to JOHN McTUIE of Tryon Co., for ₤ 20 proc. money...land on both sides of Broad River, including his and THOMAS WILLSONs improvements, 400 A adj. SIMS line...JOHN HIGHTOWER (⋀) (SEAL), Wit: SAMUEL WILKINS, JOHN COOK, THOMAS COOK. Rec. July term 1774.

Pp. 35-36: 23 Feb 1774, ABRAHAM EREHARD of Tryon Co (formerly Mecklenburg) to GEORGE MOOSGINNING of same, for ₤ 30 proc. money...140 A granted to sd. EREHARD 28 Apr 1768...ABRAHAM EARHART (SEAL), Wit: ____ ____ [German signature], ARCHIBALD FLEMING. Rec. July term 1774.

Pp. 36-37: 18 Mar 1773, PRESTON GOFORTH of Tryon Co., to THOMAS POLK of Mecklenburg Co., for ₤ 75 proc. money...land on S side Catawba on Crowders Creek known as SAML COBURNS Camp, 220 A, granted 3 Apr 1753 to JOHN LITTLE; 9 Dec 1755, from JOHN to ARCH. LITTLE, and to PRESTON GOFORTH 1 Oct 1762...PRESTON GOFORTH (X) (SEAL), Wit:

SPRUCE MACAY, JOHN BIGGER (J). Rec. July term 1774.

Pp. 37-38: 30 May 1774, JOHN CARROL of Tryon Co., to ALEXR PATTERSON of same, for ₤ 30
        proc. money...200 A on S side S fork Catawba including his own improvements
adj. PATTERSON line, granted to sd. JOHN CARROL 22 May 1772...JOHN CARROL (X) (SEAL),
Wit: JAMES PATTERSON, WILLIAM PATTERSON, JOHN BRISON. Rec. July term 1774.

Page 38: 1 Dec 1773, GEORGE BLACK to ROBT PORTER, both of Tryon Co., for ₤ 50...150 A
        on S fork Camp Creek conveyed by deed to GEORGE BLACK[confusing title]...
part of GEORGE CLAYTON tract adj. MOSES MOORE...GEORGE BLACK (SEAL), Wit: ALEXR McGAUGHY,
JAMES BLACK. Rec. July term 1774.

Page 39: 4 June 1773, PRESTON HAMPTON of Dist. of Ninety Six, Prov. of So. Carolina,
to THOMAS POTTER of Tryon Co., for ₤ 37 proc., landon Green River granted 26
Nov 1771...PRESTON HAMPTON (SEAL), Wit: WILLIAM CAPSHAW, BENJAMIN GINKINS, RICHARD
JENKINS[?]. Rec. July term 1774.

Pp. 39-40: 22 July 1773, JOHN MULLINAX & wf SARAH of Craven County, S. C. to JAMES
        PATTERSON of Tryon Co., for ₤ 50 proc. money...land in Tryon Co., on a
branch of Kings Creek, 400 A...JOHN MULLENAUX (SEAL), SARAH MULLINAX (+) (SEAL), Wit:
ROBT. McAFEE, JOHN LOGIN. Rec. July term 1774.

Pp. 40-41: 7 Apr 1773, ALEXANDER DICKSON of Duplin Co., to PETER QUINN of Craven County,
        S. C., for ₤ 60 proc. money...land on So fork of second broad River, formerly
surveyed for WILLIAM MECKLENBURG [sic] adj. FREDERICK HAMBRIGHT, granted 16 Dec 1769...
ALEXANDER DICKSON (SEAL), Wit: ROBT McAFEE, HUGH QUIN (H). Rec. July term 1774.

Pp. 41-42: 4 Sept 1772, SAML WITHROW & wf JEAN of Tryon Co., to ROBT RANKIN of same, for
        ₤ 10 proc. money...300 A granted to SAMUEL WITHROW 28 Apr 1768 on both sides
Hunting Creek below Walkers waggon road & JAMES ANSLEYs survey...SAML WITHROW (SEAL),
JANE WITHROW (O) (SEAL), Wit: JOHN DENY, ALEXR. McGAUGHY. Rec. July term 1774.

Pp. 42-43: 21 Oct 1773, CHRISTOPHER WALBERT of Tryon Co., planter, to PATRICK SCOTT
        of same, for ₤ 60 proc. money...land on both sides Walnut Creek, N side
Green River about two miles above TH: REYNOLDS including a large bottom & cane break,
granted to JN. PHIFER 29 Apr 1768 and conveyed to sd. WALBERT by deed 29 Oct 1772...
CHRISTOPHER WALBERT (SEAL), Wit: DAVID DICKEY, JOHN SCOTT, JAMES SCOTT. Rec. July
term 1774.

Pp. 43-44: 23 Oct 1773, PAUL WIZENHUNT of Tryon Co., to MICHAEL SEITS of same, for
        ₤ 20...75 A, the patent granted to JACOB FORNEY, DEVOL CITES, & PAUL
WIZENHUNT for 225 A, 9 Apr 1770...PAUL WIZENHUNT (PW), (SEAL), Wit: GEORGE LAMKIN,
JACOB SEITS, JOHN FORNEY. Rec. July term 1774.

Pp. 44-45: 26 Feb 1772, JOHN CUNES of Tryon Co., to JOHN SCOTT of same, for ₤ 33 proc.
        money...land on both sides of Keen[sic] Creek, 300 A on the side of a moun-
tain...granted to JOHN WITHROW 25 Apr 1768, and conveyed to JOHN COUNTS 18 Mar 1771...
JOHN CUNES (I)(SEAL), Wit: ALEXR McGAUGHY, MICAJAH PROCTOR. Rec. July term 1774.

Pp. 45-46: 15 Aug 1773, JOHN PHILIP FILE of Tryon Co., to JOHN SHUFFERT of same, for
        ₤ 40 proc. money...land on N side S fork Catawba on piney old field branch,
adj. DERRICK RAMSOUR, 100 A granted to JOHN LAUNCE[?], and conveyed by him & his wife
MARY to sd. JOHN PHILIP FILE 17 Apr 1773...JOHAN PHILIP PFEIL [German signature] (SEAL),
Wit: WILLIAM TOUCHSTONE,RATH[?] CONRAD, ROBT BLACKBURN. Rec. July term 1774.

Pp. 46-47: 23 July 1774, JAMES COLLINS of Tryon Co., to WILLIAM SAILOR of same, for ₤ 30
        proc. money....land on W side Buffalo Creek, 100 A...JAMES COLLINS (‡) (SEAL),
Wit: ROBT. McAFEE, JAMES McAFEE, JAMES LOGIN, Rec. July term 1774.

Pp. 47-48: 19 May 1773, THOMAS WARREN, planter, of Craven Co., S. C., to JOHN STANFORD
        of Tryon Co., for ₤ 40 proc. money...land in Tryon Co., on first broad River
adj. JOHN GRADYS corner, 200 A granted 1 Nov 1768...THOMAS WARRIN (SEAL), Wit: ABRAHAM
HARGISS, WILLIAM BRADLEY, GEORGE WHITEHEAD. Rec. July term 1774.

Pp. 48-49: 5 Apr 1773, JONAS BEDFORD to CALEB TAYLOR, both of Tryon Co., for ₤ 50...
        land on both sides Mountain Creek, 150 A excepted the line of a McFADDEN JUNR
by virtue of an older patent...adj. DICKEYs line...JONAS BEDFORD (SEAL), MARY BED-
FORD (SEAL), Wit: WILLIAM GILBERT, JOSEPH DOBSON, DAVID DONNOWAN[?] (X), JOSHUA TAYLOR,
SAREY TAYLOR (X). Rec. July term 1774.

Pp. 49-50: 23 July 1774, JAMES CAPSHAW of Tryon Co., to RICHARD TUB of same, for Ŀ 50
proc. money...land on S side White Oak Creek, granted to GEORGE ALEXANDER &
conveyed to ALEXR KILPATRICK, then to JACOB WAMACK, patent dated 25 ___ 1766...70 A adj.
POTTS ford...JAMES CAPSHAW (SEAL), Wit: ESSIX CAPSHAW, SAMUEL FANNER (S), JAMES CARGILE.
Rec. July term 1774.

Pp. 50-51: 25 July 1774, JOHN STANFORD of Tryon Co., to GEORGE TUB of same, for Ŀ 50
proc. money...land on first little Broad River, 195 A, patent dated 22 Dec
1765, for 200A...sd. STANFORD reserving 5 A for himself, conveyed by WHITLEY to NICHOLAS
FISHER, then to THOMAS WARREN, adj. JOHN GRADY...JOHN STENFORD (SEAL), Wit: WILLIAM
CAPSHAW, ABRAHAM HARGIS, JOHN FISHER (J), Rec. July term 1774.

Pp. 51-52: 22 Feb 1774, JOHN MOFFAT of Craven Co., S. C. to DAVID THOMPSON of same, for
Ŀ 26...land on little broad River including VIPES old survey, 100 A...JOHN
MOFFAT (SEAL), Wit: JOHN GAMBLE, ARCHIBALD HOGSTONE. Rec. July term 1774.

Pp. 52-53: 10 June 1774, WILLIAM BARNET of Tryon Co., to DAVID THOMPSON of same...whereas
sd. BARNET obtained patent 14 Nov 1771 on both sides little Broad River, 240
A adj. JOHN LUSK, sold to sd. THOMAS for Ŀ 44...WILLIAM BARNET (SEAL), Wit: JOHN LUSK
JOHN STANFORD. Rec. July term 1774.

Pp. 53-54: 26 July 1774, JOHN ASHLEY of Tryon Co., to JAMES UPTON of same, for Ŀ 85 proc.
money...land on both sides Warrens branch, granted to JOHN CLUPS 25 Sept 1766,
and conveyed to THOMAS PALLAM(PULLION), then to JOHN ASHLEY, 100 A, part of sd. tract...
JOHN ASHLEY (I) (SEAL), Wit: JAMES CAPSHAW, JAMES SMITH. Rec. July term 1774.

Pp. 54-55: 16 Nov 1772, DANIEL McCARTY of Tryon Co., to RICHD WALKER of same, for Ŀ 50
proc. money...200 A adj. JAMES FOSTER, JACOB RODES...DANIEL McCARTY (SEAL),
Wit: ROBERT RITCHELL[?] (O), CANDIS McCARTY (C), SUSANNAH McCARTY. Rec. July term 1774.

Pp. 55-56: 25 July 1772, THOMAS HARROD of Tryon Co., to JOHN WADE of Craven Co., S. C.
for Ŀ 40 proc. money...land granted to sd. HARROD 9 Apr 1770 on little
hickory Creek...THOMAS HARROD (SEAL), Wit: JOHN LUSK, JOSEPH JOHN WADE. Rec. July term
1774.

Page 56: _____ 1774, JACOB MOONEY of Tryon Co., for Ŀ 25 proc. money to ADAM WHITESIDES
...land on N fork of frist Broad River, 200 A granted to MOONEY 25 Apr 1760...
JACOB MOONEY (X) (SEAL), Wit: DAVIS WHITESIDE, ROBERT WHITESIDES. Rec. July term 1774.

Page 57: OCTOBER COURT A. D. 1774.

15 Aug 1774, LEWIS LINEBARGER of Tryon Co., Blacksmith, & wf BARBARA to ROBERT
ABERNATHY of same, for Ŀ 18...land on S side Kuykendalls Creek, 100 A...LUDWIG
LINEBARGER (SEAL), BARBARA LINEBARGER (+) (SEAL), Wit: DAVID ABERNATHY, JAS. GRAHAM.
Rec. Oct. term 1774.

Pp. 57-58: 27 Dec 1773, PHILIP EREHART & wf CATHERINE of Fincastle County, Colony of
Virginia to ROBERT ABERNATHY of Tryon Co., for Ŀ 60 proc. money...100 A,
which was granted to him adj. his own land that he bought of MATTHIAS CLOUS...PHILIP
EREHART (P) (SEAL), CATHARINE EREHART (C) (SEAL), Wit: JOHN ABERNATHY, JAMES FALK (I).
Rec. Oct. term 1774.

Pp. 58-59: 27 Dec 1773, PHILIP EREHART & wf CATHERINE to ROBERT ABERNATHY for Ŀ 100...
land EREHART bought of MATHIAS CLOUS, which sd. CLOUSE bought of SAML. COBURN
400 A. [Same signatures and wit. as preceding deed]. Rec. Oct. term 1774.

Pp. 59-60: 27 Aug 1774, WM. GREEN of Craven County, S. C. and JAMES McAFEE of Tryon Co.,
to JONAS BEDFORD of Tryon Co., for Ŀ 25...200 A on both sides Mountain Creek
about 3/4 mile below GEORGE DICKEYS plantation...WM. GREEN (SEAL), JAMES McAFEE (SEAL),
Wit: ESSEX CAPSHAW, JAS. McENTIRE. Rec. Oct. term 1774.

Page 60: SARAH ROBERSON of Rowan Co., do assign my claim to a waggon and a regro wench
Pender , and cattle to ABEL BEATY...7 Sept 1774...SARAH ROBERSON (W) (SEAL),
Wit: WILLIAM DREW, JAMES WILLSON. Rec. Oct. term 1774.

Page 61: 27 Oct 1774, HENRY LANDESS of Tryon Co., to ABEL BEATY for Ŀ 150 proc. money...
land on waters of Buffalo Creek that runs into Broad River, 250 A...HENRY
LANDESS (W) (SEAL), Wit: AND. POLK, THOS. PEARSON. Rec. Oct. term 1774.

Pp. 62-63: 5 Oct 1774, THOMAS BEATY & HUGH BEATY of Rowan Co.   ROBT. ARMSTRONG of
Tryon Co., & all of Prov. of N. C. & Executors of Estate of FRANCIS BEATY

late of Mecklenburg, Decd., as appears by the L. W. & T. of sd. BEATY dated 23 June
1773...to JOHN BRADLEY of Tryon Co., for Ⱡ 50 proc. money...land in Tryon Co., in the
forks of Potts Creek adj. DANL. WARLEIGHs & SHERILLS lines, granted to FRANCIS BEATY
(decd) 6 Apr. 1765...THOMAS BEATY (SEAL), HUGH BEATEY (SEAL), ROBERT ARMSTRONG (SEAL),
Wit: JAMES TATE, JAMES BEATEY, WALLACE BEATEY. Rec. Oct. term 1774.

Pp. 63-64: 3 July 1773, WM. SHARP of Rowan Co., N. C. Yeoman, to HUGH CUMMINS of Tryon
Co., for Ⱡ 20 proc. money...land on S fork White Oak, a branch of Green River
above BLYTHS survey, originally made for JAMES MILLER, north of HOWARDS old Cabin, granted to JAMES MILLER 22 Dec 1768, and conveyed to WM. SHARP by deed 25 Jan 1769...WM.
SHARP (SEAL), Wit: WALTER SHARP, GEORGE POTTS. Rec. Oct. term 1774.

Pp. 64-65: 3 July 1773, WM. SHARP of Rowan Co., to JOHN CUMMING of Tryon Co., for Ⱡ 20
proc. money...125 A subdivided from a tract of 250 granted to JAMES MILLER
22 Dec 1768, & sold to sd. SHARP 5 Jan 1769...[Same sign. and wit.] Rec. Oct. term 1774.

Pp. 65-66: 22 Aug 1773, PETER AKER SENR. to PETER CARPENTER, both of Tryon Co., for Ⱡ
139...land on S branch of Indian Creek, being a Branch of S fork Catawba by
LAWRENCE KYZERs land, including his own improvements, granted to PETER AKER 10 Apr 1761,
250 A...PETER AKER (X) (SEAL), Wit: CHRISTIAN CARPENTER (CⱢ), LUDWIG ___[Germ. signature],
VALENTINE MAUNEY. Rec. Oct. term 1774.

Pp. 66-67: 2 Jan 1769, MOSES ALEXANDER of Mecklenburg Co., to WM. CLEGHORN of Tryon Co.,
for Ⱡ 5 s 10 proc. money...land on E side main Broad River, 100 A granted to
MOSES ALEXANDER 22 Dec 1768...MOSES ALEXANDER (SEAL), Wit: WILLIAM SHARP, JNO. McKNITT
ALEXANDER. Rec. Oct. term 1774.

Pp. 67-68: 15 Oct 1774, LEWIS LINEBARGER of Tryon Co., to WM. ELDER & SAML ELDER of
same, for Ⱡ 53 proc. money...land on E side Kuykendalls Creek, 200 A granted
to JOHN STANLEY 10 Apr 1764, rec. in Secrys. Office in Book No. 10, page 333...LUDWIG
LINEBURGER (SEAL), Wit: JACOB SEITS, ROBERT ABERNATHY, DANIEL MATTHEW. Rec. Oct. term
1774.

Pp. 68-69: 25 June 1773, HENRY WRIGHT & wf AYLIS of Rowan Co., to NATHANIEL EWING, for
s5...land on W side Catawba River adj. PETER HARPOLS, Anderson branch of
Fishers Creek, granted to ARCHIBALD McLEAN 30 Apr 1762, and from him to JAMES WOODS by
virtue of a power of attorney bearing date New Hanover, Oct. court 1769, and from WOODS
to HENRY WRIGHT by L & R 19 Apr 1770, 250 A...HENRY WRIGHT (SEAL), AYLES WRIGHT (A)
(SEAL), Wit: MOSES WINSLEY, JEAN WINSLEY. Rec. Oct. term 1774.

Pp. 69-70: 29 Aug 1774, JOHN McKNITT ALEXANDER of Mecklenburg to WM. EDGAR of Craven
Co., S. C. for Ⱡ 190 NC money...350 A on both sides second broad River,
granted to ALEXANDER 28 Oct 1765 & another tract of 170 A adj. the other tract, granted
to sd. ALEXANDER 29 Apr 1768...JOHN McKNITT ALEXANDER (SEAL), Wit: JOHN ROBINSON, ARCHI-
BLE EDGAR, HUGH EDGAR. Rec. Oct. term 1774.

Pp. 70-71: 21 Feb 1774, LEWIS WIDNER to JACOB FORNEY, both of Tryon Co., for Ⱡ 20...land
on both sides Long Creek adj. JAMES CARUTHS land, HOFSTATLERS line, 200 A...
LUDWIG _____ [Germ. signature] (SEAL), Wit: JOSEPH BUFFINGTON, VALENTINE MAUNEY, HANS
ZIMMERMAN. Rec. Oct. term 1774.

Pp. 71-72: 21 Jan 1774, LEWIS WIDNER to JACOB FORNEY, for Ⱡ 20 proc. money...land on
both sides Long Creek, 300 A granted to WEIDNER 28 Apr1768...[Same sign. and
wit.] Rec. Oct. term 1774.
Attested to 16 Sept 1774 both deeds and wit. by JOHN RETZHAUPT, _____
[GErm. signature], PETER SIDES (+), THOMAS CASTNER (TC), JOST ____ [Germ. signature].

Pp. 73-74: 18 Oct 1774, GEORGE FREELAND of Tryon Co., to JOSEPH GLADDIN of Surry Co.,
same prov., for Ⱡ 50 proc. money...100 A granted to sd. FREELAND by ALEXR.
KYLE including the improvements the sd. GEORGE FREELAND now lives on, 100 A out of a
tract of 400 A granted to ALEXR KYLE SENR by patent 5 May 1769...GEORGE FREELAND (SEAL),
Wit: ALEXANDER KYLE (A), WILLIAM GUSSON[?] (X). Rec. Oct. term 1774.

Pp. 74-75: 24 Oct 1774, MOSES MOORE of Tryon Co., planter, and wf to WM. GOING of same,
for Ⱡ 26 ş 14 proc. money...150 A...granted to ROBERT COLLINWOOD and by deed
made by GEORGE LAMKIN ESQR., late Sheriff of Tryon Co., by a writ of fiere facias from
the inferior court of Tryon Co., at the suit of BENJAMIN BRACKET against the goods &
chattles of sd. COLLINSWOOD...MOSES MOORE (SEAL), Wit: GEORGE LAMPKIN, SAML SPENCER.
Rec. Oct. term 1774.

Pp. 75-76: GEORGE SHEEL of New Britain Township, Bucks Co., Pennsylvania, yeoman, appoint
my loving friend HENRY HILLEMAN of Tryon Co., NC my lawful attorney to sell
a tract of land in Tryon Co., 250 A adj. CHRISTOPHER RENCHART, PHILIP GROSS[?]...GEORG
SCHIELE [German signature] (SEAL), Wit: GEORGE HILDEBRAND, ANTHONY HOLLMAN, _____
[German signature]. Rec. Oct. term 1774. Dated 13 Spet 1773.

Pp. 76-77: 21 Dec 1772, THOMAS McKNIGHT of Rowan Co., to JAMES HENDERSON of Tryon Co.,
for ₤ 22 s 10 proc. money...land in the forks of the Catawba River, part of
a tract granted to JAMES CARTER, land was taken from sd. CARTER by a writ of fiere facias
against him by JOHN BRANDON in due from __ Feb 1761[?] at Superior Court held at Wilmington for the Counties of New Hanover, Duplin, Onslow, and Cumberland &C by JOHN HAMER,
Sheriff, and from sd. BRANDON to THOMAS McKNIGHT 7 Jan 1763, 119 A...THOMAS McKNIGHT
(SEAL), Wit: JOHN GILLESPIE, THOMAS HENDERSON, JAMES ASTON. Rec. Oct. term 1774.
[For deed from BRANDON to McKNIGHT, see my Mecklenburg County, N. C. Deed Abstracts, Vol.
I, p. 32. The within named JOHN HAMER was Sheriff of Anson County, N. C.]

Pp. 77-78: 13 Aug 1770, THOMAS McKNIGHT of Rowan Co., to JAMES HENDERSON of Tryon Co.,
for ₤ 30 proc. money...169 A in Mecklenburg Co., on W side Catawba River, on
both sides S fork, adj. GEORGE ERWINGS, granted to sd. McKNIGHT 16 Nov 1764...THOMAS
McKNIGHT (SEAL), Wit: WILLIAM SMITH (X), GEORGE EWING, JOHN GILLESPIE. Rec. Oct. term
1774.

Pp. 79-80: 20 Oct 1774, JOHN HARRIS of NC, Tryon Co., to WM HARRIS of same, for ₤ 40 proc.
money...240 A on S side S fork Catawba River on the south side of little
Catawba, being a creek formerly called third creek, near to ROBT. PATTERSONs survey, part
of a tract granted to WM. McCONNELL[?] by patent 23 Feb 1754, made over by him to JOHN
WILSON his lawful attorney, then to JOHN HARRIS by deed 17 Sept 1765, also a tract on W
side Catawba on waters of Little Catawba adj. JOHN HARRIS old line, granted to JOHN HARRIS
14 May 1772...JOHN HARRIS (SEAL), Wit: JONATHAN GULLICK, JOHN GULLICK. Rec. Oct. term
1774.

Pp. 80-81: 31 Aug 1772, JOHN HARRIS & wf JEAN of Tryon Co., to ISAAC HOLLAND of same, for
₤ 30 proc. money...136 A in Tryon Co., on little Catawba Creek adj. JOHN
GULLICK, ANDREW ARMOUR...JOHN HARRIS (SEAL), JEAN HARRIS (C) (SEAL), Wit: JONATHAN
GULLICK, WILLIAM HARRIS. Rec. Oct. term 1774.

Pp. 81-82: 16 Jan 1773, PATRICK McDAVID of Tryon Co., to JOHN MOORE of same, for ₤ 50
proc. money...100 A below Hoyles Mountain, granted to JACOB JOHNSTON 26 Oct
1767 & deeded to sd. McDAVID...PATRICK McDAVID (SEAL), Wit: JOHN McELROY, WILLIAM MOORE,
ALEXANDER MOORE. Rec. Oct. term 1774.

Pp. 82-83: 22 Oct 1774, WM CARPENTER to BENJAMIN KUYKENDALL, both of Tryon Co., for ₤ 70
...300 A on a branch of Broad River including JOHN ISONS own improvements adj.
WILLIS' line...WILLIAM CARPENTER (V₤) (SEAL), Wit: UEL LAMKIN, WILLIAM GARDNER (M),
JOSEPH HARDEN. Rec. Oct. term 1774.

Pp. 83-86: 22 May 1773, GEORGE LAMKIN, Esq., Sheriff of Tryon Co., to MOSES MOORE,
planter to same...by a writ of fiere facias from the Court of Pleas and Quarter
Sessions from Tryon Co., January and April terms 1773...BENJAMIN BRACKET against ROBERT
COLLINWOOD...200 A on W side Wards Creek...GEORGE LAMKIN Shff (SEAL), Wit: SAML SPENCER,
WILLIAM GOING. Rec. Oct. term 1774.

Pp. 86-87: 16 Feb1774, JAMES HARRIS JR. of Meck., to JOHN HARRIS of Tryon Co., for ₤ 40
proc. money...223 A near ROBERT PATTERSON, part of a tract granted to WILLIAM
McCONNEL 23 Feb 1754, and by his attorney JOHN WILSON sold to JAS. HARRIS 18 Jan 1764...
JAMES HARRIS (SEAL), Wit: JONATHAN GULLICK, JESSE GULLICK. Rec. Oct. term 1774.

Pp. 87-88: 23 Feb 1773, PATRICK McDAVID of Tryon Co., to JNO. MOORE of same, for ₤ 50
proc. money...100 A granted to THOMAS RAY...PATRICK McDAVID (SEAL), Wit:
JOHN GILLESPIE, WILLIAM MOORE, ALEXANDER MOORE. Rec. Oct. term 1774.

Pp. 88-89: 26 Oct 1774, WM GARDNER & wf HANNAH of Tryon Co., to GEORGE CHRISTOPHER
NESHINGER of same, for ₤ 17 proc. money...land on a long branch of Howards
Creek, at the head of Leonards fork, 300 A granted to sd. WILLIAM GARDNER 22 Sept 1773...
WILLIAM GARDNER (M) (SEAL), Wit: AND. NEIL, JOSEPH RICHEY. Rec. Oct term 1774.

Pp. 89-90: 26 Oct 1774, DANL McCLAREY of Craven Co., S. C. to MICAJAH PROCTOR for ₤ 50
proc. money...land on both sides a large fork of Catheys Creek, granted to sd.
CLAREY 16 Dec 1769...DANIEL McCLARY (SEAL), Wit: JAMES WILLIAMS. Rec. Oct. term 1774.

Pp. 90-91: 10 June 1774, JOHN MARTIN of Tryon Co., to THOMAS PRICE, planter, for ₤ 40
        proc. money...200 A on both sides a branch of Crowders Creek...JOHN MARTIN
(SEAL), Wit: JOHN BARBAR, DAVID ALEXANDER, JOHN WILLSON. Rec. Oct. term 1774.

Pp. 91-92: 16 July 1773, JOHN BLYTH of Rowan Co., to GEORGE POTTS of Tryon Co., for ₤ 30
        proc. money...land on both sides S fork of White Oaks Creek, below JAMES
MILLERS survey, 200 A granted to sd. BLYTH, 22 Dec 1768...JAMES BLYTH (SEAL), Wit
JAS. HUGHES, WM. SHARP. Rec. Oct. term 1774.

Pp. 92-93: 12 Sept 1774, DANIEL SHIPMAN of Tryon Co., to THOMAS REYNOLDS JR. of same, for
        ₤150 proc. money...200 A on both sides Sandy Run, N side Broad River...DANIEL
SHIPMAN (L) (SEAL), Wit: TIMO. RIGGS, SAMUEL GRAY. Rec. Oct. term 1774.

Pp. 93-94: 19 Aug 1774, THOMAS BEATTEY & wf MARGARET of Tryon Co., to DAVID ROBINSON of
        Rowan Co., for ₤ 45 NC money...land formerly in Mecklenburg Co., on W side
Cataba on both sides Littles Creek, adj. THOMAS LITTLE, 200 A granted to THOS BEATY, 25
Apr 1767...THOMAS BEATTY (SEAL), MARGRET BETTY (SEAL), Wit: SAMUEL HUNTER (S), DAVID
HODSON. Rec. Oct. term 1774

Pp. 94-96: 9 Aug 1774, ZACHARIAH BULLOCK of Craven Co., SC yeoman, to CHRISTIAN REINHART
        of Tryon Co., planter, for ₤ 20 proc. money...land on S side S fork Catawba,
adj. BEATY, 112 A granted to sd. BULLOCK 26 Oct 1767, Rec. in Secretary Office, Bk. 13
...ZACHARIAH BULLOCK (SEAL), Wit: JAMES HUNTER (J), ROBERT BLACKBURN. Rec. Oct. term 1774.

Pp. 96-97: 2 Mar 1773, FRANCIS BEATY of Mecklenburg Co., to GEORGE LEONARD SAILOR of
        Tryon Co., for ₤ 30 proc. money...land below Leonard SAILORS on a fork of
Killions Creek, above GEORGE RUNNOLDS old survey, granted to WM. HAGAR and JACOB FORNEY
26 Nov 1757, and conveyed to FRANCIS BEATY 8 Sept 1758...FRANCIS BEATY (SEAL), Wit: HUGH
BEATY, WALLACE BEATY. Rec. Oct. term 1774.

Pp. 97-98: 7 Sept 1774, JAMES LOGAN of Tryon Co., planter, to PETER SUMMY SENR., of same,
        yeoman, for ₤ 60 proc. money...land in Mecklenburg, now Tryon Co., on Jacobs
River, a S fork of S fork Catawba, 200 A granted to WM. REED 25 Apr 1767, and sold 11
Feb 1772 to ANSON REYNOLDS, then to JAMES MITCHELL 29 Mar 1773, and then to LOGAN 18 May
1773...JAMES LOGAN (SEAL), Wit: BENJAMIN HARDIN, JACOB COSTNER. Rec. Oct. term 1774.

Page 99: 15 Aug 1774, JAMES CARRUTH of Mecklenburg Co., to JOHN SLOAN Jr. of same, for
        ₤ 35 proc. money...200 A on both sides Muddy fork of Buffalo Creek including the
old mill shoals, granted to sd. CARRUTH and SLOAN by ALEXANDER KYLE...by deed 1770...
JAMES CARRUTH (SEAL), Wit: ROBERT SLOAN, JOHN SLOAN, JOHN CARRUTH. Rec. Oct. term 1774.

Page 100: 7 Sept 1774, WOOLRICH CARPENTER of Tryon Co., to PETER SITES of same, for ₤ 20
        proc. money...land on the shoal branch of muddy fork of Buffalo Creek adj.
MOSES MOORE, 200 A granted to BENJAMIN SHAW 16 Nov 1764...WOOLRIGH CARPENTER (V₤) (SEAL),
Wit: VALLENTINE MAUNEY, JACOB COSTNER. Rec. Oct. term 1774.

Page 101: Tryon County, N. C. inferior court of Pleas and Quarter Sessions, July term
        1774....NICHOLAS WELCH, exr. of L. W. & T. of JOHN WELCH, decd is due ₤ 35 s 8
d 8...You are to expose to sale the plantation on which MARGARET WHITLY, late the wife
and relict of JOHN WELCH, decd, now lives...26 July 1774. AND. NEEL, C. C.

Pp. 101-102: 8 Oct 1774, THOMAS WILLIAMS SENR. of Georgia, to WM. WILSON of Sandy Run,
        Tryon Co., NC, for ₤ 20 proc. money...land on both sides S fork of Sandy
Run, 150 A...THOMAS WILLIAMS (SEAL), Wit: TIMO. RIGGS, JOHN ASHWORTH. Rec. Oct. term
1774.

Pp. 102-103: 20 Dec 1773, JAMES COZART of Tryon Co., to JOSEPH WOOTENBURG of same, for
        ₤ 80 proc. money...52 A, part of a tract which ORASMUS RUPER in his life
time granted to DAVID JENKINS by a deed 15 Jan 1769...JAMES COZART (SEAL), Wit: ABSALOM
AGER, JOHN WELLS (+++). Rec. Oct. term 1774. Also wit. FREDERICK HAMBRIGHT.

Pp. 103-104: 20 Dec 1773, JAMES COZART to JOSEPH WOOTENBURG, for ₤ 80 proc. money...land
        on both sides Long Creek that JOHN MOORE sold to MICHAEL RUDISIL, 300 A,
that JOHN NICHOLAS sold unto JAMES COZART, 7 July 1770...JAMES COZART (SEAL), Wit:
FREDERICK HAMBRIGHT, ABSALOM AGER, JOHN WELLS (+++). Rec. Oct. term 1774.

Page 104: 26 Oct 1774, ANDREW HOYLE of Tryon Co., to JAMES WYATT JUR. of same, for ₤ 40
        proc. money...200 A on both sides Little Long Creek including the great shoals
granted to sd. HOYLE 28 Apr 1768...ANDREW HOYLE (SEAL), Wit: JAMES HENDERSON, SAMUEL
MARTIN. Rec. Oct. term 1774.

Pp. 104-105: 8 Aug 1774, WM. WILSON of Tryon Co., to THOMAS WILSON of same, for Ⱡ 50 proc.
        money...200 A including the plantation whereon sd. WM. WILSON now lives...
WILLIAM WILSON (W) (SEAL), Wit: SAMUEL SARRATT JUR., SAMUEL SARRATT SENR., JOHN SARRATT.
Rec. Oct. term 1774.

Pp. 105-106: 14 Oct 1774, JAMES PATTERSON & wf SARAH of Tryon Co., to JOHN WEST of same,
        for Ⱡ 60 NC money...land on a branch of Kings Creek...JAMES PATTERSON (SEAL),
SARAH PATTERSON (SEAL), Wit: None. Rec. Oct. term 1774.

Pp. 106-107: 12 Aug 1774, JOHN McINTIER of Tryon Co., to MOSES WHITLEY of same, for Ⱡ 64
        ...land on Hintons Creek, 300 A...JOHN McTIER (SEAL), Wit: WILLIAM McLINEY
(X), JUDITH McENTIRE, JAMES McENTIRE. Rec. Oct. term 1774.

Pp. 107-108: 20 July 1773, FRANCIS BEATTY of Mecklenburg Co., NC to JOHN ARMSTRONG of
        Tryon Co., for Ⱡ 50 proc. money...300 A in two surveys lying in the forks
of Catawba River adj. WM. CRONELY[?] corner, JOHN ARMSTRONG, CHRONICLE...FRANCIS BEATY
(SEAL), Wit: WALLACE BEATY, FRANCIS BEATEY JUNR., W. TATE. Rec. Jan. term 1775.

Page 108: SIMON KUYKENDALL for s 1 sterling pd. by ROBERT ARMSTRONG...I do formally rati-
        fy a sale made by my uncle JOSEPH HARDEN, 200 A that formerly belong to my
father JOHN KUYKENDALL, decd, adj. to W side Cataba, 15 Feb 1771...SIMON KUYKENDALL (SEAL),
Wit: JOHN BEATY. WILLIAM ELDER. Rec. Jan. term 1775.

Page 109: ____ 1773, JAMES McENTIRE & wf ANN of Tryon Co., to WM. BOOTH of same, for Ⱡ 35
        proc. money...450 A on both sides Buffalo Creek about a mile above BEATYs...
JAMES McENTIRE (SEAL), ANN McENTIRE (SEAL), Wit: MOSES WHITELY, DANIEL SINGLETON. Rec.
Jan. term 1775.

Pp. 109-111: 24 Jan 1775, NICHOLAS WISENANT of Tryon Co., to CHRISTIAN CARPENTER of same,
        for Ⱡ 60 proc. money...300 A where sd. NICHOLAS now lives, granted to ADAM
WISENANT 30 Oct 1765...____ [German signature] (SEAL), Wit: None. Rec. Jan. term 1775.

Pp. 111-112: 20 Jan 1775, GEORGE MOORGRUNG of Tryon Co., to ADAM DICK of same, for Ⱡ 34
        proc. money...land on S side Catawba on Killions Creek adj. ABRAM EREHART,
ADAM DICK, granted to ABM. EREHART 140 A, 28 Apr 1768...[German signature] (SEAL), Wit:
JOHN DELLINGER _____ [German signature]. Rec. Jan. term 1775.

Pp. 112-113: 20 July 1773, ARCHD. FLEMING & wf AGNIS of Rowan Co., to JAMES FLEMING of
        Tryon Co., for Ⱡ 20 NC money...200 A on Mountain Creek adj. JOHN LITTLE,
and FRANCIS...ARCHIBALD FLEMING (SEAL), AGNIS FLEMING (+) (SEAL), Wit: GEORGE MOSSGUNG
[German signature]. Rec. Jan. term 1775.

Pp. 113-114: 8 June 1774, ANDREW GOFORTH & RICHARD GULLICK of Tryon Co., yeoman, to JOHN
        GOFORTH of same, yeoman, for Ⱡ 72 proc. money...300 A...ANDREW GOFORTH (SEAL),
RICHARD GULLICK (SEAL), Wit: DAVID JENKINS, PRESTON GOFORTH (X). Rec. Jan. term 1775.

Pp. 114-116: 19 Dec 1774, BENJAMIN HYDE of Rowan Co., to REBECAH GILKIE of same, (lease
        s5, release Ⱡ 100)...300 A on a branch of Camp Creek adj. MOORE, BLACK, grant-
ed to HYDE 4 May 1769...BENJAMIN HIDE (SEAL), Wit: WILLIAM NEVENS, ROBERT NEVINS. Rec.
Jan. term 1775.

Pp. 117-119: 19 & 20 Jan 1767, WILLIAM CLEGHORN, Smith, of Mecklenburg Co., to JAMES
        HENDERSON of same (lease s5, release Ⱡ 80)...300 A on S side Catawba, adj.
WIDOW McKENDRICK, granted to CLEGHORN 6 Apr 1765...WILLIAM CLEGHORN (SEAL), MARY CLEGHORN
(SEAL), (X), Wit: GEORGE EWING, CATHARINE EWING (X), JONATHAN LOW, ALEXANDER COULTER.
Rec. Jan. term 1775.

Pp. 119-120: 1 Sept 1774, DANIEL JARRETT of Rowan Co., joiner, to SAMUEL JARRETT for Ⱡ 50
        proc. money...part of a tract sd. DANIEL JARRETT purchased of JOHN FONDREN,
Esq. 1 Sept 1774, 250 A...DANIEL JARROTT (SEAL), CHARLERENA GARRETT (+) (SEAL), Wit:
JACOB NOTZEL, MARTIN NORGAL. Rec. Jan. term 1775.

Pp. 120-121: 20 Oct 1774, THOMAS CAMPBELL of Tryon Co., to SAMUEL LOFTEN of same, for
        Ⱡ 66 s 14 d 4...200 A granted to sd. CAMPBELL on a S branch of Little
Catawba...THOMAS CAMPBELL (SEAL), Wit: THOS NEEL, JOSEPH NEEL, JOHN NEEL. Rec. Jan. term
1775.

Pp. 121-122: 11 Jan 1775, THOMAS HESLIP of Tryon Co. to JOSEPH JACK of same, for Ʇ 75...
           land on S side Catawba adj. to the river in Hasleps Bend, granted to THOMAS
ROBINSON, 150 A, conveyed to JAMES HUGGINS, then to ANDREW HASLEP, from ANDREW HASLEP, to
JOHN HASLEP, now deceased, to THOMAS HASLEP...THOMAS HESLIP (SEAL), Wit: JAMES JOHNSON,
BENJAMIN CORKRAN, JANE JOHNSTON. Rec. Jan. term 1775.

Page 123: 24 Jan 1775, NICHOLAS WISENANT of Tryon Co., to LAWRENCE KOIZER for Ʇ 11 proc.
           money...150 A on both sides N fork Buffalo Creek a Broad River..._____
[German signature] (SEAL), Wit: None. Rec. Jan. term 1775.

Pp. 123-124: 1 Sept 1774, DAVID JARROTT of Rowan Co., to MARTIN LOOKINGLASS of same, for
           Ʇ 50 proc. money...land purchased of JOHN   FROHOCK, 250 A...DAVID JARROTT
(SEAL), CHOALERENE JARROTT (X) (SEAL), Wit: JACOB ____ [German signature], SAMUEL[?]
JARROTT, Rec. Jan. term 1775.

Pp. 124-125: 3 Sept 1774, DAVID BYARS of Rowan Co., to MICHAEL McELRATH of Tryon Co., for
           Ʇ 40...land on N side Main Broad River, on E side Mountain Creek...on the
mill branch adj. THOMAS JOHNSTONs land, granted to sd. BYARS 29 Apr 1768...DAVID BYARS
(SEAL), Wit: JAMES BYERS, JOSEPH BYARS, MARY McGUIRE. Rec. Jan. term 1775.

Pp. 125-126: 3 Sept 1774, JAMES BYERS & wf MARGARET of Rowan Co., to MICHAEL McELWRATH of
           Tryon Co., for Ʇ 50 proc. money...land on Mill Creek, an East branch of
Mountain Creek adj. DAVIS BYARS, granted to JAMES BYERS 18 Apr 1771...JAMES BYERS (SEAL),
MARGRET BYERS (SEAL), Wit: DAVID BYARS, JOSEPH BYARS, MARY McGUIRE. Rec. Jan. term 1775.

Pp. 127-128: 17 Jan 1775, FRANCIS McCORKLE & wf SARAH of Rowan Co., to ROBERT McCASLAND
           of Tryon Co., for Ʇ 67 proc. money...land on waters of Mountain Creek adj.
line of FRANCIS McCORKLES land that he lives on, commonly known as Hob Creek, 250 A,
granted to sd. McCorkle 16 Dec 1763...FRANS. McCORKLE (SEAL), SARAH McCORKLE (SEAL), Wit:
ARCHIBALD FLEMING, LETTIS REED (0). Rec. Jan. term 1775.

Pp. 128-129: 7 Dec 1774, JAMES KELLY of Tryon Co., to JACOB MOONEY of same, for Ʇ 120
           proc. money...200 A on muddy fork of Buffalo Creek below MOSON[MOSES] MOORES
land...JAMES KELLY (I) (SEAL), MARY KELLY (0) (SEAL), Wit: PETER EKER (X), SIMEON KUYKEN-
DALL. Rec. Jan. term 1775.

Pp. 129-130: 28 Dec 1774, ROBERT EVANS of Tryon Co., yeoman, to JOHN MATTACKS of same,
           farmer, for Ʇ 7 s 10 proc. money...75 A on the S branch of Cataba River
adj. JAMES LEEPER (deceased), JOS. BEATTY, ROBERT CAMPBELL, granted ___ Apr 1768...ROB-
ERT EVANS (SEAL), Wit: JOHN GLEN, THOMAS ROBINSON. Rec. Jan. term 1775.

Pp. 130-131: 10 Oct 1774, JOHN FALLS of Mecklenburg Co., planter, to HENRY McWHARTER of
           same, for Ʇ 40...land on S fork Catheys Creek, 300 A granted to sd. FALLS
5 May 1769...JOHN FALLS (SEAL), MARTHA FALLS (N) (SEAL), Wit: SAMUEL PICKENS, WM. WRAY,
WILLIAM FALLS, Rec. Jan. term 1775.

Pp. 132-133: 25 Feb 1771, WILLIAM MACKEY of Mecklenburg Co., cooper, to WILLIAM PATTERSON
           of Tryon Co., Taylor, for Ʇ 40...land on W side S fork Cataba, adj. JAMES
PATTERSON, 1/2 of 478 A, conveyed by GEO. CATHEY & wf FANNY to JOHN BRAVARD & JOHN LUCKIE,
in trust for use of WILLIAM MACKEY (decd), 7 & 8 Dec 1758...WILLIAM MACKEY (SEAL), Wit:
FRANCIS BEATY JR., FRANCIS BEATY SR., WALLACE BEATY, ALEXANDER PATTERSON. Rec. Jan. term
1775.

Pp. 133-134: 2 Nov 1774, JOHN SLOAN of Tryon Co., to JOHN SARTAIN of same, for Ʇ 25 proc.
           money...land on E side little Braod River adj. FRANCIS BEATY, 200 A...JOHN
SLOAN (SEAL), JANE SLOAN (0) (SEAL), Wit: JOHN SLOAN, WILLIAM McKINEY, MARGARET McKINEY,
JAMES HENDERSON. Rec. Jan. term 1775.

Pp. 134-135: 5 Dec 1774, SAMUEL BARNET of Tryon Co., to WILLIAM STEVENSON of Camden Dist.,
           S. C., for Ʇ 45 proc. money...100 A on a branch of Crowders Creek adj.
EPHRAIM McLEAN, granted to SAML BARNET 18 May 1771...SAMUEL BARNET (SEAL), Wit: JOHN
BARBER, JOHN WILLSON. Rec. Jan. term 1775.

Pp. 135-136: 2 Sept 1774, HENRY JOHNSTON & wf CATHERINE of Tryon Co., to JOSEPH SCOTT of
           Rowan Co., for Ʇ 100...260 A on bank of Catawba River, granted to SAMUEL
COBURN 29 Sept 1750...HENRY JOHNSTON (SEAL), CATHERN JOHNSTON (SEAL), Wit: JAMES JOHNSTON,
JAMES DAVIS, WM. DAVIES. Rec. Jan. term 1775.

Page 137: 14 Sept 1774, HUGH BEATY of Rowan Co., planter, to THOMAS TOWNSIN of Tryon Co.,
for ₺ 30 proc. money...land on Broad River below the mouth of a large creek,
granted to sd. BEATY 6 Apr 1765...HUGH BEATY (SEAL), Wit: CHARLES EVENTON (T), JOEL
BLACKWELL (X). Rec. Jan. term 1775.

Pp. 138-140: 19 Dec 1774, WILLIAM HIDE of Rowan Co., to JOSEPH THOMSON of same (lease
s5, release ₺ 60)...200 A on branches of Cane Creek, granted to WILLIAM
HYDE, 18 Apr 1771...WILLIAM HIDE (SEAL), JEANE HIDE (SEAL), Wit: WILLIAM NEVENS, JOHN
GILKEY. Rec. Jan. term 1775.

Pp. 140-141: 24 Dec 1774, JAMES MOORE of Craven Co., S. C., planter, to THOMAS TOWNSON
of Tryon Co., for ₺ 300...land on S side Broad River, granted to sd. MOORE
5 Apr 1766, 200 A...JAMES MOORE (SEAL), Wit: RICHD COBRUN[?], CHRISTOPHER HICKS, SAML
HENER (T). Rec. Jan. term 1775.

Pp. 141-142: 1 Sept 1774, DANIEL JARRATT of Rowan Co., to JACOB WETSAIL of same, for ₺ 50
proc. **money**...part of a tract purchased by sd. JARRATT from JOHN FROHOCK,
250 A...DANIEL JARRETT (SEAL), CHEATERENA JARRATT (X) (SEAL), Wit: MARTIN _____, SAMUEL
TARREL. Rec. Jan. term 1775.

Pp. 142-144: JOHN CARSON of Rowan Co., for ₺ 150 proc. money pd. by JOHN WITHROW of
Tryon Co., 23 Dec 1775...land on Kane Creek, a branch of Second Broad River,
near Moses MOORE, HUDDLESTON adj. JAMES MARTIN, 520 A granted to sd. CARSON 6 Apr 1765...
JOHN CARSON (SEAL), Wit: WILLIAM NEVENS, JOHN GILKEY. Rec. Jan. term 1775.

Pp. 144-145: APRIL COURT AD 1775.
8 Apr 1775, WILLIAM GRAHAM of NC to JOHN ALTRUIN[?] of same, for ₺ 35...land
on N side Broad River on a branch of Buffalo Creek about two miles from the place where
THOMAS CALDWELL now lives adj. JAMES SLOANs survey, 200 A granted to JOHN TAGERT 22 May
1770, and conveyed to GRAHAM 8 Nov 1774...WILLIAM GRAHAM (SEAL), Wit: JOHN LUSK, WILLIAM
WHITESIDE, _____ [German signature]. Rec. Apr. term 1775.

Pp. 145-146: JAMES ALLEY for love, good will and affection to my sons THOMAS ALLEY and
JAMES ALLEY JUNR...land on both sides Indian Creek, 200 A I now live on,
granted 1772 also cattle [enumerated]...29 Mar 1775...JAMES ALLEY (SEAL), Wit: MELCHIOR
OYLER, FRANCIS OYLER, SARAH ALLEY (ʒ). Rec. Apr. term 1775.

Pp. 146-147: 11 Mar 1775, WILLIAM GOFORTH of Tryon Co., planter, to JOHN BAIRD JUNIOR of
Craven Co., S. C., for ₺ 60 proc. money...land on Buck Branch of Crowders
Creek, 200 A granted to PRESTON GOFORTH, 26 Sept 1776, and to sd. WILLIAM GOFORTH by deed
26 Jan 1773...WILLIAM GOFORTH (SEAL), Wit: ANDW NEEL, ROBERT SHANNAN. Rec. Apr. term 1776.

Pp. 147-148: 25 Dec 1773, NICHOLAS LEEPER & wf MARY of Tryon Co., to JONAS BEDFORD, Esq.,
for ₺ 80 proc. money...land on N side Broad River, on both sides Richlands
Creek, granted to MATTHEW FLOYD, 2 Nov 1764....NICHOLAS LEEPER (SEAL), Wit: THOMAS NEEL,
ANDREW NEEL. Rec. Apr. term 1775.

Pp. 148-149: 17 Apr 1773, JOHN LAME[?] & wf MARY of Tryon Co., yeoman, to JOHN PHILIP
FILE, of same, for ₺ 50 proc. money...land on N side S fork Cataba, adj.
DERICK RAMSOURs lower line...JOHANNES LAHME[?] [German signature], MARY LAME (X) (SEAL),
Wit: JACOB RAMSOUR, CHRISTIAN REINHARDT. Rec. Apr. term 1775

Pp. 149-150: 20 Apr 1775, THOMAS BEATY, HUGH BEATY & ROBERT ARMSTRONG Exrs. of L. W. & T.
of FRANCIS BEATY, Gent., late of Mecklenburg Co., to WILLIAM FAIRES of Tryon
Co., planter, for ₺ 40 proc. money...land above McDOWELLS or AIDENTONS land, part of a
tract granted to FRANCIS BEATY decd., 600 A, 19 Apr 1763...THOMAS BEATY (SEAL), HUGH
BEATY (SEAL), ROBERT ARMSTRONG (SEAL), Wit: FRANCIS BEATY, WILLIAM MORRISON, MATHEW _____
[German signature]... Rec. Apr. term 1775.

Page 151: 8 Nov 1774, JOHN TAGERT of Prov. of S. C. to WILLIAM GRAHAM of Tryon Co., for
₺ 20 NC money...land on N side Broad River, on a branch of Buffalo Creek...
200 A granted to sd. TAGERT 22 May 1770...JOHN TAGERT (SEAL), Wit: WILLIAM TATE, GAVIN
BLACK, SAMUEL BARNS. Rec. Apr. term 1775.

Pp. 151-152: 13 Feb 1775, EDWARD HOGAN of Tryon Co., to THOMAS HASLEP of same, for ₺ 45
NC money...land on both sides Green River between WHITESIDES and REYNOLDS,
granted to JAMES CRAFFORD 22 Dec 1768, conveyed to WM SHARP 10 Apr 1769, then to sd.
HOGAN 13 Nov 1772...EDWARD HOGAN (ᘯ) (SEAL), Wit: JOHN McFADDEN (₥), ANTHONY METCALF.
Rec. Apr. term 1775.

Page 153: 3 Dec 1773, WILLIAM ALSTON of Tryon Co., to THOMAS HUNT of same, for ₺ 40
proc. money...land on both sides Dutchmans Creek, known by the name of Davis's
Mill place, part of a tract granted to JOSEPH DAVIES (decd), 6 May 1769...WM. ALSTON (SEAL)
Wit: JAMES HANKS, ABRAHAM DUNAWAY, SAMUEL KUYKENDALL. Rec. Apr. term 1775.

Page 154: 28 Jan 1774, JOHN LUSK of Tryon Co., to ANDREW HASLEP of same, for ₺ 33.15...
by virute of a patent 1766 to ALEXANDER McENTIRE, conveyed to JOHN LUSK 23 Jan
1770...200 A on the mouth of Brushy Creek of little Broad River...JOHN LUSK (SEAL), SARAH
LUSK (S) (SEAL), Wit: THOMAS HESLIP, BENJAMIN ALLIN[?] (B), NICHOLAS FISHER. Rec. Apr.
term 1775.

Pp. 155-156: 26 Apr 1775, WALTER SHARP of Rowan Co., to WILLM. MILLS of Tryon Co., for
₺ 50 proc. money...land on Green River and both sides Panther Creek, 300 A
granted to WALTER SHARP 28 Apr 1768...WALTER SHARP (SEAL), Wit: WM. SHARP, WM. BUTLER.
Rec. Apr. term 1775.

Pp. 156-157: 15 Aug 1774, SAMUEL SHARP of Cecil Co., Md., to WILLIAM SHARP of Tryon Co,
for ₺ 10...land on both sides Walnut Creek of Green River, granted to JOHN
McKNITT ALEXANDER, 200 A, 29 Apr 1768, and conveyed to sd. SHARP by deed...SAMUEL SHARP
(SEAL), SOPHIA SHARP (SEAL), Wit: WALTER SHARP, DANIEL REESE JR., Rec. Apr. term 1775.

Pp. 157-158: 25 Apr 1775, JOHN MOORE of Tryon Co., to WILLIAM MOORE his son, for ₺ 100
proc. money...land on both sides Duharts Creek of S fork Catawba, part of a
grant to JOHN MOORE 25 Jan 1773...JOHN MOORE (SEAL), Wit: WM. CHRONICLE, JONATHAN GULLICK.
Rec. Apr. term 1775.

Pp. 158-159: 20 Apr 1775, JOHN BEARD SR. of Tryon Co. to EDWARD MELLON of same, for ₺ 30
...land on Mill Creek including BRADEYs improvements adj. JAMES LEWIS, 140
A adj. to JOHN BEARD 4 May 1769...JOHN BEARD (SEAL), Wit: AND NEEL, WILLIAM PATTERSON.
Rec. Apr. term 1775.

Pp. 159-160: 8 Jan 1775, MOSES MOORE of Tryon Co., to BENJAMIN MOORE for ₺ 300 proc.
money...land on N side Second Broad River including two forks and the
Buffalo Road, 400 A granted to MOSES MOORE 16 Nov 1764...MOSES MOORE (M) (SEAL), Wit:
JOHN DUNN, AND NEEL. Rec. Apr. term 1775.

Pp. 160-161: 25 Mar 1775, WILLIAM TANKERSLEY of Tryon Co., to JACOB MASTERS of same, for
₺ 60...land on S branch of Leepers Creek adj. PHILIP TILLINGER, 200 A granted to TANKERSLEY by TILLINGER, and to TELLINGER by patent 26 Sept 1766...WILLIAM TANKER-
SLEY (MT), (SEAL), Wit: MATTHIAS DEVOL, LEMUEL SAUNDERS. Rec. Apr. term 1775.

Pp. 161-162: 1 Feb 1775, JAMES DOUGHERTY of Tryon Co., to JAMES MILLER of same, for ₺ 50
...land on both sides Maple Creek of Mountain Creek, granted to sd. DOUGH-
ERTY May 1772...JAMES DOUGHERTY (SEAL), Wit: ALEXANDER COULTER, MARGARET WOOLF (+). Rec.
Apr. term 1775.

Pp. 162-163: 13 Feb 1775, ROBERT JOHNSTON of Tryon Co., to FREDERIC NESTER of same, for
₺ 25...50 A conveyed to him by PETER COSTNER, granted to MARTIN DELLINGER
28 Apr 1768...on Sights branch...Johnstons springs branch...ROBT JOHNSTON (SEAL), Wit:
LEMUEL SAUNDERS, MICHAEL _____ [German signature]. Rec. Apr. term 1775.

Pp. 163-164: 27 Apr 1775, CHRISTOPHER WALBERT of Tryon Co., to THOMAS ROBINSON of same,
for ₺ 51 proc. money...land on both sides Wards Creek, granted to JOHN PHI-
FER of Mecklenburg County, 18 Apr 1771, & by sd. JOHN PHIFER & wf CATHERINE to WALBERT,
23 Dec 1772, Rec. in Book 7., 200 A...CHRISTOPHER WALBERT (SEAL), Wit: JOHN BROWN SKRIM-
SHIRE, JOHN ALEXANDER, JOHN HEYEL. Rec. Apr. term 1775.

Pp. 164-165: 24 Mar 1775, PETER SMITH & wf ELIZABETH of Guilford Co., to ROBERT RAMSEY
of Bux[sic] Co., Pennsylvania, for ₺ 20 proc. money...land on SW side S
fork Catawba, on the mountain branch including a shoal above RAMSOURS line, 300 A....
_____ [German signature] (SEAL), Wit: THOMAS McCOLLOUGH, DAVID THRONBERGER[?],
DAVID RAMSEY. Rec. Apr. term 1775.

Pp. 165-166: 5 Feb 1775, JAMES SCOTT & wf MARY of Cumberland Co., Pa., to ROBERT SHANNON
of Tryon Co., for ₺ 20 proc. money...200 A on a ridge between little Catawba
and Crowders Creek...granted to sd. SCOTT 28 Apr 1768...JAMES SCOTT (SEAL), MARY SCOTT
(SEAL), Wit: JOHN CREAG. Rec. Apr. term 1775.

Pp. 166-167: 11 Mar 1775, HUGH SHANNON of Tryon Co., to JAMES SHANON, for Ⱡ 20...land
            on N side Duharts Creek of S fork Cataba, near JAS. WALLACE, 200 A, granted
to HUGH SHANNON 15 May 1772...HUGH SHANAN (SEAL), Wit: AND NEEL, ROBERT SHANNON. Rec.
Apr. term 1775.

Pp. 167-168: 14 Nov 1774, JOHN MOORE of Tryon Co., to ZECHARIAH SPENCER of same, for Ⱡ 40
            proc. money...land on S side S fork Cataba, near the foot of Hoyles Mountain
50 A, part of a grant to JOHN ALEXANDER 9 Nov 1764...JOHN MOORE (SEAL), Wit: WILLIAM MOORE,
WILLIAM ADAIR. Rec. Apr. term 1775.

Pp. 168-169: 18 Apr 1775, ABEL LEE, SENIOR of Tryon Co., to THOMAS WELCH of same, yeoman,
            for Ⱡ 54 proc. money...land on middle fork of Sandy Run of Broad River,
granted to DANIEL SHIPMAN, 5 Jan 1772...100 A...ABEL LEE (A) (SEAL), Wit: TIMO. RIGGS,
WILLIAM REYNOLDS (M). Rec. Apr. term 1775.
                            APRIL COURT ENDED

Pp. 169-171: JULY COURT AD 1775.
            22 Mar 1775, HENRY WRIGHT of Craven Co., S. C., to JOHN KIRKCONELL of Tryon
Co., for Ⱡ 100 proc. money...land on both sides main branch of Kings Creek including
SHEARSES mill place, 500 A granted to WRIGHT ___ July 1774 & another tract on both sides
Shoal Creek of first Broad River, including JONAS WELLS cabin and all improvements JOHN
LOGAN made...near McKNITT ALEXANDERs line, 400 A granted to WRIGHT 28 Feb 1775...HENRY
WRIGHT (SEAL), Wit: AND NEEL, JOHN BAIRD. Rec. July term 1775.

Page 171: HENRY WRIGHT to JOHN KIRKCONELL...bed, kitchen items, books [enumerated]...29
          Oct 1774...[Same signatures and wit.] Rec. July term 1775.

Pp. 171-173: 24 July 1775, THOMAS BEATY, HUGH BEATY & ROBERT ABERNATHY, Exrs. of L. W. &
            T. of FRANCIS BEATY, decd, to BENJAMIN COCHRAN for Ⱡ 40 proc. money...149 A
granted 15 May 1772 adj. HASLEPS corner on W side Cataba...Wit: FRANCIS BEATTY, JOSEPH
BYERS, AGNESS ARMSTRONG. Rec. July term 1775.

Pp. 173-174: 4 Feb 1775, BOSTON BEST & wf CATRIN of Tryon Co., to GEORGE CATHEY of Meck-
            lenburg Co., for Ⱡ 160 Proc.money....land on E side S fork Catawba adj. sd.
BOSTON BEST, WYATT, 100 A...BOSTIAN BEST (SEAL), CATRON BEST (O) (SEAL), Wit: GEORGE
LAMKIN, ANDREW CATHEY. Rec. July term 1775.

Pp. 174-175: 14 Apr 1775, BARTLETT HENSON of Tryon Co., to JACOB CLEMENTS of same, for
            Ⱡ 85 proc. money...land adj. THOMAS HOPPER, granted to PHILIP HENSON 26 Oct
1767 and deeded by him to ABRAHAM CLEMENTS, then to BARTLETT HENSON...BARTLETT HENSON
(SEAL), Wit: THOMAS DILL, (C), ISHAM SAFOLD. Rec. July term 1775.

Pp. 175-176: 5 Mar 1774, JAMES CAPSHAW of Tryon Co., to JOHN CUMMINS of same, for Ⱡ 3
            proc. money...land on both sides of White oak Creek including a small plant-
ation on the S side of sd. creek, a mile and a half above the cherokee ford of White
oak, part of a tract granted by patent to GEORGE ALEXANDER and by several conveyances
the property of JAMES CAPSHAW, granted 25 Sept 1766...GLOVERS camp...JAMES CAPSHAW (SEAL),
Wit: ESSIX CAPSHAW, JAMES UPTON, WILLIAM LEE (X). Rec. July term 1775.

Pp. 176-177: 26 July 1774, CHRISTIAN CARPENTER of Tryon Co., to his son JOHN CARPENTER
            for Ⱡ 5 proc. money...300 A on waters of Buffalo Creek...CHRISTIAN CARPENTER
(CɪꞦ) (SEAL), Wit: None. Rec. July term 1775.

Pp. 177-178: 16 Feb 1775, JOHN McFADDEN JUR. of Tryon Co., planter, to JOHN DENNARD of
            South Carolina, Ninety sixth [sic] District, for Ⱡ 85 proc. money...land on
William Robbins' Creek on the S side of N fork of Broad River including BARTLETT HENSONS
Camps, granted to WM. ADAMS, and conveyed to PHILIP HENSON, then to JNO. McFADDEN, 200 A
...JOHN McFADDON (ᵼᵼᵼ) (SEAL), Wit: JAMES MURPHEY, SAML McFADIN, JOHN FELTS (X). Rec.
July term 1775.

Pp. 178-179: 9 May 1775, JAMES COZART of Granville Co., N. C., to JOHN GRAHAM of Tryon
            Co., for Ⱡ 30 proc. money...300 A on Kettle Shoal branch of the S fork of
Catawba including the improvements COZART bought of FIELDS, granted to JAMES COZART, 19
May 1772...JAMES COZART (SEAL), Wit: RICHARD FOSTER, HENRY CHAMLES (O), WILLIAM GRAHAM.
Rec. July term 1775.

Pp. 179-180: 10 Sept 1773, LUDOWICK WRAY of Tryon Co., to WM GILBERT of same, for Ⱡ 70...
            300 A on Catheys Creek adj.WM WRAYS line, granted to WM. WRAY 5 May 1769,
and conveyed to LODOWICK WRAY 5 Apr 1770...LODOWICK WRAY (SEAL), Wit: JAMES COOK, HENRY
WRIGHT, WM. WRAY. Rec. July term 1775.

Pp. 180-181: 24 Oct 1774, JOHN REED of Tryon Co., to SAMUEL HUNTER of same, for s5...
land on W side Cataba, granted to JOHN BEATEY, then conveyed to JOHN CONNELY
then to JOHN REED, 200 A...JOHN REED (SEAL), MARTHA REED (SEAL), Wit: MALCOM CURRIE,
MATTHEW ARMSTRONG. Rec. July term 1775.

Pp. 181-182: 20 Sept 1774, DANIEL McCARTEY of Tryon Co., to JAMES HENDERSON of same,for
₴ 40 proc. money...250 A on both sides Catheys Creek...DANIEL McCARTY (SEAL),
Wit: DANL WIOT (E), THOMAS HUNT (T), Rec. July term 1775.

Pp. 182-183: 27 Mar 1774, WM. GLENN & wf JENET of Tryon Co., to JAMES HENDERSON of same,
for ₴ 95 proc. money...200 A on S side of S fork Catawba, granted to sd. WM
GLENN 25 Apr 1767...WILLIAM GLENN (O) (SEAL), GENET GLENN (o) (SEAL), Wit: WILLIAM MOORE,
JAMES GILLESPIE, WILLIAM GILMON. Rec. July term 1775.

Pp. 183-184: 20 Sept 1774, DANIEL McCARTY of Tryon Co., to JAMES HENDERSON of same, for
₴ 100 procl. money...land on both sides Catheys Creek...DANIEL McCARTY
(SEAL), Wit: WILLIAM GILMORE, DANIEL WIAT (S), THOMAS HUNT (T). Rec. July term 1775.

Pp. 184-185: 8 Dec 1772, WILLIAM CLEGHORN of Tryon Co., planter, to JOHN HUDDLESTONE of
same, for ₴ 20 proc. money...land on both sides Cleghorns Creek adj. to sd.
CLEGHORN, 97 A granted to SAMUEL BRIGHT 24 Dec 1770...WILLIAM CLEGHORN (SEAL), Wit: JOHN
McCUEN[?], JACOB HADEN (+). Rec. July term 1775.

Pp. 185-186: 1 Feb 1775, WILLIAM CLEGHORN of Tryon Co., to HENRY HAYES of Craven Co., SC,
for ₴ 60...land on both sides Catheys Creek of second broad River above
DANIEL McCARTYS survey, granted to JOHN BENNET 29 Apr [no year given] and conveyed to
WM. ANDERSON 7 Jan 1769...WILLIAM CLEGHORN (SEAL), Wit: ANDW. HAMPTON, ANDREW NELLSON (A)
Rec. July term 1775.

Pp. 186-187: 27 July 1775, JOSEPH ENGLAND of Tryon Co., to JACOB HOFSTATLER of same, for
₴ 20 proc. money...land on the high shoal branch of Kings Creek above JOHN
McNITT ALEXANDER and FREDERICK HAMBRIGHTs land, granted to JAMES FANNING 26 Oct 1767...
JOSEPH ENGLAND (SEAL), Wit: None. Rec. July term 1775.

Pp. 187-188: 15 May 1775, JOHN FLEMING, JOHN McCLURE & wf JANE of Tryon Co., to HUGH
KILLPATRICK of same, for ₴ 60...200 A, part of 400 A on N fork of Main
Broad River, granted to THOMAS BEATY 16 Nov 1764 & transferred to sd. FLEMING & McCLURE
by deed 6 Sept 1771...JOHN FLEMING (SEAL), JOHN McCLURE (SEAL), JANE McCLURE (X) (SEAL),
Wit: JAME. GRAY, JAMES SCOTT. Rec. July term 1775.

Pp. 188-189: 27 July 1775, THOMAS WELCH of Tryon Co., to JOHN LANDIS of same, for ₴ 80
proc. money...250 A on waters of Buffaloe Creek adj. GEORGE DAVIS line,
granted to sd. WELCH 22 May 1772...THOMAS WELCH (T) (SEAL), Wit: None. Rec. July term
1775.

Pp. 189-191: 25 May 1775, PATRICK MILLER of Mecklenburg Co., to JAMES MILCORN for ₴ 20
s 18 proc. money...land granted to PETER SUMMY 13 Oct 1765, 400 A...PATK.
MILLER (SEAL), JAMES MILCORN (╫╫) (SEAL), Wit: HEZ. ALEXANDER, WILLIAM MERCAKEN. Rec.
July term 1775.

Page 191: 11 Feb 1775, PHILIP HENSON of Tryon Co., planter, to JOHN McFADDEN of same, for
₴ 75 proc. money...land on WM. ROBBINS Creek on the S side of N fork Broad
River, granted to WM. ADAMS and conveyed to PHILIP HENSON...PHILIP HENSON (X) (SEAL),
Wit: SAML McFADDIN, BURREL SIMS, FIRNEY GREEN NORMAN.Rec. July term 1775.

Pp. 192-193: 26 July 1775, JACOB CASTNER, High Sheriff of Tryon Co., to MAURICE ROBERTS
of same, Planter, for ₴ 10 proc. money with interest from 16 Nov 1769...by
a writ of fiere facias from inferior court of pleas and quarter sessions April Session
1774...JOHN WADE, late of your county...adjudged to HUGH MONTGOMERY...300 A on both sides
of little Hickory Creek...JACOB CASTNER, Sheriff (SEAL), Wit: ALEX. MARTIN, AND NEEL.
Rec. July term 1775.

Pp. 193-194: 10 June 1775, JOHN FLEMING of Tryon Co., to JOHN McCLURE of same, for ₴ 20...
part of tract of 400 A on N fork Main Broad River, granted to THOMAS BEATY
16 Nov 1764, and by deed from THOMAS & wf MARGARET, 200 A sold 6 Sept 1771 to sd. FLEMING
...JOHN FLEMING (SEAL), Wit: JAMES SCOTT, SAME. GRAY. Rec. July term 1775.

Pp. 194-195: 27 July 1775, ROBT RANKIN of Tryon Co., to ANDREW NEWBERRY of Westfellow
Township, Chester Co., Pennsylvania, for ₴ 25...land on both sides a branch
of Second Broad River, adj. DAVID HUDDLESTONE...ROBERT RANKIN (SEAL), Wit: None. Rec.
July term 1775.

Pp. 195-196: 30 Dec 1773, EPHRAIM McLEAN of Tryon Co., to DAVID NESEET of Rowan Co., NC, for Ⱡ 25 proc. money...420 A on middle fork of Crowders Creek...EPHRAIM McLEAN (SEAL), ELISABETH McLEAN (SEAL), Wit: JOHN BARBER, WILLIAM MORRISON. Rec. July term 1775.

Pp. 196-197: 19 July 1775, SAML WALKER of Tryon Co., to WM. PICKREL of same, for Ⱡ 100 proc. money...land on both sides Broad River including the said WALKERS own improvements...100 A...SAMUEL WALKER (SEAL), MARY WALKER (+) (SEAL), Wit: SAML McFADDEN, SARAH HOGAN (+), JAMES PICKRELL. Rec. July term 1775.

Page 197: 20 Sept 1773, SAML COBURN of Tryon Co., to BABTIS SCOTT of same, for Ⱡ 20 proc. money...land on the Cataba River, adj. HASLIPS line, granted to sd. COBURN 80 A, 30 Jan 1773...SAMUEL COBURN (X) (SEAL), Wit: GEORGE LAMKIN, SARAH LAMKIN (2). Rec. July term 1775.

Pp. 198-199: 30 June 1774, WM. CLEGHORN of Tryon Co., yeoman, to JOHN SCOTT of same, for Ⱡ 10 proc. money...land on E side Main Broad River on both sides Richardsons Creek about a mile and a half above RICHARDSONS land, 100 A granted to MOSES ALEXANDER, 22 Dec 1768 and conveyed to CLEGHORN 2 Jan 1769...WILLIAM CLEGHORN (SEAL), Wit: DAVID DICKEY, JOHN SCOTT. Rec. July term 1775.

Pp. 199-200: 25 Jan 1775, GEORGE BLACK of Tryon Co., planter, to JANE WITHROW widow of same, planter, for Ⱡ 32 proc. money...153 A, part of a tract which sd. BLACK purchased from one GEORGE CLAYTON...GEORGE BLACK (SEAL), Wit: B. BOOKE, AD. OSBURN. JANE WITHROW...the within deed was issued in trust to my sons JAMES and SAMUEL WITHROW until the youngest of them attains the age of 21 years...28 Jan 1775. JANE WITHROW (SEAL), Wit: JOHN WALKER, JOHN GRAY (7). Rec. July term 1775.

Page 200: WILLIAM TWITTY of Tryon Co., to SAMUEL WALKER, bound in the penal sum of Ⱡ 400 ...18 Mar 1774...to make title to 200 A on both sides of Broad River adj. BERDS[sic] land, and including the improvement that EZEKIEL SMITH lived on...WILLIAM TWITTY (SEAL), Wit: JAMES BRIDGES, WILLIAM PICKRELL. Rec. July term 1775.

Pp. 200-201: 20 July 1775, PETER KUYKENDALL of Craven Co., S. C. to WILLIAM WEBB of Tryon Co., for Ⱡ 600...land on N side Second little Broad River including the mouth of a small creek about a mile below KUYKENDALLS old survey at the Indian path, granted to PETER KUYKENDALL, 300 A, 21 Apr 1767...PETER KUYKENDALL (SEAL), Wit: DENNY WINBORNE, ROBT McMINN. Rec. July term 1775.

OCTOBER COURT AD 1775.

Pp. 201-202: 3 Oct 1775, JOHN BEARD SENR of Tryon Co. to JOHN BEARD JUR. for Ⱡ 200 proc. money...land on S side Catawba, on Crowders Creek, known by the name of SAML COBURNS camp, 220 A granted to JOHN LITTLE 3 Apr 1753...JOHN BEARD (SEAL), Wit: AND NEEL, HUGH HOUSTON. Rec. Oct. term 1775.

Page 203: 2 Mar 1775, PETER COSTNER of Tryon Co., to ANDREW CASTNER of same, for Ⱡ 20 proc. money...300 A on the W side S fork Catawba adj. PETER LABOONS line... PETER CASTNER (PC) (SAEL), Wit: VALLENTINE MAUNEY, PETER SEITS (P). Rec. Oct. term 1775.

Pp. 203-204: Sept. 8, 1775, I do hereby give JONATHAN GULLICK liberty to conveye to JOHN GLENN a right to that tract of land which I formerly lived on in North Carolina Tryon County...HEZEKIAH BALCH. Wit: DAVID ELDER, JOHN GLEN. Rec. Oct. term 1775.

Pp. 204-205: 25 Oct 1775, JONATHAN GULLICK of Tryon Co., to JOHN GLEN for Ⱡ 85 NC currency...land on waters of Crowders Creek adj. JAMES LEWIS land now in Tryon County, granted 18 Feb 1764 to sd. JONATHAN GULLICK...JONATHAN GULLICK (SEAL), Wit: JAMES BEATY, WM. BERRY. Rec. Oct. term 1775.

Page 205: 8 Oct 1775, PATRICK McDAVID of Tryon Co., to ANDREW HAMPTON of same, for Ⱡ 200 proc. money...278 A adj. JOHN ADMISTONS[?] line granted to JAMES KUYKENDALL, 1754 and conveyed to HUGH KELLY by L 7 R 10 July 1755, and by a lawful power of attorney to PATRICK McDAVID 20 Mar 1768...PATRICK McDAVID (SEAL), Wit: ADAM HAMPTON, JAMES McDAVID. Rec. Oct. term 1775.

Page 206: ___ 1775, DANEIL McCARTY and JOHN McCARTY, Joint tenants, to LEWIS LINEBURGER of Tryon Co., for Ⱡ 30 proc. money...land on little long creek and big long creek, 487 A...DANIEL McCARTY (SEAL), JOHN McCARTY (SEAL), Wit: SAMUEL JOHNSTON, WM. ARFIL[??]. Rec. Oct. term 1775.

Pp. 206-208: 30 Jan 1775, PETER SUMMY SENR. & wf MARGARET of Tryon Co., farmer, to
PATRICK MILLER of Mecklenburg Co., for ₤ 120 proc. money...land on both sides
long creek, granted to sd. PETER SUMMY SENR. 30 Oct 1765, Rec. in the Secretaries Office
in Book 12, p. 247, 400 A...PETER SUMMY (PS)(SEAL), MARGARET SUMMY (W) (SEAL), Wit: Two
German siguntures, and ROBERT BLACKBURN. Rec. Oct. term 1775.

Pp. 208-209: 26 Aug 1774, WM. CLEGHORN of Tryon Co., to DAVID McBRIDE of same, planter,
for ₤ 120 proc. money...land on both sides Green River adj. GEORGE FARIS,
granted to sd. CLEGHORN 20 Sept 17666...WILLIAM CLEGHORN (SEAL), Wit: JOHN SCOTT, JAMES
McBRIDE (C). Rec. Oct. term 1775.

Pp. 209-210: 4 May 1775, ROBERT LEE of Tryon Co., to JOHN McINTIRE of same, for ₤ 50
NC money...200 A on S fork of Sandy Run of Broad River...ROBERT LEE (SEAL),
Wit: JACOB SHIPMAN (A), TIMO. RIGGS. Rec. Oct. term 1775

Pp. 210-211: 19 Sept 1775, PATRICK MILLER & wf MARY of Mecklenburg Co., to JAMES MEBURN
of same, for ₤ 45 proc. money...land granted to PETER SUMMy 30 Oct 1765,
conveyed to sd. MILLER by deed 30 Jan 1775., 400 A...PATK MILLER (SEAL), MARY MILLER
(SEAL), Wit: ALEXR. McGINTY, ANDREW MILLER. Rec. Oct. term 1775.

Page 212: 18 June 1774, NATHANIEL HENDERSON of Tryon Co., to JAMES McREYNOLDS, for ₤ 35
proc. money...200 A on both sides Camp Branch of little Catawba Creek adj.
JOHN GULLICKS, granted to NATHL HENDERSON 26 Jan 1773...NATHANIEL HENDERSON (SEAL), Wit:
JONATHAN GULLICK, JOHN GULLICK. Rec. Oct. term 1775.

Page 213: 15 Aug 1775, JOHN DELLINGER of Tryon Co., to WM. TANKERSLEY of same, for ₤ 50
proc. money...land on N side S fork Catawba River on a creek called Hoyles
Creek about three or four miles above HOILS plantation, 300 A granted to EDWARD BOLE,
and by different conveyances became the property of PAUL WISENANT and now in the custody
of JOHN DELLINGER...JOHN DELLINGER (SEAL), Wit: LEMUEL SAUNDERS, HEINRICH[?] DELLINGER
[German signature]. Rec. Oct. term 1775.

Page 214: 6 Oct 1775, STEPHEN LANGFORD of Tryon Co., to SAMUEL WILLSON of same, for ₤ 100
...land on middle fork of First Broad River, 200 A granted to LANGFORD 3 May
1772...STEPHEN LANGFORD (SEAL), Wit: JOSEPH GRAYSON, JOHN SCOTT (₤). Rec. Oct. term 1775.

Page 215: 23 Oct 1775, JONATHAN POTTS of Tryon Co., to JOHN WATERSON of same, for ₤ 80
proc. money...land 200 A granted to JONATHAN POTTS 24 Apr 1765 on a branch of
Buffalo Creek called Gullesons[?] Creek...JONATHAN POTTS (SEAL), Wit: WILLIAM GRAHAM,
ALEXANDER KYLE (A), NICHOLAS WALTON. Rec. Oct. term 1775.

Pp. 215-216: 2 Aug 1775, JACOB SHATLEY of Tryon Co., to MICHAEL WILLIAMS of same, for
₤ 10...land on a branch of Hyl[?] Creek of S fork Catawba, 100 A about the
great road..._____ [German signature]. (SEAL), Wit: GEORGE LAMKIN, CHRISTIAN ARNEY (+).
Rec. Oct. term 1775.

Pp. 216-217: 24 Oct 1775, ANDREW HAMPTON of Tryon Co., to JOHN WELLS of same, for ₤ 50
proc. money...228 A on main fork of Kings Creek, adj. JOHN ADMISTONS,
granted to JAMES KUYKENDALL 1754, and from him to HUGH KELLY 1755, to PATRICK McDAVID
1768, and to ANDREW HAMPTON 1765...ANDW HAMPTON (SEAL), Wit: JACOB COSTNER, ALEXANDER
GILLELAND. Rec. Oct. term 1z75.

Pp. 217-218: 19 July 1775, JAMES ALLEY SENR of Tryon Co., to VALENTINE WARLICK of same,
for ₤ 12 proc. money...land in Tryon Co. when conveyed but now in So.
Carolina, situate on both sides of Pacolet River by the patent bearing date 1771...JAMES
ALLEY (SEAL), Wit: THOS ALLEY, JAMES ALLEY JUR. MELCHER OYLER (M). Rec. Oct. term 1775.

JANUARY COURT 1776.

Pp. 218-219: 22 Dec 1776, JESSE FINN of Tryon Co., to JOHN ALEXANDER of same, for ₤ 20
proc. money...land on both sides a branch of S fork Catawba adj. WADDELLS
line, 200 A granted to FINN 22 May 1772...JESSE FINN (J) (SEAL), Wit: MATHAN DEEHON,
GEORGE DNANT[?]. Rec. Jan. term 1776.

Pp. 219-220: 15 Oct 1775, JOSEPH HIGHTOWER of Co. of Lun [Lunenburg?], Virginia, to
JOHN FREEMAN JR. of Mecklenburg Co., Virginia, for ₤ 300 proc. money...390
A on W side Catawba including a survey made for THOMAS ROBINSON, granted to ANDREW HASLEP
16 Nov 1764...JOSEPH HIGHTOWER(SEAL), Wit: BENJN. WHITEHEAD, JAMES FREEMAN, SAMUEL
PETERS. Rec. Jan. term 1776.

Pp. 220-221: 2 Nov 1775, JOHN FREEMAN JR. of Mecklenburg Co., Virginia, to JAMES FREEMAN
          JR. of Tryon Co., for Ŀ 300 proc. money...390 A [same tract as in preceding
deed]...JOHN FREEMAN (SEAL), Wit: DAVID WILLSON, SAMUEL WILLSON, GEORGE LAMKIN. Rec.
Jan. term 1776.

Page 221: GEORGE SIZEMORE of Tryon Co., for Ŀ 100 proc. money, paid by WM. GILBERT...
          negro Frank, aged 25 years...26 Aug 1775...GEORGE SIZEMORE (SEAL), Wit: THOMAS
MORRIS, DAVID GEORGE (T). Rec. Jan. term 1776.

Pp. 221-222: 8 Sept 1772, ANDREW HASLEP & wf MARY & THOMAS HASLEP of Tryon Co., to
          JOSEPH HIGHTOWER of Amelia Co., Virginia, for Ŀ 300 proc. money...390 A on
W side Cataba [same land in deeds pp. 219-221]...ANDREW HASLEP (SEAL), THOMAS HASLEP
(SEAL), Wit: GEORGE LAMKIN, WM. ALSTON, SAML KUYKENDALL.

Pp. 222-223: 21 June 1775, THOMAS HIGHTOWER of Tryon Co., to GEORGE MORGAN SR. for Ŀ 30
          proc. money...160 A on W side Broad River...THOMAS HIGHTOWER (X) (SEAL),
Wit: JOSHUA HIGHTOWER (X), EBENEZER FLOYD (E), ELISHA FORD. Rec. Jan. term 1776.

Pp. 223-224: 4 Dec 1775, MOSES MOORE of Tryon Co., to JOHN WALKER of same, for Ŀ 100
          proc. money...land at the mouth of Cane Creek of Second broad River, 400 A
granted to MOORE 16 Nov 1764....MOSES MOORE (M) (SEAL), Wit: WILLIAM GRAHAM, ROBERT
PORTER, CHARLES McLEAN. Rec. Jan. term 1776.

Pp. 224-225: 22 Nov 1775, GEORGE MICHAEL WISENANT of Tryon Co., to ADAM WISENANT of same,
          for Ŀ 100 proc. money...300 A on branch of Indian Creek, Leonards fork
above THOMAS ROBINSONS adj. HARPILL, granted to WILLM. MOORE decd, 16 Nov 1764..._____
____ [German signature]. Wit: _____ WARLICK [?] [German signature], VALLENTINE MAUNEY.
Rec. Jan. term 1776.

Pp. 225-226: 22 Nov 1775, GEORGE MICHAEL WISENANT to ADAM WISENANT for Ŀ 50...land on
          waters of Indian Creek adj. his own land, 200 A...[Same signatures and wit.
as preceding]. Rec. Jan. term 1776.

JANUARY COURT 1777.

Pp. 226-227: 14 Oct 1775, JOHN BAXTER of Craven Co., S. C. to JOHN McLEAN of Tryon Co.,
          for Ŀ 80...640 A on both sides N fork of Main Broad River above his other
survey near the mountains, granted to BAXTER 16 Apr 1765...JOHN BAXTER (SEAL), Wit:
JOS. TABIAS, NICHS. LEE, SAML McFADEN. Rec. Jan. term 1777.

Pp. 227-228: 25 Apr 1774, JOHN McFADDEN JR. & wf RUTH of Tryon Co., planter, to JOHN
          McFADDEN SENR. of same, for Ŀ 80 proc. money...land on both sides Mountain
Creek of Broad River including the mouth of Maple Creek, 200 A, granted to JOHN McFADDEN
Jr. 15 May 1772...JOHN McFADDEN (Ŧ) (SEAL), RUTH McFADON (R) (SEAL), Wit: ELIAS McFADIN,
BENJAMIN LEUGHD[?] (X), JONATHAN HAMPTON. Rec. State of North Carolina, July [sic]
Court AD 1777. [N. B. This is the first recording which reads State rather than Province.]

Pp. 228-229: 14 Oct 1775, JOHN BAXTER of Craven Co., S. C. to ALEXR MACKEY of Tryon Co.,
          for Ŀ 50 NC money...300 A on N fork Main Broad River, 3 or 4 miles above
the mouth of Mountain Creek, granted to sd. BAXTER 16 Apr 1765...JOHN BAXTER (SEAL), Wit:
NICHS. LEE, JOS. TOBIAS, SAML McFADDEN. Rec. Jan. term 1777.

Page 229: State of North Carolina, Tryon County: The foregoing is a compleat[sic] register
          of all deeds and other conveyances tendered to me to be registered from Octo-
ber Court 1774 till January Court 1777. Certified the 26th day of July 1777. AND. NEEL
Register.

JULY COURT ANNO DOMINI 1777.

Pp. 229-230: 18 July 1777, BENJAMIN HARDIN of Tryon Co., to UEL LAMPKIN of same, for Ŀ
          50 proc. money...105 A on Knobb Creek, adj. BENJAMIN HARDINS old line,
granted to FRANCIS BEATY, 6 Apr 1765...BENJAMIN HARDEN (SEAL), Wit: GEORGE LAMKIN, CATREN
HARDEN (X). Rec. July term 1777.

Pp. 230-231: 7 Mar 1777, WM. McKENNY to JOHN ANDERSON of Tryon Co., for Ŀ 50 proc. money
          ...land on both sides first Broad River including his own improvement, 200
A...WILLIAM McKINNEY (C) (SEAL), MARY McKENY (+) (SEAL), Wit: JOHN POLK, JAMES CHITWOOD,
JOHN BOYD, ROBERT ANDERSON. N. B. By a free and voluntary consent of his wife MARY.
WILLIAM GRAHAM, C. C. JONATHAN HAMPTON, C. C. Rec. July term 1777.

Pp. 231-232: 1 Feb 1776, WILLIAM LASSWELL of Tryon Co., to WILLIAM JOHNSON of same, for
ḷ 160...land on both sides Sandy Run, a branch of Broad River...200 A...
WILLIAM LASSWELL (W) (SEAL), MARYAN LASSWELL (M) (SEAL), Wit: EDWARD DUAS (X), LEAR DUAS
(X), JOHN STAFFORD. Rec. July term 1777.

Pp. 232-233: 28 Mar 1777, THOMAS BRIDGES of Camden District, S. C. to THOMAS WHITESIDES
of Tryon Co., for ḷ 50 proc. money...land on N fork first Broad River, 300 A
granted to WM. SIMS and HADEN PRIOR 20 Apr 1768, and by SIMS & PRIOR conveyed to THOMAS
BRIDGES 28 Nov 1775...THOMAS BRIDGES (SEAL), Wit: JAMES WHITESIDES, SAMUEL WHITESIDES.
Apr. 23, 1777, Sd. deed was proved by JAMES & SAMUEL WHITESIDES.

Pp. 233-234: 18 July 1777, JOSEPH ENGLAND of Tryon Co., carpenter, to ADAM KUYKENDALL of
same, for ḷ 96 s 18 proc. money...400 A on both sides Knobb Creek...JOSEPH
ENGLAND (SEAL), Wit: JOSEPH HARDIN, JAMES WILSON. Rec. July term 1777.

Pp. 234-235: 10 Apr 1776, WILLIAM ALSTON of Guilford Co., N. C. to ROBERT ALEXANDER of
Tryon Co., for ḷ 90 proc. money...274 A on S side Cataba, adj. JOHN SCOTTS
line...JOHNSONS corner...TROYS line...WIDOW KUYKENDALLS line...WM. ALSTON (SEAL), Wit:
GEORGE LAMKIN, JOHN SKRIMSHIRE. Rec. July term 1777.

Pp. 235-236: 21 June 1777, WILLIAM GILBERT, farmer, of Tryon Co., to ISAAC COOPER, farmer,
for ḷ 35 proc. money...land on both sides Bullins Creek of Green River,
granted to GILBERT 2 Mar 1775...WM. GILBERT (SEAL), Wit: JAMES COOK, JERORP[?] EGERTON,
JOHN BAIN (Ŧ). Rec. July term 1777.

Pp. 236-237: 26 June 1777, JOHN SCOTT JR. & wf LETTUCE & SARAH McHENDRICK, all of Tryon
Co., to WILLIAM ALSTON of Wake Co., N. C., for ḷ 300 proc. money...land on
S side Cataba River, including the Tuckasiege ford below the mouth of the Dutchmans
Creek, granted to SAMUEL COBURN 24 Sept 1754, 302 A...JOHN SCOTT (SEAL), LETTIS SCOTT (Y),
SARAH McKENDRICK (+) (SEAL), Wit: GEORGE LAMKIN, JOHN SCOTT. Rec. July term 1777.

Page 237: April 23, 1777. At a court held for the county of Tryon on a motion of WM.
ALSTON ordered that GEO. LAMKIN & FREDERICK HAMBRIGHT on private examination
of LETTICE SCOTT, wife of JOHN SCOTT JR... concerning relinquishing the right of her
dower to the land given her by her fathers Last will and testament. LETTICE SCOTT
relinquished dower 25 June 1777. Rec. July term 1777.

Page 238: 3 Feb 1777, LAWRENCE KOIZER to PETER SEITS, both of Tryon Co., for ḷ 12 NC
money...150 A on both sides N fork of Buffalo Creek, granted to NICHOLAS WISEN-
ANT 15 May 1772..._____ [German signature] (SEAL), Wit: SAMUEL CARBENDER, CHRISTIAN
CARPENTER (C Ŧ). Rec. July term 1777.

Pp. 238-239: 21 June 1777, WILLIAM GILBERT of Tryon Co., to ISAAC COOPER, planter, for ḷ
35 proc. money...200 A on Bullens Creek of Green River, granted to sd.
GILBERT 2 Mar 1775...WM. GILBERT (SEAL), Wit: JAMES COOK, SCROOP EGERTON, JOHN PEIN (Ŧ).
Rec. July term 1777.

Pp. 240-241: 2 Mar 1774, JAMES HENDERSON & wf VIOLET of Tryon Co., to WILLIAM ALSTON of
same, for ḷ 64 s 16 proc. money...162 A adj. ROBERT SCOTT, WIDOW McKENDRICK,
part of land bought of WM. CLEGHORN...JAMES HENDERSON (SEAL), Wit: JACOB HERNDON, WILLIAM
GLENN (O). Rec. July term 1771

Pp. 241-242: 13 Mar 1777, THOMAS WELCH of Tryon Co., to ROBERT FERGUSON of State of South
Carolina, for ḷ 100 NC money...200 A on SW of CHRISTIAN SIMMERMANS & Beaver
dam Creek, granted 19 Apr 1763...146 A on both sides of a branch of long creek...THOMAS
WELCH (SEAL), NANCY WELCH (+) (SEAL), Wit: DAVID ALLEN, WM. LIVELY (⤙⤙⤙), JOHN HILL.
Nancy Welch signed in presence of AND NEEL. Rec. July term 1777.

Pp. 242-244: 7 Oct 1774, ALEXANDER HEMPHILL & wf MARY of Camblin [sic] Co., S. C. to
BENJAMIN ARMSTRONG of Craven Co., S. C., for ḷ 82 proc. money...land on S
side Cataba in Mecklenburg Co., part of 100 A granted to JOHN KILLION 30 Sept 1749, and
conveyed to JACOB BROWN by L & R, 1 & 2 Jan 1754, and then to JOHN HILL 20 July 1757,
250 A...adj. PHILIP EREHART...ALEX HEMPHILL (SEAL), MARY HEMPHILL (S) (SEAL), Wit: JOHN
KENCEAD, JAMES ARMSTRONG. Rec. July term 1777.

Pp. 244-245: 1 Jan 1776, NATHANIEL HENDERSON & wf ELIZABETH of Tryon Co., to JAMES
PATTERSON of same, for ḷ 40 proc. money...150 A on a branch of Joharts[sic]
Creek, granted to ABRAHAM ALEXANDER 9 Nov 1764 and conveyed 23 July 1772...NATHANIEL
HENDERSON (SEAL), ELIZABETH HENDERSON (Φ) (SEAL), Wit: WILLIAM PATTERSON, JONATHAN
GULLICK, ALEXANDER PATTERSON. Rec. July term 1777.

Pp. 245-246: 20 July 1777, HUGH SHANNON of Tryon Co., to ROBERT SHANNON for Ł 80 proc.
money...200 A, part of a tract granted to EVAN LEWIS 5 Apr 1752, and made
over to HUGH SHANNON by L & R 5 Nov 1763...HUGH SHANAN (SEAL), Wit: ALEXANDER MOORE,
JONATHAN GULLICK. Rec. July term 1777.

Pp. 246-247: 1 Jan 1776, NATHL HENDERSON & wf ELIZABETH of Tryon Co. to JAMES PATTERSON
of same, for Ł 200 proc. money...450 A on S side Catawba River, about three
miles below the lower mount, granted to ALLEN ALEXANDER 4 Sept 1753, and conveyed to sd.
HENDERSON by L & R 20 Nov 1762...NATHANIEL HENDERSON (SEAL), ELIZABETH HENDERSON (✿)
(SEAL), Wit: WILLIAM PATTERSON, JONATHAN GULLICK, ALEXANDER PATTERSON. Rec. July term
1777.

APRIL COURT 1777.

Pp. 247-248: 5 July 1777, WILLIAM ALSTON of Wake Co., NC to WM. STERRILL of Tryon Co., for
Ł 80 NC money...300 A on W side Catawba on both sides of a branch falling
into the Catawba, granted to JOHN ALSTON by ROBT ABERNATHY by indenture 3 Oct 1771,
patent dated 28 Feb 1774 [sic]...WM. ALSTON (SEAL), Wit: ROBT. ALEXANDER, JOHN SKRIMSHIRE.
Rec. July term 1777.

Pp. 248-249: 5 July 1777, WILLIAM ALSTON to WM. STERRILL, for Ł 20 NC money...300 A on
S side Cataba, part of a grant to WM. HENRY 28 Feb 1754. [same signature and
wit. as preceding deed]. Rec. July term 1777.

Pp. 249-250: 5 July 1777, WILLIAM ALSTON to WM. STERRILL, for Ł 120...130 A on W side
Catawba adj. SAMUEL YOUNGS corner, granted to ANDW. McNABB 6 Apr 1765...WM.
ALSTON (SEAL), Wit: ROBT. ALEXANDER, JOHN SKRIMSHIRE. Rec. July term 1777.

Page 250: 5 July 1777, WM. ALSTON to WM. STERILL for Ł 50...land adj. ROBERT DELMER,
including the broken islands...[Same signature and wit. as preceding. Rec. July
term 1777.

Page 251: 5 July 1777, WM. ALSTON to WM. STERALL, for Ł 50 North currency...250 A on W
side of Catawba near Tuckasiege Ford, adj. ANDW. McNABB, WM. HENRY, SAML.
COBURN, & JUDITH COBURNS, a survey formerly made for SAML YOUNG, patent bearing date 26
Nov 1757...WM. ALSTON (SEAL), [Same wit.] Rec. July term 1777.

Pp. 251-252: MARTIN GRIDER & HENRY GRIDER of Augusta Co., Va., for Ł 100 Va. money pd.
by NICHOLAS CLAY and PETER STOTHER of Tryon Co., sale of cattle, swine,
waggon & gears, etc...MARTIN GREIDER (SEAL), HENRY GREIDER (SEAL), Wit: JACOB GOWDYR[?]
JUR., HENRY GROSS. Rec. July term 1777.

Pp. 252-253: 7 Oct 1775, WILLIAM KING of Tryon Co., to ROBERT KNOX of same, for Ł 52 s 10
proc. money...land on branches of Killions Creek, adj. KAMSEYS line,
granted to THOMAS POLK[?] 22 Dec 1761, and conveyed to WILLIAM CROCKETT 6 Mar 1771, then
to sd. KING 2 July 1774, 160 A...WM. KING (SEAL) (X). Wit: VINCENT COX, ___ JOHNSON, JOHN
CALDRIDGE. Rēc. July term 1777.

Page 253: 5 July 1777, WM. ALSTON to WM. STERRILL, for Ł 20 NC money...[instrument not
completed].

Pp. 253-254: 11 Mar 1777, JOHN SCOTT of Tryon Co., to WILLIAM ALSTON of Wake Co., NC,
for Ł 50 proc. money...land on N side Catawba River adj. WIDOW McKENDRICK,
CLEGHORNs, 200 A, granted to JOHN McNITT ALEXANDER 28 Oct 1765...JOHN SCOTT (SEAL), Wit:
JAMES MILLER, ALEXANDER COULTER, JACOB WEUCANT[?], GEORGE LAMKIN. JUR. Rec. July term
1777.

Pp. 254-255: 8 Oct 1776, THOMAS THOMPSON of Rowan Co., to ROBERT PATON of same, for Ł 50
NC money...land on N branch of Catheys Creek adj. JOHN WALKER, confirmed to
sd. THOMPSON by patent dated 2 Nov 1771...THOMAS THOMPSON (SEAL), Wit: ROBERT ALEXANDER,
WM. CHRONICLE. Rec. July term 1777.

Pp. 255-256: 15 Feb 1777, HENRY MASTON of Tryon Co., to JOHN KINCADE of same, for Ł 30
NC money...land on Lepers Creek of Catawba River adj. KILLIONS corner, 200
A...HEINRICH MASTEN [German signature] (SEAL), Wit: PETER CLUB (P), BENJAMIN ARMSTRONG.

Pp. 256-257: 1 Jan 1776, NATHL HENDERSON & wf ELIZABETH of Tryon Co., to JAMES PATTERSON
of same, for Ł 60 proc. money...160 A above his own house, granted to
sd. HENDERSON 16 Nov 1764 on W side Catawba adj. his own and JOHN BEARDS new survey...NA-
THANIEL HENDERSON (SEAL), ELIZABETH HENDERSON (✿) (SEAL), Wit: WILLIAM PATTERSON, JONA-
THAN GULLICK, ALEXANDER PATTERSON. Rec. July term 1777.

Pp. 257-258: 13 Nov 1775, SAMUEL RANKIN of Tryon Co., to ROBERT PARK of same, for ₺ 100
proc. money...202 A granted to JOHN WALKER 26 Sept 1766, and then to ALEXR.
GILLELAND, then to SAMUEL RANKIN...land on a branch of Crowders Creek...SAMUEL RANKIN
(SEAL), Wit: ALEXR. GILLILAND, ROBT. ALEXANDER.

Pp. 258-259: 20 May 1777, JOHN McFADEN SENR. of Tryon Co., to JAMES McFADEN of same, for
₺ 105 proc. money...land on both sides Mount Creek, the mouth of Maple Creek
...200 A being the land between the branch and the mill...JOHN McFADEN (SEAL), Wit:
BENJAMIN HIDER, JAMES MELLON. Rec. July term 1777.

Pp. 259-260: 17 Jan 1777, MARTIN PHIFER SEN. of Mecklenburg Co., to JAMES MILLICAN of
Tryon Co., for ₺ 50...200 A granted to sd. PHIFER 30 Oct 1760 on both sides
S fork Main Broad River...MARTIN PHIFER (SEAL), Wit: D. DICKEY, MARTIN ____. Rec. July
term 1777.

Pp. 260-261: 22 July 1777, JOHN GOFORTH of Tryon Co., to GEORGE PETERSON of same, for ₺
50...300 A granted to DANIEL McCARTY & conveyed to ANDREW GOFORTH and RICHARD
GULLICK, and by them to JOHN GOFORTH...JOHN GOFORTH (SEAL), Wit: JOHN BARBER, AND. NEEL.
Rec. July term 1777.

OCTOBER COURT 1777.

Page 262: 1 July 1776, GEORGE LAMPKIN of Tryon Co., to WILLIAM ALSTON of Guilford Co.,
for ₺ 30...land on McNabbs branch, adj. McKENDRICK, JOHN SCOTT, 136 A...
granted to sd. LAMKIN 25 Jan 1773...GEORGE LAMPKIN (SEAL), Wit: ROBT. ALEXANDER, Rec. Oct.
term 1777.

Pp. 262-263: 29 Oct 1777, GEORGE LAMPKIN of Tryon Co., to PETER LAMPKIN MATHAS of Mecklenburg Co., for ₺ 50...200 A in the fork of Dutchmans Creek and Catawba River,
adj. DAVIS, RANKIN...GEORGE LAMPKIN (SEAL), Wit: ROBERT ALEXANDER, AND. NEEL. Rec. Oct.
term 1777.

Pp. 263-264: 22 Oct 1777, CHRISTIAN CARPENTER to his son CHRISTIAN CARPENTER, both of
Tryon Co., for ₺ 5...300 A on both sides Buffalo Creek above his own land,
granted to sd. CHRISTIAN CARPENTER 28 Feb 1775...CHRISTIAN CARPENTER (C₤) (SEAL), Wit:
AND NEEL, JAMES HOLLAND. Rec. Oct. term 1777.

Pp. 264-265: 19 Aug 1777, JOHN MORRIS of Tryon Co., to JOHN POTTS of same, for ₺ 55...200
A on both sides Cove Creek of Broad River including his own improvements,
granted to sd. MORRIS 2 Mar 1775...JOHN MORRIS (SEAL), Wit: D. DICKEY, JAMES MILLER[?].
Rec. Oct. term 1777.

Pp. 265-266: 22 Oct 1777, CHRISTIAN CARPENTER to son JOHN CARPENTER, both of Tryon Co.,
for ₺ 5...30 A on both sides Cuffalo Creek, granted to CHRISTIAN CARPENTER
2 Mar 1775...CHRISTIAN CARPENTER (C₤) (SEAL), Wit: AND NEEL, JAMES HOLLAND. Rec. Oct.
term 1777.

Pp. 266-267: 1 Sept 1777, JAS. HENDERSON & wf VILOT of Tryon Co., to JOHN McCORD of
Bedford Co., Virginia, for ₺ 130...land on E side S fork Catawba, adj.
McKNIGHT, 200 A...JAMES HENDERSON (SEAL), VILOT HENDERSON (SEAL), Wit: JAMES McCORD,
WILLIAM McCLEARY, JOHN MOORE. Rec. Oct. term 1777.

Pp. 267-268: 26 Sept 1777, JOHN MOORE of Tryon Co., to ZACHARIAH SPENCER of same, for ₺
10 proc. money...land on S side S fork Cataba, 57 A, granted to JOHN MOORE
28 Feb 1775, adj. SPENCER...JOHN MOORE (SEAL), Wit: ALEXR MOORE, ROBERT SHANNON, JOHN
MOORE JUNR. Rec. Oct. term 1777.

Pp. 268-269: 30 Oct 1777, PERRYGREEN MAGNESS of Tryon Co., to JOHN SILES of same, for
₺ 80 proc. money...200 A on E fork Knobb Creek, above JOSEPH GOOD, granted
to sd. MAGNESS...PERRYGREEN MACKNESS (SEAL), Wit: AND NEEL, JAMES HOLLAND. Rec. Oct.
term 1777.

Pp. 269-270: 1 Mar 1777, DAVID THOMPSON of Tryon Co., to WILLIAM TUBB of same, for ₺ 100
...DAVID THOMPSON obtained by deed from WILLIAM BARNETT, 10 June 1774, land
on both sides little Broad River adj. JOHN LUSK, 240 A...DAVID THOMPSON (SEAL), Wit:
JOHN LUSK, GEORGE TUBB (H), JOHN TUBB. Rec. Oct. term 1777.

Pp. 270-271: 20 Oct 1777, THOMAS MORRISS of Tryon Co., to GEORGE WILLIAMS of same, for
₺ 40 proc. money...land on both sides Grassy Branch of Cedar Creek of Broad
River...THOMAS MORRIS (SEAL), Wit; JONATHAN HAMPTON, ADAM HAMPTON. Rec. Oct. term 1777.

JANUARY COURT 1778.

Pp. 271-272: 22 Aug 1777, JACOB SIMERLY to JOHN DITRICH BEAME, both of Tryon Co., for Ł
16 proc. money...land on branches of Beaver Dam of S fork Catawba, 300 A,
granted to BENJAMIN SHAW, 25 Oct 1774...JACOB ZIMMERL (SEAL), Wit: JAMES WHITE, JOHN
DELLINGER. Rec. Jan. term 1778.

Pp. 272-273: 19 Jan 1778, JOHN MOORE of Tryon Co., to WILLIAM HAMILTON of same, for Ł 100
proc. money...100 A on S side S fork below Hoyls Mountain, granted to JACOB
JOHNSON 26 Oct 1767, by him conveyed to PATRICK McDAVID, then to JOHN MOORE...JOHN MOORE
(SEAL), Wit: ALEXANDER MOORE, JOHN MOORE JR. Rec. Jan. term 1778.

Pp. 273-274: 20 Jan 1778, JOHN NEIGHBOURS & wf SARAH of Tryon Co., to GEORGE BLANTON of
Craven County, S. C., for Ł 60 proc. money...100 A on E side Broad River...
JOHN NEIGHBOUR (X) (SEAL), SARAH NEIGHBOUR (X) (SEAL), Wit: JOSEPH CAMP, JOHN JOHNSON,
JOHN WILSON (Ŧ). Rec. Jan. term 1778.

Pp. 274-275: 28 Nov 1777, JOHN LOW of Caswell Co., N. C. to EDMUND WYATT of Tryon Co.,
for Ł 17 north currency...100 A on both sides Rudisils Creek adj. RUDISAILs
line...granted to WILLIAM WYATT 29 Aug 1768...JOHN LOW (SEAL), Wit: GEORGE LAMKIN, JEAN
LAMKIN, FREDERICK HAMBRIGHT. Rec. Jan. term 1778.

Page 275: THOMAS BULLIN of Ninety Six District, S. C., for Ł 40 prc. by JOHN HENRY of
State of N. C....sale of cattle...27 July 1777. THOMAS BULLION (SEAL), Wit:
ROBERT SHELTON (X), JONATHAN HOLCOM (X). Proven in Ninety Six District by ROBERT SHEL-
TON before JOHN THOMAS JR., J. P., 25 Aug 1777. Rec. Jan. term 1778.

Page 276: 14 Oct 1777, JONAS BEDFORD of Tryon Co., to JOHN MOREGAN of same, for Ł 40...
land on N side Mountain Creek, near MOORES line, granted to sd. BEDFORD 28 Feb
1775...JONAS BEDFORD (SEAL), Wit: JAMES MILLER, DAVID MILLER. Rec. Jan. term 1778.

Page 277: 8 Sept 1777, WILLIAM STERRETT & wf RUTH of Tryon Co., to JOHN BOHANNON of same,
for Ł 75 north currency...157 A on a branch of Moores Creek adj. NEWTON line...
WM. STRRETT (W) (SEAL), RUTH STERRETT (X) (SEAL), Wit: GEORGE LAMKIN, THOMAS BUCHANON.
Rec. Jan. term 1778.

Pp. 277-278: 16 Feb 1766, GEORGE RUTLEDGE of Mecklenburg Co., to WILLIAM CLEGHORN of
same, for Ł 18...land on S side Enoree River on Rocky Creek below DAVID
TEMPLETONs, 400 A, granted to sd. RUTLEDGE 24 Sept 1754...GEORGE RUTLEDGE (SEAL), Wit:
JOHN MOORE, ANDW HAMPTON, PATRICK McDAVID. Rec. Jan. term 1778.

Page 279: 26 June 1777, NATHAN DAVIS of Tryon Co., to WILLIAM SMITH SR., for Ł 45 north
currency...250 A on head of Ducharts Creek, granted to sd. DAVIS 25 Jan 1773...
NATHAN DAVIS (SEAL), Wit: JOHN ASHLEY (Ŧ), WILLIAM SMITH (X). Rec. Jan. term 1778.

Pp. 279-281: 26 July 1774, JAMES BYERS of Rowan Co., to ALEXANDER COULTER of Tryon Co.,
for Ł 100 proc. money...300 A on N side Broad River on Claghorns Creek...
JAMES BYERS (SEAL), Wit: WILLIAM DAVIDSON, JOSEPH BYERS. Rec. Jan. term 1778.

Pp. 281-282: 11 Dec 1777, WM. ALSTON of Wake County, to JOHN McFARLING of Tryon Co., for
Ł 500 proc. money...land on W side Cataba including the Tuckaseige Ford
below the mouth of Dutchmans Creek, granted to SAMUEL COBURN 24 Sept 1754, 300 A...WM.
ALSTON (SEAL), Wit: GEORGE LAMKIN, ROBT ALEXANDER. Rec. Jan. term 1778.

Pp. 282-283: 15 Jan 1778, GEORGE TROUT of Tryon Co., planter, to DEBORAH BEATY, FRANCIS
BEATY, and JAMES BEATY of same, for Ł 200...200 A on both sides Shoaly
Branch of Muddy fork of Buffalo Creek, granted to JAS. KELLY 26 Sept 1766, conveyed to
FRANCIS BEATY 22 May 1767, then to GEORGE TROUT 20 Mar 1770...GEORGE TROUT(SEAL), Wit:
MARY TROUT (E) (SEAL), Wit: JAMES WHITE, JAMES PALLEY. Rec. Jan. term 1778.

Pp. 283-284: 22 Jan 1778, JOHN HARRIS of Tryon Co., to JAMES MILLER of same, for Ł 100
proc. money...200 A on both sides Maple Creek near Dickeys corner...granted
to JOHN HARRIS 28 Feb 1775...JOHN HARRIS (SEAL), Wit: JONAS BEDFORD, D. DICKEY. Rec. Jan.
term 1778.

Pp. 284-285: 2 Aug 1777, ABSALOM WATERS of Tryon Co., to AMBROSE COBBS of Halifax Co.,
Virginia, for Ł 400 proc. money...200 A granted by deed 21 Dec 1763 on W
side Catawba...ABSALOM WATERS (SEAL), Wit: SAMUEL JOHNSON, JOHN WATERS, ALEXANDER JOHNSON.
Rec. Jan. term 1778.

Pp. 285-286: 19 Jan 1778, JOHN MOORE of Tryon Co., to WILLIAM HAMILTON of same, for ₺ 100
        proc. money...50 A granted to THOMAS WRAY 26 Apr 1767, conveyed to PATRICK
McDAVID 16 Jan 1773, then to sd. MOORE...JOHN MOORE (SEAL), Wit: ALEXANDER MOORE, JOHN
MOORE JUR. Rec. Jan. term 1778.

Page 287: 4 Dec 1777, WILLIAM YANCEY of Tryon Co., to ALEXANDER DAVIDSON of same, for
        ₺ 130...land in the fork of Broad River and First little Broad River, 150 A
on a creek called Yanceys Creek...WILLIAM YANCEY (SEAL), Wit: JOHN ANDERSON, JOSEPH
CAMP. Rec. Jan. term 1778.

Pp. 287-288: 28 Nov 1777, JOHN LOW of Caswell Co., to JAMES WEYETT of Tryon Co., for ₺ 17
        north currency...100 A on both sides Long Creek of S fork Catawba, adj. JACOB
RHINES, GEORGE HOOUSES, granted to THOMAS WRAY...JOHN LOW (SEAL), Wit: GEORGE LAMKIN,
EDMOND WEYATT (ꟼ), FREDERICK HAMBRIGHT. Rec. Jan. term 1778.

Pp. 288-290: 20 Jan 1777, CHARLES FREDERICK FROLICK of Tryon Co., to PAUL HAUL, for ₺ 30
        ...land on waters of Hoyls Creek, including FRELOCKS improvement...SHUTS
corner, 250 A, granted to FRELOCK 15 Mar 1775...CHARLES FREDERICK FROELICKE (SEAL),
CHRISTENE FROELOCK (X) (SEAL), Wit: JOHN BROWN SKRIMSHIRE, JOHN DELLINGER. Rec. Jan.
term 1778.

Pp. 290-291: 8 Oct 1777, BENJAMIN ELLIS of Tryon Co., to JACOB VINZANT of same, for ₺ 150
        proc. money...300 A on S side Broad River, adj. BEATIES, ALEXANDER McENTIRE
...BENJAMIN ELLIS (ᴆ) (SEAL), Wit: WM. GREEN, JAS. McENTIRE.

Pp. 291-292: 26 Nov 1777, JOSEPH CAMP of Tryon Co., to JOSEPH BOREN of same, for ₺ 80
        proc. money...land on a branch of Certains Mill Creek, 270 A granted 15 May
1772, adj. THOMAS BROTHERS...JOSEPH CAMP (SEAL), SUSANNAH CAMP (+) (SEAL), Wit: THOS
HARRY (+), GEO. BLANTON, EATON HAWKINS. Rec. Jan. term 1778.

Page 292: 11 Dec 1777, WILLIAM ALSTON of Wake Co., to JOHN McFARLEN of Tryon Co., for
        ₺ 100 proc. money...land on W side Cataba adj. WIDOW McKENDRICK, below the
Tuckeyseige Ford, adj. CLEGHORN, SCOTT, FRANCIS BEATY, 200 A...WM. ALSTON (SEAL), Wit:
GEORGE LAMKIN, ROBT. ALEXANDER. Rec. Jan. term 1778.

Page 293: 8 Apr 1777, JOHN ASHELY of Tryon Co., to CATHARINE SMITH of same, for ₺ 60 proc.
        money...land on both sides Jumping branch of Long Creek, granted to JEREMIAH
& CATHERINE SMITH 28 Feb 1775, and made over to sd. JOHN ASHLEY by deed 7 Apr 1777...JOHN
ASHLEY (Ɨ) (SEAL), Wit: JOHN MOORE, JONATHAN GULLICK, ALEXANDER MOORE. Rec. Jan. term
1778.

Page 294: 23 July 1777, JAMES COLLINS of Tryon Co., Blacksmith, to HEZEKIAH COLLINS of
        same, for ₺ 30...land on both sides Calfpen branch of Buffaloe Creek, 200 A...
JAMES COLLINS (Ɨ)(SEAL), Wit: GEORGE BARCLAY, JACOB COLLINS. Rec. Jan. term 1778.

Page 295: 19 Sept 1777, LEONARD WEBB of Tryon Co., to WILLIAM CATHEY of same, for ₺ 30
        proc. money...150 A near the Dutchmans Creek, waters of Catawba River, granted
to sd. WEBB 1773...LEONARD WEBB (X) (SEAL), Wit: JAMES JOHNSTON, JANE JOHNSTON. Rec.
Jan. term 1778.

Pp. 295-297: 19 Jan 1778, ARCHIBALD McDOWEL of Meclenburg Co., to GEORGE RUSSELL of Tryon
        Co., for ₺ 65 proc. money...land on both sides Broad River above THOMAS
HERRONS land, granted to sd. McDOWEL 13 Oct 1765...ARCHIBALD McDOWEL (SEAL), Wit: THOMAS
WHITESIDES, HEZ. ALEXANDER. Rec. Jan. term 1778.

Pp. 297-298: 28 Oct 1777, GEORGE RUTLEDGE of Tryon Co., to JOHN WALKER, for ₺ 10 proc.
        money...land on Ducthmans Creek, granted to sd. RUTLEDGE 5 May 1769, 159 A
...GEORGE RUTLEDGE (SEAL), Wit: JAMES HENDERSON, JACOB SEITS, JAMES RUTLEDGE. Rec. Jan.
term 1778.

Pp. 298-299: 20 Jan 1778, GEORGE LAMKIN of Tryon Co., to GEORGE WEST of same, for ₺ 40
        north currency...98 A on W side Catawba on a branch falling into sd. river,
granted to SAMUEL COBURN 26 Oct 1767, part of sd. grant...GEORGE LAMPKIN (SEAL), Wit:
ROBT. ALEXANDER. Rec. Jan. term 1778.

Pp. 299-300: 17 Jan 1778, WILLIAM YANCEY of Tryon Co., to MOSES BRIDGES of same, for ₺ 40
        proc. money...land on first little Broad River, part of tract granted to
MATHEW FLOYD 2 Nov 1764...WILLIAM YANCEY (SEAL), Wit: JOHN ANDERSON, ALEXANDER DAVIDSON.
Rec. Jan. term 1778.

Pp. 300-301: 29 Apr 1776, BENJAMIN COCHRAN of Tryon Co., Weaver, to JOHN HENDERSON,

planter, for ₺ 50 proc. money...140 A adj. W side Cataba river and HESLEPS land, granted
15 May 1772 to FRANCIS BEATY, and by his Exrs sold to BENJAMIN COCHRAN...BENJAMIN COCHRAN
(SEAL), Wit: JOHN HILL, JOHN HENDERSON, WILLIAM HENDERSON. Rec. Jan. term 1778.

Pp. 301-302: 1 Nov 1777, WILLIAM WADDEL & wf JANE of Rowan Co., to JAMES MILLER of Tryon
Co., for ₺ 100 proc. money...land on N side Broad River on McDowells Creek,
1/2 a mile above HUGH BERRYS survey, granted to JACOB SIMERLE, 200 A, 25 Apr 1767...
WILLIAM WADDEL (SEAL), JANE WADLE (SEAL), Wit: _____ [German siganture], PETER EAKER (X).
Rec. Jan. term 1778.

Pp. 302-304: 11 Aug 1776, WM. BALDRIDGE & JOHN BALDRIDGE, yeomen, sons & heirs of JOHN
BALDRIDGE of Pennsylvania (decd), both of Tryon Co., to JOHN HILL of same,
for ₺ 40...land on S side Catawba on Indian Camp Creek, granted to ANDREW ALLISON 3 Apr
1752, by ALLISON conveyed to ALEXANDER McENTIRE 17 Dec 1754, and then to JOHN BALDRIDGE
12 May 1765...WILLIAM BALDRIDGE (SEAL), JOHN BALDRIDGE (SEAL), Wit: WM. GRAHAM, ROBERT
EWART. Rec. Jan.term 1778.

Pp. 304-305: 20 Feb 1777, THOMAS HARROD of Tryon Co., to THOMAS BRIDGES of Camden District,
S. C. for ₺ 60 N. C. proc.money...land on both sides Brushy Creek of First
Broad River adj. JAMES McENTIRE, 640 A granted 2 Mar 1775...THOMAS HARROD (SEAL), Wit:
JAS. McENTIRE, GEORGE RUSSELL. Rec. Jan. term 1778.

Pp. 305-306: 21 Jan 1778, ARTHUR TAYLOR, planter, to WILLIAM GILBERT of Tryon Co., for
₺ 50...land on both sides Bryants Creek of Catheys Creek of Second Broad
River near the path from Shepherds Mill to WILLIAM GILBERTS store, granted to sd. TAYLOR
22 Feb 1775...ARTHUR TAYLOR (SEAL), Wit: JAMES HOLLAND, D. DICKEY. Rec. Jan. term 1778.

Pp. 306-307: 28 Nov 1777, FREDERICK HAMBRIGHT of Tryon Co., to JOHN LOW of Caswell Co.,
for ₺ 40 north currency...300 A on waters of little Long Creek of S fork
Catawba, granted to HAMBRIGHT 28 Feb 1775...FREDERICK HAMBRIGHT (SEAL), Wit: GEORGE
LAMKIN, JAMES WYATT, EDWARD WYATT (૭). Rec. Jan. term 1778.

Pp. 307-308: 8 July 1776, THOMAS COSTNER of Tryon Co., to JOHN DODERROU of same, for ₺ 27
proc. money...300 A on Cosners branch of S fork adj. JACOB COSNER, granted
to JOHN WOOLING CARPENTER, 28 Apr 1768...THOS COSTNER (TC) (SEAL), Wit: JNO. SKRIMSHIRE,
_____ COSTNER [German signature]. Rec. Jan. term 1778.

Pp. 308-309: ___ Jan 1778, JOHN ASHLEY of Tryon Co., planter, to JAMES SANDERS of same,
for ₺ 100 proc. money...150 A on both sides Jumping branch of Long Creek
near Fergusons, granted 28 Feb 1775 to JEREMIAH & CATHERINE SMITH, by them to sd. ASHLEY
17 Apr 1777...JOHN ASHLEY (±) (SEAL), Wit: DAVID DAVIS, JAMES WELLS. Rec. Jan. term 1778.

Pp. 309-310: 7 June 1775, ARCHIBALD FLEMING of Rowan Co., to JOHN FLEMING of same, for ₺
20...lnad on waters of Second Broad River below THOMAS ROBINSONS Creek...
granted to THOMAS FLEMING 25 Apr 1767...ARCHIBALD FLEMING (SEAL), Wit: HUGH KILLPATRICK,
FRANCS. McCORKLE. Rec. Jan. term 1778.

Pp. 310-311: 25 July 1777, THOMAS BRIDGES of Camden District, S. C. to WILLIAM GREEN of
Tryon Co., for ₺ 100 proc. money...land on both sides Brushy Creek of Second
Broad River, 640 A adj. JAMES McENTIRE...THOMAS BRIDGES (SEAL), Wit: JAMES McAFEE, BURRELL
BLANTON (X).

Pp. 311-312: 1 Feb 1777, BENJAMIN SHAW of Tryon Co., to JACOB SIMERLE of Tryon Co., for
₺ 16 proc. money...land on branches of Beaver Dam of S fork Catawba, granted
to sd. SHAW 300 A, 25 Oct 1774...BENJAMIN SHAW (SEAL), Wit: THOS PEARSON, MOSES MOORE
(M). Rec. Jan. term 1778.

Pp. 312-313: 15 Apr 1777, JOHN BRISON of Tryon Co., to JAMES HOLLAND of same, for ₺ 65
proc. money...100 A on S side Little Catawba, conveyed to BRISON by deed
23 Apr 1774, granted to JOHN GULLICK by patent 26 Sept 1766...JOHN BRISON (SEAL), Wit:
WM. BERRY, JONATHAN GULLICK.[No rec. date.]

Pp. 313-314: 7 Apr 1777, JEREMIAH & KATHERINE SMITH of Tryon Co., to JOHN ASHLEY, for
₺ 30 proc. money...land on both sides Jumping branch of Long Creek, granted
to them 300 A, 28 Feb 1775...JERIMEAH SMITH (SEAL), CATHERINE SMITH (SEAL), Wit: JOHN
MOORE, JONATHAN GULLICK., ALEXANDER MOORE. Rec. Jan. term 1778.

Pp. 314-315: 6 July 1772, ANDREW HAMPTON of Tryon Co., to HUGH JENKINS of same, yeoman,
for ₺ 200 proc. money...300 A which ADAM HAMPTON died seized of, to ANDREW
HAMPTON as heir at law, his brother...also 150 A, the place that MATHEW KUYKENDALL lived

on, granted by patent 1 Apr 1750 and conveyed to ANDREW HAMPTON 4 & 5 Mar 1754...ANDW
HAMPTON (SEAL), Wit: DAVID JENKINS, JOSEPH JENKINS. Rec. January term 1775[sic].

APRIL COURT 1778.

Pp. 315-316: 11 Apr 1778, JAS. PATERSON of Tryon Co., to ANDREW FLOID of same, for ₺ 100
            proc. money...150 A on a branch of Dutchmans Creek, South of ALEXANDERS sur-
vey...near NATHANIEL HENDERSON, granted to ABRAHAM ALEXANDER 9 Nov 1764, and conveyed to
NATHANIEL HENDERSON 22 July 1772, and to sd. PATERSON 1 Jan _____....JAMES PATTERSON (SEAL),
Wit: JONT. GULLICK, THOMAS THOMAS. Rec. Apr. term 1778.

Pp. 316-317: 25 Oct 1776, JAMES COBUN & wf MARY of Tryon Co., to MILES ABERNATHY, planter,
            for ₺ 300...400 A on S side Cataba, adj. JOSEPH WISHART...JAMES COBUN (SEAL),
MARY COBUN (O) (SEAL), Wit: JOHN DEVAUX, WILLIAM ₤ARTHEY (W), BENJAMIN WALLER (W). Rec.
Arp. term 1778.

Page 318: 21 Apr 1778, JOHN STROUD of Tryon Co., to MILES ABERNATHY of same, for ₺ 200
            north currency...257 A on a branch of Cobuns and Leopards Creek adj. MORRISON,
JOHN HILL, DUNKIN, part of 2 patents...one to JOHN COBUN, the other to JOHN STROUD...
JOHN STROUD (X) (SEAL), Wit: JESSE FINN (J), GEORGE LAMKIN. Rec. Apr.term 1778.

Pp. 318-319: 2 May 1777, VALENTINE MAUNY to PETER CARPENTER, both of Tryon Co., for ₺ 20
            NC money...land on both sides Indian Creek, granted to LEWIS WEIDNER, 16
Dec 1769...VALLENTINE MAUNY (SEAL), Wit: DAVID RAMSEY, MICHAEL HOEFSELDSTER (MH), Rec.
Apr. term 1778.

Pp. 319-320: 12 Jan 1775, GEORGE LAMKIN of Tryon Co., to SAMUEL RANKIN for ₺ 170 proc.
            money...300 A adj. HITOWERS, McKENDRICK, ROBERT ALEXANDER, on Dutchman Creek
part of grants to WILLIAM CLEGHORN, JAMES HENDERSON, & GEO. LAMKIN...LAMKIN (SEAL),
Wit: ROBT. HEANDEY[?], JOSEPH FRIDER[?]. Rec. Apr. term 1778.

Pp. 320-321: 28 Jan 1777, ANDREW HOYLE of Tryon Co., to VENSANT WYAT of same, for ₺ 47
            north currency...270 A on little log Creek adj. HOYLES Line, JOHN HOYLES
line, granted to JOHN MIERS 26 Oct 1767...ANDREW HEYEL (SEAL), TAWEENA HEYEL (X) (SEAL),
Wit: GEORGE HOVIS (Ꮹ), WILLIAM SPENCER. Rec. Apr. term 1778.

Pp. 321-322: 11 Apr 1778, JOHN MOORE of Tryon Co., to ISAAC WEST of same, for ₺ 40 north
            currency...land on N side Doctors Creek, and a branch of Dutchmans Creek,
part of a grant to JOHN BEATY for 200 A...JOHN BEATY, Schoolmaster, conveyed to EDWARD
HOGAN, then conveyed to JOHN MOORE...JOHN MOORE (SEAL), Wit: GEORGE LAMKIN, GEORGE LAMKIN
JR. Rec. Apr. term 1778.

Pp. 322-323: 22 Apr 1778, PETER ACRE of Tryon Co., to SAMUEL GORDAN, Blacksmith, of
            Camden District, S. C. for ₺ 20 NC money...land on both sides Duncans Creek,
550 A, granted to PETER ACRE 24 Sept 1766...PETER ACRE (X) (SEAL), Wit: ADAM HAMPTON,
RICHARD SINGLETON. Rec. Apr. term 1778.

Pp. 323-324: 19 Feb 1778, JAMES BEATY of Tryon Co., planter, to JOHN CARRUTH of Mecklen-
            burg Co., for ₺ 100...300 A on Buffaloe Creek, waters of Broad River, about
2 miles from GUTHREYS old place, including JAMES ANDHERS[?] improvement...granted to
JAMES BEATY 6 Apr 1765 No. 12....JAMES BEATY (SEAL), Wit: ROBT BEATY, JOHN BEATY. Rec.
July[sic] term 1778.

Pp. 324-325: 14 Oct 1777, JOSEPH RICHEY of Tryon Co., to SAMUEL WALLIS of same, for ₺ 85
            proc. money...200 A adj. HARDEN...JOSEPH RICHEY (SEAL), Wit: UEL LAMKIN,
WILLIAM DAVIDSON. Rec. Apr. term 1778.

Page 325: 7 Nov 1777, STEPHEN LANGFORD of Tryon Co., to DAVY WHITESIDE, for ₺ 32 s 10
            proc. money...100 A granted to sd. LANGFORD, 28 Feb 1775 on First little Broad
River...STEPHEN LANGFORD (SEAL), Wit: WILLIAM MONROE, DANIEL SINGLETON, WILLIAM BARNET
(ℨ). Rec. Apr. term 1778.

Page 326: 25 Sept 1777, JOHN ALEXANDER of Tryon Co., planter, to BENJAMIN SHAW, yeoman,
            for ₺ 75 proc. money...land on both sides First Broad River, granted to
sd. ALEXANDER 26 Sept 1766...JOHN ALEXANDER (SEAL), Wit: MOSES MOORE (M), THOS PEARSON.
Rec. Apr. term 1778.

Pp. 326-327: 11 Apr 1778, JOHN MOORE to WM WEST, both of Tryon Co., for ₺ 35 north curren-
            cy...part of a grant to JOHN BEATY, Schoolmaster, 200 A, by an old School
house branch, conveyed to EDWARD HOGAN, then sd. MOORE...JOHN MOORE (SEAL), Wit: GEORGE

LAMKIN, GEORGE LAMKIN JR. Rec. Apr. term 1778.

Pp. 327-328: 22 Feb 1774, SAMUEL GRAY of Tryon Co., to WILLIAM GRAY of same, for ₤ 20...
300 A...SAML GRAY (SEAL), Wit: DAVID HAYS, THU[?] GRAY. Rec. Apr. term 1778.

Pp. 328-329: 4 Mar 1777, WILLIAM ALSTON of Wake Co., to ROBERT ALEXANDER of Tryon Co.,
for ₤ 10...land on waters of Kuykendalls Creek adj. KUYKENDALLS, LAMKIN &
TROY, 50 A, patent to ALSTON 24 Nov 1774...WM. ALSTON (SEAL), Wit: SAMUEL REAHKEY, THOMAS
CLARK. Rec. Apr. term 1778.

Pp. 329-330: 21 Apr 1778, LEWIS LINEBARGER of Tryon Co., for ₤ 100 proc. money pd. by
ROBERT BOYED...land on big and little long Creeks adj. JOHN JENKINS, 480
A granted to JOHN & DANIEL McKENTNEY[?], 15 May 1770...LUDWIG LINEBURGER [German sign.]
(SEAL), _____ [German signature] (SEAL), Wit: _____ [German singautre], THOMAS
McGILL. Rec. Apr. term 1778.

Pp. 330-331: 16 Dec 1777, ROBERT McCOMB of Tryon Co., to MOSES WILLIAMS of same, for ₤ 40
north currency...240 A on waters of Dutchmans Creek of Catawba, granted to
sd. McCOMB 2 Mar 1775...ROBERT McCOMB (SEAL), Wit: MILES ABERNATHY, JESSE FINN (J). Rec.
Apr. term 1778.

Pp. 331-332: 20 Mar 1773, WM SHARP of Rowan Co., to GEORGE PARRY of Tryon Co., for ₤ 40
proc. money...land on both sides Calb or Club Creek, S side Green River,
200 A, granted to JOHN FRANKLIN 22 Dec 1768, conveyed to WM. SHARP 10 Apr 1769...WM.
SHARP (SEAL), Wit: SAML GRAY, WM. GRAY, RICHARD PAGE. Rec. Apr. term 1778.

Pp. 332-333: 6 Mar 1778, MARTIN PHIFER SR. of Mecklenburg Co., to JOHN FULLENWIDER of
Rowan Co., for ₤ 200...land on S side Catawba adj. WM. ARMSTRONG, MARTIN
PHIFER, 371 A...MARTIN PHIFER (SEAL), Wit: JASON FRISSELL, THOMAS CARSON, JACOB RAMSOUR.
Rec. Apr. term 1778.

Pp. 333-334: 6 Apr 1778, SAMUEL KUYKENDALL of Tryon Co., to JOHN WEST of same, for ₤ 30
proc. money...60 A on Kuykendalls Creek adj. WM. MOORE, BELL, KUYKENDALL,
granted 2 Mar 1775...SAMUEL KUYKENDAL (SEAL), Wit: JONTH. KUYKENDALL, FRANCIS GASCORGN.
Rec. Apr. term 1778.

Pp. 334-335: 30 Aug 1777, MICHAEL HOLLSHOUSER of Rowan Co., planter, to GEORGE REEL of
Tryon Co., for ₤ 50...part of a grant to LAWRENCE SNAP, late of Rowan, since
deceased, and will by him to his daughter CHRISTIANNA SNAPP, now wife of MICHAEL HOLLS-
HOUSER, 200 A...MICHEL HOLZHAUSER (SEAL), Wit: JOHN LEWIS BEARD, JAMES ROBINSON, AD:
OSBORN. Rec. Apr. term 1778.

Pp. 335-336: 6 Mar 1778, MARTIN PHIFER SR. of Mecklenburg Co., to JOHN FULWIDER[sic] of
Rowan Co., for ₤ 200...land on both sides S fork Catawba, about 2 miles
below SAMUEL BICKERSTAFF, 450 A...MARTIN PHIFER (SEAL), Wit: JASON FUISSELLE, THOMAS
CARSON. Rec. Apr. term 1778.

Pp. 336-337: 21 Nov 1777, JAMES REES of Tryon Co., to VESTER(VIOLET) TAGERT of same, for
₤ 100 proc. money...land on a branch of Crowders Creek, granted to JOHN
TAGERT 28 Apr 1768 and conveyed to JAMES REES 25 July 1771...REES (SEAL), Wit: JOHN
ROBINSON, ALEXR ROBINSON. Rec. Apr. term 1778.

Pp. 337-338: HUGH JENKINS of Rowan Co., for parental love to JOSEPH JENKINS, his Legiti-
mate son...land on long Creek, 202 A which FRANCIS BEATY conveyed to DAVID
STANDLEY 16 Oct 1764, and another tract adj. HAMRIGHT, granted to STANLEY 26 Oct 1766,
200 A, conveyed by STANLY to HUGH JENKINS 30 June 1768...HUGH JENKINS (SEAL), Wit:
JAMES LENKINS, MATTHEW STEWART. Rec. Apr. term 1778.

Pp. 338-339: 25 July 1771, JOHN TAGERT of Tryon Co., to JAMES RICE of Orange Co., for
₤ 30 proc. money...land on a branch of Crowders Creek, granted to TAGERT
28 Apr 1768 adj. ALEXANDER ROBINSON...JOHN TAGERT (SEAL), Wit: WILL REED, THOS NEEL. Rec.
Apr. term 1778.

JULY COURT AD 1778.

Pp. 339-340: 20 Apr 1775, THOMAS BEATY, HUGH BEATY & ROBERT ARMSTRONG, Exrs. of FRANCIS
BEATY decd of Mecklenburg Co., to JOSEPH DICKSON of Rowan Co., for ₤ 94
proc. money...land on popler branch and Lick fork of Buffaloe, 1 1/2 miles above BENJ.
SHAW and on the path from LEONARD SAFFERETS to JAMES KELLYs, 300 A, granted to sd.
FRANCIS BEATY, 16 Nov 1764...Wit: JAMES BEATY, FRANCIS ARMSTRONG, ROBT. BEATY. Rec.

July term 1778.

Pp. 341-342: 1 Aug 1772, THOMAS McKNIGHT of Rowan Co., to THOMAS HENRY of Tryon Co., for
ᵬ 50...land on W side Catawba River near FRANCIS BEATY, 195 A granted to
sd. McKNIGHT, 22 Feb 1764...THOMAS McKNIGHT (SEAL), Wit: JOHN McELROY, CHARLES McKNIGHT,
JAMES HENDERSON, THOMAS BEATY, JOSEPH HENRY. Rec. July term 1778.

Pp. 342-434: 10 Mar 1777, WILLIAM ALSTON of Tryon Co., to JOHN BEATY of same, for ᵬ 50
proc. money...land on waters of Doctors Creek adj. JOHN SAILOR, 184 A...WM.
ALSTON (SEAL), Wit: ROBT. ABERNATHY. Rec. July term 1778.

Pp. 343-344: 15 Sept 1777, GEORGE POTTS of Tryon Co., to JAMES HUGGINS of same, for ᵬ 60
proc. money...200 A on both sides Potts Creek of Buffelow Creek, granted to
GEORGE POTTS 22 Dec 1768...GORGE POTTS (X) (SEAL), Wit: JOHN SLOAN, WALTER CARRUTH, Rec.
July term 1778.

Pp. 344-345: 2 Feb 1777, DEVALD CRYTS & wf SOPHIAH, planter, to JACOB FORNEY of Tryon
Co., planter, for ᵬ 100 proc. money...by certain deeds bearing date 7 Sept
1763 and 1770, formerly the Plantation of JACOB FORNEY...200 A on S side Catawba and on
ANDREW KILLIONS Creek and 75 A on a branch of ANDREW KILLIONS Creek adj. JACOB FORNEY,
GEORGE DICK, PAUL WHISNANT...DAVID CRYTS (X) (SEAL), SOPHYAH CRYTS (I) (SEAL), Wit:
ABM MIERS (O), JOHN BEATY. Rec. July term 1778.

Page 346: 20 Oct 1775, JOHN GRAHAM, late of Tryon Co., to WILLIAM GRAHAM of said county,
for ᵬ 30...300 A on waters of S fork Catawba River including the Improvement
of JAMES COZART, SHITTLES, granted to JAMES COZART 19 May 1772...JOHN GRAHAM (SEAL),
Wit: JACOB MONEY (X), ELIZABETH CARLON (𝓛). Rec. July term 1778.

Page 347: 20 Aug 1773, RICHARD BARRY of Mecklenburg Co., to JOHN McKNIT ALEXANDER of
same, for ᵬ 60 proc. money...640 A granted to sd. BARRY 26 Sept 1766 on E side
Little Broad River...RICHD BARRY (SEAL), Wit: JOHN SMITH, WILLIAM SIMPLE, THOMAS BEATY,
JOHN HILL. Rec. July term 1778.

Pp. 348-349: 26 Jan 1778, JOHN McDOWEL of Burke Co., to ARTHUR PATTERSON of Tryon Co.,
for ᵬ 200 proc. money...land on the Main No. Fork of Kings Creek, N side
Broad River, near the Long Mountain, 600 A granted to JOHN EDINTON 30 Aug 1753, conveyed
from sd. NICHOLAS EDINTON to sd. JOHN McDOWEL 9 July 1772...JOHN McDOWEL (SEAL), Wit:
GEORGE PATTERSON, JAMES PATTERSON. JO. McDOWELL. Rec. July term 1778.

Page 349: 11 July 1778, WILLIAM SMITH JUR. of Tryon Co., to DANIEL GRAY of same, for ᵬ 50
north currency...150 A on both sides Duharts Creek, granted to SAMUEL COBUN
25 Nov 1771, to conveyed to sd. SMITH 6 July 1773...WILLIAM SMITH (SEAL), Wit: GEORGE
LAMPKIN, GEORGE LAMKIN JUR. Rec. July term 1778.

Pp. 349-350: 25 Jan 1777, MILES ABERNATHY & wf SARAH ANN of Tryon Co., to ARTHUR BENOM
of Pittsylvania Co., Va., for ᵬ 150...land on a branch of Killians Creek,
200 A...MILES ABERNATHY (SEAL), SARAH ANN ABERNATHY (+) (SEAL), Wit: WM. BERRY, JOSEPH
ABERNATHY, JOSEPH BERRY. Rec. July term 1778.

Pp. 350-351: 8 Mar 1775, FRANCIS GASKINS of Tryon Co., to JOHN BEALE of same, for ᵬ 40
proc. money...land on banks of Doctors Creek, 150 A granted to sd. GASKINS
16 Feb 1773...FRANCIS GOSCOGER (SEAL), Wit: WILLIAM MASSEY, NANCY SHARP (--), DAVID
BLALOCK, GEORGE LAMKIN. Rec. July term 1778.

Pp. 351-352: 18 July 1778, JOHN MOORE of Tryon Co., to ALEXANDER MOORE his son of same,
for ᵬ 200 proc. money...land on Beaver Dam Creek that runs into the South
Fork of the Catawba, 229 A granted to JAMES ARMSTRONG 30 Aug 1753, and conveyed to WM.
SMITH 5 Jan 1739[sic]...JOHN MOORE (SEAL), Wit: WILLIAM MOORE, JOHN MOORE, JUR. Rec.
July term 1778.

Pp. 352-353: 28 Apr 1775, WILLIAM SMITH of Tryon Co., Blacksmith, to JOHN MOORE of same,
for ᵬ 156 s 6 d 8 proc. money...land on Beaver Dam Creek that runs into the
South Fork of Catawba, granted to JAMES ARMSTRONG 30 Aug 1753, and conveyed to sd. WILLIAM
SMITH 5 Jan 1759, 150 A...WILLIM S___ [German signature] (SEAL), Wit: JOSEPH BUFFINGTON,
JONAN. COATES, JACOB ZIM____. Rec. July term 1778.

Pp. 353-354: 7 June 1773, ROBERT ELDER of Tryon Co., planter, to SAMUEL ELDER of same,
Taylor, for ᵬ 15 proc. money...land adj. W side Catawba and adj. DAVID
ELDER, JAMES CUNNINGHAM, JAMES BRADY, CATHEY, CHRONICLE, HINES, 92 A, part of 200 A
granted to ROGER COOK 30 Oct 1765...conveyed by COOK to FREDERICK HAMBRIGHT, then to

WILLIAM PATTERSON, then to sd. ELDER...ROBERT ELDER (E) (SEAL), Wit: ROBT. ARMSTRONG, DAVID ELDER. Rec. July term 1778.

Pp. 354-355: 7 July 1778, JOHN PHILIP DELLINGER & wf BARBARA of Tryon Co., to JOHN FINGER for ₺ 100...[grantee later appears to be TRINGER]...100 A adj. to his own and SHULSES land...JOHN DELLINGER (SEAL), BARBARA DELLINGER (X) (SEAL), Wit: DAVID RAMSEY, _____ [German signature]. Rec. July term 1778.

Pp. 355-356: 29 Dec 1777, JAMES WYATT of Tryon Co., to GEORGE HORTON of same, for ₺ 28 north currency...100 A on both sides S fork Catawba adj. JACOB NINES[?], GEORGE HAVAS, granted to THOMAS WRAY 26 Oct 1767...JAMES WYATT (SEAL), JAMES WITHERS[?], Wit: DANIEL GRAY, SAMUEL RANKIN. Rec. July term 1778.

Pp. 356-357: 22 July 1778, CHRISTIAN CARPENTER of Tryon Co., to JOSEPH GOODS of same, for ₺ 100 proc. money...land on both sides Knobb Creek near the Cherokee path, granted to sd. CARPENTER 29 Apr 1768...CHRISTIAN CARPENTER (C₺) (SEAL), Wit: JOSEPH HARDING, AND NEEL. Rec. July term 1778.

Pp. 357-358: 17 July 1778, JOHN PHILIP DILLINGER & wf BARBARA of Tryon Co., to JOHN FINGERS[?] of same, for ₺ 200...land on lick branch of Lepers Creek, 300 A... JOHN DELLINGER (SEAL), BARBRA DELLINGER (+) (SEAL), Wit: DAVID RAMSEY, _____ [German signature]. Rec. July term 1778.

Pp. 358-359: 22 Aug 1777, VALENTINE MONEY to JOHN McENTIRE for ₺ 10 proc. money...land on both sides Magness's Creek of Broad River...VALLENTINE MAUNY (SEAL), Wit: AND NEEL. Rec. July term 1778.

Pp. 359-360: 10 Oct 1777, MOSES FERGUSON (Schoolmaster) & wf MARTHA of Camden District, S. C., to JOHN McMICHAEL, Distiler of same, for ₺ 310...land in Tryon Co., on Long Creek on the W side Catawba near ADAM MEEKS corner, THOMAS WELSHES line, granted to sd. FERGUSON 28 Oct 1765...MOSES FERGUSON (SEAL), MARTHA FERGUSON (S) (SEAL), Wit: WILLIAM McMICHAEL, PATRICK McGONNEGEL, DAVID KNOX. Rec. July term 1778.

Pp. 360-361: 5 Nov 1776, JAMES MURPHEY of Tryon Co., to JOHN WERE of same, for ₺ 30 proc. money...200 A granted to OWEN MURPHEY, 28 Apr 1768 on both sides Buffaloe Creek...JAMES MURPHEY (₤) (SEAL), Wit: JOSEPH GLADEN, JOHN SLOAN. Rec. July term 1778.

Pp. 361-362: 21 July 1778, THOMAS BEATY of Rowan Co., planter, to HUGH BEATY of Tryon Co., for ₺ 100...320 A on the N side of first Little Broad River including the mouth of Hickory Creek, granted to FRANCES & JOHN BEATY for 640 A, 30 Oct 1768...THOMAS BEATY (SEAL), Wit: ROBERT BEATY, WALLACE BEATEY, FRANCES BEATY. Rec. July term 1778.

Pp. 362-363: 21 July 1778, JOHN McMICHAEL of Camden District, South Carolina, to JAMES WHITE of Tryon Co., for ₺ 100 NC money...land on waters of Long Creek on the W side of the South Fork Waggon Road near ADAM MEEKS corner, near THOMAS WELCHES line, granted to MOSES FERGUSON 28 Oct 1765...JOHN McMICHAEL (SEAL), Wit: THOS PEARSON, ALEXAN-DER GILLILAND. Rec. July term 1778.

Pp. 363-364: 23 July 1778, THOMAS BEATY of Rowan Co., and ROBERT ARMSTRONGof Tryon Co., Exrs. of FRANCIS BEATY of Mecklenburg Co., decd, to HUGH BEATY, for ₺ 50... land on N side Little Broad River on Hickory Creek, granted to FRANCES & JOHN BEATY, for 640 A, part of sd. tract, 30 Oct 1765...THOMAS BEATY (SEAL), ROBT ARMSTRONG (SEAL), Wit: JAMES PULLEY, ADAM NICKLE[?], ROBERT BEATY. Rec. July term 1778.

Pp. 364-365: 21 July 1777, STEPHEN LYON of Tryon Co., to DAVID BLALOCK of same, for ₺ 30 ...land on S side Catawba on Robersons Creek, 150 A including his own im-provements adj. LINK[?]...STEPHEN LYON (SEAL), Wit: DAVID ABERNATHY. Rec. July term 1778.

Pp. 365-366: 23 July 1778, THOMAS BEATY of Rowan Co., & HUGH BEATY & ROBERT ARMSTRONG of Tryon Co., Exrs. of FRANCIS BEATY, decd, to WALLACE BEATY of Tryon Co., for ₺ 50...160 A on N side of first Little Broad River, granted to FRANCIS & JOHN BEATY, 30 Oct 1765...Wit: JAMES PULLEY, ROBERT BEATY, ADAM NIELE. Rec. July term 1778.

Pp. 366-367: 23 July 1778, JAMES WEYET JUNR. of Tryon Co., to JAMES WEYAT SENR, for ₺ 20 north currency...100 A on Little Long Creek, granted to ANDW HOYLE 28 Apr 1768...JAMES WYATT (SEAL), Wit: DANIEL WEYATT (E), GEORGE PALMER. Rec. July term 1778.

Pp. 367-368: GEORGE MORGAN to EDWARD CAMP, former of Tryon Co., for ₺ 50...land on S side Broad River, granted to THOMAS HIGHTOWER 1773, 160 A...19 Dec 1777...GEORGE MORGAN (SEAL), Wit: JOSHUA HITOWER (₤), JOSEPH COFELL, ROBERT CHILDRESS. Rec. July term 1778.

Pp. 368-369: 2 Jan 1778, WILLIAM KINKAID of Tryon Co., to JOHN KINKAID of same, for Ł 146
...150 A on Killions Creek adj. KILLION, KINCAID...WILLIAM KINKAID (SEAL),
Wit: JAMES JOHNSON, BENJAMIN ARMSTRONG. Rec. July term 1778.

Pp. 369-370: 7 July 1778, THOMAS HUNT to ROBERT ALEXANDER, both of Tryon Co., for Ł 54...
93 A known as DAVIS Mill seat...near a pond...granted to JOSEPH DAVIS, decd,
6 May 1769, and made over to WILLIAM ALSTON by sd. DAVIS 3 Oct 1772, and to sd. HUNT by
deed 3 Dec 1773...THOMAS HUNT (X) (SEAL), Wit: JAS HOLLAND. Rec. July term 1778.

Page 370: 21 July 1778, WILLIAM MASSEY of Tryon Co., to GEORGE LAMKIN of same, for Ł 80
proc. money...200 A on W side Catawba, adj. WIDOW McKENDRICK, granted to WM.
CLEGHORN and one granted to JAMES HENDERSON 15 May 1772...WILLIAM MASSEY (SEAL), Wit:
JOHN GILLAM, FRANCIS GASCOIGN, WILLIAM NICHOLAS (W). Rec. July term 1778.

Pp. 371-372: 11 Mar 1778, ANDREW KELLER & RAHUN[?] his wife of Tryon Co., to ANDREW NEEL
of same, for Ł 100 proc. money...land on branches of Long Creek adj. MICHAEL
HOSTATLERS, KYZERS, granted to PETER PLUNKLEY, 9 Apr 1770...ANDREW KELLER (*) (SEAL), RA-
HUNE KELLER (+) (SEAL), Wit: ____ [German signature], JOHN BRADLEY. [Rec. date not given.]

Pp. 371-372: 11 Mar 1778, ANDREW KELLER & wf RAHUNA to ANDREW NEEL, for Ł 100 proc. money
...land on a branch of Long Creek including his improvement, 100 A granted
to sd. ANDW KELLER 28 Feb 1775...Wit: ____ [German signature]. Rec. July term 1778.

Pp. 373-374: 6 July 1774, BOSTON BEST of Tryon Co., to DAVID JENKINS of same, for Ł 50...
170 A...BOSTIAN BEST [German signature] (SEAL), Wit: FREDERICK HAMRIGHT,
JACOB CASTNER. Rec. July term 1778.

Pp. 374-375: 22 Apr 1778, PETER SITES of Tryon Co. to ADAM NEEL of same, for Ł 100 proc.
money...land on Muddy fork of Buffalow Creek adj. MOSES MOORE, 200 A,
granted to BENJAMIN SHAW 16 Nov 1764...PETER SITES (X) (SEAL), Wit: Two German signatures.
[No rec. date given].

Pp. 375-376: 24 July 1778, NATHANIEL ALDRIDGE of Tryon Co., to JOHN McFARLAND of same, for
Ł 50...land on the waters of Bridge Branch of Crowders Creek, 180 A granted
to sd. ALDRIDGE 28 Feb 1775...NATHANIEL ALDRIDGE (A) (SEAL), Wit: JONATHAN GULLICK,
AMBROSE FOSTER. Rec. July term 1778.

Pp. 376-377: 23 July 1778, FREDERICK HAMBRIGHT of Tryon Co., to THOMAS MORRIS for Ł 150
...land on both sides Catheys Creek, waters of Second Broad River, 200 A
granted to sd. HAMBRIGHT 1768...FREDERICK HAMBRIGHT (SEAL), Wit:WM. NEVIL, JAMES JOHN-
STON. Rec. July term 1778.

Pp. 377-378: 21 July 1778, JONAS BEDFORD of Tryon Co., to DAVID MILLER of same, for Ł 15
proc. money...500 A on Mountain Creek, 28 Feb 1775 granted to sd. BEDFORD...
JONAS BEDFORD (SEAL), Wit: AD OSBORN, AND NEEL. Rec. July term 1778.

Pp. 378-379: 5 June 1778, JOHN McLEAN to THOMAS WHERRY, for Ł 950...320 A on N side Main
Broad River, part of tract surveyed for JOHN BAXTER by WILLIAM DICKSON 20
Aug 1764, granted to JOHN BAXTER 16 Aug 1765...JOHN McLAIN (SEAL), Wit: DAVID LEWIS,
DAVID MILLER, JOHN SCOTT. Rec. July term 1778.

Pp. 379-380: 5 Aug 1777, JOHN WHITESIDE to JOSEPH McDONALD of Tryon Co., for Ł 100...
250 A on both sides Green River about two miles above JOHN HITOWERs survey,
which fell to JOHN WHITESIDE by heirship, being the only son of WILLIAM WHITESIDE, granted
to sd. WILLIAM WHITESIDE 25 Sept 1766...JOHN WHITSED (SEAL), Wit : JNO. EARLE, WM. NEVIL,
JEREMIAH McDONALD. Rec. July term 1778.

Page 380: 22 June 1778, HENRY HAYS of South Carolina, Ninety Six District, to JOHN
FLACK of Tryon Co., for Ł 350...300 A on Catheys Creek, granted to JOHN BENNETT
29 Apr 1769...HENRY HAYS (SEAL), Wit: JONATHAN HAMPTON, ANDW HAMPTON. Rec. July term
1778.

Page 381: 25 Sept 1777, JOHN ALEXANDER of Tryon Co., planter, to STEPHEN LANGFORD,
planter, for Ł 87 s 10 proc. money...land on both sides Little Broad River
adj. ROBERT WHITESIDES, granted to sd. ALEXANDER 2 Mar 1775...JOHN ALEXANDER (SEAL), Wit:
THOS PEARSON, MOSES MOORE (M). Rec. July term 1778.

Pp. 381-382: 25 Sept 1777, BENJAMIN SHAW of Tryon Co., to STEPHEN LANGFORD of same, for
Ł 25 proc. money...land on both sides first Little Broad River, granted to
sd. SHAW 26 Sept 1766...BENJAMIN SHAW (SEAL), Wit: MOSES MOORE (M), THOS PEARSON. Rec.

July term 1778.

Pp. 382-383: 3 Dec 1776, THOMAS ANDERSON SENR. & wf MARY of Tryon Co. to THOMAS ANDERSON
JUNR., planter, for Ł 10 NC money...land on both sides Andersons Creek,
gr'anted to sd. THOMAS ANDERSON 10 Apr 1761...100 A...THOMAS ANDERSON (SEAL), MARY ANDER-
SON (M) (SEAL), Wit: JOHN COIT[?], STEPHEN LYON, JOHN DEVAUX. Rec. July term 1778.

Pp. 383-384: 27 Apr 1778, ARCHIBEL McDOWEL of Mecklenburg Co., to MICHAEL McELWRATH, for
Ł 25 proc. money...land on both sides North fork of Main Broad River, granted
to sd. McDOWEL 30 Oct 1765, 300 A...ARCHIBALD McDOWELL (SEAL), Wit: HEZ. ALEXANDER,
ELIAS MCFADEN. Rec. July term 1778.

Pp. 384-385: 19 Apr 1778, JOHN McFADEN of Tryon Co., to WILLIAM LUSK of same, for Ł 60
...land on both sides Maple Creek of Mountain Carrek, part of 150 A conveyed
to McFADEN 18 Apr 1778 by JNO. KIRKONNEL...JOHN McFADIN (₩) (SEAL), Wit: AND NEEL,
RICHARD SINGLETON. Rec. July term 1778.

Pp. 385-386: 20 Mar 1778, JOHN WALKER of Tryon Co., to WILLIAM GILBERT of same, for Ł 50
...land on N branch of Catheys Creek, granted to WALKER __ Oct 1767...JOHN
WALKER (SEAL), Wit: ANDW HAMPTON, WILLIAM HENRY, JONATHAN HAMPTON. Rec. July term 1778.

Page 387: 14 July 1778, ELIAS McFADEN of Tryon Co., to SAMUEL McFADEN, for Ł 140..
land on S side Main Broad River above JOHN BAXTERS land, 100 A granted to
ARCHIBALD McDOWEL, 30 Oct 1765, and conveyed to ELIAS McFADEN 27 Apr 1778...ELIAS McFADEN
(SEAL), Wit: JONATHAN HAMPTON, JOHN McLEWER. Rec. July term 1778.

Pp. 388-389: 13 Apr 1778, WILLIAM ADAMS of Cambden[sic] Dist., S. C. to HUGH GORDON of
Tryon Co., for Ł 100 proc. money...land on S side Crowders Creek adj.
ALLISONS Survey, 115 A, granted to JOHN McDOWELL 30 Aug 1753...WILLIAM ADAMS (SEAL), Wit:
BENJAMIN McFARLEN, HENRY GORDON, ALEXR. GILLELAND. Rec. July term 1778.

Pp. 389-390: 9 Jan 1777, WILLIAM PATTERSON of Tryon Co., to JACOB BEKERof same, for Ł125
proc. money...250 A on S side Catawba on Cobruns Creek adj. ABRAM SCOTT,
part of a grant to JOHN KILLON 13 Sept 1759, conveyed to EREHART, then to ANDW CATHEY,
then to THOMAS YEATES, then to DAVID CROCKET, then to sd. WILLIAM PATERSON...WILLIAM
PATTERSON (SEAL), Wit: JACOB SEITS, ALEXANDER PATTERSON. Rec. July term 1778.

Pp. 390-391: 27 Apr 1778, ARCHIBALD McDOWEL of Mecklenburg Co., to ELIAS McFADEN of Tryon
Co., for Ł 80 proc. money...land on both sides Main Broad River above JOHN
BAXTERS land, granted 30 Oct 1765 to sd. McDOWEL, 200 A...ARCHIBALD McDOWEL (SEAL), Wit:
HEZ. ALEXANDER, MICHAL McELWRATH. Rec. July term 1778.

Pp. 391-392: 23 July 1778, WILLIAM HENRY of Tryon Co., to JAMES HENRY of Craven Co., SC,
for Ł 100 NC money...land on N side Second Broad River adj. WILLIAM HENRYs
corner...WILLIAM HENRY (SEAL), Wit: ALEXANDER HENRY, JAMES COBUN, ROBERT EWART. Rec.
July term 1778.

Page 392: 23 July 1778, WILLIAM HENRY to JAMES HENRY, for Ł 200 NC money...land on both
sides Second Broad River, 335 A near WALKERS corner [Same siganture and wit.
as preceding deed.] Rec. July term 1778.

Pp. 392-393: 3 June 1778, JOHN McLEAN of Tryon Co., to JOHN MORRISS of same, for Ł 550
...350 A on S side Main Broad River, part of land surveyed for JOHN BAXTER
by WILLIAM DIXON 20 Aug 1764, granted 640 A...JOHN McLANE (SEAL), Wit: DAVID LEWIS, JOHN
RUSSELL, DAVID MILLER. Rec. July term 1778.

Pp. 393-394: 24 Aug 1777, ARCHIBALD McDOWEL of Mecklenburgh Co., to JOHN McFADEN of Tryon
Co., for Ł 80...land on both sides Main Broad Tiver, 200 A...ARCHIBALD
McDOWELL (SEAL), Wit: SAML MARTIN, WM. GRAY, WILLIAM HALE. Rec. July term 1778.

Page 395: 14 July 1778, JOHN McFADEN of Tryon Co., to WILLIAM HALL of same, for Ł 40...
land on S side Main Broad River, granted to ARCHIBALD McDOWEL 30 Oct 1765,
conveyed by him to JOHN McFADEN 24 Aug 1777...JOHN McFADEN (₩) (SEAL), Wit: JONATHAN
HAMPTON, MARGARET HAMPTON (X). Rec. July term 1778.

Pp. 395-396: 4 June 1778, ELIZABETH SNAPP's Executors, GEORGE HENRY BERGER and LEWIS
BEARD, both of Rowan Co., to GEORGE REAL of Tryon Co., for Ł 90 s 10...795
A on both sides Lepers Creek, granted to LAWRENCE SNAPP decd, and by his L. W. & T.
divided in four parts unto four of his children, so that sd. ELIZABETH SNAPP, his daughter, decd, became owner of 200 A and by her L. W. & T., dated 14 June 1774...JOHN LEWIS

BEARD (SEAL), GEORGE HENRY BERGER (LS), Wit: JACOB MOSTER (X), JOHN RIRCHELMAN. Rec.
July term 1778.

Pp. 396-397: 20 Oct 1778, JOHN SLOAN ESQR. of Tryon Co., to GEORGE PALMER of same, for
Ᏸ 60 North currency...land on both sides Little Long Creek of Catawba ADJ.
HYLES land, granted to sd. SLOAN 24 Dec 1770...JOHN SLOAN (SEAL), Wit: AND NEEL. Rec.
Oct. term 1778.

Pp. 397-398: 28 Mar 1778, JOHN HUGGINS JUNR. of Tryon Co., to JOHN HUGGINS SENR. of same,
for Ᏸ 130 proc. money...100 A on Little Catawba, granted to HUGH BERRY 20
Apr 1767, conveyed to JAMES LOGAN ____, then to sd. HUGGINS 10 Jan 1770...JOHN HUGGINS
(SEAL), Wit: JONTH GULLICK, ELIZABETH HUGGINS. Rec. Oct. term 1778.

Pp. 398-399: 22 Oct 1778, JACOB MOONEY JUR. of Tryon Co., to WILLIAM OATS of same, for
Ᏸ 200 proc. money...land on Muddy fork of Buffaloe below MOSES MOORES land,
200 A granted to JAMES KELLY 16 Nov 1764, then to JACOB MOONEY JR. 7 Dec 1774...JACOB
MOONEY JUR. (X) (SEAL)Wit: AND NEEL. Rec. Oct. term 1778.

Pp. 399-400: 21 Oct 1778, JAMES SLOAN of Tryon Co., to JACOB CONNEL, for Ᏸ 250...land on
a branch of Buffalow Creek, including EBENEZER FLOYDS Improvement, 200 A
granted to sd. JAMES 9 Apr 1770...JAMES SLOAN (SEAL), Wit: JAMES HENDERSON, BENJAMIN
ORMAND. Rec. Oct. term 1778. Also wit. WILLIAM OATS.

Page 401: 2 Sept 1778, JOHN CUSTER & wf ELIZABETH to CHRISTIAN EAKER, both of Tryon Co.,
for Ᏸ 35 proc. money...land on both sides Buffaloe Branch of Indian Creek adj.
NICHOLAS WELCH, 300 A granted to NICHOLAS WELCH 20 Mar 1772...JOHN CUSTER (SEAL), ELASA-
BETH CUSTER (SEAL), Wit: VALLENTINE MAUNY, PETER ACKER (+). Rec. July term 1778.

Pp. 401-402: 16 Oct 1778, JAMES REES of Tryon Co., to WILLIAM REES of same, for Ᏸ 30
proc. money...174 A on North Branches of Crowders Creek adj. ALEXANDER ROBIN-
SONS corner, granted to AMBROSE FOSTER 9 Apr 1770...REES (SEAL), Wit: JOHN GULLICK,
JONATHAN GULLICK. Rec. Oct. term 1778.

Pp. 402-403: 12 Aug 1778, WILLIAM HARRIS & wf ANNA of Tryon Co., to JOHN McCLURE of same,
for Ᏸ 20 proc. money...40 A on W side his own land on waters of Little
Catawba Creek, granted to JOHN HARRIS 14 May 1772...WILLIAM HARRISS (SEAL), ANNA HARRISS
(X) (SEAL), Wit: JOHN HARRIS, JOSEPH NEEL, JONATHAN GULLICK. Rec. Oct. term 1778.

Pp. 403-404: 21 Oct 1778, GEORGE DAVIS of Tryon Co., to GEORGE PATTERSON of same, for
Ᏸ 100 proc. money...land on a large branch of Buffaloe Creek 200 A granted
to GEORGE DAVIS 28 Apr 1778...GEORGE DAVIS (+) (SEAL), Wit: JAMES HENDERSON, JAMES
PATTERSON, CHAS. MEDLOCK. Rec. Oct. term 1778.

Page 405: PHILIP WISENANT of Tryon Co., have mortgaged unto ADAM WISENANT and HENRY HIL-
DEBRAND...parcel of Blacksmith tools...14 Feb 1778...PHILIP ____ [German sig-
nature] (SEAL), Wit: THOS PEARSON.

Pp. 405-406: 28 Mar 1778, HEZEKIAH COLLINS of NC to WILLIAM GRAHAM of same, for Ᏸ 40 NC
money...200 A on both sides Calfpen Branch of Buffalo Creek, granted to
JAMES COLLINS 25 Jan 1773, and conveyed to sd. HEZEKIAH COLLINS...HEZEKIAH COLLINS (X)
(SEAL), Wit: WILLIAM GUTER (W), ARCHIBALD GRAHAM, SUSANNA TWITTY. Rec. Oct. term 1778.

Page 406: 29 Aug 1777,GEORGE LAMKIN of Tryon Co., to CHARLES MATTOX of same, for Ᏸ 30
north currency...land on branches of S fork Catawba, adj. HENDERSON, granted
to sd. LAMKIN 28 Feb 1775...GEORGE LAMKIN (SEAL), Wit: WM CHRONICLE, JOHN MATTOX.
Rec. Oct. term 1778.

Pp. 406-407: 2 Sept 1778, JOHN CUSTARD & wf ELIZABETH to CHRISTIAN AKER, both of Tryon
County, for Ᏸ 100 proc. money...land on both sides Buffaloe Branch including
his own improvement, 300 A, granted to sd. CUSTARD 28 Feb 1775...JOHN CUSTER (SEAL),
ELASABETH CUSTER (SEAL), Wit: VALLENTINE MAUNY, PETER ACKER (X). Rec. Oct. term 1778.

Pp. 407-408: 27 Nov 1776, ADAM CLONINGER of Tryon Co., to GERHARD WILL, for Ᏸ 25 proc.
money...200 A on waters of Lepers Creek on Armstrong Branch of the Dutchmans
Creek of the Catawba River including his own improvement, granted to sd. ADAM CLONINGER,
25 Apr 1773...ADAM CLONINGER (SEAL), Wit: JACOB SEITS, JOHN EDELMAN (IE), JOHANNES WILL.
Rec. Oct. term 1778.

Pp. 408-410: 19 Mar 1778, JOHN POLK & wf AGNESS of Tryon Co., to WILLIAM HANNA of Camden
Dist., S. C., for Ᏸ 100...land on both sides of Crooked Run of First Broad
River including his own Improvement near a path leading from to POLK to DAVISES, 400 A...

JOHN POLK (SEAL), AGNIS POLK (O) (SEAL), Wit: UEL LAMKIN, SAMUEL WALLACE. Rec. Oct. term 1778.

Page 410: 29 Nov 1774, WILLIAM NEVAN of Rowan Co., to ARCHIBALD WHITE of Mecklenburg Co., for Ƚ 60 NC money...land on S fork Camp Creek, 250 A...WILLIAM NEVANS (SEAL), Wit: JOSEPH WALKER, SAMUEL WHITE, ARCHIBALD WHITE. Rec. Oct. term 1778.

Pp. 411-412: 9 Mar 1773, THOMAS BETTY, wf MARGARET,ABEL BETTY & MARY BETTY of N. C. to JAMES KERR of Rowan Co., for Ƚ 45...land granted to CHARLES BETTY, now decd, but became THOMAS BETTY, ABEL BETTYS & MARY BETTYS by his L. W. & T., granted 31 Mar 1753...land on S side Catawba River on waters of & on Stony Creek, part of a tract surveyed for CHARLES BEATY & THOMAS BEATY adj. near JOHN BETTYS land, & bought of JOHN CHITALM, 400 A...THOMAS BEATY (SEAL), MARGARET BEATY (Ƚ) (SEAL), ABEL BEATY (SEAL), MATTHEW ARMSTRONG (SEAL), MARY ARMSTRONG (SEAL), Wit: MATTHEW McCORKEL, JOHN RICE. Rec. Oct. term 1778.

Page 412: 21 Nov 1776, JACOB DEVOLD of Guilford Co., Miller to GARROTT WILL of Tryon Co., Farmer, for Ƚ 28 proc. money...land on Goxy Branch of Killion Creek, 243 A ...JACOB DAVOLD (X) (SEAL), Wit: JOHANNES WILL, ADAM STARR, MARGARET STARR (X). Rec. Oct. term 1778.

Page 413: 25 May 1776, WALLACE BEATY of Tryon Co., planter, to ROBERT CARRUTH of same, planter, for Ƚ 30 proc. money...land on muddy fork of Buffalo Creek, granted to sd. WALLACE BEATY by the L. W. & T. of FRANCIS BEATY decd, granted to sd. FRANCIS 13 Oct 1765...WALLACE BEATEY (SEAL), Wit: HUGH BEATY, WALTER CARRUTH. Rec. Oct. term 1778.

Pp. 413-414: 12 Aug 1778, WILLIAM HARRIS & wf ANNA of Tryon Co., to JOHN McCLURE, for Ƚ 400 proc. money...240 A on S side S Fork Catawba near ROBERT PATTERSON, part of a tract granted to WILLIAM McCONNELL 23 Feb 1754, conveyed to JAMES HARRIS by L & R 18 Jan 1764, then to JOHN HARRIS by deed 17 Sept 1765, then to WILLIAM HARRIS Oct 1774...WILLIAM HARRIS (SEAL), ANNA HARRIS (+) (SEAL), Wit: JOHN HARRIS, JOSEPH NEEL, JONATHAN GULLICK. Rec. Oct. term 1778.

Pp. 415-416: 1 Apr 1778, JOHN McKNITT ALEXANDER of Mecklenburg Co., to CHARLES STICE of Tryon Co., for Ƚ 90 circulating currency...land, part of one tract of 640 A pattened in the name of RICHARD BERRY 26 Sept 1766, and conveyed to sd. ALEXANDER 20 Aug 1775, & the other tract of 200 A pattened in the name of sd. ALEXANDER 4 Mar 1775... JN. Mc. ALEXANDER (SEAL), Wit: SAMUEL HAMRICK, WILLIAM COPELAND. Rec. Oct. term 1778.

Page 416: 17 Jan 1778, STEPHEN SHELTON of Tryon Co., to THOMAS MURRY of same, for Ƚ 90 ...land on W side First Little Broad River, part of a tract granted to sd. SHELTON 22 May 1772 adj. JAMES LOGAN, including the plantation where sd. SHELTON lives, 100 A...STEPHEN SHELTON (SEAL), Wit: JOHN ANDERSON, ALEXANDER DAVIDSON. Rec. Oct. term 1778.

Pp. 417-418: 9 Mar 1773, THOMAS BEATY & wf MARGARET,ABEL & MARY BETTY, of Tryon Co., to JAMES KERR of Rowan Co., for Ƚ 46 proc. money...land granted to CHARLES BETTY (now deceased), but became THOS BETTYS,ABEL BETTYS & MARY BETTS by his L. W. & T. ...land on S side Catawba on waters of Long Creek and Hogans Creek, including a Buffaloe Lick adj. JOHN JACHARDS, KILLIONS, HOGANS...THOMAS BEATY (SEAL), MARGRET BETTY (X) (SEAL), ABEL BETTY (SEAL), MATHEW ARMSTRONG (SEAL), MARY ARMSTRONG (SEAL), Wit: _____, JOHN REED. [illegible name may be MATTHEW McCORCLE]. Rec. Oct. term 1778.

Pp. 418-419: 9 Mar 1773, JAMES KERR of Rowan Co., to WILLIAM TATE of Orange Co., NC, for Ƚ 50 proc. money...land granted to CHARLES BETTY & THOS BETTY, adj. near JOHN BETTYS, & Bought of JOHN CHISOLM, conveyed by Heirs of sd. CHARLES BETTY to sd. JAMES KERR...JAMES KERR (SEAL), Wit: MATHEW McCORKELL, JOHN REED. Rec. Oct. term 1778.

Pp. 419-420: 9 Mar 1773, JAMES KERR to WILLIAM TATE of Orange Co., for Ƚ 50...land conveyed to sd. KERR by heirs of CHARLES BETTY on waters of Lantys and Hogans Creek including a Buffaloe Lick adj. JOHN JACKARD, KILLION, HAGARS[?]...[same signature and wit.] Rec. Oct. term 1778.

Pp. 420-421: 28 Sept 1778, ADAM SMITH of Tryon Co., to THOS WARDEN of same, for Ƚ 40... land on both sides Howards Creek below NICOLAS FRIDAYS land including the shoals on sd. creek, 300 A granted TETER HAVNER 29 Apr 1768, and conveyed by sd. HAVNER to HENRY HILDEBRAND 21 Oct 1768, and to ADAM SMITH 28 __ 1774...ADAM SMITH (+) (SEAL), Wit VALLENTINE COON, MARGET COON (X). Rec. Oct. term 1778.

Pp. 421-422: 22 Oct 1778, JAMES HENDERSON of Tryon Co., to WILLIAM PORTER of same, for
Ł 400 NC money...300 A granted to DANIEL McCARTY 26 Oct 1767, then to JAMES
HENDERSON...JAMES HENDERSON (SEAL), Wit: JAMES COOK, JACOB CARPENTER, MICHAEL EAKER.
Rec. Oct. term 1778.

Pp. 422-423: 17 July 1778, JOHN CATHEY SENR. of Mecklenburg Co., to THOMAS ROBINSON of
Tryon Co., for Ł 250 proc. money...621 A between the North and South Forks
of the Catawbar River near the waggon road leading the Tuckaseege Ford near JAMES BEATEYS
corner, granted to JOHN CATHEY 12 Mar 1753...JOHN CATHEY (SEAL), Wit: CHARLES MATTOX,
ROBERT BERKLEY, ARCHIBALD CATHEY. Rec. Oct. term 1778.

Pp. 423-424: 17 Jan 1776, THOMAS HESLIP of Tryon Co., to WILLIAM BURGESS of same, for Ł
20 proc.money...land on S side Green River, 40 A, adj. EDWARD HOGANS, granted
to JAMES CRAWFORD 22 Dec 1768, granted to WILLIAM SHARP by deed 10 Apr 1769, then to
EDWARD HOGAN 18 Nov 1772, then to HESLIP 1775...THOMAS HESLEP (SEAL), Wit: ANTHONY MET-
CALF, EDWARD HOGAN (S), Rec. Oct. term 1778.

Page 424: 19 Oct 1778, ROBERT McMINN of Tryon Co., to ABRAHAM KUYKENDAL, for Ł 80...land
on both sides Sandy Run of Broad River, 100 A granted to AARON BURLISON 1766,
...ROBERT McMINN (SEAL), Wit: JOHN KUYKENDALE, WALLACE JOHNSON. Rec. Oct. term 1778.

Page 425: 11 Sept 1777, REBECCAH GILKEY of Tryon Co., to JOHN GILKEY of same, for Ł 80
proc. money...300 A granted to sd. REBECCAH GILKEY 9 Dec 1774 adj. MOORE, on a
branch of Camp Creek...REBECCAH GILKEY (N) (SEAL), Wit: WILLIAM PORTER, ROBERT GILKEY.
Rec. Oct. term 1778.

Page 426: 25 Oct 1777, WILLIAM EAGER of Mecklenburgh Co., to GEORGE BLACK Esqr. of Tryon
Co., for Ł 500 proc. money...350 A on both sides Second Broad River, granted
to JOHN MCKNIT ALEXANDER 28 Oct 1765, # 48, and 170 A adj. to other tract, granted to sd.
ALEXANDER, conveyed 29 Aug 1774...WILLIAM EGER (SEAL), Wit: ADAM EDGER, ROBT. HARRIS.
Rec. Oct. term 1778.

Pp. 426-427: 21 Oct 1778, WILLIAM HENRY of Tryon Co., to SAMUEL BELL of same, for Ł 100...
200 A on both sides E branch of Mountain Creek, granted to JAMES DOUGHERTY
2 Dec 1770...WILLIAM HENRY (SEAL), Wit: ARTHER TAYLOR, WILLIAM YANCEY. Rec. Oct. term
1778.

Pp. 427-428: 30 Dec 1776, JOHN BEEMAN of Rowan Co., to SAMUEL McMURRY, yeoman, of Tryon
Co., for Ł 80 NC money...250 A on both sides Robinsons Creek...JOHN BEEMAN
(SEAL), Wit: HENRY CALLAHAN, EDWARD CALLAHAN (X). Rec. Oct. term 1778.

Pp. 428-429: 11 Oct 1777, ARCHIBALD WHITE of Mecklenburg Co., planter, to WILLIAM DUNN
of Tryon Co., for Ł 80 NC money...land on S fork Camp Creek...ARCHIBALD
WHITE (SEAL), MARY WHITE (X) (SEAL), Wit: SAMUEL[LEMUEL?] WHITE, ADAM EDGER. Rec. Oct.
term 1778.

Pp. 429-430: 21 Oct 1778, PETER JOHNSON of Mecklenburg Co., to JOHN KIRKCONNEL, for Ł 100
proc. money...land on Grassy branch of Camp Creek adj. BRADLEY, granted to
sd. JOHNSTON 2 Mar 1775, 300 A...PETER JOHNSTON (SEAL), Wit: AND NEEL, JAMES BAIRD.
Rec. Oct. term 1778.

Pp. 430-431: 21 Oct 1778, PETER JOHNSTON to JOHN KIRKCONNEL, for Ł 100 proc. money...land
on both sides Knobb Creek adj. JOSEPH ENGLAND, JAMES ADAMS, granted to sd.
JOHNSTON 28 Feb 1775, 300 A...PETER JOHNSTON (SEAL), Wit: AND NEEL, JAMES BAIRD. Rec.
Oct. term 1778.

Pp. 431-432: 21 Oct 1778, PETER JOHNSTON to JOHN KIRKCONNELL, for Ł 100 proc. money...
350 A granted to sd. JOHNSTON 2 Mar 1775, on branches of Nob Creek of Broad
River, adj. GOOD, JOSEPH RICHEY, JOSEPH GOOD...[Same signature and wit]. Rec. Oct. term
1778.

Pp. 432-433: 21 Oct 1778, PETER JOHNSTON to JOHN KIRKCONNELL, for Ł 100 proc. money...
land on N fork White Oak Creek of Green River on or near JOEL BLACKWELLS
line, 250 A granted to sd. JOHNSTON 2 Mar 1775...PETER JOHNSTON (SEAL), [Same wit.] Rec.
Oct. term 1778.

Pp. 434-435: 21 Oct 1778, PETER JOHNSTON to JOHN KERKCONNELL for Ł 100 proc. money...
200 A granted to sd. JOHNSTON, 2 Mar 1775 on both sides south fork of First
Broad River...[Same signature and wit.] Rec. Oct. term 1778.

Pp. 435-436: 21 Oct 1778, PETER JOHNSTON to JOHN KIRKCONNELL, for Ł 100 proc. money...
land on S side of the east fork of Robinsons Creek of Broad River including
the meadow, granted to sd. JOHNSTON 2 May 1775, 200 A...[Same signature and wit.] Rec.
Oct. term 1778.

Pp. 436-437: 28 Mar 1778, ANDREW NEEL of Tryon Co., to JOHN KIRKCONNEL of Beaufort Co.,
same state, for Ł 100 proc. money...land on a branch of Catheys Creek including RILEYS improvement, 400 A granted to sd. NEEL 2 Mar 1775...ANDW NEEL (SEAL), Wit:
PETER JOHNSTON, WM. GILBERT. Rec. Oct. term 1778.

Pp. 437-438: 28 Mar 1778, ANDREW NEEL to JOHN KIRKCONNEL, for Ł 40 proc. money...land on
N side Broad River including AARON RYLEYS improvements, 60 A granted to
sd. NEEL 2 Mar 1775...[Same signature and wit]. Rec. Oct. term 1778.

Pp. 438-439: 28 Mar 1778, ANDREW NEEL to JOHN KIRKCONNEL for Ł 100 proc. money...land on
both sides S fork Broad River, 200 A granted to sd. NEEL 2 Mar 1775...[same
signature and wit.] Rec. Oct. term 1778.

JANUARY COURT 1779.

Pp. 439-440: 20 Dec 1775, THOMAS HESLIP of Tryon Co., to EDWARD HOGAN of same, for Ł 19
proc. money...10 A on N side Green River, part of a tract conveyed to sd.
HOGAN 13 Feb 1775...THOMAS HESLIP (SEAL), Wit: JOHN MORRISS, ANDW. HAMILTON, DAVID LEWIS,
JR. Rec. Jan. term 1779.

Page 440: 21 Jan 177_, WM. CALLAHAN of Tryon Co., to WILLIAM WHITE, for Ł 150...land on
both sides Hunting Creek below WITHROWS, 200 A granted to JAMES ANDREWS 9 Apr
1770...WILLIAM CALLAHAN (SEAL), Wit: WILLM ROBERTSON, EDWARD CALAHAN. Rec. Jan. term
1779.

Page 441: 16 Jan 1779, DAVID McBRIDE of Tryon Co., to WILLIAM NEVELL of same, for Ł 150
proc. money...land on both sides Green River, adj. lands of GEORGE PEARIS,
250 A...DAVID McBRIDE (SEAL), MARGET McBRIDE (SEAL), Wit: GEORGE WOLF (G), JEREMIAH Mc-
DONAL. Rec. Jan. term 1779.

Pp. 441-443: 22 Nov 1778, JONES WILLIAMS of Tryon Co., to MARY BRADLEY of same, for Ł 50
proc.money...100 A, part of a grant to WM. SHARP...JONES WILLIAMS (X) (SEAL),
Wit: JONATH. HAMPTON, THOMAS WILLIAMS (X). Rec. Jan. term 1779.

Page 443: 22 Dec 1778, JAMES McCOMB & wf MARY of Tryon Co., to JOHN BEALE of same, for
Ł 150...land on W side Catawba on W side Killions Creek, 157 A & another
tract of 78 A adj. sd. McCOMBS old survey & adj. HAGAR...JAMES McCOMB (SEAL), MARY Mc-
COMB (⌒) (SEAL), Wit: RICHARD BEALE, JAMES NEWLY. Rec. Jan. term 1779.

Pp. 443-445: 14 Nov 1778, JAMES MILLER of Tryon Co., to ISAAC LEDBETTER of same, for Ł
130 proc. money...land on both sides Broad River including the mouth of two
Creeks, 200 A granted to WM. BASSETT 20 Apr 1767, conveyed to JAMES MILLER 1 Aug 1772...
JS MILLER (SEAL), Wit: WM. GILBERT, THOMAS MORRISS, WILLIAM DUNN. Rec. Jan. term 1779.

Pp. 445-446: 23 July 1778, THOMAS BEATY, HUGH BEATY & ROBERT ARMSTRONG, Exrs. of FRANCIS
BEATY, to JAMES PALLEY, all of Tryon Co., for Ł 40...400 A on Shoally branch
of Muddy fork of Buffalo Creek, MOORES corner, granted to BENJAMIN SHAW 26 Sept 1766...
THOMAS BEATY (SEAL), HUGH BEATY (SEAL), ROBERT ARMSTRONG (SEAL), Wit: ADAM NELL[?],
JAMES BEATEY, WALLACE BEATY. Rec. Jan. term 1779.

Pp. 446-447: 1 Feb 1770, JOHN TEMPLETON & wf MARGARET of Rowan Co., to JAMES DICKEY of
Tryon Co., for Ł 27...land on N side Broad River, on W side Mountain Creek,
on the Polk Branch, granted to JOHN TEMPLETON 25 Sept 1766...JOHN TEMPLETON (SEAL),
MARGARET TEMPLETON (SEAL), Wit: ABRAHAM YELTON[?], HUGH KILPATRICK. Rec. Jan. term 1779.

Pp. 447-448: 12 Dec 1778, CHRISTIAN CARPENTER of Tryon Co., to ISAAC WHITE of same, for
Ł 200 proc. money...300 A, the land NICHOLAS WISENANT lived on, granted to
ADAM WISENANT, 30 Oct 1765, purchased by sd. CARPENTER to NICHOLAS WISENANT, 24 Jan 1775,
adj. HAGER...CHRISTIAN CARPENTER (CB)(SEAL), Wit: JAMES WHITE, HENRY HOGEN (X). Rec. Jan.
term 1779

Pp. 448-449: 21 Jan 1779, PHILIP WISENANT of Tryon Co., to JOHN HARRIS of same, for Ł 200
...land on waters of Indian Creek, adj. ADAM WISENANTS land, HOWARD lands...
granted to sd. PHILLIP 14 Nov 1771..._____ [German signature] (SEAL), Wit: AD: OSBORN,
ANDW NEEL., B. BOOTH. Rec. Jan. term 1779

Pp. 449-450: 19 Sept 1778, DAVID NESBET, merchant in Rowan Co., to JOHN WILSON of Tryon
Co., for Ł 250 proc. money...416 A on S side Cataba on middle fork of Crow-
ders Creek adj. WM. INHINS[?]...DAVID NESBIT (SEAL), Wit: JONAS BEDFORD, JOHN HILL, TIMO.
RIGGS. Rec. Jan. term 1779.

Pp. 450-451: 27 Mar 1776, ROBERT HESLIP of Tryon Co., to CHRISTOPHER HOYLE, planter, of
same, for Ł 60 proc. money...370 A on W side S fork Cataba, adj. JACOB
HORSES corner, adj. WADDLES line, PALMERS line...ROBERT HESLIP (R) (SEAL), MARY HESLIP (X)
(SEAL), Wit: DAVID RAMSEY and Two German signatures. Rec. Jan. term 1779.

Pp. 451-452: 19 Oct 1778, JOHN WALKER Esq. to JAMES COOK SENR., for Ł 70 proc. money....
tract of 79 A, part of 300 A on Catheys Creek between WALKERs and COOKS land,
adj. BARR...granted to WALKER 23 Dec 1768, No. 514. JOHN WALKER (SEAL), Wit: WM. POLER,
WM. ROBERTSON, JOHN GLACK. Rec. Jan. term 1779.

Pp. 452-453: 7 Dec 1778, JAS. SWAFFORD of Tryon Co., to PERRYGREEN MAGNIS, by virute of
a patent 8 Feb 1774,, land on both sides Brushy Creek of First little Broad
River, 300 A...JAMES SWAFFORD (J) (SEAL), Wit: UEL LAMKIN, JOEL BAUGHAN. Rec. Jan. term
1779.

Pp. 453-454: 20 May 1778, SAMUEL HUNTER of Camden Dist., S. C. to EATON HOKINGS[?], of
Tryon Co., for Ł 25...150 A on S side First little Broad River, part of a
grant to STEPHEN SHELTON, 22 May 1772...SAM: HUNTER (SEAL), Wit: GEO. BLANTON, THOS
HARRIS (X), Rec. Jan. term 1779.
[The remaining deeds in this volume were recorded in Lincoln County].

Pp. 454-455: 20 Nov 1778, MARY ORMOND of Mecklenburg Co., widow, to BENJAMIN ORMOND of
Tryon Co., for Ł 30 proc. money...land on S side S fork Catawba, on the
head of Long Creek adj. the little mountain, 400 A granted to JAMES ORMOND, decd, 30 Mar
1754...MARY ORMOND (𝒪) (SEAL), Wit: ISAAC PRICE, JOHN FLENNIKEN. Rec. Apr. term 1779.

Pp. 455-456: 27 Aug 1777, ROBERT SHANNON of Tryon Co., to THOMAS NORMAN of same, for Ł 36
...200 A on the dividing ridge between Little Catawba and Crowders Creek, in
or near HUGH TORRENCES line, NATHANIEL ALDRIDGES line, granted to JAMES SCOTT 28 Apr
1768, conveyed to sd. SHANNON by deed 5 Feb 1775...ROBERT SHANNON (SEAL), Wit: JOHN MOORE,
HUGH TORRANCE, WILLIAM CAIRNS. Rec. Apr. term 1779.

Pp. 456-457: 20 Sept 1778, JAMES HENDERSON to JAMES MILKERAN of Tryon Co., for Ł 40 NC
money...land on S side S fork Catawba, a little below EWINS ford, adj.
DEHARTS Creek, near GILMORES line...JAMES HENDERSON (SEAL), Wit: WILLIAM McCORD, JOHN
MOSHALZ[?], ANDREW BARRY. Rec. Apr. term 1779.

Pp. 457-458: 2 Jan 1779, JOHN WELLS to JOHN CARPENTER JUNR, both of Tryon Co., for Ł 22
proc. money...land on the Kettle Shoal, branch of the S fork Catawba River,
adj. KETTLES corner, 200 A granted to sd. WELLS 28 Feb 1775...JOHN WELLS (ℋℋ (SEAL),
Wit: JOHN DELLINGER, ISAAC WHITE. Rec. Apr. term 1779.

Page 458: 25 Jan 1779, MICHAEL SEITS of Tryon Co., to HENRY McMILIEN of same, for Ł 20
proc. money...75 A granted to JACOB FORNEY, DAVID CRITS, and PAUL WISENHUNT
for 225 A...MICHAEL SEITS (SEAL), Wit: RICHARD BEALE, JOHN BEALE. Rec. Apr. term 1779.

Page 459: 19 Apr 1779, WILLIAM GRAHAM of Lincoln Co., to PETER LABOON of same, for Ł 300
....land on S fork Catawba River, on Kettle Shoal, 300 A, granted to JAMES
COZART, 19 May 1772...W. GRAHAM (SEAL),, Wit: ANDW NEEL, _____ [German signature], WILLIAM
TWITTY. Rec. Apr. term 1779.

Page 460: 27 Feb 1779, HENRY VERNOR of Tryon Co., to JOHN GRAHAM of same, for Ł 20 proc.
money...300 A on waters of Crowders Creek, adj. sd. VERNORS, WALKERS, & COBURNS
...HENRY VARNER (N) (SEAL), Wit: JON. DUNWOODY, JAMES MARTEN, ALEXANDER GILLELAND. Rec.
Apr. term 1779.

Pp. 460-462: 15 Apr 1779, JAMES HENDERSON of Lincoln to JOHN EWING of same, for Ł 50...
land in the forks of the Catawba River, granted to JAMES CARTER[?], and by
fyre facias against him by JOHN BRANDON, in the term of February XXII by the proceedings
of a court of then county of New Hanover, Bladen, Onslow, &c....sold by BRANDON to THOMAS
McKNIGHT, 6 & 7 Jan 1763...JAMES HENDERSON (SEAL), Wit: GEORGE LAMKIN, SAMUEL RANKIN,
JAMES PALLEY. Rec. Apr. term 1779.

Pp. 462-463: 23 Apr 1779, JOHN HOUFSTATLER of Lincoln Co., to ROBERT FERGUSON of same,
for Ł 30 NC money...300 A granted to sd. HUFSTATLER 26 July 1774..._____
_____ [German signature]. Wit: JNO WILSON, THOS ESPEY, SAMUEL DUNAWAY. Rec. Apr. term
1779.

Pp. 463-464: 20 Apr 1779, CHARLES McLEAN of Lincoln Co., to JOHN OATS of same, for Ł 375
...land on upper fork of Crowders Creek, 243 A, part of 300 A granted to
JONATHAN NEWMAN, 21 Apr 1764 and conveyed to sd. McLEAN...CHARLES McLEAN (SEAL), Wit:
ARCHIBALD ALLISON, SAMUEL ESPY. Rec. Apr. term 1779.

Pp. 464-465: 11 Mar 1779, JAMES WHITE of Lincoln Co., yeoman, to THOMAS WHITE of same,
yeoman, for Ł 300 continental money...land on W side of South Fork Waggon
Road near ADAM MEEK, THOMAS WELCH, granted to MOSES FERGUSON 28 Oct 1765, 300 A...
JAMES WHITE (SEAL), Wit: JOSEPH NEEL, JONATHAN THOMAS GIVENS. Rec. Apr. term 1779.

Pp. 465-466: 29 Dec 1778, ROBERT MECOMB & wf MARGARET of Tryon Co., to ROBERT ABERNATHY
JR. of same, for Ł 80 proc. money...land at the mouth of Mecombs Springbranch
adj. WISHART, 150 A...ROBT MECOMB (SEAL), MARGARET MECOMB (SEAL), Wit: RICHARD BEALE,
MILES ABERNATHY. Rec. Apr. term 1779.

Pp. 466-467: 28 Mar 1778, JOHN MARTEN, cooper & wf MARY of Tryon Co., to JAMES MARTEN,
planter, for Ł 100 NC money...208 A on waters of Crowders Creek adj. JOHN
MARTIN...JOHN MARTEN (SEAL), MARY MARTEN (M) (SEAL), Wit: JOHN BARBER, ROBERT ALLISON.
Rec. Apr. term 1779.

Page 467: 28 Aug 1778, JAMES SAUNDERS of Anson Co., to RICHARD SAUNDERS of Tryon Co., for
Ł 100 north currency...150 A near FERGUSON, granted to JEREMIAH & KATHERINE
SMITH, 25 Feb 1775...JAMES SAUNDERS (SEAL), Wit: GEORGE LAMKINS, DANIEL GRAY (D). Rec.
Apr. term 1779.

Page 468: 21 Nov 1778, WILLIAM SMITH JR of Tryon Co., to JOHN ASHLEY of same, for Ł 50
north currency...land on head branches of Duharts Creek, adj. DAVIS, part of
a grant to NATHAN DAVIES for 250 A, 25 Jan 1773...WILLIAM SMITH (SEAL), Wit: GEORGE LAM-
KINS, GEORGE LAMKINS JR., JOSEPH MASSEY. Rec. Apr. term 1779.

Pp. 468-469: 19 Sept 1778, WILLIAM SMITH JR. of Tryon Co., to WILLIAM DAVIES of same, for
Ł 20 north currency...100 A on W side S fork Catawba and on head branches
of Duharts Creek, adj. to sd. SMITH part of 250 A granted to NATHAN DAVIES, 25 Jan 1773...
WILLIAM SMITH (SEAL), Wit: GEORGE LAMKINS, JEAN LAMKIN. Rec. Apr. term 1779.

Pp. 469-470: 22 Mar 1779, JACOB HUFSEDLER to CHRISTIAN MAUNY, both of Tryon Co., for Ł
24...land on both sides Jacob Fork of Long Creek including his own improvement where he now lives...200 A granted to HOOFSTEDLER 28 Mar 1775...JACOB HOOFSTEDLAR
(Ϫ) (SEAL), Wit: ROBT FERGUSON, JACOB MONEY (X). Rec. Apr. term 1779.

Pp. 470-471: 4 Jan 1779, MICHAEL SEITS of Tryon Co., to HENRY McMILON of same, for Ł 100
proc. money...200 A on S branch of Killians Creek, granted to sd. SEITS 23
Dec 1763...MICHAEL SEITS (SEAL), Wit: RICHARD BEALE, JOHN BEALE. Rec. Apr. term 1779.

Pp. 471-472: 13 July 1778, DAVID ELDER of Tryon Co., farmer to JAMES PATTERSON, of same,
Taylor, for Ł 100 proc. money...land on W side Catawba, adj. ROBERT ARMSTRONG,
CHRONICLE, & ELDER, part of a tract conveyed by SAMUEL YOUNG, then to JOHN KUYKENDAL,
decd, then to JOSEPH HARDIN, then to FREDERICK HAMBRIGHT, then to ROGER COOK, then to
WILLIAM PATTERSON, then to DAVID ELDER...DAVID ELDER (SEAL), Wit: JONATHAN GULLICK, AND.
HOIL[?]. Rec. Apr. term 1779.

Pp. 472-473: 29 Jan 1779, THOMAS NORMAN of Tryon Co., to NATHANIEL ALDRICH of same, for
Ł 55 proc. money...200 A on the dividing ridge between Little Cataba and
Crowders Creek, granted to JAMES SCOTT 28 Apr 1768, conveyed to ROBERT SHANNON 5 Feb
1775, to THOMAS NORMAN 27 Aug 1777...THOS NORMAN (SEAL), Wit: ALEXR ROBINSON, JONATHAN
GULLICK. Rec. Apr. term 1779.

Pp. 473-474: 10 Feb 1778, JOHN MOORE SR. of Tryon Co., to JAMES GRAHAM of same, for Ł 50
proc. money...190 A on W side Catawba on Kuykendalls Creek, between JAMES
ARMSTRONG & JAMES KUYKENDALL, granted to JOHN MOORE 24 Sept 1754...JOHN MOORE (SEAL),
Wit: WILLIAM MOORE, WILLM McCLERY. Rec. Apr. term 1779.

Pp. 474-475: 17 Aug 1777, WILLIAM STERRETT & wf RUTH of Tryon Co., to EBENEZER NEWTON
of same, for Ł 185 proc. money...216 A , part of 3 patents (1) granted to
WM. HENRY 28 Feb 1754 (2) granted to ANDREW McNABB 6 Apr 1765 (3) to SAMUEL YOUNG 26
Nov 1757...on McNabbs branch falling into Cataba, a little belww the Tuckesiege ford...
WILLIAM STARET (SEAL), RUTH STERRETT (X) (SEAL), Wit: GEORGE LAMKIN, ROBT. ALEXANDER,
ABM. SCOTT. Rec. Apr. term 1779

Pp. 475-476: 10 July 1779, JOSEPH ABERNATHY of Lincoln Co., to DAVID ABERNATHY, for ₤ 60 ...land on a fork of Hoyles Creek, a little above WILLIAM SMITH...JOSEPH ABERNATHY (SEAL), Wit: ROBT ABERNATHY, JAS. FREEMAN. Rec. July term 1779.

Pp. 476-477: 23 Nov 1776, NATHANIEL EWING of Roan Co., to JOSEPH ABERNATHY of Tryon Co., for ₤ 40 proc. money...land on the fork of Hoils Creek, a little above WILLIAM SMITH, granted to WILLIAM ANDERSON 16 Nov 1764...NATHL EWING (SEAL), Wit: DAVID ABERNATHY, THOMAS WAGGENER, MILES ABERNATHY. Rec. July term 1779.

Page 477: 10 July 1776, RICHARD WALKER of Tryon Co., to WILLIAM ALSTON of Guilford Co., for   for ₤ 50 proc. money...land on both sides Long Creek adj. JACOB ROPNOD[?], 200 A...RICHARD WALKER (SEAL), Wit: DANIEL WALKER (N), MARY WALKER (R), GEORGE LAMKIN, GEORGE LAMKIN, JR. Rec. July term 1779.

Pp. 477-478: 14 Oct 1778, NATHAN DAVIS of Tryon Co., planter, to JOHN BOIDE of same, planter, for ₤ 25 proc. money...93 1/2 A on W side Dutchmans Creek, about a mile from the mouth, on road leading from Tuckasiege ford to a dreen[sic] falling into Beaver Dam Creek by SARAH KUYKENDALL, granted to JOSEPH DAVIS ELDER, 6 May 1769...NATHAN DAVIS (SEAL), Wit: JOHN BROWN SKRIMSHIRE, JOHN STURRET, JAMES BUCKNAN. Rec. July term 1779.

Pp. 478-480: 14 Jan 1778, JAMES MILCUM & wf MARTHA of Tryon Co., to JOHN McGILL and JOSEPH BLACKWOOD of Mecklenburg Co., for ₤ 200 proc. money...land granted to PETER SUMMEY, 13 Oct 1765 & conveyed to PATRICK MILLER 30 Jan 1775, to JAMES MILCUM __ May 1775, on both sides Long Creek...JAMES MILCUM (HH) (SEAL), Wit: WM. BLACKWOOD, JOHN CARSON, WM. KERR. Rec. July term 1779.

Page 480: 24 Oct 1777, GEORGE LAMKIN of Tryon Co., to VINCENT COX of same, for ₤ 40 north currency...98 A on W side Cataba, adj. MOSES BOWERS, part of a grant to SAMUEL COBURN 26 Oct 1767...GEORGE LAMKIN   (SEAL), Wit: JAMES COBRUN, GEORGE LAMKIN. Rec. July term 1779.

Pp. 480-481: 21 July 1778, GEORGE WEST of Tryon Co., to VINCENT COX of same, for ₤ 60... 100 A on W side Catawba, adj. COX, part of a grant to SAML COBURN, 26 Oct 1767...GEORGE WEST (+) (SEAL), Wit: JACOB SEITS, MARY ABERNATHY. Rec. July term 1779.

Pp. 481-482: 30 Aug 1778, JOHN STROUD & wf MARTHA of Tryon Co., to PETER DUNKIN of same, for ₤ 20 proc. money...109 A on waters of Leepers Creek, adj. MORRISON, STROUD, part of a grant to sd. STROUD 25 Jan 1773...JOHN STROUD (X) (SEAL), Wit: MARTHA STROUD (0) (SEAL), Wit: MILES ABERNATHY, BATTEE ABERNATHY. Rec. July term 1779.

Pp. 482-483: 21 June 1777, MARTIN SHUTTS of Tryon Co., Doctor, & wf JULIANNA, to NICHOLAS STRUM & HENRY DELLINGER of same, for ₤ 70...land on waters of Leepers Creek & Lick Run, adj. JOHN DELLINGER, 300 A granted to HENRY DELLINGER 6 Apr 1765, and conveyed to SHUTTS 15 Jan 1767..._____, _____ [Both German signatures]. Wit: ROBERT JOHNSTON, _____ [German signature]. Rec. July term 1779.

Page 484: 13 July 1778, JAMES PATTERSON of Tryon Co., Taylor to DAVID ELDER of same, for ₤ 100 proc. money...140 A on S side S fork Catawba adj. JAMES PATTERSONs old corner, granted to ADEN[sic] ALEXANDER 4 Sept 1753, conveyed to NATHANIEL HENDERSON, 20 Nov 1762, then to sd. PATTERSON 1 Jan 1776...JAMES PATTERSON (SEAL), Wit: JONATHAN GULLICK, ANDW FLOID. Rec. July term 1779.

Pp. 484-485: 30 July 1778, JAMES PATTERSON to DAVID ELDER, for ₤ 100...160 A adj. NATHL HENDERSON, JAMES BAIRD, granted to NATHANL HENDERSON 16 Nov 1764, and conveyed to PATTERSON 1 Jan 1776...JAMES PATTERSON (SEAL), Wit: JONATHAN GULLICK, AND. FLOID. Rec. July term 1779.

Pp. 485-486: 6 May 1778, JOHN FULENWIDER of Rowan Co., to MARTIN PHIFER of Mecklenburg Co., for ₤ 40...part of land made over to sd. FULENWIDER by MARTIN PHIFER, on S fork Catawba, 46 A...JOHN FULENWIDER (SEAL), Wit: JASON FRISSELL, JOHN DUNN. Rec. July term 1779.

Pp. 486-487: 21 Apr 1779, CHARLES McLEAN of Lincoln Co., to PETER HAMMON of same, for ₤ 25...57 A, part of 300 A granted to JONATHAN NEWMAN 21 Apr 1764, and conveyed to sd. McLEAN...CHARLES McLEAN (SEAL), Wit: ANNE LELAND, JAMES McCEFY (₤) [McAFEE?]. Rec. July term 1779.

Page 488: 14 May 1779, JOHN KINKAID of Lincoln Co., to JAMES KINKAID of same, for Ł 100
        proc. money...150 A on Killions Creek adj. KILLIAN,KINKAID formerly ROBISON...
JOHN KINKAID (0) (SEAL), Wit: JAMES JOHNSTON, JAMES LACKEY, BENJAMIN ARMSTRONG. Rec. July
term 1779.

Pp. 488-489: 18 July 1778, JOHN BOYD of Tryon Co., planter, to SARAH KUYKENDALL of same,
        for Ł 60 proc. money...93 1/2 A on W side Dutchmans Creek about a mile from
the mouth...JOHN BOYD (SEAL), Wit: JAMES KUYKENDALL, SAMUEL RANKIN. Rec. July term 1779.

Pp. 489-490: 28 Nov 1778, JOHN HILL & wf of Tryon Co., to JAMES LUCKY of same, for Ł 480
        ...350[?] A on a branch of Coborns Creek...JOHN HILL(SEAL), Wit: JOHN KIN-
KAID, JOSEPH ABERNATHY. Rec. July term 1779.

Pp. 490-491: 28 Nov 1778, JOHN HILL to JAMES LUCKY, for s 5...___ A on a branch of
        Coborns Creek, adj. KILLIAN, ALEXANDER BALDRIDGE...JOHN HILL (SEAL), Wit:
JOHN KINKAID, JOSEPH ABERNATHY. Rec. July term 1779.

Page 491: 10 Jan 1779, GEORGE LAMKIN of Lincoln Co., to GEORGE LAMKIN JR. of same, for
        Ł 100 North currency...100 A on the head of Nowlens branch, part of a grant to
JOSEPH DAVIES, 400 A, 28 Apr 1768...GEO LAMKIN (SEAL), Wit: AND NEEL. Rec. July term
1779.

Page 492: 21 July 1779, JOHN MOORE of Lincoln Co., to GEORGE LAMKIN of same, for Ł 240...
        400 A where JOSEPH DAVIS late lived, on branches of S fork Catawba, granted to
DAVIES 28 Apr 1768 and conveyed to sd. MOORE...JOHN MOORE (SEAL), Wit: FRED. HAMBRIGHT,
THOMAS ESPEY. Rec. July term 1779.

Pp. 492-493: 21 Jan 1779, DANIEL GRAY of Tryon Co., to JOHN MASSEY of Bute Co., N. C.,
        for Ł 500...150 A on both sides Duholts[sic] Creek adj. BAISEL, granted to
SAMUEL COBURN, and sold to WILLIAM SMITH JR., then to DANIEL GRAY...DANIEL GRAY (0)
(SEAL), Wit: WILLIAM MASSEY, RALPH COBBS. Rec. July term 1779.

Pp. 493-494: 29 Dec 1778, ALEXANDER THOMPSON of Tryon Co., to WILLIAM NANCE of same, for
        Ł 400...200 A on S side Catawba, adj. JOHNSTON, BAULDRIDGE, granted to
JOSEPH SCOTT 25 Apr 1767, conveyed to ALEXANDER WELLS, 25 Oct 1771...ALEXANDER THOMPSON
(X) (SEAL), Wit: ROBT ABERNATHY, RICHARD BEALE, MILES ABERNATHY. Rec. July term 1779.

Pp. 494-495: 27 Feb 1779, JOHN GRAHAM of Tryon Co., to ROBERT PARKES of same, for Ł 70
        proc. money...land granted to HENRY VERNOR 4 May 1769 on waters of Crowders
Creek, adj. HENRY VERNER, WALKER & COBORN, 300 A...JOHN GRAHAM (SEAL), Wit: ISAAC HOLLAND,
MOSES HENDRY, JAMES PARK. Rec. July term 1779.

Pp. 495-496: 4 Mar 1778, WILLIAM TANKERSLEY & wf BARBARA of Tryon Co., to FREDERICK
        RODES of same, for Ł 125 proc. money...land on N side S fork Cataba, on
Hoyles Creek, 300 A, granted 20 Mar1775 to EDWARD BOLE...WILLIAM TANKERSLEY (WT) (SEAL),
BARBARA TANKERSLEY (X) (SEAL), Wit: LANCELOT ARMSTRONG, NICHOLAS FRYDAY, HENRY ROADS.
Rec. July term 1779.

Page 496: 10 Mar 1778, WILLIAM VERNER of Tryon Co., planter, to JOHN SMITH of same,for
        Ł 100...263 A granted to HENRY VERNOR, 29 Apr 1768, and conveyed to WILLIAM
VERNER, adj. WALKER...WILLIAM VERNER (SEAL), Wit: SAMUEL DUNAWAY, MARY DUNAWAY (Ł). Rec.
July term 1779.

Page 497: 23 May 1777, ROBERT ABERNATHY JR. & wf MARY of Tryon Co., to GEORGE SEITS of
        same, for Ł 150...land on S side Catawba on Leepers Creek adj. DAVID ABERNATHY,
BOLDRIDGE, 200 A granted to GEORGE LAMKIN, 15 Apr 1771, and conveyed to sd. ABERNATHY...
ROBERT ABERNATHY (SEAL), MARY ABERNATHY (SEAL), Wit: JACOB SEITS, JOHN WATERS. Rec. July
term 1779.

Page 498: 1 Oct 1778, ROBERT ABERNATHY JR. & wf MARY to GEORGE SEITS, for Ł 200...land
        on branches of Leepers Creek including ROCKERTS improvements, adj. KINDARDS
[sic], ROBERT ABERNATHY. Wit: MILES ABERNATHY, RICHARD BEALE, HARMON DANIEL. Rec. July
term 1779.

Pp. 498-499: 19 Nov 1778, EDWARD WYATT of Tryon Co., to STEPHEN CENTER of same, for Ł 60
        north currency...100 A on Rudesels Creek, adj. RUDASEL, granted to WM.
WYATT 29 Aug 1778...EDWARD WYATT (p) (SEAL), Wit: ANER SENTER (J-her mark), KEZZIAH
SENTER (+). Rec. July term 1779.

Pp. 499-500: 25 Aug 1778, LEWIS LINBARGER & wf BARBARA of Tryon Co., to WILLIAM TANKERS-
LEY of Craven Co., S. C., for ₤ 47...land on Hoils Creek, a little below
Sailers branch...LEWIS LINEBERGER (SEAL), BARBARY LINEBARGER (X) (SEAL), Wit: GASPER
CLOB, MICHAEL MARTER (M). Rec. July term 1779.

Page 500: 2 Mar 1779, PETER LeBON of Tryon Co., to SAMUEL WHITE of same, for ₤ 300 proc.
money...300 A on Licks Branch on SW side S fork Catawba, granted to sd. PETER
LeBON 6 Apr 1765...PETRE LeBON (SEAL), Wit: FREDERICK HAMBRIGHT, ISAAC WHITE. Rec. July
term 1779.

Page 501: 7 Feb 1777, JAMES RUTLEDGE of Tryon Co., to JAMES COBURN of same, for ₤ 10...
land on waters of Kuykendalls Creek, 37 A, part of 300 A granted to JAMES
ARMSTRONG decd, 30 Aug 1753...JAMES RUTLEDGE (SEAL), Wit: JAMES JOHNSTON, JACOB SEITS.
Rec. Oct. term 1779.

Pp. 501-502: 12 Feb 1779, GEORGE LAMKIN of Tryon Co., to JESSE FEATHERSTON of Granville
Co., State aforesd., for ₤ 50 continental money...200 A granted to LAMKIN 2
Mar 1775...Wit: GEORGE COX, SUANOWATH[?] SMITH ( ), JEAN LAMKIN. Rec. Oct. term 1779.

Pp. 502-503: 18 Dec 1777, MATTHEW TROY Esq., & wf ANNE of Rowan Co., fo JAMES McCAVER of
Orange Co., for ₤ 265 proc. money...land on S side S fork Catawba, S side
Long Creek, 350 A granted to sd. TROY 25 Jan 1773...MATT TROY (SEAL), ANNE TROY (X) (SEAL),
Wit: JOHN McCALL, BENJAMIN NEWTON. Rec. Oct. term 1779.

Pp. 503-504: 18 Dec 1777, MATTHEW TROY & wf ANNE of Rowan Co., to JOHN McCALL of Orange
Co., for ₤ 135 proc. money...land on S side McNabbs Creek, on S side
Cataba adj. JOHN ALSTON, PHILIP ALSTON, granted to sd. TROY 25 Jan 1773...Wit: LACUFF
McCAVANT[?], BENJAMIN NEWTON. Rec. Oct. term 1779.

Pp. 504-505: _____ 1779, GEORGE LAMKIN of Lincoln Co., to WILLIAM SMITH JR., fo same,
for ₤ 100...100 A adj. sd. LAMKIN, part of a grant of 400 A to JOSEPH
DAVIS, and conveyed to JOHN MOORE, then to sd. LAMKIN...Wit: GEORGE LAMKIN JR., RALPH
COBB. Rec. Oct. term 1779.

Page 505: 27 July 1779, STEPHEN SENTER of Lincoln Co., to RALPH COBB of same, for ₤ 500
north currency...100 A adj. RUDISAL, granted to WM. WYETT 29 Aug 1768...STEPHEN
SENTER (SEAL), Wit: GEORGE LAMKIN JR., Rec. Oct. term 1779.

Page 506: 26 Sept 1778, JOSEPH GLADEN of Tryon Co, to ALEXANDER KILE for ₤ 150 proc.
money...100 A by deed from GEORGE FREELAND to JOSEPH GLADEN, part of 400 A
granted to ALEXANDER KILE, 5 May 1769...JOSEPH GLADEN (SEAL), Wit: ABEL BEATTY, JOHN
LUSK. Rec. Oct. term 1779.

Pp. 506-507: 19 Oct 1779, ALEXANDER KILE of Lincoln Co., to ROBERT WEER for ₤ 200...100
A [same land in preceding deed]...ALEXANDER KILE (A) (SEAL), Wit: JONATHAN
GULLICK, THOMAS PEARSON, PEREGREEN MAGNES. Rec. Oct. term 1779.

JANUARY COURT 1780.

Pp. 508-509: 2 Oct 1777, THOMAS BEATY & HUGH BEATY of Rowan Co., & ROBERT ARMSTRONG of
Tryon Co., Exrs. of FRANCIS BEATY decd of Mecklenburg Co., for ₤ 57 s 16,
to SAMUEL CARPENTER...land on Nobb Creek near the Nobb, granted to sd. FRANCIS BEATY,
6 Apr 1765...Wit: DAVID BEATY, FRANCIS BEATY, ROBT BEATY. Rec. Jan. term 1780.

Pp. 509-510: 26 Sept 1779, WILLIAM MORRISON of Lincoln Co., to ANTHONY CLARK of same,
for ₤ 1950 NC money...200 A on both side middle fork of Crowders Creek,
granted to sd. MORRISON 16 Dec 1769...WILLIAM MORRISON (SEAL), Wit: GEO: DEMSY, JOHN
KENSLAR, JEAN DEMSY. Rec. Jan. term 1780.

Pp. 511-512: 21 Sept 1778, JAMES HOLLAND of Tryon Co., to JOHN McREYNOLDS of same, for
₤ 75 proc. money...100 A adj. JOHN BRESON, SAMUEL GINGLES, part of a grant
to JOHN GULLICK, 26 Sept 1766 and conveyed to JOHN BRESON 23 Apr 1774, and to sd. HOLLAND
15 Apr 1777...JAS. HOLLAND (SEAL), Wit: ISAAC HOLLAND, JAMES SHANNON. Rec. Jan. term
1780.

Pp. 510-511: 8 Aug 1777, THOMAS DICKSON of Tryon Co., to WILLIAM HENRY of Craven Co.,
S. C., for ₤ 200 NC money...land partly in Tryon County, on both sides of
the boundary line, on W side Cataba, and S fork Crowders Creek, adj. HANCE McWHERTER,
640 A...THOMAS DICKSON (SEAL), Wit: JOHN CHITTIM, MALCOLM HENRY, WILLIAM HENRY. Rec.
Jan. term 1780.

Page 512: 1 Sept 1779, JAMES JOHNSTON of Lincoln Co., to JAMES COBUN of same, for Ł 50
proc. money...land in the forks of Catawba River, on a branch of the Dutchmans
Creek, 200 A granted to SAMUEL RANKIN, 22 Dec 1768...JAMES JOHNSTON (SEAL), Wit: WM.
BERRY, JAMES WILLIAMS, BATTEE ABERNATHY. Rec. Jan. term 1780.

Pp. 512-513: 1 Sept 1779, JAMES JOHNSTON of N. C. to JAMES COBURN of same, for Ł 100 proc.
money...land on Kuykendalls Creek, adj. THOMAS RINES, 183 A...JAMES JOHNSTON
(SEAL), Wit: WM. BERRY, JAMES WILLIAMS, BATTEE ABERNATHY. Rec. Jan.term 1780.

Pp. 513-514: 24 Aug 1779, JOHN McFARLIN of Lincoln Co., to WILLIAM DAVIES of Mecklenburg
Co., for Ł 500 NC money...land on Catawba River adj. WIDOW McKENDRICK,
CLEGHORN, 200 A granted to JOHN McKNITT ALEXANDER, 28 Oct 1765, and conveyed to JOHN
SCOTT, then to WILLIAM ALSTON, then to JOHN McFARLIN...JOHN McFARLIN (SEAL), Wit: JAMES
JOHNSTON, ROBERT BEATEY, ABM. SCOTT.

Pp. 514-515: 24 Aug 1779, JOHN McFARLIN of Lincoln to WILLIAM DAVIES of Mecklenburg Co.,
for Ł 1000 NC money...302 A on S side Catawba, including an Indian path
below the mouth of Dutchmans Creek, granted to SAMUEL COBURN 24 Sept 1754...JOHN McFAR-
LIN (SEAL), Wit: JAMES JOHNSTON, ROBERT BEATEY, AM. SCOTT. Rec. Jan. term 1780.

Page 516: 13 Sept 1779, JOSEPH WISHARD of Mecklenburg Co., to ROBERT ABERNATHY JR. of
Lincoln Co., for Ł 500 NC money...110 A adj. ABERNATHY, SAMUEL JOHNSON...JOSEPH
WISHARD (SEAL), Wit: JOHN BROWN SKRIMSHIRE, SAMUEL JOHNSTON. Rec. Jan. term 1780.

Pp. 516-517: 8 Jan 1780, JOHN DOZER of Lincoln Co., to THOMAS HORTON of same, for Ł 1800
proc. money...100 A on S side Catawba River adj. JOSEPH WISHARD, JAMES
COBURN, JOHN COBURN, SAML COBURN, Part of a grant to SAMUEL COBURN, 176 A, 6 Oct 1767...
and by deed to sd. DOZER 1 Oct 1771...JOHN DOZER (SEAL), Wit: JOHN BROWN; SKRIMSHIRE,
MILES ABERNATHY. Rec. Jan. term 1780.

Pp. 517-518: 19 Jan 1780, RICHARD VENABLES of Lincoln Co., to RICHARD VENABLES JR. of
same, for Ł 200...land on middle fork of Crowders Creek, part of a grant to
EPHRAIM McLEAN, and conveyed to VENABLES 16 Dec 1768...RICHARD VENABLES (X) (SEAL), Wit:
JOHN BARBER, ANTHONY CLARK, JOHN WILSON. Rec. Jan. term 1780.

Pp. 518-519: 19 Jan 1780, JAMES FANNING, son and heir at law of JAMES FANNING of Craven
Co., S. C., to JOHN CURRY of Lincoln County, for _____...300 A on both
sides Kings Creek, granted to JAMES FANNING, 26 Sept 1766...JAMES FANNIN (SEAL), Wit:
JAS STROTHER, SAMUEL BARNET. Rec. Jan. term 1780.

Pp. 519-520: 10 Sept 1779, ROBERT McCOMB of Lincoln Co., to ROBERT ABERNATHY JR., for
Ł 1000 north currency...part of a tract sold by JOSEPH WISHEART to sd.
McCOMB, 50 A...ROBERT McCOMB (SEAL), Wit: JOHN BROWN: SKRIMSHIRE, SAMUEL JOHNSTON. Rec.
Jan. term 1780.

Pp. 520-521: 8 Jan 1780, JOHN STROUD of Lincoln Co., to JOHN DOZER of same, for Ł 400...
land on waters of Coborns Creek, adj. HILL, DUNCAN, part of a grant to
STROUD 28 Feb 1775...JOHN STROUD (P) (SEAL), Wit: JOHN BROWN: SKRIMSHIRE, MILES ABERNATHY.
Rec. Jan. term 1780.

Pp. 521-522: 18 Jan 1780, LAWRENCE KOISER to his son JOSEPH KOISER, both of Lincoln Co.,
for Ł 5...land on a branch of Long Creek near MICHAEL HOFSTEDLARS, & adj.
LAWRENCE KOISER, 300 A granted to sd. LAWRENCE KOISER 250 A, and now the remaining 50
A..._____ [German signature] (SEAL), Wit: ANDW NEEL, JAS. WHITE. Rec. Jan. term 1780.

Page 522: 20 Feb 1777, JOSEPH WISHART of Mecklenburg Co., to ROBERT McCOMB of Tryon
Co., for Ł 240 proc. money...land that he formerly lived on, bought of JOHN
RICHMAN, 16 Jan 1768...JOSEPH WISHEAT (SEAL), Wit: JAMES JOHNSTON, MILES ABERNATHY. Rec.
Jan. term 1780.

Page 523: 6 Jan 1780, ROBERT WIER of Lincoln Co., to JOHN SLOAN of same, for Ł 100...land
granted to ALEXANDER HOYLE [perhaps mistaken for KYLE?], 17 Apr 1769, on muddy
fork of Buffalo Creek adj. to sd. WIER...ROBERT WIER (SEAL), Wit: JAMES DOUGHERTY, JOHN
LEQUEIR. Rec. Jan. term 1780.

Pp. 523-524: 24 Dec 1779, ANDREW PATRICK of Lincoln Co., to ROBERT MARTIN of same, for
Ł 45...land on waters of Little Cataba, adj. JAMES CRAIG & OSBURNS old
survey, granted to ANDREW ARMOUR 26 Oct 1767, and conveyed to sd. PATRICK 25 Feb 1769...
ANDREW PATRICK (SEAL), Wit: WILLIAM McCORDE, JNO. GULLICK. Rec. Jan. term 1780.

Pp. 524-525: 18 Jan 1780, JOHN GULLICK SENR. of Lincoln Co., to JOHN GULLICK JR. of same,
for natural love and affection...land on a creek called Little Catawba,
part of two grants to ROBERT PATTERSON 3 Feb 1754 and conveyed to MOSES ALEXANDER by
Sheriff Deed, 10 Jan 1766 to NATHANIEL ALEXANDER, then to JOHN GULLICK SR. 12 Jan 1766...
JOHN GULLICK (SEAL), Wit: JNO GULLICK, ROBT BEATY. Rec. Jan. term 1780.

Pp. 525-526: 26 Oct 1779, MARTIN HOYLE of Lincoln County, to JOHN HOYLE of same, for
Ł 200 NC money...land on S side S fork Catawba 60 A, part of a grant to
PETER HOYLE 17 Mar 1754, and sd. PETER HOYLE dying intestate, sd. land fell to his
eldest son JACOB, and he likewisde dying intestate, fell to sd. MARTIN HOYLE, his only
son...MARTIN HOIL (SEAL), Wit: JOHNATHAN GULLICK, _____ [German signature]. Rec. Jan.
term 1780.

Pp. 526-527: 26 Oct 1779, MARTIN HOYLE to JOHN HOYLE, for Ł 300 NC money...land granted
to PETER HOYLE on N side Long Creek, 17 May 1754 [same chain as preceding]
[Same signature and wit.] Rec. Jan. term 1780.

Pp. 527-528: 26 Oct 1779, MARTIN HOYLE to ANDREW HOYLE, for Ł 300 NC money...land granted
to PETER HOYLE 17 May 1754 [same chain as preceding]...Wit: JONATHAN GULLICK,
JOHN HEYEL. Rec. Jan. term 1780.

Pp. 528-529: 5 Apr 1780, JOHN RAMSEY of Lincoln Co., to JOHN BOLDRIGE of same, for Ł 5000
north currency...388 A on Dutchmans or Lepords Creek including part of a
grant to ANDREW KEILLING [KILLIAN], 1000 A, 30 Sept 1749....JOHN RAMSEY (D) (SEAL), Wit:
GEORGE LAMKIN, ROBERT KNOX. Rec. Apr. term 1780.

Pp. 529-530: 16 Mar 1778, JAMES WYATT JR. of Tryon Co., to WM. VERNON of same, for Ł 250
proc. money...land on both sides little long creek, near ANDERSONs,including
WYATTS mill and improvements, part of a grant to ANDREW HOYLE, 28 Apr 1768, and conveyed
to WYATT 26 Oct 1774...JAMES WYATT (SEAL), Wit: JONATHAN GULLICK, GEORGE PALMER. Rec.
Apr. term 1780.

Page 530: 18 Jan 1780, NICHOLAS TARTER to JOHN KIMBRO, both of Lincoln Co., for Ł 3 NC
money...200 A on branches of Long Creek, granted to GEORGE MICHAEL WISENANT,
13 Oct 1765...NICKLOS TARTAR (SEAL), MARY TARTER (X) (SEAL), Wit: THOMAS ESPEY, ROBT.
FERGUSON. Rec. Apr. term 1780

Pp. 530-531: 18 Jan 1780, NICHOLAS THARTER to JOHN CIMBOR, both of Lincoln Co., for Ł
100 NC money...land on SW side S fork Catawba, on branches of Long Creek,
45 A adj. HAGAR, granted to LAURENCE KOISER 9 Oct 1764...[Same signature and wit.] Rec.
Apr. term 1780.

Pp. 531-532: 1 June 1779, JACOB STROUP & wf of Lincoln Co., to ADAM STROUP of same, for
Ł 74...land on both sides Sailors branch of Hoÿles Creek, 200 A...JACOB
STROUP (SEAL), Wit: ANDW NEEL. Rec. Apr. term 1780.

Pp. 532-533: 4 Apr 1780, JOHN McKNITT ALEXANDER of Mecklenburg to JENKIN JENKINS of
Lincoln Co., for Ł 300...300 A on both sides Hoyles Mill path, adj. RICHARD
SPAIGHT...JNO McK. ALEXANDER (SEAL), Wit: JOHN POTS[?], JOHN JENKINS. N. B. The
Depreciation is now at fifty for one, therefore I have received no more than six pounds
value. JNO. McK. ALEXANDER. Rec. Apr. term 1780.

Pp. 533-534: 28 July 1773, JOHN RAMSEY & wf AGNES of Tryon Co., to RICHD JONES of same,
for Ł 5000 north currency...land adj. the place whereon they now live, 162
A...JOHN RAMSEY (SEAL), AGNES RAMSEY (X) (SEAL), Wit: JOHN CALDRIDGE, JOHN JONES. Rec.
Apr. term 1780.

Page 534: 5 Apr 1780, JOHN RAMSEY of Lincoln Co., to JOHN JONES of same, for Ł 5000 north
currency...274 A on Dutchmans or Leepords Creek, adj. JOHN BOLDRIDGE, part of
1000 A granted to ANDREW KEILLON 30 Sept 1749...JOHN RAMSEY (O)(SEAL), Wit: GEORGE LAMKIN,
ROBERT KNOX.

Pp. 534-535: 10 Dec 1779, PHILIP KENSELER & wf YOULEY of Lincoln Co., to PHILIP NOULL,
for Ł 1000...land on NE side S fork Catawba, on the path between SAMUEL
BICKERSTAFF & DERRICK RAMSOUR, 320 A granted to FRANCIS BEATY 16 Nov 1764 and conveyed
to AARON BICKERSTAFF then to PHILLIP KENSLAR...PHILIP KENSLAR (SEAL), YOULEY KENSYLER(+)
(SEAL), Wit: DAVID RAMSEY, CHRISTIAN RENHART. Rec. Apr. term 1780.

Pp. 535-536: 31 Mar 1780, JAMES CUNNINGHAM of Lincoln Co., planter, to ROBERT ALEXANDER
of same, for Ł 4000 NC money...200 A on the head of his own branch of waters

S fork Catawba adj. WILLIAM CRONICLE, JOHN CATHEY...JAMES CUNNINGHAM (SEAL), Wit: GEORGE
EWING, JOHN BEATEY. Rec. Apr. term 1780.

Pp. 536-537: North Carolina, Tryon County: 29 Dec 1778, ROBERT ABERNATHY JR. to ABRAM
EARHART, Blacksmith...by certain ____ 10 May 1754, 400 A on S side Catawba,
Cheagles Creek, about half a mile above a fall, land formerly surveyed for PETER EARHART
and also 100 A adj. to sd. TRACT, now property of sd. ABERNATHY and on E side Snyders
Creek...part of a grant to PHILIP EARHART 26 Oct 1767...STANKARD corner...for ₺ 250...
ROBERT ABERNATHY (SEAL), Wit: RICHARD BEALE, MILES ABERNATHY. Rec. Apr. term 1780.

Pp. 537-538: 1 Apr 1779, ROBERT ABERNATHY & wf SARAH of Lincoln Co., to JOSEPH ABERNATHY
of same, for ₺ 130...400 A on a branch of Lepards & Keillons Creek...ROBT
ABERNATHY (SEAL), SARAH ABERNATHY (X) (SEAL), Wit: MILES ABERNATHY, JOHN ABERNATHY. Rec.
Apr. term 1780.

Pp. 538-539: 2 Feb 1780, JOHN WELLS of Lincoln Co., to JAMES WILSON of same, for ₺ 146
NC money...131 A on both sides Sims' spring branch of Crowders Creek, a
little above JOHN WALKERS, granted to sd. JOHN WELLS 21 July 1774...JOHN WELLS (HH)
(SEAL), Wit: JAMES GRAHAM, WILLIAM RIDLEY, JNN. GULLICK. Rec. Apr. term 1780.

Pp. 539-540: 3 Apr 1780, MICHAEL WILLIAMS of Lincoln Co., to JACOB HOFFMAN of same, for
₺ 40 proc. money...land on a branch of Hoyles Creek, conveyed from JACOB
SHILLEY to MICHAEL WILLIAMS 28 Aug 1775, adj. to a corner of the place where he now lives,
granted to JACOB SHILLEY 23 Feb 1773, adj. JACOB STROUP...MICHAEL WILLIAMS(MX) (SEAL),
Wit: ALEXR MOORE, Rec. Apr. term 1780.

Pp. 540-541: 18 Apr 1780, MICHAEL WILLIAMS of Lincoln Co., to JACOB HOOFMAN of same, for
₺ 100...150 A granted to JACOB SHATELY 29 Apr 1768 & conveyed to sd. WILLIAMS
12 July 1771, on Hoyles Mill Creek...MICHAEL WILLIAMS (MX) (SEAL), Wit: GEORGE LAMKIN,
ANDW NEEL. Rec. Apr. term 1780.

Pp. 541-542: 6 Nov 1778, JAMES WALLACE of Mecklenburg Co., to JOHN DICKSON of same, for
₺ 140 proc. money...188 A on S side Catawba on Duharts Creek adj. ALEXANDER
LEWIS, granted to sd. WALLACE 9 Nov 1764...JAMES WALLACE (SEAL), Wit: ADAM BAIRD, THOMAS
DICKSON, ANDW NEEL. Rec. Apr. term 1780.

Pp. 542-543: 19 Apr 1780, JAMES COBURN of Lincoln Co., to SAMUEL RANKIN of same, for ₺
1000...land on waters of Kuykendalls Creek, 37 A, part of 300 A granted to
JAMES ARMSTRONG 30 Aug 1753...JAMES COBUN (SEAL), Wit: ANDW NEEL, ROBT ALEXANDER, FREDER-
ICK HAMBRIGHT. Rec. Apr. term 1780.

Pp. 543-544: 19 Apr 1780, JAMES COBURN to SAMUEL RANKIN, for ₺ 1000...land on Kuykendalls
Creek on W side Catawba, THOMAS RHINES corner, 183 A, part of 300 A granted
to JAMES ARMSTRONG 2 Oct 1751...[Same signature &wit.] Rec. Apr. term 1780.

Pp. 544-545: 19 Apr 1780, JAMES COBURN to SAMUEL RANKIN, for ₺ 3000...land on a branch
of Dutchmans Creek near SAMUEL RANKINS, adj. RUTLEDGE, 200 A granted to
RANKIN 22 Dec 1768, and conveyed to PHILIP ALSTON, then to JAMES JOHNSTON, then to
JAMES COBURN. [Same signature and wit.] Rec. Apr. term 1780.

Pp. 545-546: 25 Dec 1779, JOHN MOORE of Lincoln Co., to ALEXANDER MOORE of same, for
natural love and affection to his son...189 A granted to WILLIAM SMYTH, 5
May 1769 and conveyed to JOHN MOORE 3 Nov 1778...JOHN MOORE (SEAL), Wit: JNO GULLICK,
TOM. DUNWODEY, THOMAS CAMPBELL. Rec. Apr. term 1780

Pp. 546-547: 27 Dec 1779, JOHN MOORE to son JOHN MOORE, for natural love and affection...
189 A on Beaver Dam, granted to JAMES ARMSTRONG 30 Aug 1753, and conveyed
to WILLIAM SMITH 5 Jan 17[69]and to JOHN MOORE 3 Nov 1778...Wit: THOMAS CAMPBELL, WILLIAM
MOORE, JNO. GULLICK. Rec. Apr. term 1780.

April Term 1781.

Pp. 547-548: 6 Jan 1781, HENRY DELLINGER & NICHOLAS SKRURN of Lincoln Co., to HENRY CAUN
of same, for ₺ 80...land on Leepers Creek on Lick Run adj. DELLINGERS, 300
A granted to sd. DELLINGER 6 Apr 1765, and by him conveyed to MARTIN SHULTS, 24 Dec 1772
and then to sd. DELLINGER & SMITH...HEINRICH DELLINGER [German signature] (SEAL), NICHO-
LAS SKRUN (£) (SEAL), Wit: DAVID RAMSEY, MICHAEL _____ [German signature]. Rec. Apr.
term 1781.

July Term 1781.

Pp. 548-549: 9 Apr 1781, GEORGE PATTERSON of Lincoln Co., to DAVID ELLIOTT of same, for
Ђ 1000...300 A granted to DANIEL McCARTY and conveyed to ANDREW GOFORTH &
RICHARD GULLICK, then to JOHN GOFORTH, then to sd. GEORGE PATTERSON...GEORGE PATTERSON
(SEAL), Wit: ISAAC WHITE, DEREMIAH SMITH. Rec. July term 1781.

Pp. 549-550: 23 Feb 1780, ROBERT CHERRY of Lincoln Co., to WILLIAM NIXON of Charlotte
Co., Va., for Ђ 3000 proc. money...200 A on S side Cataba, granted to
LEONARD KILLION, conveyed to GEORGE BROWN 6 Jan 1754, and to JOHN WATKINS 20 July 1757,
then to JOANNA HUMPHRIES 25 Oct 1764...ROBERT CHERRY (SEAL), Wit: JAMES JOHNSTON, JOHN
KINKAID, JAMES LUCKY. Rec. July term 1781.

Pp. 550-551: 9 Oct 1781, JOHN ASHLEY of Lincoln Co., to WILLIAM SMITH SR., of same, for
Ђ 30 north currency...100 A on branches of Duharts Creek, adj. WM. DAVIS
corner, part of a grant to NATHAN DAVIS, 250 A, 25 Jan 1773, and conveyed to WM. SMITH,
JR, then to WILLIAM DAVIS....JOHN ASHLEY (Ɨ) (SEAL), Wit: GEORGE LAMKIN, ANNHIA[?]
LAMKIN. Rec. Oct. term 1781.

Pp. 551-552: 14 May 1781, SAMUEL ELDER of Lincoln Co., to WILLIAM CHRONICLE of same, for
Ђ 800...92 A on S side Catawba, adj. BARNET, HAMBRIGHT, granted to ROGER
COOK 30 Oct 1765...SAMUEL ELDER (SEAL), Wit: JAMES HENDERSON, FRANCIS BEATY. Rec. Oct.
mter 1781.

Pp. 552-553: 26 Oct 1779, MARTIN HOYLE of Lincoln Co., to MICHAEL HOYLE of same, for Ђ
200...196 A on N side S fork Catawba, part of a grant to PETER HOYLE 17 May
1754, sd. PETER dying intestate, land feel to his eldest son JACOB, and he dying intestate, fell to his only son MARTIN...MARTIN HOYLE (SEAL), Wit: JONATHAN GULLICK, JOHN
HEYEL. Rec. Oct. term 1781.

Page 553; 24 Jan 1779, JAMES JOHNSTON of Lincoln Co., to ABRAHAM SCOTT of same, for Ђ260
...land in fork of Catawba River, by the waggon Road, adj. JOHN CATHEY, THOMAS
HENRY, BOLES, McNABB, 600 A...JAMES JOHNSTON (SEAL), Wit: ROBT ALEXANDER, SAML RANKIN.
Rec. Oct. term 1781.

Page 554: 18 Apr 1780, SAMUEL RANKIN of Lincoln Co., to GEORGE COX of same, for Ђ 6000
continental money...300 A on the Dutchmans Creek adj. DAVIES formerly McKEN-
DRICK, ROBERT ALEXANDER...SAML RANKIN (SEAL), Wit: GEORGE LAMKIN, ROBT ALEXANDER. Rec.
Apr. term 1780.

Pp. 554-555: 2 Nov 1779, JOHN DICKSON of Mecklenburg Co., to THOMAS DIXON of same, for
Ђ 100 proc. money...188 A on Duharts Creek adj. ALEXR LEWIS, granted to
JAMES WALLACE 9 Nov 1764 and conveyed to JOHN DICKSON 6 Nov 1778...JOHN DICKSON (SEAL),
Wit: ROBERT BEATEY, THOS ALEXANDER, JOSEPH DICKSON. Rec. Apr. term 1780.

Pp. 555-556: January Term 1782.
ANDREW HESLIP of Lincoln Co., planter, to son THOMAS HESLEP of same, negro
Ned and his wife Peg, and half of all furniture...to my daughter MARY McFADDEN, widow of
Rutherford Co., negro Charly and mulatto boy Josh & others...14 Nov 1781...ANDREW HESLEP
(SEAL), Wit: ROBERT SCOTT, SAML McCOMBS. Rec. Jan. term 1782.

Pp. 556-557: 29 Sept 1781, WILLIAM CHRONICLE of Lincoln Co., to NATHANIEL PORTER of same,
for Ђ 4000...land on S side Catawba, adj. CUNNINGHAM, 92 A, granted to ROGER
COOK, 30 Oct 1765...WILLIAM CHRONICLE (SEAL), Wit: GEORGE EWING, HUGH EWING, JAS. McKEE.
Rèc. Jan. term 1782.

Pp. 557-558: 20 Mar 1779, COL. CHARLES McLEAN & wf SUSANNAH of Lincoln Co., to ROBERT
FERGUSON of Camden District, S. C., planter, for Ђ 1000 NC money...300 A
on S side Catawba on N fork Crowders Creek above Jacob COBURNS...CHARLES McLEAN (SEAL),
SUSANNAH McLEAN (SEAL), Wit: JOHN BARBAR, JOHN FALLS, JNO. WILSON. Rec. Jan. term 1782.

Pp. 558-559: 2 Jan 1782, JOHN ALEXANDER of Lincoln Co., planter, & wf SARAH to PHILIP
HULL of same, Gentleman, for Ђ 50...land in WADDELS lines, 200 A granted to
JESSE FINN 22 May 1772...JOHN ALEXANDER (SELA), SARE ALEXANDER (b) (SEAL), Wit: JOHN
SLOAN, JOHN DELLINGER.

Pp. 559-560: 16 May 1780, CHARLES McLEAN of Lincoln Co., to SAMUEL BARNET of same, for
Ђ 500...37 A on N fork Crowders Creek, part of a grant to JACOB COBORN 16
Nov 1764, and conveyed 27 Aug 1768...and another tract adj. to it, 240 A on both sides
Crowders Creek, adj. WALLACE, COBURN, granted to sd. JACOB COBURN 25 Apr 1767, and con-
veyed to sd. McLEAN 27 Aug 1768...CHARLES McLEAN (SEAL), Wit: JNON. GULLICK, JOHN WILSON

JOHN DUNWODEY. Rec. Jan. term 1782.

Pp. 560-561: 25 Feb 1778, JOHN SHUFERT of Rowan Co., planter, & wf MARY CLEVE SHUFERT
to MARTIN FRIDAY of Tryon Co., for Ᵽ 50...land on N side S fork Catawba on
piney old fields branch, adj. lower line of a grant to DERRICK RAMSOUR...100 A granted
to JOHN LARIM 21 Dec 1763, conveyed to JOHN PHILIP FILE 12 Apr 1773, and to JOHN SHU-
FERT 15 Aug 1773 _____ [German signature] (SEAL), MARY CLAVE SHUFERT (+) (SEAL), Wit:
HENRY HOLLMAN, ROBT BLACKBURN. Rec. Jan. term 1782.

Pp. 562-563: 11 Mar 1777, NICHOLAS FRIDAY of Tryon Co., farmer, & wf ELIZABETH to MARTIN
FRIDAY of same, for Ᵽ 50...land near NICHOLAS FRIDAYS new dwelling house,
150 A, the south side of two grants to DERRICK RAMSOUR 24 Sept 1754 and 26 Oct 1767,
and conveyed to sd. NICHOLAS FRIDAY 21 Apr 1770...[Both German signatures]. Wit: ROBT
McCASLAND, Proved; _____ [German signature]. Rec. Jan. term 1782.

Pp. 563-564: 25 Mar 1782, MARTIN HOYLE of Lincoln Co., to PETER BEST of same, for Ᵽ 100
NC money...land on N side S fork Catawba, adj. his grand-fathers old line,
part of a tract granted to JOHN HOYLE 6 Apr 1765...MARTEN HOIL (SEAL), Wit: JNO MOORE,
ELIZABETH MOORE. Rec. Apr. Term 1782.

Page 564: 12 Mar 1782, MARTEN HOYLE of Lincoln Co., to PETER BEST, for Ᵽ 100...29 A,
part of PETER HOYLEs old tract, on stony branch, granted to PETER HOYLE 8
May 1753 [Same signature and wit.] Rec. Apr. term 1782.

Page 565: 12 Apr 1782, JOHN WELLS of Lincoln Co., to JOHN HAMBRIGHT for Ᵽ 500 specie...
178 A on the main fork of Kings Creek, part of a grant to JAMES KUYKENDALL,
1754, and conveyed to HUGH KELLY 1755, and to PATRICK McDAVID 1768, and to ANDREW
HAMPTON 1775, and then to sd. JOHN WELLS...JOHN WELLS (+++) (SEAL), Wit: GEORGE LAMKIN,
FREDK. HAMBRIGHT, ISAAC HOLLAND. Rec. Apr. term 1782.

Pp. 565-566: 15 Apr 1782, FREDERICK HAMBRIGHT SR. of Lincoln Co., to JAMES WELLS of
same, for Ᵽ 500 specie...136 A in the fork of Long Creek & on still House
branch, granted to sd. HAMBRIGHT 5 May 1769, No. 382...FREDERICK HAMBRIGHT (SEAL), Wit:
GEORGE LAMKIN, GEORGE LAMKIN JR. Rec. Apr. term 1782.

Pp. 566-567: 20 Feb 1777, WM. ELDER & SAML ELDER, both of Tryon Co., to ADAM CLOLINGER
of same, for Ᵽ 65 NC money...land on E side Kuykendalls Creek, 200 A
granted to JOHN STANLEY 10 Apr 1761, patent recorded in Secretaries office Book 10,
p. 333...WILLIAM ELDER (SEAL), SAMUEL ELDER (SEAL), Wit: JOSEPH ABERNATHY, JACOB SEITS,
Rec. Apr. term 1782.

Page 567: 22 Apr 1780, VALENTINE MAUNY to FREDERICK ATHERHOLD, both of Lincoln Co., for
Ᵽ 30...200 A granted to RICHARD WARD, __ Sept 1766...VALLENTINE MAUNY (SEAL),
Wit: GEORGE ____ [German signature]. Rec. Apr. term 1782.

Pp. 567-568: 18 Feb 1782, JOSEPH SCOTT of Lincoln Co., to JOHN STROUD of same, for
Ᵽ 2000...260 A on S side Catawba, granted to SAML COBURN 29 Sept 1750...
JOSEPH SCOTT (SEAL), Wit: ____ SMITH, JOEL SMITH (XX), Rec. Apr. term 1782.

Pp. 568-569: 6 Feb 1782, THOMAS ANDERSON & wf PEGGY of Lincoln Co., to JOHN POSTON of
Rowan Co., for Ᵽ 160 "Hard money or Old Trade"...300 A on S side Catawba,
granted to THOMAS ANDERSON 1 Apr 1761, No. 88...THOMAS ANDERSON ( ) (SEAL), PEGGY
ANDERSON (Ϩ) (SEAL), Wit: JOHN POSTON JUNR. FRS. CUNNINGHAM. N. B. The interlining
words in the above deed was wrote before signing also there is 100 A of the above
boundary lines which THOMAS ANDERSON sold to his son THOMAS ANDERSON in that part where
URBAN ASHEBRAUER now lives. Rec. Apr. term 1782.

Pp. 569-570: 7 Jan 1777, JAS. JOHNSTON of Tryon Co., to THOMAS RHINE for Ᵽ 100 proc.
money...land on Kuykendalls Creek adj. JAMES ARMSTRONG, 202 A granted to
JOHN ARMSTRONG 25 Apr 1762 and part of a tract conveyed by JAMES ARMSTRONG, 30 Aug 1753
...JAMES JOHNSTON (SEAL), Wit: JAMES COBURN, ROBT ABERNATHY, JACOB SIETS. Rec. Apr.
term 1782.

Pp. 570-571: 7 Feb 1777, JAMES RUTLEDGE of Tryon Co., to THOMAS RHINE of same, for Ᵽ 10
...37 1/2 A, part of 300 A granted to JAMES ARMSTRONG, 30 Aug 1753...JAMES
RUTLEDGE (SEAL), Wit: JAMES COBURN, JACOB SEITS, ROBT ABERNATHY. Rec. Apr. term 1782.

Pp. 571-572: 11 Aug 1782, CORNELIUS McCARTY of Lincoln Co., to HUGH BLAIR & DANIEL Mc-
CARTY of same, for Ᵽ 800...2185 A on the S side Catawba, in the State of
South Carolina and known by the name of Harris's Island, which was originally granted

in different parts and parcels to one RICHD HARRIS and one RICHARD STEPHENS & afterwards
by virute of diverse means conveyed and became vested in the late JOHN BULL decd who
by his L. W. & T. divised the same to his grandson WILLM MIDDLETON (decd) on whose
intestate became vested in his sisters co-heiresses, MARY BUTLER, wife of Major PIERCE
BUTLER, and SARAH GUIRRARD, wife of BENJN. GUERRARD, Esq., who conveyed same to
ALEXANDER ROSE, and by ROSE conveyed to CORNELIUS McCARTY (decd) on whose death intestate passed to CORNELIUS McCARTY of N. C., eldest son to DANIEL McCARTY, who was eldest
brother of CORNELIUS McCARTY decd...CORNELIUS McCARTY (O) (SEAL), Wit: JAMES RUTLEDGE,
LEONARD ADCOCK, JAMES WRIGHT. Rec. Oct.term 1782.

Pp. 572-574: Same deed as preceding for ₺ 1000 in gold and silver. It appears to be
the other part of a lease and release, but it is not so stated.

Pp. 574-575: GEORGE LAMKIN & GEORGE LAMKIN JR. of Lincoln Co., to ROBERT ALEXANDER, for
₺ 100 specie...negro Sharper, 25 years old...4 Oct 1782...GEORGE LAMKIN
SR (SEAL), GEO. LAMKIN JR. (SEAL), Wit: JAMES HENDERSON, HUGH BLAIR.

Page 575: 9 Apr 1782, JOHN CARPENTER to son JOHN CARPENTER, both of North Carolina,
for ₺ 5...land on both sides Beaverdam, on S side S fork Catawba, 288 A,
granted to JOHN CARPENTER SR. 26 Nov 1757...HANZ ZIMMERMAN [German signature] (SEAL),
Wit: None. Rec. Oct. term 1782.

Pp. 575-576: 20 Apr 1782, JOHN KIMBRO of Lincoln Co., to JOHN BULLOCK of same, for ₺
200 NC money...200 A on branches of Long Creek, granted to GEORGE MICHAEL
WISENANT, 13 Oct 1765, and 45 A adj. to it, formerly belonging to NICHOLAS THARTER &
conveyed to JOHN KIMBRO 18 Jan 1780...JOHN KIMBRO (ﾂ) (SEAL), Wit: EBENEZER NEWTON,
JOHN STARIT, THOS NEWTON. Rec. Oct. term 1782.

Pp. 576-577: 26 Oct 1779, JOHN HOYLE of Lincoln Co., to MARTIN HOYLE of same, for ₺
200 NC money...100 A on N side S fork Catawba, granted to sd. JOHN HOYLE
28 Feb 1775...JOHN HEYLL (SEAL), Wit: JONATHAN GULLICK, _____ [German signature]. Rec.
Oct. term 1782.

Page 577: A Deed of Gift. HENRY REYNOLDS of Lincoln Co., planter, to daughter MARY
REYNOLDS...negro Tud, 2 1/2 years old...2 Mar 1782...HENRY REYNOLDS (SEAL),
Wit: JOHN SLOAN, ROBERT GLENN. Rec. Oct. term 1782.

Page 578: A deed of Gift. HENRY REYNOLDS to daughter RACHEL REYNOLDS...negro Silva
2 years old...2 Mar 1782. [Same sign and wit.] Rec. Oct. term 1782.
January Term
Pp. 578-579: 16 Nov 1782, DUNCAN OCHILTREE, SAML MARTIN, ADLAI OSBURN, of Charlotte,
N. C., merchants to JOHN MOORE for ₺ 150...land on main fork of Kings
Creek near JOHN KUYKENDALL, 300 A and also a tract adj. to it 90 A...DAN OCHILTREE
(SEAL), SAM MARTIN (SEAL), Ochiltree, Martin & Co. Wit: EDWARD HUNTER, SAMUEL WHITE.
Rec. Jan. term 1783.

Pp. 579-580: JONATHAN JONES of Lincoln Co., to JOHN BARDLEY of same, for ₺ 20 specie...
and ₺ 40 to be paid in horses on or before 25 Dec next, and ₺ 40 in hard
money or trace before 25 Dec 1784, and ₺ 40 to be paid by 25 Dec 1785...tract on both
sides Potts Creek, excluding 40 A sold to THOMAS HOOVER, formerly held and occupied by
JOSEPH MILLIGAN, 400 A...6 Jan 1783...JONATHAN JONES (SEAL), Wit: DANL McKISSICK, WIL-
LIAM ADAMS. Rec. Jan. term 1783.

Pp. 580-581: 16 Sept 1782, JOHN LANDERS of Lincoln Co., planter, to JAMES McALLEN of
same, for ₺ 2600 proc. money...250 A on N side Buffalo Creek, adj. GEORGE
DAVISES, granted to THOMAS WELSH 22 May 1772...JOHN LANDERS (SEAL), Wit: Wit: GEORGE
PATTERSON, JAMES WILSON. Rec. Oct. term 1782.

Page 581: 6 Jan 1783, RICHARD JONES of Lincoln Co., to JOHN RAMSEY of same, for s5...
150 A on both sides Dutchmans Creek adj. RAMSEY...RICHARD JONES (SEAL), Wit:
JOHN CALDRIDGE, JOHN JONES. Rec. Jan. term 1783.

Pp. 581-582: 19 Jan 1778, WM WRAY & wf of Rowan Co., to ROBERT CARUTHERS of Orange Co.,
NC, for ₺ 140...448 A in Tryon Co., on S side Catawba, including the place
that JOHN THOMAS hath a deed for, 17 May 1754, and made conveyance to ELIJAH MASSEY 13
Feb 1754, conveyed to THOMAS HUFF...adj. LARGES corner, BEATIES, ANDREW KILLIAN...WM
WRAY (SEAL), JEAN WRAY (SEAL), Wit: JOHN COCHRAN, JAMES HENDRY. Rec. Jan. term 1783.

Pp. 582-583: 8 June 1782, JOHN STROUD & wf PATTY of Lincoln Co., to JAMES DOZIER of same,
for ₺ 190...land on S side Catawba, 150 A granted to SAML COBORN, 29 Sept

1750...JOHN STROUD (X)(SEAL), PATTY STROUD (X) (SEAL), Wit: SHAROD[?] STROUD, ARCHIBALD
LITTLE, ROBERT CARUTHERS. Rec. Jan. term 1783.

Pp. 583-584: 19 Dec 1782, JOHN WALKER of Lincoln Co., to JAMES RUTLEDGE of same, for Ł5
          specie...land on W side Catawba on both sides Dutchmans Creek, near the
mouth of sd. Walkers spring branch, 23 A, part of 154 A granted to GEORGE RUTLEDGE (decd)
and conveyed to sd. WALKER...JOHN WALKER (Ɨ W) (SEAL), Wit: JOHANN PFILL, WM MATTHES
(Կᗺ). Rec. date not given.

Pp. 584-585: 16 Nov 1781, JOHN SIGEL of Lincoln Co. to JOHN COCHRAN of Rowan Co., for
          Ł 50...land on head waters of Duharts Creek including his improvements...
JOHN SIGEL (SEAL), MARGARET SIGEL (X) (SEAL), Wit: ROBERT CARUTHERS, DAVID CHERRY. Rec.
date not given.

Page 586: 11 Oct 1779, JOHN BROWN SKRIMSHIRE of Lincoln Co., to SAMSON LAMKINS of
          Rutherford Co., for Ł 75...land on W side S fork Catawba, granted to sd.
JOHN BROWN SKRIMSHIRE, 200 A...JOHN BROWN SKRIMSHIRE (SEAL), Wit: GEO LAMKIN JUR.,
VINT. COX, JAS FREEMAN. Rec. date not given.

Pp. 586-587: 31 Aug 1782, JACOB FORNEY of Lincoln Co., to BENJAMIN ORMOND of same, for
          Ł 20...land on waters of Crowders Creek, 200 A granted to FORNEY 14 Nov
1771...JACOB FORNEY (SEAL), Wit: ABRAHAM FORNEY, ZECHARIAH SALLYR, LEONARD SAILOR (LS),
Rec. date not given.

Pp. 587-589: 1 Oct 1782, FREDERICK HAMBRIGHT of Lincoln Co., to EDWARD HUNTER of same,
          for Ł 500 in gold and silver...3 tracts (1) 258 A adj. JAMES WELLS, FREDER-
ICK HAMBRIGHTs old line (2) 156 A adj. JAMES WELLS line on the still House branch (3)
300 A adj. JOSEPH JENKINS, LINEBARGERS...FREDERICK HAMBRIGHT (SEAL), Wit: JO DICKSON,
JAMES JOHNSTON. Rec. Jan. term 1783.

Pp. 589-590: 16 Nov 1782, JOHN MOORE of Charlotte, N. C. to THOMAS POLK, Esq., of same,
          for Ł 150...land on main fork of Kings Creek near JOHN KIRKENDALL, 300 A
and tract of 90 A adj. to it...JOHN MOORE (SEAL), Wit: EDWARD HUNTER, SAMUEL WHITE.
Rec. Jan. term 1783.

Pp. 590-591: 16 Nov 1782, DAN OCHILTREE, SAML MARTIN, ADLAI OSBURN & WILLIAM POLK,
          the company of OCHILTREE, MARTIN & Co., merchants of Charlotte, N. C. to
JOHN MOORE, Esq., for Ł 100...land on waters of Howards Creek & waters of N fork Indian
Creek, 500 A...DANIEL OCHILTREE (SEAL), SAML MARTIN (SEAL), Wit: EDWARD HUNTER, SAMUEL
WHITE. Rec. Jan term 1783.

Page 591: Deed of Gift. JOSEPH SCOTT of Lincoln Co., waggon marker to son ABRAHAM
          SCOTT...tract in Wilkes County, State of Georgia, on Saffords fork of Long
Creek, above SAFFORDS survey, 200 A & a negro boy Jesse...9 Dec 1782...JOSEPH SCOTT
(SEAL), Wit: ABM SCOTT, Rec. Jan. term 1783.

Pp. 591-592: Deed of Gift. JOSEPH SCOTT to daughter MARGERY SCOTT...negro Benn...9
          Dec 1782...[same sign. and wit.] Rec. Jan. term 1783.

Page 592: Deed of Gift. JOSEPH SCOTT to daughter OSTREN SCOTT...negro Hanna...9 Dec
          1782...[same sign. and wit.] Rec. Jan. term 1783.

          Deed of Gift. JOSEPH SCOTT to daughter ANN SCOTT...negro Limrick...9 Dec
1782...[same sign. and wit.] Rec. Jan. term 1783.

Pp. 592-593: Deed of Gift. JOSEPH SCOTT to daughter ESTHER SCOTT...negro Sam...9 Dec
1782   1782...[same sign. and wit.] Rec. Jan. term 1783.

Pp. 593-594: 16 Nov 1782, JOHN MOORE, Esq., of Charlotte, N. C. for Ł 100 to SAML MAR-
          TIN...[same property in deed on pp. 590-591]...JOHN MOORE (SEAL), Wit:
EDWARD HUNTER, SAMUEL WHITE. Rec. Jan. term 1783.

                         April Court Anno Domini 1783.

Pp. 594-595: 28 Oct 1780, JOHN WEST of Lincoln Co., to WM WEST of same, for Ł 35 north
          currency...80 A on S side Doctors Creek, granted to JNO. BAILEY, School
Master, for 200 A adj. WM MOORE, conveyed by BAILY to EDWARD HOGAN, then to JOHN MOORE
...WILLIAM WEST (X) (SEAL), Wit: VINCENT COX, LUCY COX (V). Rec. Apr. term 1783.

Page 595: Lincoln Co.: This day cam WILLIAM STROUD SENR & under oath sayeth that
          JOHN STROUD is his eldest son by his first wife, born in Wedlock...1 Feb 1783

WILLIAM STROUD (M). Wit: JAMES JOHNSTON, J. P., JOHN HILL. Rec. Apr. term 1783.

Pp. 595-596: 28 Oct 1782, JAMES CALWELL of Lincoln Co., to JOHN SLOAN of same, for
Ŀ 50...250 A on Lick fork of Indian Creek & waters of Muddy fork of Buff-
alo Creek, granted to THOMAS CALWELL 11 Nov 1774, No. 256...JAMES CALWELL (X) (SEAL),
Wit: JOHN ALEXANDER, JOHN SLOAN SEN (J). Rec. Apr. term 1783.

Pp. 596-597: 12 July 1782, PETER SEITS of Lincoln Co., planter, to WILLM DAVIES, of
same, for Ŀ 120 NC money...land on N fork of Buffaloe Creek, 150 A granted
to NICHOLAS WISENANT 15 May 1782[should be 1772]...PETER SEITS (*) (SEAL), Wit: CHRIST-
OPHER CARPENTER (CE), ANN CARPENTER, FERNEY GREEN NORMAN. Rec. Apr. term 1783.

Page 597: JOHN TUCKER of Lincoln to ALEXANDER BALDRIDGE...land on N side Gilmores branch,
adj. DAVID ABERNATHY, part of land which JOHN **BALDRIDGE** bought of JNO. ARM-
STRONG...30 Jan 1783...JOHN TUCKER (SEAL), Wit: JOSEPH ABERNATHY, WM. BALDRIDGE. Rec.
Apr. term 1783.

Pp. 597-598: 11 Apr 1783, AMOS SPEECE of Ninety Sixth District, S. C., to MARTIN FRIDAY
of Lincoln Co., for Ŀ 130 in gold or silver...land adj. JAMES WILSON,
THOMAS CAHOON, WARLICK, 225 A, conveyed from ANTHONY HOLMAN & wf to sd. SPEECE..._____
[German signature] (SEAL), Wit: EDWARD HUNTER, JAMES HENDERSON, JOHN CHITTIM. Rec.
date not given.

Pp. 598-599: 7 May 1782, HENRY HOLMAN of Burke Co., N. C., planter, to MICHAEL POTTS of
Lincoln Co., for Ŀ 50...land on E side Clarks Creek about a mile east of
RAMSOURS land, 250 A granted to WILLIAM WELSH 15 Nov 1762, and conveyed to GEORGE SHIPE
23 & 24 July 1768, & to HOLMAN as attorney 13 Sept 1773...leter of attorney proved in
Tryon Court October tern 1774...HENRY HOLLMAN (SEAL), Wit: ROBERT BLACKBURN, HENRY
GROSE. Rec. Apr. term 1783.

Pp. 599-600: 15 Feb 1783, BOSTON BEST SR., of Lincoln Co., to WIRELY RUDICIL of **same**,
for Ŀ 60 in gold & silver...land in Fork of Catawba, on branches of Hoyles
Mill Creek adj. HOYLE, LINEBURGER...BOSTON BEST (X) (SEAL), Wit: JO. DICKSON, JAMES
RUTLEDGE. Rec. Apr. term 1783.

Pp. 600-601: 8 Apr 1783, ROBERT CARUTH & JOHN CARUTH of Lincoln Co., to JAMES LOGAN of
same, for Ŀ 40...land on both sides of Little Catawba above JAMES LOGAN
granted 10 May 1772 to JOHN SLOAN, and conveyed to ADAM CARUTH, sd. JOHN & ROBERT
CARUTH, heirs of sd. ADAM CARUTH (decd)...ROBERT CARUTH (SEAL), JOHN CARUTH (SEAL), Wit:
ROBERT ALEXANDER, JOHN SLOAN. Rec. Apr. term 1783.

Pp. 601-602: 26 Aug 1782, CHRISTOPHER HAVER of Burke Co., N. C. to JOSHUA SHERILL of
Lincoln Co., for Ŀ 200...189 A on W side Catawba, adj. WM. SIMPSON, granted
to sd. HAVER from Earl Granville 10 May 1762...CHRISTER HAVER (SEAL), Wit: WILLIAM
SHERRILL (X), JACOB SHERRILL. Rec. Apr. term 1783.

Page 602: 7 Apr 1783, NICHOLAS CLAY of Lincoln Co., to JACOB SEBACK of same, for Ŀ 150
...land on Potts' Creek, 150 A granted to THOMAS POTTS 30 Aug 1753, and by
his L. W. & T. conveyed to JOHN POTTS, who with his wife MARY conveyed to NICHOLAS
CLAY 6 & 7 Jan 1769..._____ [German signature] (SEAL), Wit: _____ [German signature],
ROBERT BLACKBURN. Rec. Apr. term 1783.

Page 603: JOHN MARTIN of Lincoln Co., for love & affection to son JOSIAS MARTIN of same,
...360 A on N fork Crowders Creek, granted to JOHN MARTIN 2 July 1766 (except
30 A already to JAMES MARTIN)...20 Mar 1782...JOHN MARTIN (SEAL), Wit: JOHN WILSON,
MARY MARTIN (M). Rec. Apr. term 1783.

Pp. 603-604: 6 Mar 1782, RICHARD SAUNDERS to JAMES HENDERSON, both of Lincoln Co., for
Ŀ 30,000...150 A near FERGUSON, granted to JEREMIAH & CATHERINE SMITH 25
Feb 1775...RICHARD SAUNDERS (R) (SEAL), Wit: FREDK HAMBRIGHT, JAMES HILLHOUSE, JOHN
HAMBRIGHT. Rec. Apr. term 1783.

Pp. 604-605: 22 Dec 1782, JAMES TAYLOR of Ninety Sixth District, S. C. to JOHN SLOAN of
N. C., for Ŀ 60 proc. money...land on both sides N fork of Long Creek,
...JAMES TAYLOR (SEAL), Wit: EDWARD CORNWIL, JOHN ALEXANDER. Rec. Apr. term 1783.

Pp. 605-606: 20 Jan 1779, NICHOLAS WELCH of Tryon Co., to JOHN ROWLAND of Rowan Co.,
for Ŀ 400 proc. money...200 A granted to sd. WELSH 22 May 1772...NICHOLAS
WELSH (SEAL), Wit: THOMAS PEARSON, HENRY CADLOCK. Rec. Apr. term 1783.

Pp. 606-607: 3 May 1782, JOHN WORK of Rowan Co., to WILLIAM KERR & JAMES KERR of same,
        for Ь 450...land in Burke County, on both sides Mountain Creek adj.
ROBERT BINGHAM PERKINS, 336 A granted to THOMAS ANDERSON 10 May 1762, and conveyed to
sd. WORK 22 Feb 1774...JOHN WORK (SEAL), Wit: JAS BYERS, JOSEPH BYERS. Rec. Apr. term
1783.

Book #13. July Term 1783.

Pp. 607-608: 17 May 1776, HENRY GROSS of Rowan Co., planter, & wf ELIZABETH to JOHN
        GROSS, yeoman, of same, for s5...land in formerly Tryon, now Rowan Co.,
adj. lands formerly HENRY RAMSOURS now DAVID RAMSOURS, 225 A, part of a grant to
THOMAS WELCH 10 Apr 1761...conveyed to sd. HENRY GROSS 10 Aug 1773...HENRY GROSS (SEAL),
ELISABETH GROSS (X) (SEAL), Wit: JOHANN PHILLIP _____ [German signature], ROBERT
BLACKBURN. Rec. July term 1783.

Pp. 608-610: 17 May 1776, HENRY GROSS & wf ELIZABETH to CHRISTIAN GROSS JR., for s5...
        75 A, part of a tract granted to THOMAS WELCH 10 Apr 1761, and another
survey of 150 A adj. to sd. tract adj. GRISSMORE, granted to ROBERT BLACKBURN 28 Apr
1760 and conveyed to THOMAS WELCH, 20 July 1769, and to HENRY GROSS 10 Aug 1773...
[Same signatures and wit.] Rec. July term 1783.

Pp. 610-611: 18 Mar 1783, JACOB FORNEY of Lincoln Co., to GEORGE DECK of same, for s5...
        land on both sides Long Creek adj. HOOFSTATLER, CARUTH, 200 A granted to
LEWIS WEIDNER 28 Apr 1768...JACOB FORNEY (SEAL), Wit: ARTHUR BREN[?], WILLIAM LUCKY,
PETER FORNEY. Rec. July term 1783.

Pp. 611-612: 21 June 1783, JOHN WYATT of Lincoln Co., to ELIZABETH WYATT of same, for
        Ь 15 specie...100 A on S fork Catawba, adj. JAMES WYATT, part of a grant
to JAMES WYATT for 392 A, and conveyed to DANIEL WYATT JR., and sd. DANIEL dying without heir to his body, the land fell to sd. JOHN WYATT...JOHN WYATT (C) (SEAL), Wit:
GEORGE LAMKIN, JAMES WYATT. Rec. July term 1783.

Page 612: 18 Mar 1783, GEORGE DECK of Lincoln Co., to JACOB FORNEY of same, for s5...
        land on S side Catawba, adj. CHEAGLES, 190 A granted to MATTHIAS DECK, 3 Apr
1752..._____ [German signature] (SEAL), Wit: ARTHUR BYNUM, WILLIAM LUCKEY, PETER FORNEY.
Rec. July term 1783.

Pp. 612-613: 17 Dec 1781, MOSES WILLIAM of Lincoln Co., to HUGH BLAIR of same, for Ь
        7000...240 A on waters of Dutchmans Creek, granted to ROBERT McCOMB 2
Mar 1775...MOSES WILLIAMS (D) (SEAL), Wit: JAMES RUTLEDGE, SARAH RUTLEDGE. Rec. July
term 1783.

Pp. 613-614: 12 May 1780, JOHN BARBER of Lincoln Co., to JOHN WILSON of same, for Ь 20
        ...land on waters of Crowders Creek, adj. EPHRAIM McLANE, granted to sd.
BARBER 25 Jan 1773...JOHN BARBER (SEAL), Wit: THOMAS WHITE, ISAAC WHITE. Rec. July
term 1783.

Pp. 614-615: 28 May 1779, THOMAS POLK Esq. of Mecklenburg Co., to JOSEPH DICKSON of
        Rowan Co., for Ь 7000...four tracts, 825 A (1) land conveyed by WILLIAM
CLEGHORN to WILLIAM MOORE 14 Dec 1762, 328 A adj. SAMUEL COBURN (2) 300 A conveyed by
WM. ADAIR to MOORE 14 Dec 1762 adj. CABEENS[?] (3) land conveyed by ROBERT ABERNATHY
to MOORE 13 July 1770, 102 A (4) 45 A granted to MOORE 11 Feb 1763 on waters of Dutchmans Creek...THOS POLK (SEAL), Wit: JOSEPH MOORE, _____ POLK. Rec. July term 1783.

Pp. 615-616: 8 July 1783, MARTIN HOYLE of Lincoln Co., to WIRRY RUDISILL of same, for
        Ь 3...land on Hoyles Creek, granted to PETER HOYLE 27 May 1754...MARTIN
HOIL (SEAL), Wit: JOHN MOORE, ELIZABETH MOORE. Rec. July term 1783.

Pp. 616-617: 11 June 1783, JAMES MILLICAN of Rutherford Co., to ROBERT JOHNSON of same,
        for Ь 400 in gold and silver...536 A conveyed from ROBERT ALEXANDER to
JAMES MILLICAN 6 Feb 1767, 96 A on N side Doctors Creek (2) land conveyed by SIMON
KUYKENDALL to MILLICAN 12 Dec 1769, 300 A (3) 200 A granted to sd. MILLICAN 10 Dec 1769
adj. WM. MOORE...JAMES MILLICAN (Ŧ) (SEAL), Wit: ROBT ALEXANDER, WILLIAM JOHNSON, ROBT
JOHNSON. Rec. July term 1783.

Pp. 617-618: 29 Mar 1783, WILLIAM HARRIS of Camden District, S. C. to JOHN McCLEUR of
        Lincoln Co., for Ь 50 specie...40 A on Little Catawba adj. JOHN HARRIS,
granted to JOHN HARRIS 14 Mar 1772 & conveyed to sd. WILLIAM HARRIS...WM. HARRIS (SEAL),
Wit: JONN. GULLICK, MARGARET GULLICK. Rec. July term 1783.

Pp. 618-619: 27 Feb 1782, JOHN BEARD of Lincoln Co., to JAMES BEARD of same, for ₤ 1000
          ...136 A on waters of little Catawba & Duharts Creek, granted to sd. JOHN
BEARD 6 Apr 1765...JOHN BEARD (SEAL), Wit: JONN. GULLICK, JOHN BAIRD JR., ZACH SPIERS.
Rec. July term 1783.

Pp. 619-620: 15 Feb 1783, WILLIAM THOMPSON & wf SARAH of Lincoln Co., to HENRY THOMPSON
          of same, for ₤ 120 proc. money...land on N side Mountain Creek, adj. ROBT
McKISSICK, 157 A conveyed by ABRAHAM COLLETT to HENRY THOMPSON SR 5 & 6 Jan 1765 & by
his L. W. & T. of sd. WILLIAM on 22 May 1777...WILLIAM THOMPSON (SEAL), SARAH THOMPSON
(S) (SEAL), Wit: ROBERT McCUSICKE, SAML THOMPSON. Rec. July term 1783.

Pp. 620-621: 28 Apr 1783, JOHN WELLS SR. of Rutherford Co., planter, to JOHN WILLISON
          of Lincoln Co., for ₤ 30...150 A granted to JOHN WELLS 21 July 1774, on
both sides Simms Branch of Crowders Creek, a little above JOHN WALKERS, adj. THOMAS
BULLENGS, JOHN NUCKELLS lines...JOHN WELLS (ℍ) (SEAL), Wit: DAVID ELLIOTT, JAMES
WELLS. Rec. July term 1783.

Pp. 621-622: 7 July 1783, GEORGE CATHY of Mecklenburg Co., to his son GEORGE CATHEY of
          same, for ₤ 20...land adj. BOSTON BEST, JAMES WYATT, 100 A with the grist
mill & utensils...GEORGE CATHY (SEAL), Wit: JOHN CARRUTH, JOSEPH JENKINS. Rec. July
term 1783.

Pp. 622-623: 9 July 1783, ROBERT ALEXANDER Esq. to SAML CALDWELL, planter, both of
          Lincoln Co., for ₤ 150 specie...200 A in Lincoln Co., in the fork of
Catawba on head of JAMES CUNNINGHAMS branch, adj. WM. CHRONICLE, HENRY, JOHN CATHY...
ROBT ALEXANDER (SEAL), Wit: JOHN CARRUTH, JNO MOORE, Rec. July term 1783.

Page 623: 20 May 1783, PHILIP DELLINGER of Lincoln Co., to HENRY DELLINGER, son of sd.
          PHILIP, for natural love and affeciton...land on which I now live, 185 A,
granted to MARTIN TELLINGER, 30 Aug 1755 and conveyed to sd. PHILIP 3 Sept 1757...
PHILIP DELLINGER [German signature] (SEAL), Wit: JNO MOORE, JACOB _____. Rec. July
term 1783.

Pp. 623-624: PHILIP DELLINGER, for natural love & affeciton to son JOHN DELLINGER....
          gift of cattle, still & vessels, furniture, etc...22 May 1783...JOHANN
PHILIP DELLINGER [German signature] (SEAL), [Same wit. as preceding]. Rec. July term
1783.

                         October Term 1783.

Pp. 624-626: 17 May 1776, CHRISTIAN GROSS SENR of Rowan Co., planter, to HENRY GROSS
          of same, yeoman, for s5...land in (formerly Tryon) Rowan Co., on N side
S fork Catawba, both sides Clarks Creek, adj. CARSONERS, part of 2 surveyed 227 A granted to DANIEL WARLICK 28 Mar 1751 & 23 Dec 1768, conveyed to VALENTINE WARLICK, 16 Oct
1769, and then to sd. CHRISTIAN GROSS 18 Feb 1774..._____ [German signature],MARTLENA
GROSS (O) (SEAL), Wit: ROBT BLACKBURN. Rec. Oct. term 1783.

Pp. 626-627: 7 May 1783, JOHN TUCKER of Lincoln Co., to JOHN BALDRIDGE of same, for ₤
          5 specie...48 A on Beaver Dam branch of Dutchmans Creek, adj. DAVID
ABERNATHY, JACOB SIDES, BALDRIDGE, & COX, granted to TUCKER 28 Oct 1782...JOHN TUCKER
(SEAL), Wit: JAMES RUTLEDGE, PETER FORNEY. Rec. Oct. term 1783.

Page 627: 7 Oct 1783, GEORGE LAMKIN of Lincoln Co., to GEORGE COX of same, for ₤ 80
          specie...land on both sides Dutchmans Creek, 100 A near JAMES ALEXANDER,
PHILLIPS, granted to sd. LAMKIN for 300 A...GEORGE LAMKIN (SEAL), Wit: CHARNICK COX,
JOHN RUSTS. Rec. Oct. term 1783.

Pp. 627-629: 18 Dec 1779, JEMIMA SHARP, widow of Mecklenburg Co., to NATHAN MENDINGHALL
          of Craven Co., S. C., for ₤ 600 NC money...land on both sides North fork
Crowders Creek adj. SAML INGLES, JAMES BALDRIGE, 100 A granted to ANDREW McNABB 29 Apr
1768 & conveyed to JEMIMA 10 Dec 1769...JEMIMA SHARP (X) (SEAL), Wit: JOHN SHARP, JNO.
McK. ALEXANDER, THOS. PRICE. Rec. Oct. term 1783.

Page 629: 2 Mar 1782, GEORGE ROMONGER of Lincoln Co., to SAMUEL JOHNSTON of same, for
          ₤ 20 hard money...land on his own brances of Dutchmans Creek, 150 A on the
head of sd. branch, the waggon road and the Dutch meeting house, granted to sd. ROMON-
GER 11 May 1773...GEORGE ROMONGER (R) (SEAL), MARY ROMONGER (M) (SEAL), Wit: WILLIAM
GOODSTON (Λ), DANIEL JONSTON (D). Rec. Oct. term 1783.

Page 630: 7 May 1770, JAMES PRICE of Tryon Co., to GEORGE DENNY of same, for Ł 100
    proc. money...250 A on the waters of Crowders Creek, granted to ARCHD. HOU-
STON & conveyed to JAMES PRICE...JAMES PRICE (SEAL), Wit: THOMAS PRICE, ALEXANDER
DENNY. Rec. Oct. term 1783.

Pp. 630-631: 2 Oct 1783, JAMES HILLHOUSE of Lincoln Co., to JOHN PINNER of same, for
    Ł 40...200 A on Big Long Creek adj. to his 200 A entry, #72 including a
part of JOHN PINNERS improvement & a spring near the ridge road, granted to HILLHOUSE
13 Aug 1779, & also 100 A, part of 200 A granted to sd. HILLHOUSE 13 Aug 1779, adj.
KATHERINE SMITH, WILLM MASSEY, JAMES HILLHOUSE, WILLIAM SMITH...JAMES HILLHOUSE (SEAL),
Wit: JAS LOGAN, JOHN MOORE, MARY LOGAN. Rec. Oct. term 1783.

Pp. 631-632: 1 Jan 1783, ROBERT ARMSTRONG of Lincoln Co., & HUGH BEATY of Rutherford
    Co., exrs. of L. W. & T. of FRANCIS BEATY of Mecklenburg Co., for Ł 30 pd.
by THOMAS BENTLEY, 100 A on both sides Indian Creek, granted to FRANCIS BEATY 22 Dec
1768 & No. 101...ROBERT ARMSTRONG (SEAL), HUGH BEATY (SEAL), Wit: FRANCIS BEATY, WALLACE
BEATY. Rec. Oct. term 1783.

Page 633: 7 Oct 1783, THOMAS PERKINS of Lincoln Co., to ABSOLAM WRIGHT of Guilford Co.,
    for Ł 25 proc. money...(grantee later ABSOLAM KNIGHT)...100 A adj. WILLIAM
REVAN[?]...THOMAS PERKINS (T) (SEAL), Wit: EDWARD HUNTER, JUDITH SCOTT HUNTER. Rec.
Oct. term 1783.

Pp. 633-635: 9 Oct 1783, JOSEPH HENRY Sheriff of Lincoln Co., to JAMES HENDERSON of
    same, ...where on 10 Jan 1783 at the court of P & QS for Lincoln Co.,
against JAMES BELL...writ of fiere facias...land on Dutchmans Creek adj. SAML KUYKEN-
DALL, WM. MOORE...200 A....JOSEPH HENRY Sheriff (SEAL), Wit: THOMAS ESPEY, JAMES
LITTLE, JOHN BARBER. Rec. Oct. term 1783.

Page 635: 2 Mar 1782, GEORGE ROMONGER of Lincoln Co., to SAML JOHNSTON of same, for Ł
    80 hard money...150 A on both sides PETER ROMONGERS branch, granted to sd.
GEORGE 9 June 1766...GEORGE ROMONGER (R) (SEAL), MARY ROMONGER (M) (SEAL), Wit: WILLIAM
GOODSTON (Λ), DANIEL JOHNSTON (D). Rec. Oct. term 1783.

Page 636: 1 Jan 1783, THOMAS WILSH of Lincoln Co., planter, to THOMAS BENTLEY of same,
    for Ł 20...120 A on both sides Indian Creek, part of 200 A granted to THO-
MAS WELSH 5 May 1769 & No. 343, & the remainder of the tract is lost by an older
right...THOMAS WELSH (T) (SEAL), Wit: FORNEY G. NORMAN, WALLACE BEATEY. Rec. Oct. term
1783.

Pp. 636-638: 8 Jan 1780, JOSEPH HENRY Esq., Sheriff of Lincoln Co., to WM JOHNSTON of
    Orange Co....by a writ from the Superior Court for the district of Hills-
borough, to levy of the goods & CHattells of EDMUND FANNING (late of Lincoln Co.)...
Ł 1000 specie which WILLIAM WYLY lately in superior court of Law & Equity recovered
against for damages...witness PLEASANT HENDERSON, Clerk of our said Court 1 Oct 1783...
land on both sides Little Creek in Lincoln Co., granted by L & R from JOHN DUHART &
wife of JOHN WALKER 29 Dec 1762 & from sd. WALKER to sd. FANNING, 17 Apr 1765...Wit:
JO. DICKSON. Rec. Jan. term 1784.

Pp. 638-639: 1 Dec 1766, WILLIAM CUMMING of Edenton, Chowan Co., to EDMUND FANNING of
    Childsburg, Orange Co., for Ł 30 proc. money...land in Mecklenburg, former-
ly Anson Co., which a certain JOHN ANDERSON by L & R conveyed to sd. WILLIAM CUMMING
& one JOHN DUNN equal moities, on NE side S fork Catawba, adj. ANDERSON, Clarks Creek
...WILLIAM CUMMING (SEAL). Dec. L, 1766: Then came WILLM CUMMINGS before me his
Majesties Chief Justice of Province and acknowledged said deed. JAS. HASELL. Rec. Jan.
term 1784.

Page 639: 15 Mar 1783, VALENTINE CROTS of Lincoln Co., to GEORGE RUMINGER of same, for
    s5...150 A granted to sd. CROTS by a certain MATTHIAS CLOWERS, and granted
to JOHN BUMGARNER by patent 20 Dec 1763...VALENTINE CROTS (Ŧ) (SEAL), Wit: GEORGE
TAYLOR(2), THOS SAUNDERS. Rec. Jan. term 1784.

Pp. 639-640: 20 Mar 1783, GEORGE DICK of Lincoln Co., to MATHIAS PETERSON of same, for
    Ł 18...66 A on waters of Killians Creek adj. DICKS old line, part of a
grant to sd. DICK 19 June 1772...____ [German signature] (SEAL), Wit: ARTHER BYNUM,
WILLIAM LUCKEY, PETER FORNEY. Rec. Jan. term 1784.

Pp. 640-641: 27 Sept 1782, MARTIN HOYL & wf MARY of Lincoln to JOSEPH AKER of same,
    for Ł 60 in gold or silver...185 A adj. PHILIP DELLINGER, near LAWRANCE
SNAPP, part of 370 A granted to MARTIN DELLINGER 30 Aug 1753...MARTIN HEIL [German

signature], Wit: JNO MOORE, _____ [Germansignature]. Rec. Jan. term 1784.

Pp. 641-642: 29 July 1783, ROBERT BLACKBURN of Lincoln Co., farmer, & wf MARTHA to
DANIEL ERNEST of same, yeoman, for Ŀ 50...land on E side Clarks Creek adj.
HENRY SUMMEROUR, HENRY GROISSES, sd. BLACKBURNS old survey, 66 A granted to sd. BLACK-
BURN 29 Oct 1767...ROBT BLACKBURN (SEAL), MARTHA BLACKBURN (SEAL), Wit: HENRY SUMMER-
OUR, _____ [German signature]. Rec. Jan. term 1784.

Page 642: We, chosen as arbitrators of a land dispute between LEWI LINEBARGER and
ALEXANDER MOORE, our judgement is as follows...the line run from a black oak,
sd. MOORES corner & runs So 8 Wt. until it strikes sd. LINEBARGERS line...LUTWIG
LEINBURGER, ALEXANDER MOORE; ROBT ANDER, NICKLESS RUM[?], JONATHAN GULLICK, WM.
CHRONICLE. Rec. Jan. term 1784.

APRIL COURT Anno Domini 1784.

Pp. 642-643: 26 Jan 1778, JOSEPH JACK of Tryon Co., to WILLIAM BRADSHAW of Mecklenburg
Co., for Ŀ 250...land in Tryon Co., 150 A granted to THOMAS ROBISON...
JOSEPH JACK (SEAL), Wit: ROBERT EWART, JAMES JOHNSTON. Rec. Apr. term 1784.

Pp. 643-644: 20 Jan 1784, JOHN SENTER of Lincoln Co., to JAMES MILLICAN of same, for
Ŀ 500 north currency...150 A on branches of Moores Creek falling into
Dutchmans Creek, part of a grant to JAMES SENTER for 628 A, 20 Feb 1775...JOHN SENTER
(SEAL), Wit: THOS BUCHANAN, JAS. ALEXANDER. Rec. Apr. term 1784.

Pp. 644-645: 3 Apr 1784, JAMES LUCKEY of Lincoln Co., to ROBERT LUCKEY of same, for Ŀ
100 specie...125 A on waters of Catawba River adj. JAMES LUCKEY...JAS.
LUCKEY (A) (SEAL), Wit: PETER FORNEY, JACOB SIDES. Rec. Apr. term 1784.

Pp. 645-646: 28 Nov 1776, BAPTIS SCOTT of Tryon Co., planter, to JAMES ABERNATHY of
same, planter, for Ŀ 300 proc. money...land on S side Catawba River oppo-
site the great shoals, granted to MARTIN SCHUCHMAN 23 Feb 1754, conveyed to ABRAM KUY-
KENDALL by L & R 27 Aug 1757, to BAPTIS SCOTT 23 Apr 1772 & also 80 A granted to SAML
COBON 13 Feb 1772 and conveyed to sd. SCOTT & another tract granted to sd. SCOTT 25
Jan 1773 208 A...BAPTIS SCOTT (SEAL), Wit: ROBT ABERNATHY, GEORGE SCOTT, JANE LAMKIN.
Rec. Apr. term 1784.

Pp. 646-648: 7 Apr 1784, JOSEPH HENRY, Sheriff of Lincoln Co....by a writ from the
Court of P & QS...to levy from RACHEL MATTIX, admx. of Estate of JOHN
MATTIX decd, Ŀ 36 specie, which JOHN HILL recovered...75 A on the S branch of Catawba,
adj. JAMES LEEPER (decd), CHITTAM, granted to ROBT EVANS, and conveyed to MATTIX 25
Dec 1774...Wit: SAM MARTIN, JAMES JOHNSTON, JAMES LITTLE, JNO. WORK. Rec. Apr. term
1784.

Page 648: 19 Aug 1780, JINKIN JINKINS of Lincoln Co., to CHARLES MATTIX of same, for
Ŀ 4000...300 A surveyed for JOHN McKNIT ALEXANDER, upon waters of S fork
Catawba on both sides Hoyles Mill path adj. WM. STERRETT, RICHARD SPAIGHT...JINKIN
JINKINS (SEAL), Wit: JOHN MATTOX, WILLIAM MATTOX (X). Rec. Apr. term 1784.

Pp. 648-649: 20 July 1775, DAVID NISBITT of Rowan Co., merchant, to WILLIAM STEVENSON
of Tryon Co., for Ŀ 5 proc. money...4 1/2 A on head of middle fork of
Crowders Creek, part of a grant to EPHRAIM McLEAN & conveyed to sd. NISBITT...DAVID
NISBIT (SEAL), Wit: JOHN BARBER, JOHN WILLSON. Rec. Apr. term 1784.

Pp. 649-650: 5 Apr 1784, HUGH BRISON of Cambden District, S. C. to JAMES HENRY of
Lincoln Co., for Ŀ 60 NC money...land on both sides Crowders Creek adj.
JOHN WALKER, McLEAN, granted to WILLIAM HENRY 25 Jan 1773, & conveyed to MOSES HENRY,
then to sd. BRISON...HUGH BRISON (SEAL), Wit: JNO. WILSON, JAMES THOMSON, JNO. BARBER.
Rec. Apr. term 1784.

Pp. 650-651: 6 Apr 1784, JOSEPH DICKSON of Lincoln Co., to JNO RUTLEDGE of same, for
Ŀ 140 proc. money...300 A on Lick fork of Buffaloe about 1 1/2 miles above
BENJAMIN SHAWS survey on the path from LEONARD SAFFERETS to JAMES KELLYS...granted to
FRANCIS BEATY 17 Nov 1764...JO. DICKSON (SEAL), Wit: JAMES RUTLEDGE, EDWARD HUNTER,
Rec. Apr. term 1784.

Pp. 651-652: 24 May 1781, STEPHEN SENTER of Lincoln Co., to JOHN SENTER of same, for
Ŀ 500 north currency...151 A on branches of Moores Creek, falling into
Dutchmans Creek, part of a grant to JAMES SENTER 628 A, 20 Feb 1775...STEPHEN SENTER
(SEAL), Wit: ABNER SENTER, ANTHONY SENTER (O). Rec. Apr. term 1784.

Page 652: 16 Nov 1778, ADAM STROUP of Tryon Co., to HENRY TANKERSLEY of Craven Co.,
S. C., for Ł 30...200 A on Leepers Creek...ADAM STROUP (SEAL), Wit: GASPER
CLOB, JOSEP ABERNATHY. Rec. Apr. term 1784.

Page 653: 20[?] Dec 1783, HENRY CARLOCK of Lincoln Co., planter, to FRANCIS GUTHRIE of
same, for Ł 70 north currency...land on both sides Buffalo Creek including
his own improvements where he now lives adj. THOMAS WELSHES, 200 A...HENRY CARLOCK
(SEAL), Wit: FORNEY NORMAN, GEORGE PATTERSON. Rec. Apr. term 1784.

Pp. 653-654: 7 Apr 1784, JOHN KINCAID of Lincoln Co., to THOMAS KINCAID for love & good
will to his son...100 A on W side Catawba on Killians Creek, part of a
granted to ANDREW KILLION 30 Sept 1749, and conveyed to sd. JOHN KINKAID...JOHN KINKAID
(O) (SEAL), Wit: JO: DICKSON. Rec. Apr. term 1784.

Pp. 654-655: 14 Nov 1783, ELISABETH WYATT of Lincoln Co., to JAMES WYATT JR., of same,
for Ł 12 proc. money...100 A on E side S fork Catawba, adj. JAMES WYATT
with DANIEL WYATT's improvement, part of a grant to JAMES WYATT for 392 A, 26 Oct 1767
...ELISABETH WYATT (SEAL), Wit: NATHL JACKAN, AARON TEMPLEMAN. Rec. Apr. term 1784.

Pp. 655-656: 7 Apr 1784, JOHN KINKAID of Lincoln Co., to ROBERT KINKAID for Love & good
will to his son...100 A on Killians Creek, part of a grant to ANDREW KILL-
ION 30 Sept 1749& conveyed to sd. JOHN KINKAID 20 Oct 1765...JOHN KINKAID (.) (SEAL),
Wit: JO: DICKSON. Rec. Apr. term 1784.

Pp. 656-657: 18 Oct 1783, SAMUEL JOHNSTON & wf OLIVE of Lincoln Co., to WILLIAM TILLMAN
of same, for Ł 250 in gold or silver...land on N side of Dutchmans Creek,
adj. JAMES KUYKENDALL, 280 A granted to MARY KUYKENDALL now wife of MARTIN ARMSTRONG,
26 Mar 1755 & conveyed by sd. ARMSTRONG to ANDW HAMPTON by single deed 25 Nov 1763...
SAMUEL JOHNSTON (SEAL), OLLEY JOHNSTON (O) (SEAL), Wit: ROBT. ALEXANDER, THOMAS BURKE,
JOHN BEALE. Rec. Apr. term 1784.

Pp. 657-658: 18 Nov 1783, JAMES WYATT of Lincoln Co., to JENKEY JENKINS of same, for
Ł 200...land on waters of Long Creek, a branch of S fork Catawba, 100 A
granted to ANDREW HOYLE 25 Apr 1768...JAMES WYATT (SEAL), Wit: EDWARD HUNTER, EDWARD
JENKINS, JOHN JENKINS (+). Rec. Apr. term 1784.

Pp. 658-659: 7 Apr 1784, JOHN KINCAID of Lincoln Co., to JOHN KINCAID JR. of same, for
love & good will to his son...100 A, part of a grant to ANDREW KILLION,
30 Sept 1749, and conveyed to KINCAID 20 Oct 1765...JOHN KINCAID (C) (SEAL), Wit: JO:
DICKSON. Rec. Apr. term 1784.

Pp. 659-660: 27 Mar 1784, GEO. LAMKIN of Lincoln Co., to WM. TILLMAN of same, for Ł 50
specie...100 A on head of Nowlins branch, part of a grant to JOSEPH DAVIES
400 A, 28 Apr 1768...GEOR. LAMKIN (SEAL), Wit: ROBT ABERNATHY, JNO. TAYLOR. Rec. Apr.
term 1784.

Page 660: 19 Jan 1784, ALEXANDER LOCKHEART of Lincoln Co., & wf AGNESS to NICHOLAS
FRIDAY, for Ł 55...land on both sides Clarks Creek, adj. his own, DANIEL
WARLUCKS lines, 154 A granted to sd. LOCKHEART 5 May 1769...ALEXANDER LOCKHEART (E)
(SEAL), AGNESS LOCKHEART (A) (SEAL), Wit: SARAH CUMBEDAN, ROBERT BLACKBURN. Rec.
Apr. term 1784.

Page 661: JOHN HOLLAND of Lincoln Co., to JOHN HUGGINS JR., of same, for Ł 45...cattle,
furniture, guns etc. [items listed]...6 Feb 1784...JOHN HOLLAND (SEAL), Wit:
JAS. LOGAN. Rec. Apr. term 1784.

Pp. 661-662: 8 Jan 1784, JOSEPH HENRY Sheriff of Lincoln Co., to WM. JOHNSTON of Orange
Co., NC....by a writ from Superior Court of Hillsborough...to levy from
goods & chattels of EDMUND FANNING, Ł 1000, which WILLIAM WYLY recovered in court...
150 A on NE side S fork Catawba, adj. JOHN ANDERSON, part of 300 A which JOHN ANDERSON
conveyed to WILLIAM CUMMING & JOHN DUNN in equal moities & WM. CUMMING conveyed to sd.
FANNING 1 Dec 1766...Wit: JO: DICKSON. Rec. Apr. term 1784.

Page 663: 17 May 1783, JOHN BEALE of Lincoln Co., to GEORGE SEITS for s5...land on
waters of Docters Creek, 184 A adj. SAILERS...JOHN BEALE (SEAL), Wit: JOS.
ABERNATHY, MATHEW ROBERSON, JOHN EDELMAN (X). Rec. Apr. term 1784.

Pp. 663-664: 7 May 1783, JOHN BEALE of Lincoln to JACOB SEITS, for s5...150 A on
Doctors Creek, granted to BEALE by WM. ALSTON 8 Mar 1775...JOHN BEALE
(SEAL), Wit: JO ABERNATHY, MATHEW ROBERSON, JOHN EDELMAN (X). Rec. Apr. term 1784.

Pp. 664-665: 10 Mar 1784, WILLM. TILLMAN of Lincoln Co., to HUGH BLAIR of same, for
Ł 280 specie...land on N side Dutchmans Creek, granted to MARY KUYKENDALL,
26 Mar 1755, who married MARTIN ARMSTRONG & conveyed to ANDREW HAMPTON, then to SAMUEL
JOHNSTON, then to sd. TILLMAN...near ABRAM KUYKENDALL, 280 A...WM. TILLMAN (SEAL), Wit:
JO: DICKSON, ADAM BAIRD. Rec. Apr. term 1784.

Pp. 665-666: 7 Mar 1782, HENRY HOLLMAN & wf ELISABETH to HENRY SUMMEROR of Burk Co.,
NC, for Ł 200...land in Burk Co., on E side Clarks Creek, 200 A, part of
a grant to SAMUEL BEASON 30 Sept 1749, conveyed to JOHN RAMSOUR 13 & 14 June 1754, and
by JACOB & DAVID RAMSOUR (heirs of sd. JOHN by his L. W. & T.) conveyed to HENRY
HOLLMAN 21 Nov 1767...HENRY HOLLMAN (SEAL), ELISABETH HOLLMAN (O) (SEAL), Wit: ROBERT
BLACKBURN, HENRY GROSE. Rec. Apr. term 1784.

Pp. 666-667: 5 Dec 1783, CHARLES MATTOX of Lincoln Co., to SAML CALWELL of same, for
Ł 50 specie...80 A granted to GEORGE LAMKIN 20 Feb 1775, conveyed to MATTOX
on a branch of S fork Catawba...CHARLES MATTOX (SEAL), Wit: JAS McKEE, JAMES ROBINSON.
Rec. Apr. term 1784.

JULY COURT Anno Domini 1784.

Pp. 667-668: 7 June 1784, JOHN CARSON of Mecklenburg Co., NC to WILLIAM KILLION of
Lincoln Co., for Ł 40...land on both sides Buffaloe Creek above a parcel
of land formerly the property of JAMES KELLY 200 A granted to DAVID McCREE 16 Dec 1769,
and conveyed to sd. JOHN CARSON 1771[?]...JOHN CARSON (X) (SEAL), Wit: ROBT ALEXANDER,
JOHN SENTLER, Rec. July term 1784. Proven by ROBERT ALEXANDER.

Pp. 668-669: 15 Mar 1783, JOHN POSTON of Rowan Co., to GEORGE GOODWIN of Lincoln Co.,
for Ł160 hard money or old trade...300 A including the falls on Leonard
Sailors Creek, granted # 88, to THOMAS ANDERSON 1 Apr 1761...JOHN POSTON (SEAL), Wit:
MATTHEW GOODWIN, JESSE LANIER. Rec. July term 1784.

Pp. 669-670: 18 ___ 1784, PETER CLOBB SR., of Lincoln Co., to MICHAEL MASTER of same,
for s5...land on Leepers Creek...PETER CLOBB (PC) Wit: JOS. ABERNATHY,
JACOB SEIDS. Rec. July term 1784.

Pp. 670-671: 22 Mar 1783, CHRISTOPHER LISTER & wf ESTHER of Lincoln Co., to JACOB
SEITS of same, for Ł 30...100 A adj. JACOB SEITS, KILLION, LISTER, part of
a grant to THOMAS OURICK 24 Sept 1754, the said THOMAS OURICK dying & leaving no
other heir but the said ESTHER, wife of CHRISTOPHER LISTER...._____ [German signature]
(SEAL), ESTHER LISTER (+). Wit: JOHN WALKER, JOHANNES ULMAN[?] [German signature]. Rec.
July term 1784.

Pp. 671-672: 6 Jan 1784, GODFREY LIPE of Mecklenburg to NICHOLAS FRYDAY & NICHS. SCRUM
for Ł 30 specie...land on the shoal branch falling into the high shoals
adj. REINHARDTS, DELLINGER, 250 A...[Signed in German and English]. Wit: HEINRICH
DELLINGER [German signature], PHILLIP NIELL. Rec. July term 1784.

Page 672: 3 Nov 1783, JOHN RUTLEDGE of Lincoln Co., to ROBERT McCOMB for Ł 80 specie...
land on both sides Dutchmans Creek, adj. GEORGE RUTLEDGE, JAMES COBUN, JAMES
GRAHAM, HUGH JENKINS, & THOMAS GHENT, including his own improvements, 300 A granted to
sd. RUTLEDGE 24 Mar 1780...JOHN RUTLEDGE (SEAL), Wit: GEORGE RUTLEDGE, ADAM NIELL. Rec.
July term 1784.

Pp. 672-674: 5 July 1784, JOSEPH HENRY, Sheriff of Lincoln Co., to ROBERT ABERNATHY...
by a writ from the Court of P & QS of Lincoln Co....to levy from JOHN
BROWN SKRIMSHIRE, a sum recovered against him by ROBERT ABERNATHY...date of writ, 21
Nov 1783...109 A on waters of Leepers Creek, adj. MORRISONS corner, part of a grant to
JOHN STROUD, conveyed to PETER DUNKIN & then to JOHN BROWN SKRIMSHIRE. Rec. July term
1784.

Pp. 674-675: 5 July 1784, PETER LABOON of Lincoln Co., planter, to WILLIAM CALDWELL of
Mecklenburg Co., for Ł 200...300 A on Kettle Shoal Creek, granted to JAMES
COZART 19 May 1772, conveyed to WM. GRAHAM & then to sd. PETER LABOON...PETER LeBON
(SEAL), Wit: _____ GRAHAM, JAMES JOHNSTON, PETER FORNEY. Rec. July term 1784.

Pp. 675-676: 7 July 1784, GEORGE LAMKIN of Lincoln Co., to ROBERT ALEXANDER of same, for
Ł 25 specie...50 A adj. BATES, McKENDRICKS...GEORGE LAMKIN (SEAL), Wit:
ROBT ABERNATHY, ROBERT MCCOMB. Rec. July term 1784.

Pp. 676-677: 13 Mar 1784, GEORGE LITTLE of Lincoln Co., planter, & wf NANCY to JOHN
ALLEN of Lincoln Co., for Ł 20 proc. money...land on both sides Killions

Run, adj. FRANCIS BEATY, FLEMMING, 250 A granted to JOHN LITTLE 22 Dec 1768...GEORGE
LITTEL (SEAL), NANCY LITTLE (C) (SEAL), Wit: JOHN WAGGONER, JOHN REED. Rec. July term
1784.

Pp. 677-678: 3 July 1784, HENRY TANKERSLEY of Lincoln Co., to ROBERT MITCHEL of Mecklenburg Co., for Ł 100 specie...land on both sides GEORGE REACES [REAVES?]
branch of Lepers Creek...HENERAY TANKERSLEY (+) (SEAL), Wit: JOHN CARUTH, RALPH COBBS.
Rec. July term 1784.

Pp. 678-679: THOMAS SALTER of the Northern Liberties of the City of Philadelphia, Pa.,
merchant, for natural love & affection to JAMES SULLIVAN, late of the State
of New Jersey, & wf MARY & her two eldest sons SAMUEL and JOHN SULLIVAN and of their
going to and residing on the premises herein after granted and for the sum of s 10....
land on S side S fork Catawba, 600[?] A (being the second described of two tracts
which PETER HARPILL of Lincrum[?] Township, in the County of Bucks, Pa., yeoman, by deed
20 Feb 1768, recorded in Mecklenburg Co., granted to sd. THOMAS SALTER, by two distinct
patents both dated 28 Mar 1751, granted to sd. HARPELL)...4 Sept 1783....THOS SALTER
(SEAL), Wit: BURTON HATHAWAY, PETER CARSON, R. WHITEHEAD. Rec. July term 1784.

Pp. 679-680: 23 Apr 1782, THOMAS SALTER of Philadelphia, merchant to JOHN COXE of
Middlesex Co., N. J., yeoman, the half brother of sd. THOMAS SALTER & AARON
COXE, PAUL COXE, ELISHA COXE & ELIJAH COXE, the sons of sd. JOHN COXE, for natural love
& affection...and for s5....land on N side S fork Catawba on S branch of Fishers Creek,
part of grant to PETER HARPILL, 100 A, by L & R 19 & 20 1768, recorded in Mecklenburg
Co...THOS SALTER (SEAL), Wit: RACHEL COXE, NANCY COX, R. WHITEHEAD. Rec. July term
1784.

Pp. 681-682: 25 Feb 1784, JOHN FLEMING of Rutherford Co., to ARCHIBALD FLEMING of
Lincoln Co., for s 10 specie...67 A, part of 594 A granted by EARL GRAN-
VILLE to FRANCIS BEATY, 10 May 1762 & by sd. BEATY conveyed to JOSEPH CRONKLETON, by
deed 11 Dec 1770...JOHN FLEMING (SEAL), Wit: FRAS. CUNNINGHAM, FRAS. McCORKEL. Rec.
July term 1784.

Pp. 682-683: 19 July 1784, JAMES HENMAN of Burke Co., to ELIZABETH HENMAN, for Ł 12
specie...land on waters of Clarks Creek, 223 A, part of 777 A granted to
sd. HENMAN 28 Oct 1782...JAMES HENMAN (SEAL), Wit: JO: DICKSON, JAMES JOHNSTON. Rec.
July term 1784.

Page 683: ROBERT OLIPHANT of Lincoln Co., for Ł 65 s 4 to ____ BRYSON...150 A on
Littens Mill Creek, adj. lands of JAMES McLEAN, WILLM SHERRILL, & WM. SIMPSON,
& also cattle, furniture, etc [listed]...26 June 1784...ROBERT OLIPHANT (SEAL), Wit:
GEORGE BROTHERTON. Acknowledge before FRS. CUNNINGHAM, J. P. 28 June 1784.

Pp. 683-684: 16 June 1784, ROBERT ALEXANDER of Lincoln Co., to JOHN SUMTER of same, for
Ł 40...200 A on waters of Groves branch of Crowders Creek adj. JOHN Mc-
FARLANDS entry...ROBT ALEXANDER (SEAL), Wit: ROBERT WIER. Rec. July term 1784.

Pp. 684-685: 22 Jan 1784, JOSEPH HENRY Sheriff of Lincoln Co., to ABRAHAM FORNEY of
same...by a writ from Court of Lincoln Co...to levy from ADAM DECK,
FREDERICK HAGAN, MICHL SIDES, EDWD TURNER & HENRY MASTER Ł 660 s 17 specie, which JACOB
FORNEY recovered against them...write dated 23 Nov 1783...190 A on S side Catawba, on
Cheagles Creek, now Killions Creek, part of a tract granted to MATHIAS DECK, 3 Apr
1752 & conveyed to ADAM DECK...Wit: WM. GRAHAM, JOHN CARUTH, JO. DICKSON. Rec. July
term 1784.

Pp. 685-687: 22 Jan 1784, JOSEPH HENRY Sheriff to SUSANAH FORNEY...[same court case as
in preceding deed]...140 A on W side Killians Creek, granted to GEORGE
MUSKIMUCK, and conveyed to ADAM DIKES, 20 Jan 1775...Wit: JOHN KINKAID (0), ROBERT
LUCKEY, WM. LUCKEY. Rec. July term 1784.

Pp. 687-688: 22 Jan 1784, JOSEPH HENRY, Sheriff, to ABRAHAM FORNEY [same court case
as in preceding deeds]...141 A, part of grant to ADAM DIKE...Wit: THO.
WHITE, ROBT ALEXANDER, JOHN CARUTH. Rec. July term 1784.

Pp. 688-689: 1 May 1783, JONATHAN POTTS & wf RACHEL of Mecklenburg Co., to JOHN FARTRIES
of same, for Ł 80...land on a branch of Haywards Creek, granted to THOMAS
POTTS, father to sd. JOHN,. by patent 28 Mar 1755, & conveyed to sd JOHN by his L. W.
& T., 244 A adj. DANIEL KINGERYS, JOHN BOLINGERS...JONT. POTTS (SEAL), RACHEL POTTS (1)
(SEAL), Wit: LUDWIG WINFL[?] [German signature], JOHN ALEXANDER. Rec. July term 1784.

October Court A. D. 1784

Pp. 689-690: 20 July 1784, JOHN HILL of Lincoln Co., to JOHN MATTOXES heirs, for s 5...
                75 A on S branch of Catawba adj. JAMES BEATY, CHITTAM, ROBERT CAMPBELL...
granted to ROBERT EVANS and conveyed to sd. JOHN MATTOX, 28 Dec 1784...JOHN HILL (SEAL),
Wit: ROBT ALEXANDER, THOMAS ROBINSON. Rec. Oct. term 1784.

Pp. 690-691: 1 Oct 1784, JAMES McAFEE of Lincoln Co., to sons JAMES McAFEE JR., ABNER
                McAFEE, & ROBERT McAFEE, minors, for natural love and affection...150 A
including the improvements the said JAMES McAFEE now lives on...to involve in the sd.
JAMES JR. at the death of JAMES SR & wf MARY...to ABNER & ROBT, tract on Indian Creek,
called the Greesy Cove in Washington Co., N. C., purchased in co-partnership with his
brother ROBERT McAFEE from MARTIN DUDWILER & others...also negroes [named]...JAMES
McAFEE (SEAL), Wit: WM. GRAHAM, JO. DICKSON. Rec. Oct. term 1784.

Pp. 691-692: GEORGE LAMKIN SR. & GEORGE LAMKIN JR. of Lincoln Co., to THOS RINE...negro
                Ben, aged 21 years, for ℔ 135 specie, 1 Apr 1784...GEORGE LAMKIN (SEAL),
GEORGE LAMKIN JR. (SEAL), Wit: WM. CALDWELL. Rec. Oct. term 1784.

Pp. 692-693: 16 Aug 1784, JACOB WEAVER of Lincoln Co., to JACOB FIFFER of same, farmer,
                for ℔ 35...land in formerly Burke, now Lincoln Co., adj. LUTES, on N fork
Long Branch adj. ALEXANDER, GEORGE KEPNER, JAMES WILSON, DANL McKISSICK, granted to sd.
WEAVER 14 Mar 1780...J. G.[?] WEAVER (SEAL), MARGARETHA WEAVER (+) (SEAL), Wit: MARTIN
_____ [German signature]. Rec. Oct. term 1784.

Pp. 693-694: 23 May 1778, ABRAHAM KEENER & wf JULIANA of Tryon Co., to PETER FINGER of
                same, for ℔ 135...part of a tract sold to JAS ABERNATHY, 170 A granted to
GASPER KEENER, father of sd. ABRAHAM 25 May 1754, and 100 A granted to sd. ABRAHAM 28
Feb 1775... _____ KEENER [German signature] (SEAL), JULIANA KEENER (+) (SEAL), Wit:
RICHARD JOHNSTONE, ROBT BLACKBURN. Rec. Oct. term 1784.

Pp. 694-695: 1 Oct 1784, SAMUEL COLLINS SENR. of Lincoln to ABRAHAM COLLINS of same,
                for ℔ 40...100 A on waters of Buffaloe Creek adj. lands of JAMES COLLINS,
including SAML COLLINS JR. improvement...granted to SAMUEL COLLINS SR., 25 Mar 1780...
SAMUEL COLLINS (SEAL), Wit: WM GRAHAM, JAMES McAFEE, ISAAC PHILLIPS. Rec. Oct. term
1784.

Pp. 695-696: 25 Feb 1784, JOHN FLEMING of Rutherford Co., to ARCHD FLEMING of Lincoln
                Co., for s 10 specie...part of 594 A granted by EARL GRANVILLE to FRANCIS
BEATY & by BEATY to sd. JOHN FLEMING 4 July 1765...JOHN FLEMING (SEAL), Wit: FRS.
CUNNINGHAM, SAML LONG. Rec. Oct. term 1784.

Pp. 696-697: 29 May 1784, THOMAS McCORMACK of Lincoln Co., to SAMUEL McMINN, for ℔ 100...
                land on waters of Sigels Creek adj. JOHN SIGEL, YOCKARD, 200 A granted to
sd. McCORMACK, 25 Mar 1780...THOS McCORMACK (𝟚) (SEAL), Wit: FRS CUNNINGHAM, JOHN
CUNNINGHAM. Rec. Oct. term 1784.

Pp. 697-698: 3 Sept 1784, ROBT ARMSTRONG of Lincoln Co., to JOHN HILL of same, for ℔
                100...land on N side S fork Catawba adj. JOHN ARMSTRONG, granted to ROBERT
CAMPBELL 26 Oct 1767, and conveyed to FRANCIS ARMSTRONG, then to ROBERT ARMSTRONG by
bond...ROBERT ARMSTRONG (SEAL), Wit: JAMES HILL, SARAH ARMSTRONG. Rec. Oct. term 1784.

Pp. 698-699: 4 Oct 1784, MICHAEL HECKELMAN & wf ELIZABETH of Lincoln Co., to VALENTINE
                LITTLE of same, for ℔ 150...land on both sides Leopards Creek adj. THOMPSON,
granted to sd. HECKELMAN, 300 A 22 Dec 1768...MICHAEL HECKELMAN (M) (SEAL), ELISABETH
HECKELMAN (+). Wit: HENRY SUMMEROUR, ROBT BLACKBURN.

Pp. 699-700: 4 Aug 1784, ALEXR LOCKHART & wf ANN of Lincoln Co., planter, to FELIX
                CLOTSETLER of aowan Co., for ℔ 55...land on E side Clarks Creek, 150 A,
part of a grant to ALEXR LOCKHART 23 Dec1768...ALEXANDER LOCKHART (SEAL), ANN LOCKHART
(A) (SEAL), Wit: ROBT BLACKBURN, JACOB DICK[?] [German signature]. Rec. Oct. term 1784.

Pp. 700-701: 19 Dec 1782, JAMES RUTLEDGE of Lincoln Co., to JOHN WALKER of same, for
                ℔ 5 specie...land on waters of Dutchmans Creek, 73 A granted to JAMES
RUTLEDGE, 25 Jan 1773, and part of a new survey for which he has not yet obtained the
grant, 45 A...JAMES RUTLEDGE (SEAL), Wit: JOHANNES WILL, WM. MATHIS (WM). Rec. Oct. term
1784.

Pp. 701-702: 12 Sept 1778, JOHN BEARD, son & heir to WM. BAIRD, decd, planter, to Meck-
                lenburg Co., N. C., to JAMES WITHERSPOON of same, Taylor, for ℔ 60...land
in Tryon Co., about 2 miles SW of JOHN BEARD on a branch of Little Catawba, 147 A....

granted to WM. BAIRD decd, 6 Apr 1765...JOHN BEARD (O) (SEAL), Wit: JOHN FLENNIKIN, SAML FLENNIKEN. Rec. Oct. term 1784.

Pp. 702-703: 2 Oct 1784, JAMES McAFEE & WILLIAM GREEN of Lincoln Co., to THOMAS MARTIN of same, for ₤ 100...290 A, formerly the property of JOSEPH GREEN, on both sides of the province line, on a branch of Buffalo Creek, adj. JOSEPH GREEN...JAMES McAFEE (SEAL), WILLIAM GREEN (SEAL), MARY McAFEE (M) (SEAL), Wit: JACOB COLLINS, WILLIAM MESRAM [?] (X). Rec. Oct. term 1784.

Pp. 703-704: 13 Sept 1784, WILLIAM JOHNSTON of Orange Co., N. C. to JOSHUA WILSON of Lincoln Co., for ₤ 45 specie...150 A beginning at a corner formerly JOHN ANDERSONS, one undivided moiety of 300 A conveyed by JOSEPH HENRY Sheriff of Lincoln Co. to WILLIAM JOHNSTON 8 Jan 1784...WILLIAM JOHNSTON (SEAL), Wit: None. 7 Oct 1784, Acknowledged before JNO. WILLIAMS.

Pp. 704-705: THOMAS McKNIGHT of Craven Co., S. C., farmer, for ₤ 130 proc. money pd. by SAMUEL YOUNG of Rowan Co...land in Tryon Co., on S fork CAtawba, 350 A, part of a tract executed & taken from JAMES CARTER, Esq., by a writ of fiere facias against him by JOHN BRANDON & issued in February term 1762[?] at Supreme Court in Wilmington & by sd. BRANDON conveyed to McKNIGHT by L & R 6 & 7 Jan 1763....12 Sept 1772...THOMAS McKNIGHT (SEAL), Wit: WM. McKNIGHT, SARAH McKNIGHT (ζ). Proved by WM. McKNIGHT 10 Mar 1778, before SAML SPENCER. March term, Salisburg District.

January Court 1785.

Pp. 706-707: 16 Mar 1784, JOSEPH HENRY, Sheriff of Lincoln Co., to DANIEL McKISSICK, Esq., of same, ...by a writ issued from Court of P & QS of Lincoln Co., ...to levy against goods & chattels of JOHN MILLS, ₤ 160...writ dated 8 Oct 1783...606 A on waters of Clarks Creek including his deceased father's WILLIAM MILLS improvements adj. JOHN WELSH, JOHN RAMSOUR, granted to sd. JOHN MILLS, 23 Apr 1768...JOSEPH HENRY, Sheriff (SEAL), Wit: JOHN BARBER, SAMUEL CLOUNEY, JNO. WILSON. Rec. Jan. term 1785.

Page 707: LEONARD SAILOR of Lincoln Co., for ₤ 50 pd. by JOSEPH DICKSON of same, one negro Sam which is now in the hands of the Commrs. of confiscated property... 17 Sept 1781...LEONARD SAYLOR (L) (SEAL), Wit: RALPH COBBS. Rec. Jan. term 1785.

Pp. 707-708: 13 Dec 1784, WILLIAM HENRY SR. of Camden Dist., S. C. to JOHN BARBER of Lincoln Co., for ₤ 125 specie...land on S branch of Crowders Creek & middle branch of sd. creek adj. WM HENRY JR., 224 A...WILLIAM HENRY (SEAL), Wit: JNO. WILSON, WM HENRY JUR., JAS LAUGHLIN. " N. B. The said WILLIAM HENRY is not bound hereby to warrant any part of the above described land that may be interlocked with or covered by the courses of WM. ADAMS' patent or THOMAS PRICE's." Rec. Jan. term 1785.

Pp. 708-710: 31 Dec 1784, THOMAS PRICE of Lincoln Co., to NATHAN MENDINGHALL of same, for s 5 sterling...land on waters of Crowders Creek adj. to sd. MENDING-HALL, part of a grant to JOHN MARTIN...THOMAS PRICE (SEAL), Wit: JOHN WILSON, ISABELLA PRICE (/). Rec. Jan. term 1785.

Page 710: 14 June 1777, JOHN STROUD & wf PATTY of Tryon Co., farmer, to THOMAS HESLIP of same, for ₤ 32 s10 NC money...116 A on S side Catawba...JOHN STROUD (+) (SEAL), PATTEE STROUD (X) (SEAL), Wit: DANL HIIVOY [?], JOSEPH SCOTT, JESSE FINN (J). Rec. Jan. term 1785.

Pp. 710-711: 10 Sept 1777, THOMAS HESLIP of Tryon Co., to THOMAS BELL of same, for ₤ 63 ...land on W side Catawba adj. GRAHAM, HENRY JOHNSTON, ARCH. LITTLE, granted to JOHN STROUD, 25 Jan 1773 & conveyed to sd. HESLIP...THOMAS HESLIP (SEAL), Wit: JOSEPH SCOTT, ARCHIBALD LITTLE. Rec. Jan. term 1785.

Pp. 711-712: 29 Sept 1784, JAMES HUGGINS of Lincoln Co., to SAMUEL DYER of same, for ₤ 80 specie...200 A on Potts Creek of Buffaloe...JAMES HUGGINS (SEAL), Wit: WILLIAM YANCEY, JOHN _____ [German signature]. Rec. Jan. term 1785.

Pp. 712-713: 6 Oct 1781, HENRY JASPER of Lincoln Co., to WILLIAM GORDON of same, for ₤ 70 hard money...land on a branch of Kings Creek, granted to sd. JASPER 2 Mar 1775, adj. GEORGE PINKLEY, 136 A, including sd. JASPERS improvment...HENRY JASPER (X) (SEAL), Wit: WILLIAM YANCEY, EDWARD CORNWIL. Rec. Jan. term 1785.

Page 713: 20 Nov 1784, WM CORDEN of Lincoln Co., to ROBERT WIER of same, for ₤ 120 specie...136 A (same tract in preceding deed)...WILLIAM GORDEN (SEAL), Wit: WILLIAM YANCEY, JOHN WEER. Rec. Jan. term 1785.

Page 714: 3 Nov 1784, HENRY THOMPSON of Lincoln Co., to THOMAS WHEELER of same, for
Ł 60...land on S side Mountain Creek, 67 A, part of a tract conveyed by
ABRAHAM COTTELL to HENRY THOMPSON Sr. 5 & 6 Jan 1765 & then to ALEXANDER THOMPSON, and
by ALEXANDER & Henry Sr. by deed 7 May 1772 to sd. HENRY THOMPSON JR...HENRY THOMPSON
(SEAL), Wit: FS. CUNNINGHAM, JAMES LITTEN. Rec. Jan. term 1785.

Page 715: 2 May 1782, GEORGE LEONARD SAILOR of Lincoln Co., to GEORGE SEITS of same,
for Ł 30...37 A, part of a grant to GASPER KEENER on a branch falling into
Leepers Creek..._____ [German signature] (SEAL), Wit: ROBT JOHNSTON, GEORGE LAMKIN,
MICHAL RUDISIL [German signature]. Rec. Jan. term 1785.

Pp. 715-716: 12 Oct 1784, GEORGE LEONARD SAILOR of Lincoln Co., to JOHN RUDISILL of
same, for Ł 160...380 A part of a grant to GASPER KEENER 12 May 1754, &
the other part granted to JAMES ABERNATHY, 28 Feb 1775...GEORGE LEONARD SAILOR (LS),
Wit: MICHEL RUDISEL [German signature], LEMUEL SAUNDERS. Rec. Jan. term 1785.

Pp. 716-717: 30 July 1784, JAMES HENDERSON of Lincoln Co., to JOHN TAYLOR of same, for
Ł 60...land on both sides Dutchmans Creek adj. SAML KUYKENDALL, WILLIAM
MOORE, conveyed to sd. HENDERSON by JOSEPH HENRY, Sheriff, 9 Oct 1783...JAMES HENDERSON
(SEAL), Wit; AARON BOGS, JAMES BOGS. Rec. Jan. term 1785.

Pp. 717-718: 10 Jan 1783, FRANCIS GILMORE of Lincoln Co., to JOHN MOORE of same, for
Ł 200 hard money...land on Duharts Creek, near NATHL HENDERSON, DAVIES,
250 A granted to JOHN McKNITT ALEXANDER 9 Nov 1764...FRANCIS GILMORE (SEAL), Wit:
JOHN MOORE, JOHN McCORD, SAML STEWART. Rec. Jan. term 1785.

Pp. 718-719: 8 Mar 1784, DAVID ELDER of Lincoln Co., to ANDW FLOYD, for Ł 130 specie...
227 A on S side S fork Catawba, about 3 miles below the lower Mount, granted to ALLEN ALEXANDER 16 Nov 1764, & conveyed to NATHL HENDERSON, then to JAMES PATTER-
SON, and then to sd. ELDER...DAVID ELDER (SEAL), Wit: WILLIAM KINKEAD, JONA. GULLICK.
Rec. Jan. term 1785.

Pp. 718-719: 1 Mar 1777, JAMES ABERNATHY & wf ELISABETH of Tryon Co., to GEORGE LEONARD
SAYLOR of same, for Ł 150...land on both sides Leepers Creek adj. ABRAHAM
KEENER 280 A part of a grant to GASPER KEENER 20 May 1754 & also 200 A granted to sd.
ABERNATHY, 28 Feb 1775...JAMES ABERNATHY (SEAL), ELISABETH ABERNAHTY (SEAL), Wit: ROBT
JOHNSTON, ELISABETH KEENER (+). Rec. Jan. term 1785.

Pp. 720-721: 17 May 1784, PETER CLOBB SR., PETER CLOBB JR., & MICHAEL MASTER, all of
Lincoln Co., to JACOB SEITS of same, for Ł 112...167 A adj. MICHL MASTER...
PETER CLOBB SEN (P) (SEAL), PETER CLOBB JR (PC) (SEAL), MICHL MASTER (M) (SEAL), Wit:
JOS. ABERNATHY, _____ [German signature]. Rec. Jan. term 1785.

Pp. 721-722: 27 Oct 1783, JOHN RUTLEDGE of Lincoln Co., to JEAN RUTLEDGE of same, for
Ł 40 proc. money...200 A, granted to ROBERT WALKER 25 Apr 1767 & afterwards
deeded to GEORGE RUTLEDGE, adj. ANDREW HAMPTON, HOGAN...JOHN RUTLEDGE (SEAL), Wit:
JAMES RUTLEDGE, GEORGE RUTLEDGE. Rec. Jan. term 1785.

Pp. 722-723: 15 Dec 1783, SAMUEL LOFTON of Lincoln Co., to FRANCIS ADAMS of same, for
Ł 150...300 A granted to THOMAS CAMPBELL, 2 Mar 1775, near the old waggon
road, adj. HARRIS, BROWN...the contents of 2 patents, conveyed by CAMPBELL to sd.
LOFTON...SAMUEL LOFTON (SEAL), Wit: ANDW FLOID, ISAAC HOLLAND, JOHN BERRY. Rec. Jan.
term 1785.

Pp. 123-124: 30 Dec 1784, FRANCIS ADAMS of Camden District, to ROBERT CAMPBELL of
Lincoln Co., for Ł 160...300 A [same land as in preceding deed]...FRANCIS
ADAMS (SEAL), Wit: WM MOORE, WM. BERRY, JOHN GLEN. Rec. Jan. term 1785.

April Court A. D. 1785

Page 724: Grant to JOSEPH KENNADY, 300 A Tryon Co., on W side Mountain Island joining
his own land...4 Mar 1775. JO. MARTIN. Rec. Apr. term 1785.

Pp. 724-725: 10 Dec 1783, THOMAS BEATY, HUGH BEATY, & ROBERT ARMSTRONG, Exrs. of L. W.
& T. of FRANCIS BEATY, to JOSEPH HENRY of Lincoln Co., for Ł 100 specie...
500 A on India Creek of S fork Catawba, about 3 miles above THOMAS REYNOLDS including
the old Indian Camp....Wit: GEORGE EWING, JAMES BEATEY, FRANCIS BEATY. Rec. Apr. term
1785.

Pp. 725-726: 21 Feb 1785, JOHN AREND of Lincoln Co., to PHILIP KENSLER of same, for Ł

70[?] NC currency...land the sd. JOHN AREND now lives upon on SE end of his plantation on both sides Leepers Creek...JOHN ARENDK (SEAL), Wit: VALLENTINE MAUNY, ROBT JOHNSTON. Rec. Apr. term 1785.

Pp. 726-727: 30 Oct 1784, JOSEPH HENRY Sheriff of Lincoln Co., to JOSEPH DICKSON, Esqr., by virtue of a writ from the court of P & QS of Lincoln Co., to levy of JOEL HELTON at the suit of JOHN HILL...land on S side S fork Catawba, granted to JOHN BROWN SKRIMSHIRE, 2 Mar 1775 & by him to SAMPSON LARKIN, & by him to sd. JOEL JELTON... ____ Jan 1784...Wit: WM. MOORE, THOS BUCKHANNON. Rec. Apr. term 1785.

Pp. 727-728: 12 Oct 1784, NICHOLAS FRIDAY of Lincoln Co., to CHRISTOPHER ARNEY for ₺ 20 ...land on S side Dellingers Creek belwo ARNEYS land, 200 A...NICHOLAS FRIDAY (SEAL), Wit: MICHAEL RIDISIL [?] [German signature]. Rec. Apr. term 1785.

Pp. 728-729: 1 Jan 1785, WILLIAM GARNER of Rutherford Co., planter, to TOBIAS JAMES of Lincoln Co., for ₺ 16...land on both sides Reynolds Mill Creek, 300 A... WILLIAM GARNER (M) (SEAL), Wit: NATHL CLARK, JOHN REYNOLDS (‡R). Rec. Apr. term 1785.

Pp. 729-730: 11 Jan 1785, ISAAC KIMBOL of Lincoln Co., to WILLIAM CROCKETT of same, for ₺ 50 specie...land on Kings Creek adj. HENRY JASPER, granted to KIMBALL 13 Oct 1783...ISAAC KIMBAL (SEAL), Wit: JOHN WILSON JUR., SARAH WILSON, JOHN WILSON. Rec. Apr. term 1785.

Page 730: 5 Apr 1785, NICHOLAS GOSNELL of Lincoln Co., to CHARLES GOSNELL JR., of same, for ₺ 150...50 A on Long Creek adj. HORTON, granted to sd. GOSNELL 1 Nov 1784...NECLES GOSNELL (SEAL), Wit: GEORGE LAMKIN. Rec. Apr. term 1785.

Page 731: 1 Apr 1785, NICHOLAS GOSNELL of Lincoln Co., to CHARLES GOSNELL JR., of same, for ₺ 100 specie...100 A being the place where sd. CHARLES GOSNELL JR. now lives on Long Creek adj. HOVISES corner, granted to sd. NICHOLAS GOSNELL 1 Nov 1784... NECLIS GOSNELL (SEAL), Wit: GEORGE LAMKIN, SAMUEL LAMKIN. Rec. Apr. term 1785.

Pp. 731-732: 12 Mar 1785, JAMES WALLACE of Orange Co., N. C. to JOHN HUFFMAN of Lincoln Co., for ₺ 70 specie...200 A adj. JAMES FOSTER, WILLIAM LINNS[?], JACOB ROADS, Granted to DANIEL McCARTY ____ Jan 1775...JAMES WALLACE (SEAL), Wit: GEORGE LAMKIN, RICHARD VANDIKE. Rec. Apr. term 1785.

Pp. 732-733: 12 Feb 1779, DERRICK RAMSOUR of Tryon Co., to JOHN SIGMAN of same, Blacksmith, for ₺ 50...land on both sides Clarks Creek, 200 A part of a grant to PETER BROIL 3 Sept 1753 and conveyed to sd. RAMSOUR 3 June 1758...DERRICK RAMSOUR (X) (SEAL), Wit: JACOB RAMSOUR, ROBT BLACKBURN. Rec. Apr. term 1785.

Pp. 733-735: 12 Mar 1777, PETER SUMMY of Tryon Co., farmer, to DAVID RAMSOUR of same, yeoman, for ₺ 20...land on N side S fork Catawba, adj. WARLICK, RAMSOUR, part of a grant to PETER SUMMY 29 Apr 1768, 41 1/4 A...PETER SUMMY (PS) (SEAL), Wit: ____ WARLICK [?] [German siganture], ANDREAS HÜTIG (English, ANDREW HEDICK); ROBT BLACKBURN. Rec. Apr. term 1785.

Pp. 735-736: 27 Apr 1784, ROBERT JOHNSTON of Lincoln Co., to WILLIAM McQUOWN of same, for ₺ 145 specie...land on both sides Doctors Creek adj. WILLIAM MOORE, MILLICAN, HOGAN, 200 A...ROBERT JOHNSON (SEAL), Wit: JO. DICKSON, JAMES DICKSON. Rec. Apr. term 1785.

Page 736: 4 Jan 1785, WILLIAM DAVIS of Lincoln Co., to ROBERT ALEXANDER of same, for ₺ 50...11 1/2 A & 8 poles adj. to ALEXANDER...WM. DAVIES (SEAL), Wit: JOHN HUNTER [?], HENRY DAVIES. Rec. Apr. term 1785.

Page 737: 2 Aug 1779, STEPHEN LYON of Tryon Co., planter, to URBAN ASHEBURN of same, for ₺ 1500...land on both forks of Andersons Creek, part of a grant to THOS ANDERSON SENR., 16 Apr 1761 & sold to THOMAS ANDERSON JR. 3 Dec 1776, then to sd. LYON 18 May 1778...STEPHEN LYON (SEAL), Wit: LEMUEL SAUNDERS, THOMAS ANDERSON JR., Rec. Apr. term 1785.

Pp. 737-738: 24 Mar 1785, JONATHAN JONES, Blacksmith, of Lincoln Co., to PHILIP NULL of same, for ₺ 120 NC money...land on both sides Potts Creek, part of a grant to JOSEPH MILLICAN, & conveyed by MILLICAN to his daughter CATHREN who is wife of sd. JONES, 250 A adj. POTTS...JONATHAN JONES (X) (SEAL), Wit: DAVID RAMSEY, THOMAS ANDERSON (T). Rec. Apr. term 1785.

Pp. 738-739: 25 Mar 1785, JOHN BATES & wf MARGARET of Lincoln Co., to JOHN HILTEBRANT of same, for Ł 50...land on waters of Howard Creek, adj. REINHART, WELCH, 300 A granted HENRY HILTEBRANT 22 Dec 1768 & transferred to sd. BATES...JOHN BATES (E) (SEAL), MARGARET BATES ( ) (SEAL), Wit: ROBT BLACKBURN, LEWIS WARLICK. Rec. Apr. term 1785.

Pp. 739-740: 6 Dec 1784, DANIEL CAMPBELL & wf MARGARET of Lincoln Co., to GEORGE MISCO-
NONK of same, for Ł 40 specie...land on both sides Little Creek of Catawba, adj. FLEMMING, BARNET LOCKMAN 270 A granted to LEONARD KILLING & conveyed to NETHEAS KILLING, then to sd. CAMPBELL...DINALE CAMPBELL (SEAL), MARGARET CAMPBELL (#) (SEAL), Wit: FRAS. McCORKLE, _____ [German signature]. Rec. Apr. term 1785.

Pp. 740-741: 11 Mar 1784, THOMAS WINKLER & wf ANN MARY of Burk Co., to JOHN KILLIAN Of
same, for Ł 170 specie...land in Burk Co., formerly Rowan, on both sides Clarks Creek, adj. JOHN KILLION, 200 A _____ [German signature] (SEAL), ANN MARY WINKLER (X) (SEAL), Wit: THOS: WHITROW[?], JACOB KILLION, _____ WINKLER[?] [German signature]. Rec. Apr. term 1785.

Pp. 741-742: 16 Feb 1785, MICHAEL INGEL of Licoln Co., to PHILIP KINSLER of same, for
Ł 7 s 2...part of a grant sd. INGLE now lives on, near the Shoal on Leopards Creek, 9 A & 40 poles...MICHAEL INGEL (MƗ) (SEAL), Wit: DAVID RAMSEY, JOHN AREND. Rec. Apr. term 1785.

Page 742: 27 Nov 1784, SAMUEL CARPENTER of Rutherford Co., planter, to REUDOLPH BEN of
Lincoln Co., for Ł 32...land on both sides Buffalo Creek of Broad River, adj. CHRISTIAN CARPENTER, WILLIAM REYNOLDS, 200 A...SAMUEL CARBENDER (SEAL), CEABREN CARPENTER ( ) (SEAL), Wit: ROBERT GLENN, _____ ZIMMERMAN [German signature]. Rec. Apr. term 1785.

Page 743: 13 Aug 1784, WILLIAM REED of Mecklenburg Co., to JOHN HILTEBRANT of Lincoln
Co., for Ł 40...land on waters of Potts Creek, adj. JOHN BRADLEY, granted to sd. REED 8 Apr 1768...WILL REED (SEAL), Wit: JOSEPH JOHNSON, DANIEL _____. Rec. Apr. term 1785.

Pp. 743-744: 2 May 1782, GEORGE ADAM SITS of Lincoln Co., to JOHN GODFREY AREND of
Rowan Co., for Ł 80...land on both sides of Leepers Creek adj. JASPER KEENERS, decd, granted to sd. GEORGE ADAM SITS, 16 Nov 1764 ...already in consequence with land of LEONARD SAYLOR & settled by a deed 2 May 1782, total 200 A...GEORGE SIDES (GS), Wit: JACOB FORNEY, ABRAHAM EARHART, PETER FORNEY. Rec. Apr. term 1785.

Page 745: 15 Feb 1785, GEO. DENNY of Lincoln to WILLIAM PRICE of same, for Ł 150...land
on N fork Crowders Creek, 148 A being an undivided moiety of grant to ARCHIBALD HOSTOUN, & conveyed to JAS PRICE, then to GEO. DENNY...GEORGE DENNY (SEAL), Wit: SARAH WILSON, MARY WILSON, JNO. WILSON. Rec. Apr. term 1785.

Pp. 745-746: 6 Apr 1785, GEORGE LAMKIN of Lincoln Co., to RICHARD VENDIKE of same, for
Ł 70 in gold & silver...200 A on a branch of Long Creek adj. STEPHEN SENTER, DAVIS, Tan Trough branch, granted to JOSEPH DAVIS 28 Apr 1768...GEORGE LAMKIN (SEAL), HANNAH LAMKIN (H)(SEAL)Wit: ANN LAMKIN (A), STEPHEN SENTER. Rec. Apr. term 1785.

Pp. 746-747: 16 Jan 1781, HUGH SHANNON of Lincoln Co., to ROBERT SHANNON of same, for
Ł 8000...100 A adj. HUGH SHANNON, part of a grant to EVAN LEWIS 7 Apr 1752 & conveyed to sd. HUGH 5 Nov 1763...HUGH SHAAN (SEAL), Wit: JOHN MOORE, JONATHAN GULLICK. Rec. Apr. term 1785.

Pp. 747-748: 2 Apr 1785, JOSHUA SHERRILL of Lincoln Co., to JAMES HOLDSCLAW of same,
for Ł 200...land on W side Catawba, at the mouth of Burtchfields Creek, 103 1/4 A, granted to sd. SHERILL by EARL GRANVILLE 10 May 1762...JOSHUA SHERILL (SEAL), Wit.: ELISHA SHERELL, ELIAS WHITE. Rec. Apr. term 1785.

Pp. 748-749: 4 Jan 1785, PETER SUMMY of Lincoln Co., farmer, to ANDREW HEADY of same,
planter, for Ł 5...land on N side S fork Catawba, 64 A, part of a grant to sd. SUMMY 29 Apr 1768...PETER SUMMY (PS) (SEAL), Wit: JACOB RAMSOUR, HENRY HOKE. Rec. Apr. term 1785.

Pp. 749-750: 15 Feb 1785, FREDERICK SUMMY & wf PLANTENA of Lincoln Co., to JACOB SUMMY
of same, for Ł 150...100 A on S side S fork Catawba, part of a grant to ABINGTON SHERILL 4 Apr 1756, & sd. ABINGTON SHERILL died intestate & fell to his oldest son REUBEN SHERILL & conveyed to sd. FREDERICK SUMMY 1 Apr 1778...FREDRICH SUMY [German signature], PLANTEENA SUMY (X) (SEAL), Wit: JACOB _____ [German signature], ROBT. BLACKBURN. Rec. Apr. term 1785.

Pp. 750-751: ____ 1777, LAWRENCE SNAPP of Rowan Co., to GEORGE REAL of Tryon Co., for
₺ 40 proc. money...195 A, part of a grant to LAWRENCE SNAPP, SR., father of
sd. LAWRENCE SNAPP JR., & by the L. W. & T. of SNAPP SR. fell to SNAPP JR....LAWRENCE
SNAPP (SEAL), Wit: MICHEL RUDISILI [German signature], ALEXANDER LONG. Rec. Apr. term
1785.

Pp. 751-752: 26 Feb 1785, CORNELIUS McCARTY of Lincoln Co., to JACOB RINE of same, for
₺ 45...130 A on W side S fork Catawba, on waters of Big Long Creek, adj.
RINE, ROADS, JOHN HOYLE, including his own improvement...CORNELIUS McCARTY (⅃) (SEAL),
Wit: JO. DICKSON, JAMES RUTLEDGE. Rec. Apr. term 1785.

Pp. 752-753: 4 Apr 1785, JOSEPH GLADEN of Lincoln Co., to SAMUEL AUTHUR for ₺ 40....
125 A on long branch of Beasons Creek, granted 8 Oct 1783 & 25 A part of
200 A granted to GLADEN 25 Mar 1780...JOSEPH GLADEN (SEAL), Wit: None. Rec. Apr. term
1785.

Pp. 753-754: 15 Mar 1783, ROBERT MONTGOMERY of 96th Dist., S. C. to HENRY CLARK Of
Rutherford Co., N. C., for ₺ 100 proc. money...land in Lincoln Co., on
both sides Rudisells Creek, adj. RUDISELL, granted to WM. WYATT 29 Aug 1768...ROBERT
MONTGOMERY (SEAL), ISBEL MONGTOMERY (↰) (SEAL), Wit: EPHRAIM CLARK, JESSE CLARK (Γ).
Rec. Apr. term 1785.

Page 154: 2 Apr 1785, JACOB SEITS of Lincoln Co., to GEORGE SEITS of same, for ₺ 60...
150 A granted to JACOB SEITS by JOHN BEALE 7 May 1783...JACOB SEIDS (SEAL),
Wit: JO DICKSON, JNO BARBER, Rec. Apr. term 1785.

Pp. 754-755: 7 Aug 1784, CHARLES FREDERICK GLANCE of Frederick Co., Md., to WILLIAM
VERNON of Lincoln Co., for ₺ 50 specie...100 A on W side S fork Catawba,
adj. VERNOR[?], JACOB GLANCE, JOHN SMITH, part of a grant to sd. CHARLES FREDERICK
GLANCE for 400 A, 25 Mar 1780...CHARLES FREDERICK GLANCE (SEAL), Wit: JOHN HUFMAN. Rec.
Apr. term 1785.

Pp. 755-756: 11 Mar 1785, BENJAMIN PERKINS of Wilks Co., Georgia, to JOSHUA SHERILL of
Lincoln Co., for ₺ 200...land on both sides Mountain Creek, 347 1/2 A,
granted to sd. PERKINS by deed from EARL GRANVILLE 21 Dec 1761...BENJAMIN PERKINS
(BP) (SEAL), Wit: JAMES HOLSCLAW, JOSEPH HAWKINS. Rec. Apr. term 1785.

Pp. 756-757: 21 Sept 1784, JOSEPH HENRY, Sheriff of Lincoln Co., to FRANCIS CUNNINGHAM
Esqr., of same...by a writ of the court of P & QS of Lincoln Co., to levy
of REUBEN SIMPSON, at the suit of JAMES RANKIN, ₺ 54 s4 d7...land on Beaver Dam Branch
on W side Catawba, adj. STEPHEN FISHER, FRANCIS CUNNINGHAM, 500 A, part of 640 A granted
to REUBEN SIMPSON, 11 Oct 1783 # 581...Wit: ROBERT RANKIN, DAVID HODSON, AGNESS CLARK
(1). Rec. Apr. term 1785.

Pp. 757-758: JAMES ROBINSON of Lincoln Co., planter, for love & affection to son DAVID
ROBINSON, planter, tract purchased of EARL GRANVILLE 1 Dec 1753, 184 A...
17 Mar 1785...JAMES ROBINSON (SEAL), Wit: W. W. JOHNSON, JESSE ROBINSON. Rec. Apr. term
1785.

Pp. 758-759: 15 Dec 1785, BENNET OSBORN of NinetySix District, [S. C.], to JAMES LITTON
of Lincoln Co., for ₺ 400...land on S side Catawba on a small creek that
falls in below Sherills ford, adj. JAMES CLARK, JAMES LITTEN, granted to sd. OSBORN 28
Oct 1782...BENNET OSBURN (SEAL), Wit: ELISHA SHERRILL, JAMESHOLSCLAW. Rec. Apr. term
1785.

Pp. 759-760: 2 Apr 1785, ROBERT JOHNSON of Lincoln Co., to ALEXANDER JOHNSON of same,
for ₺ 25...land on Doctors Creek adj. JOSEPH DICKSON, WILLIAM McEWINS[?],
granted to WILLIAM MOORE & conveyed to ROBERT ALEXANDER, then to JAMES MILLICAN, then
to ROBERT JOHNSTON...ROBERT JOHNSTON (SEAL), Wit: JO DICKSON, EDWD HUNTER. Rec. Apr.
term 1785.

Pp. 760-761: 4 Mar 1783, JOHN DUDEROW of Lincoln Co., to JOHN SMITH of same, for ₺ 20...
land on S side Causners branch of S fork Catawba adj. sd. DUDEROW, granted
to WOOLEY CARPENTER 28 Apr 1768...JOHANNES DOTTERO [German signature] (SEAL), Wit:
JOHN HUFMAN, JACOB COSTNER, GEORGE LAMKIN. Rec. Apr. term 1785.

Pp. 761-762: 1 Nov 1784, JOHN STROUD & wf MARTHA of Lincoln Co., to LEWIS HILL of
Franklin Co., N. C., for ₺ 110...110 A on bank of Catawba River, adj. JAMES
DOZER, JOHNSONS Creek, BELL, LITTLE...JOHN STROUD (X) (SEAL), MARTAH STROUD (X) (SEAL),
Wit: SHARED STROUD, JAMES NIXSON, JOHN STROUD. Rec. Apr. term 1785.

Page 762: 7 Aug 1784, CHARLES FREDERICK GLANTZ, of Frederick Co., Md., to JOHN SMITH of N. C., for Ʞ 60 specie...304 A on W side S fork Catawba, adj. JACOB GLANTZ, CONRED KERNDER, GERARD VINZANTS, & nearly VERNERS, DUDEROWS, granted to sd. GLANTZ, 25 Mar 1780...CHARLES FREDERICK CLANCE (SEAL), Wit: JOHN HUFMAN. Rec. Apr. term 1785.

July Court A. D. 1785.

Page 763: 12 Apr 1785, ABRAHAM CLARK of Lincoln Co., to WILLIAM GRAHAM of same, for Ʞ 100 specie...200 A on waters of Beatons Creek, adj. WILLIAM MOORE, WIDOW COLLINS, granted to sd. CLARK 25 Apr 1780...ABRAHAM CLARK (SEAL), Wit: GEO. COCKBURN, JONATHAN HARDIN (h), Rec. July term 1785.

Pp. 763-764: 12 July 1784, ROBERT BURCHFIELD of Burk Co., N. C. to FRANCIS CUNNINGHAM of Lincoln Co., for Ʞ 40...land granted to ROBERT BURCHFIELD SR., 14 Mar 1780 adj. JOHN HAWKINS, crossing Isaacs Creek, 350 A...ROBERT BURCHFIELD (Robe)(SEAL), Wit: THOS WHEELER, WM. COUNLY[?], BENJN. CORNELIUS. Rec. July term 1785.

Pp. 764-765: 22 June 1785, JEAN PATTERSON of Lincoln Co., to THOMAS THOMAS of same, for Ʞ 15...100 A on Duharts Creek adj. sd. PATTERSON, granted to JAMES PATTERSON, decd, 9 Oct 1783...JEAN PATTERSON (X) (SEAL), JOHN PATTERSON. Wit: WILLM RANDLES, SAMUEL CLOWNEY. Rec. July term 1785.

Pp. 765-766: 16 June 1785, JOHN BULLOCK of S. C. to JAMES COLEMAN of same, for Ʞ 500 sterling...245 A on W side S fork Catawba, 200 A granted to GEO. MICHAEL WISENANT, 13 Oct 1765...JOHN BULLOCK (SEAL), Wit: JAS DAWSON, DANL BULLOCK. Rec. July term 1785.

Pp. 766-767: 27 June 1785, JOHN BULLINGER of Lincoln Co., to DANIEL BULLINGER of same, for Ʞ 5...part of a grant to FRANCIS MACKILWEAN 17 May 1754 & part of 2 tracts granted to SAMUEL HOWARD, on Howards Creek, formerly known as Fishers Creek, 257 A...JOHANNES ____ [German signature] Wit: FRS. CUNNINGHAM, WILLIAM ____. Rec. July term 1785.

Pp. 767-768: 22 June 1785, JOHN SEFFRET to CHRISTIAN HEGAR, both of Lincoln Co., for ____ land on S side S fork Catawba, 300 A granted to LEONARD SEFFRED,decd, father of sd. JOHN, 17 Feb 1760...JOHN SEFFRET (SEAL), Wit: JOHN LONG, PETER FORNEY. Rec. July term 1785.

Pp. 768-769: 19 June 1785, JOHN CARRUTH of Lincoln Co., planter, to POLEY CHIRNEY of same, for Ʞ 12...land on S fork Buffaloe Creek, adj. ANDREW HESLIP, granted to CARUTH 1 Nov 1785 & No. 98...JOHN CARRUTH (SEAL), Wit: ROBT JOHNSTON, GEORGE WISTENHUNT. Rec. July term 1785.

Pp. 769-770: 6 June 1785, MARTIN HOYLE of Lincoln Co., to GEORGE DELLINGER of same, for Ʞ 20...land on Leepers Creek adj. his own & LAWRENCE SNAPPS lines, 180 A granted to HOYLE 22 Apr 1763...MARTIN HEIL (SEAL), Wit: JNO MOORE, NECLES GOSNELL. Rec. July term 1785.

Pp. 770-771: 22 Jan 1785, THOMAS ROBINSON of Rutherford Co., to JACOB HERRE & LEONARD HERRE of Lincoln Co., for Ʞ 30...land on both sides Leonards fork of Indian Creek adj. CLOUD, ROBINSON, 100 A granted to THOMAS ROBINSON 25 Jan 1773...THOMAS ROBINSON (SEAL), Wit: JOHN CARUTH, VALENTINE MAUNEY. Rec. Apr. term 1785.

Page 771: 6 July 1785, JACOB RINE of Lincoln Co., to PETER RINE, for Ʞ 50...land on both sides Long Creek, adj. JACOB RINE, 170 A surveyed for JACOB RINE, granted 6 Apr 1765...JACOB REIN [German signature] (SEAL), Wit: JO DICKSON, EDWARD HUNTER. Rec. July term 1785.

Page 772: State of N. C., Lincoln Co., June 23, 1785. This day came AGNES REED before me and made oath that she delivered the wife of WILLIAM ALEXANDER decd of a female child ANN ALEXANDER, now the wife of JAMES FLEMING, & known by the name of ANN FLEMING. AGNES REED (+). Before JAMES LITTLE, J. P. Wit: JO DICKSON, C. C. Rec. July term 1785.

Pp. 772-773: 2 July 1785, WILLIAM SHERRILL SEN., of Lincoln Co., to WM. SHERRILL JR., for natural love & affection to his son...land on W side Catawba adj. ADAM SHERRILL   Wit: MOSES SHERILL, ADAM SHERILL (A). Rec. July term 1785.

Pp. 773-774: North Carolina, Lincoln Co.:WILLIAM MOORE of Washington Co., on the night

of 1 Apr 1785, at JACOB RAMSOURS, in Lincoln Co., behave myself very ill in abusing
[verbally] CAPT. ROBERT ALEXANDER, for which I am very sorry...8 Apr 1785. WILLIAM MOORE.
Wit: JNO WILSON, JAS BARBER. Rec. July term 1785.

Pp. 774-775: 22 Mar 1780, WILLIAM CATHY of Lincoln Co., to FRANCIS SNELL of same, for
Ł 550...land near Dutchmans Creek, adj. orphans line, granted to sd.
CATHEY by Indenture 1777...WILLIAM CATHY (W) (SEAL), Wit: JAMES COBURN, SAMUEL RANKIN,
Rec. July term 1785.

Page 775: 5 July 1785, ROBERT SHANNON of Lincoln Co., to DAVID McCORD, for Ł 150...
160 A on Duharts Creek, adj. JOHN MOORE...ROBERT SHANNON (SEAL), Wit: WILLIAM
MOORE, JOSEPH MESSESS. Rec. July term 1785.

Pp. 775-776: 13 Nov 1784, PHILIP CLONINGER, of Lincoln Co., to MATHIAS PETERSON, for
Ł 60...land on both sides Sheagles Creek..._____ [German signature] (SEAL),
Wit: JOS. ABERNATHY, ADAM CLONINGER, Rec. July term 1785.

Pp. 776-777: 29 Dec 1783, AMBROSE FOSTER of Lincoln Co., to ANDREW FALLS of Lincoln Co.,
for Ł 160...200 A granted to ALEXR DIXON, 18 Apr 1771, & conveyed to sd.
FOSTER on watersof Crowders Creek, in the forks of Bridges Branch, Bairds Mountain...
AMBROSE FOSTER (SEAL), Wit: JAS LOGAN, STEPHEN SENTER, JNO BARBER. Rec. July term 1785.

Pp. 777-778: 8 July 1785, JOHN SUTTON JR., of Lincoln Co., to PHILIP NULL of same, for
Ł 250...negroes [named] intrust...JOHN SUTTON the elder hath bond for his
appearance at Morgan District Superior Court in Burke Co., 1 Sept next...JOHN SUTTON
(SEAL), Wit: EDWARD HUNTER, W. GRAHAM, GEORGE RISH. Rec. July term 1785.

Pp. 778-779: 26 June 1785, STEPHEN SENTER of Lincoln Co., to ANDREW TAYLOR of same, for
Ł 35...land in fork of Catawba on both sides path from Spencers ford to
COL. DICKSON, 77 A...STEPHEN SENTER (SEAL), Wit: JO DICKSON, JO HENRY. Rec. July term
1785.

Pp. 779-780: 2 July 1785, WILLIAM SHERILL of Lincoln Co., to ADAM SHERILL of same, for
Ł 55...land between the plantations where sd. WILLIAM & ADAM now liveth,
138 1/2 A...WILLIAM SHERILL (X) (SEAL), Wit: MOSES SHERRILL, JAMES CLARK[?]. Rec. July
term 1785.

OCTOBER COURT

Pp. 780-781: 27 Aug 1783, MATTHEW BROWN, Gunscmith, late of Lincoln Co., to JAMES
HENDERSON of same, for Ł 2000...land on a branch of Little Catawba, adj.
lands formerly sd. MATTHEW BROWNS, adj. JOHN BAIRD & WM BEARDS survey, granted to sd.
BROWN 25 Mar 1780...MATTHEW BROWN (SEAL), Wit: ROBT ALEXANDER, JAMES ALEXANDER. Rec.
Oct. term 1785.

Pp. 781-782: 6 June 1774, GEORGE LEONARD SAILOR of Tryon Co., to DEVOLD CRITES of same,
for Ł 100 proc. money...land on middle fork of Killions Creek, adj. FRAN-
CIS BEATY, 240 A purchased by SAILOR of ULRICK CROWDER, & sd. CROWDER of PETER SEALOR
JR., and granted to PETER SEALOR SR., 10 Apr 1761..._____ [German signature] (SEAL),
Wit: JACOB SEIDS, PETER CREITS [German signature], JOHANNES WILL. Rec. Oct. term, 1785.

Pp. 782-783: 8 Oct 1785, PHILIP NULL of Lincoln Co., to JOHN SUTTON JR., for Ł 250...
negroes [named]...PHILIP NULL (SEAL), Wit: EDWARD HUNTER, ARTHUR BYNUM.
Rec. Oct. term 1785.

Page 783: 24 July 1784, DANIEL WILL of State of Pa., to MATTHIAS DEVALD of N. C., for
Ł 50 NC. money...land on both sides toddy branches of Killions Creek adj.
SEIDS, 243 A...DANIEL WILL (SEAL), Wit: [all 3, German signatures]. Rec. Oct. term
1785.

Page 783: June 30, 1785. BENJAMIN ARMSTRONG acknowledges that what he said of JOHN
BOGS in regard of scandal is false..BENJA. ARMSTRONG. Wit: JNO REED, JOHN
BALDRIDGE. Rec. Oct. term 1785.

Page 784: 30 Sept 1785, JNO McKNITT ALEXANDER of Mecklenburg Co., to MICHAEL RUDACELL
SR., of same, for Ł 20...200 A on Rudasells Creek adj. & interfering with
MICHAEL RUDASELLS old patent, granted to JOSEPH CARSON 26 Oct 1767, #197, conveyed to
JOHN McK. ALEXANDER, 2 Sept 1769...J. M. ALEXANDER (SEAL), Wit: WM SHARPE, _____.
Rec. Oct. term 1785.

Pp. 784-786: 5 Oct 1785, WM SHARPE of Rowan Co., to JOHN MILLER of same, for ₺ 100...
        land in Lincoln Co., late Burke, on both sides Jacobs fork S fork Catawba,
adj. JOSEPH JOHNSON, in the edge of WARDS bottom, granted to sd. SHARPE,28 Oct 1782...
WM. SHARPE (SEAL), Wit: JO DICKSON, R. WOOD.

Page 786: 27 June 1785, PHILIP NULL of Lincoln Co., to GEORGE RUSH of same, for ₺200...
        320 A on path between SAML BICKERSTAFFS & DERRICK RAMSOURS & another tract of
30 A...PHILLIP NULL & wf MARGARET...PHILLIP NULL (SEAL) [Margaret did not sign]. Wit:
EDWARD HUNTER, ROBERT WEER. Rec. Oct. term 1785.

Page 787: 11 Jan 1785, ROBERT KNOX of Lincoln Co., to JOHN BOGGS, for ₺ 87 specie...
        land on branches of Killions Creek, at an old corner of WILLIAM CATHEYS land,
adj. SEITS, KINKAID, 160 A...granted to THOMAS YEATS, 22 Dec 1765 & conveyed to WM.
CROCKET 6 Mar 1761, & to WILLIAM KING 2 July 1774, to ROBERT KNOX 7 Oct 1775...ROBERT
KNOX (SEAL), Wit: JAMES JOHNSTON, BENJAMIN ARMSTRONG. Rec. Oct. term 1785.

Pp. 787-788: _____ 1785, WILLIAM PERKINS SEN., to BENJAMIN PERKINS, for ₺ 5...part of
        a tract sd. PERKINS now live upon on Mountain Creek, 120 A...WILLIAM
PERKINS (SEAL), SARAH PERKINS (X) (SEAL), Wit: JAMES LEE, JAMES GALLESMORE. Rec. Oct
term 1785.

Pp. 788-789: 16 Feb 1785, JOHN SAILLOR of Ninety Sixth Dist., S. C. to JAMES BRYSON of
        Lincoln Co., for ₺ 60...land on S fork of Mountain Creek adj. JAMES MARTIN,
part of a tract granted to SAILLOR 300 A, 8 Oct 1782...JOHN SAILLORS (₮S) (SEAL), Wit:
WILLIAM GANT, LUKE BLADE (X), JOHN GANT. Rec. Oct. term 1785.

Pp. 789-790: 2 May 1782, GEORGE LEONARD SAILOR of S. C., to JOHN CUTFREETERANT of same,
        for ₺ 8...53 A on both sides Leopards Creek, adj. KEENERS, GEORGE SIDES...
part of a grant to GASPER KEENER...____ [German signature] (SEAL), Wit: GEORGE LAMKIN,
ROBERT JOHNSTON, MICHAEL _____ [German signature]. Rec. Oct. term 1785.

Pp. 790-791: 10 Sept 1785, URBAN ASHYBRAUER & wf MARY of Lincoln Co., to JOHN SEGEL of
        same, for ₺ 90...200 A granted to sd. ESHYBRAUER, 26 Oct 1767...URBAN
ESHYBRAUER (AB) (SEAL), MARY ESHYBRAUER (+) (SEAL), Wit: JOHN HILDEBRAND, ROBT.
BLACKBURN. Rec. Oct. term 1785.

Pp. 791-792: 1785, WM PERKINS SR., to JAMES LEE JONES for ₺ 19 s 10...99 1/2 A, part of
        tract sd. PERKINS live on, on waters of Mountain Creek...WILLIAM PERKINS
(SEAL), Wit: RICHARD ALEXANDER, (RA), RACHEL ALEXANDER (RA). Rec. Oct. term 1785.

Pp. 792-793: 21 Sept 1785, THOMAS BEATTY & ROBERT ARMSTRONG of Lincoln Co., to CHRISTIAN
        CARPENTER of same, for ₺ 50...250 A on Shoal branch of 3 forks of Buffaloe
Creek, granted to FRANCIS BEATY 26 Sept 1766...THOS BEATY (SEAL), ROBERT ARMSTRONG
(SEAL), Wit: JAMES BEATEY, JOHN BEATY. Rec. Oct. term 1785.

Pp. 793-794: 6 July 1785, THOMAS BEATY of Rowan Co. and JOHN BEATY of Mecklenburg Co.,
        to JAMES MURPHEY of Lincoln Co., for ₺ 70...land on Shoal branch of 3
forks of Buffaloe Creek, granted to FRANCIS BEATY 26 Sept 1766...THOMAS BEATY (SEAL),
JOHN BEATY (SEAL), Wit: ROBERT ARMSTRONG, JAMES BEATY. Rec. Oct. term 1785.

Pp. 794-795: 15 Mar 1785, JOHN McCARTY of Lincoln Co., to THOMAS HEARTON, Hatter, for
        ₺ 80...land on waters of Coburns Creek including his own improvement adj.
BENJ. ARMSTRONG, WM. CATHEY, & JOHN RAMSEY, granted to McCARTY 1 Nov 1784...JOHN Mc-
CARTEY (SEAL), Wit: ROBT KINKEAD, SAML BLYTH, WILLIAM McTINCAILL[?]. Rec. Oct. term
1785.

Page 795: 1 June 1782, JOHN COX & AARON COX of Lincoln Co., to DEDER HEFFNER of same,
        for ₺ 10...10 A adj. the mill pond...JOHN COX (SEAL), AARON COX (SEAL), Wit:
ROBERT ABERNATHY, PAUL COX. Rec. Oct. term 1785.

Pp. 795-796: 4 Oct 1785, PETER SUMMEY SR., of Lincoln Co., farmer, to JACOB ROADS of
        same, for ₺ 50...land on S fork Howards Creek, adj. THOMAS WELCHES old
corner, 300 A granted to SUMMY 29 Oct 1767...PETER SUMMY (PS) (SEAL), Wit: _____,
ROBT BLACKBURN. Rec. Oct. term 1785.

January Court 1786

Pp. 796-797: JOHN JONES & MARTHA JONES of Rowan Co., to HUGH ROBISON of same, farmer,
        for ₺ 50...land in Lincoln Co., including SOLOMON HOVERS improvement, on
W side Catawba, on W side N branch of Killions Creek, adj. WILLIAM HAGAR, 135 A granted
to SOLOMON HOOVER 13 Oct 1756...13 July 1784...JOHN JONES (SEAL), MARTHA JONES (M)

(SEAL), Wit: JOHN MONTGOMERY, GEORGE ROBISON. Rec. Jan. term 1786.

Pp. 797-798: JOHN PITTILLO of Lincoln Co., to ROBERT CRUTHERS of same,...a negro Ned,
            3 years od...14 Nov 1785...JOHN PITTILLO (SEAL), Wit: THOMAS LITTLE,
FRANS. McCORKLE. Rec. Jan. term 1786.

Page 798: LEONARD SAYLORS to THOMAS ESPEY & JOHN CARRUTH, one Negro Milly, for Ł 20...
            2 May 1783...LEONARD SAYLOR (LS) Wit: SAML ESPEY. Rec. Jan. term 1786.
LEONARD SAILOR of Rutherford Co., for Ł 60 to ROBERT WEER of Lincoln Co., negro Milla
in the Custody of THOMAS ESPEY...14 Oct 1785... _____ [German signature] (SEAL), Wit:
WM GRAHAM, D. DICKEY. Rec. Jan. term 1786.

Pp. 798-799: LYDIA MASSEY of Lincoln Co., for Ł 87 specie to JOHN BARBER...negro
            Rebecca....26 Dec 1785...LYDIA MASSEY (+) (SEAL), Wit: WM. RICE, JOHN
ROBISON. Rec. Jan. term 1786.

Pp. 799-800: 12 Aug 1784, JOSEPH HENRY Esq., Sheriff of Lincoln Co., to JOSEPH HENRY
            of same, by a writ to levy Ł 10 from goods & chattels of JAMES GRAHAM, 10
Apr 1784...for Ł 31...190 A, granted to JOHN MOORE 24 Sept 1754, conveyed to JAMES
GRAHAM 10 Feb 1778...JOSEPH HENRY, Sheriff (SEAL), Wit: WM. RANKIN, JAMES RUTLEDGE,
ROBERT JOHNSTON, Rec. Jan. Sess. 1784 "(sup'd. 1786)."

                        END OF VOLUME 2.

The following are lists of probates from the Secretary of State's papers. N. C. Archives S. S. 884.

"A list of letters Testamentary granted in Tryon County from April Term 1769 till October Term the Same Year."

What Court	Deceased		Exr. or Admn.	Security
April Term 1769	Robt Shaw	Intestate	Margaret Shaw) & Samuel Watson)	John Jordan &) John Hall)
	John Langham	Testator	Comford Langham	---------------
July Term 1769	Joseph Sailor	Intestate	Katharine Sailor	Leonard Sailor &) Ulrick Crowder)
	John Welsh	Testator	Nicholas Welsh	--------------------
Octor. Term 1769	Nicholas Henson	Intestate	Phillip Henson	William Sims &) Zachh. Bullock)
	Jeremiah Potts	Intestate	Jno. Potts	Hugh Quinn, Solomon Beson[?], Saml. Davison, & Jno. Stephenson
	William Karr	Intestate	Charity Karr	Geo. Gibson &) Henry Smith)
	John Kannon	Testator	Henry Clark	--------------------

"A List of Letters Testamentary & of Administration Granted by Tryon County Court in one Year Preceding the 26th day of October 1770 Together with the names of the Testator or Intestates & of their Securities & the Sums bound in."

Deceaseds Names		Admn. to whom granted	Securities names	Sums bound in
Jacob Wilfong	Testator	George Willfond & Robt. Blacburn [sic]	---------------	------------
Roger Cook	Intestate	Jane Cook	Robt. Swann & Wm. Henry Tayr.	₤ 200
Jacob Fink	Intestate	Barbara Fink	Michl Rudisel & Geo. Fink	₤ 200
Adam Loony	Intestate	Robert Loony	Jno. Nuckols & Patrick Moor	₤ 250
John Gready	Intestate	Nicholas Fisher	Wm. Yancey, Jno. Stanford & Jos. Neel	₤ 500
William Hanna	Intestate	Margaret Hanna	Jno Hardin, Benja. Do., & Jno. McIntire	₤ 200
Henry Willis	Intestate	Margaret Willis	Jno. Hardin, Benja. Do., & Jno. McIntire	₤ 200
Mattw. Shearer	Intestate	Sarah Shearer	Lewis Witener & Christy Carpenter	₤ 100
John McCormack	Testator	Joseph Bradner & Jas. Campbel	--------------------	------

"[A Li]st of Letters Testamentary and of Administra[tion] ordered to be Granted in Tryon County by the Inferior Court of Said County from January Term 1771 till July Term 1771 both Terms Inclusive"

Deceased	Executors	Administrators	Securities
John Potts	Ezchl. James & George Potts	--------------	----------
James McAfee	Robert McAfee & Joseph Hardin	--------------	----------
James Watson	William & Samuel Watson	--------------	----------
John Summy	Peter Sumy & Robert Blackburn	--------------	----------
Wm Froneburger	-----------------	Mary Fronebergr.	Peter Aker & Larence Kyzer ₤ 500
A True Copy	Test	Ezek. Polk, C. C.	

"North Carolina, Tryon County. November 25th 1772. A List of Probates for Granting Letters Testamentary and of Administration in Tryon Court in One Year Preceeding the Date hereof together with the parties names and of their Executors or Administrators and Securities."

Name of the Deceased		Exr. or Admn.	Securities
William Moore	Testator	Mary Coulter	
David Robison	Testator	Frances Robison	
Joseph Green	Testator	Mary Green & Jas. McEntire	
Jeremiah Smith	Intestate	Katherine Smith	James Logan & James Armstrong
William Litle	Testator	Thomas Litle	
George Bounds	Testator	Francis Prince	
Daniel Warlock	Intestate	Nicholas Warlock	Henry Holman & Xr. Rinchart
William Shepherd	Intestate	George Sizemore	George Winters & John Morris
Christopher Pettie	Intestate	Sarah Pettie	James Martin & Leonard Sailor
George Watts	Intestate	Frances Watts	Robt. McAfee & William Yancy
Robert Abernathy	Testator	Miles Abernathy	
James Kelly	Intestate	William Wray	John Walker & James Coulter

A True List   Test Andw. Neel, C. C.

"An Account of the Letters Testamentary and of Administration, granted for Tryon County in the Year One Thousand Seven Hundred and Seventyfour."

Date of Letters	To Whom Granted	On Whose Estate	Securities	Bond	Court
26 Apr 1774	(Hannah Henry & (John Robinson	William Henry	(David Alexander & (Alexr. Gilliland	₺300	April
27 Apr 1774	(Robert Ewart & (James Johnston	Alexander Wells	Testator		Ditto
Ditto	Elice Alexander	Robert Alexander	(John Walker & (John McKinney	₺ 150	Ditto
Ditto	Jane Withrow	Samuel Withrow	(James Wilson & (John Walker	₺ 600	Ditto
28 Apr 1774	Elizabeth Coyle	Alexander Coyle	(Thos Colwell (Thos. Welch & (John McEntire	₺ 500	Ditto
29 Apr 1774	-----Christmas[?]	R---Felker[?]	(-----Miller & (Michael Felker	₺ 120	Ditto
26 July	James Davison	John Oaks	Testator		July
27 July	Jane Lamkin	William Lamkin	William Moore	₺ 200	Ditto
28 July	Phebe Collins	John Collins	Testator		Ditto
25 October	(Mary Harman & (Anthony Harman	John Harman	Testator		

Tryon County) I do certify the above to be a true List Witness my hand this 31st Day of October A. D. 1774. Andw. Neel, C. C.

"An Account of the Letters Testamentary and of Administartion, Granted for Tryon County, in the Year One Thousand Seven Hundred and Seventy-Eight."

Date of Letters	To Whom Granted	On Whose Estate	Securities	Bond	Court
19 Jan 1778	(Joseph Camp& (George Blanton	William Wilson	Testator		Jan.
21 Jan	James Miller Jur.	John Johnston	(Wm. Henry & (Alexr. Coulter	₺ 300	Jan.
29 Apr 1778	George Pearis	Jacob Swank	James Miller, Jur.	₺ 150	Apr.
20 July 1778	Francis Ross	John Hartness	(John Walker & (Abrm. Scott	₺ 400	July
Same date	Thomas Potts	George Potts	(Jonathan Potts & (Peter Quin	₺ 500	Same
19 Oct 1778	(John Will, Adam (Cloninger & Jacob Sides	Girard Will	Testator		Oct.
20 Oct 1778	(Mary Bradley & (Richard Ledbetter	John Bradley	Testator		Same
20 Oct 1778	Thomas Beatey	John Beatey	Testator		Oct.
23 Oct 1778	(Katherine Statler & (Conrad Statler	Peter Statler	(Joseph Harden & (Benjn. Harden	₺ 1200	Same.

A True List Test Andw. Neel, C. C.

TRYON COUNTY WILLS

[Some of these wills are filed with the Lincoln County Wills in North Carolina Archives,
C. R. 060.801.1-28; others are found in the Tryon County Miscellaneous Box, C. R. 094.
901.1]

Will of ROBERT ABERNATHY SENR. of Tryon County...to my loving wife, the labour of two
negroes during her life, to wit, Will and Sue, after her death, to my daughter ANN TURNER
...to my son JOHN five shillings...likewise to my son D[?]____ five shillings...to my
daughter ELIZABETH WILLIAMS five shillings...to my wife aforesd. her choice of my beds
and furniture, also the use of what part of my stock as will be sufficient...to my son
MILES seven Negro Slaves...son MILES aforsd. Sole Executor...31 Jan 1772...ROBERT
ABERNATHY SR. (R). Wit: JAMES ABERNATHY, Jurate; DAVID CRITES (D), DAVID ABERNATHY (A).

Will of CHRISTIAN AKER of County of Tryon, planter...to my dearly beloved wife the bed
and furniture belonging to it, also one third of my whole Estate exclusive of my lands...
to my well beloved Son PETER AKER, all the Land on the So. side of the Creek with the
Improvements, the other part to be to CHRISTIAN AKER, also a piece of land, that the
pattent is not set[?], but the fees paid, to be to my son CHRISTIAN AKER, then they[sic]
whole Land to be Valued By the Executor (or three possible men) When the oldest Boy
Comes of age...Then the whole Valuation of the whole said lands to be Equally Deposited
among My three Sons Viz., PETER AKER, CHRISTIAN AKER, & DANIEL AKER...to my daughter
BARBARY AKER the sum of ℔ 10 of our said Province Currency...to my well-beloved daughter
CATHERINE AKER, the sum of ℔ 10 proc....PETER AKER SEN., CHRISTIAN CARPENTER SR[?], &
JOHN AKER Sole Executors of this my last will & Testament...my wife EVE to have the third
part of said place as long as she lives a Widdow...25 June 1776...CHRISTIAN AKER (X)
(SEAL), Wit: WILLIAM GRAHAM, BARBERY AKER (O), MARY AKER (X). Proved July Term 1777.

Will of GEORGE BOUNDS of the Parish of St. Thomas County of Tryon...to my daughter SARAH
WADLINGTON one Negro Girl Lyda...to my Grandson GEORGE BOUNDS WADLINGTON, one Molatto
Boy named Solomon...to my Grandson WILLIAM WADLINGTON...to my grandson GEORGE BOUNDS WAD-
LINGTON, one Mare...to my daughter SARAH PRINCE one Molattoe Girl named Rose...to my son
in law FRANCIS PRINCE, all the rest of my Estate Real & Personal, provided that the sd.
PRINCE or his Heirs shall pay unto NANCY ASHBY the Daughter of HENRY ASHBY & NELLY his
wife when the sd. NANCY shall arrive at the age of eighteen or on the day of her marriage
the sum of ℔ 20 cash or hard money...Provided also that the sd. FRANCIS or His Heirs
shall pay the sum of ℔ 20 cash or hard money unto SINAH CLAYWELL ASHBY, the daughter of
the aforesaid HENRY & NELLY when she the sd. SINAH CLAYWELL shall arrive at the age of
eighteen years or at the day of her marriage...to daughter NELLY ASHBY may have out of
my Estate a decent mourning Gown, Hat[?] & Gloves...son in law FRANCIS PRINCE,Exr....
22 Dec 1771...GEORGE BOUNDS (X) (SEAL), Wit: JOSEPH JONES, THOS. BROWN, JOSEPH BROWN.

Will of JOHN BRADLEY of the County of Tryon...to my daughter SARAH MORGAN, five shillings
sterling...to my daughter ANNA JONES, five shillings...to my son by my first wife JOHN
BRADLEY five shillings...to my son RICHARD BRADLEY...to my son JOHN BRADLEY, my son by my
Second wife five shillings...to my son GEORGE WARTON BRADLEY, five shillings...to my
daughter MARY BRADLEY, my son EDWARD BRADLEY, my son ISAAC BRADLEY, my son JAMES TERRY
BRADLEY, my son JOHN W.[?] BRADLEY, five shillings sterling to be payed to Each of them...
to my loving wife MARY BRADLEY, 100 A being part of the tract belonging to JONES WILLIAMS,
likewise 400 A lying Near ____?____ in Burke County, my Negro Wench Nan & her children,
two mares, one colt & one horse, 17 head of cattle...wife, Extx., also as Exr. RI_____
[Richard Ledbetter]...24[?] June 1778...JOHN BRADLEY (X) (SEAL), Wit: JONATHAN HAMPTON,
ANDW. HAMPTON, JONES WILLIAMS (X). Proved & filed Oct. Court 1778.

25 Feb 1775, Will of WILLIAM CLEGHORN of Tryon County, Freeholder...to LETTICE CLEGHORN
me dearly beloved wife, the plantation tools and house furniture, and the plantation
I now live on her lifetime if she sees fit to Live on it, three Negroes during her lifetime if unmarried, and if married after that the said three Negros I give and Bequeath
to my Three Sons WILLIAM JAMES and JOHN CLEGHORN to be divided equally among them when
they become of age...to my well Beloved Daughters REBECKAH and JANE CLEGHORN 400 A on
the warriers Creek, South Carolina...to my well Beloved Daughter MARY CLEGHORN, 200 A
on Lawsons fork South Carolina...to my Well Beloved Daughter LETTICE CLEGHORN, 350 A on
Fishing Creek, part in the Indian Line...to my well Beloved Sons WILLIAM JAMES and JOHN
CLEGHORN...land I live on[?]...250 A on South Pacolet to be sold at the Expiration of
Three Years after my Dicease, one half to my well beloved Freind JOHN SCOTT JUNR....to
well beloved daughter SARAH HUDDLESTON, s5 sterling, all Bills Notes and Debts I allow
to be collected...wife LETTICE and JAMES HEMPHILL, my well beloved friend, Exrs...WILLIAM
CLEGHORN (SEAL), Wit: D. DICKEY, Jurate., HUGH WILLSON (H).

28 March 1774, Will of JOHN COLLINS of Tryon County...to PHEBY me Dearly and Well Beloved
Wife my Whole Estate if in Case She Mary[sic] the Will is that my Whole Estate Be divided

between her and all my Children excepting BATHIAH GEORGE my beloved Daughter my Will is
that if in Case her mother Mary that then she the Said BATHIAH Shall Received the sum
of five shillings sterling...my Brother JAMES COLLINS and my Wife PHEBY Exrs...JOHN
COLLINS (‡) (SEAL), Wit: ROBERT McAFEE, Jurt.; WILKERSON TURNER (T), ABIGAIL TURNER (+).

Will of JAMES GORDAN...unto my beloved Wife ANNE GORDAN, one first Choice of my slaves,
and also of six Cows from my stock, and one horse, her Bed and furniture, and my pewter
and other Kitchen furniture, Together with her Living in my Dwelling house and on my
plantation as Long as she may live, unless she marry, in which Case I do will that the
said house and Land do revert to the benefit of my son HUGH that my said Wife do retain
to her use for the Benefit of the Junior Legatees Two horses and my other Implements of
husbandry...to my son SAMUEL GORDON, one house Bible with the Marginal notes of the value
of five Shillings Sterling money...to my daughter MARY JONES, one house Bible...to my son
WILLIAM GORDON, one house bible...to son HENRY GORDON, one plantation or tract of land
bounding Westward on the land formerly by me sold to WILLIAM WRAY and extending towards
Crowders Creek...to my son JOHN GORDON, two stills with their appurtenances...to my daughter ANNE GORDON, one good bed and furniture together with one Slave of the value of
Ь 100...to my son JAMES GORDAN, one horse of the value of Ь 20, a Sett of Blacksmiths
Tools, one thousand Weight of Iron and a Half a Faggot of Steel...to my daughter ELEANOR,
a good Bed and furniture with one Slave of the Value of Ь 100...to my daughter MARGARET
one good bed and furniture and Ь 100...to my son HUGH, my plantation I now live on, to
revert to him on the marriage or death of my wife...to my grandson JAMES GORDON, son of
WILLIAM GORDON, my plantation on Beaver Dam Bounding NE on Land sold by me unto WILLIAM
WRAY, and that my son WILLIAM if he think meet do Occupy the said Land until my said
Grandson attain the age of 21 years...to my deceased son ROBERT GORDONS children Ь 5each
and put out to Interest untill they attain to the age of 15, each...to my Grandson JOHN
JAMES a Horse and Saddle of the value of Ь 23...wife ANN, & son HENRY, Exrs...23 Nov
1774...JAMES GORDON (SEAL), Wit: EZEK POLK, NATHAN MENDENHALL JUNR., FENEY[?] ANDERSON.

22 April 1775, Will of SAMUEL GRAY of Tryon County...to son JOHN GRAY, all the land on
the North West Square on that side the River he paying Ь 5 towards the schooling of the
Children...to my son WILLIAM GRAY, one bay mear [sic] and colt formerly Called his...the
remainder of my land and movable Estate to my son JAMES GRAY except one bay mear to my
son DAVID...to wife AGNESS GRAY a sufficent[sic] and Decent Maintainance during her
Widowhood and is Likewise to raise and school all the children decently...SAML. GRAY
(SEAL), Wit: WM. GRAY, JOHN McELVEN JUR.[Jurate or Junior?].

20 Sept 1771, Will of JOSEPH GREEN of Tryon Co., planter,..to wife MARY Ь 100...to WILL-
IAM GREEN, my Dearly and Well beloved Son, Ь 100...to ANNE GREEN, my daughter...to son
ABRAHAM GREEN...to ISAAC GREEN, my son Ь 100...to daughter MARY GREEN...to son JACOB
GREEN...to son JOSEPH GREEN...ABRAHAM, ISAAC, JACOB, MARY & JOSEPH to be schooled...
to be learnt to Read and Write a Good Commendable hand and to Cypher...JOSEPH GREEN (‡)
Wit: HENRY REYNOLDS (X), ALEXANDER MEANDER, ROBT McAFEE, Jurate.

Will of JOHN HANNAH of County of Macklenburg...to MARY me Beloved Wife all my Lands and
all Household furniture and two mares and two cows and calves...to ICHABUD HANNA, my Son
four mares...to my Sun RICHARD HANNAH, five mares...to my Daughter HANNAH, one Cow and
Calf and two mairs[sic]...to my daughter ELEZEBETH two yearling heffers[sic], two mares
and a colt and one yearling...my Brother in law HENRY CORK, Exr...1 Aug 1767...JOHN
HANNAH (I H), Wit: WILLM McKOWN, ICHABOD CLARK[?], GEORGE McKOWN.

Will of JOHN HARMAN of Tryon Co., Yeoman...to MARY my dearly beloved Wife, one third of
my estate...to my three sons JOHN, ANTHONY & DAVID my land Estate, but when it is divided the old improv'd part of the Estate to be for my son ANTHONY...my five daughters
and one son namely CHRISTINA, MARY, SUSANNAH, ELIZABETH, ANNA and DANIEL, to be divided
when the youngest becomes of age...wife MARY & son ANTHONY, Exrs...12 Feb 1774...JOHN
HARMAN (H), Wit: THOS PEARSON, [other name illegible.]

Will of WILLIAM LITTLE in Meclingburg County...500 A of land that is lying on or near to
JOHN DUHEARTS place on the south side of the fork to be Equally devided between my
Brothers and Sister which is THOMAS LITTLE, JOHN LITTLE, ARCHIBALD LITTLE, and MARTHA
LITTLE lying on the south side of Lantys Creek...to my brother THOMAS, Ь 9...to MARTHA
LITTLE one feather bed...to Brother ARCHIBALD, Ь 5...to my Brothers and sister JAMES and
ALLEXANDER and MARGRAT LITTLE, Ь 9 to be equally divided...to brother THOMAS Ь 11 s5 that
JAMES HENERY is due with one Black Mare and Colt and four Steers...4 August 1764...
WILLIAM LITTLE (SEAL), Wit: ABEL BEATTY, ARCHIBALD LITTLE, JOHN BEATTY.

[N. B. The will of WILLIAM HAGER (1775) and will of JAMES McAFFEE (1769) are missing
from Archives.]

8 Sept 1770, Will of JOHN McCORMICK of Tryon Co., Farmer...the Plantation I now live on to my Dear and loving wife AGNESS McCORMICK ...if she marries again, then no more than the law allows her and at her death or marriage the land to be sold and equally divided among all my children...leave my said wife her riding Saddle and the horse called Roger and if my wife is with child that it shall have an Equal dividend with my other children ...to my Son JOSEPH the young mare call'd the Brock faced mare...my wearing apparel to my son JOHN and also the little Bay mare...JOSEPH BREDNER and JAMES CAMPBELL, Exrs... JOHN McCORMICK (O) (SEAL), Wit: JOHN COOPER, JAMES PURSLEY, MOSES FERGUSON.

25 March 1776, JOHN McFADDIN of North Carolina in the County of Tryon...unto HANNAH my dearly beloved wife plantation I now live on...unto WILLIAM McFADDIN my Beloved and oldest son, one Cow...to my Sons JAMES, JOHN, SAML., and ELIAS and ANDREW McFADIN each s 5...unto STEPHEN and to ALEXANDER McFADIN my Sons, the plantation I now live on at the decease of their mother...to son STEPHEN the side of the Creek we now Live on being the West side...unto my daughter MARGARET McFADIN, one Bed and furniture...son ALEXANDER & wife EXRS...JOHN McFADIN (SEAL), Wit: D. DICKEY, Jurt., THOMAS WALKER (X). Proved in Court July A. D. 1777.

Oct 19th 1770...Will of WILLIAM MOORE of Tryon County...to wife MARY, all my Goods and Chattles...to son JOSEPH MOORE, the plantation I now live on and I do allow him to pay to his Brother JOHN when of age the sum of ₺ 20 proc. money...to my son JOHN MOORE, my plantation on Green River and a black mare of four years old...to my daughter MARY MOORE one sorrel mare and ₺ 30 proc. to be leavied out of her mothers shear[sic]...wife MARY and friend WILLIAM CLEGHORN, Exrs...WM. MOORE (X) (SEAL), Wit: D. DICKEY, JOSEPH HART, SAML. GRAY.

Will of OWEN MURPHY...wife ABIGAIL for the Term of her life this house where I now dwell ...at her death to my son JEAMES MURPHY...unto my Eldest son WILLIAM MURPHY one shilling good Money of old England...to my beloved Grandson JOHN one heifer...son JAMES MURPHY and Mother my only Exrs...6 Dec 1775...OWEN MURPHY (O) (SEAL), Wit: RICHD LANSDELL, ALEXANDER CUILR (A), HENERY WILLIAMS. Proved and Filed Jany Court 1776.
    January ye 24th 1776. I ABIGAIL MURPHY Being the wife of OWEN MURPHY Lately Deceased by his will I do hereby ordain this my son JEAMES MURPHY to act for me...ABIGAIL MURPH (X) (SEAL), Test: JAMES CHITWOOD.

Will of WILLIAM MURPHY of Tryon County, Planter...to ELISABETH my Dearly beloved Wife, all and singular the Plantation whereon she now Lives...and afterward to possess her third only one Bay mare four years old Branded on the Near Shoulder thus W and on the near Buttock thus M making her the sole Extx...to my son JOHN MURPHEY all the other two thirds except the Child now in the womb should be a son and if so then the land shall be equally divided between them both...WILLIAM MURPHEY (SEAL), Wit: PHILIP WISENANT, REUBEN WARREN[?].

Will of JOHN OAKS...[will in very poor condition]...estate to be divided among my five children...JAMES DAVISON...Wit: JACOB MOONEY, JONATHAN PRICE.

Will of WALTER POLLARD of Dale Parish and county of Chesterfield [Virginia], planter... to SARAH HASSKINS [HAWKINS?] my feather bed and furniture...to MORRISS ROBERT JR., son of JANE PRIDE, and to his wife UNITY ROBERTS three negroes [named] and after MORRIS ROBERTS and his wifes decease to MORRISS ROBERTS JR. six children named SUSANNAH ROBERTS, MARTIN ROBERTS, JOSHUA ROBERTS, MARY ROBERTS, JANE ROBERTS, and JOHN ROBERTS...11 Nov 1768...WALTER POLLARD (X) (SEAL), Wit: JOHN TAYLOR, ELENDR. MASON (X).
    In Chesterfield county court March Term 1769. Will of WALTER POLLARD decd, was proved by the two subscribing wit. Teste BENJN. WATKINS, Clk.
    PARKE POINDEXTER clerk of the county court of Chesterfield in Virginia, do certify the forgoing[sic] will of WALTER POLLARD decd is correctly copies from the records in my office...30 Sept 1831..
    I, ELEAZAR CLAY, presiding Justice of the peace for County of Chesterfield, do certify that PARKE POINDEXTER is the legal clerk of the county court...30 Sept 1831.

19 Jan 1771 Will of JAMES WATSON of Trion[sic] County...unto my son WILLIAM ₺ 10 sterling ...to my Eldest Daughter SUSANNAH s5 sterling...to my second daughter ELSE 150 A that joyns thomas Skotes land [THOMAS SCOTT]...to my third daughter ELESABETH s5 sterling... to my grandson JAMES WALKER ₺ 10 proc. money...to my grandson THOMAS SKOOT [SCOTT] the Whole money I have paid for him for Which I have Got a Detachment for his land and Sume other things all Which I Desire my Executors to Return to him if he Comes Personally to Enjoy them if not to be Sold and Devided among WILLIAM and ELSE...son WILLIAM WATSON and SAMUEL WATSON, Exrs...JAMES WATSON Wit ROBERT ALEXANDER, VIOLAT WATSON, SAMUEL WATSON.

Will of WILLIAM WHITESIDE of Tryon County...unto my well Beloved wife ELISABETH my household goods and my plantation during her life...my children DAVIS WHITESIDE & ROBERT & TOMAS & JOHN & MARGARET and WILLIAM, THOMAS and SAMUEL & ADAM and if She should depart this life before my Son FRANCIS WHITESIDE comes of age my children above mentioned to have the Benefit of the plantation and So Soon as my Son FRANCIS comes of age he may enter in possession of the same and also to pay my daughter ELISABETH ₤ 20...to my daughter SARAH ₤ 20...to my son JAMES WHITESIDE my land on the South mountain in Virginia, Augusta County allowing him to pay ₤ 15 Va. currency towards the discharge of my debts... son WILLIAM WHITESID and THOMAS WHITESIDE Exrs...24 Oct 1777...WILLIAM WHITESIDE (0) (SEAL), Wit: DAVIS WHITESIDE, JAMES WHITESIDE.

Will of GERHARD WILL of Tryon County farmer...to MARY BABARA[sic] my Dearly Beloved wife ...all my Money, but in case she marry again, she is to have her Thirs and no more...to my son DANIEL ₤ 10 and to my son JACOB ₤ 10...to my Daughters ELISABETH and MAGDALENA s 10 each...to my daughters EVE, CHRISTINA and FRONICA two Cows and calfs and a Bed Each...to my youngest son CONROD, the plantation I now live on and the tract of land bought of ADAM CLONNINGER and when he is at the age of 16 years he is to have two horse creturs wago plow....JOHN WILL, JACOB SEITS, ADAM CLONINGER Exrs...3 July 1778...GERHARD WILL (W) (SEAL), Wit: JAMES ROUTLEDGE, JAMES COBURN, MICHAL CLONINGER [German signature].

22 Oct 1765, Will of JOHN LANHAM of County of Meclinburgh [sic] Shewmaker [sic]...to COMFORD my Dearly beloved wife the one part of Land which I now possess...to my daughter SARAH HAGARTY s 5 proc. money...to my daughter EASTER DEAN s 5 proc. money...to my daughter COMFORD OSBURN s 5 proc. money...to my Daughter JEAN McCOY s 5 proc. money...to my Sons WILLIAM LANGHAM and ABEL LANGHAM all the remainder of my lands at their mothers death...wife COMFORD, Extx...JOHN LANHAM (‿∧), Wit: PETER KUYKENDAL Jurate, ABRAHAM KUYKENDAL (Z), RICHMAN FLENMAN.

WILLIAM TWITTY's nuncupative Will made in presence and proved by the Oath of THOMAS JOHNSON to have been made and pronounced a few Hours before his Death on the River Kentucke in the Indian lands on the 27 March 1775.
To wit, That it was his Will that his Wife SUSANNAH TWITTY should keep the Children and what there was together to give them Good Education and do well by them
THOMAS JOHNSON (2). Sworn in Open Court July Sess. 1775. Test ANDW NEEL, C. C.

Will of WILLIAM WILSON of Tryon Co....all my personal Estate in the Ceare of my Trusty and Well Beloved Friends JOSEPH CAMP and GEORGE BLANTON, whom I appoint my Executors... to the only support of my wife ANNER and my youngest daughter MOLLEY one Cow and Calf, one Black mare...to daughter MOLLEY at the decease of my widdow, I do give to be divided Equally Betwen JOSEPH CAMPS and JOSEPH HOPPERS Children...29 May 1777...WILLIAM WILSON (W) (SEAL), Wit: ALEXR McDOUGAL, JOSEPH CAMP, JAMES WEBB.

Will of JOHN POTTS of Tryon Co....unto beloved brother EZEKIEL one half of tract I have on Bullocks Creek...to my brother GEORGE, the other half...to my sister SUSANNA one Cow and calf...to my sister SARAH one Cow and Calf...to my sister ISBEL one Cow and Calf... to my three Brothers EZEKIEL, JAMES and GEORGE, Exrs., the rest of my personell estate... the last day of November 1770...JOHN POTTS (SEAL), Wit: JAMES MACKBEE, PATRICK HENNES (0), jurates; MARY POTTS.

Will of JOHN WELSH of Tryon Co....to MARGARET WELSH my wife the best of my young creature of horse kind...to my Ouldest daughter REBECCAH two pewter Dishes and six plates, mare & saddle...to my son JOHN one mare and saddle and two saws one Cross Cut and one Whip Saw... one tract to be sold namely Camp Creek also my daughter MARGARET one young mare and to my wife ₤ 5 for her in Child bearing...5 June 1769...JOHN WELSH (SEAL), Wit: ALEXANDER LOCKHART, JOHN LINDSAY JUR. Executors: MARGARET WELSH, THOMAS WELSH, NICHOLAS WELSH. Certified to be a true copy from the original will Test. ANDW NEEL, C. C.

Will of GEORGE RUTLIG of North Carolina and Living in Tryon County...to JEAN my wife, her bed and furniture two horses of her choice...to son JAMES a track of land of 150 A... to my second son JOHN, the place on the douchmans [Creek?], 200 A below ANDREW HAMPTON... to my third son GEORGE a place on Turkey Creek of 22_ A...my fourth son CHARLES the place I now live on...my oldest daughter MAREY hir choice of the horse or mair that gows by hir name and ₤ 20...to my second daughter SUSANA hir Choice of aney Crater[sic] that gows by hir name...also JEAN my third daughter I give ₤ 25 also 75 A and one track of land on Broad river got from JAMES CRESOT...wife JEAN and WILLIAM GLAGHORN [CLEGHORN] Exrs...21 Mar 1770...GEORGE RUTLEDGE (SEAL), Wit: WILLIAM _____, ANDREW HESLEP, JOHN BROWN, Skrimshire[?].

Will of DAVID ROBERTSON of Tryon Co....to wife FRANCES ROBERTSON, 400 A where I now live a Negro George and all cattle & stock...my children MATTHEW ROBERTSON, MOLLY ROBERTSON, ISRAEL ROBERTSON, ISAAC ROBERTSON, ISHAM ROBERTSON, JAMES ROBERTSON, DAVID ROBERTSON, ABNER ROBERTSON, SALLY ROBERTSON, JOHN ROBERTSON & BETTY ROBERTSON...and as touching the Estate of my Brother CHARLES ROBERTSON, I give to GEORGE ROBERTSON the Youngest of my Brothers after the said Estate pays to my wife ₤ 20 Va. money...IRBY DEWBERRY and wife FRANCES, and WILLIAM MARCHBANKS, Exrs...8 July 1771...DAVID ROBERTSON Wit: VARDRY Mc BEE, ADAM BURCHFIELD (A), MATTHEW ROBERTSON (T), WILLIAM ARVIN[?]. Proved by VERDRY MAGBEE Oct. court 1771 EZEK. POLK, C. C. Certified to be a true copy 8 Dec 1774 ANDW NEEL, C. C.

TRYON COUNTY ESTATES

[The following are abstracts of the only estate papers extant from Tryon County. They are filed with Lincoln County Estates at N. C. Archives, Raleigh. The call numbers for these at N. C. Archives are given.]

C. R. 060.508.135

Henry Willis
"An Inventory of the Estate of Henry Willis Decd"
Jany the 5th 1771. Margerit Willis (X).

C. R. 060.508.136

Samuel Withrow
April 19th 1774
"The Inventory of the Goods & Chattles Belonging to the Estate of Samuel Withrow Deceasd."
Includes: "1 Acct. in Wm Henrys hands"
Jane Witherow (↵).

C. R. 060.508.52

William Hannah
Jany 5th 1770 "An Inventory of the Estate of Willm Hannah"
Margerit Willis (X)

C. R. 060.508.75
[no date] "An Inventory of the Goods & Chattles of Alexander Kyle Decd"
The above returned Tryon Court April Session 1774.
Eliz. Coyle (( )).

C. R. 060.508.87
"The Inventory of the Goods and Chattels of James Mcafee deceased"
April the 15th 1778
Joseph Hardin, Robert McAfee, Exrs.

C. R. 060.508.72
"A True Invitory of the Goods and Chattle of William Keer Late Deceed"
given Registry of Tryon
24th October 1769
Charity Kerr (X).
Teste Saml Spencer.

C. R. 060.508.89
"An Inventory of the Goods and Chattels of John McCormack Deceased"
Decr 6, 1770
[Marked sale on reverse]
    Buyers: Alexr Eaken, Widow McCormack, Thos Morgan, John McMicheal, John Dalton, Joseph McCormack, John Leard, Willm Patrick, Willm Hegerty, Thos Dalton, Richd Whiteacre, Joseph Clark, David Davis, Alexr Currey, James Pursley, William McDowel, James Ferguson, "1 Common Prayer Book---Richd Whiteacre," David Duff, Thos. Neasmith, Joseph Bradner, James Duff, James Patterson, William Eakin, Rubin Dowland, James Alcorn, John Bigar, David Neel, Willm Howe, John Howe, Joseph Henderson, Thos Patton, James Dursley, John Leard, Daniel Shaw, Samuel Weathers, Samuel Quinton, Samuel Watson, John Cooper, Jeramiah Demas, John Kimbere, James Campbell.

[Another sheet]
James Campbell & Joseph Bradner, Exrs.

[Another sheet]
    "The Estate of John McCormack Deceased Dr. to Sundry accompts."
David Neel, Jas. Patrick, John Craig, Robt. Birney, John Tagart, Mr. Balch, Ezekl Polk, Moses Ferguison, John Watson, Joseph Hous, Robt. Adams, Rebeca Friley, Robt. Patrick, John Berry, Robt. Bigar, Andw Callys, James Pursley, Willm Barnet, David Duff, Colonel Neel.

C. R. 060.508.104
    April ye 5th 1771
    "An Inventory of the goods of Cristefor Pitty desceased" Sarah Petty (ɤ), Admx.
[on back]
    To the Care of John Dunn, Esqr.

C. R. 060.508.124
   William Slavin
[one document]
"We or Either of us Do promise to pay or Cause to be paid unto Andrew Allison or William
Luckie Executors of the Estate of William Slavin Decsd. on their Order the just Sum of
Six pounds seven Shillings and three pence prock. Money to be Paid at or against the tenth
Day of January Next for Value Received as witness our hands the Eleventh Day of March
1764" Samuel Withrow (Seal) John Withrow (8) (Seal). Testes: James Gillespie, John
Irwin.

C. R. 060.508.131
   Wm Twitty

"An Inventory of the Effects of William Twitty Decest & Apraised by John Walker & Andrew
Hampton"
returned Octr. CT. 1775 signed SUSANNA TWITTY

October ye 14th 1775
Then Recived of Susannah Twitty one pound Ten Shillings prock money...Thomas Johnson
Test, David Miller.

Recived in full...Willim Lee (X) Present, David Miller.

Then Recd of Mrs. Susannah Twitty Two pound one Shilling prock money. I say Recd by Me
Micheal Mcwrath 19 Apr 1776

I promis to pay...unto Smol Mcfadon...ninteen poind one Shilling prock money...18 Day
of December next...16 October 1775 Susannah _____. Present, David Miller.

I promise to pay or Cause to be paid unto William Lee...one Hundred pounds South Carolina
Currance [sic] on or before the Twenty fifth day of December next...first April 1774
William Twitty.

State of North Carolina
We, William Graham, Fredk Hambright, Geo. Winters, Geo. Lamkin, James Patterson, Miles
abernathy, Robt. Abernathy & David Abernathy all of the County of Lincoln are bound for
Ten Thousand Pounds Lawful Money...22d April A. D. 1779.
Whereas the above bound William Graham has been chosen by William Twitty, Susanna and
Allen Twitty as their Guardian and has also been appointed Guardian to Mary Twitty,
Russell, Arabella, Bellariah[?] and Charlotte orphans and minors of Wm Twitty decd.
W Graham (LS), Frederick Hambright (LS), George Winters (+) (LS), George Lamkin (LS),
James Patterson (LS), Miles Abernathy (LS), Robt Abernathy (LS), David Abernathy (LS),
Wit: Ad: Osborn, Andw Neel.

The State of William Twitty Decd to Alexander Kilpatrick, January 1775.

96 Destrict) Alexander Kilpatrick Made Oath before me a Majestrate for said
So Carolina) District & Province...before me John Tagert 23rd Octr 1777.
                                                        Alescr kilpatrick
John Tagert JP
Octr 23rd 1777) Recd of William Graham in full...P Alescr kilpatrick
Test Jno Nuckols

Contra Cr.
1. By Alexander Kilpatrick Acct
2. By Wm Lees note assigned to Saml McFadden
   paid Susanna Twity
3. By John Boys accompt P Do
4. By Michl McElwraths acct
5. By Jabez Evans act.
6. By Thomas Johnstons
7. By Joseph Byers

Recd of Mrs[?] Twity Eight pound South Carolina Corency in full...acompt Agenst Mr.
William Twitys Esteat this Jenuar 17th 1777 John Boys.

Then Recd of Mrs. Susannah Twitty Eighteen pound Nine Shilling Currant money of Virginia
                         John Russell 22 April 1776

July the 17 Day 1776
Received of Souzana Twity the Some of one Pound thirteen Shilins...Joseph Byers.

Then Recd of Mrs. Susannah Twitty Nineteen pound one Shillings Currant money of North
Carolina ...Samuel Mcfaddin 18 April 1776

Effects Appraisd by Andrew Hampton Jas Mcfaddin
1776
Jany 5[?] Day   One Rone Horse
                 One Black Bald Mare
April 18   One Negro fellow Tobey
                 Samuel Walker Bond
                 John Steen Bond
                 Joseph McDaniel Note hand

William Twitty Del to Jabius Eviens

Two Beaver Traps

Robert Willikins account

South Carolina   )   Personaly Appeared Jabex Evins Before me John Tagert a Justice
Ninety Six District)   of the Peace for said District...fifth Day of December
1776 John Tagert JP   Jabez Evans

The Administrators of the Estate of William Twitty deceased
to Inventory and Valuation returned
to Tryon Court October Term 1775

April Sess 1779
        Widows Third part   ₤ 405.3
                 W. Graham
Test Ad: Osborn

[William Twitty made a nuncupative will 7 March 1775; it is in Tryon Co. Misc. at Archives]

C. R. 060.508.78
July the 17th 1769
John Carrol & Thos Morgn appraised the Goods and Chattle of John Lanham Decd...
Inventory

"A Just and true account of Abel Lees estate"
April 23 1778   Roart[?] Lee

C. R. 060.508.83
   William Little

28 October 1771
"An Account of ye goods and Chartels Belonging to Ye Estate of William Littel [sic]
Deceased Sold by Thomas Littel Executor"

Buyers: James Reduck, James Bell, Thomas Little, Petter Lenberey, John Reed, Peter
       Linbarger.

[Another page]
Paid Francis Lock for Publick Taxes 1765
Paid Moses Alexander for Publick Taxes
Paid William More for Publick Taxes 1772
Paid to Alexander Martin for fees.

Received 30 Aug 1771
Names: Thomas Litle, Jas. Henery, Jas. Beell, David Robeson, John moore.

Page 1: 26 Apr 1779, WILLIAM DUNN to SAMUEL REED, both of Rutherford Co.,
for ₤ 75 NC money...180 A on both sides of a small branch of fare
Camp Creek...WILLIAM DUNN (SEAL), Wit: JOHN SMITH, WM. HUDDLESTON.

Page 2: 18 Feb 1779, JAMES MILLER of Tryon Co., to JOHN WHERRY of same,
for ₤ 250 proc. money...200 A on N side Broad River, on _____
Creek granted 5 Apr 1767 to JAMES SIMERAL and conveyed to JEAN EARVEN,
then to JAMES MILLER...JAS. MILLER (LS), Wit: STEPHEN WILLIS, ELIZTH GALT-
NEY (X).

Page 3: 25 July 1779, RICHARD HIX JUNR of Rutherford Co., to ELIAS ALEXAN-
DER of same, for ₤ 200 proc. money...a tract on both sides of Rock-
ey branch of Floyds Creek, just above the great flat rock...RICHARD HIX
JUNR (X) (SEAL), Wit: JAMES NORRIS, WM. JOHNSON (‡).

Pp. 4-5: 28 Mar 1778, BENJAMIN KUYKENDALL to JOSEPH KUYKENDALL, both of
Tryon Co., for ₤ 75...300 A on a branch of Broad River including
JOHN JEANS own improvement adj. WILLISES line...BEN KUYKENDALL (LS), Wit:
W. J. LAMKIN, BENJAMIN HARDIN (B).

Pp. 5-6: 27 July 1779, ROBERT PORTER of Rutherford Co., to WILLIAM SMART
JUNR., for ₤ 20 NC money...29½ A on both sides Camp Creek adj.
WM. SMARTS line...ROBERT PORTER (SEAL), Wit: LODOWICK WRAY, ALEXR McGAUGHY.

Pp. 7-8: 2 Mar 1779, JOHN WITHROW of Rutherford County, to JAMES WITHROW
(county not stated), for ₤ 50 proc. money...200 A on Cane Creek
of Second Broad River, granted to JOHN CARSON, 6 Apr 1765, conveyed to
JOHN WITHROW by deed...JOHN WITHROW (W) (SEAL), Wit: JONATHAN GULLICK.

Pp. 8-9: 24 Dec 1778, JOHN EVINS & wf MARGET of Roan Co., to PATRICK WAT-
SON, for ₤ 150...250 A in Tryon Co., on S fork Cane Creek...grant-
ed to JOHN NEVINS 27 Apr 1767...JOHN NEVINS (X) (SEAL), MARGARET NEVINS(X)
(SEAL), Wit: JOHN WATSON, WILLIAM BARR, JOHN BARR.

Pp. 10-11: 11 Dec 1771, THOMAS PRICE of Tryon Co., to JAMES DAVISON of
same, for ₤ 75 NC money...land on Loves Creek of Broad River,
200 A granted to sd. PRICE 22 Dec 1769...THOS PRICE (SEAL), Wit: THOS
BRANDON, ARTHUR DUDNEY.(X).

Pp. 12-13: 20 Jan 1779, THOMAS MORRIS of Tryon Co., to GIDEON RUCKER of
same, for ₤ 300...land on both sides Cathey Creek on Second
Broad River, 200 A granted to FREDERICK HAMBRIGHT 20 Apr 1768...THOMAS
MORRIS (SEAL), Wit: ADAM HAMPTON, FRANCIS McCALL, RICHARD DOUHORTY (☒).
Proven July 27, 1779.

Page 13: John McLEAN of Rutherford County, farmer, for love and good will
to my son DAVID McCLAIN, a minor living with myself...negro Jacob
...Wit: JOHN EARLE, GEORGE PEARIS. Dated 16 July 1779.

Pp. 14-15: 23 Nov 1778, WILLIAM STOCKTON of Tryon Co., to WILLIAM WILLIS
Junr., of same, for ₤ 20 proc. money...land on Little Broad
River adj. JOHN SMITH, part of tract granted 29 Apr 1768, 24 A...WILLIAM
STOCKTON (SEAL), Wit: DAVIS WHITESIDES, JOHN WHITESIDES, THOMAS STOCKTON.

Page 15: JOHN McCLAIN of Rutherford Co., for love and good will to minor
son CHARLES McCLAIN...negro Ben...16 July 1779. Wit: JOHN EARLE,
GEORGE PEARIS.

Page 16: JOHN McCLAIN of Rutherford Co., for love and good will to my
daughter REBECCA McCLAIN living with myself...one Black Horse,
and other cattle (enumerated)...16 July 1779...Wit: JOHN EARLE, GEORGE
PEARIS.

Page 17: JOHN McCLAIN of Rutherford Co., to son EPHRAIM McCLAIN, a minor...
negro Isaac...16 July 1779...Wit: JOHN EARLE, GEORGE PEARIS.

Pp. 18-19: 19 July 1779, ANDREW HASLEP to WILLIAM McELMURRY both of Ruther-
ford County, for ₤ 400...land on both sides First Little Broad
River, at the mouth of Brushy Creek adj. JOHN LUSKS, 200 A granted to
ALEXANDER McENTIRE in 1766, & conveyed to JOHN LUSK by deed 23 Jan 1770,

then to ANDREW HASLEP 8 Jan 1774...ANDREW HASLEP (SEAL), Wit: JONATHAN
HAMPTON, FRED. HAMBRIGHT. Proven July term 1779.

Page 20: JOHN McCLAIN to daughter MARGARET living with me...one grey gild-
ing, other cattle (enumerated)...& bed & furniture...16 July 1779
...Wit: JOHN EARLE, GEORGE PEARIS.

Page 21: JOHN McCLAIN to daughter MARY McCLAIN of lawful age living with
me...black mare & cattle (enumerated)...also 200 A on Nob(sic)
Creek adj. JOHN McFADDEN as by a survey made by JOSEPH HENRY doth show...
16 July 1779...Wit: JOHN EARLE, GEORGE PEARIS.

Pp. 22-23: 3 Nov 1778, WILLIAM STOCKTON & wf JEAN of Tryon Co., to JOHN
SMITH of same, for Ł 100 No. currency...229 A on both sides
First Little Broad River, part of a patent to THOMAS BLACK, 29 Apr 1768
adj. SHAWS line...WILLIAM STOCKTON (SEAL), (Jean did not sign). Wit:
BEN KUYKENDALL, ABSALOM FORVIS(?).

Pp. 23-24: 27 July 1779, SAMUEL McMURRY Sen. of Rutherford Co., to JOHN
GOFORTH and ANDREW GOFORTH of same, for Ł 60 proc. money...200
A on both sides fare Camp Creek of Second Broad River above WARDS land...
SAMUEL McMURRY (SEAL), Wit: JAMES ROBERTSON, JOSEPH DUNN. Prov. July term.

Pp. 25-26: 11 May 1778, ROBERT NEVANS & wf ANN, JOHN NEVANS, WILLIAM NEVANS
and HENRY NEVANS of Rowan Co., farmers, to SAMUEL ANDREW of
Tryon Co., for Ł 65...land granted to JAMES NEVANS by patent 25 Apr 1767...
ROBERT NEAVANS (SEAL), ANN NEAVANS (X) (SEAL), JOHN NEVANS (X) (SEAL),
WILLIAM NEVANS (SEAL), HENRY NEVANS (SEAL), Wit: JOHN CARSON, ROBERT PORTER.

Pp. 26-27: 19 Nov 1778, WILLIAM HALL of Tryon Co., to MARY JONES (county
not stated), for Ł 200...land on S side Main Broad River...
WILLIAM HALL (SEAL), Wit: JAMES MILLER, WILLIAM STEGALL (X), JOHN McFADDING
(⊢Ð, WM. BRANT (X).

Page 28: 26 July 1779, JOHN MORRIS & JOHN McLEAN to JOHN LEWIS for Ł 500
and a negro boy...3 tracts, 550 A on branches of Mountain Creek
(excepting or reserving to HENRY TROUT and DAVID LEWIS 35 A)...granted to
sd. MCCLAIN & JAMES ENSLOW by patents & to JOHN MORRIS by deed...JOHN
McCLEAN (SEAL), JOHN MORIS (X) (SEAL), Wit: JONATHAN HAMPTON, THOS ROWLAND.

Page 29: 9 Feb 1778, JOHN THOMASON SENR. of Tryon Co., to RICHARD HIX JUNR
of same, for Ł 70 proc. money...land on both sides Rocky branch
of Floyds Creek, 300 A...JOHN THOMASON (SEAL), Wit: JONAS BEDFORD, SHAD-
RICK ATKINS (O).

Pp. 30-31: 12 Apr 1767, JOHN WALKER of Mecklenburg Co., to WILLIAM CLEG-
HORN of same...256 A in Mecklenburg Co., on S side Catawba,
on N branch of Fishing Creek adj. MATTHEW TOOLS, granted to THOMAS WALKER
30 Aug 1753, conveyed to JAMES HENDERSON by L & R, 1 & 2 Dec 1755, then to
JOHN WALKER 3 & 4 May 1763...JOHN WALKER (SEAL), Wit: HENRY VERNER,
REBECCA VERNER, JAMES HENDERSON. Rec. July term 1779.

Pp. 31-32: 24 Apr 1779, JONAS BEDFORD of Rutherford Co., to WILLIAM HAWKINS
of Halifax Co., Va., for Ł 1100...land on N side Main Broad
River, on both sides Richland Creek, granted 2 Nov 1764, 200 A...JONAS
BEDFORD (SEAL), Wit: JOEL RIGGS, JOHN CARMICLE (X), PHILIMON HAWKINS.

Pp. 33-34: 5 Jan 1779, ADAM WHITESIDE of Tryon Co., to SAMUEL STOCKTON of
same, for Ł 250 proc. money...land on N fork of first Broad
River, granted to JACOB MONEY 28 Apr 1760...ADAM WHITESIDE (SEAL), Wit:
RICHARD SINGLETON, JAMES WHITESIDE, DAVIS WHITESIDE.

Pp. 34-36: 7 Nov 1778, JOHN McFADDING of Tryon Co., to ISHAM REAVIS of same,
for Ł 40...100 A on both sides Main Broad River...JOHN McFADDING
(⊣Ð, Wit: DAVID LEWIS JUNR., DAVID GEORGE (+), WILLIAM BRYANT.

Pp. 36-37: 23 Jan 1778, JOSEPH RICHEY of Tryon Co., to JAMES HAMBLE of same,
for Ł 80 proc. money...400 A on Nob Creek adj. HARDIN...JOSEPH
RICHEY (SEAL), Wit: UEL LAMKIN, JOSEPH HARDIN.

Pp. 38-39: 29 Spet 1779, HUGH KILLPATRICK of Rutherford co., to JOHN Mc-
        CLURE of same, for Ł 100...400 A on N fork Main Broad River, gra
granted to THOMAS BEATY 16 Nov 1764, transferred to JOHN FLEMING and JOHN
McCLURE by deed from THOS BEATY & wf MARGARET 6 Sept 1771, and to sd. KILL-
PATRICK 15 May 1775, 200 A on S side River, lower part of tract...HUGH
KILLPATRICK (SEAL), Wit: D. DICKEY, J. GRY(?).

Pp. 39-40: ___ July 1779, ANDREW HAMPTON of Rutherford Co., to NOAH HAMPTON
        of same, for Ł 300 proc. money...300 A on Mountain Creek of
Broad River, granted to ANDREW HAMPTON, 15 ____ 1772, #67...ANDW. HAMPTON
(SEAL), Wit: JONATHAN HAMPTON, JOEL PARIS (X).

Pp. 41-42: 21 Jan 1779, PATRICK HAMILTON & wf MARGARET of Rowan Co., to
        BENJAMIN ADAMS SR. of Tryon Co., for Ł 35 NC money...300 A grant-
ed to sd. HAMILTON 15 May 1772, on both sides Mount (sic) Creek of Second
Broad River...PATRICK HAMILTON (SEAL), MARGARET HAMILTON (SEAL), Wit:
BENJAMIN ADAMS SR., JAS COOK, MUNFORD WILSON.

Pp. 42-43: Grant of SAMUEL SPENCER 300 A on N fork White Oak Creek including
        JOHN NICKOLS folly. 3 Mar 1779. Plat dated 7 Dec 1768. JONATHAN
GULLICK, Surv.

Page 44: Grant to THOMAS SPRIGGS, 100 A in Tryon Co., on both sides North
        Pacolet River including the mouth of lawns(?) Creek, 3 Mar 1779.
Plat dated 10 Dec 1778. JONATHAN GULLICK, Surv.

Page 45: Grant to SAMUEL SPENCER, 200 A in Tryon Co., on the upper Skiewicker
        a branch of North Pacolet River, 3 Mar 1779. Plat dated 10 Dec
1778. JONATHAN GULLICK, Surv.

Page 46: Grant to JAMES LOGAN, 136 A on laws creek, both sides North Pacolet,
        3 Mar 1779. Plat dated 10 Dec 1778. JONATHAN GULLICK, Surv.

Page 47: Grant to THOMAS SPRIGGS in Tryon Co., 100 A on North Pacolet inclu-
        ding little cane break, 3 Mar 1779. Plat dated 10 Dec 1778, JONA-
THAN GULLICK, Surv.

Page 48: Grant to JOSEPH McDOWELL, 400 A on both sides Green River, adj.
        WHITESIDES, 3 Mar 1779, plat dated 12 Dec 1778, JONATHAN GULLICK,
Surv.

Book A#1

Page 49: 28 Nov 1780, JAMES MILLICAN of Lincoln Co., to JULIOUS CLARKSON
        of Rutherford Co., for Ł 15, 000...200 A granted to MARTIN PHIPHER
30 Oct 1766, #92, conveyed to JAMES MILLICAN 17 Jan 1777, on both sides
South fork Main River (Broad River?) called the Poplar bottom including
some Indian camps...JAMES MILLICAN (SEAL), Wit: JAMES HAMPTON, ROBT. LEWIS,
ANDREW HAMPTON, ANDR. MILLICAN.

Page 50: 4 Jan 1780, THOMAS SPRIGGS of Rutherford Co., to JAMES LOGAN of
        Lincoln Co., for Ł 300 continental currency...100 A on both sides
North Pacolet River including mouth of lows(?) Creek, granted 3 Mar 1779...
THOMAS SPRIGGS (SEAL), Wit: JOSHUA LOPER, JABEZ EVANS, SAMUEL COLDWELL.

Page 51: 11 Dec 1778, JOHN FLEEMAN of Tryon Co., planter, to WILLIAM LANG-
        HORN of same, for Ł 50 proc. money...200 A on Second Broad River
on the first Creek that runs in on the E side of the River below THOMAS
ROBERTSON Creek, being the Creek that runs in at the Cherokey(sic) path...
300 A granted to THOMAS FLEEMAN 1767 & conveyed by deed to sd. JOHN...
JOHN FLEYMAN (SEAL), Wit: JOHN MORGAN, JOSEPH CARTWRIGHT, WILLIAM McGAUGHY.

Pp. 52-53: 22 Jan 1780, WILLIAM MONROE of Rutherford Co., to JAMES WHITE-
        SIDE of same, for Ł 5...land on both sides First Little Broad
River, near JOHN KERCONNEL, 200 A granted to sd. MONROE 8 Feb 1775...WILLIAM
MONROE (SEAL), Wit: THOMAS WHITESIDES, DAVIS STOCKTON.

Pp. 53-54: 25 Jan 1780, WILLIAM GILBERT and wife SARAH of Rutherford Co., to
        RITCHARD LEADBETTER of same, for Ł 200...land on both sides Cedar
Creek, waters of Broad River, 220 A granted 9 Mar 1768...WM. GILBERT (SEAL),
SARAH GILBERT (SEAL), By ALEXR McGAUGHY, Regr.

Pp. 54-55: 26 Oct 1780, GEORGE BLACK, weaver, Rutherford Co., to JOHN BROWN
for Ł 400 NC currency, 200 A granted to sd. BLACK 1 Mar 1774,
on a branch of Keen(sic) Creek of Second Broad River...by the side of a
path that leads to RANKINS and JOHN DEVENEYS, adj. JOHN WITHROW...GEORGE
BLACK (SEAL), Wit: ALEXANDER McGAUGHY, JOHN GUFFY (X).

Pp. 56-57: 25 July 1781, FREDERICK HAWKINS of Rutherford Co., to WILLIAM
GILBERT of same, for Ł 100...land on both sides Puzzel Creek adj.
JACOB KUYKENDALL, MARY ARMSTRONG, 132 A, part of a grant to JACOB KUYKENDALl
conveyed to HAWKINS by deed 20 Mar (year not given)...FREDRICK HAWKINS
(SEAL), Wit: JAMES MILLER, THOMAS MORRIS, STEPHEN WILLIS.

Page 57: May 5, 1781, N. C. Rutherford Co.: THOMAS ROBERSON of co. aforesd.
to JAMES ARMSTRONG of S. C....sale of negroes & cattle, swine, etc.
...THOMAS ROBERSON (SEAL), Wit: DAVID McCLESKY, GEORGE McCLESKY.

Page 58: 2 Jan 1781, JOHN ASHLEY of Lincoln Co., to THOMAS FRENCH of Ruther-
ford Co., for Ł 60...100 A on both sides of Greens Creek of White
Oak, granted to sd. ASHLEY 2 Mar 1775...JOHN ASHLEY (Ɫ) (SEAL), Wit: UEL
LAMKIN, GEORGE LAMKIN.

Page 59: 6 Sept 1780, ANTHONY MITCALF of Rutherford Co., to JAMES LATTO of
same, for Ł 75 proc. money...100 A on both sides Green River....
ANTHONY MITCALF (SEAL), Wit: ISHAM RAVIS, JOHN FRENCH, JAMES REN (X), BEN-
JAMIN LAUGHTER (Z).

Page 60: 6 Dec 1778, WILLIAM LIVELY of Tryon Co., to LEWIS PRICE of same,
for Ł 160...200 A on both sides Duncans Creek...granted to CHRIST-
IAN CARPENTER & conveyed to sd. LIVELY, 13 Oct 1765...WILLIAM LIVELY (X)
(SEAL), Wit: JAMES WHITESIDES, WILLIAM MONROE.

Pp. 61-62: 10 Mar 1781, WILLIAM GILBERT of Rutherford Co., to GILES WILLIAMS
of same, for Ł 500...land on both sides Knobb Creek of Broad
River, including a cabbin, 100 A granted to JOHN McFADDEN 16 July 1774 &
conveyed to sd. GILBERT 26 Oct 1779...WM. GILBERT (SEAL), Wit: JAMES MILLER,
WM. PORTER.

Pp. 62-63: 22 Oct 1781, ADAM HEMPTON of Rutherford Co., to JOHN MILLAR of
same, for Ł 100 specia(sic)...100 A on both sides Maple Creek of
Mountain Creek, part of 150 A granted to HUGH KILPATRICK, conveyed to JOHN
McFADDEN 18 Mar 1778, then to WILLIAM LUSK 19 Apr 1778, then to sd. HAMPTON
agreeable to a survey made by JOHN KERCONNEL...ADAM HAMPTON (SEAL), Wit:
D. DICKEY.

Pp. 64-65: 21 Sept 1781, WILLIAM NEVIL of Rutherford Co., planter, to JOHN
PURVIS of Ninety Six Dist., S. C., for Ł 250 proc. money...land
on both sides Green River, adj. GEORGE PARIS...granted to WILLIAM CLEGHORN
20 Sept 1766...WILLIAM NEVIL (SEAL), Wit: B. TUTT, SPELCOVE MAN BROWN.
DANIEL BROWN (X).

Pp. 65-66: 23 July 1781, WILLIAM LUSK of Rutherford Co., to ADAM HAMPTON
of same, for Ł 10...part of 150 A on Maple Creek of Mountain
Creek, granted to HUGH KILPATRICK, conveyed to JOHN McFADDEN 18 Mar 1778,
to sd. LUSK 19 Apr 1778...surveyed made by JOHN KIRCONNEL...adj. DAVID
GEORGE...WILLIAM LUSK (SEAL), Wit: JONATHAN HAMPTON, ROBERT LEWIS.

Pp. 66-67: 4 Mar 1780, JOHN WOOD of Rutherford Co., to GEORGE WOOD of same,
for s 10...land in Rowan County, then Tryon, now Rutherford, on
a south branch of Gilshot Thomas branch or Creek, now called Greens Creek,
below JAMES WOOD, 150 A, part of 400 A granted to JOHN LYON and conveyed
to sd. JOHN WOOD...JOHN WOOD (OO)(SEAL), Wit: CHARLES ASHLY, PATRICK VANCE,
WM. WOOD.

Pp. 68-69: 4 Mar 1780, JOHN WOOD of Rutherford Co., to WILLIAM WOOD of same,
for s 10...land on a S branch of Gilshot Thomas Creek, now
Greens Creek below JAMES WOOD, 250 A, part of 400 A granted to JOHN LYON...
JOHN WOOD (OO) (SEAL), Wit: Dd. JACKSON, GEORGE WOOD (+), ANTHONY MATHAS.

Pp. 70-71: 7 Sept 1781, BENJAMIN HARDEN of Washington Co., N. C. to HENRY
CLARKE of same, for Ł 10...260 A in Rutherford Co., on W fork

of Knob Creek, granted 5 May 1769 to sd. HARDEN...BENJAMIN HARDEN (SEAL), Wit: BENJAMIN CLARK, RICHD WALTON.

Pp. 71-72: 25 Sept 1781, JOHN BEATY of Meclinburg Co., to WILLIAM GRAHAM of Lincoln Co., for Ƚ 80 "in the old rate"...400 A in Rutherford Co., on W side First Little Broad River, granted to BEATY 30 Oct 1765... JOHN BEATY (SEAL), Wit: JOHN GULLICK, WM. TWITTY, SAML LOFTON.

Pp. 72-73: 25 Sept 1781, ROBERT ARMSTRONG of Lincoln Co., to WILLIAM GRAHAM of same, for Ƚ 80 "in gold and silver at the old rate" ...300 A on S side first Little Broad River...ROBERT ARMSTRONG (SEAL), Wit: JOHN GULLICK, WM. TWITTY, SAML LOFTON.

Page 74: 17 June 1782, GEORGE BALL of Rutherford Co., to JOHN ELMS of same, for Ƚ 60...land on both sides Turkey otter of Cove Creek, granted to sd. BALL 23 Feb 1775...GEORGE BALL (SEAL), Wit: WILLIAM GRANT, LEWIS MUSICK, WILLIAM WATSON.

Page 75: 2 Mar 1782, SAMUEL FRENCH of Rutherford Co., to MATHEW HARPER JR. of Ninety Six District, S. C., for Ƚ 250 proc. money...land on both sides Green River, above the Cherokey Ford, 200 A granted to JOSEPH CLARK, 25 Sept 1766...SAMUEL FRENCH (SEAL), Wit: PETER LEWIS, ROBERT HARPER, EPHRAIM LEWIS.

Page 76: 17 Oct 1782, MICHAEL McELWRATH of Rutherford Co., to THOMAS MORRIS of same, for Ƚ 60 "hard money"...land on N side Main Broad River, on E side Mountain Creek on the mill branch adj. THOMAS JOHNSON, 300 A, granted to DAVID BYERS 29 Apr 1768...MICHAEL McELWRATH (SEAL), No wit.

Page 77: 17 Oct 1783, MICHAEL McELWRATH to THOMAS MORRIS, for Ƚ 60 "Hard money"...land on E side Mountain Creek adj. DAVID BYERS, 300 A, granted to sd. BYERS 18 Apr 1771...MICHAEL McELWRATH (SEAL), No wit.

Pp. 78-79: 17 Sept 1781, BENJAMIN HARDEN of Washington Co., N. C. to HENRY CLARK of same, for Ƚ 10...land in Rutherford County on Nobb Creek at the Cherocee path, granted 6 Apr 1765 to FRANCIS BEATY...BENJAMIN HARDIN (SEAL), Wit: BENJAMIN CLARK, RICHD WALTER.

Page 79: 13 Feb 1779, ELISABETH ROAN of Wilmington, (New) Hanover Co., to JOHN WALKER of Rutherford Co., for Ƚ 200...land in the fork of Broad River, 302 A granted 28 Sept 1754, to MAJOR ROBERT ROWAN...ELISABETH ROWAN (SEAL), Wit: FELIX WALKER, THOMAS WALKER.

Pp. 80-81: 15 Sept 1779, WILLIAM WHITESIDES of Rutherford Co., to JAMES WHITESIDES of same, for Ƚ 125...200 A on both sides Little Broad River, granted to HUGH BEATY, 6 Apr 1765, including sd. WM. WHITE-SIDES improvement, NATHANIEL TRACY and ELISABETH WHITESIDES their improve-ments...WILLIAM WHITESIDES (SEAL), Wit: SAMUEL STOCKTON, THOMAS WHITESIDES, THOMAS EVANS.

Pp. 81-82: 6 Dec 1780, JOSEPH BLACK of Rutherford Co., to JOHN ANDREWINGLE (JOHN ANDREW INGLE?) of same, for Ƚ 80 NC currency...200 A, granted to sd. JOSEPH BLACK 24 May 1770, #351 on both sides Catheys Creek, adj. JOHN BENNETT, JAMES BLACK...JOSEPH BLACK (⊕) (SEAL), Wit: ALEXD Mc_ GAUGHY, WILLIAM SMART.

Page 82: Grant to SAMUEL HAYS, 200 A on both sides Green River, adj.JOSEPH McDOWNELD, EDWARD HOGAN 28 Oct 1782. ALEX MARTIN.

Page 83: Grant #206, to SAMUEL HAYS, 50 A on N side Green River, adj. JOSEPH McDONNELDS, and his own...28 Oct 1782. ALEX MARTIN.

Pp. 83-84: 18 Oct 1779, ADAM KIRGKENDOLL of Rutherford Co., to JOSEPH CAR-PENTER for Ƚ 800...292 A...ADAM KUYKENDOLL (SEAL), MARGET KUY-KENDALL (SEA), Wit: SAMUEL CARPENTER, JAMES STEVENSON, SAMUEL YOUNG.

Pp. 84-85: 26 Dec 1781, GILES WILLIAMS of Rutherford Co., to JONATHAN HAMPTON of same, for Ƚ 50 specia currency...100 A on both sides Knobb Creek, granted to JOHN McFADDEN 16 July 1774, to WILLIAM GILBERT by deed 26 Oct 1779, then to sd. WILLIAM 10 Mar 1781...GILES WILLIAMS (SEAL), Wit: ANDREW HAMPTON SR., ANDREW HEMPTON JNR.

Pp. 85-86: 22 Jan 1780, ROBERT ARMSTRONG of Lincoln Co., & HUGH BEATY of
        Rutherford Co., to THOMAS WHITESIDES of Rutherford Co., for Ł
40...land on both sides Little Broad River, including the mouth of the
North fork, adj. BENJAMIN SHAW, 300 A granted to ARMSTRONG & BEATY, 23 Dec
1768...ROBERT ARMSTRONG (SEAL), HUGH BEATY (SEAL), Wit: WILLIAM WHITESIDE,
FRANCIS BEATY, THOM HAKTO.

Pp. 87-88: 27 Oct 1779, JOHN KIRKCONNEL of Beaufort Co., N. C., to SAMUEL
        KING of Rutherford Co., for Ł 65 proc. money...land on both
sides S fork Broad River, 200 A granted to sd. KIRKCONNEL by deed from
ANDREW NEEL, 28 Mar 1778, and to sd. NEEL by patton (sic) 2 Mar 1775...
JNO KIRKCONELL (SEAL), Wit: WM. GILBERT, WILLIAM MILLS.

Page 88: 23 July 1778, WILLIAM HENRY of Tryon Co., to JAMES HENRY of Cre-
        van (sic) Co., S. C., for Ł 200 NC money...land on both sides
Second Broad River near WALKERS corner, 330 A...WILLIAM HENRY (SEAL),
Wit: ALEXANDER HENRY, JAMES COBURN. ROBERT EWART.

Page 89: 23 July 1778, WILLIAM HENRY to JAMES HENRY, for Ł 100 NC money
        ...land on N side Second Broad River adj. WM HENRY, WALKER, 64
A...Wit: ALEXANDER HENRY, JAMES COBURN, ROBERT EWART.

Page 90: 5 Sept 1782, UEL LAMKIN of Rutherford Co., to JOHN WHEALER of
        same, for Ł 100 specy...105 A on Knobb Creek, part of 2 pattons
(1) granted to FRANCIS BEATY 6 Apr 1765 (2) granted to BENJAMIN HARDIN 5
May 1769...UEL LAMKIN (SEAL), Wit: HENRY CLARK, JAMES PETTERSON, WILLIAM
CORNELUS.

Page 91:   1783, TIMOTHY RIGGS SEN. of Rutherford Co., to GEORGE
        MOOR of same, for Ł 160 specy...land on both sides Sandy Run of
Second Broad River, 640 A...TIMI RIGGS (SEAL), Wit: MOSES BRIDGES (B),
ISAIAH BLACKWELL (X).

Page 92: 26 Apr 1778, JOHN WILSON of Rowan Co., N. C. to JOHN EARLES of
        Tryon Co., for Ł 100 proc. money...land on both sides North
Packolet River, 300 A...JOHN WILSON (SEAL), Wit: BAYLIS EARLE, GEORGE
NEAWETHY, PETER RENTFRO (P).

Page 93: 13 Dec 1776, RICHARD TUB of Tryon Co., to JOHN STANFORD of same,
        for Ł 50...land on S side White Oak Creek about 2 miles above
the mouth, adj. JAMES CAPSHAW, 70 A, part of a grant to GEORGE ALEXANDER,
26 Sept 1766...RICHARD TUB (SEAL), Wit: JAMES WHITESIDES, JAMES BRADLEY
(X).

Pp. 94-95: 11 Nov 1782, ELISABETH BICKERSTAFF of Rutherford co., to JOHN
        JONES of same, for Ł50...land on waters of Robertsons Creek of
Second Broad River adj. PETER EAKER, granted to sd. ELISABETH BICKERSTAFF
14 Nov 1771...ELISABETH BICKERSTAFF (X), Wit: RICHARD SINGLETON, PHILIP
MONROE (X).

Page 95: Grant to JOHN GOODBREAD, 150 A on Main Cove Creek including the
        mouth of first creek below PHILIP GOODBREAD's claim, including
his owm improvements...25 Mar 1780. RD. CASWELL.

Page 96: Grant to ALEXANDER MACKEY, 510 A on Hone(?) Creek of North Packo-
        lett including HOWARDS improvement...13 Aug 1779. RD. CASWELL.

Pp. 96-97: Grant to ALEXANDER MACKEY, 100 A on N side Main Broad River,
        adj. his own and DAVID LEWIS land...28 Oct 1782. ALEX MARTIN.

Page 97: Grant to ALEXANDER MACKEY in Tryon Co., on Wheats Creek, 200 A...
        28 Oct 1782. ALEX MARTIN.

Page 98: 16 Apr 1783, THOMAS MORRIS of Rutherford Co., planter, to WILLIAM
        EVES Of same, for Ł 100 specie...land on N side Broad River on
Mountain Creek, the mouth of Maple Creek adj. JOHN McFADDEN SEN. 200 A,
and also a piece of land that JOHN McFADDEN conveyed to JAMES McFADDEN,
and conveyed by sd. JAMES to JAMES LAUGHTER, between the branch and the
mill...conveyed to MORRIS by LAUGHTER 17 Apr 1782...THOMAS MORRIS (SEAL),
Wit: ANDW HAMPTON, DAVID MILLER.

Page 99; 20 ____ 1779, JOHN LEWIS & wf SUSANNA to THOMAS ROWLAND, both of
    Rutherford Co., for Ł ____...175 A...JOHN LEWIS SEN (SEAL),
SUSANNA LEWIS (SEAL), Wit: DAVID MILLER, ALEXANDER McFADIN.

Pp. 99-100: Grant to ANDREW HEMPTON, 200 A adj. his own land in Tryon Co.,
    on both forks of Mountain Creek...28 Oct 1782...ALEX MARTIN.

Page 100: Grant to WILLIAM EVES, 100 A in Tryon Co., on Mountain Creek
    including the race paths and muster ground adj. HEMPTON, JOHN
MORRIS 13 Aug 1779. RD. CASWELL.

Page 101: Grant to THOMAS GOODBREAD, 100 Ain Tryon Co., on Duncans Creek
    of Cove Creek 28 Oct 1782. ALEX MARTIN.

Pp. 101-102: Grant to JOSEPH HENRY, 100 A on Long Branch of Jenkins fork
    of White Oak...25 Mar 1780. RD CASWELL.

Page 102: Grant to JOSEPH HENRY, 200 A on N fork White Oak including HENRY
    ADKINS cabbin, near ALLISONS...28 Oct 1782. ALEX MARTIN.

Page 103: Grant to GEORGE DICKEY, 100 A in Tryon Co., on Main Broad River,
    adj. JOHN McLEAN and nearly adj. to his own land...13 Aug 1779.
RD CASWELL.

Pp. 103-104: 28 July 1779, JONAS BEDFORD of Rutherford Co., to GEORGE
    WILLIAMS of same, for Ł 150...land on both sides Buffaloe
Creek, including the Rock House bottom, 300 A granted to sd. BEDFORD, 16
Feb 1774...JONAS BEDFORD (SEAL), Wit: RD SINGLETON, RICHARD LEDBETTER,
WM. LEDBETTER.

Page 105: 21 Mar 1783, CHRISTOPHER HICKS of Orangeburg District, S. C. to
    THOMAS CAMP of Rutherford Co., for Ł 100 proc. money...land on
S side Main Broad River, including his own improvement and mouth of Horse
Creek, 200 A granted to sd. HICKS 16 July 1774...CHRISTOPHER HICKS (H),
Wit: CRANSHAW CAMP, DANIEL CAMP (D).

Page 106; Grant to THOMAS DONALSON 100 A in Tryon Co., on Middle fork of
    Catheys Creek adj. JAMES BLACK, including his own improvements
...28 Oct 1782. ALEX MARTIN.

Pp. 106-107: Grant to CHRISTIAN HOGAN, 90 A in Tryon Co., on N side Green
    River, on EDWARD HOGANS springs branch adj. sd. HOGAN...28
Oct 1782. ALEX MARTIN.

Page 107: 20 Mar 1783, THOMAS ROBESON of Rutherford Co., to GRAVES EVES
    of same, for Ł 55 NC money...land on both sides Puzel Creek of
Second Broad River...granted to sd. ROBERSON 28 Feb1775...THOMAS ROBERSON
(SEAL), Wit: JAMES LINN, JAMES LINN JR.

Page 108: 16 Dec 1782, JAMES WILSON of Rutherford Co., to WILLIAM CORNELIUS
    of same, for Ł 50 state currency...300 A on Beaver Dam Branch of
Knobb Creek, including his improvement...JAMES WILSON (SEAL), Wit: ROBERT
ANDERSON, JOHN McADAMS, JOHN ANDERSON.

Page 109: 7 Apr 1782, JAMES LAUGHTER of Rutherford Co., to THOMAS MORRIS
    of same, for Ł 200 proc. money...land on Mountain Creek at the
mouth of Maple Creek, adj. JOHN McFADDEN SR, 200 A and also a piece of
land the sd. JOHN McFADDEN sold to JAMES McFADDEN by my own survey, and
sd. JAMES McFADDEN sold to THOMAS MORRIS...JAMES LAUGHTER (Ɪ) (SEAL),
Wit: JAMES SARTAIN, JESEY NEVEL.

Page 110: Grant to JOHN HUGGINS 250 A on waters of Wilkes Creek adj. lands
    of JOHN RITCHMOND, including JAMES BRADLYS improvement...25 Mar
1780. RD CASWELL.

Pp. 110-111: 31 July 1782, WILLIAM DUNN of Rutherford Co., yeoman, to
    JOSEPH DUNN, yeoman, for Ł 20...land on both sides of Camps
Creek, granted to WILLIAM NEAVIN, 7 Aug 1765...WILLIAM DUNN (SEAL), Wit:
TIMO RIGGS, SIMEON DUNN.

Pp. 111-112: Grant to THOMAS JUSTICE, 300 A including the Rock House and
down toward REILEYS entry...28 Oct 1782. ALEX MARTIN.

Page 112: Grant to JOHN HUGGINS, 250 A in Tryon Co., on Wilkes Creek of
Beaver Dam, including GEORGE BARKLEYs improvement...25 Mar 1780
RCH CASWELL.

Page 113: 5 Nov 1782, PETER QUIN of Rutherford Co., to THOMAS MORRIS of
same, for Ⴑ 80 specie...200 A on both sides Catheys Creek, being
a parcel of land that was formerly known by WILLIAM McMURRYS, adj. FREDER-
ICK HAMBRIGHT, granted to DIXSON 1769...PETER QUIN (SEAL), Wit: None.

Page 114: Heirs of JOHN BATTLES of Tryon Co., decd: ye widow SARAH BATTLES,
JOHN BATTLES, NANNY AGELENTALIS BATTLE, WILLIAM BATTLE, ANGELIK-
EY BATTLE, with assistance of WILLIAM ROBERTS , BENJAMIN ADAMS, & ALEXR
McGAUGHY...agreement to division of slaves and property...5 Dec 1776...
SARAH BATTLE (X) (SEAL), JOHN BATTLE (SEAL), ANGELLIKEY BATTLE (O) (SEAL),
NANNY ARGENLITINE (SEAL), WILLIAM BATTLES (X) (SEAL), Wit: WM. ROBERTSON,
BENJAMIN ADAMS, ALEX McGAUGHY.

Page 115: 19 Mar 1783, SAMUEL FRENCH of Rutherford Co., to JOHN BAPTISTEER
of same, for Ⴑ 40 proc. money...land on S side Green River, adj.
SAMUEL FRENCH SR. line...SAMUEL FRENCH (X) (SEAL), Wit: JAMES WADLINGTON,
BEATY ANDERSON.

Pp. 115-116: Grant to JOHN ANDERSON 195 A on Grassy Branch of First Broad
River, adj. JOHN POLK & his own land...28 Oct 1782. ALEX
MARTIN.

Page 116: Grant to JOHN ANDERSON, 100 A on Crooked Run of First Broad River
adj. JOHN POLK, JOHN KIRCONNEL...28 Oct 1782. ALEX MARTIN.

Page 117: Grant to JOHN McKINNY, 400 A in Tryon Co., waters of Little
Broad River including the high shoal and JERRYMIAH WILKES improvements...28 Oct 1782. ALEX MARTIN.

Pp. 117-118: 30 July 1783, JOHN HUGGINS of Lincoln Co., to HUGH McVEY of
Rutherford Co., for Ⴑ 60...250 A on Wilkes Creek adj. RITCH-
MANS line...JOHN HUGGINS (SEAL), Wit: JAS HUGGINS, JOHN McVEY.

Page 118: Grant to WILLIAM GRAHAM, 100 A in Tryon Co., on North Packolet
adj. SPRIGS, MILLARS entries...13 Aug 1779. RD. CASWELL.

Page 119: Grant to WILLIAM GRAHAM 156 A on the fork of White Oak, adj.
JOHN CUMMINS line...13 Aug 1779. RD CASWELL.

Pp. 119-120: Grant to THOMAS CAMP, 100 A on S side Main Broad River, about
pools branch, including JOHN WILSON improvements...28 Oct
1782. ALEX MARTIN.

Page 120: Grant to THOMAS CAMP, 200 A on S side Main Broad River...FOREST
HACKSIN shoal, and including his own improvements...28 Oct 1782
ALEX MARTIN.

Pp. 120-121: Grant to THOMAS CAMP on N side Main Broad River including
CAMPS landing and improvements...28 Oct 1782. ALEX MARTIN.

Page 121: Grant to NATHAN CAMP, 200 A in Tryon County on Sandy Run of
Main Broad River, adj. ABRAM. KUYKENDALL & including where sd.
CAMP now lives...28 Oct 1782. ALEX MARTIN.

Page 122: Grant to THOMAS POTTER, 100 A in Tryon Co., on both sides Green
River, including part of his own improvements...28 Oct 1782.
ALEX MARTIN.

Pp. 122-123: Grant to WILLIAM BANTON, 100 A on White Oak Creek of Green
River, adj. JAMES CAPSHAW, including a shoal & his improvement...28 Oct 1782. ALEX MARTIN.

Page 123: Grant to JOHN LUSK on E side Little Broad River, adj. his own land & a small improvement..-25 Mar 1780. RCH CASWELL.

Page 124: Grant to JAMES WHITESIDES, 100 A in Tryon Co., on First Broad River, adj. MOSES MOOR, WILLIAM WHITESIDES & his own land...25 Mar 1780. RCH CASWELL.

Pp. 124-125: Grant to JAMES WHITESIDES, 200 A in Tryon Co., on waters of First Broad River, adj. WILLIAM WHITESIDES, & his own land... 25 Mar 1780. RCH CASWELL.

Page 125: Repeat of preceding grant.

Page 126: Grant to WILLIAM GILBERT 400 A in Rutherford Co., on middle fork of Salud(a) River, above his other survey...11 Oct 1783. ALEX MARTIN.

Pp. 126-127: Grant to WILLIAM GILBERT, 640 A, in Rutherford Co., on both sides of S fork Saluda River, above his other land...11 Oct 1783. ALEX MARTIN.

Page 127: Grant to WILLIAM GILBERT 640 A on both sides Saluda about a mile below the mouth of the middle fork...11 Oct 1783. ALEX MARTIN.

Page 128: Grant to WILLIAM GILBERT, 640 A, on both sides Beaver Dam Creek, a branch of Chickaroa, adj. his other line...11 Oct 1783. ALEX MARTIN.

Pp. 128-129: Grant to WILLIAM GILBERT, 640 A on both sides Chichoa, a North fork of Saluda about 40 poles from the mouth of Beaver Dam Creek...11 Oct 1783. ALEX MARTIN.

Page 129: Grant to WILLIAM GILBERT, 640 A on both sides Middle fork of Saluda River, adj. his other line that includes the mouth... 11 Oct 1783. ALEX MARTIN.

Page 130: Grant to WILLIAM GILBERT, 640 A, on both sides Middle fork of Saluda...11 Oct 1783. ALEX MARTIN.

Pp. 130-131: Grant to WILLIAM GILBERT, 400 A on both sides Middle fork of Saluda...above JOHN HOLLANDS survey...11 Oct 1783. ALEX MARTIN.

Page 131: Grant to WILLIAM GILBERT, 640 A on both sides S fork Saludy River above the Old Town...11 Oct 1783. ALEX MARTIN.

Page 132: Grant to WILLIAM GILBERT, 640 A on both sides Chickoa, a North fork of Salude...11 Oct 1783...ALEX MARTIN.

Pp. 132-133: Grant to WILLIAM GILBERT, 640 A on both sides S fork Saludy River...11 Oct 1783. ALEX MARTIN.

Page 133: Grant to WILLIAM GILBERT, 640 A on both sides Middle fork Saludy near BRIDGES line...11 Oct 1783. ALEX MARTIN.

Page 134: Grant to WILLIAM GILBERT, 640 A on both sides S fork Saludy River, near 3/4 mile above the mouth of the middle fork...11 Oct 1783. ALEX MARTIN.

Pp. 134-135: Grant to WILLIAM GILBERT on both sides Chickeroa, 640 A, including the old Indian town house...11 Oct 1783. ALEX MARTIN.

Page 135: Grant to WILLIAM GILBERT, 640 A on S fork Saludy including the mouth of the middle fork...11 Oct 1783. ALEX MARTIN.

Page 136: Grant to WILLIAM GILBERT, 640 A on both sides of the Chickaroa a north fork of Saluda...11 Oct 1783. ALEX MARTIN.

Pp. 136-137: Grant to WILLIAM GILBERT, 200 A on the shoal branch of Catheys Creek, adj. his own land...28 Oct 1782. ALEX MARTIN.

Page 137: Grant to WILLIAM GILBERT, 300 A in Tryon Co., including the forks of Shepards Creek, adj. his own line...15 Aug 1779. RD CASWELL.

Page 138: Grant to HUGH BEATY, 200 A in Tryon Co., adj. WALLIS BEATY, JOHN SHAW, NATHANIEL KEIS, MAGNESS...28 Oct 1782. ALEX MARTIN.

Pp. 138-139: N. C. Rutherford County: JAMES HOLLAND, JAMES WHITESIDES, JOHN FLECK, WILLIAM PORTER, THOMAS WESH, ROBERT PORTER, RITCHARD SINGLETON & FELIX WALKER, arbitrators chosen by SAMUEL ANDREWS & JAMES WITHROW, concerning land on Cain Creek claimed by each party between the plantations where the sd. ANDREWS & WITHROW now live...do find that sd. ANDREWS a patton grant to JAMES MARLING...ANDREWS to make title to sd. WITHROW to land on which WITHROW has improvements...13 Sept 1783.

Page 139: Grant to JAMES HUDDLESTON, 50 A on Cean (sic) Creek of Second Broad River, adj. JOHN WALKER, DAVID HUDDLESTON, entry #341, including his own improvements...28 Oct 1782. ALEX MARTIN.

Page 140: Grant to JONATHAN FAUCH, 100 A on E side Little Broad River, adj. PEPES & including his own improvements...28 Oct 1782. ALEX MARTIN.

Pp. 140-141: Grant to ALLEN HINSON, 50 A on Bullions Creek of Green River, about a mile from the mouth of said creek, including his own improvement...28 Oct 1782. ALEX MARTIN.

Page 141: Grant to JOHN BLACK, 100 A in Tryon County in the Cove, a little below PHILIP GOODBREADS claim or old improvement...28 Oct 1782. ALEX MARTIN.

Pp. 141-142: Grant to GEORGE PARRIS, 100 A in Tryon Co., on Allesons Creek of Green River...3 Mar 1779. RC CASWELL.

Page 142: Grant to JOHN WALKER, 100 A on Cain Creek of Second Broad River, adj. his own land between DAVID HUDDLESTON & ARON DEVINEY...25 Mar 1780. RC CASWELL.

Page 143: Grant to JAMES LOGAN in Tryon Co., 50 A on North Packolet River adj. and above THOMAS SPRIGS entry...30 Aug 1779 RC. CASWELL.

Pp. 143-144: Grant to JAMES LOGAN, 100 A on North Pacolet River above his other entry including HOOPER Camp...30 Aug 1779. RC. CASWELL.

Page 144: Grant to JAMES LOGAN, 200 A on North Pacolet River adj. & below JAMES MILLARS entry near including SPRIGGS improvement...20 Aug 1779. RC CASWELL.

Pp. 144-145: Grant to JAMES LOGAN, 50 A on Vanes Creek adj. SPRIGGS entry...30 Aug 1779. RC CASWELL.

Page 145: Grant to JAMES LOGAN, 200 A near the North and South fork of White Oak...30 Aug 1779. RC CASWELL

Page 146: Grant to JAMES LOGAN, L00 A on middle fork of Schuiwicker, a branch of North Pacolet...30 Aug 1779. RC CASWELL.

Pp. 146-147: Grant to JOHN MOORE, L50 A in Tryon Co., on both sides Hinsons Creek of N Pacolet including HINSONs improvement...30 Aug 1779. RC CASWELL.

Page 147: Grant to JONATHAN GULLICK, 100 A on Little Creek of North Pacolet, 30 Aug 1779. RC CASWELL.

Pp. 147-148: Grant to JONATHAN GULLICK, 100 A on waters of Mountain Creek, adj. JAMES LARGENT...28 Oct 1782. ALEX MARTIN.

Page 148: Grant to JONATHAN GULLICK & JAMES LOGAN, 200 A on two branches
of Shippards Creek lying between WILLIAM GILBERT & JAMES ADAIR
...28 Oct 1782. ALEX MARTIN.

Page 149: Grant to JONATHAN GULLICK, 100 A on Nawns Creek of North Pacolet near 2 miles from the mouth, including GILSON (GIBSON?)s
Camp...30 Aug 1779. RC CASWELL.

Page 149: Grant to ALEXANDER McDONALD, 100 A on both sdies of the Cove
Creek, adj. his own land...25 Mar 1780. RC CASWELL.

Page 150: Grant to JOHN POTTS, 100 A on N fork Cedar Creek, adj. RICHARD
LEDBETTER...28 Oct 1782. ALEX MARTIN.

Pp. 150-151: Grant to JOHN POTTS, 100 A on Youngs Creek, a fork of Cedar
Creek, adj. JOHN WINTERS...28 Oct 1782. ALEX MARTIN.

Page 151: Grant to JOHN POTTS, 100 Aon Morrises(?) Creek of Cove Creek,
including JAMES McNEALYS improvement...28 Oct 1782. ALEX MARTIN.

Pp. 151-152: Grant to JOHN POTTS, 100 A including where he now lives &
the meeting house...25 Mar 1780...ALEX MARTIN.

Page 152: Grant to JOHN POTTS, LOO A on Cedar Creek of Main Broad River,
adj.JONES WILLIAMS, including the mouth of Jumping Branch...
25 Mar 1780. ALEX MARTIN.

Page 153: Grant to JAMES HOLLAND, 640 A in Rutherford County on both sides
Ulenoy Creek, a west branch of Saluda River...11 Oct 1783.
ALEX MARTIN.

Pp. 153-154: JAMES HOLLAND, 640 A on both sides S fork Saluda below
Watticoes Improvement...11 Oct 1783. ALEX MARTIN.

Page 154: Grant to JAMES HOLLAND 100 A on both sides S fork Saluda below
WATTICOOS improvement...11 Oct 1783. ALEX MARTIN.

Pp. 154-155: Grant to JAMES HOLLAND, 300 A on W fork Saluda...11 Oct
1783. ALEX MARTIN.

Page 155: Grant to JAMES HOLLAND, 500 A on both sides Ulenoy above his
other survey...11 Oct 1783. ALEX MARTIN.

Page 156: Grant to JAMES HOLLAND, 640 A on both sides the Ulenoy Creek,
above a mile above the old town...11 Oct 1783. ALEX MARTIN.

Pp. 156-157: Grant to JAMES HOLLAND, 300 A on both sides Ulenoy, above
the old town...11 Oct 1783. ALEX MARTIN.

Page 157: Grant to JOHN HOLLAND, 300 A on both sides the Checheroa...11
Oct 1783. ALEX MARTIN.

Page 158: Grant to JOHN HOLLAND, 640 A on both sides Checoroa, a North
fork of Saluda...11 Oct 1783. ALEX MARTIN.

Pp. 158-159: Grant to JAMES HOLLAND, 640 A on the Saluda below his other
survey...11 Oct 1783. ALEX MARTIN.

Page 159: Grant to DANIEL THATCHER, 300 A on both sides South Pacolet
close by the path that leads from WYERS improvement to the
Blackhouse...__ Oct 1783. ALEX MARTIN.

Page 160: Grant to DANIEL THATCHER, 300 A on both sides the Chicaroa
...11 Oct 1783. ALEX MARTIN.

Pp. 160-161: Grant to DANIEL THATCHER, 300 A on both sides Chicora...11
Oct 1783. ALEX MARTIN.

Page 161: Grant to DANIEL THATCHER, 640 A on both sides Chiceroa, 11 Oct
1783. ALEX MARTIN.

Page 162: Grant to ABNER NASH 640 A on both sides Chicaroa...11 Oct 1783.
ALEX MARTIN.

Pp. 162-163: Grant to ROBERT MILLAR, 200 A on both sides S fork Saluda
including WALTICOOS improvements & the mouth of a small
Creek...11 Oct 1783. ALEX MARTIN.

Page 163: Grant to ABNER NASH, 640 A on both sides Checaroa...11 Oct 1783.
ALEX MARTIN.

Page 164: Grant to DAVID DICKEY, 640 A on both sides Ulenoy Creek, about
3 miles above the old town...11 Oct 1783. ALEX MARTIN.

Pp. 164-165: Grant to JAMES GLASGOW, 640 A on NE side Saluda River, above
the mouth of Georges Creek...11 Oct 1783. ALEX MARTIN.

Page 165: Grant to JAMES GLASGOW, 640 A on both sides Saluda, below the
mouth of Chicoroa...11 Oct 1783. ALEX MARTIN.

Pp. 165-166: Grant to JAMES GLASGOW, 640 A on both sides Saluda, above
the mouth of Chicoroa...11 Oct 1783. ALEX MARTIN.

Page 166: Grant to JAMES GLASGOW, 640 A on both sides Saludy below the
mouth of Checora about a mile...11 Oct 1783. ALEX MARTIN.

Page 167: Grant to JAMES GLASGOW, 640 A on both sides Ulenoy below the
Nanows...11 Oct 1783. ALEX MARTIN.

Pp. 167-168: Grant to PHILEMON HACKINS (HAWKINS), 640 A on both sides Saluda, including GEORGE PARIS half Breeds improvements...11
Oct 1783. ALEX MARTIN

Page 168: Grant to JOHN BRYAN, 400 A on middle fork Saluda above WILLIAM
GILBERT...11 Oct 1783. ALEX MARTIN.

Page 169: 3 July 1783, DAVID LEWIS to GEORGE MUSICK, for b 10...100 A on
Wheats Creek, part of tract adj. THOMAS ROWLAND, ABRAHAM MUSICK
...DAVID LEWIS (SEAL), Wit: THOMAS MUSICK, JOSEPH WILLIAMS, JEHOIDAY
MUSICK.

Pp. 169-170: 20 Apr 1776, JOHN HUDDLESTON of Tryon Co., to JOHN BATTLE of
Sussex Co., Va., for b 30 proc. money...150 A on Second Broad
River adj. DAVID HUDDLESTON...JOHN HUDDLESTON (SEAL), SARAH HUDDLESTON
(X) (SEAL), Wit: CALEB TAYLOR, JOHN MORGAN, JOSHUA TYLER.

Pp. 170-171: 27 Jan 1783, EDWARD CALLIHAN of Rutherford Co., planter, to
JESSY RAKESTRAW, Black Smith, of same, for b 100 proc. money
...land on hunting Creek, near THOMAS ROBERSONs improvement, including
where Walker's Road crosses sd. Creek, adj. SAMUEL WITHROW, granted to
GEORGE PEE, then of Tryon County, 8 Apr 1768, & conveyed to EDWARD CALLI-
HAN, 29 Aug 1772...EDWARD CALLIHAN (E) (SEAL), Wit: WILLM ROBERTSON,
ROBERT RANKIN.

Page 171: 28 Nov 1774, JAMES CHEEK of North Carolina, to WILLIAM HANNON
for b 60 proc. money...land on N side of Main Pacolett River,
granted to RITCHARD HENDERSON, 26 Oct 1767, adj. JAMES CHEEK...JAMES
CHEEK (SEAL), Wit: JOHN EARLES, JOHN NEEL (E).

Page 172: 7 Apr 1783, GEORGE WINTERS of Rutherford Co., planter, to
JONAS BEDFORD JUN., of same, for b 150...300 A on a branch of
Floyds Creek of Broad River...GORG WINTERS (X) (SEAL), Wit: JAMES COOK,
ELIAS ALEXANDER.

Page 173: 10 Apr 1783, JAMES WEBB of Rutherford Co., to NATHAN BYERS of
Caswell Co., for b 150...200 A on N side main Broad River adj.
McCLANNAHANS...JAMES WEBB (+) (SEAL), Wit: WILLM HACKINS, JOHN WEBB,
WILLIAM COOPER.

Page 174: 10 Sept 1783, ELIAS MORGAN of Rutherford Co., to THOMAS TRAMMELL
of same, for b 40...land on both sides First Broad River,

including ye waggon Road that leads from ye flint hills to Kings Mountain...ELIAS MORGAN (SEAL), Wit; JOEL BLACKWEL (X).

Pp. 174-175: 27 Oct 1779, JOHN KIRKCONNELL & WM GILBERT of Rutherford
          Co., to ALEXANDER McDONNALD of same, for ₤ 50...land on
both sides Cove Creek, including the mouth of Turkey Otter, 200 A granted
to sd. KIRKCONNELL & GILBERT, 5 Mar 1775...JNO KIRKCONELL (SEAL), WM
GILBERT (SEAL), Wit: D. DICKEY, JOHN CUMMINS.

Pp. 175-176: 28 July 1779, ALEXANDER COULTER of Rutherford Co., to
          ROBERT SHIPLEY of same, for ₤ 400...300 A on Cleghorns
Creek, formerly Sheppards Creek, JAMES BYARS pattentee...ALEXANDER
COULTER (SEAL), Wit: D. DICKEY, RICHARD SINGLETON.

Page 177: 23 Apr 1779, HUGH TODD Of Mecklenburg Co., to ARTHER TYLER of
          Rutherford Co., for ₤ 350 proc. money...land on N branch of
Catheys Creek of 2nd Broad River, about 3/4 a mile from WILLIAM GILBERT,
granted 5 Jan 1773 to JAMES BELL, and conveyed to SAMUEL CARROL...HUGH
TODD (SEAL), Wit: HUGH KILPATRICK, ROBERT SHIPLY.

Page 178: 17 Mar 1777, STEPHEN HOWARD of Tryon Co., to THOMAS BAKER of
          same, for ₤ 40 proc. money...150 A on both sides 2nd Broad
River...STEPHEN HOWARD (SEAL), Wit: JOHN ASHWORTH, WM. WEBB, FEREBAH
HOWARD (X).

Page 179: 24 Jan 1780, GEORGE WILLIAMS of Rutherford Co., to RICHARD
          LEDBETTER of same, for ₤ 100...land on both sides Grassy branch
of Cedar Creek of Broad River, including his own improvement, 200 A...
GEORGE WILLIAMS (SEAL), Wit: "No body."

Page 180: 9 Feb 1783, SAMUEL WALLACE of Rutherford Co., to JAMES WILSON
          of same, for ₤ 100...land in Rutherford Co., on Nobb Creek of
Little Broad River, 200 A...SAMUEL WALLACE (SEAL), Wit: BENJAMIN HARDIN,
WILLIAM CORNELIUS.

Pp. 180-181: 25 Jan 1780, WILLIAM GILBERT & wf SARAH of Rutherford Co.,
          to RITCHARD LEDBETTER fo same, for ₤ 200...land on Cedar
Creek, of Broad River, on N side Young Mountain, joining above WRAY,
200 A granted to WILLIAM ADAMS 9 Mar 1768...WM GILBERT (SEAL), SARAH
GILBERT (SEAL), No wit.

Page 182: 27 Sept 1783, WILLIAM MILLS of Rutherford Co., to WILLIAM
          TWITTY of same, for ₤ 200 specia...150 A on N side Green River,
part of a tract conveyed to AMBROSE MILLS & falling to sd. WILLIAM by
heirship...POWELS Cabin...WILLIAM MILLS (SEAL), Wit: ANN MILLS, JOHN
MILLS.

Page 183: 22 Oct 1779, JOHN MORRIS & wf MARTHA to DAVID LEWIS, each of
          Rutherford Co., for ₤ 50...30 A, part of a tract now in poss-
ession of JOHN LEWIS on Mountain Creek & hath been improved by HENNERY
TROUT...JOHN MORRIS (SEAL), Wit: NONE.

Pp. 183-184: 21 July 1783, JAMES DOUDLE of South Carolina, to MILES
          GOFORTH of Rutherford Co., for ₤ 30...100 A granted by
patent to JOHN DEVENY 25 NOv 1771, and by deed to sd. DOWDLE, 25 July
1772, on flat branch of fare Camps Creek, adj. WM. McCAUGHY...JAMES DOU-
DLE (SEAL), Wit: HU BEATY, ZECKRIAH GOFORTH (X).

Pp. 184-185: 23 Sept 1783, JOHN MOORE of Dist. of Ninety Six, S. C. to
          JAMES LOGAN of Lincoln Co., N. C., for ₤ 45...land on both
sides of hinsons Creek of N Packolet River, including Hinsons improvement, granted to JOHN MOOR 13 Aug 1779...JOHN MOORE (SEAL), Wit: WILLIAM
ATSENY, ROBERT YOUNG, ELISABETH ARMSTRONG (X).

Pp. 185-186: 13 Oct 1783, WILLIAM TWITTY of Rutherford Co., to SAMUEL
          WALKER of same, for ₤ 200 proc. money...land on both sides
Broad River, 200 A...WILLIAM TWITTY (SEAL), Wit: WM. GRANT, JOHN McCLIND.

Pp. 186-187: 7 Mar 1780, JOSEPH CLEMENS of Rutherford Co., to ARTHER
          TYLER of same, for ₤ 1000 proc. money...200 A on both sides

hunting creek, below WITHROWS land, granted to JAMES ANDREW 9 Apr 1770...
JOSEPH CLEMENS (SEAL), Wit: THOMAS ROBERSON, JESSY WEBB.

Pp. 187-188: 9 Nov 1777, JOHN McFADDEN of Tryon Co., to WILLIAM PICKRFLL
            of Bute Co., N. C., for ₺ 60...land on both sides Main Broad
River, part of tract that sd. McFADDEN now lives on...JOHN McFADDEN (X)
(SEAL), Wit: SAMUEL WALKER, LOOMSFORD BAGWELL (X).

Pp. 188-189: 30 Sept 1783, JONATHAN FOUCH of Rutherford Co., to ABRAHAM
            HARGIS of same, planter, for ₺ 40 proc. money...100 A on E
side Little Broad River, adj. PEPES & including his own improvement...
JONATHAN FOUCH (X) (SEAL), Wit: PETER QUIN, DANIEL QUIN.

Pp. 189-190: 20 Mar 1783, ANDREW HAMPTON of Rutherford Co., to WILLIAM
            GRANT...on 7 Jan 1783 at Court of P & QS for Rutherford Co.,
by a writ of Fiere facias against JOHN MORRIS, Planter, late of Rutherford
Co....350 A on N side Main Broad River, grant to JOHN BANER 17 Apr 1765...
ANDREW HAMPTON (SEAL), Wit: None.

Pp. 191-192: 15 Oct 1783, ANDREW HAMPTON to GEORGE BLACK...on 14 Jan 1783,
            at Court of P & QS for Rutherford Co., writ of fiere facias
against BENJAMIN ADAMS, late of Rutherford Co., planter,...300 A on both
sides of Mount Creek of 2nd Broad River,granted to sd. ADAMS 21 Jan 1779...
ANDREW HAMPTON (SEAL), Wit: JONATHAN HAMPTON, SAMUEL WALKER.

Pp. 192-193: 10 Sept 1779, JOHN BERRY of Dist. of Ninety Six, S. C. to
            JAMES GRAY of N. C., for ₺ 2000 S. C. money...land on N side
Broad River, on McDonalds Creek, adj. JAMES BYARS...JOHN BERRY (SEAL), Wit:
RICHARD McCLURE, ANDREW THOMSON.

Pp. 193-194: 12 Oct 1779, JAMES HENDERSON of Lincoln Co., to GEORGE FLEE-
            MAN of Rutherford Co., for ₺ 150...land on both sides Catheys
Creek of 2nd Broad River...JAMES HENDERSON (SEAL), Wit: T. WALKER, JOHN
WALKER.

Pp. 194-195: 21 Oct 1779, ISHAM RAVIS of Rutherford Co., to MARY JONES of
            same, for ₺ 3000 proc. money...land on both sides Main Broad
River, granted by deed from ARCHIBALD McDOWELL & JOHN McFADDIN 24 Aug 1777,
200 A...ISHAM RAVISH (SEAL), Wit: WILLIAM BRIANT (W), HERRIS BEAVES (H).

Pp. 195-196: 25 Oct 1779, SAMUEL STOCKTON of Rutherford Co., planter, &
            wf PRUDENCE to WILLIAM WHITESIDE of Washington Co., N. C.,
for ₺ 300...land on W side Wards Creek, granted to ROBERT COLLINWOOD, and
by deed from GEORGE LAMKIN, Esqr., late Sheriff of Tryon Co., at the suit
of BENJAKIN BRACKET, sold to MOSES MOOR, 22 ___ 1773 & another tract on
both sides Wards Creek, granted to WILLIAM GOING 2 Mar 1775...SAMUFL
STOCKTON (SEAL), PRUDENCE STOCKTON (SEAL), Wit: JAMES WHITESIDE, DAVIS
WHITESIDES.

Pp. 196-197: 23 Aug 1779, WILLIAM GOING of Rutherford Co., planter, & wf
            HESTER to SAMUEL STOCKTON of same, planter, for ₺ 3000...
(same tracts in preceding deed)...WILLIAM GOING (SEAL), HESTER GOING (X).
Wit: THOMAS WHITESIDES, DAVIS WHITESIDES.

Pp. 198-199: 10 Jan 1775, SAMUEL GIVENS & wf MARGARET Of Mecklenburg Co.,
            to WILLIAM JOHNSTON of Tryon Co., for ₺ 85...land on 2nd
Broad River, above HUDDLESTONS survey, granted to GIVEN by deed 25 Apr
1767...SAMUEL GIVENS (SEAL), MARGARET GIVENS (O) (SEAL), Wit: BENJAMIN
ADAMS, JOHN GIVINS.

Page 199: Grant to JONATHAN HARDIN, 100 A where WALLACE BEATYS line crosses
            DAVID HARDINS, adj. DAVID HARDIN, FRANCIS BEATY, & WALLACE BEATY
...28 Oct 1782. ALEX MARTIN.

Page 200: Grant to JONATHAN HARDIN, 600 A on Little Hickry Creek, adj.
            JAMES CROW, MORRIS ROBERTS, including his own improvement...25
Mar 1780. RICHD CASWELL.

Pp. 200-202: 30 Aug 1780, HENRY MONTFORD of Halifax Co., N. C. to PETER
            MALETT, THOMAS TULLOCK, & JOHN ESTES of Orange Co., N. C., for

Ł 100, 000 N. C. currency...land in Rutherford County on the Rich cove, North fork Broad River, 4700 A, described in 11 deeds granted to JOSEPH MONTFORD [apparently these are actually grants]...(numbers, acreage, and dates of each given)...HENRY MONTFORD (SEAL), Wit: WM LYTLE, MATHEW McCOULLY.

Page 202: 26 Dec 1783, JAMES MILLAR of Rutherford Co., to BENJAMIN JOHN-
             STON of same, for Ł 50...50 A on N side Green River, granted to
sd. MILLAR, part of a grant for 100 A...JAS MILLAR (SEAL), Wit: FELIX
WALKER.

Page 203: Grant to JOHN CAMP, 150 A on N side Little Broad River, adj.
             and below RITCHARD HENDERSON, including his own improvement,
also adj. MR. HILL...28 Oct 1782. ALEX MARTIN.

Pp. 203-204: Grant to JAMES LINN, 150 A on Second Broad River adj. CATHEY
             & NATHAN PROCTORS...28 Oct 1782. ALEX MARTIN.

Page 204: Grant to JAMES SCOTT, 100 A on Walnut Creek of Green River,
             below ALEXANDER CARUTH, adj. COULTER & GRIFFITH RUTHERFORD...
25 Mar 1780. RCD. CASWELL.

Pp. 204-205: Grant to ROBERT MELONE, 100 A on Ballo branch of Catheys
             Creek, adj. WILLIAM GILBERT & BAR...13 Aug 1779. RCD CASWELL.

Page 205: Grant to JONATHAN HEMPTON, 640 A on both sides N fork Saluda
             called Checkoroa...11 Oct 1783 ALEX MARTIN.

Page 206: Grant to ELIAS ALEXANDER, 100 A on Floyds Creek of Broad River,
             above his land...25 Mar 1780. RCD CASWELL.

Pp. 206-207: 4 Nov 1783, JOHN HUDLESTON of Rutherford Co., to JAMES SCOTT
             of same, for Ł 130 specia...land on both sides Cleghorns
Creek of Broad River, adj. WILLIAM CLEGHORN, 97 A granted to SAMUEL BRIGHT,
24 Dec 1770, and conveyed to WM. CLEGHORN 24 Apr 1771...JOHN HUDDLESTON
(SEAL), SARAH HUDDLESTON (O) (SEAL), Wit: JOHN SCOOT, SR., JOHN SCOTT,
JAMES CLEGHORN (✗).

Pp. 207-208: 14 Jan 1784, THOMAS MORRIS of Rutherford Co., to THOMAS
             DOVE of same, for Ł 100...200 A on both sides Catheys Creek,
known formerly by WILLIAM McMURRYS, adj. FREDERICK HAMBRIGHT, granted to
DICSON, 1769 and conveyed from PETER QUEEN to THOMAS MORRIS 5 Nov 1782...
THOMAS MORRIS (SEAL), Wit: FRANCIS LOGAN, ALEXR McGAUGHY.

Page 208: Grant to ABSALOM GREGORY 150 A on Little Broad River, on the
             Long branch, including both his own improvements...25 Mar 1780.
RCD CASWELL.

Page 209: 9 Jan 1784, BENJAMIN PRICE of Rutherford Co., to JAMES BRADLEY
             for Ł 40...land on E side Little Broad River, adj. BENJAMIN
RICE, bought of ABSALOM GREGORY, on both sides the Long Branch, including
the improvement that ABSALAM GREGORY now lives on where his fathers lived,
adj. DAVID THOMPSON...Benjamin Rice (X) (SEAL), Wit: PETER QUIN, ABRAHAM
HARGISS.

Page 210: Grant to JOHN HOLAND, 640 A on both sides Checkoroa, a North
             fork of Saluda above his other ladn...11 Oct 1783. ALEX MARTIN.

Pp. 210-211: Grant to WILLOUGHBY WILLIAMS, 640 A on both sides Middle
             fork of Saluda River, about 1/2 mile above BRIDGES improve-
ment...11 Oct 1783. ALEX MARTIN.

Pp. 211-212: 14 Mar 1783, JOHN ANGELS of Rutherford Co., to ROBERT CHERRY
             of Lincoln Co., for Ł 35...land on both sides Catheys Creek,
below JAMES BLACKS land, adj. JOHN BENNETs corner, granted to JOSEPH
BLACK, & by him conveyed to JOHN ANGEL...JOHN ANGEL (SEAL), Wit: JOHN
BLACK, D. DICKEY.

Pp. 212-213: 24 Mar 1779, JAMES McFADIN of Rutherford Co., to JAMES LATTO
             of same, for Ł 200...land on N side Broad River on both sides

Mountain, mouth of Maple Creek...200 A that JOHN McFADDIN sold to JAMES McFADDIN of his old survey, between he branch and the mill, adj. JOHN McFADIN...JAMES FADIN (I) (SEAL), Wit: ISHAM REAVES, _____ CARUTH(?)(torn).

Page 213: 19 Jan 1778, JOHN DENARD of Tryon Co., to WILLIAM NETTLES of
  same, for ₺ 85 proc. money...land on WILLIAM ROBINS Creek, on
S side N fork Broad River, including BARTLET HENSONs camps, 200 A, grant-
ed to WILLIAM ADAMS & conveyed to PHILIP HENSON then to JOHN McFADDIN
JUNR., and then to sd. JOHN DENNARD...JOHN DENNERD (I) (SEAL), Wit:
JOHN McKINNE SENR., JOHN McKINNER JUNR.

Page 214: 15 July 1775, ABRAHAM KIRKENDALL of Tryon Co., to JOHN WEBB of
  same, for ₺ 35...land on W side SEcond Broad River, 300 A...
ABRAHAM KIRKENDALL (A) (SEAL), Wit: JOHN BYAS (J), ROBERT BYAS.

Page 215: Tryon Co.: 3 Feb 1776, JOHN NIEGHBOURS & wf SARAH of Tryon Co.,
  to JOSEPH CLARK of same, planter, for ₺ 20...land on floyds
Creek of Broad River, 200 A granted 28 Feb 1775...JOHN NEIGHBOURS (I)
(SEAL), SARAH NEIGHBOURS (X) (SEAL), Wit: TOWNSEND ROBERTSON, MATHIAS
DAVIS TURNER, PETER DILL (P).

Page 216: 9 Jan 1784, ABSALOM GREGORY of Rutherford Co., to BENJAMIN RICE
  of same, for ₺ 80...150 A on both sides Long Branch of Little
Broad River, including both his own improvements...adj. DAVID THOMSON,
granted 20 Mar 1780...ABSOLOM GREGORY (A) (SEAL), Wit: PETER OUIN, JAS
BRADLEY (ᘯ),ABRAHAM HARGIS.

Page 217: 17 Jan 1780, WILLIAM BURGESS of Rutherford Co., to WILLIAM Mc-
  CAFFERTY of Mecklenburg Co., for ₺ 38 NC currency...40 A on S
side Green River adj. EDWARD HOGAN, granted to JAMES CRAWFORD, 22 Dec
1768, and by deed to WILLIAM SHARP 10 Apr 1769, and by EDWARD HOGAN to
THOMAS HESLIP, and from HESLIP to WILLIAM BURGESS, 17 Jan 1776...WILLIAM
BURGESS (SEAL), ELINOR BURGESS (ς) (SEAL), Wit: JAMES MILLAR, JO. MOORE.

Page 218: 12 Aug 1783, WILLIAM McCAFFERTY of Mecklenburg to ANDREW MILLAR
  pf Rutherford Co., for ₺ 38 NC currency...(same tract as preceding)...granted by deed to EDWARD HOGAN, from him to WILLIAM SHARP,
18 Nov 1772...WM. McCAFFERTY (SEAL), Wit: JOSEPH MOORE, DAVID MILLAR.

Page 219: Grant to GEORGE RUSSEL, 100 A on Main Broad River between his
  own and WILLIAM NETTLES land...28 Oct 1782...RD CASWELL.

Pp. 219-220: Grant to GEORGE RUSSEL, 100 A on N fork Main Broad River
  on Jeffs Branch, adj. his own land...28 Oct 1782. RD CASWELL.

Page 220: Grant to GEORGE RUSELL, 50 A on N fork Broad River above his
  other entry including SHERDERICK NETTLES improvements...18
Oct 1782. ALEX MARTIN.

Page 221: Grant to JOHN COLLINS, 100 A on Little Hickry Creek, above
  BENJAMIN HARDIN, including his own improvement...25 Mar 1780.
RD. CASWELL.

Pp. 221-222: Grant to JOHN COLLINS, 100 A on Little Hickry Creek of Little
  first Broad River, adj. his other entry...25 Mar 1780.
RD. CASWELL.

Page 222: Grant to JAMES CAMP, 200 A on Sizemores Creek of Second Broad
  River below JOHN THOMSONS entry...25 Mar 1780. RD. CASWELL.

Page 223: Grant to SAMUEL SPENCER, 200 A on N side Green River, in the
  Little Cove thereof, in the lower line of his 600 A entry...
11 Oct 1783. ALEX MARTIN.

Pp. 223-224: Grant to SAMUEL SPENCER, 100 A on both sides Alstons Creek
  of Green River, about 1 1/2 miles above ALSTONS land...11
Oct 1783. ALEX MARTIN.

Page 224: Grant to SAMUEL SPENCER, 400 A on both sides of upper Buffalow
  Creek of Main Broad River, near the foot of Ball Mountain, adj.

WILLIAM BASSET, JONAS BEDFORD...11 Oct 1783. ALEX MARTIN.

Page 225: Grant to SAMUEL SPENCER, 600 A on N side Green River on the
Little Cove...11 Oct 1783. ALEX MARTIN.

Pp. 225-226: Grant to THOMAS ROWLAND, 100 A on Balls branch of Catheys
Creek of Second Broad River, adj. JOHN MELONES Entry...11
Oct 1783. ALEX MARTIN.

Page 226: Grant to THOMAS ROWLAND, 200 A on Main Broad River including
JOHN LITTLES Improvements, adj. DAVID LEWIS...13 Aug 1779 RD
CASWELL.

Page 227: Grant to ABRAHAM KIRKENDOL, 100 A on Grogg Creek, on the path
from his house to ABEL HILLS including JOHN TURNERs cabbin...
25 Mar 1780. RD CASWELL.

Pp. 227-228: Grant to ABRAHAM KIRKENDOLL, 200 A on Sandy Run of Broad
River, below the wagon Road that leads from CORONAL(sic)
WALKERS to Charlestown, including his own improvement where he now lives
...25 Mar 1780. RD CASWELL.

Page 228: Grant to ANTHONY DICKEY, 400 A on Mill Creek of Broad River,
adj. his own land, BYERS...13 Oct 1783. ALEX MARTIN.

Page 229: Grant to WILLIAM SMITH, 200 A on waters of Big Hickry adj.
BEATYS, JOHN WATERSONS, including his own improvement...28
Oct 1782. ALEX MARTIN.

Pp. 229-230: Grant to ALEXANDER DAVIDSON, 75 A on Main Broad River adj.
his own land, including GUTHERIES improvement...28 Oct 1782
ALEX MARTIN.

Page 230: Grant to MOSES BRIDGES, 90 A near the mouth of Little Broad
River, adj. STEPHEN SHITTANCE, & his own, ALEXANDER DAVIDSONS
...25 Mar 1780. RD CASWELL.

Page 231: Grant to JAMES KITCHERSIDES, 100 A on Grogg Creek of Sandy
Run of Main Broad River, about 1 1/2 miles below the path
from the High Shoal to CAPT KEYKENDOL, including the flat Rock Shoal...
25 Mar 1780. RD CASWELL.

Pp. 231-232: Grant to JAMES SATERFIELD, 100 A on Beavour Dam Creek of
Little Broad River, above JAMES LOGAN, including his own
improvement...28 Oct 1782. ALEX MARTIN.

Page 232: Grant to MATHEW GUTHREY, 100 A on Main Broad River including
the Island Shoal ford and his own improvement...28 Oct 1782.
ALEX MARTIN.

Pp. 232-233: Grant to DENNIS HERN, 100 A on N side Main Broad River,
including WILLIAM PORTERS improvement...28 Oct 1782. ALEX
MARTIN.

Pp. 233-234: 15 Dec 1783, ELIAS MORGIN to WILLIAM PELL, both of Ruther-
ford Co., for Ł 60 NC money...200 A on both sides Little
Mountain Creek of Broad River, granted to ELIAS MORGAN, 2 Mar 1775...
ELIAS MORGAN (SEAL), Wit: GEORGE LEDBETTER, WILLIAM SELF (✗), GEORGE
WALTON BRADLY.

Pp. 234-235: 14 Dec 1784, JOHN WITHROW of Rutherford Co., to GEORGE
BLACK of same, for Ł 6...200 A in South Carolina, Ninety
Six District, on waters of Little River of Long Keen, in Granville Co.,
adj. WILLIAM CRAWFORD & vacant land, granted to JOHN WITHROW out of the
office of Charlestown, 7 May 1767...JOHN WITHROW (W) (SEAL), Wit: ALEX-
ANDER McGAUGHY, MILES GOFORTH.

Page 235: Grant to JAMES LINN, 50 A on E side Second Broad River, adj.
his own line...11 Oct 1783. ALEX MARTIN.

Pp. 235-236: Grant to WILLIAM HUDDLESTON, 100 A on S side Cain Creek adj. JAMES HUGHEYS Entry & his own land...13 Oct 1783. ALEX MARTIN.

Page 236: Grant to DAVID PORTER, 100 A on a branch of Camp Creek of Second Broad River adj. his own land, WILLIAM PORTER...28 Oct 1782 ALEX MARTIN.

Page 237: Grant to WILLIAM PORTER, 100 A on a branch of Camp Creek of Second Broad River, adj. his own land...28 Oct 1782. ALEX MARTIN.

Pp. 237-238: Grant to THOMAS MORRIS, 200 A on waters of Shippards Creek, adj. WILLIAM GILBERTS late Entry, his own survey...27 Oct 1784. ALEX MARTIN.

Page 238: Grant to GEORGE PARRIS, 100 A on N side Green River adj. his own land...13 Oct 1783. ALEX MARTIN.

Page 239: Grant to JAMES HUEY, 92 A on both side Cane Creek of Second Broad River, adj. JOHN WITHROW, WILLIAM HUDDLESTON, including his own improvement...13 Oct 1783. ALEX MARTIN.

Pp. 239-240: Grant to ISHAM RAVESS, 100 A on Godfreys branch of Main Broad River, adj. WALKER, including where there was a large Cabbin built...28 Oct 1782. ALEX MARTIN.

Page 240: Grant to ADLAI OSBURN, 150 A on North Pacolet, on little Cane Creek above LOGANS Entry...13 Oct 1783. ALEX MARTIN.

Page 241: Grant to JAMES MILLAR, 100 A on both sides Green River adj. DIXON, including McGUIRES & ISHAM HINSONs Improvements...28 Oct 1782. ALEX MARTIN.

Pp. 241-242: Grant to JOHN SMYTHE, 100 A on First Broad River adj. WILLIAM MILLES JUN., COLLINWOOD, including a shoal...13 Oct 1783. ALEX MARTIN.

Page 242: Grant to BENJAMIN WILLIAMS, 200 A Yanceys Branch of First Broad River, about 1 1/2 miles above ALEXANDER DAVIDSONS, including the improvement he bought of MOSES BRIDGES...28 Oct 1782. ALEX MARTIN.

Page 243: Grant to JOSEPH CAMP, 400 A on a branch of Wades Mill Creek, adj. land of JOSEPH BONING(?), including the Improvement where GEORGE BLANTON now lives, adj. BENJAMIN BRIDGES, 25 Mar 1780...RD CASWELL.

Pp. 243-244: Grant to JOSEPH CAMP, 250 A on W side Main Broad River, opposite the mouth of First Broad River, including JOSEPH CAMPS Improvement...13 Oct 1783. ALEX MARTIN.

Page 244: Grant to JOHN McCLURE, 150 A on Main Borad River adj. JOHN McCLURE, ALEXANDER COULTER, JOSEPH MOORE..13 Aug 1779. RD CASWELL.

Page 245: Grant to JOHN McCLURE, 64 A on Main Broad River adj. JOHN McCLURE, JAMES MILLAR, HUGH KILPATRICK...13 Aug 1779. RD CASWELL.

Pp. 245-246: Grant to ELIAS ALEXANDER, 200 A on both sides Floyds Creek... 11 Oct 1783. ALEX MARTIN.

Page 246: Grant to RITCHARD SCRUGGS, land on N side Main Broad River in the forks of Main and Second Broad River, including his own improvements...28 Oct 1782. ALEX MARTIN.

Page 247: Grant to JAMES HENDERSON, 200 A on Sandy Run of First Broad River adj. JAMES SWOFFORD, THOMAS WELCH, & LOGAN, including HARGERTYS improvement...13 Oct 1783. ALEX MARTIN.

Pp. 247-248: Grant to ROBERT WIER, 200 A in Lincoln Co., on First Broad
          River, adj. HENDERSON, including ABSOLUM OTRIES improvement
...9 Oct 1782. ALEX MARTIN.

Page 248: Grant to JAMES LOGAN, 150 A on Sandy Run, including FORNEGREEN
          NEWMANS improvements...13 Oct 1782. ALEX MARTIN.

Page 249: Grant to JAMES LOGAN, 100 A on a branch of Robersons Creek,
          above AARON BICKERSTAFF...13 Oct 1783. ALEX MARTIN.

Pp. 249-250: Grant to JAMES LOGAN, 150 A on Horse Creek of Main Broad
          River, including RICHARD HICKS improvement...13 Oct 1783.
ALEX MARTIN.

Page 250: Grant to JAMES LOGAN, 50 A on Vauns branch of North Packolet
          above SPRIGS Entry...13 Oct 1783. ALEX MARTIN.

Page 251: Grant to JAMES LOGAN, 150 A on a branch of Glaghorns Creek,
          adj. JAMES MILLAR...13 Oct 1783. ALEX MARTIN.

Pp. 251-252: Grant to JAMES LOGAN, 100 A on Suck fork of First Broad
          River, adj. SEMSES land...13 Oct 1783.ALEX MARTIN.

Page 252: Grant to WALLACE BEATY, 100 A on N side Big Hickry Creek, adj.
          his own land, including the path from MAGNESSES to TUBBS...13
Oct 1783. ALEX MARTIN.

                              "Book C"
Pp. 253-254: 26 Aug 1784, JOHN LEWIS of Rutherford Co., (Sheriff), Esq.,
          to MATHEW HOLLAND...whereas on 15 Apr 1784 at the Court of
P & QS, against JOSEPH UNDERWOOD, JOHN GOODBREAD, JOHN ASHWORTH, THOMAS
TOWNSEND, JOHN CAMP & THOMAS CAMP & RITCHARD LEDBETTER, late of Ruther-
ford Co., planters, Ł 740 s 19 adjudged to WILLIAM GILBERT...220 A on
Cedar Creek, above EPHRAIM McCLAIN and below WILLIAM ADAMS, granted to
WILLIAM WRAY, 28 Apr 1768...JOHN LEWIS (SEAL), Wit:JAS HOLLAND, BENJAMIN
LANGFORD, MATHEW HOLLAND.

Page 255: Grant to JOSEPH HENRY & ROBERT ANDERSON, 640 A on Wilkeys
          Creek of First Little Broad River, adj. COL. WILLIAM GREENLEE
...27 Oct 1784. ALEX MARTIN.

Pp. 255-256: Grant to JOSEPH BURNET, 150 A adj. THOMAS ROBERSON, inclu-
          ding BURWELL SIMMS Improvement...25 Mar 1780. RD CASWELL.

Page 256: 10 July 1784, JOHN LEWIS, Sheriff of Rutherford Co., to DAVID
          MILLAR...by a writ from the Court of P & QS, against JAMES
LOGAN & WILLIAM ADAMS, 2nd Monday of April 1784...200 A on Main Mountain
Creek...J. LEWIS (SEAL), Wit: FELIX WALKER.

Pp. 257-258: Grant to DENNIS DUFF, 100 A on Darnels Creek of Cove Creek,
          including the little Cane Break...13 Oct 1783, ALEX MARTIN.

Page 258: Grant to JOHN FLECK, 80 A on both sides Catheys Creek, adj.
          FLEMMING...28 Oct 1782. ALEX MARTIN.

Page 259: Grant to WILLIAM DUNN, 100 A on waters of upper Camp Creek,
          adj. his own line...28 Oct 1782. ALEX MARTIN.

Pp. 259-260: Grant to RICHARD BRADLEY, 50 A on Turkey Otter Creek, in
          or near McCALS line...11 Oct 1783. ALEX MARTIN.

Page 260: Grant to ELIAS ALEXANDER, 200 A on FLoyds Creek of Main Broad
          River, adj. his own land, WILLIAM NETTLES....27 Oct 1784. ALEX
MARTIN.

Page 261: Grant to WILLIAM ARMSTRONG, 200 A on main fork of White Oak,
          adj. ISAC CAPSHAW & including 2 improvements...27 Oct 1784.
ALEX MARTIN.

Pp. 261-262: Grant to WILLIAM COLLINS, 100 A on Rocky Branch of Second

Broad River, and including his own improvement...10 Oct 1783. ALEX MARTIN.

Page 262: Grant to PETER QUIN,323 A on NW side little Broad River adj.
ARMSTRONG and including his own two improvements...13 Oct 1783.
ALEX MARTIN.

Page 263: Grant to WILLIAM GRANT, 150 A on Grants Creek of Cove Creek,
known by the name of NEELYS timber tree...13 Oct 1783. ALEX
MARTIN.

Pp. 263-264: Grant to WILLIAM GRANT, 50 A on Grants Creek adj. POTTS...
11 Oct 1783. ALEX MARTIN.

Page 265: Grant to SAMUEL TURNER, 100 A on N side Main Broad River, including his own improvement...13 Oct 1783. ALEX MARTIN.

Page 264: Grant to WILLIAM GRANT, 100 A adj. his own line...11 Oct 1783.
ALEX MARTIN.

Pp. 265-266: Grant to THOMAS WARNER, 100 A at the mouth of Ashworths
Creek, 13 Oct 1783. ALEX MARTIN.

Page 266: Grant to WILLIAM GILBERT, 200 A on the head waters of Sheppards
Creek adj. his other entry. 13 Oct 1783. ALEX MARTIN.

Page 267: Grant to JOHN McKINNEY, 100 A on S side Main Broad River, adj.
his own line...27 Oct 1784. ALEX MARTIN.

Pp. 267-268: Grant to JOHN McKINNEY, 100 A on S fork White Oak, adj.
GEORGE POTTS...10 Nov 1784. ALEX MARTIN.

Pp. 268-269: 2 ___ 1783, JOHN WITHROW of Rutherford Co., to JAMES HUGHEY
of same, for Ł 30...70 A on Cane Creek a branch of Second
Broad River, part of a grant to JOHN CARSON, 6 Apr 1765 & conveyed to sd.
WITHROW...JOHN WITHROW (W) (SEAL), Wit: ANDREW GOFORTH, JAS WITHROW.

Page 269: Grant to CHRISTOPHER WALVERT, 200 A on both sides Wards Creek,
adj. THOMAS ROBERSON, & EDWARD FRANCES, including the forks &
his own improvement. 13 Oct 1783. ALEX MARTIN.

Page 270: Grant to BENJAMIN BRIDGES, 400 A on little Shoal Creek of First
Broad River, adj. JOHN McKNITT ALEXANDER, and including his
own improvement... Oct 1783. ALEX MARTIN.

Pp. 270-271: Grant to JAMES LOGAN, 100 A on Beaver Dam Creek of First
Broad River...adj. SHELTON...13 Oct 1783. ALEX MARTIN.

Pp. 271-273: 26 Aug 1784, JOHN LEWIS (Sheriff) of Rutherford Co., to
WILLIAM WILLIAMS...on 2nd Monday in April 1784, and the
Court of P & QS, recovered against JOSEPH UNDERWOOD, JOHN GOODBREAD,
JOHN ASHWORTH, THOMAS TOWNSEND, JOHN CAMP & THOMAS CAMP, Planters....to
WILLIAM GILBERT...200 A, property of THOMAS TOWNSEND, on S side Main
Broad River, including the old Cane Break, granted to JAMES MOOR, 5 Apr
1766, Rec. in Clarks office Jan. term 1775...JOHN LEWIS (SEAL), Wit:
JAS HOLLAND, BENJAMIN LANGFORD, HENRY HOLLAND.

Pp. 273-274: JOHN LEWIS, Sheriff of Rutherford Co., for Ł 45 s 5, pd. by
JAMES HOLLAND, for a Slave Poll, 45 years old and two chil-
dren (named) [same case as preceding]...26 Aug 1784. J. LEWIS (SEAL),
Wit: BENJAMIN LANGFORD, HENRY HOLLAND, MATHEW HOLLAND.

Pp. 274-275: Grant to JOHN McFADDEN, 200 A on Nobb Creek of Broad River,
adj. JOHN McLAIN & BEARD, including JOHN CRAWFORDs improvement...28 Oct 1782. ALEX MARTIN.

Pp. 275-276: 29 Oct 1783, JOHN WHEELER of Rutherford Co., to HUGH IVESTER
of Lincoln Co., for Ł 70...105 A on Knobb Creek adj. BEN-
JAMIN HARDIN, part of 2 patents, one granted to FRANCIS BEATY, 6 Apr
1765, the other to BENJAMIN HARDIN 5 May 1769...JOHN WHEELER (X) (SEAL),
Wit: SAMUEL CARPENTER, NATH CLARK.

Page 276: Grant to JOSEPH BRADLEY, 100 A on waters of Williams Creek of
First Broad River, adj. SPENCER...20 Oct 1784. ALEX MARTIN.

Pp. 277-278: 26 Aug 1784, JOHN LEWIS Sheriff of Rutherford Co., to
HENRY HOLLAND...[same case as pp 271-3 & 273-4]...200 A,
property of RICHARD LEDBETTER, on N fork Main Broad River called Cedar
Creek, N side Youngs Mountain, adj. WM WREY, granted to WILLIAM ADAMS,
28 Apr 1768...J. LEWIS (SEAL), Wit: JAS HOLLAND, BENJAMIN LANGFORD,
MATHEW HOLLAND.

Pp. 279-280: 26 Aug 1784, JOHN LEWIS Sheriff of Rutherford Co., to
WILLIAM WILLIAMS...234 A on N side Main Broad River, adj.
McCLANIHANS, granted to HUGH BEATY, 6 Apr 1765...[same case as preceding]
...150 A, property of JOHN CAMP, on both sides Second Broad River, adj.
RICHARD HENDERSON, McHILL, including his own improvement...granted 28
Oct 1782, No. 253...J. LEWIS (SEAL), Wit: JAS HOLLAND, BENJAMIN LANGFORD,
HENRY HOLLAND.

Pp. 283-285: 20 Mar 1783, ANDREW HAMPTON of Rutherford Co., to GEORGE
BLACK of same...by writ of fiera facias to levy ₺ 55 s14
d3 specia from goods and chattels of BENJAMIN ADAMS, & another case
recovered against ADAMS by WAITSELL AVERY...land on both sides Mountain
Creek of Second Broad River, 300 A granted to sd. ADAMS, 21 Jan 1779...
ANDW HAMPTON, Sheriff. Wit: LOUDERIWCK WRAY, RUBEN WOOD.

Pp. 285-286: 26 Aug 1784, JOHN LEWIS Sheriff of Rutherford Co., to JAMES
HOLLAND, for ₺ 40...[same case as pp. 279-280]...negro Joe,
age 26...Wit; HENRY HOLLAND, MATHEW HOLLAND.

Pp. 286-287: 27 Aug 1784, JOHN LEWIS Sheriff of Rutherford Co., to
DAVID DICKEY, for ₺ 40...negro Nell, 22 yrs old and 2 chil-
dren (named)...[same case as preceding] Wit: JONATHAN HAMPTON, ANTHONY
DICKEY.

Pp. 287-288: 26 Aug 1784, JOHN LEWIS Sheriff to ANDREW HAMPTON, for ₺ 30
specia...slave woman Lett and children (named)...of goods
and chattels of JOSEPH UNDERWOOD...[same case as preceding]...Wit:
BENJAMIN LANGFORD, HENRY HOLLAND, MATHEW HOLLAND.

Page 289: 10 Mar 1780, JOHN McENTIRE of Rutherford Co., to ROBERT LEE
of same, for ₺ 500 proc. money...land on Sandy Run of Main
Broad River, adj. TIMOTHY RIGGS, 300 A...JOHN McENTIRE (SEAL), Wit:
TIMO RIGGS, ROBERT WIER.

Page 290: 24 Mar 1785: ALEXANDER McFADDEN of Rutherford Co., to MOSES
FERGUSON of same...whereas JOHN MCFADDEN, formerly of Rutherford Co., having removed himself to the county of Davidson and since
his removal having sold a tract to MOSES FERGUSON & having given power
of attorney to sd. ALEXANDER...land on Nobb Creek adj. JOHN McLAIN,
BEARD & including JOHN CRAWFORDS improvement...granted to JOHN McFADDEN
28 Oct 1782...ALEX McFADDEN (SEAL), Wit: DAVID DICKEY, MARY DICKEY.

Page 291: Grant to ALEXANDER MACKEY, 200 A on N fork White Oak of Green
River, adj. QUINN & including JOHN OWENS improvement...13
Oct 1783. ALEX MARTIN.

Pp. 291-292: Grant to ALEXANDER MACKEY, 100 A on a creek that runs into
Green River at MILLS...13 Aug 1779. RD CASWELL.

Page 292: Grant to ABRAHAM MUSICK, 100 A on Wheats Creek adj. his own
survey, including JOHNTON improvement...28 Oct 1782. ALEX
MARTIN.

Pp. 292-293: 7 Feb 1785, HUGH BEATY of Rutherford Co., to WILLIAM GRA-
HAM of Lincoln Co., for ₺ 35 specia...236 A on branches of
First Borad River, adj. JOHN BEATY, ROBERT ARMSTRONG, granted to FRAN-
CIS BEATY, decd, 28 Feb 1775 & left to his son HUGH BEATY...HUGH BEATY
(SEAL), Wit: WALLACE BEATY, ALEXANDER McFADDEN, GEORGE TUBB (I).

Page 294: 16 Jan 1777, ARON BICKERSTAFF & wf MARY of Tryon Co., to
MARTHA BICKERSTAFF of same, for ₺ 120...land on Robertson

Creek of Second Broad River, adj. PETER ACRE, 250 A granted to sd.
ARON, 15 May 1772...ARON BICKERSTAFF (SEAL), MARY BICKERSTAFF (M) (SEAL),
Wit: RICHARD SINGLETON, BENJAMIN BICKERSTAFF, JESSE BICKERSTAFF (X).

Page 295: Grant to GEORGE BLACK, 60 A on Second Broad River adj. his
own land, THOMAS JONES...24 Oct 1784. ALEX MARTIN.

Pp. 295-296: Grant to GEORGE PARRIS, 100(?) A on S fork Brights Creek of
Green River, including Connoways improvement...28 Oct 1782.
ALEX MARTIN.

Page 297: Grant to WILLIAM WEBB, 150 A on N side Second Broad River
adj. his own land...13 Oct 1783. ALEX MARTIN.

Pp. 297-298: Grant to JONATHAN GULLICK, 150 A on S fork Whte Oak Creek
near CUMMINGS line, between WILEY JONES, ALSTON & PARMER...
13 Oct 1783.ALEX MARTIN.

Page 298: Grant to JOHN LOGAN, 60 A on Shoal Creek of Broad River, inclu-
ding Camp spring & WILLIAM LOGANS improvement adj. SAMUEL
BRIER, CHARLES STICE , JOHN McNITT ALEXANDER...25 Mar 1780...RICHARD
CASWELL.

Page 299: Grant to ALEXANDER ORR, 200 A on McCashlins branch of Second
Broad River adj. ARON DIVENEYS & JOHN WALKERS including his
own improvement....27 Oct 1784. ALEX MARTIN.

Pp. 299-300: Grant to JAMES WITHROW, 150 A on Cane Creek of Broad River
between his own and SAMUEL ANDREWS survey...13 Oct 1783.
ALEX MARTIN.

Page 300: Grant to GEORGE WOLFE, 200 A on North Packolet above TOWNSEND
ROBERSONS, including his own improvement...27 Oct 1784. ALEX
MARTIN.

Page 301: Grant to ANDREW NELSON, 200 A on Hinsons Creek of First Broad
River including three forks and where he now lives...13 Oct
1783. ALEX MARTIN.

Pp. 301-302: Grant to JOHN SMART, 87 A on waters of Cane Creek adj. lands
of ALEXANDER McGAUGHY, WILLIAM HUDDLESTON, WILLIAM LONG &
his own...27 Oct 1784. ALEX MARTIN.

Page 302: Grant to PATRICK WATSON, 50 A on S fork Cane Creek...11 Oct
1783. ALEX MARTIN.

Page 303: 18 Sept 1784, FRANCES ADAMS of Lincoln Co., planter, to JOHN
WALBERT of Rutherford Co., for L 50...200 A, ½ of 400 A grant-
ed 2 Mar 1775, adj. JOSEPH ENGLAND...FRANCIS ADAMS (SEAL), Wit: CHRISTO-
PHER WALBERT, AMBROSE COBBS (X).

Pp. 304-305: 18 Mar 1785, THOMAS WALLIS, plaintiff, of Rutherford Co.,
& wf MARGARET to WILLIAM GOINGS, for L 30...200 A on both
sides First Broad River...THOMAS WALLAS (X) (SEAL), MARGARET WALLAS (X)
(SEAL), Wit: MATHEW BLACK, WILLIAM GOING.

Page 305: 5 Jan 1785, JOHN PURVIS of Ninety Six District, S. C. to WILL-
IAM NEVEL of Rutherford Co., for L 50 proc. money...land on S
side Green River adj. GEORGE PARRIS, 250 A...JOHN PURVIS (SEAL), Wit:
JOHN MILLER, THOMAS TURNER.

Page 306: 8 Jan 1785, THOMAS CAMP of Rutherford Co., planter, to THOMAS
HARRISON of 96 District, S. C., for L 100...land on S side
Main Broad River, against THOMAS HAWKINS Shoal, including THOMAS CAMPS
improvement, granted 28 Oct 1782, 200 A...THOMAS CAMP (SEAL), Wit:
CRENSHAW CAMP, ISAIAH BLACKWELL (X), WILLIAM CAMP.

Pp. 307-308: 17 Feb 1784, JAMES COOK of Rutherford Co., farmer & wf
CATHERINE, to WILLIAM PORTER, farmer, for L 300...land on
btoh sides Catheys Creek of Second Broad River, 392 A, adj. JAMES

BIGLOTONS, WALKERS...JAS COOK (SEAL), CATHERINE COOK (X), Wit: ROBERT GILKEY, JOHN HAYNE, THOMAS DONNELSON.

Pp. 308-309: 18 Dec 1783, SAMUEL SMITH of Rutherford Co., to HENRY DOOLEY of same, for Ь 55...land on N side First Broad River, including the mouth of Maple Creek, adj. JOHN LONDON, 200 A granted to HENRY RUNNELS, 28 Feb 1775...SAMUEL SMITH (SEAL), Wit: JAMES WILLSON, ANDR WILLSON.

Pp. 309-310: 13 Jan 1783, ABRAHAM KUYKENDOL of Washington Co., N. C. to WILLIAM WEBB of Rutherford Co., for Ь 30 specia...300 A on Second Broad River above old field called RICHMOND FLEMENS...ABRAHAM KUYKENDALL (SEAL), Wit: JAMES MILLER, WM. GRAHAM.

Pp. 310-311: 27 May 1783, JOHN SWAN of Rutherford Co., to WILLIAM WEBB of same, for Ь 150 specia...475 A on both sides Second Broad River, granted to ROBERT SWAN 14 Nov 1771 & fell to JOHN SWAN by heirship ...JOHN SWAN (SEAL), Wit: RICHARD COLEMAN SR., WM WEBB SR. (X), MARY COLEMAN (M).

Pp. 311-312: 13 Sept 1783, JAMES MILLER of Rutherford Co., to HUGH KIL-PATRICK of same, for Ь 130...236 A on both sides N fork of Main Broad River adj. JOHN McLEUR, including his own improvement, near McDON-ALD, KELLY, granted to JAMES MILLER SEN., 28 Oct 1782...JAS MILLER (SEAL), Wit: ROBT LEE, JOHN EARLE.

Pp. 312-313: 6 Mar 1785, BENJAMIN BRACKET & wf ANN of Rutherford Co., to HUGH SMITH of same, land on a branch of Broad River, 300 A adj. WILLIS...BENJAMIN BRACKET (SEAL), Wit: WILLIAM GOINGS, SAMUEL WHITE-SIDES.

Pp. 313-314: 20 Sept 1784, JAMES BRADLEY of Rutherford Co., to ABRAHAM HARGIS of same, for Ь 40...79 A land sd. RICE bought of ABSALUM GREGORY, including the Improvement NATHANIEL RICE now lives on, adj. THOMAS THOMAS...JAMES BRADLEY (X) (SEAL), Wit: PETER QUIN, JOHN TATE.

Pp. 314-315: 11 Nov 1778, JACOB KUYKENDALL & MARY ARMSTRONG of Tryon Co., to ROBERT CLINTON of same, for Ь 130 proc. money...168 A, part of a grant to sd. KUYKENDALL & ARMSTRONG 24 Sept 1754, on both sides Second Broad River, including Clarks ford, adj. WILLIAM BAKER, Puzzel Creek...JACOB KUYKENDALL (SEAL), MARY ARMSTRONG (X) (SEAL), Wit: WM. LANHAM, MARTIN ARMSTRONG.

Pp. 315-316: 15 Dec 1784, JOHN FLACK of North Carolina, to JOHN ANDERSON of Guilford Co., N. C., for Ь 200 North money...land on S fork Camp Creek, adj. SMART, 250 A...JOHN FLACK (SEAL), Wit: ROBERT CHERRY, DAVID McLAIN.

Page 316: 15 Dec 1784, JOHN FLACK to JOHN ANDERSON, for Ь 50 north money ...100 A adj. his own land...Wit: ROBERT CHERRY, DAVID McLEAN (X).

Page 317: 25 Oct 1784, PETER QUIN of Rutherford Co., to JOHN TATE of South Carolina...for Ь 150 proc. money...land on S side First Broad River, granted to JOHN GRADY 1768, and from JOHN GRADY decd, to NICHOLAS FISHER, Admr., and from FISHER to sd. QUIN...PETER QUIN (SEAL), Wit: JAMES BRADLEY (X), WILLIAM BRADLEY (X).

Pp. 317-318: 9 Mar 1784, ANTHONY MIDCALD of Rutherford Co., to ELIZABETH LAUGHTER of same, for Ь 50...land on N side Green River, adj. EDWARD HOGAN and below his own land, 41 A...ANTHONY MEDCALF (SEAL), Wit: ISHAM REVIS, ISAAC BRIANT (X).

Page 319: 5 Jan 1785, GEORGE BLANTON of Rutherford Co., to AARON BRIDGES of same, for Ь 100..land on E side Broad River, 100 A granted to GEORGE HEATHLY by Gov. Wm. Tryon...GEORGE BLANTON (SEAL), Wit: MOSES BRIDGES (B), BIRWELL BLANTON.

Page 320: 3 Jan 1785, GEORGE PARRIS of Rutherford Co., to ALEXANDER THOMAS of same, for Ь 36...land on one of the forks of White

Oak, a little below Tryon Mountain...HINESES old place, granted 13 Aug 1779, 130 A...GEORGE PARRIS (SEAL), Wit: WM NEVEL, SAML McFADDEN.

Page 320½: 11 Nov 1784, LETITIA CLEGHORN of Rutherford Co., to JAMES
        SCOTT of same...whereas WILLIAM CLEGHORN did in his lifetime sell to JOHN HUDDLESTON 53 A, part of 400 A, sd. CLEGHOPN then lived on ...in will of sd. WILLIAM CLEGHORN in Lincoln County, authroise his Ear (sic) LETTICE to make title...sd. JOHN HUDDLESTON having sold said land to JAMES SCOT...53 A, part of a grant to JOHN McDOWELL, 6 Nov 1764...and conveyed to CLEGHORN...LETTICE CLEGHORN (X). Wit: ROBERT MILLICAN, THOMAS MILLICAN.

Pp. 321-321½: 29 Sept 1779, WILLIAM MILLS Of Rutherford Co., to THOMAS
        WADLINGTON of same, for Ŀ 200 proc. money of N. C....land on both sides Walnut Creek, waters of Green River, adj. JOHN FISHFR, granted to JOHN McKNITT ALEXANDER 29 Apr 1769, and conveyed to SAMUEL SHARP, then to WILLIAM MILLS...WILLIAM MILLS (SEAL), ELINOR MILLS (SEAL), Wit: JOHN EARLE, WM NEVIL.

Page 321½: 7 Feb 1784, JOHN WITHROW of Rutherford Co., to JAMES WITHROW
        of same, for Ŀ 300...land in the County of Anson then, now in South Carolina, Camden District, on N side Broad River, on the mouth of Buffalow Creek, 300 A granted to JOHN WITHROW 4 Sept 1753...JOHN WITHROW (W) (SEAL), Wit: JOHN LEWIS, WILLIAM COLE.

Page 322: 1 Jan 1785, GEORGE WINTERS of Rutherford Co., to JOHN BRADLEY
        of same, for Ŀ 100...300 A on both sides Youngs Creek of Broad River, adj. McLAIN, granted to WINTERS 21 July 1774, No. 176...GEORGE WINTERS (X), Wit: THOMAS DOVE (P), LENNARD SAYLOR (S).

Page 323: 21 Nov 1784, JOHN WOOD and GEORGE WOOD, both of Rutherford Co.,
        to JAMES RYDINGS of same, for Ŀ 200...land on Greens Creek, 150 A; also 100 A adj. to JOHN WOODS land...JOHN WOOD (Ŧ) (SEAL), GEORGE WOOD (+) (SEAL), SARAH WOOD (-) (SEAL), Wit: MOSES FRENCH (E), JOSFPH WALKER.

Page 324: 15 May 1784, JULIUS CLARKSON of Albemarle Co., Ga., to JOHN
        MECAN of same, for Ŀ 120 Va. money...200 A granted to MARTIN PHIFER, 30 Oct 1760 and conveyed to JAMES MILLICAN, 17 Jan 1777, including some Indian Camps...JULIUS CLARKSON (SEAL), Wit: JOHN DALTON, JO. TALIAFERRO, DAVID DOLTON, ROBERT LEWIS.

Pp. 325-326: 21 Oct 1776, JACOB CLEMENS of Tryon Co., to WILLIAM ROBINS
        of same, for Ŀ 100 proc. money...land on W side Broad River, including a small Island, granted to PHILIP HINSON 21 Oct 1776, and conveyed to ABRAHAM CLEMMENS, then to BARTLET HINSON, then to JACOB CLEMONS ...JACOB CLEMINS (SEAL), ELISAPETH CLEMINS (SEAL), Wit: JOHN McKINNEY, THOMAS DILLS (U).

Page 326: 22 Dec 1783, JOHN WEBB of Ninety Six District, S. C., to SAM-
        UEL SWAN of Rutherford Co., for Ŀ 130...land on W side Second Broad River, 300 A...JOHN WEBB (SEAL), Wit: FELIX WALKER.

Page 327: 5 June 1784, GEOPGE PARRIS of Rutherford Co., to MARY WHITE of
        same,..land under Tryon Mountain, on both sides of Cubb or Clarks Creek, S side Green River, 200 A...GEORGE PARRIS (SEAL), Wit: TIMO RIGGS, ROGER CARSON (O).

Page 328: 6 July 1784, TALIFERRO LEWIS of Albemarle Co., Ga., to JOHN
        LEWIS of Rutherford Co., for Ŀ 80 NC money...land on Main Creek...by lottery as agreeable to the L. W. & T. of JOHN LEWIS...TALIA-FERRO LEWIS (SEAL), Wit: FELIX WALKER.

Pp. 329-330: 15 Apr 1784, LETTICE CLEGHORN of Rutherford Co., to JOHN
        SCOTT of same, for Ŀ 130...land on S side Main Broad River, conveyed to WILLIAM CLEGHORN...part of a 400 A grant to JOHN McDOWELL, 16 Nov 1764...land adj. McCLAIN, McDOWELL...LETTICE CLEGHORN (X) (SFAL), Wit: JOHN MILLICAN, JAMES SCOTT, WILLIAM GRAY.

Page 330: Grant to DAVID THOMSON, 300 A on W side First Broad River, on

Pepes Branch, adj. WILLIAM TUBBS, JOHN FAFFET, including his own improvements...25 Mar 1780. RD. CASWELL.

Pp. 331-332: 13 Jan 1784, HENRY CLARK of Rutherford Co., to WILLIAM QUEEN of same, for ₺ 100...land on both sides W Fork Knobb Creek, granted 5 May 1769 to BENJAMIN HARDIN...HENRY CLARK (SEAL), Wit: ANDW WILSON, SAMUEL CARPENTER.

Pp. 332-333: 13 Jan 1784, HENRY CLARK to WILLIAM QUEEN, for ₺ 100...240 A on Knobb Creek, including a Great Bottom, Cherokey path and forks of the Creek, granted 6 Apr 1765 to FRANCIS BEATY...HENRY CLARK (SEAL), Wit: ANDREW WILLSON, SAMUEL CARPENTER.

Page 333: Grant to DAVID MILLER, 200 A on Hintons Creek...6 Dec 1785. RD CASWELL.

Page 334: Grant to MARVIL ELLIOT, 300 A on Buffalow Creek, near JONAS BEDFORD, adj. GATES...16 Dec 1785. RD. CASWELL.

Pp. 334-335: Grant to JOHN EARLE & DAVID MILLER, 400 A on both sides Hoopers Creek...16 Dec 1785. RD. CASWELL.

Pp. 335-336: 15 Oct 1783, ABRAHAM KIRKENDOLL of Rutherford Co., to WILLIAM BACKER of same, for ₺ 30 specia...340 A on Second Broad River...ABRAHAM KIRKENDOL (SEAL), Wit: WM. WEBB, JOHN KIRKINDOL.

Page 337: Grant to JAMES LATTA, 100 A on Nobb Creek above JOHN McLAIN... 28 Oct 1782. ALEX MARTIN.

Pp. 337-338: 16 Apr 1785, ELIAS ALEXANDER of Rutherford Co., to JOHN McKINNEY of same, for ₺ 20...land on N side Main Broad River adj. THOMAS DILLS, including GABRIEL SIMONS Improvements, 50 A granted to sd. ALEXANDER 27 Oct 1784...ELIAS ALEXANDER (SEAL), Wit: WAITSELL AVERY, F. WALKER.

Pp. 338-339: 24 Dec 1782, PETER DILLS of Ninety Six District, S. C. to JOHN McKINNEY of Rutherford Co., for ₺ 100 Proc money... land on N side Main Broad River, including his own improvement, 100 A granted to PETER DILLS 24 May 1770...PETER DILLS (P) (SEAL), Wit: J. McDERMITT, JOHN HAWKINS.

Pp. 339-340: 28 Oct 1779, WM PALMER of Hallifax Co., N. C., to JOHN McKINNEY of Rutherford Co., for ₺ 40...land on both sides Sandy Run of Broad River, 100 A granted to sd. PALMER 6 Dec 1771... WM PALMER (SEAL), Wit: CHRISTOPHER HICKS (X), ELLIS HICKS (X), JOHN KUYKONELL.

Page 341: Grant to JAMES HICKS, 200 A on a Creek that DANIEL BLACKWELL lived on, on both sides the _____ that leads from Richardsons Mill to the High Shoals...13 Oct 1783. ALEX MARTIN.

Pp. 341-343: 30 Apr 1784, WILLIE JONES, EXR. of ROBERT JONES, Decd.,& HENRY MONFORD, Exr. of JOSEPH MONTFORD decd., to LEMUEL ALSTON, son & heir at law of SOLOMON ALSTON, decd...whereas sundry tracts supposed to be in Maclinburgh (sic) County, were surveyed for ROBERT PALMER, ROBERT JONES JUNR., SOLOMON ALSTON JUNR., & JOSEPH MONTFORD have been divided...& sold to LEMUEL ALSTON...600 A on both sides Main North Fork of Packolet River, granted to JOSEPH MONTFORD, 30 Oct 1765; 200 A on Smiths Creek, granted to WILLIE JONES, SOLOMON ALSTON, & JOSEPH MONTFORD 22 Dec 1768; 300 A now in S. C. on Shoal Creek about a mile above BRIGHTS new place, granted to sd. JONES, ALSTON & MONTFORT, 22 Dec 1768; 300 A now in S. C. on Walnut Creek of Green River, granted to JONES, ALSTON & MONTFORT 22 Sept 1768...WILLIE JONES (SEAL), H. MONTFORT (SEAL), Wit: JAS MILLER, JAS WITHEROW, RICHD SINGLETON.

Page 343: 21 Feb 1785, PHILEMON HAWKINS of Rutherford Co., to WILLIAM HAWKINS of same, for ₺ 40...land on N side Main Broad River, adj. WILLIAM HAWKINS land that he bought of JONAS BEDFORD, and below PETER DILLS, granted 27 Oct 1784...PHILEMON HAWKINS (SEAL), Wit: H. M. WOOD, JACOB DAVIS (I).

Page 344: 20 Jan 1783, JAMES McFADDEN of Davidson Co., N. C. to ALEXANDER
McFadden of Rutherford Co., for ₺ 25...land on a branch of Maple
Creek, adj. WILLIAM LUSK, 150 A...JAMES McFADDEN (‡), Wit: MOSES FERGUSON,
ISAAC PENINGTON.

Pp. 345-346: 16 Feb 1785, JOHN McKNIT ALEXANDER of Mecklenburg Co., to
ENOCH HAMRICK of N. C., for ₺ 41 NC money...land on both sides
Shoal Creek, adj. CHARLES STICE, SAMUEL HAMRICK, adj. WRIGHT, 264 A, part
of two tracts...J. McKNIT ALEXANDER (SEAL), Wit: MICHL HOGAN & one German
signature.

Page 346: 1 Jan 1785, JOHN WITHEROW of Rutherford Co., to JAMES THOMPSON
of same, for ₺ 65...land on Cane Creek adj. JAMES WITHEROW, JAMES
HUGHEY, 200 A granted to JOHN CARSON of Rowan Co., 6 Apr 1765 and by deed
conveyed to JOHN WITHEROW, 20 Dec 1775...JOHN WITHROW (W) (SEAL), Wit:
JOHN STERLING, JAMES DUNBERRY.

Pp. 347-348: 13 Apr 1780, MICHAEL MUCKLEWRATH, SAMUEL NESBIT, & JOHN
MUCKLEWRATH, guardians of MICHAEL McELWRATH of 96 Dist, S. C.
to THOMAS MORRIS of Rutherford Co., for ₺ 100 specia...50 A, part of a
grant to MICHAEL McELWRATH, 2 Mar 1775...MICHAEL McELWRATH (SEAL), SAMUEL
NESBET (SEAL), JOHN McELWRATH (SEAL), Wit: WM. PORTER, ANTHONY DICKEY,
GEORGE LEDBETTER.

Pp. 348-349: 15 Apr 1785, SAME to SAME, for ₺ 1150 specie...land on both
sides N fork of Main Broad River, 300 A...Wit: WM. PORTER,
ANTHONY DICKEY, GEORGE LEDBETTER.

Page 349: 2 Nov 1784, JAMES LOGAN of Camden District, S. C., to GEORGE
BLANTON of Rutherford Co., ...land on Beavour Creek of First
Little Broad River, adj. SHELTON...JAMES LOGAN (SEAL), Wit: TIRE HAMRICK,
JOHN ADAMS.

Page 350: 21 Feb 1785, ABRAHAM CLARK of Rutherford Co., to SAMUEL QUEEN
of N. C., for ₺ 62 s 10 states currency...300 A on Beaver Dam
branch of Nobb Creek, including his improvements, adj. JOSEPH HARDEN...
ABRAHAM CLARK (SEAL), Wit: WILLIAM QUEEN (X), SAMUEL CARPENTER.

Page 351: 12 Apr 1785, WILLIAM TWITTY of Rutherford Co., to CHARLES LEWIS
of same, for ₺ 100...land on E side Mountain Creek, adj. ROWLAND,
part of tract conveyed by JOHN MORRIS to JOHN LEWIS, 12 Apr 1785, and
bequethed by the L. W. & T. of JOHN LEWIS to his daughter FRANCIS ROADS...
WILLIAM TWITTY (SEAL), FRANCES TWITTY (SEAL), Wit: JAMES MILLER, JOHN
RUSSELL.

Page 352: Grant to RICHARD HOLLOWAY, 200 A on W side First Broad River,
on both sides of the wagon Road that leads from Tryon Court
House to JOHN WALKERs, including WILLIAM GARNERS improvement...28 Oct 1782
ALEX MARTIN.

Pp. 352-353: Grant to DAVID MILLER, 240 A on both sides the S fork of
Floyds Creek, waters of Second Broad River...11 Oct 1783. ALEX
MARTIN.

Page 353: Grant to NATHAN CAMP, 100 A on the lines of the South State,
including his own improvements, on head of Gloudy(?) branch of
Surrats Creek...13 Oct 1783. ALEX MARTIN.

Page 354: Grant to GEORGE THOMPSON, 50 A on N side Main Broad River, adj.
BENJAMIN ROWLAND,..20 Oct 1782. ALEX MARTIN.

Page 355: Grant to JOEL SHELTON, 150 A on cornfield fork of Beaver Dam
above JAMES BLACKBURNS, including his own improvement...13 Oct
1783. ALEX MARTIN.

Pp. 254-255: Grant to JOEL SHELTON, 100 A on cornfield fork of Beaver Dam
Creek of Little Broad River, about 1 ½ miles above SAMUEL BLACK-
BURN, including his own improvement...13 Oct 1783. ALEX MARTIN.

Page 356: Grant to ALEXANDER McFADDEN, 150 A on Mountain Creek of Main
Broad River, adj. JOHN McFADDEN deceased land, BENJAMIN HYDER...
28 Oct 1782. ALEX MARTIN.

Pp. 356-357: Grant to JAMES GRAY, 200 A on Huddlestons Creek on W side his
own line adj. JOHN McLUER...11 Oct 1783. ALEX MARTIN.

Pp. 357-358: Grant from GEORGE III to EDWARD DICKEY, 63 A on W side Main
Broad River, including his own improvement, near HAWKINS corner...28 Feb 1775. JO MARTIN.

Pp. 358-359: 15 Dec 1780, JOHN LEWIS, Sheriff of Rutherford Co., to JOHN
CRAWFORD of same, by writ from the Court of P & OS, to levy
from the goods, chattels, etc. of THOMAS DAVIS L 8 s16 d6 which was recovered by JOHN WALBERT...300 A on both sides little Broad River...J. LEWIS
(SEAL), Wit: DAVID MILLER, THOS ROWLAND.

Pp. 359-360: Grant to JOHN SULLINS, 300 A on Hogans Branch of Second Broad
Broad River...11 Oct 1783. ALEX MARTIN

Page 360: Grant to JAMES MILLER, 200 A on the Flat Branch of Broad River
below the mouth of Keen Creek...13 Oct 1783. ALEX MARTIN.

Page 361: Grant to ROBERT COLE, 50 A on both sides Duncans Creek...11 Oct
1783. ALEX MARTIN.

Pp. 361-362: Grant to ROBERT COLE, 100 A on waters of Robersons Creek...11
Oct 1783. ALEX MARTIN.

Page 362: Grant to WILLIAM BAKER, 50 A on Choerkee branch of Second Broad
River, adj. ROBERT CLINTON & his own land, including RICHARD
FLEMENDS improvement...11 Oct 1783. ALEX MARTIN.

Page 363: Grant to FRANCIS McNAMAIR, 100 A on Chesnut Log branch of Sandy
Run adj. the upper side of the wagon Road including his own improvement...11 Oct 1783. ALEX MARTIN.

Pp. 363-364: Grant to JOHN McENTIRE, 400 A on both sides Grassy branch of
First Broad River including WM. McKINNEYS improvement & the
wagon Road...11 Oct 1783. ALEX MARTIN.

Pp. 364-365: Grant to PHILEMON HAWKINS, 70 A on N side Main Broad River,
adj. WILLIAM HAWKINS land that he bought of JONAS BEDFORD &
below PETER DILLS, on Richardsons Creek...20 Oct 1784. ALEX MARTIN.

Page 365: Grant to JONES WILLIAMS, 50 A on Gressey, adj. KUYKENDALL...11
Oct 1783. ALEX MARTIN.

Page 366: __ Apr 1784, JAMES MILLER of Rutherford Co., to FINDAL WHITWORTH
of same, for L 50 specia...land on Green River, including ISAAC
HENSONS improvement, part of a grant of 100 A to sd. MILLER 7 Oct 1782,
60 A...JAS MILLER (SEAL), Wit: FELIX WALKER.

Pp. 366-367: Grant to SAMUEL ANDREWS, 45 A on Cain Creek of Second Broad
River, adj. JOHN SCOTT & his own survey...13 Oct 1783. ALEX
MARTIN.

Page 367: Grant to JOHN McDOWELL, 640 A on French Broad River near Sugar
Loaf Mountain...21 Dec 1785. RD CASWELL.

Page 368: Grant to JOHN CARSON, 640 A on both sides French Broad River,
above JOHN McDOWELLS survey...21 Dec 1785. RD CASWELL.

Pp. 368-369: Grant to CHARLES McDOWELL, 640 A on both sides French Broad
River, including Cherry Point, Mount Pleasant...21 Dec 1785.
RD CASWELL.

Page 369: Grant to CHARLES McDOWELL, 640 A on both sides French Broad River
adj. BENJAMIN DAVIDSONS survey...21 Dec 1785. RD CASWELL.

Page 370: Grant to JAMES GREENLEE, 200 A on both sides French Broad River
...21 Dec 1785. RD CASWELL.

Pp. 370-371: Grant to THOMAS HASLEP, 50 A on both sides Main Broad River,
adj. WM ROBERSON...16 Dec 1785. RD CASWELL.

Page 371: Grant to JONAS BEDFORD, 100 A adj. BAMALAY KING...13 Aug 1779
RD CASWELL.

Page 372: Grant to JONAS BEDFORD, 200 A above KIRKONELS...28 Oct 1782.
ALEX MARTIN.

Pp. 372-373: Grant to JONAS BEDFORD, 150 A on Ashworth Creek of Second
Broad River, about ½ mile below LILES entry...28 Oct 1782.
ALEX MARTIN.

Page 373: Grant to JONAS BEDFORD, __ A on Duncans Creek, above LIVELY...
28 Oct 1782. ALEX MARTIN.

Page 374: Grant to JONAS BEDFORD, 100 A on both sides First Broad River,
three miles above JOHN SMITH, 28 Oct 1782. ALEX MARTIN.

Pp. 374-375: Grant to ISAAC HENALD, 200 A on Bills Creek of Cove Creek,
above STEPHEN SHELTONS at the foot of Youngs Mountain, including his own improvements...28 Oct 1782. ALEX MARTIN.

Page 375: Grant to STEPHEN SHELTON, 200 A on Bills Creek of Cove Creek,
above WILLIAM NETTLES, including his own improvement, adj.
HANELS line...28 Oct 1782. ALEX MARTIN.

Page 376: 25 Mar 1783, WILLIAM GREEN of Camden District, S. C. to WILLIAM
WOODS of Mecklenburg, then Tryon, now Rutherford Co., for Ł 50
NC currency.-.land on S side Green River on Mill Creek now called Greens
Creek, a branch of White Oak Creek, adj. JOHN CLARK, JOSEPH GREEN, JOHN
LYONS, by the path that leads from Green River to Thickety Creek, 200 A
...WILLIAM GREEN (SEAL), PRUSILLA GREEN (SEAL), Wit: GEORGE TYLOR (G),
DAVIS WHISELL, WILLIAM WILKINSON.

Page 377: 16 Apr 1783, GEORGE WINTERS of Rutherford Co., planter, to RAY-
MOND BADFORD, of same, for Ł 50...land granted to sd. WINTERS 2
Mar 1775 on Second Broad River near to HENDERSONS, 300 A...GEORGE WINTERS
(X) (SEAL), Wit: JAS COOK, ELIAS ALEXANDER.

Page 378: Grant to JONES BEDFORD, 100 A on Kirkconnels branch of First
Broad River, including the holy springs...28 Oct 1782. ALEX
MARTIN.

Pp. 378-379: Grant to JONES BEDFORD, L00 A on Ashworth Creek of Second
Broad River, about 3/4 mile above LILES entry...28 Oct 1782.
ALEX MARTIN.

Page 379: Grant to JONES BEDFORD, L00 A on left hand fork of Beatys Creek
of First Broad River, ½ mile above STEPHEN LANGFORD land...28
Oct 1782. ALEX MARTIN.

Page 380: Grant to JOHN McKINNEY, 299 A on Hogpen Branch of Second Broad
River...17 Dec 1785. R CASWELL.

Pp. 380-381: Grant to CHARLES TYLER, 100 A on Main Broad River adj. NICHO-
LOS HENSON...16 Dec 1785. R CASWELL.

Page 381: Grant to ABRAHAM KIRKENDALL, 50 A on Sandy Run of Broad River,
adj. his own land he bought of ROBERT McMIN on the path from
KIRKENDALES to high Shoals...11 Oct 1783. ALEX MARTIN.

Page 382: Grant to THOMAS HESLIP, 50 A on both sides Main Broad River, adj.
WILLIAM ROBINS, CHARLES TYLER...16 Dec 1785. R CASWELL.

Pp. 382-383: Grant to DAVID GAGE, 200 A on Sandy Run of Broad River adj.
PARMER or the place where RIGGS now lives, including his own
improvements, adj. THOMAS RUNOLDS...11 Oct 1783. ALEX MARTIN.

Page 383: Grant to SAMUEL HUNTER, 50 A on Main Broad River...11 Oct 1783.
ALEX MARTIN.

"D"

Page 384: Grant to JOHN GULLICK, 120 A on a branch of White Oak, adj. WIL-
LIAM CAPSHAW, including EDWARD HOLDENS improvements where he now
lives...13 Oct 1783. ALEX MARTIN.

Pp. 384-385: 1 May 1784, THOMAS SPRIGS of Ninety Six Dist., S. C. to ROB-
ERT CARUTH of Rutherford Co., for ₤ 80 specia...land on N
Pacolet known as the little Cove Break, 100 A granted to SPRIGS 2 Mar
1779...THOMAS SPRIGS (X) (SEAL), Wit: JOHN EARL, HERY DOOLEY, JO BAY'S
EARLS.

Pp. 385-386: 19 Nov 1783, ISHAM RAVIS of Rutherford Co., to SAMUEL WALKER
of same, for ₤ 20 proc. money...land on both sides Main Broad
River, adj. WALKER...ISHAM RAVIS (SEAL), Wit: BENJAMIN HIDER, ISAAC BRYANT
(X), DAVIS VANCE.

Pp. 386-387: Grant to JAMES MILLER, 50 A on Green River...16 Dec 1785.
R. C. CASWELL.

Pp. 387-388: 10 July 1786, JAMES MILLER of Rutherford Co., planter, to
SAMUEL THOMSON of same, planter, for ₤ 30...50 A on Green
River, granted to sd. MILLER 16 Dec 1786 (sic)...JAS MILLER (SEAL), Wit:
THOMAS MORRIS, JNO LEWIS, JAMES HOLLAND.

Page 388: Grant to THOMAS ROWLAND, 100 A on Brights Creek of Green River,
including ROBERT MOSELYs improvement...28 Sept 1785. R. C. CAS-
WELL.

Page 389: Grant to EDWARD KANADY, 200 A on both sides Sandy Run, adj.
THOMAS RANALDS & TIMOTHY RIGGS, including their improvements...
adj. GAGE...11 Oct 1783. ALEX MARTIN.

Pp. 389-390: Grant to JOHN LUSK, 200 A on W side First **Broad** River, adj.
DAVID THOMPSONs entry including a small improvement made by
DAVID THOMPSON & a place called the flat Rock...25 Mar 1785. R. C. CASWELL.

Pp. 390-391: Grant to DAVID MILLER, 120 A on both sides middle fork of
Bills Creek at the foot of Youngs Mountain...12 Dec 1786...
R. C. CASWELL.

Page 391: Grant to DAVID MILLAR, 100 A on both sides Cedar Creek, including
two fording places on said Creek...12 Dec 1786. R. C. CASWELL.

Page 392: Grant to WILLIAM GOINGS & DAVID MILLER, 200 A on the head of a
branch of Wards Creek...12 Dec 1786. R. C. CASWELL.

Pp. 392-393: Grant to ABSOLUM TATUM & DAVID MILLER, 200 A on S fork Mountain Creek adj. ANDREW HAMPTON...12 Dec 1786. R. C. CASWELL.

Pp. 393-394: Grant to ABRAHAM MUSICK & DAVID MILLER, 100 A on both sides
Skywicke, at or near ABRAHAM MUSICKS or JOSEPH THOMAS corner
...12 Dec 1786. R. C. CASWELL.

Page 394: Grant to WILLOUGHBY WILLIAMS & DAVID MILLER, 200 A on both sides
north fork of Mountain Creek...12 Dec 1786. R. C. CASWELL.

Page 395: Grant to BEALES EARLS, THOMAS WADSWORTH, SAMUEL EARL, WILLIAM
TURPIN, FELIX WALKER & DAVID MILLER, land on S side North Paco-
let River on both sides Colt Creek, Alice Camp Creek, 640 A...12 Dec 1786.
R. C. CASWELL.

Page 396: Grant to JOHN McDONNALD, 100 A on waters of Mountain Creek, adj.
HIDERS...12 Dec 1786. R. C. CASWELL.

Pp. 396-397: Grant to DAVID MILLER, 50 A on S side Chakhill Mountain on
both sides the Cove Road that leads from HAMPTONS to the Cove,
near McDONNALDS improvements...12 Dec 1786. R. C. CASWELL.

Page 397: Grant to DAVID MILLER & JAMES MILLER JUNIOR, 100 A on middle
        fork of Walnut Creek, below the gap of the Mountain...12 Dec
1786. R. C. CASWELL.

Page 398: Grant to THOMAS POOLMAN(?) & DAVID MILLER, 150 A on Camp branch
        of White Oak near SAMUEL McBRIERS...12 Dec 1786. R. C. CASWELL.

Pp. 398-399: Grant to DAVID BOYS & KEER BOYS, 200 A on both sides of
           Guffs(?) branch, adj. GEO. RUSHELS...12 Dec 1786. R. C. CAS-
WELL.

Pp. 399-400: Grant to ANDREW MILLER, 100 A on S side Green River, adj.
           McDONNOLDS...12 Dec 1786. R. C. CASWELL.

Page 400: Grant to ROBERT WEIR 200 A on E side First Little Broad River on
        both sides Simmons Creek, adj. WILLIAM SIMS...28 Sept 1785. R.
C. CASWELL.

Page 401: Grant to SAMUEL ANDREWS, 30 A on Cane Creek adj. his own land
        he bought of MARTIN...28 Oct 1785. Rc. CASWELL.

Pp. 401-402: Grant to JOHN MILLAR, 640 A on both sides French Broad River,
           12 Dec 1786. R. C. CASWELL.

Pp. 402-403: Grant to JOHN CRAWFORD, 150 A on both sides Richardsons Creek
           ...28 Sept 1785. R. C. CASWELL.

Page 403: Grant to WILLIAM PORTER, 50 A on cabin branch of Catheys Creek
        ...11 Oct 1783. ALEX MARTIN.

Pp. 403-404: Grant to WILLIAM PORTER, 100 A on S side Catheys Creek, adj.
           COOK & his own land, including WILLIAM DAVIS improvements...
13 Oct 1783. ALEX MARTIN.

Pp. 404-405: Grant to GEORGE WILLIAMS, 50 A on Jumping Branch adj. THOMAS
           MORRIS...11 Oct 1783. ALEX MARTIN.

Page 405: Grant to GEORGE WILLIAMS, 100 A on Youngs Creek...11 Oct 1783.
        ALEX MARTIN.

Page 406: Grant to JOSEPH LOGAN, 200 A on First Broad River adj. BEATY,
        including his own improvement...11 Oct 1783. ALEX MARTIN.

Pp. 406-407: Grant to JAMES WEBB, 200 A on Ashworths Creek of Second Broad
           River adj. HILL...13 Oct 1783. ALEX MARTIN

Pp. 407-408: Grant to JAMES HOLLAND, 200 A on Mountain Creek of Main Broad
           River, adj. JOHN SARRELS...13 Oct 1783. ALEX MARTIN.

Page 408: Grant to WILLIAM CAMP, 150 A on N side Main Broad River, adj.
        THOMAS BROTHERS...11 Oct 1783. ALEX MARTIN.

Page 409: Grant to DAVID LILES, 150 A on N side Second Broad River adj.
        SWAN, including MOSELYS OWENS improvements...27 Oct 1785. ALEX
MARTIN.

Pp. 409-410: Grant to JAMES KITCHSIDES, 200 A on both sides Grog Creek,
           including KIRENDALS(sic) Muster Ground...27 Oct 1785. ALEX
MARTIN.

Page 410: Grant to JOHN McLEAN, 200 A on Nob Creek, adj. JOHN McFADIN,
        including JOHN STAFORDS improvements...13 Oct 1783. ALEX MARTIN.

Page 411: 14 Nov 1784, GEORGE TUB of Rutherford Co., to WILLIAM GRAHAM
        of Lincoln Co., for £ 100...195 A on both sides First Little
Broad River, granted to MOSES WHITLEY, for 200 A, of which 5 A was recovered being a neck adj. HARGESSES line, granted to sd. WHITLEY 22 Dec
1768, adj. JOHN GREGORY, GRADY...GEORGE TUB (I) (SEAL), MARY TUB (M)
(SEAL), Wit: MORRIS ROBERTS, WM. Mc_____.

Page 412: 9 Sept 1785, SAMUEL SPENCER, Esq., of Anson Co., to JAMES MILLAR
          of Rutherford Co., and JOSEPH HENRY of Lincoln Co., for Ŀ 100...
200 A on N side Green River in the little Cove thereof, adj. sd. SPENCERs
600 A entry...SAMUEL SPENCER (SEAL), Wit: BENJM CLEVELAND, WM. GRAHAM, WM.
LENOIR.

Pp. 412-413: 9 Sept 1785, SAMUEL SPENCER, Esq., to JAMES MILLAR and JOSEPH
             HENRY, for Ŀ 160...400 A on Buffalow Creek of Main Broad River
near the foot of Bald Mountain, adj. WILLIAM BASSELS survey, JONAS BEDFORD
...Wit: WAIGHTSTILL AVERY, BENJM CLEVELAND, W. GRAHAM.

Pp. 413-414: 9 Sept 1785, SAMUEL SPENCER, Esq., to JAMES MILLAR and JOSEPH
             HENRY, for Ŀ 200...600 A on both sides Green River in the
little Cove...Wit: BENJN CLEVELAND, W. GRAHAM, WM. LENOIR.

Pp. 414-415: 1 Dec 1785, ENOCH HAMRICK of Rutherford Co., planter, to JAMES
             HAMRICK of same, for Ŀ 35...100 A on both sides Shoal Creek
of First Broad River, adj. HENRY WRIGHT, granted to JOHN McKNITT ALEXANDER
4 Mar 1775...ENOCH HAMRICK (SEAL), Wit: GEO BLANTON, ABEDNEGO ADAM (X).

Pp. 415-416: 2 Nov 1785, JOHN LOGAN Of State of S. C., to JAMES HAMRICK
             of Rutherford Co., for Ŀ 20...60 A on a branch of Shoal Creek,
adj. SAMUEL McBRIER, JOHN McKNITT ALEXANDER, HENRY WRIGHT, granted to
JOHN LOGAN 21 Mar 1780...JOHN LOGAN (SEAL), Wit: GEO BLANTON, MOSES
BRIDGES (X), JOHN MORGAN (X), JAMES CACUM(?).

Page 416: Grant to ELISHA HARDCASTEL...100 A on both sides Middle fork of
          Sandy Run...28 Sept 1785. RC CASWELL.

Page 417: 25 Nov 1775, MARY ARMSTRONG, JACOB KUYKINDOL & MARTIN ARMSTRONG
          of Tryon Co., to WILLIAM BAKER, for Ŀ 100...land granted to MARY
ARMSTRONG & JACOB KUYKENDOL 24 Sept 1754, 300 A on both sides Second Broad
River...MARY ARMSTRONG (SEAL), JACOB KUYKENDOL (SEAL), MARTIN ARMSTRONG
(SEAL), Wit: JOHN STAFORD (X), DAVID GAGE, JOHN TOMESON (3).

Pp. 418-419: 27 Oct 1779, JOHN KIRKCONELL of Beaufort Co., N. C., to JOHN
             GOODBREAD of Rutherford Co., for Ŀ 60...land on both sides
Cedar Creek, adj. THOMAS MORRIS, BRADLEY...JNO KIRKCONELL (SEAL), Wit:
WM. GILBERT, D. DICKEY, ALEX MONAL(?).

Pp. 419-420: 20 Feb 1786, LETTICE CLEGHORN, admr. of WM. CLEGHORN decd.,
             & WILLIAM CLEGHORN, son of sd. LETTICE, to JOHN FISHER of
Rutherford Co., for Ŀ 80...land on S fork White Oak Creek, below JAMES
BLYTH & above JOEL BLACKWELL, 200 A granted to HENRY HOLEMAN 22 Dec 1768
...LETTICE CLEGHORN (X) (SEAL), WILLIAM CLEGHORN (SEAL), Wit: JAMES SCOOT,
WILLIAM TOMSON.

Page 420: 28 Oct 1783, JAMES SATERFIELD of Rutherford Co., to GEORGE
          BLANTON, for Ŀ 50...100 A on Beaverdam Creek of Little Broad
River...JAMES SATERFIELD (SEAL), Wit: MOSES BRIDGES (X), ENOCH HAMRICK.

Page 421: 28 Aug 17[8]6, OBEDIAH ROBERTS of Spartinburg(sic) County, S. C.
          to DAVID MILLER of Rutherford Co., whereas RALPH FLEEMAN, a
recindenture(sic) of Davison Co., N. C., by letters of attorney to sd.
ROBERTS dated 13 June 1785...land on Indian Creek of Broad River, 250 A
granted to RALPH FLEEMAN, 24 Dec 1770, No. 288, for Ŀ 20 NC currency...
OBEDIAH ROBERTS (SEAL), Wit: D. DICKEY, WM. NEVEL.

Pp. 422-423: 10 Jan 1787, JOHN LEWIS, Sheriff of Rutherford Co., to DAVID
             MILLS of same...by writ from Court of P & QS to levy from
the goods & chattels of JEREMIAH McDONNALD, Ŀ 29 s4...at the suit of
JACOB CARPENTER...200 A adj. TWITTY, on S side Main Broad River & adj. sd.
McDONNALD...JNO LEWIS (SEAL), No wit.

Pp. 423-424: 30 Sept 1784, BENJAMIN BRIDGES of Camden District, S. C. to
             JOHN BRIDGES of Rutherford Co., for Ŀ 50 proc. money...land
on waters of First Little Broad River, on S fork Shool Creek, part of a
grant to BENJAMIN BRIDGES 13 Oct 1783, adj. JOHN McKNITT ALEXANDER, 200 A
...BENJAMIN BRIDGES (X) (SEAL), Wit: JAS CAMP, MOSES BRIDGES (X), A.
McGAUGHY.

Pp. 424-425: 20 Apr 1786, JOHN STANFORD of Rutherford Co., to ABRAHAM
KIRKENDALL of same, for Ⱡ 200...land on N side First Little
Broad River, below the mouth of Hickory Creek, granted to JAMES NICKELSON,
200 A, 26 Oct 1767...JOHN STANFORD (SEAL), Wit: HUGH BEATY, ESSEX CAPSHAW,
JOHN STANFORD JUNIOR.

Pp. 425-426: 3 Jan 1786, JOSEPH HENRY & ROBERT ALEXANDER, Esqrs., of Lincoln Co., to WILLIAM GRAHAM, Esqr., of Lincoln Co., for Ⱡ100
...land on Wilkeys Creek of First Little Broad River adj. WILLIAM GRIMBERS
"(so spect for GREHAM)" 600 A...JOSEPH HENRY (SEAL), ROBERT ALEXANDER (SEAL)
Wit: WM. SHARP, ROBERT WEIR.

Pp. 426-427: 13 Sept 1785, STEPHEN LANGFORD of Rutherford Co., to JOHN
SMITH of same, for Ⱡ 300...land on both sides First Little
Broad River, granted to BENJAMIN SHAW, 21 Sept 1766...STEPHEN LANGFORD
(SEAL), Wit: MALCOM HENRY, ROBERT SMITH, ALEXANDER McCAUGHY.

Pp. 427-428: 29 Oct 1775, HENRY McWHIRTER & wf MARY of Tryon Co., to
LOUDWICK WREY, planter, of same, for Ⱡ 70...land on uppermost
south fork of Catheys Creek, 300 A...HENRY WHIRTER (X) (SEAL), MARY WHIRTER
(X) (SEAL), Wit: MICHOGEY PROCTOR, PATRICK BLACK, JOHN DORNELSON (X).

Pp. 428-429: Grant to DAVID DICKEY, 100 A on Cleghorns Creek above BERRYs
land...13 Oct 1783. ALEX MARTIN.

Pp. 429-430: 13 Sept 1785, STEPHEN LANGFORD of Rutherford Co., to JOHN
SMITH of same, for Ⱡ 80...land on both sides Little Broad
River adj. ROBERT WHITESIDES granted to JOHN ALEXANDER, 2 Mar 1775...STE-
PHEN LANGFORD (SEAL), Wit: ROBERT SMITH, MILCOM HENRY.

Pp. 430-431: 1 Apr 1786, HUGH BEATY of Rutherford Co., planter, to ABRAHAM
KIRKENDOL of same, for Ⱡ 212 s10...300 A on N side First
Little Broad River, on Hickory Creek, granted to FRANCIS & JOHN BEATY,
for 640 A, 30 Oct ____, #346...HUGH BEATY (SEAL), Wit: GEO BLANTON, JOHN
STANFORD, JOHN STANFORD JR.

Pp. 431-432: 5 Apr 1785, RICHARD RANDLES of Lincoln Co., to ABRAHAM CLARK
of same, for Ⱡ 50 prock money...land on both sides First
Little Broad River, granted to RANDLES ____ Mar 1775...RICHARD RANDLES (X)
(SEAL), Wit: SAMUEL CARPENTER, FRANCIS GUTTERY.

Pp. 432-433: 5 Dec 1783, THOMAS FRENCH of Rutherford Co., to GEORGE WOOD
for Ⱡ 50...land on Greens Creek, south of White Oak Creek,
adj. PULLAM, ASHLEY, JOHN WOODS, granted to JOHN ASHLEY and by him conveyed to THOMAS FRENCH, 50 A, patent for 100 A...THOMAS FRENCH (SEAL),
BETSY SORREL FRENCH (SEAL), Wit: WILLIAM WOOD, ZACHARIAH SPENCER.

Pp. 433-434: 18 June 1783, THOMAS FRENCH of Rutherford Co., to GEORGE WOOD
of same, for Ⱡ 150 proc. money...land on S side White Oak
Creek, part of a grant to JOHN CLARK & conveyed to THOMAS PULLAM then to
JOHN ASHLEY, then to JOHN DAVIS, then to THOMAS FRENCH, granted 21 Sept
1766...THOMAS FRENCH (SEAL), Wit: WM WOOD, ISAAC NENSO(?).

Pp. 434-435: 8 Nov 1785, GEORGE WINTERS of Rutherford Co., planter, to
JAMES COOK, planter, of same, for Ⱡ 100 proc. money...land on
Shepherds Creek of Catheys Creek of Second Broad River, 200 A granted to
sd. WINTERS, 21 July 1774...GEORGE WINTERS (X) (SEAL), Wit: JACOB WOMACK,
JAMES BRITTON, _____ (German signature?).

Page 436: 6 Apr 1786, CHRISTOPHER WALBERT of Rutherford Co., to JACOB
CARPENTER of Lincoln Co., for Ⱡ 70...land on both sides Wards
Creek, adj. THOMAS ROBINSON, EDWARD FRANCIS, including the forks and inclu-
ding an Improvement...CHRISTOPHER WALBERT (SEAL), Wit: WILLM JOHNSON,
ARTHUR GRAHAM.

Pp. 436-437: 24 Nov 1786, WILLIAM GOINGS of Rutherford Co., to PETER
WOODWARD of same, for Ⱡ 100...200 A on both sides First Broad
River adj. COLLINGWOODS...WILLIAM GOING (SEAL), Wit: DANIEL GAGE, DANIEL
LASWELL (X).

Page 438: 26 Dec 1783, WILLIAM BUNTIN of Rutherford Co., to JAMFS WADLING-
          TON of same, for ₤ 30 proc. money...land on White Oak Creek, adj.
JAMES CAPSHAW, including his owm improvement, 100 A...WILLIAM BUNTIN (K)
(SEAL), Wit: ALEXANDER McFADDIN, ANDREW HAMPTON.

Page 439: 13 Oct 1783, JOHN BLACK to WILLIAM HERRIS, both of Rutherford
          Co., for ₤ 30...100 A on a branch of Cove Creek, below PHILLIP
GOODBREADS claim or old improvement...granted to sd. BLACK 28 Oct 1787(sic)
...No. 169...JOHN BLACK (SEAL), Wit: EZEKEL POTTS, WOOTEN HERRIS (X).

Page 440: Grant to DAVID HARDING, 100 A in Lincoln Co., on the head of the
          cabbin branch of Buffaloe, adj. JONATHAN HARDINS entry...9 Oct
1783. ALEX MARTIN.

Pp. 440-441: 8 July 1785, BENJAMIN BRECKET of Rutherford co., planter, &
             ANN to EDWARD FRANCIS of same, for ₤ 40...200 A on both sides
Wards Creek, including the mouth of Coxes Creek & his own improvement...
granted to sd. BRECKET 25 July 1774...BENJAMIN BRACKET (SFAL), ANN BRACKET
(X) (SEAL), Wit: WILLIAM GOINGS SR., WILLIAM GOINGS JR.

Page 442: Grant to JOHN WHERRY, 100 Aon Gleghorns Creek adj. RALPH WILSON,
          WILLIAM GILBERT, & his own line...28 Sept 1785. R.C. CASWELL.

Pp. 442-443: 6 Jan 1786, THOMAS MORRIS to JOSHUA TYLOR, both of Rutherford
             Co., for ₤ 80...land on N side Main Broad River on F side
Mountain Creek, adj. THOMAS JOHNSTON, granted to DAVID BYERS, 29 Apr 1768
...THOMAS MORRIS (SEAL), Wit: MOSES WRIGHT, JAMES JAFFREY.

Pp. 443-444: 11 Apr 1786, THOMAS MORRIS of Rutherford Co., to JOSHUA TYLOR
             of same, for ₤ 100...150 A that WILLIAM DORTIN now lives on.
½ of 300 A granted to BYERS 29 Apr 1768...THOMAS MORRIS (SEAL), Wit: JOHN
WHERRY, EDWARD MORRIS.

Page 445: 2 Jan 1786, THOMAS MORRIS of Rutherford Co., to DAVID DORTIN of
          same, for ₤ 50...land on both sides North fork Broad River, 70
A, part of a grant to MICHAEL MUCKLEWORTH (sic) 2 Mar 1775, No. 295...
THOMAS MORRIS (SEAL), Wit: ISHAM REVIS, THOMAS DORTIN (X).

Pp. 446-447: 10 Jan 1787, JOHN LEWIS, Sheriff of Rutherford Co., to FRAN-
             CIS LOGAN of same...by writ from Court of P & OS, to levy of
goods and chattels of GEORGE WINTERS, ₤ 62...at the suit of FRANCIS LOGAN
...210 A including his own improvement, adj. CREAGS corner, where sd.
WINTERS formerly lived, adj. WALKER, granted 21 July 1774...JNO LEWIS
(SEAL), No wit.

Pp. 447-448: Grant to JOHN SCOOT, on both sides Walnut Creek of Green
             River, adj. JOHN PHIPHER, decd., & WILLIAM MILLS survev...
25 Mar 1780. RC. CASWELL.

Page 448: Grant to WILLIAM SMITH, 100 A on Camps branch of Buffaloe, in-
          cluding BENJAMIN HARDINS improvement...13 Oct 1783. ALEX MARTIN.

Pp. 448-449: Grant to JAMES SLOAN, 200 A on Williams Creek of First Broad
             River, including JOHNATHAN WILSON improvement, adj. ALEXANDER
McENTIRE, JOHN HIGHTOWER...11 Oct 1783. ALEX MARTIN.

Pp. 449-450: Grant to ALEXANDER McENTIRE, 200 A on E side Main Broad River,
             on Johnsons branch, Dyches ford, including his own improve-
ment...13 Oct 1783. ALEX MARTIN.

Pp. 450-451: 18 Apr 1786, THOMAS DOVE of Rutherford Co., to THOMAS LAY of
             same, for ₤ 140 specy...200 A on both sides Catheys Creek,
part of land formerly surveyed by WILLIAM McMURRY, adj. FREDERICK HAMBRIGHT
granted 1769...THOMAS DOVE (X) (SEAL), Wit: JOHN HOLLAND, ELIZABETH
HOLLAND.

Pp. 451-452: 10 Aug 1786, THOMAS LAY of Rutherford Co., to HUGH GREENWOOD
             of same, for ₤ 170...200 A granted to WILLIAM McMURRY, adj.
FREDERICK HAMBRIGHT, granted 1769...THOMAS LAY (X) (SEAL), Wit: JAMES
HOLLAND, SARAH GILBERT.

Page 453: 5 Apr 1787, JOHN GULLICK of Lincoln Co., to DAVID MILLAR of
Rutherford Co., for ₺ 30...land on a branch of Whitoak(sic),
adj. WILLIAM CAPSHAW, 120 A, including EDWARD HOLDENS improvement....
JOHN GULLICK (SEAL), Wit: AD OSBURN, WM SHARP.

Page 454: Grant to WILLIAM BAKER, 100 A on Webbs Creek of Second Broad
River, adj. KUYKINDALLS, including an improvement made by DAVID
GAGE...13 Oct 1783. ALEX MARTIN.

Pp. 454-455: 16 Feb 1787, FELIX WALKER of Rutherford Co., to SETH LEWISH
of same, for ₺ 60...land on both sides Green River adj. JAMES
WALKERS fence, granted to JAMES MILLAR, 28 Oct1782, & conveyed to BENJAMIN
JOHNSTON & FENDALL WANSWORTH in two separate deeds, and then to FELIX
WALKER...FELIX WALKER (SEAL), Wit: LUCY HALL (X).

Page 456: 11 Mar 1785, FENDALL WHITEWORTH of Rutherford Co., to FELIX
WALKER for ₺ 50...land on Green River, granted to JAMES MILLER,
28 Oct 1782, 60 A...FENDALL WHITWORTH (SEAL), Wit: JAMES WALKER.

Page 457: 18 June 1784, BENJAMIN JOHNSTON to FELIX WALKER for ₺ 50...
part of 100 A on Green River, 50 A granted to JAMES MILLAR...
BENJAMIN JOHNSTON(X) (SEAL), Wit: FENDALL WHITWORTH, JAMES WALKER.

Page 458: 18 Jan 1787, WILLIAM GRAHAM of Rutherford Co., to ALEXANDER
CARRUTH of same, for ₺ 50...100 A on North Pacolete River, adj.
SPRIGGS & MILLAR, granted to sd. GRAHAM 13 Aug 1779...WILLIAM GRAHAM
(SEAL), Wit: JOHN McCLEAN, WM. WEBB.

Page 459: Grant to PETER JOHNSTON, 110 A on both sides Green River including the improvement JOHN CASEMON lives on...25 May 1787. R.C.
CASWELL.

Page 460: Grant to PETER JOHNSTON 200 A on N side Broad River adj. BAXTER,
& formerly BAXTER, now THOMAS WHERRY...25 May 1787. RC CASWELL.

Page 461: Grant to RALPH WILSON, 100 A on Gleghorns Creek of Main Broad
River adj. JAMES MILLAR JUR....13 Oct 1783. ALEX MARTIN.

Page 462: 28 Apr 1786, PATRICK MARTIN of Halifax Co., N. C. to GEORGE
WILLIAMSON of Halifax Co., N. C. for ₺ 100 proc. money...land on
both sides First little Broad River, 640 A...PATRICK MARTIN (SEAL), Wit:
W. MONFORD, WM. JONES.

Pp. 463-464: 25 Oct 1786, JAMES WEBB JUN. of Rutherford co., to ELIZABETH
ARMSTRONG of same, for ₺ 40...150 A on both sides Ashworths
Creek of Second Broad River, including MOOB OWENS improvement...JAMES
WEBB (X) (SEAL), Wit: DANEIL WEBB (X), CHAS MULLER(?).

Page 464: Grant to ISHAM RIVES, 193 A on long branch of Main Broad River,
including the mouth of said branch & a school house...13 Oct
1783. ALEXANDER MARTIN.

Page 465: Grant to JOHN BRADLEY, 50 A on Turkey Otter Creek, 28 Sept 1785.
RICHARD CASWELL.

Pp. 465-466: Grant to ISHAM REAVES, 100 A on both sides Main Broad River,
adj. his own land he bought of JOHN MCFADDEN, near to LAUGH-
TERS land...28 Oct 1782. ALEXANDER MARTIN.

Pp. 466-467: Grant to WILLIAM HALL, 100 A on S side Main Broad River, adj.
his own land, opposite McFADDINS House...28 Oct 1782. ALEX
MARTIN.

Page 467: Grant to JOHN JONES, 100 A on Suckhole branch of Mountain Creek,
28 Oct 1782. ALEX MARTIN.

Page 468: Grant to JOHN BRADLEY, 50 A on Turkey Otter Creek...28 Sept 1785.
RC CASWELL.

Pp. 468-469: Grant to JOHN FRANKLIN, 100 A on both sides Sandy Run, adj.
JAMES BLACKBURNs...27 Sept 1785. RC CASWELL.

Pp. 469-470: Grant to SAMUEL LUM, 100 A on Cow Creek of Sandy Run, adj.
BENJAMIN McNESS, ROBT McMIN, WILLIAM RASSE...25 May 1787.
RC CASWELL.

Pp. 470-471: 29 Nov 1784, WILLIAM GOING of Rutherford Co., to MARK BROWN
of same, for Ł 24...150 A on both sides Wards Creek, below
the land he lives on...WILLIAM GOING (SEAL), HASTER GOING (SEAL), Wit:
UEL LAMKINS, BENJ. BRICKET (B), ABRAHAM COBB (S).

Pp. 471-472: Grant to JAMES KITCHSIDES, 400 A on Grog Creek adj. his own
land...28 Sept 1785. RC. CASWELL.

Pp. 472-473: 5 Dec 1785, GRAVES EAVES, of Rutherford Co., to ABEL LEWIS
of same, for Ł 60 NC currency...land on E side Second Broad
River, including his own improvements, near Catheys line, granted to sd.
EAVES 28 Feb 1775, 109 A...GRAVES EVES (X) (SEAL), Wit BURREL EVES,
THOMAS DAVIS (X).

Pp. 473-474: 6 Dec 1786, THOMAS ROBERTSON, of Rutherford Co., to MARTHA
MORGAN for Ł 60...land on Robertsons Creek, granted 20 Feb
1771, 250 A...THOMAS ROBERTSON (SEAL), Wit: DAVID MILLAR, EZEL. ENLOE.

Pp. 474-475: 1 Oct 1785, JAMES BLACK of Rutherford Co., to JOHN HERRIS of
same, for Ł 80...100 A on middle fork of Catheys Creek, adj.
JOHN ENNIS, THOMAS DONNELSON, including his own improvement...granted to
BLACK 28 Oct 1782...JAMES BLACK (SEAL), Wit: GEORGE FLEMING, LOUDWICK
WREY.

Pp. 475-476: 30 Nov 1785, JOHN TATE of Spartanburg Co., S. C. to NATHAN
HAMRICK of Rutherford Co., for Ł 200...land on S side First
Broad River...JOHN TATE (SEAL), Wit: TIMO RIGGS, JERE HAMBRICK.

Pp. 476-477: 1 July 1785, GEORGE WOOLF of 96 District, S. C. to GEORGE
BARKLEY of Rutherford Co., for Ł 70...land on a branch of
North Pacolett River...GEORGE WOOLF (SEAL), Wit: TIMO RIGGS, JOHN EARL.

Page 477: 12 July 1779, GEORGE HERRIS of Rutherford Co., to JOSEPH LOGAN
of same, for Ł 70...land on both sides Buck Creek of First Broad
River, including his onw improvements...GEORGE HERRIS (X) (SEAL), Wit:
SAMSON LAMKIN, ELIAS MORGIN, MARTHA LAMKIN (X).

Page 478: 5 Jan 1787, WILLIAM PORTER of Rutherford Co., to ROBERT GILKEY
of same, for Ł 40...100 A on S side Catheys Creek, adj. COOKS
& his own land, including WILLIAM DAVIS improvement...granted to PORTER
13 Oct 1783...ditto 50 A on cabbin branch of Catheys Creek, granted to
PORTER 13 Oct 1783...ditto 150 A on Catheys Creek on cabbin branch, part
of a tract sd. PORTER bought of JAMES HENDERSON 22 Oct 1778, the whole
300 A...WM PORTER (SEAL), Wit: HENRY CALLAHAN, ROBERT FINLEY.

Page 479: 8 Sept 1784, ELIAS ALEXANDER of Rutherford Co., to ELIZABETH
THOMESON of same, for Ł 100...300 A on Rockey Branch of Floyds
Creek...ELIAS ALEXANDER (SEAL), No wit.

Pp. 479-480: 9 July 1787, JOHN SMITH of Rutherford Co., to ROBERT SMITH
of same, for Ł 20 NC money...land on Little Broad River,
granted to JOHN ALEXANDER 2   1775 & part of a grant to BENJAMIN SHAW
21 Sept 1766...JOHN SMITH (SEAL), Wit: T. WALKER, C. C.: WM JOHNSTON.

Pp. 480-481: 13 Apr 1787, ALEXANDER DAVIDSON to ROBERT ELLIOT of Maryland
for Ł 50...75 A on N side Main Broad River, granted to
DAVIDSON, 28 Oct 1782...ALEXANDER DAVIDSON (SEAL), Wit: AD OSBURN, WM.
SHARP.

Pp. 482-483: 13 Apr 1787, ALEXANDER DAVISON to ROBERT ELIOT of Maryland,
for Ł 100...land in fork of Main Broad River & Little Broad
River, Yanceys Creek...150 A, part of a grant to MATHEW FLOYD, 200 A
2 Nov 1764...and by him conveyed to PETER or HUGH OUIN, and then to WILLIAM
YANCEY, then to sd. DAVIDSON...ALEXANDER DAVIDSON (SEAL), Wit: AD OSBORN,
WM SHARP.

Page 483: Grant to DAVID MILLAR, 100 A on both sides Charles Creek, upon
          GLEGHORNS line...9 Aug 1787 RC. CASWELL.

Page 484: Grant to DAVID MILLAR, 100 A on Greens branch of Mountain Creek,
          waters of Main Broad River, including RITCHARD DAUGHFRTYs improve-
ment...22 Nov 1783. ALEX MARTIN.

Pp. 484-485: Grant to DAVID MILLAR, 30 A on Main Broad River, adj. BASSETS
          old corner...9 Aug 1787 RC CASWELL.

Page 485: Grant to ABRAHAM KIRNEGO, 200 A on N side South fork of Mountain
          Creek, adj. DAVID MILLAR, WILLIBY WILLIAMS...9 Aug 1787 RC CAS-
WELL.

Page 486: Grant to WILLOUGHBY WILLIAMS, 400 A on Camp creek of Green River
          ...9 Aug 1787 RC CASWELL.

Pp. 486-487: Grant to SPRUCE McCAY, 150 A on both sides Magness Creek, in-
          cluding SAMSON TRAMBLES old improvement, near WILLIAMS line...
9 Aug 1787. RC CASWELL.

Page 487: Grant to JAMES HOGAN, 25 A on the North Pacolet adj. his own
          land...28 Setp 1785. RC CASWELL.

Page 488: Grant to MARTHA DOUGLAS 100 A on a fork of Barans Creek,
          adj. HUGH QUIN, including his improvement...11 Oct 1783. ALEX
MARTIN.

Page 488: Grant to SPRUCE McCOY, 150 A on long branch of Jinkins Creek...
          9 Aug 1787. RC CASWELL.

Page 489: Grant to SPRUCE McCOY & WILLIAM GOINGS, 200 A on head of Stoney
          Run...9 Aug 1787 RC CASWELL.

Page 489: Grant to SPRUCE McCOY, 200 A...9 Aug 1787 RC CASWELL.

Page 490: Grant to ADILY OSBORN, 62 A adj. THOMAS PULLAMS...7 Aug 1787.
          RC CASWELL.

Page 490: Grant to SPRUCE McCOY & WILLIAM GOINGS, 500 A...   KINS old
          improvement...Crooked Run, MOORS LINE...9 Aug 1787 RC CASWELL.

Page 491: Grant to SPRUCE McCOY, 150 A adj. HOGAN...9 Aug 1787 RC CASWELL.

Pp. 491-492: Grant to SPRUCE McCOY, 250 A on both sides Adams Creek, adj.
          JAMES HAWKINS...7 Aug 1787 RC CASWELL.

Page 492: Grant to JOHN EARL, 640 A on the upper cove of Green River,
          cabbin branch....9 Aug 1787 RC CASWELL.

Page 493: 9 Aug 1782, THOMAS BAKER of Rutherford Co., to THOMAS HARRISON
          of same, for L 60 proc. money...150 A on Second Broad River,
granted to STEPHEN HOWARD, 21 Mar 1775 and by him sold to sd. BAKER...
THOMAS BAKER (SEAL), Wit: JOHN SWANN, FRANCES PARKER (X-his mark).

Page 494: 28 June 1786, THOMAS WASHINGTON of Rutherford Co., to JOHN
          WHITESIDE, for L 30 proc. money...land on a branch of Walnut
Creek of Green River above MOORS cabbin, granted to JOSEPH MORE, &
conveyed to THOMAS WASHINGTON...THOMAS WASHINGTON (SEAL), No wit.

Page 495: Blank.

END OF Deed Bk. A.D.

ERRATUM: P. 42 (586-588) line three should read sold to SAMUEL RICHARDSON....

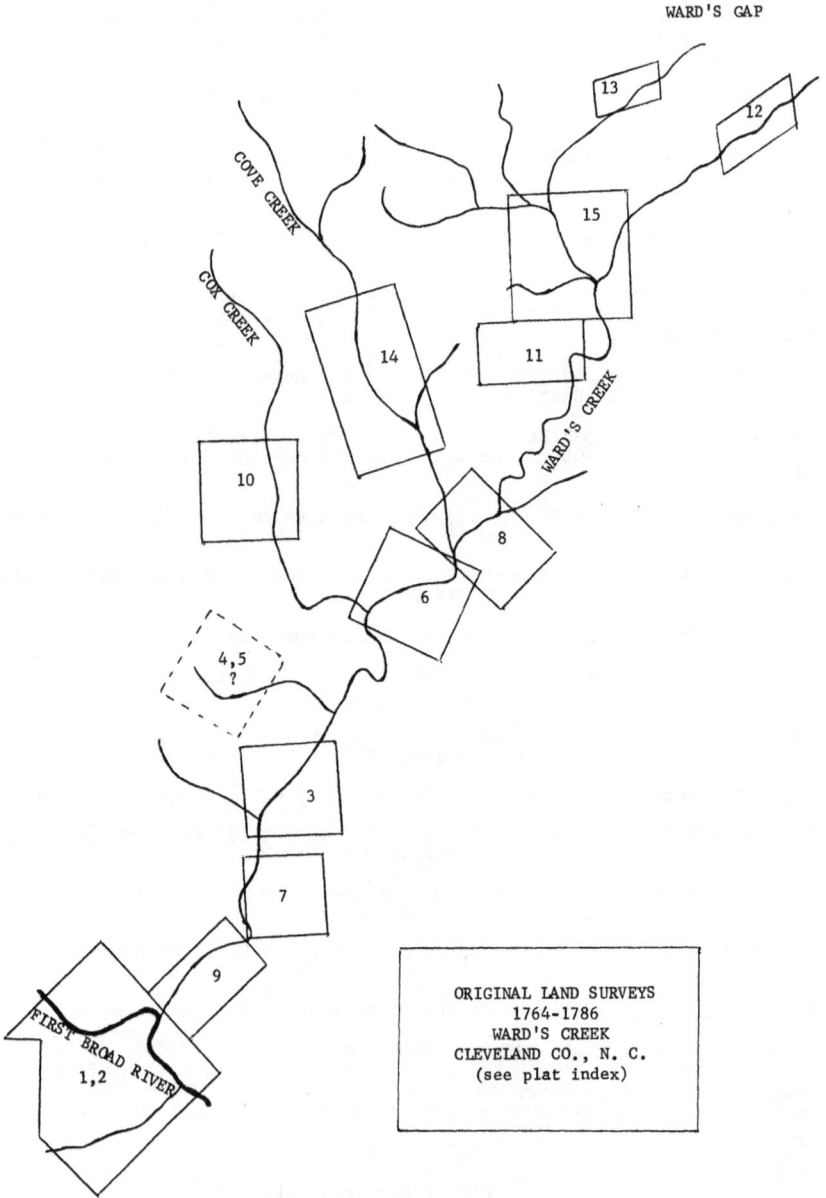

WARD'S GAP

13

12

COVE CREEK

COX CREEK

15

14

11

WARD'S CREEK

10

8

6

4,5
?

3

7

9

FIRST BROAD RIVER

1,2

ORIGINAL LAND SURVEYS
1764-1786
WARD'S CREEK
CLEVELAND CO., N. C.
(see plat index)

ORIGINAL LAND GRANTS, WARD'S CREEK, 1764-1786, Plat Index:

A tributary of First Broad River, Ward's Creek lies entirely in present-day Cleveland Co., N. C., in the northwestern section, heading at Ward's Gap. The accompanying plat is an approximation taken from a more detailed map which I have constructed. Constructing plat maps is a tenuous art and Ward's Creek presents virtually every situation. As an examination of the plat index which follows illustrates, this land was granted when Ward's Creek was part of Mecklenburg, Tryon, Burke, and Rutherford Counties, N. C. Numerous other grants in the area were made subsequent to 1786, even after the area became part of Cleveland County. Thus, to trace ownership of land in what was once Tryon County, one may need to search deeds recorded in several counties.

The following list, corresponding numerically to the plat map, gives information in the following order: name of grantee; county in which originally surveyed; dates: surveyed (sur.), entered (ent.), granted (gr.); chainbearers (CB); and other pertinent information.

1. Peter Duncan, Mecklenburg, gr. 16 November 1764; This tract was mis-surveyed, having First Broad River running northeast to southwest. Nevertheless Duncan sold it, part to Richard Ward (from whom the creek took its name) and part to Thomas Black (Meck. Deed Bk. 2, p. 171, p. 146). Thomas Black then received a corrected grant for the same tract (see 2 below). However, in 1818 Duncan's grandson Hiram Duncan, son of Mark Duncan, sold the tract to Thomas Parker! (Rutherford Deed Bk. 29-31, p. 431) No survey in packet in Land Grant Office.

2. Thomas Black, Mecklenburg, sur. 19 March 1768; gr. 29 April 1768; CB Jacob Moaney, Henry Willis.

3. Robert Collinwood, Tryon, gr. 22 December 1768; no survey in packet.

4. John Fifer, Tryon, sur. 10 November 1769, gr. 18 April 1771; CB Richard Ward, William Sims; This tract has the same survey description as 5 below and I am not able to give a precise location for either.

5. William Shepherd, Tryon, sur. 8 February 1771, gr. 18 April 1771; CB William Sims, William Shepherd.

6. Benjamin Brackett, Tryon, sur. 29 May 1773, gr. 21 July 1774; CB David Loyles, Christopher Walbert; Tryon Land Entries: "about a Quarter of a Mile above Shepperds including an improvement at the mouth of Cooks Creek".

7. William McGowing, Tryon, gr. 2 March 1775; packet empty; members of this family appear in other records of the period as Going, etc.

8. Christopher Walbert, Tryon, ent. 14 March 1779, sur. 10 July 1779, gr. 13 October 1783; CB Edward Francis, Christopher Walbert Sr.

9. Frederick Hambright, Tryon, sur. 8 April 1782, gr. 13 October 1783; CB William Goins, William Killen; Hambright speculated in land in a wide area.

10. John Smith, Rutherford, sur. 27 January 1783; gr. 4 January 1792; CB W. Killen; "Lying on Both Sides of Cokeses Creek Inclouding William Bricketes Inprovment"; Estate file of Thomas Black, Lincoln Co., N. C., shows his widow Elizabeth married Morris Cox. Cox Creek may have been named for this family.

11. John Walbert, Rutherford, sur. 24 July 1784; gr. 28 November 1792; CB Christopher Walbert Jr., Jesse McGlammery.

12. Christopher Knartzer, Burke, ent. 5 January 1779, sur. 13 January 1786, gr. 18 May 1789; CB Jos. Bullin, Jacob Knartzer; Note that George Christopher Natzer was naturalized at Rowan Co., N. C., Superior Court, 23 September 1765. His daughter Margaret married Daniel Wortman (Date of bond: 13 September 1779) in Rowan County and they founded the Wortman family in northwestern Cleveland Co. Cornatzer in Davie Co., N. C., was named for this family.

13. Joseph Bullin, Burke, ent. 4 August 1784, sur. 13 January 1786, gr. 18 May 1789; CB Jno. Queen, Jno. Craigo.

14. Christopher Walbert, Burke, ent. 20 October 1778, sur. 14 January 1786, gr. 10 July 1788; CB Chr. Walbert, John Walbert; entry made to John Wolbrt: "Lying on Cove Creek Including Bengaman Hinson Cove a Campe and Cabin".

15. George Walker, Burke, ent. 4 May 1781, sur. 11 April 1786, gr. 10 July 1788; CB Zac. Downs, Thos. Downs; entry: "Including the Improvments whare on the folkinberys now Lives".

Miles S. Philbeck, Jr.
Bostic, North Carolina
18 September 1976

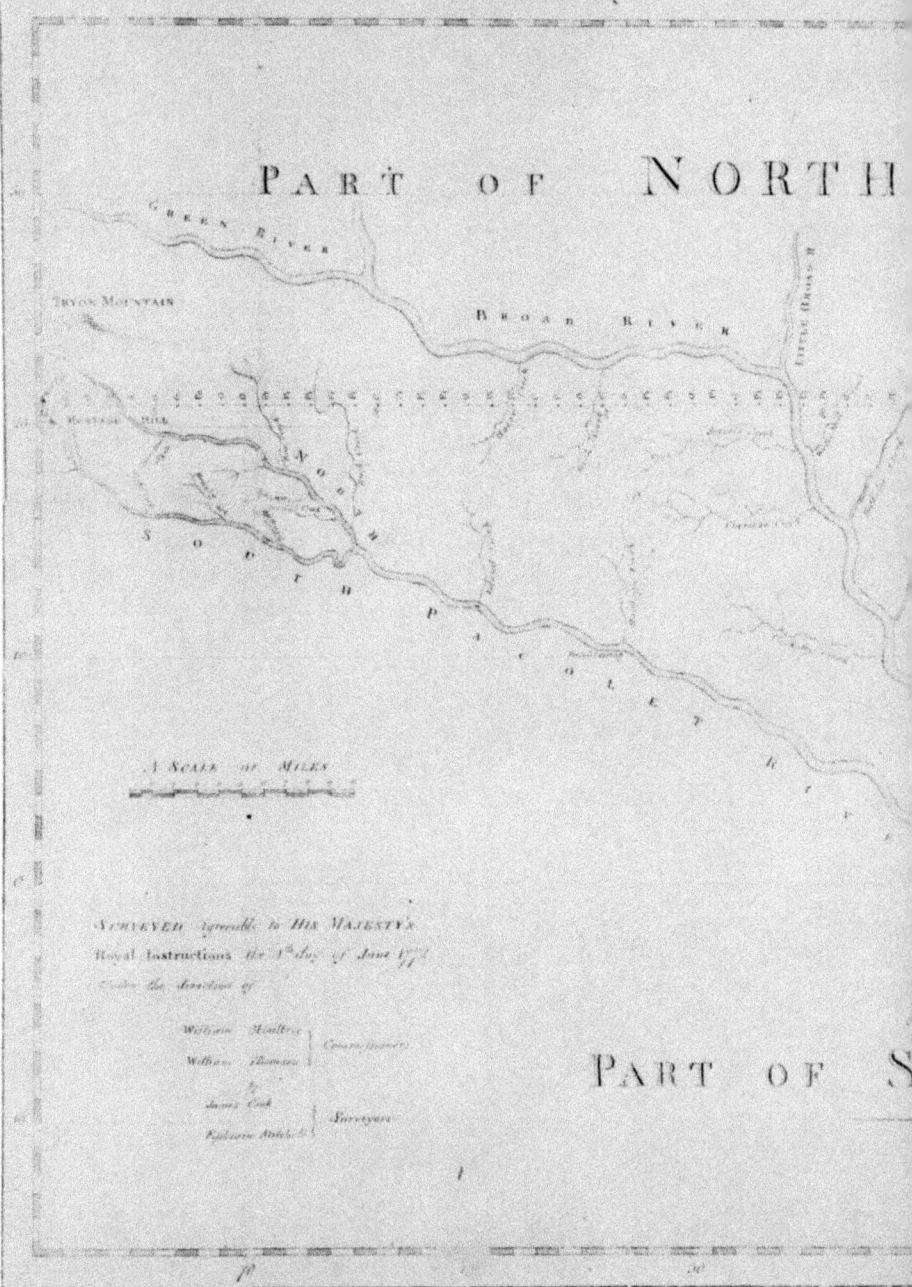

A MAP OF PART OF THE COUNTIE

LATELY ADDED TO THE PROVI

PART OF NORTH

GREEN RIVER

TRYON MOUNTAIN

BROAD RIVER

LITTLE HORS R

NORTH

SOUTH

PACOLET

RIVER

A SCALE OF MILES

SURVEYED agreeable to HIS MAJESTY'S
Royal Instructions the 1st day of June 17—
under the direction of

William Moultrie }
Commissioners
William Thomson }
&
James Cook }
Surveyors
Ephraim Mitchell }

PART OF S

MECKLENBURG AND TRYON

OF SOUTH CAROLINA By H. Mouzon Junr.

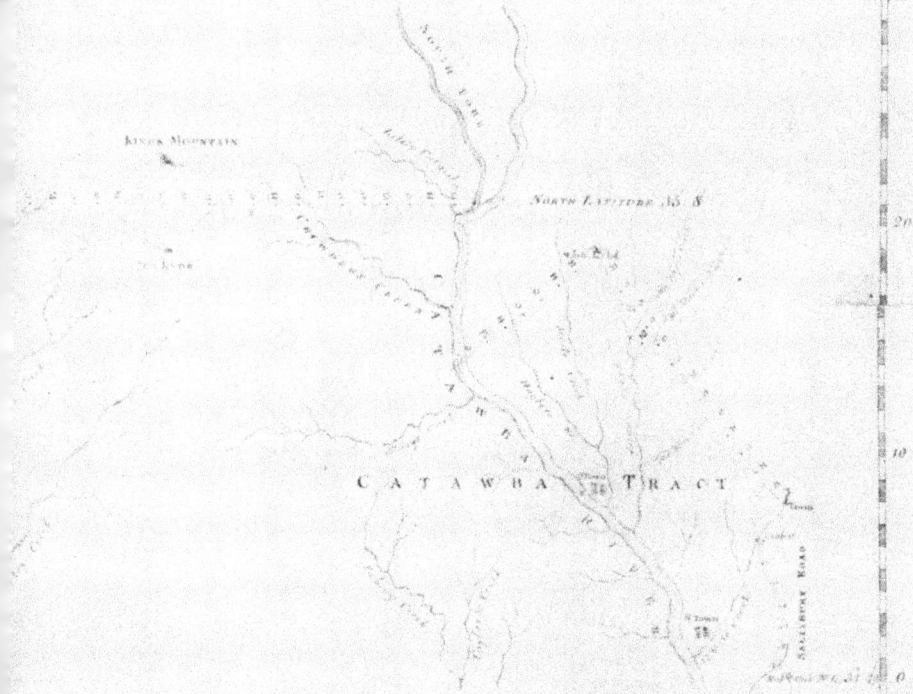

AROLINA

KINGS MOUNTAIN

NORTH LATITUDE 35. 8

CATAWBA TRACT

TH CAROLINA

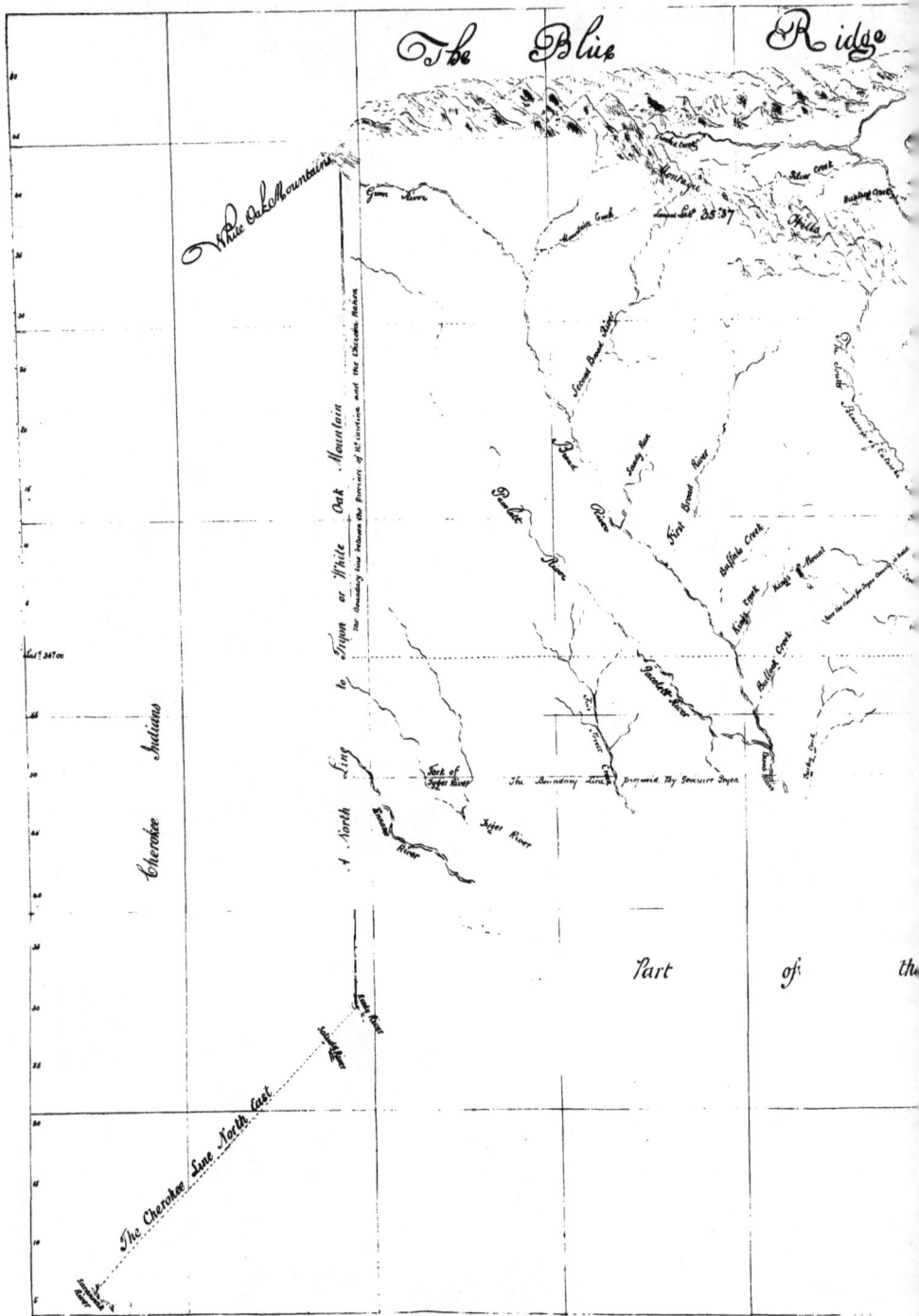

The Blue Ridge

White Oak Mountains

Green River

Montague

S'Hills

Second Broad River

First Broad River

Broad River

Pacolet River

Pacolet River

Lat. 35°00′

Cherokee Indians

A North Line to Tryon or White Oak Mountain

The Boundary line between the Province of N. Carolina and the Cherokee Nation

The Boundary Line proposed by Governor Tryon

Fork of Tyger River

Tyger River

Part of the

The Cherokee Line North East

Saluda River

Province of North Carolina

This dotted Line marks the Parallel of 35°:00' North Lat.° and is consequently the true place of the Boundary Line

opened first in Latitude 34°:49.½° being at the Road where the Crown's Left off a due East Line

Corner Stake by the

Province of South Carolina

www.ingramcontent.com/pod-product-compliance
Lightning Source LLC
Chambersburg PA
CBHW021903020426
42334CB00013B/453